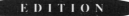
EDITION

6

D0406346

CRIMINAL JUSTICE: LAW & POLITICS

EDITION

6

CRIMINAL JUSTICE: LAW & POLITICS

EDITED BY GEORGE F. COLE
University of Connecticut

Wadsworth Publishing Company
Belmont, California
A Division of Wadsworth, Inc.

Library of Congress Cataloging-in-Publication Data
Criminal justice : law and politics / edited by George F. Cole. — 6th
    ed.
        p. cm.
    Includes bibliographical references.
    ISBN 0-534-19686-1
    1. Criminal justice, Administration of—United States.   I. Cole,
George F., [date].
KF9223.A75C753   1992
345.73'05—dc20
[347.3055]   92-28401
                                                                                          CIP

ISBN 0-534-19686-1

Sponsoring Editors: *Cynthia C. Stormer, Peggy Adams*
Editorial Associate: *Cathleen S. Collins*
Production Editor: *Marjorie Z. Sanders*
Interior Designer: *Lisa Berman*
Cover Designer: *Susan Haberkorn*
Art Editor: *Susan Haberkorn*
Permissions Editor: *Mary Kay Hancharick*
Copy Editor: *Carol Beal*
Technical Illustrator: *Susan Haberkorn*
Cover Printer: *Phoenix Color Corporation*
Compositor: *GTS Graphics*
Printer: *Arcata Graphics/Fairfield*

While preparing this sixth edition of *Criminal Justice: Law and Politics,* I had an opportunity to reflect on the changes in criminal justice research during the past two decades. The contents of the first edition, published in 1972, reflected the fact that the field was characterized by articles advocating reform and by case studies of individual agencies of criminal justice. At that time social scientists had very little understanding of the operations of the police, prosecution, defense, courts, and corrections. The heavy funding of criminal justice research since that time has enabled scholars to describe ongoing practices systematically, to use the tools of empirical methodologies, and to contribute to criminal justice policies. As a result, much of the conventional wisdom has been challenged. Research has also led to new theoretical perspectives, to interdisciplinary studies, and to an expanded research community, so that in addition to academic studies there are investigations by members of governmental agencies, nonprofit organizations, and private research companies.

As the editor of this book I am pleased that it has received such wide and continuing use in political science, criminal justice, law, and sociology courses. Because I am also aware of the responsibility of maintaining a collection that is current, academically sound, and readable, I have included articles that reflect the developments noted above. To do this, I have had to drop several favorite but dated pieces. I have rewritten the introductory sections so that they are up-to-date and serve to integrate the individual articles; as a result, the book is more than a mere assemblage of readings. The changes in this edition are consistent with the original theme: criminal justice can be understood as a relationship between law and politics that operates within the context of an administrative system.

Special thanks are extended to the following reviewers: Michael Blankenship, Memphis State University; Nolan Jones, National Governors' Association; Larry Mays, New Mexico State University; and Robert G. Seddig, Allegheny College. Each made helpful suggestions. Cindy Stormer, criminal justice editor at Brooks/Cole, was an important source of encouragement. Working with these people made my tasks most pleasant.

George F. Cole

CONTENTS

PART ONE

Politics and the Administration of Justice......1

PART TWO

Police......71

PART FIVE
Courts......275

PART SIX
Corrections......397

PART SEVEN
Policy Perspectives......483

Politics and the Administration of Justice

The close relationship between law and politics has been recognized since ancient times. Yet it has taken the social conflicts of the past quarter century to make us aware that the way criminal justice is allocated reflects the values of the individuals and groups that hold the power in the political system. Consider the changes over the past decade. Policies toward crime and justice, formulated in a more liberal political era, have changed along with the attitudes of the American public. Consequently, the ways that government tries to deal with the problem of crime and justice have also changed to policies that are much more conservative.

Crime and justice are crucial policy issues in a country such as the United States in which a tension exists between the need (1) to maintain public order and (2) to protect such precious values as individual liberties, the rule of law, and democratic government. One might hope that citizens in the "land of the free" could live without having to devote great physical and psychological energies, let alone resources, to personal protection, but for many Americans the possibility of being victimized by criminals is ever-present. When in 1973 the National Advisory Commission on Criminal Justice Standards and Goals set as a target the reduction of crime over the ensuing ten years, it stated that a time would come in the immediate future when:

- A couple can walk in the evening in their neighborhood without fear of assault and robbery.
- A family can go away for the weekend without fear of returning to a house ransacked by burglars.
- A woman can take a night job without fear of being raped on her way to or from work.
- Every citizen can live without fear of being brutalized by unknown assailants.

Two decades later, however, these goals are still illusive.

Ours is neither the best nor the worst of times. There has always been too much crime, and virtually every generation since the founding of the Republic has felt threatened by it. This does not mean that the amount and types of crime have been the same over time. During the labor unrest of the 1880s and 1930s, pitched battles

1

took place between strikers and company police. Organized crime became a special focus during the era of Prohibition. The murder rate, which reached a high in 1933 and a low during World War II, has actually decreased since 1982, even though the rate in some cities has risen dramatically during the last several years with the war on drugs.

What is striking about crime in the United States is that the problem is so much greater than it is in other industrialized countries. In per capita terms, about ten American men die by criminal violence for every Japanese, German, or Swedish man; about fifteen die for every English or Swiss man; and over twenty for every Dane. More than 150 countries, developed and undeveloped, have lower murder rates than the United States. When we look at robbery, the data are even more dismaying. The robbery rate in New York City is five times greater than London's and, incredibly, 125 times higher than in Tokyo. In the 1980s crime in the United States stabilized at a very high level; however, in the 1990s arrests for drug sales and drug-related violence have skyrocketed, causing dislocations in many parts of the criminal justice system.

The Rise of Crime as a Political Issue

Crime as a national issue leaped on the American scene during the late 1960s as acts of violence, measured by the FBI's *Uniform Crime Reports,* skyrocketed. As crime increased, so did the public's awareness of it. In a 1968 Gallup survey, "crime and lawlessness" were mentioned as a cause of apprehension more often than any other local problem. This finding may be contrasted with the results of a similar poll taken in 1949 when only 4 percent of big-city residents felt that crime was their communities' worst problem. In the 1968 presidential election, "law and order" became a highly explosive slogan that politicians found aroused voters. Since that time the public has continued to cite crime as one of the four major problems confronting the United States.

With street crime beginning to rise in 1965, President Lyndon Johnson appointed a commission to look at the crime problem. In its 1967 report, the President's Commission on Law Enforcement and Administration of Justice declared that crime was caused essentially by disorganization in U.S. society; that agencies of law enforcement, adjudication, and corrections lacked resources; and that rehabilitation had not been used enough as a means of treating offenders. The overriding theme of the report was that efforts must be made to eliminate the social conditions that bring about crime. There must be an end to social and racial injustices so that the ideals of the American ethic could be achieved and so that persons convicted of crimes could be reintegrated into their communities. Congress responded to these recommendations in 1968 by establishing the Law Enforcement Assistance Administration (LEAA) to experiment with new approaches in dealing with crime and to help the states with crime-prevention and crime-control efforts. Yearly appropriations for the LEAA exceeded $850 million by 1974; before its demise in 1982, it had spent more than $5 billion.

These actions reflected a general consensus. Richard Nixon, Gerald Ford, and Jimmy Carter held similar views on crime policies; many state legislatures adopted a moratorium on new prison construction; the U.S. Supreme Court under chief justices Earl Warren and Warren Burger extended the rights of defendants in criminal trials, and social agencies at all levels of government emphasized rehabilitating offenders by reintegrating them into the community.

This consensus broke down in the later 1970s as conservative critique of the established liberal policies gained credence. Findings of criminal justice researchers cast doubt on many of the earlier ideas. Debate about "what works" forced a reconsideration of rehabilitation as the primary goal of the criminal sanction. Research was published that began to question many traditionally held assumptions about police work. Reformers recommended that greater weight be given to the goals of incarceration and deterrence. Questions were raised about the granting of bail to repeat offenders, the sentencing discretion of judges, parole release policies, and the broader efforts to reduce crime through social reform.

The election of Ronald Reagan in 1980 and his reelection in 1984 solidified the shift in federal crime control policies that had been evolving over some time. Speaking before the annual convention of the International Association of Chiefs of Police in 1981, Reagan defined the crime problem as one that would not be solved by more money, more police, or more prosecutors. As he asserted:

> The war on crime will only be won when an attitude of mind and a change of heart take place in America—when certain truths hold again and plant their roots deep into our national consciousness. Truths like: right and wrong matter; individuals are responsible for their actions; retribution should be swift and sure for those who prey upon the innocent.

Just before the 1984 elections, bipartisan majorities in Congress passed, and President Reagan signed, the Comprehensive Crime Control Act of 1984, which incorporated many of the proposals—tightening of the insanity defense, harsher sentences, abolition of parole release, and preventive detention of dangerous persons awaiting trial—advanced by those who had been urging a new "tougher" approach to crime. Such federal legislation affects only a small portion of criminal cases, since 95 percent of all crimes are prosecuted by the states. But many states had already adopted tougher policies themselves.

The drug problem was high on the public's agenda throughout the presidential campaign of 1988. On reaching office, President Bush pressed Congress to appropriate $7.9 billion in the first year to aid in drug enforcement to build new prisons for drug offenders, to extend criminal penalties, to give military aid to drug source countries, and to create additional treatment and education programs.

At both the state and federal levels of government crime has remained a policy concern during the early 1990s. With the continuing war on drugs, escalating incarceration rates, and limited fiscal resources, political leaders have continued to try to fashion policies that will meet the public's demand that crime be dealt with in ways that will ensure the maintenance of law and order within the context of the rule of law.

Politics and the Criminal Justice System

Dramatic events and major shifts in public policies illumine the most obvious connections between criminal justice and the political system, yet even the most mun-

dane criminal justice decisions, such as the allocation of police resources, have political ramifications because influential people in the community work to ensure that
the law will be applied in ways that are consistent with their perception of local
values. Because laws are often ambiguous, full enforcement may be both impossible
and undesirable, and many laws no longer have public support. In addition, the actors
in the legal system, who have a wide range of discretionary powers, determine who
will be arrested, on what charges they will be prosecuted, and how their cases will
be decided. Should police be instructed to keep vagrants on skid row and away from
the "better" hotels? Should gambling be allowed to flourish? Do defendants with
counsel get more lenient treatment from the prosecutor's office than indigents? Are
suburban juveniles who steal cars sent home for parental discipline while juveniles
from the ghetto are sent to reformatories? Such questions make it clear that criminal
justice is not a neatly structured, impartial decision-making process in which the rule
of law always prevails and each individual is treated equally.

Like all legal institutions, the criminal justice system is "political"; it is engaged
in the formulation and administration of public policies, where choices must be made
among such competing values as the rights of defendants, protection of persons and
property, justice, and freedom. Various groups in society interpret these values differently. The effect of community norms on the criminal justice machinery can be
seen by comparing the disposition of criminal cases in different cities, or sentences
handed out by judges in small towns, and in metropolitan areas. What a rural judge
may perceive as a crime wave is often viewed as routine by that judge's urban counterpart. Definitions of what is criminal are applied by members of society who have
the power to shape the enforcement and administration of criminal law. Thus, judicial
personnel are engaged in the "authoritative allocation of values" just as are other
governmental decision makers whose positions are generally perceived as political.

Besides the pervasiveness of politics in the administration of justice, political
influences permeate the legal system. Political parties have a great influence on
recruitment of judges, prosecutors, and other legal personnel. In many cities the road
to a judgeship is paved with deeds performed for a political party. Prosecuting attorneys are recognized as political actors of consequence. Because of their discretionary
powers, because they are usually elected with party support, and because of the
patronage they have at their disposal, prosecutors are key figures that have ties both
to the internal politics of the justice system and to local political organizations. Likewise, appointment of the police administrator is a political decision that determines
the style of law enforcement a community can expect.

It is difficult to speak of a single criminal justice system in the United States,
for there are many systems. Every village, town, county, city, and state has its own
criminal justice system, and there is a federal one as well. All operate somewhat
alike, but never precisely alike. Community influences, as well as the historical evo-
lution of the federal system, which gives the states freedom to create and direct their
own basic institutions, lead to differences in criminal justice systems.

The FBI and the Justice Department are much in the news, but the executive
branch of the federal government plays a minor role in the broad perspective of
criminal justice. Most crimes are violations of state laws, but enforcement is left to
a multitude of local agencies that have wide powers of discretion. Few states have
a unit to coordinate activities among law-enforcement officials. Likewise, the inde-

pendent election or appointment of judges means that the state appellate courts have little formal authority over the lower courts headed by local judges.

It is at the local level that the individual has contact with the legal process. Most citizens are not destined to appear in court or at the police station, but their perception of the quality of justice meted out there to others greatly affects their willingness to abide by the laws. Robert Kennedy noted that the "poor man looks upon the law as an enemy, not as a friend. For him the law is always taking something away." Thus, if it is widely assumed that the police can be bribed, that certain groups are singled out for harsh treatment, or that lawbreaking will not result in the punishment of offenders, the political system loses much of its dominion over the behavior of the affected populace. As Roscoe Pound once said, criminal law "must safeguard the general security and the individual life against abuse of criminal procedure while at the same time making that procedure as effective as possible for the securing of the whole scheme of social interests."

Although there is a tendency to divide administration of criminal justice into enforcement, adjudication, and corrections, this distinction neglects the very close interrelationship and overlapping among the various actors. Within the justice system, the outputs of one decision-making section, such as the police, become the inputs of another, such as the prosecutor. Likewise, the court, coroner, grand jury, bondsman, and defense counsel have continuing relationships concerning a wide variety of actions that have an impact on the allocation of justice. Similarly, the work of correctional officials is influenced by the sentencing behavior of the judges and the decisions of parole agencies. As a result, the internal politics of the criminal justice bureaucracy immerses officials in a network of interpersonal contacts that emphasize their dependence upon one another. Each actor in the judicial system has goals and values related to his or her own job situation. To achieve these goals, each needs the cooperation of others. Bargaining among judicial officials over the conditions governing the disposition of each case appears to be typical of decision making. To view the justice process as a machine in which decisions are made solely on the basis of "rational" criteria, such as evidence, is to overlook the very personal ways in which justice is individualized.

The confluence of law, administration, and politics results in a system in which officials who are sensitive to the political process make decisions at various points concerning the arrest, charges, conviction, and sentences of defendants. The local legal subsystem is very much involved in the allocation of costs and benefits of the political system. Thus the judicial process induces conditions that are important to the political needs of actors in the legal system. Criminal prosecutions provide opportunities for the political system to affect judicial decisions and for the judicial process to provide favors that nourish political organizations.

The Crisis of Criminal Justice

No one can seriously question that crime is prevalent in the United States. What is in question is the amount of crime, the types of crime, the causes of crime, and the policies that will or will not be effective in dealing with the problem of crime. Law-enforcement officials and much of the public have a picture of a nation under siege by criminals being pampered by the civil-libertarian bias of court decisions, by sentences that are merely a slap on the wrist, and by correctional practices that do not work. But critics of this assessment say that the amount of crime is actually decreasing, that the criminal justice system discriminates against the poor, that due process rights are being neglected, and that correctional facilities often turn minor offenders into criminals.

Although references are made to the increase of crime, it should be emphasized that it is primarily "visible" crime rather than "upper-world" or "organized" crime that makes the headlines, arouses the community, and attracts the major thrust of law-enforcement resources. *Upper-world crimes* are violations committed in the business world—tax evasion, price fixing, consumer fraud, health and safety infractions—activities that are often thought of as shrewd business practices rather than crimes. Such offenses are highly profitable but rarely come to the attention of the public. Much of society does not perceive upper-world crime the way that it views purse snatching. The term *organized crime* describes a social framework for committing criminal acts, rather than specific types of offenses. Organized criminal groups participate in illegal activities that offer maximum profit at minimum risk of interference from law enforcers. These groups offer goods and services that millions of Americans desire even though they have been declared illegal. With minor exceptions, organized crime seldom provides input to the criminal justice process. *Visible crimes* are committed primarily by the poor and run the gamut from shoplifting to homicide. They are the least remunerative violations and, because they are visible, the least protected. These are the crimes that are used for the statistics in the *Uniform Crime Reports;* they are the acts that most of the public considers criminal.

Much crime goes unreported. On the basis of data collected by the National Crime Surveys, an estimated 45 percent of rape victims, about half of robbery victims, and 55 percent of those experiencing simple assault do not report the event to the police. Many reasons have been advanced for nonreporting, such as the fear of public embarrassment by rape victims, the fear of police involvement, and the belief by some Americans that the police will do nothing. In addition, because much violent behavior occurs among people who know each other, some victims do not call the police because they regard the offense as a private matter or do not want to hurt the perpetrator, especially if he or she is a family member.

The number of court officials and the size of facilities have been based on the premise that up to 90 percent of defendants will plead guilty. Attorneys have learned that court congestion can be used to their clients' advantage so that their cases will be dropped or they will receive lighter sentences. When the defense adopts an adversarial stance, invoking due process criteria and requesting a jury trial or continuances, the fine balance that keeps the justice system in equilibrium may be upset. Demands that formal procedures be followed slow down the process, often creating turmoil in courts that must dispose of cases as quickly as possible to prevent a backlog. Delaying cases usually weakens prosecution efforts, because evidence becomes "stale," witnesses are lost, and public interest lapses.

To cope with the pressures of a higher crime rate and a lack of resources, the criminal justice system has placed greater emphasis on administrative decision making in the pretrial period, when the primary objective of law officials is to screen out cases that do not contain the elements necessary for a speedy prosecution and conviction. Such practices require that society choose between the need for order and the individual's civil liberties. This precarious balance is subject to political influences, because various groups have different conceptions of the rights and duties of those who are part of the judicial system. The defendant is often caught between demands for order and the inadequacies of the criminal justice machinery.

Defining Criminal Behavior

Since the beginning of Western law, forcible rape has been defined as criminal behavior and is almost universally condemned. In the United States, the women's movement has focused attention on the treatment of rape victims by the police and courts, so that these incidents often take on the aura of political symbolism. However, it can be shown that the precise definition of the act, the defenses that may be used by the accused, and the sanctions prescribed allow for considerable latitude in applying the law. For example, rape is generally understood to be sexual intercourse by a male with a female who is not his wife against her will and under conditions of threat or force. However, in a ruling the English House of Lords has stated that if a man believes that the woman has given consent, he cannot be convicted of rape, no matter how unreasonable his belief may be. Until declared unconstitutional by the U.S. Supreme Court in 1977, death was the penalty for rape in some states. In some areas of the world, rape is not charged if certain classes of women are involved; among the Gusii tribe of Kenya, forcible rape is an accepted form of sexual relations for unmarried males. What must be emphasized is that even though this behavior has been declared wrong almost everywhere in the world since ancient times, there is considerable variation in the way the criminal act has been defined and in the sanctions prescribed by law.

As with the range of definitions and sanctions applied to rape, one might ask why the consumption of alcohol in the United States during the 1920s was considered a criminal act when it is not so considered now. Why are the penalties for possession of marijuana severe in some states, while little attention is paid to the act in Oregon, Alaska, and Maine? What was it about Puritan Massachusetts that caused certain ways of behaving to be called witchcraft, the penalty for which was death? It appears that in different locations and times certain behaviors have been defined as criminal and other behaviors have not. What are the social and political forces that determine the law? It is important to remember that laws are written by legislators and emerge from human experience. There are usually disagreements in society about the exact nature of the laws defining behavior as criminal.

As the common law of crimes emerged in England during the twelfth century, one of the primary distinctions made was between offenses considered *mala in se*— "ordinary crimes," acts bad in themselves (murder, rape, arson, theft)—and offenses considered *mala prohibita*—acts that were crimes because they were prohibited by the positive law (rioting, poaching, vagrancy, drunkenness). "Ordinary crimes" were considered felonies that could be prosecuted in the central criminal courts; acts that were *mala prohibita* were proclaimed by legislation, considered misdemeanors, and enforced by justices of the peace. By and large the types of crimes classified as *mala in se* have remained static and those known as *mala prohibita* have greatly expanded.

Modern legislatures have added three major groups to the traditional offenses: crimes without victims, political crimes, and regulatory offenses. Today there are many more arrests and prosecutions for the total number of offenses belonging to these latter categories than for the traditional violations of the criminal law.

The distinction between ordinary crimes and those that are prohibited serves the useful purpose of pointing to the sources of the criminal law. Scholars of the sociology of law have developed two major theories to explain the focus and functions of criminal laws and the processes by which they evolve: a "consensus model," wherein a group or society expresses its will or values through the criminal law, and a "conflict model," which emphasizes the role of political interests in the formulation of the law.

The consensus position asserts that the criminal law reflects societal values that transcend the immediate interests of particular groups and individuals; it is an expression of the social consciousness of the whole society. From this perspective, legal norms emerge through the dynamics of cultural processes to meet certain functional needs and requirements that are essential for maintaining the social fabric. It assumes that the society has achieved a well-integrated and relatively stable agreement on basic values.

In contrast to the view of the criminal code as a product of the consensus of values in society, a relatively new approach emphasizes that it is through the conflict of political power that interest groups affect the content of the code. Power, force, and constraint, rather than common values, are the fundamental organizing principles of society. Because political influence is unequally distributed, some groups have greater access to decision makers and use their influence to ensure the enactment of legislation that protects their interests. According to this approach, wrongful acts are characteristic of all classes in society, and the powerful not only shape the law to their own advantage but also are able to dictate the use of enforcement resources in such a way that certain groups are labeled and processed by the criminal justice system.

At this point in the development of a sociology of law, it is impossible to reach a conclusion about the theoretical value of the consensus and conflict models. In the case of some laws, especially those prohibiting crimes that are *mala in se,* there is a consensus in most Western societies as to the values espoused. It is also easy to show how the laws prohibiting cattle rustling, the consumption of alcohol, vagrancy, and the sale of pornography—crimes *mala prohibita*—have their source in the political power of special interests. Because the great bulk of criminal violations now are those of the latter type, attention logically focuses on the conflict model.

The Supreme Court and Criminal Justice

The U.S. Supreme Court under the chief justiceship of Earl Warren will be remembered for its insistence that constitutional guarantees be extended throughout the administration of criminal justice. Long concerned with individual rights in the courtroom, the justices directed their attention during the 1960s to *pretrial* rights in a series of decisions that had the intention of bolstering adversary elements during the crucial periods between commission of a crime and the defendant's appearance in court. These decisions concerned citizens' rights in the areas of search and seizure, interrogation, confessions, jury trial, and cruel and unusual punishment—issues addressed in the Fourth, Fifth, Sixth and Eighth Amendments to the U.S. Constitution.

Until 1961, when it ruled that states could not use evidence obtained in violation of the Fourth Amendment's restrictions on unreasonable searches and seizures, the Supreme Court had insisted essentially that states maintain standards of "fundamental fairness" in the criminal justice process. This meant that only the most blatant examples of injustice in criminal administration were outlawed by the Court. Thus the 1923 murder convictions of five black men sentenced to death after a forty-five-minute trial dominated by a mob were overturned. The Court also disallowed a confession beaten out of two Mississippi defendants by deputies using metal-studded belts. As Justice Cardozo noted, the test for determining the legitimacy of state action was to ask if due process of law had been denied to a citizen by practices that violated those "fundamental principles of justice which lie at the base of our civil and political institutions." From the 1920s until the 1960s the Court adhered to this dictum, only gradually giving citizens Bill of Rights protection against state actions.

The leading critic of the fairness doctrine was Justice Black, who believed that it was unconstitutional because it did not provide for absolute protection of civil liberties and meant that the Supreme Court had to apply uncertain standards to each case. Black argued that the Fourteenth Amendment made the entire Bill of Rights binding on the states and that the courts had a duty to enforce these rights. Although First Amendment rights and the right to counsel in capital cases were incorporated by earlier Courts, the Warren Court began the piecemeal incorporation of most of the remaining basic rights in the first ten amendments. These new decisions focused primarily on the pretrial actions of the police and the prosecutor. By 1969 the safeguards had been applied to all the civil-liberties provisions, with the exception of questions concerning capital punishment, excessive bail, and grand jury indictments.

The decision that has caused the greatest public interest is that of *Miranda v. Arizona* (1966), in which the Chief Justice outlined a code of conduct for police interrogation. The decision requires that accused persons be told that they have the right to remain silent, that statements they make may be used as evidence against them, and that they have a right to the presence of an attorney, either appointed or retained. In effect, the Warren Court said that it is not enough for the states to follow procedures that allow for "fundamental fairness" in criminal proceedings; there must also be absolute compliance by state and local officials with the provisions of the Bill of Rights.

The political reaction to the Warren Court decisions was immediate and vociferous, especially to those that concerned restrictions on police activities. Law-enforcement groups such as the International Association of Chiefs of Police and the National District Attorneys Association claimed that the presence of counsel during all phases of the interrogation process would burden the system and reduce the number of convictions. This view was supported by most of the representatives of police and prosecutors on the President's Crime Commission. In a supplement to the final report, these members wondered whether "the scales have tilted in favor of the accused and against law enforcement and the public further than the best interest of the country permits."

Many observers believed that the 1969 appointment of Warren Burger as Chief Justice and the reconstitution of the Court by Richard Nixon would bring an end to the due process revolution, but this was not to be the case, particularly with regard to provision of counsel. In *Argersinger v. Hamlin* (1972) the right to counsel was extended to persons charged with misdemeanors where imprisonment might result. After ruling the death penalty as then administered to be unconstitutional (*Furman v. Georgia*, 1972), the Court approved revised statutes under which the sentencing judge or jury could take into account specific aggravating or mitigating circumstances in deciding whether a convicted murderer should be put to death (*Gregg v. Georgia*, 1976). Also, since the Burger Court, the importance and legitimacy of plea bargaining has been recognized (*North Carolina v. Alford*, 1970), and rules have been drawn up to ensure that the promises made to defendants are fulfilled (*Santobello v. New York*, 1971).

Cases arising out of the exclusionary rule and the protections against unreasonable search caused libertarians the most concern about the Burger Court. *Mapp v. Ohio* (1961) applied provisions of the Fourth Amendement to the states, but the facts in that case were more straightforward than in most law-enforcement situations. The U.S. Constitution does not prohibit searches, but only "unreasonable searches and seizures." It is the ambiguity of this phrase and the complexity of some arrest and investigation incidents that have created problems for the Court. It is clear that a search based on a warrant issued by a magistrate is reasonable. The more difficult cases involve searches without a warrant that are made "incident to a lawful arrest." What is a lawful arrest, and how much can be seized? The police justify their need for this type of search as a protection for an officer—to remove weapons from the suspect and to gain evidence before it can be destroyed. What if the officer mistakenly thought he or she was following consitutional procedures? Should a "good-faith exception" be granted to evidence illegally seized under these conditions?

The 1986 elevation of William Rehnquist to the chief justiceship and the appointment of additional conservative members to the Court by presidents Reagan and Bush have created a new six-to-three majority that appears to be at odds with many of the criminal justice decisions of the past thirty years. The new Court has begun to consider such issues as preventive detention, the exclusionary rule, administration of the death penalty, and the "good faith exception." It is with these issues that the Rehnquist Court can be expected to retreat from some of the positions of the Warren and Burger years.

Administrative Politics

Social scientists have recognized that discussing an organization solely in terms of its structure does not tell us much about its dynamic processes. Although the term *organization* suggests a certain bareness—a lean, no-nonsense construct of consciously coordinated activities—all organizations are molded by forces tangential to their rationally ordered structures and stated ends. The formal rules do not completely account for the behavior of the actors, because there is also an informal structure resulting from the social environment and the interaction of these actors. Organizations have formal decision-making processes, but these may serve mostly to legitimize organizational goals and may act to enhance the symbolic needs of authority. Emphasis on the prescribed structure may overlook the way the achievement of goals depends upon the behavior of actors who have their own agendas, which may run counter to the professed aims of the organization. In addition, the organization itself has needs that have to be fulfilled in order for it to survive. Thus, realization of system aims is only one of the several important purposes of an organization. The system adapts its responses to meet its needs, because informal arrangements arise to meet the goals of both the organization and the people in it.

The administration of criminal justice is characterized by certain essential features. First, it is an open system; new cases, changes in personnel, and different conditions in the political arena mean that it must deal with constant variations in its milieu. Second, there is a condition of scarcity within the system; shortages of such resources as time, information, and personnel are characteristic. The system's inability to process every case according to the formally prescribed criteria affects the subunits of law enforcement—police, prosecutor, courts—so that each competes with the others for the available resources. Central to this analysis is the politics of administration—the variety of interactions between an agency and its environment that augment, retain, or diminish the basic resources needed to attain organizational goals.

Observers often refer to the legal process as a continuum—an orderly progression of events. As in all legally constituted structures, there are formally designated points in the process where decisions concerning the disposition of cases are made. To speak of the system as a continuum, however, may underplay the complexity and the flux of relationships within it; although the administration of criminal justice is composed of a set of subsystems, there are no formal provisions for subordination of one unit to another. Each unit has its own clientele, goals, and norms, yet the outputs of one unit constitute the inputs of another.

Conflicts always exist among the various actors in the criminal justice process. Each actor sees the problem of crime and the administration of justice from a different perspective. The daily experiences, social background, and professional norms of the police, prosecutor, defense attorney, and judge influence the way each makes decisions. The police officer who has seen the agony of crime victims and risked his or her life to protect society may be unable to understand why defendants are released on bail or why prosecutors willingly reduce charges to gain guilty pleas. At the same time, the prosecutor may be concerned about the police officer's lack of attention to detail in collecting evidence, while the judge may be upset by a failure to maintain a defendant's civil rights. One characteristic of the criminal justice process is that all participants are dependent on others to assist them in their work. At every stage from arrest to sentencing, a variety of actors with different viewpoints and goals are involved in making decisions about the disposition of each case.

Given the fragmentation of the system, we may ask how decisions are made. As interdependent subunits of a system, each organization and its clientele are engaged in a set of exchange relationships across their boundaries. The need for participants to interact leads to the making of bargains that determine the conditions under which a defendant's case will be handled. The police, charged with making decisions concerning the apprehension of suspects, interact with the prosecutor's office when presenting evidence and recommending charges. The defendant, through counsel, may make a guilty plea in exchange for a reduction of the charges by the prosecutor. Likewise, the courts and prosecutor are linked by the decision to bring charges, by the activities in the courtroom, and by the disposition of the case.

Although the formal structures of the judicial process stress antagonistic and competitive subunits, interaction may strengthen cooperation within the system, thereby deflecting it from its manifest goals. For example, the roles of prosecutor and defense counsel are antagonistic, but continued interaction on the job, in professional associations, and in political or social groups may produce a friendship that influences how they play their roles. Combat in the courtroom, as ordained by the formal structure, may not only endanger a personal relationship but also expose weaknesses to their own clientele. Instead of promoting the unpredictability and professional insecurity stressed by the system, decisions on cases may be arranged to be mutually beneficial to the actors in the exchange.

The most distinctive feature of the administration of criminal justice is the high degree of discretion. As in few other social organizations, the amount of discretion in law enforcement, judicial, and correctional agencies increases as one moves *down* the administrative hierarchy. In most organizations, the observer usually finds the lowest-ranking members performing the most routine tasks under supervision, with various mechanisms of quality control employed to check their work. In criminal justice, personnel such as patrol officers, assistant district attorneys, public defenders, judges, and correctional officers may be viewed as street-level bureaucrats who exercise discretion on vital decisions affecting defendants.

A final characteristic of the administration of justice is that the system may be viewed as a filtering process through which cases are screened: some are advanced to the next level of decision making; and either others are rejected or the conditions under which they are processed are changed. At each stage decisions are made by officials as to which cases will proceed to the next level. Some arrestees go free because the police decide that a crime has not been committed or the evidence is not sound. The prosecutor may drop charges thinking that conviction will not be possible. Great numbers of those indicted will plead guilty, the judge may dismiss the charges against others, the jury may acquit a few defendants; while most of that small number who go to trial will be found guilty. Various options are available to the judge at the time of sentencing, and thus some offenders will go to prison while others will serve their time in the community. The "funnellike" nature of the criminal justice system results in many cases entering at the top, but owing to the filtering process, only a small portion are convicted and punished.

Criminal justice is greatly affected by the values of each decision maker, whose career, influence, and position may be more important to him or her than consideration for the formal requirements of the law. Accommodation will be sought with those in the exchange system so that decisions that are consistent with the values of the participants and the organization are reached. A wide variety of departures from the formal rules of the due process ideology are accepted by judicial actors but never publicly acknowledged. Because of the strain of an overwhelming caseload and the adversary nature of the formal structure, members of the bureaucracy can reduce stress while maximizing rewards by filtering out cases that are disruptive or potentially threatening to the established norms. Because defendants pass through the system and the judicial actors remain, the accused may become secondary figures in the bureaucratic setting. The administrative norms are so well established that judges may agree that defendants who survive the scrutiny of the police and prosecutor must be guilty.

The administration of criminal justice may be viewed as having goals that are antagonistic to the due process model. Decisions concerning the disposition of cases are influenced by the selective nature of a filtering process in which administrative discretion and interpersonal exchange relationships are extremely important. At each decision-making level, actors in the judicial system are able to determine which types of crime will come to official notice, which kinds of offenders will be processed, and how enthusiastically a conviction will be sought. It is in these day-to-day practices and policies of the criminal justice agencies that the law is put into effect, and it is out of this activity that organizations and individuals shape the law.

Suggestions for Further Reading

CURRIE, ELLIOTT. *Confronting Crime*. New York: Pantheon Books, 1985. Why is criminal violence so much worse in the United States than in other affluent industrial societies? Currie critiques both conservative and liberal prescriptions for reducing crime and offers new directions.

DAVIS, KENNETH CULP. *Discretionary Justice*. Baton Rouge: Louisiana State University Press, 1969. A seminal work exploring the nature of discretion. Davis suggests that opportunities for discretionary decisions be formalized to prevent abuse.

ERIKSON, KAI T. *Wayward Puritans*. New York: John Wiley, 1966. Analysis of three "crime waves" in Puritan Massachusetts. The findings indicate that persons are labeled deviant when the community is undergoing periods of stress.

HALL, JEROME. *General Principles of Criminal Law*. 2nd ed. Indianapolis: Bobbs-Merrill, 1947. One of the clearest texts outlining the foundations of the criminal law and the defenses that may be used.

HEIDENSOHN, FRANCES M. *Women and Crime*. New York: New York University Press, 1985. An account and critique of criminological writings on women and criminality.

LAFREE, GARY D. *Rape and Criminal Justice*. Belmont, Calif.: Wadsworth, 1989. Research on rape based on interviews with police officers, prosecutors, and judges in Indianapolis.

MUSTO, DAVID F. *The American Disease: Origins of Narcotics Control*. 2nd rev. ed. New Haven, Conn.: Yale University Press, 1987. A historical analysis of drug policy in the United States. It argues that each generation that experiences drug abuse indoctrinates the next generation to its horrors.

WILSON, JAMES Q. *Thinking About Crime*. 2nd ed. New York: Basic Books, 1983. Argues for policies to improve the criminal justice system and thus reduce crime. Wilson examines various law enforcement, sentencing, and correctional strategies.

1

Two Models of the Criminal Process

Herbert L. Packer

*In one of the most important contributions to systematic thought about the admin-
istration of criminal justice, Herbert Packer articulates the values supporting two
models of the justice process. He notes the gulf existing between the "Due Process
Model" of criminal administration, with its emphasis on the rights of the individual,
and the "Crime Control Model," which sees the regulation of criminal conduct as
the most important function of the judicial system.*

Two models of the criminal process will let us perceive the normative antinomy at
the heart of the criminal law. These models are not labeled Is and Ought, nor are
they to be taken in that sense. Rather, they represent an attempt to abstract two separate value systems that compete for priority in the operation of the criminal process.
Neither is presented as either corresponding to reality or representing the ideal to the
exclusion of the other. The two models merely afford a convenient way to talk about
the operation of a process whose day-to-day functioning involves a constant series
of minute adjustments between the competing demands of two value systems and
whose normative future likewise involves a series of resolutions of the tensions
between competing claims.

   I call these two models the Due Process Model and the Crime Control Model.
. . . As we examine the way the models operate in each successive stage, we will
raise two further inquiries: first, where on a spectrum between the extremes represented by the two models do our present practices seem approximately to fall; second, what appears to be the direction and thrust of current and foreseeable trends
along each such spectrum?

   There is a risk in an enterprise of this sort that is latent in any attempt to polarize.
It is, simply, that values are too various to be pinned down to yes-or-no answers.
The models are distortions of reality. And, since they are normative in character,

Source: Reprinted from *The Limits of the Criminal Sanction* by Herbert L. Packer,
with the permission of the publishers, Stanford University Press. © 1968 by Herbert
L. Packer.

there is a danger of seeing one or the other as Good or Bad. The reader will have his preferences, as I do, but we should not be so rigid as to demand consistently polarized answers to the range of questions posed in the criminal process. The weighty questions of public policy that inhere in any attempt to discern where on the spectrum of normative choice the "right" answer lies are beyond the scope of the present inquiry. The attempt here is primarily to clarify the terms of discussion by isolating the assumptions that underlie competing policy claims and examining the conclusions that those claims, if fully accepted, would lead to.

Values Underlying the Models

Each of the two models we are about to examine is an attempt to give operational content to a complex of values underlying the criminal law. As I have suggested earlier, it is possible to identify two competing systems of values, the tension between which accounts for the intense activity now observable in the development of the criminal process. The actors in this development—lawmakers, judges, police, prosecutors, defense lawyers—do not often pause to articulate the values that underlie the positions that they take on any given issue. Indeed, it would be a gross oversimplification to ascribe a coherent and consistent set of values to any of these actors. Each of the two competing schemes of values we will be developing in this section contains components that are demonstrably present some of the time in some of the actors' preferences regarding the criminal process. No one person has ever identified himself as holding all of the values that underlie these two models. The models are polarities, and so are the schemes of values that underlie them. A person who subscribed to all of the values underlying the other would be rightly viewed as a fanatic. The values are presented here as an aid to analysis, not as a program for action.

Some Common Ground

However, the polarity of the two models is not absolute. Although it would be possible to construct models that exist in an institutional vacuum, it would not serve our purposes to do so. We are postulating, not a criminal process that operates in any kind of society at all, but rather one that operates within the framework of contemporary American society. This leaves plenty of room for polarization, but it does require the observance of some limits. A model of the criminal process that left out of account relatively stable and enduring features of the American legal system would not have much relevance to our central inquiry. For convenience, these elements of stability and continuity can be roughly equated with minimal agreed limits expressed in the Constitution of the United States and, more importantly, with unarticulated assumptions that can be perceived to underlie those limits. Of course, it is true that the Constitution is constantly appealed to by proponents and opponents of many measures that affect the criminal process. And only the naive would deny that there are few conclusive positions that can be reached by appeal to the Constitution. Yet there are assumptions about the criminal process that are widely shared and that may be viewed as common ground for the operation of any model of the criminal process. Our first task is to clarify these assumptions.

First, there is the assumption, implicit in the ex post facto clause of the Constitution, that the function of defining conduct that may be treated as criminal is separate from and prior to the process of identifying and dealing with persons as criminals. How wide or narrow the definition of criminal conduct must be is an important question of policy that yields highly variable results depending on the values held by those making the relevant decisions. But that there must be a means of definition that is in some sense separate from and prior to the operation of the process is clear. If this were not so, our efforts to deal with the phenomenon of organized crime would appear ludicrous indeed (which is not to say that we have by any means exhausted the possibilities for dealing with that problem within the limits of this basic assumption).

A related assumption that limits the area of controversy is that the criminal process ordinarily ought to be invoked by those charged with the responsibility for doing so when it appears that a crime has been committed and that there is a reasonable prospect of apprehending and convicting its perpetrator. Although police and prosecutors are allowed broad discretion for deciding not to invoke the criminal process, it is commonly agreed that these officials have no general dispensing power. If the legislature has decided that certain conduct is to be treated as criminal, the decision makers at every level of the criminal process are expected to accept that basic decision as a premise for action. The controversial nature of the occasional case in which the relevant decision makers appear not to have played their appointed role only serves to highlight the strength with which the premise holds. This assumption may be viewed as the other side of the ex post facto coin. Just as conduct that is not proscribed as criminal may not be dealt with in the criminal process, so conduct that has been denominated as criminal must be treated as such by the participants in the criminal process acting within their respective competences.

Next, there is the assumption that there are limits to the powers of government to investigate and apprehend persons suspected of committing crimes. I do not refer to the controversy (settled recently, at least in broad outline) as to whether the Fourth Amendment's prohibition against unreasonable searches and seizures applies to the states with the same force with which it applies to the federal government. Rather, I am talking about the general assumption that a degree of scrutiny and control must be exercised with respect to the activities of law-enforcement officers, that the security and privacy of the individual may not be invaded at will. It is possible to imagine a society in which even lip service is not paid to this assumption. Nazi Germany approached but never quite reached this position. But no one in our society would maintain that any individual may be taken into custody at any time and held without any limitation of time during the process of investigating his possible commission of crimes, or would argue that there should be no form of redress for violation of at least some standards for official investigative conduct. Although this assumption may not appear to have much in the way of positive content, its absence would render moot some of our most hotly controverted problems. If there were not general agreement that there must be some limits on police power to detain and investigate, the highly controversial provisions of the Uniform Arrest Act, permitting the police to detain a person for questioning for a short period even though they do not have grounds for making an arrest, would be a magnanimous concession by the all-powerful state rather than, as it is now perceived, a substantial expansion of police power.

Finally, there is a complex of assumptions embraced by terms such as "the adversary system," "procedural due process," "notice and an opportunity to be heard," and "day in court." Common to them all is the notion that the alleged criminal is not merely an object to be acted upon but an independent entity in the process who may, if he so desires, force the operators of the process to demonstrate to an independent authority (judge and jury) that he is guilty of the charges against him. It is a minimal assumption. It speaks in terms of "may" rather than "must." It permits but does not require the accused, acting by himself or through his own agent, to play an active role in the process. By virtue of that fact the process becomes or has the capacity to become a contest between, if not equals, at least independent actors. As we shall see, much of the space between the two models is occupied by stronger or weaker notions of how this contest is to be arranged, in what cases it is to be played, and by what rules. The Crime Control Model tends to de-emphasize this adversary aspect of the process; the Due Process Model tends to make it central. The common ground, and it is important, is the agreement that the process has, for everyone subjected to it, at least the potentiality of becoming to some extent an adversary struggle.

So much for common ground. There is a good deal of it, even in the narrowest view. Its existence should not be overlooked, because it is, by definition, what permits partial resolutions of the tension between the two models to take place. The rhetoric of the criminal process consists largely of claims that disputed territory is "really" common ground: that, for example, the premise of an adversary system "necessarily" embraces the appointment of counsel for everyone accused of crime, or conversely, that the obligation to pursue persons suspected of committing crimes "necessarily" embraces interrogation of suspects without the intervention of counsel. We may smile indulgently at such claims; they are rhetoric, and no more. But the form in which they are made suggests an important truth: that there *is* a common ground of value assumption about the criminal process that makes continued discourse about its problems possible.

Crime Control Values

The value system that underlies the Crime Control Model is based on the proposition that the repression of criminal conduct is by far the most important function to be performed by the criminal process. The failure of law enforcement to bring criminal conduct under tight control is viewed as leading to the breakdown of public order and thence to the disappearance of an important condition of human freedom. If the laws go unenforced—which is to say, if it is perceived that there is a high percentage of failure to apprehend and convict in the criminal process—a general disregard for legal controls tends to develop. The law-abiding citizen then becomes the victim of all sorts of unjustifiable invasions of his interests. His security of person and property is sharply diminished, and, therefore, so is his liberty to function as a member of society. The claim ultimately is that the criminal process is a positive guarantor of social freedom. In order to achieve this high purpose, the Crime Control Model requires that primary attention be paid to the efficiency with which the criminal process operates to screen suspects, determine guilt, and secure appropriate dispositions of persons convicted of crime.

Efficiency of operation is not, of course, a criterion that can be applied in a vacuum. By "efficiency" we mean the system's capacity to apprehend, try, convict, and dispose of a high proportion of criminal offenders whose offenses become known. In a society in which only the grossest forms of antisocial behavior were made criminal and in which the crime rate was exceedingly low, the criminal process might require the devotion of many more man-hours of police, prosecutorial, and judicial time per case than ours does, and still operate with tolerable efficiency. A society that was prepared to increase even further the resources devoted to the suppression of crime might cope with a rising crime rate without sacrifice of efficiency while continuing to maintain an elaborate and time-consuming set of criminal processes. However, neither of these possible characteristics corresponds with social reality in this country. We use the criminal sanction to cover an increasingly wide spectrum of behavior thought to be antisocial, and the amount of crime is very high indeed, although both level and trend are hard to assess. At the same time, although precise measures are not available, it does not appear that we are disposed in the public sector of the economy to increase very drastically the quantity, much less the quality, of the resources devoted to the suppression of criminal activity through the operation of the criminal process. These factors have an important bearing on the criteria of efficiency, and therefore on the nature of the Crime Control Model.

The model, in order to operate successfully, must produce a high rate of apprehension and conviction, and must do so in a context where the magnitudes being dealt with are very large and the resources for dealing with them are very limited. There must then be a premium on speed and finality. Speed, in turn, depends on informality and on uniformity; finality depends on minimizing the occasions for challenge. The process must not be cluttered up with ceremonious rituals that do not advance the progress of a case. Facts can be established more quickly through interrogation in a police station than through the formal process of examination and cross-examination in a court. It follows that extrajudicial processes should be preferred to judicial processes, informal operations to formal ones. But informality is not enough; there must also be uniformity. Routine, stereotyped procedures are essential if large numbers are being handled. The model that will operate successfully on these presuppositions must be an administrative, almost a managerial, model. The image that comes to mind is an assembly-line conveyor belt down which moves an endless stream of cases, never stopping, carrying the cases to workers who stand at fixed stations and who perform on each case as it comes by the same small but essential operation that brings it one step closer to being a finished product, or, to exchange the metaphor for the reality, a closed file. The criminal process, in this model, is seen as a screening process in which each successive state—prearrest investigation, arrest, postarrest investigation, preparation for trial, trial or entry of plea, conviction, disposition—involves a series of routinized operations whose success is gauged primarily by their tendency to pass the case along to a successful conclusion.

What is a successful conclusion? One that throws off at an early stage those cases in which it appears unlikely that the person apprehended is an offender and then secures, as expeditiously as possible, the conviction of the rest, with a minimum of occasions for challenge, let alone post-audit. By the application of administrative expertness, primarily that of the police and prosecutors, an early determination of the probability of innocence or guilt emerges. Those who are probably innocent are screened out. Those who are probably guilty are passed quickly through the remaining stages of the process. The key to the operation of the model regarding those who are not screened out is what I shall call a presumption of guilt. The concept requires some explanation, since it may appear startling to assert that what appears to be the precise converse of our generally accepted ideology of a presumption of innocence can be an essential element of a model that does correspond in some respects to the actual operation of the criminal process.

The presumption of guilt is what makes it possible for the system to deal efficiently with large numbers, as the Crime Control Model demands. The supposition is that the screening processes operated by police and prosecutors are reliable indicators of probable guilt. Once a man has been arrested and investigated without being found to be probably innocent, or, to put it differently, once a determination has been made that there is enough evidence of guilt to permit holding him for further action, then all subsequent activity directed toward him is based on the view that he is probably guilty. The precise point at which this occurs will vary from case to case; in many cases it will occur as soon as the suspect is arrested, or even before, if the evidence of probable guilt that has come to the attention of the authorities is sufficiently strong. But in any case the presumption of guilt will begin to operate well before the "suspect" becomes a "defendant."

The presumption of guilt is not, of course, a thing. Nor is it even a rule of law in the usual sense. It simply is the consequence of a complex of attitudes, a mood. If there is confidence in the reliability of informal administrative fact-finding activities that take place in the early stages of the criminal process, the remaining stages of the process can be relatively perfunctory without any loss in operating efficiency. The presumption of guilt, as it operates in the Crime Control Model, is the operational expression of that confidence.

It would be a mistake to think of the presumption of guilt as the opposite of the presumption of innocence that we are so used to thinking of as the polestar of the criminal process and that, as we shall see, occupies an important position in the Due Process Model. The presumption of innocence is not its opposite; it is irrelevant to the presumption of guilt; the two concepts are different rather than opposite ideas. The difference can perhaps be epitomized by an example. A murderer, for reasons best known to himself, chooses to shoot his victim in plain view of a large number of people. When the police arrive, he hands them his gun and says, "I did it and I'm glad." His account of what happened is corroborated by several eyewitnesses. He is placed under arrest and led off to jail. Under these circumstances, which may seem extreme but which in fact characterize with rough accuracy the evidentiary situation in a large proportion of criminal cases, it would be plainly absurd to maintain that more probably than not the suspect did not commit the killing. But that is not what the presumption of innocence means. It means that until there has been an adjudication of guilt by an authority legally competent to make such an adjudication, the suspect is to be treated, for reasons that have nothing whatever to do with the probable outcome of the case, as if his guilt is an open question.

The presumption of innocence is a direction to officials about how they are to proceed, not a prediction of outcome. The presumption of guilt, however, is purely and simply a prediction of outcome. The presumption of innocence is, then, a direction to the authorities to ignore the presumption of guilt in their treatment of the suspect. It tells them, in effect, to close their eyes to what will frequently seem to be factual probabilities. The reasons why it tells them this are among the animating presuppositions of the Due Process Model, and we will come to them shortly. It is enough to note at this point that the presumption of guilt is descriptive and factual; the presumption of innocence is normative and legal. The pure Crime Control Model has no truck with the presumption of innocence, although its real-life emanations are, as we shall see, brought into uneasy compromise with the dictates of this dominant ideological position. In the presumption of guilt this model finds a factual predicate for the position that the dominant goal of repressing crime can be achieved through highly summary processes without any great loss of efficiency (as previously defined), because of the probability that, in the run of cases, the preliminary screening process operated by the police and the prosecuting officials contains adequate guarantees of reliable fact-finding. Indeed, the model takes an even stronger position. It is that subsequent processes, particularly those of a formal adjudicatory nature, are unlikely to produce as reliable fact-finding as the expert administrative process that precedes them is capable of. The criminal process thus must put special weight on the quality of administrative fact-finding. It becomes important, then, to place as few restrictions as possible on the character of the administrative fact-finding processes and to limit restrictions to such as enhance reliability, excluding those designed for other purposes. As we shall see, this view of restrictions on administrative fact-finding is a consistent theme in the development of the Crime Control Model.

In this model, as I have suggested, the center of gravity of the process lies in the early, administrative fact-finding stages. The complementary proposition is that the subsequent stages are relatively unimportant and should be truncated as much as possible. This, too, produces tensions with presently dominant ideology. The pure Crime Control Model has very little use for many conspicuous features of the adjudicative process, and in real life works out a number of ingenious compromises with them. Even in the pure model, however, there have to be devices for dealing with the suspect after the preliminary screening process has resulted in a determination of probable guilt. The focal device, as we shall see, is the plea of guilty; through its use, adjudicative fact-finding is reduced to a minimum. It might be said of the Crime Control Model that, when reduced to its barest essentials and operating at its most successful pitch, it offers two possibilities: an administrative fact-finding process leading (1) to exoneration of the suspect, or (2) to the entry of a plea of guilty.

Due Process Values

If the Crime Control Model resembles an assembly line, the Due Process Model looks very much like an obstacle course. Each of its successive stages is designed to present formidable impediments to carrying the accused any further along in the process. Its ideology is not the converse of that underlying the Crime Control Model. It does not rest on the idea that it is not socially desirable to repress crime, although critics of its application have been known to claim so. Its ideology is composed of a complex of ideas, some of them based on judgments about the efficacy of crime control devices, others having to do with quite different considerations. The ideology of due process is far more deeply impressed on the formal structure of the law than is the ideology of crime control; yet an accurate tracing of the strands that make it up is strangely difficult. What follows is only an attempt at an approximation.

The Due Process Model encounters its rival on the Crime Control Model's own ground in respect to the reliability of fact-finding processes. The Crime Control Model, as we have suggested, places heavy reliance on the ability of investigative and prosecutorial officers, acting in an informal setting in which their distinctive skills are given full sway, to elicit and reconstruct a tolerably accurate account of what actually took place in an alleged criminal event. The Due Process Model rejects this premise and substitutes for it a view of informal, nonadjudicative fact-finding that stresses the possibility of error. People are notoriously poor observers of disturbing events—the more emotion-arousing the context, the greater the possibility that recollection will be incorrect; confessions and admissions by persons in police custody may be induced by physical or psychological coercion so that the police end up hearing what the suspect thinks they want to hear rather than the truth; witnesses may be animated by bias or interest that no one would trouble to discover except one specially charged with protecting the interests of the accused (as the police are not). Considerations of this kind all lead to a rejection of informal fact finding processes as definitive of factual guilt and to an insistence on formal, adjudicative, adversary fact-finding processes in which the factual case against the accused is publicly heard by an impartial tribunal and is evaluated only after the accused has had a full opportunity to discredit the case against him. Even then, the distrust of fact-finding processes that animates the Due Process Model is not dissipated. The possibilities of human error being what they are, further scrutiny is necessary, or at least must be available, in case facts have been overlooked or suppressed in the heat of battle. How far this subsequent scrutiny must be available is a hotly controverted issue today. In the pure Due Process Model the answer would be: at least as long as there is an allegation of factual error that has not received an adjudicative hearing in a fact-finding context. The demand for finality is thus very low in the Due Process Model.

This strand of due process ideology is not enough to sustain the model. If all that were at issue between the two models was a series of questions about the reliability of fact-finding processes, we would have but one model of the criminal process, the nature of whose constituent elements would pose questions of fact not of value. Even if the discussion is confined, for the moment, to the question of reliability, it is apparent that more is at stake than simply an evaluation of what kinds of fact-finding processes, alone or in combination, are likely to produce the most nearly reliable results. The stumbling block is this: How much reliability is compatible with efficiency? Granted that informal fact-finding will make some mistakes that can be remedied if backed up by adjudicative fact-finding, the desirability of providing this backup is not affirmed or negated by factual demonstrations or predictions that the increase in reliability will be x percent or x plus n percent. It still remains to ask how much weight is to be given to the competing demands of reliability (a high degree of probability in each case that factual guilt has been accurately determined) and efficiency (expeditious handling of the large numbers of cases that the process ingests). The Crime Control Model is more optimistic about the improbability of error in a significant number of cases; but it is also, though only in part therefore, more tolerant about the amount of error that it will put up with. The Due Process

Model insists on the prevention and elimination of mistakes to the extent possible; the Crime Control Model accepts the probability of mistakes up to the level at which they interfere with the goal of repressing crime, either because too many guilty people are escaping or, more subtly, because general awareness of the unreliability of the process leads to a decrease in the deterrent efficacy of the criminal law. In this view, reliability and efficiency are not polar opposites but rather complementary characteristics. The system is reliable *because* efficient; reliability becomes a matter of independent concern only when it becomes so attenuated as to impair efficiency. All of this the Due Process Model rejects. If efficiency demands shortcuts around reliability, then absolute efficiency must be rejected. The aim of the process is at least as much to protect the factually innocent as it is to convict the factually guilty. It is a little like quality control in industrial technology; tolerable deviation from standard varies with the importance of conformity to standard in the destined uses of the product. The Due Process Model resembles a factory that has to devote a substantial part of its input to quality control. This necessarily cuts down on quantitative output.

All of this is only the beginning of the ideological difference between the two models. The Due Process Model could disclaim any attempt to provide enhanced reliability for the fact-finding process and still produce a set of institutions and processes that would differ sharply from those demanded by the Crime Control Model. Indeed, it may not be too great an oversimplification to assert that in point of historical development the doctrinal pressures emanating from the demands of the Due Process Model have tended to evolve from an original matrix of concern for the maximization of reliability into values quite different and more far-reaching. These values can be expressed in, although not adequately described by, the concept of the primacy of the individual and the complementary concept of limitation on official power.

The combination of stigma and loss of liberty that is embodied in the end result of the criminal process is viewed as being the heaviest deprivation that government can inflict on the individual. Furthermore, the processes that culminate in these highly afflictive sanctions are seen as in themselves coercive, restricting, and demeaning. Power is always subject to abuse—sometimes subtle, other times, as in the criminal process, open and ugly. Precisely because of its potency in subjecting the individual to the coercive power of the state, the criminal process must, in this model, be subjected to controls that prevent it from operating with maximal efficiency. According to this ideology, maximal efficiency means maximal tyranny. And, although no one would assert that minimal efficiency means minimal tyranny, the proponents of the Due Process Model would accept with considerable equanimity a substantial diminution in the efficiency with which the criminal process operates in the interest of preventing official oppression of the individual.

The most modest-seeming but potentially far-reaching mechanism by which the Due Process Model implements these antiauthoritarian values is the doctrine of legal guilt. According to this doctrine, a person is not to be held guilty of a crime merely on a showing that in all probability, based upon reliable evidence, he did factually what he is said to have done. Instead, he is to be held guilty if and only if these factual determinations are made in procedurally regular fashion and by authorities acting within competences duly allocated to them. Furthermore, he is not to be held guilty, even though the factual determination is or might be adverse to him, if various rules designed to protect him and to safeguard the integrity of the process are not given effect: the tribunal that convicts him must have the power to deal with his kind of case ("jurisdiction") and must be geographically appropriate ("venue"); too long a time must not have elapsed since the offense was committed ("statute of limitations"); he must not have been previously convicted or acquitted of the same or a substantially similar offense ("double jeopardy"); he must not fall within a category of persons, such as children or the insane, who are legally immune to conviction ("criminal responsibility"); and so on. None of these requirements has anything to do with the factual question of whether the person did or did not engage in the conduct that is charged as the offense against him; yet favorable answers to any of them will mean that he is legally innocent. Wherever the competence to make adequate factual determination lies, it is apparent that only a tribunal that is aware of these guilt-defeating doctrines and is willing to apply them can be viewed as competent to make determinations of legal guilt. The police and the prosecutors are ruled out by lack of competence, in the first instance, and by lack of assurance of willingness, in the second. Only an impartial tribunal can be trusted to make determinations of legal as opposed to factual guilt.

In this concept of legal guilt lies the explanation for the apparently quixotic presumption of innocence of which we spoke earlier. A man who, after police investigation, is charged with having committed a crime can hardly be said to be presumptively innocent, if what we mean is factual innocence. But if what we mean is that it has yet to be determined if any of the myriad legal doctrines that serve in one way or another the end of limiting official power through the observance of certain substantive and procedural regularities may be appropriately invoked to exculpate the accused man, it is apparent that as a matter of prediction it cannot be said with confidence that more probably than not he will be found guilty.

Beyond the question of predictability this model posits a functional reason for observing the presumption of innocence: by forcing the state to prove its case against the accused in an adjudicative context, the presumption of innocence serves to force into play all the qualifying and disabling doctrines that limit the use of the criminal sanction against the individual, thereby enhancing his opportunity to secure a favorable outcome. In this sense, the presumption of innocence may be seen to operate as a kind of self-fulfilling prophecy. By opening up a procedural situation that permits the successful assertion of defenses having nothing to do with factual guilt, it vindicates the proposition that the factually guilty may nonetheless be legally innocent and should therefore be given a chance to qualify for that kind of treatment.

The possibility of legal innocence is expanded enormously when the criminal process is viewed as the appropriate forum for correcting its own abuses. This notion may well account for a greater amount of the distance between the two models than any other. In theory the Crime Control Model can tolerate rules that forbid illegal arrests, unreasonable searches, coercive interrogations, and the like. What it cannot tolerate is the vindication of those rules in the criminal process itself through the exclusion of evidence illegally obtained or through the reversal of convictions in cases where the criminal process has breached the rules laid down for its observance. And the Due Process Model, although it may in the first instance be addressed to the maintenance of reliable fact-finding techniques, comes eventually to incorporate prophylactic and deterrent rules that result in the release of the factually guilty even in cases in which blotting out the illegality would still leave an adjudicative fact-finder convinced of the accused person's guilt. Only by penalizing errant police and prosecutors within the criminal process itself can adequate pressure be maintained, so the argument runs, to induce conformity with the Due Process Model.

Another strand in the complex of attitudes underlying the Due Process Model is the idea—itself a shorthand statement for a complex of attitudes—of equality. This notion has only recently emerged as an explicit basis for pressing the demands of the Due Process Model, but it appears to represent, at least in its potential, a most powerful norm for influencing official conduct. Stated most starkly, the ideal of equality holds that "there can be no equal justice where the kind of trial a man gets depends on the amount of money he has." The factual predicate underlying this assertion is that there are gross inequalities in the financial means of criminal defendants as a class, that in an adversary system of criminal justice an effective defense is largely a function of the resources that can be mustered on behalf of the accused, and that the very large proportion of criminal defendants who are, operationally speaking, "indigent" will thus be denied an effective defense. This factual premise has been strongly reinforced by recent studies that in turn have been both a cause and an effect of an increasing emphasis upon norms for the criminal process based on the premise.

The norms derived from the premise do not take the form of an insistence upon governmental responsibility to provide literally equal opportunities for all criminal defendants to challenge the process. Rather, they take as their point of departure the notion that the criminal process, initiated as it is by the government and containing as it does the likelihood of severe deprivations at the hands of government, imposes some kind of public obligation to ensure that financial inability does not destroy the capacity of an accused to assert what may be meritorious challenges to the processes being invoked against him. At its most gross, the norm of equality would act to prevent situations in which financial inability forms an absolute barrier to the assertion of a right that is in theory generally available, as where there is a right to appeal that is, however, effectively conditional upon the filing of a trial transcript obtained at the defendant's expense. Beyond this, it may provide the basis for a claim whenever the system theoretically makes some kind of challenge available to an accused who has the means to press it. If, for example, a defendant who is adequately represented has the opportunity to prevent the case against him from coming to the trial stage by forcing the state to its proof in a preliminary hearing, the norm of equality may be invoked to assert that the same kind of opportunity must be available to others as well. In a sense the system, as it functions for the small minority whose resources permit them to exploit all its defensive possibilities, provides a benchmark by which its functioning in all other cases is to be tested: not, perhaps, to guarantee literal identity but rather to provide a measure of whether the process as a whole is recognizably of the same general order. The demands made by a norm of this kind are likely by their very nature to be quite sweeping. Although the norm's imperatives may be initially limited to determining whether in a particular case the accused was injured or prejudiced by his relative inability to make an appropriate challenge, the norm of equality very quickly moves to another level on which the demand is that the process in general be adapted to minimize discriminations rather than that a mere series of post hoc determinations of discriminations be made or makeable.

It should be observed that the impact of the equality norm will vary greatly depending upon the point in time at which it is introduced into a model of the criminal process. If one were starting from scratch to decide how the process ought to work, the norm of equality would have nothing very important to say on such questions as, for example, whether an accused should have the effective assistance of counsel in deciding whether to enter a plea of guilty. One could decide, on quite independent considerations, that it is or is not a good thing to afford that facility to the generality of persons accused of crime. But the impact of the equality norm becomes far greater when it is brought to bear on a process whose contours have already been shaped. If our model of the criminal process affords defendants who are in a financial position to do so the right to consult a lawyer before entering a plea, then the equality norm exerts powerful pressure to provide such an opportunity to all defendants and to regard the failure to do so as a malfunctioning of the process of whose consequences the accused is entitled to be relieved. In a sense, this has been the role of the equality norm in affecting the real-world criminal process. It has made its appearance on the scene comparatively late and has therefore encountered a system in which the relative financial inability of most persons accused of crime results in treatment very different from that accorded the small minority of the financially capable. For this reason, its impact has already been substantial and may be expected to be even more so in the future.

There is a final strand of thought in the Due Process Model that is often ignored but that needs to be candidly faced if thought on the subject is not to be obscured. This is a mood of skepticism about the morality and utility of the criminal sanction, taken either as a whole or in some of its applications. The subject is a large and complicated one, comprehending as it does much of the intellectual history of our times. It is properly the subject of another essay altogether. To put the matter briefly, one cannot improve upon the statement by Professor Paul Bator:

> In summary we are told that the criminal law's notion of just condemnation and punishment is a cruel hypocrisy visited by a smug society on the psychologically and economically crippled; that its premise of a morally autonomous will with at least some measure of choice whether to comply with the values expressed in a penal code is unscientific and outmoded; that its reliance on punishment as an educational and deterrent agent is misplaced, particularly in the case of the very members of society most likely to engage in criminal conduct; and that its failure to provide for individualized and humane rehabilitation of offenders is inhuman and wasteful.[1]

This skepticism, which may be fairly said to be widespread among the most influential and articulate contemporary leaders of informed opinion, leads to an attitude toward the processes of the criminal law that, to quote Mr. Bator again, engenders "a peculiar receptivity toward claims of injustice which arise within the traditional structure of the system itself; fundamental disagreement and unease about the very bases of the criminal law has, inevitably, created acute pressure at least to expand and liberalize those of its processes and doctrines which serve to make more tentative its judgments or limit its power." In short, doubts about the ends for which power is being exercised create pressure to limit the discretion with which that power is exercised.

The point need not be pressed to the extreme of doubts about or rejection of the premises upon which the criminal sanction in general rests. Unease may be stirred simply by reflection on the variety of uses to which the criminal sanction is put and by a judgment that an increasingly large proportion of those uses may represent an unwise invocation of so extreme a sanction. It would be an interesting irony if doubts about the propriety of certain uses of the criminal sanction prove to contribute to a restrictive trend in the criminal process that in the end requires a choice among uses and finally an abandonment of some of the very uses that stirred the original doubts, but for a reason quite unrelated to those doubts.

There are two kinds of problems that need to be dealt with in any model of the criminal process. One is what the rules shall be. The other is how the rules shall be implemented. The second is at least as important as the first, as we shall see time and again in our detailed development of the models. The distinctive difference between the two models is not only in the rules of conduct that they lay down but also in the sanctions that are to be invoked when a claim is presented that the rules have been breached and, no less importantly, in the timing that is permitted or required for the invocation of those sanctions.

As I have already suggested, the Due Process Model locates at least some of the sanctions for breach of the operative rules in the criminal process itself. The relation between these two aspects of the process—the rules and the sanctions for their breach—is a purely formal one unless there is some mechanism for bringing them into play with each other. The hinge between them in the Due Process Model is the availability of legal counsel. This has a double aspect. Many of the rules that the model requires are couched in terms of the availability of counsel to do various things at various stages of the process—this is the conventionally recognized aspect; beyond it, there is a pervasive assumption that counsel is necessary in order to invoke sanctions for breach of any of the rules. The more freely available these sanctions are, the more important is the role of counsel in seeing to it that the sanctions are appropriately invoked. If the process is seen as a series of occasions for checking its own operation, the role of counsel is a much more nearly central one than is the case in a process that is seen as primarily concerned with expeditious determination of factual guilt. And if equality of operation is a governing norm, the availability of counsel is seen as requiring it for all. Of all the controverted aspects of the criminal process, the right to counsel, including the role of government in its provision, is the most dependent on what one's model of the process looks like, and the least susceptible of resolution unless one has confronted the antinomies of the two models.

I do not mean to suggest that questions about the right to counsel disappear if one adopts a model of the process that conforms more or less closely to the Crime Control Model, but only that such questions become absolutely central if one's model moves very far down the spectrum of possibilities toward the pure Due Process Model. The reason for this centrality is to be found in the assumption underlying both models that the process is an adversary one in which the initiative in invoking relevant rules rests primarily on the parties concerned, the state, and the accused. One could construct models that placed central responsibility on adjudicative agents such as committing magistrates and trial judges. And there are, as we shall see, marginal but nonetheless important adjustments in the role of the adjudicative agents that enter into the models with which we are concerned. For present purposes it is enough to say that these adjustments are marginal, that the animating presuppositions that underlie both models in the context of the American criminal system relegate the adjudicative agents to a relatively passive role, and therefore place central importance on the role of counsel.

One last introductory note: . . . What assumptions do we make about the sources of authority to shape the real-world operations of the criminal process? Recognizing that our models are only models, what agencies of government have the power to pick and choose between their competing demands? Once again, the limiting features of the American context come into play. Ours is not a system of legislative supremacy. The distinctively American institution of judicial review exercises a limiting and ultimately a shaping influence on the criminal process. Because the Crime Control Model is basically an affirmative model, emphasizing at every turn the existence and exercise of official power, its validating authority is ultimately legislative (although proximately administrative). Because the Due Process Model is basically a negative model, asserting limits on the nature of official power and on the modes of its exercise, its validating authority is judicial and requires an appeal to supralegislative law, to the law of the Constitution. To the extent that tensions between the two models are resolved by deference to the Due Process Model, the authoritative force at work is the judicial power, working in the distinctively judicial mode of invoking the sanction of nullity. That is at once the strength and the weakness of the Due Process Model: its strength because in our system the appeal to the Constitution provides the last and overriding word; its weakness because saying no in specific cases is an exercise in futility unless there is a general willingness on the part of the officials who operate the process to apply negative prescriptions across the board. It is no accident that statements reinforcing the Due Process Model come from the courts, while at the same time facts denying it are established by the police and prosecutors.

Notes

1. Paul Bator, "Finality in Criminal Law and Federal Habeas Corpus for State Prisoners," *Harvard Law Review* 76 (1963): 441–442.

2

The Politicization of Street Crime:
The Cedar City Experience

Stuart A. Scheingold

Since the mid-1960's street crime has been a "volatile, persistent, and intractable issue in American politics." In public opinion surveys Americans have placed crime as one of the top five issues about which they are most concerned. Many politicians have responded with calls for policies that would "unshackle the police" and incarcerate more offenders. But what has been the impact of increased street crime on local politics? Is "law and order" a successful issue to gain elective office? Perhaps the political will to tackle the problem of street crime is more apparent than real.

James Q. Wilson has argued that the politicization of street crime can be traced to the dramatic increase in crime beginning in the 1960s. Thus for Wilson, politicization attests to the vitality of pluralist democracy in the United States—that is, to political leaders responding to real public grievances (Wilson 1977, pp. 72–73). The findings for "Cedar City," the pseudonymous setting for this research, reveal a much more complex and problematic picture.

First, there was surprisingly little politicization of street crime in Cedar City— although there was substantial politicization of *criminal process.* A corruption scandal in the Cedar City Police Department that implicated the Park County prosecutor had broad political ramifications. So too did racial tensions stemming in part from allegations of racial bias in policing practices as well as in the hiring and promotion of police officers. But street crime, per se, was only modestly and sporadically politicized despite a significant number of efforts to do so throughout the research period.

Second, the patterns of politicization in Cedar City cast serious doubt on the reassuring consensual democratic pluralism that is at the heart of Wilson's analysis. There was not much agreement among political leaders nor within the general public on the politicization of street crime. Politicization campaigns were organized by the Cedar City Police Officers Guild and by small-business interests from the declining neighborhood of Crystal Valley, where some grass roots support was found. Con-

Source: From Stuart A. Scheingold, "The Politicization of Street Crime: The Cedar City Experience," *Studies in Law, Politics, and Society,* Vol. 10, pp. 175–215. Notes, figures, and some tables deleted. Reprinted by permission.

versely, established business and media elites in the downtown core tended to play down the issue. Except for a brief period in the 1970s, the general public was unresponsive to law and order populism, and the most crime-ridden part of the city, the predominately black central area, was clearly hostile. Thus, the political salience of street crime varied along class and race lines and established elites worked effectively against politicization. In Cedar City there was neither consensus nor grass roots democracy when it came to the politics of street crime.

Although it could be argued that these findings have to do with the particularities of Cedar City, this does not seem to be the case. On the one hand, Cedar City was subject to the same kinds of pressures that are generally associated with the politicization of street crime from 1964 to 1980. On the other hand, there are good reasons to question Wilson's consensual democratic pluralist model of politicization and to pay more attention to the role of elites and to divisions within the public.

More specifically, this paper reveals that the key distinction is not between Cedar City and other urban areas but between extensive politicization of street crime at the national level and limited politicization at the local level. This distinction stems from the differing responsibilities for street crime at the two levels of government. At the local level, where politicians and criminal process professionals must deal directly with street crime and with a divided public, politicization tends to create more problems than it resolves. At the national level, where the war on street crime is almost exclusively a symbolic activity uniting "us" against "them," politicization resonates very well with the public and is, thus, a tempting target of opportunity for politicians.

· · ·

The Setting

Cedar City is the major urban center of Park County—a medium-sized metropolitan area with a population of just over one million in the western United States. Cedar City prides itself on its "liveability"—beautiful vistas, easy access to superb four-season recreational opportunities, and a good selection of urban amenities. Despite all of these attributes, Cedar City has a fair share of urban problems with direct relevance to criminal process.

· · ·

It is true that the tensions in Cedar City were rather moderate as compared with the more stratified and strife-ridden cities of the East and the upper Midwest. It is, moreover, likely that these differences might explain variations in politicization from place to place. But on the basis of evidence and argument presented in the concluding section of the paper, it seems reasonable to believe that urban centers in general are heavily influenced by the same moderating forces operative in Cedar City but not in national politics.

Politicization

The politicization of crime is a complex process and not at all easy to describe, let alone to explain. Most simply, to politicize crime is to put it on the political agenda. But what agenda? Political scientists tend to distinguish among different kinds of political agendas—corresponding roughly to how seriously the issue is taken by the polity. Cobb and Elder (1983) contrast the systematic and institutional agendas. The systematic agenda signifies a vague sense of public awareness—to "a general set of political controversies . . . falling within the range of legitimate concerns of the polity." The institutional agenda, on the other hand, is composed of "a set of concrete, specific, items scheduled for active and serious consideration by a particular institutional decision-making body"(p. 14).

This distinction between issues that preoccupy the public in a diffuse fashion and those that present concrete policy proposals is at the heart of the understanding of politicization that will be employed in this paper. *To oversimplify, crime was fairly regularly on the systematic agenda in Cedar City politics during this period but seldom made it to the institutional agenda. Conversely, other criminal process issues, like corruption and racial bias, were seldom on the political agenda at all, but once politicized tended to be taken seriously.*

To dichotomize in this fashion is, however, to miss some important variations, or stages, of politicization. At its most limited, politicization is simply public awareness. Insofar as policy proposals are formulated, politicization reaches a second stage. Once these proposals are taken seriously, politicization has reached its penultimate stage. Finally, election of candidates campaigning on the proposals or acceptance of the proposals by governmental institutions signals the most advanced stage of politicization. Thus, politicization is separate from policy implementation, which may or may not be an objective (Edelman, 1977). *In this paper, the concern is solely with the limited politicization of street crime. . . .*

Politicization and the Public

Research on public policy at the national level reveals the barriers to politicization and also suggests that politicization is an interactive process involving both political leadership and public sentiments. Kingdon (1984) argues, for example, that the political arena is generally well supplied with policy proposals but only a few of them reach the political agenda.

> [T]he proposals that survive to the status of serious consideration meet several criteria, including their technical feasibility, their fit with dominant values and the current national mood, their budgetary workability, and the political support or opposition they might experience (p. 21).

While the public clearly is involved, there is substantial agreement among public policy analysts that political leaders have more to say about what is on the political agenda than does the general public.

Kingdon makes a further distinction between agenda items and realistic alternatives. The former are primarily attributable to *elected* government officials and the latter emerge out of the interplay of organized interest groups (p. 21). The election process forces political leaders to pay some attention to the public's mood and in this way imposes constraints on influential elites. For a number of reasons, however, these limits are rather modest.

The political leaders with whom Kingdon spoke do not, in the first place, look to public opinion polls to assess national mood. Instead, they look to attentive publics with whom they are regularly in contact. Moreover, in their relationships with the general public, political leaders are at least as likely to exert influence as to be influenced. . . .

Note that the media play a role in setting the agenda and in so doing contribute to the attenuation of the public's impact on the process. According to Kingdon, what the media choose to report tends to be taken by political leaders as a reflection of the national mood. Kingdon goes on to argue that media coverage is frequently misleading—exaggerating, for example, the importance of social movements and, thus, conveying a sense of national mood which is not an accurate reflection of public concern. Of course, media attention may in and of itself reshape public sentiments in the manner of a self-fulfilling prophecy (pp. 63, 157).

There are data suggesting that Kingdon's interactive model is directly applicable to the politicization of crime. Skogan and Maxfield's (1981) study of public reactions to crime reveals levels of fear that are much higher than would be suggested by the incidence of crime.

> The substantial disparity between the two frequencies guarantees that direct personal victimization cannot account for much of the overall variation in levels of fear in the general population, although it certainly may be linked to the fears of those who were directly victimized (p. 60).

Both political leaders and the media seem to contribute to this disparity. Gerbner and Gross (1976, pp. 173–198) argue that television leads the public to exaggerate the incidence and the severity of street crime. Skogan and Maxfield (1981) put more emphasis on vicarious victimization:

> [P]ersonal neighborhood communication networks substantially magnify the apparent volume of violence. . . . Like media coverage of crime, the processes which lead victims' stories of their personal experience to "get around" seem to accentuate the apparent volume of personal as opposed to property crime (pp. 157, 155).

Either way, the public's fear of crime and, thus, the raw material of politicization is precariously rooted in erroneous impressions. This all adds up to an anxious and malleable public responsive to political leaders who wish to politicize crime.

Politicization of crime seems to follow an interactive course based on complex relationships among elected officials, influential elites, media messages, and public perceptions. Politicization seems to occur when political leaders, in part taking their cues from the media, choose to play upon public anxieties, which are themselves inflamed by media imagery and vicarious victimization rather than by crime as such. For these and other reasons, it would seem inappropriate to think of politicization of crime as a self-generating public reaction to an increase in victimization as Wilson's analysis suggests.

· · ·

Patterns of Politicization

Given the breadth of the politicization continuum, no single empirical indicator will suffice. At the low end, politicization has to do with public attitudes—a public that is increasingly preoccupied by, and fearful of, crime. At the high end, politicization is expressed in public policy proposals to limit plea bargaining, increase the severity of sentencing, give the police more leeway, and so forth. Somewhere between each end of the continuum are political campaigns in which law and order values are salient. Analysis of politicization will, therefore, be drawn eclectically from two different sources.

In the absence of local public opinion data, newspaper reporting on crime will serve as one indicator of politicization. Content coding will be used to trace variations in the frequency and character of crime reporting. The guiding premise, consonant with the interactive understanding of politicization presented in the previous section, is that newspapers both reflect and influence the political ethos. Content coding also provides a systematic and comprehensive, if indirect, picture of politicization over the seventeen years covered by this research.

Analysis of the frequency and the success of campaigning on crime provides a more direct, but rather episodic indicator, of politicization. A cursory reading of the electoral record could easily lead to the conclusion that street crime was a pervasively prominent political issue during the years from 1964 to 1980. Early signs appeared in 1964 with candidates promising better street lighting as a way to reduce crime and with the establishment of an unofficial "police legislative committee" to introduce a police presence into electoral politics. In 1967, law and order themes surfaced more explicitly—as exemplified by one city council candidate who proposed the following program to "combat" crime violence and immortality:

C   communication between the police department and city hall
O   organization of crime control districts
M   mechanization of the police department for more efficiency
B   budgeting priorities on protection
A   awareness through a campaign to alert the public
T   timing . . . NOW

This militant note was to be struck frequently in subsequent years and as late as 1979 the initiative process was employed in an effort to stiffen felony sentencing. Thus, one could argue that there was considerable politicization of street crime in the years between 1964 and 1980.

But a close look at the events of that period suggests that the politicization of street crime was weak and sporadic. Although attempts to politicize street crime were made, these attempts were relatively infrequent. Moreover, as often as not opposing candidates were able to finesse, rather than join, the issue or the electorate failed to rally to the law and order cause. While law and order candidates were occasionally successful, it never proved possible to build on these victories. Candidates with other issues had more success and more staying power.

At any rate, content analysis of crime reporting and qualitative analysis of campaigning on crime provide two independent measures of politicization and, thus, serve as checks on one another. As it turns out, they yield matching patterns of politicization. At the same time, they reveal distinctive dimensions of the politicization process. Analysis of these patterns and dimensions is a prelude to the search for explanations in subsequent sections.

Crime Reporting

The content analysis of newspaper reporting of crime between 1964 and 1980 provides several different measures of politicization—each representing different points on the continuum between the systematic and institutional agendas. All articles on crime were tabulated and then broken down so as to distinguish:

1. reports of local crime from accounts of crime elsewhere in the country;
2. straight crime-reporting articles that raise policy issues;
3. among policy articles so as to identify those challenging or supporting current practices; and
4. among punitive, due process and/or managerial values promoted by the policy articles.

Local crime was distinguished from crime elsewhere in the country on the assumption that a local focus is suggestive of immediate concern—although still very much at the systematic end of the politicization continuum. To separate out policy articles is, of course, to move toward the institutional end of the continuum. Institutional tendencies are further revealed by looking, respectively, at the intensity of the conflict and the values at stake in the policy debate. In short, the four distinctions are indicative of ascending levels of politicization—or, in other words, movement from the systemic toward the institutional agenda.

According to these data, there is considerable variation between systemic and institutional politicization. Basic crime reporting, the weakest indicator of public concern, peaks most prominently in 1970 with significant but lesser elevations in 1965–1966, 1972, and 1976–1978. Conversely, institutional or policy relevant politicization peaked significantly only in the period 1975–1978—a period in which the articles tended to be increasingly critical and significantly, but not predominately, punitive. Thus, the first finding is that the heightening of vague public concerns occurs more frequently than does policy-relevant politicization. In other words, systematic politicization of street crime is, as might have been expected, more volatile than institutional politicization.

More curious are the variations in the frequency of local and nonlocal crime reporting. While local crime reports fairly consistently outnumbered crime reports from elsewhere in the country, the year-to-year changes tended to run in opposite directions with a clear and puzzling convergence reaching its peak in 1977 when the number of local articles actually dipped below reports from elsewhere in the country. We are thus presented with an anomaly. During the 1975–1978 period when politicization was becoming the most policy-relevant or institutional, the vague and distant messages of crime elsewhere in the country were becoming disproportionately more prominent in local news reporting.

With respect to institutional politicization, per se, further intriguing patterns emerge from the data. There are striking correlations among the policy-relevant indicators. The period from 1975 through 1978 stands out as a time during which policy issues were discussed frequently and critically and during which policy advocacy took on a decidedly punitive caste. Some qualifications to these generalizations are, however, in order. First, there is a modest peaking of policy in the 1968–1970 period—also inflected punitively and critically. Second, even when policy advocacy

T a b l e   1 / **Law and Order Policy Proposals, 1964–1980**

Year	Policy	Yes	No
1964	*Initiative:* to allow local licensing of pinball, punch cards and card games		X*
1966	*Initiative:* to increase police hiring		X
1968	*Legislation:* creating a court of appeals	X	
1970	*Bond Issue:* including a detention and rehabilitation center		X
1974	*Initiative:* to legalize possession of small amounts of marijuana		X*
1975	*Initiative:* mandatory capital punishment	X*	
1976	*Initiative:* antipornography		X
	Initiative: ban on speed traps		X*
1977	*Bond Issue:* new police precinct houses	X*	
	Bond Issue: repair of public safety building		X
	Initiative: direct mayoral appointment of chief of police (without examination)		X*
1978	*Initiative:* antigay		X
	rollback of police shooting policy	X*	

NOTE: *Indicates successful politicization of crime.

was at its most punitive, due process values continued to be strongly represented in criminal justice discourse.

Three generalizations emerge from these findings. First, there are clear and readily identifiable periods of politicization. Second, it seems much easier to get crime on the vague systemic agenda than on the more concrete institutional agenda. In only four years covered by this study was there unequivocal institutional politicization of crime. Third, when politicization occurs, its tone is distinctly critical and punitive—although the debate is hardly one-sided on either count.

These findings also raise some interesting questions. How is the relatively modest degree of politicization to be explained? After all, during a seventeen-year period when law and order seemed to figure prominently in the political ethos, institutional politicization was apparently confined 1975 through 1978. And what is it about that particular period that explains the heightened politicization of street crime? Is there, moreover, any significance to the disproportionate shift from local to nonlocal crime reporting during the four years when politicization peaked?

But before answering these questions, it is important to look at the companion indicator of politicization, campaigning on crime. As has already been suggested, this second indicator provides a rough test of how accurately crime reporting portrays the patterns of politicization. In addition, analysis of campaigning on crime puts us immediately in touch with concrete aspects of politicization.

Campaigning on Crime

There were essentially two avenues to the politicization of street crime. Candidates for public office did sometimes make street crime a campaign issue. . . . A more direct way to advance law and order values was to formulate policy proposals in the legislature or in the form of initiatives and revenue bonds presented to the electorate, as shown in Table 1. Generally speaking, the issue was joined more clearly in the latter than the former, because candidates were frequently evasive. Still in both instances, crude balance sheets can be drawn up and then embellished by narrative detail so as to reveal a nuanced picture of campaigning on crime.

Between 1964 and 1980 policy issues relating to crime arose twelve times— less than one per year. But these summary figures are misleading in a couple of ways. First, these policy proposals were not spread evenly over the period: seven of twelve instances were concentrated in the four years from 1975 through 1978. Second, not all of the questions raised bore directly on street crime. Notice that Table 1 includes bond issues for funding of criminal justice facilities: initiatives connected to the legalization of gambling, the prohibition of pornography, and the decriminalization of marijuana and restrictions on gays, as well as a proposal to create an intermediate court of appeals. These marginal issues were included because they were often attacked or defended in terms of their relationship to street crime—albeit in a partial and indirect fashion. As for hard-core street crime issues, there were only three: (1) increased police hiring (1966), (2) capital punishment (1975), and (3) police shooting policy (1978).

The advocates of law and order had a two-thirds success rate on the three hard core issues. The failure occurred in 1966 when there was insufficient support from the electorate to force the hiring of more police officers. On the other hand, a 1975 initiative requiring capital punishment for those convicted of murder in the first degree passed by a two-to-one margin. And in 1978 an initiative was passed that forced the city council to relax restrictions on police shooting policy. On the marginal matters, the outcomes were more evenly divided.

The same spotty pattern of activity and mixed rate of success applies to candidates who campaigned on crime. . . . On the average, law and order campaigning tended to be concentrated in the period between 1975 and 1978, and law and order candidates were successful about 50 percent of the time.

Clearly, the most avid proponents of politicization would be disappointed by the numbers in the table. Nonetheless, these figures probably exaggerate the extent to which street crime was politicized. Looking beneath the balance sheet to the specifics of campaigning on crime suggests that the politicization of crime was both ephemeral and idiosyncratic. It was ephemeral in that it was largely confined to a brief period in the latter part of the 1970s. It was idiosyncratic in that it seemed to be heavily based on personality and contingent circumstances.

Consider, first, the entry of rank and file police officers into electoral politics. While several tried for office, the records of three presidents of the Cedar City Police Officers Guild are most instructive, given the pivotal role of the guild in efforts to politicize street crime. When Mark Victor stepped down as guild president and was elected to the city council in 1969, it looked as if police candidates might prosper in electoral politics. Victor was the driving force behind the guild's Political Action Committee and he quickly became a person of influence on the council and in city politics. His reelection to the council in 1973 emboldened him to enter the mayoral race in 1977, but he failed even to secure enough votes in the primary to make the runoff election. After failing in an attempt to get back on the council in 1978, Victor left politics and entered private business.

Only at the end of the period did two other guild presidents try their hands at politics, and their records are instructive. One of them, Donald Martin, was twice unsuccessful in his effort to gain a seat on the city council—despite support from business and trade union groups as well as the guild and others associated with law and order values. In contrast, Wayne Michaels was elected to the state legislature in 1980. However, his own view was that it was more his childhood roots in the legislative district and his fiscal conservatism than his image as a police officer that accounted for his success. He also claimed that he was much less dependent on the work of fellow police officers than was Martin. In any case, election to the legislature did not require a city wide constituency and, thus, is not a particularly good indicator of the politicization of street crime in Cedar City.

The record of Park County prosecutorial races is also instructive. On two of three occasions, law and order candidates lost, and the single law and order victory was in 1978 during the peak period of politicization. In 1970 the law and order campaign of the machine incumbent, Dana Phillips, was largely irrelevant in a primary won by reformer Whitney Steele. The basic issue was the police payoff scandal, which cast a shadow over the prosecutor's office. Steele went on to win the general election in a close race against his Democratic rival. Four years later, this same Democrat tried to close the gap with a law and order campaign, but Steele won handily. That campaign was, nonetheless, a learning experience for Steele, who sensed a shift in the public mood, changed his policies, and began to build a law and order image— in part, because he anticipated a run for the governorship. Thus, the 1978 law and order victory of Tony Jefferson, a key Steele aide, would seem to be indicative of an earlier change in the political climate—providing further confirmation of 1975–1978 as a period of heightened politicization (for details, see Scheingold and Gressett 1987, pp. 483–491).

But even this high point of politicization cannot be taken at face value. Consider the signal event of that period: the electoral defeat of two liberal incumbent judges in 1976. These two judges had been targeted by a coalition of law and order groups led by the Cedar City Police Guild, which had also handpicked the successful challengers. Defeat of two incumbent judges was taken by both their friends and foes as an unequivocal sign of politicization. In retrospect, however, there may have been less there than met the eye. In the first place, only two of five judges targeted by the law and order coalition were defeated. Moreover, these two chose to make the election into a plebiscite on the liberal reforms that they favored, thus contributing to politicization. Finally, there seems to have been an undercurrent of anti-Semitism against the defeated incumbents who each had clearly Jewish names. In any case, there was no superior court follow-up and, indeed, one of the defeated incumbents was subsequently appointed to the state court of appeals where he sat until his retirement with the man who defeated his liberal colleague in the 1976 election (for details, see Scheingold and Gressett 1987, pp. 494–500).

The other notable successes of politicization were the two initiative campaigns already mentioned. In 1975, the electorate responded enthusiastically and positively to a capital punishment proposal. And in 1978, the police guild led a successful fight against restrictions that the city council had placed on police use of firearms. Both of these victories are certainly indicative of successful politicization. The capital punishment issue was pretty straightforward and suggested that the Cedar City electorate was in 1975 in tune with the punitive values of the broader American public, 60 percent of whom were favorably disposed to capital punishment for those convicted of murder.

The initiative on police shooting policy is still more suggestive of effective politicization. Police shootings had been an issue in Cedar City at least since 1971 when a young black man was shot while allegedly placing a bomb outside a postal substation. Although the coroner's jury held that there were grounds for pressing charges against the police officer who had fired the fatal shots, the prosecuting attorney took no action. Through the years, there were other instances of questionable police shootings—ordinarily involving blacks—and a variety of relevant proposals emerged for review boards, for the exclusion of hollow-point bullets, and so forth. It was not, however, until 1977 that the city council acted. The council's ordinance restricted the use of deadly force to situations in which police officers were defending themselves or others in imminent danger or apprehending an armed or violent suspect. Don Martin, then president of the police guild, organized the initiative campaign that successfully and significantly relaxed these restrictions—thus, directly rebuking the city council.

But once again, there is a kind of hollow quality to these victories. Don Martin was, for example, unable to parlay his instrumental role in the initiative campaign into a seat on the city council even though his opponent, a minority woman, supported the council's more restrictive ordinance. Recall also that the 1979 initiative campaign to compel judges to give prison sentences under certain circumstances did not merely fail to gain voter approval, it could not even attract enough signatures to get on the ballot. The initiative campaigns, therefore, provide yet another instance of episodic politicization with little or no generative momentum.

The crime reporting and the campaign data present consistent and puzzling pictures of the politicization of street crime. The clearest common chord is the concentration of politicization in the 1975–1978 period. Roughly two-thirds of the endorsements occurred during this period, as did twelve of the nineteen victories by law and order endorsees. This was also the period of peak activity with respect to initiatives and referenda. Another common chord is the equivocal quality of politicization. That is to say, only in the 1975–1979 period did crime reporting take on a clear policy caste—and even then the focus seemed to shift toward distant nonlocal matters.

And yet it would be an overstatement to dismiss street crime altogether as a salient issue. There was, of course, at least one four-year period when street crime was fairly successfully politicized—albeit with mixed results. More broadly, even though campaigning on street crime was seldom successful, the tone of political discourse did shift in a distinctly law and order direction during seventeen years covered in this research. Consider, for example, the increasing level of controversy in crime reporting. Moreover, even candidates who did not campaign on crime were generally careful not to appear unconcerned or soft on the issue. Consequently, due process proposals and candidates became relatively rare in the later 1970s and did not fare very well. Street crime is, therefore, best seen as a latent, rather than a manifest, issue, which cast a significant shadow across the political arena.

But however these patterns of politicization are characterized, they pose two broad questions. How is the relatively limited politicization of the 1964–1980 period to be explained? What is it about the 1975–1978 period that led to the disproportionate politicization during those four years? . . .

Public Quiescence

A major obstacle to politicization of street crime was widespread public apathy on the issue. Interviews with Cedar City political leaders revealed very little grass roots pressure with respect to street crime. As we shall see, prominent politicians seemed virtually oblivious to the issue and/or inflected it in ways that were not consistent with a sense of public urgency. Of course, the politicization data indicate that the public was not at all times apathetic. There were periods from the late 1960s to the late 1970s when the public was sufficiently responsive to make campaigning on crime a viable option. Moreover, as we shall see below, there were also constituencies in Cedar City that were more or less continuously preoccupied with crime. The objectives of this section will be to explore and explain the rather modest level of public concern about street crime.

It has already been suggested that the general rule of public apathy on street crime and the exceptions to it can be best understood by thinking about street crime as a latent rather than a manifest public concern. While the public seems to have a real and continuing fear of street crime, this fear is normally politically dormant. Accordingly, there was relatively little pressure on candidates to campaign on crime and ordinarily relatively little response to those who did. This seems to be the basic message of the Cedar City interviews that will be considered in the first portion of this section.

But to think of public concerns about street crime as latent raises two further questions. Why is it that during a period when the public's fear of crime was rather steadily increasing, street crime turned out to be such an ephemeral issue? And what about the exceptions to the general rule—the occasions when the public was sufficiently aroused to put street crime on the institutional or the systematic agenda? . . .

Street Crime as a Latent Concern

Street crime was sufficiently beside the point that it was difficult to get political leaders to address it directly in interviews. Consider, for example, the parallel patterns of response of two city council persons when asked to talk about the issue. There was, in the first place, an inclination to confuse street crime with the "tolerance policy"—that is, with the corruption scandal that rocked the city in the late 1960s.

> The concern is always up here, I think the tolerance policy hit us.
> It was always a challenge to the Chief of Police to keep organized crime out of Cedar City.

Once the focus on street crime was finally established, there was a tendency to personalize the issue rather than to think in terms of constituency pressures.

> The worst thing that happened was the other night. I had been out to a meeting. I came home and still had not hung my coat up. I was sitting there with my coat talking to my husband about midnight and somebody tries to break into the house. He [the police chief] probably gave me (his place of business) more than average attention . . . not to the point of patronage.

Finally, when pressed, both council persons make pro forma declarations lacking in conviction and hardly suggestive of an inclination to politicize street crime.

> I am not insensitive to it. I want to put it that way. We did have our law and justice issues that we got into.
> I have a great burden for the people who get robbed, who are mugged, storekeepers.

While this precise pattern was not repeated by other respondents, the low salience of street crime was consistently confirmed in a variety of ways.

Consider the rather oblique way another member of the council came to include street crime as an issue in his unsuccessful mayoral bid. The issue emerged from a kind of random search for targets of opportunity. One staff member who participated in the process described it as follows:

> One issue was bad checks. He wanted to make it a crime to knowingly—because of businessmen not being able to get enforcement against bad check writers—write more than three bad checks or something like that. And he ran into a wall, so he didn't get anywhere with that. . . . And of course he made a lot of noise about community crime-prevention programs. . . . We came up with something new every two or three days. I spent a lot of time doing basically PR work. A lot of my job was just thinking up ideas and coming up with press releases. This was maybe nine months or a year before the election and just trying to get his name in the paper as much as possible. So you would see those things—like zoos do. That's where you'd sell the elephant dung [for commercial purposes].

Presumably "zoo do" had less to contribute to a coherent campaign image than crime. But when asked what led the candidate to campaign on crime, the staffer was in some considerable doubt.

> I don't know why. Probably because he was a liberal and wanted to bolster his conservative support. . . . He takes positions for consciously political reasons quite a lot. . . . I think he was to come up with things that were—I think he was looking for ways to get a portion of the vote that responds. *Even though it's small,* there is that portion of the vote. And I think he was looking for ways to get it (emphasis added).

In other words, crime was not chosen because it was perceived as an issue of major public concern but because it served as a conservative litmus test and might provide access to a small slice of the electorate.

Even Mark Victor, the first police guild activist to seek public office, tended to steer clear of street crime as a priority issue. It is hardly surprising, therefore, that his relationships with his erstwhile associates on the guild tended to be rather cool.

> Mark did help us a lot because he came from us and he had another viewpoint in his vote. However, the presidents who followed him, in my estimation, had ego problems, and they thought it was beneath them to go to Mr. Victor. They thought Mr. Victor should come to them. So there really was not a close tie with Victor's office. . . . So a lot of members are bitter about Victor and he blames the guild.

It would thus appear that Victor continued to identify with, and speak on behalf of, law and order values. But he also seemed to keep the guild at arms' length in an effort to broaden his base of support. This once again is suggestive of the political marginality of street crime.

The most notable exception to this rule was George Walker, a longtime council member who represented the predominately black area of the city. By the time of our interview in 1983, Walker felt less pressure, but he could clearly recall when street crime was a priority problem for his constituents.

> They don't hammer away on it anymore; they have almost given up on the fact that it's going to get any better. . . . Nobody basically jumps on me anymore. . . . At this time it doesn't come up any more than any other issue, like land use. . . . There was a time that was the primary thing that came up in the early years. From the time I came on the council [1967] until we got out past the police corruption to the latter part of the Bass administration [1977]. It's gotten back to where it's just another issue like everything else now. It's not because the crime is dropping off, it's because we've sort of woke up to living in the period we are in.

Because there was a high level of concern about street crime among blacks, Walker came to the council determined to take on justice issues, but not as a law and order advocate. Instead, he saw himself as a "buffer between the police and the black community which were increasingly at each other's throat." He was, in short, less concerned with politicizing street crime than with politicizing the racial bias of policing.

The conclusion to be drawn from all of this is that street crime was consistently a *manifest issue* for only small portions of the public. This simple truth was driven home to candidates who tried unsuccessfully to build citywide law and order constituencies. For the broader public, street crime seems to have been a latent issue— perhaps a real and continuing fear but one that came to the surface only occasionally.

The Social Construction of Victimization

It is tempting, but inadequate, to explain these patterns of public response to street crime in terms of victimization. It seems to follow, for example, that blacks are preoccupied with street crime because they tend to be disproportionately victimized. Moreover, the core of the law and order constituency seems to have been drawn from Crystal Valley, another relatively high-crime area of Cedar City. But the Cedar City data as well as research elsewhere suggest that victimization is not as good a predictor of politicization as race and other socioeconomic variables.

National surveys on the fear of crime in the 1960s and 1970s regularly revealed discontinuities between victimization and reactions to it. Blacks were, for example, more victimized, more fearful, but less punitive. Women, in contrast, were less victimized, more frightened, and less punitive. Finally, the most punitive group in the American society, according to the work of Arthur Stinchcombe and his associates, was comprised of rural white males who were less victimized and less fearful. Thus, victimization provides neither a necessary nor a sufficient explanation for the kind of punitive politicization of crime associated with the politics of law and order.

Cedar City findings are compatible with these national patterns. If victimization were the key to public arousal, it would seem to follow that the crime rate would help explain the variations in crime reporting in the 1960s and 1970s, but this is not the case. There was only a weak, albeit a statistically significant, relationship between the national crime rate and national crime reporting. Indeed, a simple time trend was a somewhat better predictor of crime reporting than was the crime rate. And there was no significant relationship between the crime rate and the number of articles about crime at the local level. In other words, news reporting and the public sentiments associated with it seem to have a life of their own—quite distinct from the actual incidence of crime.

Still more revealing are the patterns of politicization in two key Cedar City neighborhoods. Both Crystal Valley and the central area are relatively high-crime areas. But the two neighborhoods are polar opposites on politicization issues. Crystal Valley, the less victimized of the two, supported initiatives which, respectively, brought a return to capital punishment and relaxed the city council's restrictions on police shooting policy. The more heavily victimized central area, in contrast, rejected the two initiatives. These data, thus indicate that it is not victimization, per se, but how that victimization is construed that determines the course of politicization.

[How do we] understand why street crime was construed differently in the two neighborhoods? The explanation is relatively simple for the central area. Law and order proposals forced a choice between controlling the police and controlling crime, and the predominately black central area was apparently more worried about racial bias in criminal process than about street crime. Certainly, this was the view of black political leaders.

The reverse seems to have been true in the Crystal Valley, although the picture seems a good deal more complex. Crystal Valley in the 1970s was a neighborhood in transition with a poverty rate that was rising faster than the citywide average and an increasing influx of blacks whose numbers doubled during the 1970s. In all probability the residents of Crystal Valley associated increasing crime and economic decline with the growing black presence in their neighborhood. Thus, law and order values drew sustenance from racial hostility and social crisis.

· · ·

This section has begun the process of explaining the modest extent of politicization in Cedar City during the high-crime years of the late 1960s and 1970s. In the first place, the Crystal Valley and central-area data suggest that the "natural constituency" for politicization, those people most victimized, was divided. More specifically, blacks were diverted from law and order populism by their fears of racial bias in criminal process and by the antiblack overtones of the law and order ethos. Conversely, for most of the residents of Cedar City, most of the time, street crime was at best a latent rather than a manifest issue. The average person in Cedar City just did not seem to think about street crime in political terms.

While this second finding adds to our understanding of the weakness of the politicization impulse, it begs the underlying question that will be considered in the next two sections. How are we to account for political quiescence on an issue about which there seems to be such strong feelings? The interactive model of politicization presented at the outset of this paper suggests that political leaders both shape and reflect public attitudes. If so, given latent public concerns about crime, there is reason to believe that committed elites could have effectively mounted a symbolic crusade on behalf of law and order values. In Cedar City, however, the established elites of the city were opposed to politicization while the leaders of the law and order campaign were relatively weak and marginalized.

The Law and Order Coalition

The politicization campaign was led by the police guild and some small-business interests in Crystal Valley. Occasionally, it was possible to work effectively on behalf of law and order values. In general, however, the law and order coalition, with limited resources, was simply no match for the established civic elites who worked together with the leadership of the black community to neutralize efforts to politicize street crime.

The Cedar City Police Guild

The guild's interest in politics was fueled during the 1970s by two different kinds of frustrations. The rank and file felt that they were not getting their fair share when it came to pay and working conditions. More generally, they felt that their status was under assault from a number of quarters. The bitterness on these two fronts allowed the new guild leadership to gain significant support from the membership for political action directed at enhancing police prestige and at improving wages and working conditions.

On the other hand, guild leaders had to contend with both apathy and resistance from the rank and file. In part, the problem was the free-rider tendencies that plague most organizations. Another problem was rooted in priorities. Although there is no reason to doubt the membership's acceptance of law and order values, only on the bread and butter issues directly related to wages and working conditions was consistent politicization of the rank and file possible. Finally, Cedar City police officers harbored the typical police distaste for politics and politicians and were thus reluctant to get involved in political action.

Politics tends to be a dirty word for police officers in Cedar City, as it is elsewhere. This basic distrust of politics is rooted in the firmly held belief that politics poses a dual threat to police professionalism. First, politicians are seen as outsiders intent on pandering to the public or doing favors for the influential. This congenital inclination of elected officials to curry favor is seen at the very least to interfere with even-handed law enforcement and, in the worst-case scenario, to deteriorate into full-scale corruption. Second, politicians are perceived as amateurs who, leaving aside their questionable probity, simply do not understand law enforcement.

Cedar City police officers were particularly sensitive to the links between politics and corruption because of the widespread police payoff system that was exposed toward the end of the 1960s. None of the respondents denied that corruption was pervasive, but they traced it, as well as its prejudicial exposure, to perfidious politicians who had introduced a "tolerance policy"—that is, a policy of selective enforcement of vice laws. . . . In other words, politicians without the courage to live by their own vice laws, whether for personal profit or campaign support, planted the seeds of corruption. Then, in an effort to escape personal responsibility for the inevitable consequences of their own policy, [they] scapegoated the police department.

The exposure of corruption had a terrific impact on the department. Its leadership was decimated, its public image shattered, and its membership wracked by conflict and recrimination. As the police saw it, both innocent and guilty officers suffered. . . . To make matters worse, the police were convinced that politicians, most notably County Prosecuting Attorney Phillips, were directly implicated in the payoff system and yet were escaping largely unscathed.

It was during this period that the guild's first unfortunate foray into politics occurred. The guild leadership, without consulting the membership, broke with a tradition of electoral neutrality to support, of all people, incumbent prosecutor Phillips when he ran for reelection in 1970. Needless to say, the rank and file guild members felt further compromised by this unilateral decision, which openly linked the department to a politician who was directly associated with the tolerance policy but seemed to be evading responsibility for its corrupting consequences. In any case, this episode further soured rank and file police officers on politics.

This residual political cynicism dogged the reform elements that took over the guild in the wake of the corruption scandal. Moreover, the members' distrust of politicians tended to extend to their own leaders whom they feared were using their guild office as a stepping-stone. Of course, Mark Victor, a prime mover in the efforts to politicize police grievances, did capitalize on his high visibility to gain election to the city council, and as we have already seen in the third section, Victor's subsequent relations with the guild were apparently not very smooth.

In addition, guild politics, like politics in general, was hardly pure, and sometimes it was deemed necessary to work with organizations that were suspect.

> We had organizations come to us that we didn't necessarily agree with their philosophy and what they did but they came to us for their own reasons and if the situation fit we'd work with them.

Thus, the guild allied with the A.C.L.U. in fighting against mandatory polygraph testing and apparently had at least tangential relations with radical right organizations. [As one guild activist put it:]

> While I viewed our position as a moderate to conservative effort, I met with some people that were so damned far out, right-wing conservative, they scared me more than the left-wing liberal-type people. God they were scary. . . . I want nothing to do with these kinds of people. They were some really scary people, vigilante types almost.

What was true of organizations was also true of candidates.

> If you have Candidate One who has such a strong political base and . . . it's obvious from the backing he has or the money behind his campaign . . . he is going to win this election hands down. As opposed to his opponent, Candidate Two, who may be a highly motivated, extremely honest, desirable candidate, one that you might personally favor. But this is a key position . . . you know for a fact that he won't win. You probably as a responsible group will actually go for Candidate One, however reluctantly, because at least you'll have the door open to that candidate.

Of course, even if the members accept that kind of logic and the endorsements that flow from it, it does not follow that they will have much enthusiasm or they will participate very actively.

Even insofar as the rank and file were sympathetic to the objectives and methods of the guild leadership, it was difficult to generate the kind of energy required for effective campaigning. A certain amount of political activity was possible without the participation of the rank and file. Ad hoc endorsements of candidates, for example, put very modest demands on organizational resources. Consider the guild's Saturday screening sessions in which candidates were questioned by a membership committee. Obviously, a relatively small group of politically committed members could bear this burden.

While endorsements were the easiest way to go, what the candidates really looked for were campaign workers who would assemble and distribute lawn signs, collect money, ring doorbells, and otherwise carry the message to the voters.

> You don't really have to do very much for each candidate to have that open door because they appreciate so much whatever they get. They need that free labor. We have the potential. A thousand members. If only a few were active, we'd be heroes.

But the membership was difficult to activate.

Like most people, police officers are reluctant to devote their free time to such work. Thus, it was particularly difficult to sustain political activity over an extended period of time—as was required, for example, from a plan for continuous monitoring of judges:

> Not when it's an everyday thing. It was another job. Another piece of paper to be filled out. And they do that all day long.

It was also difficult to turn out election workers on behalf of candidates espousing law and order values, even when these candidates were guild members. And unlike fire fighters who, according to the police, have time while on duty to assemble signs and stuff envelopes, only off-duty time is available to the guild Political Action Committee.

Adding to the reluctance of police to actively campaign was their embarrassment at having to approach strangers. The irony did not escape guild activists.

> Now here is an officer who deals with strangers all day long. Knock on the door and give a 30-second spiel. It really embarrasses them. They don't want to be confronted. They don't want to be asked hard questions. They don't want to be embarrassed. And they're not in control. On the street they're in control. It's a whole new world.

As a result, the "vast majority" of police officers would rather give money than doorbell a neighborhood. And while some could be enlisted, even with those "you have to ask each one individually. You have to lead them by the hand. You have to organize the project and lay it all out for them. It's a tremendous job with a lot of disappointments."

Crystal Valley Activism

More than any other researcher, James Q. Wilson has provided insight into the populist sentiments that have given rise to the politics of law and order. As Wilson sees it, order maintenance is distinct from but intimately related to crime control:

> A stable neighborhood of families who care for their homes, mind each other's children, and confidently frown on unwarranted intruders can change in a few years, or even a few months, to an inhospitable and frightening jungle. A piece of property

is abandoned, weeds grow up, a window is smashed. Adults stop scolding rowdy children; the children, emboldened, become more rowdy. Families move out, unmarried adults move in. Teenagers gather in front of the corner store. The merchant asks them to move; they refuse. Fights occur. Litter accumulates. People start drinking in front of the grocery; in time, an inebriate slumps to the sidewalk and is allowed to sleep it off. Pedestrians are approached by panhandlers.

At this point it is not inevitable that serious crime will flourish or violent attacks on strangers will occur. But many residents will think that crime, especially violent crime, is on the rise, and they will modify their behavior accordingly (Wilson 1985, pp. 78–79).

Irrespective of the empirical validity of Wilson's claim, a setting in which the public feels itself threatened by a diffuse and synergistic combination of disorder and crime is conducive to a politics of law and order.

This certainly seems to have been the case in Cedar City. The police guild found its organized support primarily in troubled residential–commercial neighborhoods. The analysis of one police guild activist reads like a paraphrase of Wilson.

People in the Crystal Valley . . . were literally being put out of business. The whole area was undergoing a transformation, but it was accelerated by the fact that several neighborhood groups . . . literally ran in packs out there and the Park County judges as a group simply adopted release policies that you put them in jail and within a matter of hours they're back on the street even for very serious crimes. . . . And the sentencing of those people and particularly their early release . . . led community leaders such as Betty Sawyer, who was a real estate agent in that area and candidly whose livelihood, now this is my opinion . . . if the area is allowed to go to pot, the property values drop and the business just isn't there.

In other words, small-business persons, whose economic interests and social status were directly threatened, took the lead in mobilizing locals to support and to participate in a variety of law and order programs.

For the most part, the law and order activism involved seemingly ad hoc efforts organized for particular purposes—for example, the Redwood Merchant Patrol, a Guardian Angel–like undertaking to reassure shoppers during the Christmas season; Help Eliminate Lawless Protesting (H.E.L.P.), apparently put together by a maverick downtown businessman with the covert help of dissident police officers—with the objective of unleashing the police against anti-Vietnam War protestors; Family and Friends of Missing Persons and Victims of Violent Crimes, which supported a 1975 capital punishment initiative that was accepted by the electorate, and the Civic Builders who campaigned unsuccessfully against two council members who had not been sufficiently sympathetic to the Cedar City Police Department.

Amidst this welter of ephemeral activity, only the business persons of the Crystal Valley seem to have provided the police guild with a reasonably constant ally. Sometimes presenting themselves as the Crystal Business Club and at other times as the Crystal Valley Chamber of Commerce, this group got underway in 1969. At that time, its president, Sheldon Plumber, addressed the Public Safety Committee of the Cedar City Council and complained about rising crime in general and the recent murder of a local grocer in particular. Plumber warned the council that a recent community meeting had talked of vigilante action and complained about council restrictions on the police and about the sentencing practices of judges. More specifically, he asked that restrictions be lifted on a police practice of photographing juveniles:

> Why cannot police be trusted to use their own judgement? We have here a classic example of concern for criminal sensibilities over the welfare of society.

Plumber also voiced his oppostion to lenient sentencing practices:

> It is a form of madness to turn loose a criminal with two or three previous convictions (on the 10th or 20th offence) after a short confinement. . . . We must fairly face the failure of our present parole and rehabilitation practices.

Five years later, these same Crystal Valley business persons repeated their objections to rehabilitation and, under the aegis of chamber of commerce President Betty Sawyer, oranized a "court watchers" program to monitor the sentencing practices of Park County Superior Court judges. As a columnist for the *Cedar City Tribune* put it:

> Some groups or individuals have been content to gripe about the crime situation but the Crystal Valley Chamber decided to do something about it.

The court watchers established an insistent presence, although there is no way to know how much of an impact they had on sentencing practices. Subsequently the Crystal Valley Chamber joined with several other law and order groups to put together a Courtwatch Coalition, which together with the police guild played a leading role in the successful effort to unseat two liberal judges.

The essential message of this section is that the law and order coalition was not very strong. Neither guild leadership nor the Crystal Valley business persons had significant financial capabilities or ready access to the mass media. They were both heavily dependent on the enthusiasm and commitment of volunteers who could rise to the occasion only from time to time. Crystal Valley court watchers did, for example, establish a meaningful presence in Park County courtrooms toward the end of the 1970s. The guild rank and file, for its part, was now and then mobilized—most notably in the successful efforts to relax restrictions on the use of firearms by the police and to unseat the two liberal judges who had shown little sympathy or respect for the police. But these volunteers could not be counted upon to provide the strong and consistent support required for effective politicization.

Containing Politicization

The intrinsic limitations of the law and order coalition stood in stark contrast to the formidable opposition to politicization. The core of this opposition was comprised of local government officials, corporate executives, and leading professionals who had strong incentives for promoting a salubrious image of downtown Cedar City. They were joined by the leaders and community groups representing central-area blacks who, of course, had other reasons for rejecting the politics of law and order. Under the circumstances, it is hardly surprising that the opponents usually had sufficient political clout to divert, co-opt or simply defeat the politicization of street crime.

Established Elites

For three distinct reasons, established elites resisted efforts to politicize street crime. It was, in the first place, conventional practice in Cedar City to avoid highly charged electoral campaigns. As attorney Austin Sedley, who worked in both the city council and the mayor's office during the 1970s, put it:

> [T]his is such a conservative city in a certain way.... Politicians don't attack each other directly and when they do they get in trouble. You're only supposed to talk about yourself and perhaps the issues—but no *ad hominum* at all. And you're not supposed to be incendiary. And if you are, the *Cedar City Tribune* just gets after you. So campaigns are low key.

Secondly, the downtown elites were civic boosters with a promotional program of their own. To portray Cedar City as crime-ridden was hardly consistent with this program or with efforts to woo shoppers from suburban malls and conventions from other cities. Thirdly, street crime was a racially divisive issue and once blacks became an electoral force with a distinctive anti crime agenda, the politicization of street crime became an increasingly risky strategy.

Accordingly, the established elites put most of their energies into their own long-term Campaign for Civic Excellence in which crime took a backseat to a variety of civic improvements. The campaign, begun in 1966, proposed a series of bond issues, first in 1968 and again in 1970, for such things as mass transit, a new stadium, parks and recreation, low-income housing, improved sewage systems, highways, and so forth. The 1970 bonds did include funding for construction of crime-related facilities— albeit with a rehabilitative rather than a law and order, bias.

There were also both positive and negative ways in which the established elites refocused attention and energy from the politicization of street crime to the Campaign for Civic Excellence. On the one hand, the elite supported a Community Crime Prevention Council (C.C.P.C.) that created twenty-two community councils throughout the city. On the other hand, they withheld support from candidates who were inclined to politicize crime. As attorney Austin Sedley saw things:

> [I]t's a lot easier to go out there and positively be an advocate for the neighborhoods and in connection with that you can certainly advocate a community crime prevention program. That's great and they have had a lot of support. But to charge that somebody is soft on crime is not a nice thing to say about somebody and it's probably not true. So I think it has to do with the nature of politics in this town.

Thus, the Community Crime Prevention Council, while not particularly successful, did provide a noncontroversial alternative to more radical law and order proposals to empower the police and constrain the judges. Tensions with the police department were in part a result of the refusal of the C.C.P.C. to adopt a hard line on crime. As for candidates intent on politicizing street crime, they were unable to get the endorsement of the established elite's Good Government League. More informally, the liberal judicial incumbents in the 1976 election were admonished to evade rather than respond to law and order charges, and the conservatives who defeated them were not readily accepted into the establishment.

The newspaper data reported earlier also sheds some light on the containment of crime as a political issue. It will be recalled that as politicization reached its peak in the 1975-to-1978 period, the proportion of local crime reporting decreased to the point where it actually fell beneath reports of crime elsewhere in the country. There is no way of knowing whether this was intentional or not, but the diversion of public attention from the immediate street crime problems of Cedar City was surely consistent with the depoliticization objectives of the established elites.

Central Area Blacks

The street crime concerns of central area blacks were, as we have seen, expressed in the priority given to public safety issues by George Walker, the black member on the city council. Community groups also regularly spoke out on criminal justice issues. But, of course, black distrust of the police put them at odds with the law and order coalition. For blacks, police reform was the necessary precondition to effective police service and this took initial precedence over crime control, as such.

Consequently, the black community was seriously out of step with politicized whites on the street crime issue. Recall that street crime did not become a significantly salient issue in Cedar City until roughly 1975, but according to Walker it was the "primary thing" for blacks from the late 1960s into the late 1970s. Thus, just as the rest of the community was turning on to street crime, blacks seemed to be turning off. More specifically, black leaders opposed the capital punishment initiative, which was at the expressive core of the politicization campaign. And throughout the period, blacks complained about the police who were, of course, the spiritual and organizational leaders of the law and order coalition. As early as 1969, the Negro Voters League met with the mayor and asked him to replace the chief of police. Blacks were also among the earliest proponents of citizen participation in the struggle against crime. Finally, blacks supported and/or initiated proposals for giving the community a voice in police disciplinary proceedings dealing with excessive force and other harassment of citizens.

As it turned out, black concerns with fairness and citizen participation were much more influential than the law and order values associated with the politicization of crime—except, perhaps in the 1975–1978 period. This was, in part, because Walker and some other black leaders were willing to play the kind of mediative role that was consistent with the concerns of the established elites. In addition, black votes were crucial to the two mayors who governed the city throughout the 1970s. Consider, for example, the departure of a law and order police chief, Dale Stalker, who was a hero to hard-line rank and file police officers but had a reputation for being unresponsive, even hostile, to the black community. His successor, Charlie Scobel, was chosen primarily because there was no doubt that he would comply more readily with Mayor Berger's wishes than his independent predecessor but also because he got along well with blacks. As one of Berger's senior staffers put it:

> If it hadn't been for Berger's support in the black area, he wouldn't have been mayor and Scobel wouldn't have been chief.

The reforms begun by Berger and Scobel were taken up and extended by their successors, Tim Godwin and Joseph Haley, who established police discipline as a priority issue and also created an effective program of affirmative action hiring and promotion. As a consequence, police–community relations improved dramatically throughout the course of the 1970s.

The balance of political power in Cedar City clearly ran against politicization. The law and order coaltion, working on its own, was seldom strong enough or sufficiently savvy to mobilize latent public fears of crime. Nor was the coalition in a postion to reach out to blacks or to gain the acceptance of established elites. Blacks, although genuinely concerned about street crime, felt themselves threatened by the policies and values of the law and order coalition—especially the pro-police and pro–capital punishment proposals. Established elites were loath to portray Cedar City as a crime-ravaged city and preferred the kind of low-key approach to crime control that precluded politicization.

Conclusions

The sporadic success of efforts to politicize street crime in Cedar City can be traced to two major obstacles. First, support for politicization among the general public seems to have been fragmented, lukewarm, and latent. Second, there seems to have been a tacit agreement among community leaders not to exploit latent opportunities.

It might seem that these findings are idiosyncratic, telling us more about the peculiarities of Cedar City than about the politicization of street crime. Certainly, each setting is special and it is important to be sensitive to the particularities of Cedar City. But both the empirical record and the logic of politicization, presented in the introductory section, suggest that Cedar City experiences reveal important generalizations about the politicization of street crime in the United States.

The Lessons of Cedar City

Perhaps the central finding of the Cedar City research is that street crime was not a particularly promising target of opportunity for local political entrepreneurs. The rate of success was poor both for individual candidates who campaigned on street crime and for other kinds of electoral efforts on behalf of law and order values. Still, crime was effectively politicized from time to time—thus raising questions about how and why politicization does occur.

There are some indications that the occasional politicization of crime was a direct response to social disorganization. The two areas of the city most responsive to politicization, the central area and Crystal Valley, were, after all, high-crime areas where people were most likely to feel the effects of street crime. There also seemed to be a class dimension to politicization insofar as these were areas characterized by low income, unemployment, and other indicia of poverty.

At first glance, these findings on class and victimization seem to imply a direct and unproblematic linkage between material conditions and politicization. Accordingly, it might reasonably be inferred that the low levels of politicization in Cedar City were due to its acceptably safe streets and relatively prosperous circumstances. This inference would, however, be at best a misleading oversimplification.

Other findings indicate that the relationship between material conditions and politicization are complex and contingent. Recall, . . . that a simple time trend provided a better explanation for the patterns of politicization than did the crime rate. More specifically, . . . the 1975-to-1978 period of peak politicization was not characterized by corresponding elevations in the crime rate. Figures for murder and burglary were not particularly high during those four years, although robbery rates did increase some and assault figures were significantly higher. In other words, criminal victimization, as such, did not seem to provide an adequate explanation for the aberrant levels of politicization during the 1975-through-1978 period.

The alternative argument is that politicization is dependent on an indeterminate variety of material conditions and on how these conditions are construed. Thus, while poverty and victimization seemed to work together to influence politicization, race was a cross-cutting factor—leading to sharply contrasting ways of expressing street crime as a political issue. The priority for the predominately black central area was police reform, while racially divided Crystal Valley supported law and order candidates and their program. More broadly, established elites with incentives to cool public concerns about street crime and the resources to shape campaign practices and public debate were generally successful at resisting and/or co-opting politicization.

Thinking about politicization in terms of the construction of street crime rather than as its direct reflection also suggests an explanation for the relatively effective politicization of the 1975-to-1978 period. . . . The politicization of street crime may be associated with perceptions of social crisis which transcend street crime as such. . . .

The point is that our culture tells us that punishment is a simple, effective, and morally compelling response to crime. Accordingly, there are obvious temptations to redirect anxieties stemming from more elusive and intractable problems to the ostensibly simple and manageable problem of crime.

Double-digit inflation in Cedar City as well as elsewhere in the county occurred during the period from 1975 to 1978. This was also a period during which the explosive issue of school desegregation, and more explicitly a 1978 anti-busing initiative, divided the city. In this context the data on assault may be instructive insofar as assault tends to have more to do with social disorder than with the kind of predatory activity associated with more conventional crimes like robbery and burglary.

Accordingly, street crime may well have become a tempting condensation symbol during this period. Given the moral dilemmas of busing, the technical complexities of inflation, and the pervasiveness of urban disorder, the attractions of a relatively straightforward problem like street crime may have been sufficient to undermine the moderating influences of established elites. If so, high crime may have been a necessary, but hardly a sufficient, pre-condition to politicization—thus helping to explain the long lag time between increased street crime in the 1960s and politicization in the late 1970s.

Cedar City in Context

The best available data for putting Cedar City in context comes from a major research project on the governmental responses to crime in ten cities between 1948 and 1978 (see Jacob 1984; Jacob and Lineberry, 1983; Jacob and Lineberry, with Heinz, Beecher, Moran, and Swank 1982). The findings from this research reveal striking similarities between the patterns of politicization uncovered in Cedar City and those to be found elsewhere in the United States—thus suggesting that the lessons of Cedar City are more generally applicable. At the same time, this research suggests that by national standards the level of politicization in Cedar City was relatively, *but not uniquely,* low—thus providing some insight into the circumstances that promote moderation in the politics of street crime. In short, both the Cedar City variations and its more typical tendencies help to explain when, why, and to what extent street crime is likely to become politically salient.

The overall patterns of politicization in the ten cities studied in the governmental responses to crime project are virtually identical to what was found in Cedar City. That is to say, politicization emerged rather belatedly, tended to be sporadic, and was concentrated in the period between 1974 and 1978. Herbert Jacob, one of the principal investigators for the project put it this way.

> [F]rom the middle 1960s—when official crime rates were rising most markedly—
> the political agendas of cities were crowded with issues. . . . Crime thus had stiff
> competition from other issues. . . . Only during the last period (1974–1978) did
> crime reach the number-one position; budget and tax problems and the economy
> continued to rank near the top (Jacob 1984, pp. 20–21).

Jacob's findings are also consistent with the idea of crime as a condensation symbol. He points out that while crime was just one issue among many, its salience "may have been related to the public's attention to school desegregation, race relations, and civic disorders, matters that some persons linked to crime (Jacob 1984, p. 23).

With all that said, the governmental responses to crime research suggests a more moderate level of politicization in Cedar City than elsewhere in the country. While their data are not directly assimilable to the Cedar City findings, some informed speculation is possible. It seems unlikely, for example, that the salience of street crime in Cedar City ever reached the levels uncovered in Indianapolis, Newark, and Philadelphia. Nor does crime seem to have intruded into the politics of Cedar City as consistently as it did in Boston and Minneapolis. Conversely, the other middle-sized Western cities like Phoenix, Oakland, and San Jose reveal a moderation comparable to Cedar City's. In short, the moderation of politicization in Cedar City seems to distinguish it from about two-thirds of the ten cities in the governmental responses to crime project.

There is, however, another way of looking at all of this. An examination indicates that moderation is really the rule rather than the exception. Most of the time in most places, the politicization of crime was not very intense, and the Cedar City findings help us explain the underlying strength of the forces of moderation. On the other hand, given the right combination of circumstances, intense politicization did develop in a number of cities—although not really in Cedar City, which, therefore, provides some insight into the conditions likely to contain politicization. In short, Cedar City teaches us something about the basic tendencies that promote moderation and also about the special circumstances that reinforce moderation when it is under pressure.

Perhaps the best way to appreciate the underlying strength of the forces of moderation is to contrast the appeals of politicization at the national level to its drawbacks at the local level. For national politicians, the politicization of crime provides a unifying theme and thus a valence issue. While victimization is experienced differentially according to class, race, gender, and geography, the *threat* that victimization poses to property and person evokes comparable fears throughout the society. National political leaders can, therefore, deploy the fear of crime to unify the public against the criminal. In this way, attention can be diverted *from* structural problems for which the government has responsibility, but inadequate capabilities, to individual failings for which outrage and denunciation are ordinarily sufficient responses.

At the local level, where there is direct responsibility for criminal process, the picture is significantly different with the incentives running distinctly against politicization. First, local political leaders and criminal process professionals must to some extent answer for a failure to control crime. Since street crime poses insoluble policy problems, politicization generates expectations that cannot be met. Second, politicization of street crime in urban areas tends to exacerbate social divisions because racial minorities are disproportionately represented in arrest conviction, and incarceration rates. Insofar as these minorities have a significant political voice, politicization is divisive. Finally, politicization of street crime is also likely to have an adverse impact on the local business climate. In short, politicization at the local level tends to impose burdens while at the national level it is likely to confer benefits. To a significant extent, then, the underlying dynamics of moderation in Cedar City are typical rather than special. . . .

References

Cobb, R. W., and C. D. Elder. 1983. *Participation in American Politics: The Dynamics of Agenda-Building,* 2nd ed. Baltimore, MD: The Johns Hopkins University Press.

Edelman, M. 1967. *The Symbolic Uses of Politics.* Champaign-Urbana: University of Illinois Press.

――――― 1977. *Political Language: Words That Succeed and Policies That Fail.* New York: Academic Press.

Gerbner, G., and L. Gross. 1976. "Living with Television: The Violence Profile." *Journal of Communications* 26: 173–197.

Heinz, A., H. Jacob, and R. L. Lineberry, eds. 1983. *Crime in City Politics.* New York: Longman.

Jacob, H. 1984. *The Frustrations of Policy: Responses to Crime by American Cities.* Boston: Little, Brown.

Jacob, H., and R. L. Lineberry. 1983. "Crime, Politics, and the Cities." In *Governmental Responses to Crime: Crime on Urban Agendas,* edited by H. Jacob and R. L. Lineberry, with A. M. Heinz, J. A. Beecher, J. Moran, and D. H. Swank. Washington, DC: National Institute of Justice.

Jacob, H., and R. L. Lineberry, with A. M. Heinz, J. A. Beecher, J. Moran, and D. H. Swank. 1982. *Governmental Responses to Crime: Crime on Urban Agendas.* Washington, DC: National Institute of Justice.

Kingdon, J. 1984. *Agendas, Alternatives, and Public Policy.* Boston: Little, Brown.

Rubin, L. B. 1988. *Quiet Rage: Bernie Goetz in a Time of Madness.* Berkeley: University of California Press.

Scheingold, S. A. 1984. *The Politics of Law and Order: Street Crime and Public Policy.* New York: Longman.

Scheingold, S. A., and L. A. Gressett. 1984. "The Politics of Law and Order: Politicizing Amorphous Public Concerns." Paper presented at the annual meeting of the American Political Science Association, Washington, DC, August 30–September 2.

Scheingold, S. A., and L. A. Gressett. 1985. "The Politics of Police Policy Making." Paper presented at the annual meeting of the Law and Society Association, San Diego, June 6–9.

SCHEINGOLD, S. A., AND L. A. GRESSETT. 1987. "Policy, Politics, and the Criminal Courts." *American Bar Foundation Research Journal:* 461–505.

SKOGAN, W. G., AND M. G. MAXFIELD. 1981. *Coping with Crime: Individual and Neighbor-hood Reactions.* Beverly Hills, CA: Sage.

WILSON, J. Q. 1977. *Thinking about Crime.* New York: Vintage.

———— 1985. *Thinking about Crime,* rev. ed. New York: Vintage.

ARTICLE

3

Toward a Theory of Street-Level Bureaucracy

Michael Lipsky

Most people employed by criminal justice organizations can be described as street-level bureaucrats. They are public employees who interact constantly with nonvoluntary clients and have a considerable amount of discretion about how to deal with them. Michael Lipsky argues that street-level bureaucrats must do their jobs in spite of inadequate resources and in an environment where their authority is regularly challenged and where expectations about how they should be doing their job are contradictory and/or ambiguous.

I. Street-Level Bureaucracy and the Structure of Work

This essay is an attempt to develop a theory of the political behavior of street-level bureaucrats and their interactions with clients. Street-level bureaucrats, defined below, are those men and women who, in their face-to-face encounters with citizens, "represent" government to the people. The essay is also an effort to inquire into aspects of organizational life common to various urban bureaucracies, so that we may begin to develop generalizations about urban bureaucratic behavior that transcend discussions of individual bureaucratic contexts. We seek answers to the general question: What behavioral and psychological factors are common to such bureaucratic roles as teacher, policeman, welfare worker, lower-court judge? To identify such common elements would be to make a start toward theory in the study of urban bureaucracy.

Concentrating on the reactions of some urban bureaucrats to conditions of stress, this essay also draws attention to various structural factors that may contribute to the inherent inability of some urban bureaucracies to provide objective, nondiscriminatory service, to recognize the existence of biased behavior, and to respond to pres-

Source: Reprinted from Michael Lipsky, "Street-Level Bureaucracy and the Analysis of Urban Reform," *Urban Affairs Quarterly*, Vol. 6 (June 1971), pp. 391–409. Copyright © 1971 by Sage Publications. Reprinted by permission of Sage Publications, Inc.

sures from some client groups. These assertions are matters of public urgency at a time when police departments, school systems, welfare offices, and urban legal systems increasingly have come under severe criticism.

The discussion is focused upon two types of urban public-service employees currently experiencing considerable pressure from many groups: policemen and teachers. The example provided by lower-court judges is also utilized considerably, and other urban bureaucracies are referred to when relevant.

While we concentrate on the relationship of some urban bureaucrats to conditions of stress, the term *street-level bureaucrat* is used throughout to draw attention to individuals in organizational roles requiring frequent and significant contacts with citizens. Specifically, a "street-level bureaucrat" is defined as a public employee whose work is characterized by the following three conditions:

1. He is called upon to interact constantly with citizens in the regular course of his job.

2. Although he works within a bureaucratic structure, his independence on the job is fairly extensive. One component of this independence is discretion in making decisions; but independence is not limited to discretion. The attitude and general approach of the street-level bureaucrat toward the citizen may affect the individual significantly. These considerations are broader than the term *discretion* suggests.

3. The potential impact on citizens with whom he deals is fairly extensive.

This paper will concentrate on the interaction of street-level bureaucrats and the nonvoluntary clients with whom they deal in the course of their jobs.

In American cities today, their work environments frequently require street-level bureaucrats to confront problems stemming from lack of organizational and personal resources, physical and psychological threat, and conflicting and/or ambiguous role expectations. People in these bureaucratic roles both deliberately and unconsciously develop mechanisms to cope with these problems. Street-level bureaucrats are also receptive to and supportive of organizational structural mechanisms that simplify and reduce the burdens of office. We will attempt to describe and assess the impact of selected bureaucratic resolutions of these problems on job performance and community relations.

A few other job conditions common to street-level bureaucrats should be mentioned here. They perform their jobs with nonvoluntary clients, and, no doubt related, these clienteles for the most part do not serve as primary bureaucratic reference groups. These points may be illustrated by considering the nature of police interactions with offenders and suspects, teachers' interactions with pupils, and lower-court judges' interactions with individuals charged with criminal or deviant behavior.

Another condition commonly characterizing street-level bureaucrats is that they have limited control—although extensive influence—over clientele performance, accompanied in part by high expectations and demands concerning that performance. Police and lower-court judges are charged with controlling behavior that has profound social roots. Teachers are asked to compensate for aspects of children's upbringing for which they are not responsible.

Still another condition characterizing street-level bureaucracies is the difficulty in measuring job performance in terms of ultimate bureaucratic objectives. Work standards may be established and attempts made to determine if those standards are being achieved. For example, when policemen are asked to make a certain number of arrests per month, or social workers are asked to maintain a certain size caseload, they are being asked to measure up to work standards. But these measures are only problematically related to public safety or clients' ability to cope with problems, which are the ultimate objectives in police–citizen or social worker–client interactions. The practical impossibility of accurately measuring job performance, in combination with wide discretion, contributes to substantial problems in controlling or shaping these organizations from above.

Although the theoretical aspects of this essay to some degree are generally applicable to interactions between street-level bureaucrats and citizens, they are most applicable to interactions with low-income and minority-group clients. Poor people and minority-group members tend to command fewer personal resources than more favored individuals and thus are more dependent upon governmental bureaucratic structures for fair treatment or provision of basic services.

In this brief essay I will not be able to provide a comprehensive analysis of street-level bureaucratic groups. Nor can the jobs or professions be described in monolithic fashion; they encompass a wide range of variation. In attempting to develop a parsimonious theory of governmental organizational behavior and client interaction, I am interested rather in making more understandable certain problems of these bureaucratic structures and in initiating critical analysis of certain aspects of governmental organizational behavior at the point of consumption.

The discussion will apply to aspects of street-level bureaucracy when the following conditions are relatively salient in the job environment:

1. Available resources are inadequate.
2. Work proceeds in circumstances where there exists clear physical and/or psychological threat and/or the bureaucrat's authority is regularly challenged.
3. Expectations about job performance are ambiguous and/or contradictory and include unattainable idealized dimensions.

Although to some extent these conditions prevail in most bureaucratic contexts, they are *relatively salient* in street-level bureaucracies in the contemporary American urban setting. They are the result of (and I will suggest they are in some ways the causes of) what is known as the urban "crisis." Evidence of the existence of these conditions may be found in contemporary discussions of these professions and to some degree in general analyses of organizational behavior. The conditions do not invariably obtain, and they are less salient in some bureaucratic contexts than in others. In some settings street-level bureaucrats are relatively free from these conditions. This fact does not invalidate the argument. It only suggests that at times the inferences drawn here are not applicable and that it would be useful to specify those conditions under which they *are* applicable. Although the analysis is concentrated to some extent on police, teachers, and lower-court judges, it is intended to be relevant in other bureaucratic contexts when the characteristics and qualifications discussed above obtain.

The remainder of this section extends and amplifies the discussion of conditions of stress under which street-level bureaucrats often must work.

Inadequate Resources

Almost all bureaucratic decision-making contexts are characterized by limited time and information. Street-level bureaucrats, however, work in a relatively high degree of uncertainty relative to the complexity of individuals about whom they must make decisions, although they are required to act as if certainty were achievable and were regularly achieved.

Resources necessary to function adequately as street-level bureaucrats may be classified as organizational resources and personal resources. Organizationally, street-level bureaucrats must be provided with adequate technical assistance and tools and with settings conducive to client compliance. Perhaps most important, the manpower/client ratio must be such that service may be provided with a relatively low degree of stress consistent with expectations of service provision.

Typical personal resources necessary for adequate job performance are sufficient time to make decisions (and act upon them), access to information, and information itself. For the policeman in many encounters with citizens, scarce personal resources frequently make it difficult to collect relevant information or process information adequately. When breaking up a fight in a bar, a policeman may not have time to determine the initiating party and so must make a double arrest. The need to mobilize information quickly in an uncertain bureaucratic environment may account for police practices of collecting or hoarding as much information as possible on individuals and situations in which policemen may be called to intervene, even if this information is inadmissible in court. It is not only that guidelines governing police behavior are inadequate but that inadequacy of personal and organizational resources contributes to the "improvisational" ways in which law enforcement is carried out.

In big cities, lower-court judges who process tens of thousands of cases each year and have great difficulty bringing cases to trial in timely fashion hardly have time to obtain a comprehensive picture of every case on which they sit. One might attribute this pressure to lack of manpower, since more judges would permit each case to be heard more fully. But whether one attributes it to lack of time or to inadequate staffing, lower-court judges lack the resources to do their job adequately. Many big-city teachers must perform in overcrowded classrooms with inadequate materials and with clients requiring intense personal attention.

Threats and Challenges to Authority

The conditions under which street-level bureaucrats are asked to do their jobs often include distinct physical and psychological threats. This component is most clearly relevant to the police role. Police constantly work under the threat of violence that may come from any direction at any time. Threat may exist independent of the actual incidence of threat materialization. The fact that policemen spend most of their time in nonthreatening tasks does not reduce the threat affecting their job orientations.

Teachers in inner-city schools under some circumstances also appear to work under threat of physical harm. But more common may be the threat that chaos poses for a teacher attempting to perform his job. The potential for chaos, or a chaotic classroom, implies the elimination of the conditions under which teaching can take place. The threat of chaos is present whether or not teachers commonly experience chaos and regardless of whether chaotic classroom conduct is caused by students or inspired by the teacher.

Although the institutional setting in which lower-court judges conduct cases reduces the potential for threat, judges are harried by the enormous case backlogs that confront them and by the knowledge that individuals who cannot make bail spend long periods in jail without trial. They are under constant pressure from administrative judicial superiors to reduce this backlog. The imperative to "keep the calendar moving," reinforced by the (often unrealized) judicial goal of a minimum wait from arrest to trial, is distinctly dissonant with the component of the ideal judicial image, which stresses hearing each case on its merits.

Threat and authority seem reciprocally related for street-level bureaucrats. The greater the degree of personal or role authority, the less the threat. One might also hypothesize that the greater the threat, the less bureaucrats feel that authority is respected, and the more they feel the need to invoke it. These hypotheses are supported by invocations to teachers to establish classroom control as a precondition to teaching. They also tend to be confirmed by studies of police behavior. Danger and authority have been identified as the two principal variables of the police role. The authority vested in the role of policeman is seen by police as an instrument of control, without which they are endangered. Hence comes the often reported tendency to be lenient with offenders whose attitude and demeanor are penitent, but harsh and punitive to those offenders who show signs of disrespect. Indeed, policemen often appear to "test" the extent to which an offender is respectful in order to determine whether he is a "wise guy" and thus has an improper attitude.

Expectations about Job Performance

Street-level bureaucrats often must perform their jobs in response to ambiguous and contradictory expectations. These expectations in part may be unattainable. Some goal orientations may be unrealistic, mutually exclusive, or unrealized because of lack of control over the client's background and performance, as discussed above.

Role theorists generally have attempted to locate the origin of role expectations in three "places": in peers and others who occupy complementary role positions; in reference groups, in terms of whom expectations are defined, although they are not literally present; and in public expectations generally, where consensus about role expectations can sometimes be found. While we cannot specify here how role expectations are generated for various street-level bureaucrats, we can make a few points concerning conflict in urban areas over these bureaucracies.

Conflicting and ambiguous role expectations stemming from divided community sentiments are the source of considerable bureaucratic strain. As public officials, street-level bureaucrats are subject to expectations that they will treat individuals fairly and impartially. To some degree they are also subject, as public officials, to expectations that individuals and individual cases will be treated on their unique merits. Provision of services in terms of the ideal is constantly challenged by "realists," who stress the legitimacy of adjustments to working conditions and the unavailability of resources.

Apparently in direct conflict with expectations concerning equal treatment are expectations from more parochial community interests, to which street-level bureaucrats are also subject as public officials. In a real sense, street-level bureaucrats are expected by some reference groups to recognize the desirability of providing *unequal* treatment. Invocations to "clean up" certain sections of town, to harass undesirables through heavy surveillance (prostitutes, motorcycle or juvenile gangs, civil rights workers, hippies), to prosecute vigorously community "parasites" (junkies, slumlords), and even to practice reverse discrimination (for minority groups)—all such instances represent calls for unequal bureaucratic treatment. They illustrate the efforts of some community segments to use street-level bureaucracies to gain relative advantages.

Conflicts stemming from divisive, parochial community expectations will be exacerbated in circumstances of attitudinal polarization. As relative consensus or indifference concerning role expectations diminishes, street-level bureaucrats may respond by choosing among conflicting expectations rather than attempting to satisfy more than one of them. In discussing police administrative discretion, James Q. Wilson suggests that there is a "zone of indifference" in the prevailing political culture within which administrators are free to act. When values are polarized, the zone may become wider. But indifference and, as a result, discretion may be diminished as bureaucratic performance is increasingly scrutinized and practices formerly ignored assume new meaning for aroused publics.

The police role is significantly affected by conflicting role expectations. In part stemming from public ambivalence about the police, policemen must perform their duties somewhere between the demands for strict law enforcement, the necessity of discretion in enforcement, and various community mores. They must accommodate the constraints of constitutional protection and demands for efficiency in maintenance of order and crime control. They must enforce laws they did not make in communities where demands for law enforcement vary with the laws and with the various strata of the population, and where police may perceive the public as hostile yet dependent. Police role behavior may conflict significantly with their own value preferences as individuals and with the behavior and outlook of judges. They are expected to be scrupulously objective and impartial, protective of all segments of society. Speaking generally, we may expect lack of clarity in role expectations in these cases to be no less dysfunctional than in other circumstances where lack of role clarity has been observed.

In discussing the generation of role expectations in street-level bureaucracies, we should note the relative unimportance of nonvoluntary clients. This is not to say that children are unimportant to teachers, or that litigants and defendants are unimportant to judges. But they do not primarily, or even secondarily, determine bureaucratic role expectations. Some contemporary political movements that appear to be particularly upsetting to some street-level bureaucrats, such as demands for community control and community health planning, may be understood as demands for inclusion in the constellation of bureaucratic reference groups by nonvoluntary clients. It may not be that street-level bureaucracies are *generally* unresponsive, as is sometimes claimed. Rather, they have been responsive in the past to constellations of reference groups that have excluded a significant portion of the population with whom they regularly deal.

Public bureaucracies are somewhat vulnerable to the articulated demands of any organized segment of society because they partially share the ethos of public responsiveness and fairness. But street-level bureaucracies seem particularly incapable of responding positively to the new groups because of the ways in which their role expectations are currently framed. Demands for bureaucratic changes are most likely to be responded to when they are articulated by primary reference groups. When they are articulated by client groups outside the regular reference group arena, probabilities of responsiveness in ways consistent with client demands are likely to be significantly lower.

II. Adaptations to the Work Situation

In order to make decisions when confronted with a complex problem and an uncertain environment, individuals who play organizational roles will develop bureaucratic mechanisms to make the tasks easier. To the extent that street-level bureaucrats are threatened by the three kinds of problems described in the first section, they will develop coping mechanisms specifically related to these concerns. In this discussion we will focus on the ways in which simplifications, routines, and various coping mechanisms or strategies for dealing with the bureaucratic problems described earlier are integrated into the behavior of street-level bureaucrats and their organizational lives.

By simplifications, we refer to those symbolic constructs in terms of which individuals order their preceptions so as to make the perceived environment easier to manage. They may do this for reasons of instrumental efficiency and/or reasons of anxiety reduction. By routines, we mean the establishment of habitual or regularized patterns in terms of which tasks are performed. For this essay we will concentrate on routines for the purpose of, or with the effect of, alleviating bureaucratic difficulties arising from resource inadequacy, threat perception, and unclear role expectations. This essay may be said to focus on the trade-offs incurred in, and the unintended consequences of, developing such mechanisms.

Having discussed three conditions under which street-level bureaucrats frequently must work, we now examine some of the ways in which they attempt to accommodate these conditions and some of the implications of the mechanisms developed in the coping process.

Accommodations to Inadequate Resources

The development of simplifications and routines permits street-level bureaucrats to make quick decisions and thereby accomplish their jobs with less difficulty (perhaps freeing scarce resources through time saving), while at the same time partly reducing tensions with clients or personal anxiety over the adequacy of decisions made. "Shortcuts" developed by these bureaucracies are often made because of inadequate resources. Police limit enforcement because of inability to enforce constantly all laws (even if the community wanted total enforcement). Routinization of judicial activities in the lower courts is pervasive. Decisions on bail and sentencing are made without knowledge of the defendant's background or an adequate hearing of the individual cases, as judges "become preoccupied simply with moving the cases. Clearing the dockets becomes a primary objective of all concerned, and cases are dimissed, guilty pleas are entered, and bargains are struck with that end as the dominant consideration."

Not only does performance on a case basis suffer with routinization but critical decisions may effectively be made by bureaucrats not ultimately responsible for the decisions. Thus, for example, judges in juvenile courts have effectively transferred decision making to the police or probationary officers whose undigested reports form the basis of judicial action. Both in schools and in the streets, the record of an individual is likely to mark him for special notice by teachers and policemen who, to avoid trouble or find guilty parties, look first among the pool of known "troublemakers." Certain types of crimes, and certain types of individuals, receive special attention from street-level bureaucrats who develop categorical attitudes toward offenses and offenders.

Additionally, routines may become ends in themselves. Special wrath is often reserved for clients who fail to appreciate the bureaucratic necessity of routine. Clients are denied rights as individuals because to encourage exercise of individual rights would jeopardize processing of caseloads on a mass basis.

Accommodations to Threat

Routines and simplifications are developed by street-level bureaucrats who must confront physical and psychological threat. Inner-city schoolteachers, for example, consider maintaining discipline one of their primary problems. It is a particularly critical problem in "slum" schools, where "keeping them in line" and avoiding physical confrontations consume a major portion of teachers' time, detracting from available educational opportunities. Even under threatening circumstances, elementary schoolteachers are urged to "routinize as much as possible" in order to succeed.

"You gotta be tough, kid, or you'll never last" appears to be typical of the greeting most frequently exchanged by veteran officers in socializing rookies into the force. Because a policeman's job continually exposes him to potential for violence, he develops simplifications to identify people who might pose danger. Skolnick has called individuals so identified "potential assailants." Police may find clues to the identity of a potential assailant in the way he walks, his clothing, his race, previous experiences with police, or other "nonnormal" qualities. The moral worthiness of clients also appears to have an impact on judicial judgment. In this regard, the police experience may be summed as the development of faculties for suspicion.

Mechanisms may be developed to reduce threat potential by minimizing bureaucratic involvement. Thus policemen are tutored in how to distinguish cases that should be settled on the spot with minimal police intervention. Ploys are developed to disclaim personal involvement or to disclaim discretion within the situation. "It's the law," or "Those are the rules" may be empirically accurate assertions, but they are without substance when weighed with the relationship between discretion and law enforcement. Street-level bureaucrats may totally evade involvement through avoidance strategies. Thus, according to one account, failure to report incidents in ghetto neighborhoods are "rationalize[d] . . . with theories that the victim would refuse to prosecute because violence has become the accepted way of life for his community, and that any other course would result in a great loss of time in court, which would reduce the efficiency of other police functions."

Routines also serve to provide more information about potential difficulties and to protect an image of authority. "Potential assailants"are frequently approached by police in a brusque, imperious manner in order to determine if they respect police authority. Early teacher identification of "troublemakers," and the sensitivity of policemen to sudden movements on the part of a suspect (anticipating the reaching for a weapon), further illustrate the development of simplifications for the purposes of reducing the possibility of physical threat.

Threats to the systems of which street-level bureaucrats are a part also contribute to the sense of threat personally perceived. Thus street-level bureaucrats attempt to provide an atmosphere in which their authority will be unquestioned and conformity to their system of operation will be enhanced. The courtroom setting of bench, bar, and robes, as well as courtroom ritual, all function to establish such an environment. Uniforms also support the authoritative image, as do institutional rules governing conduct and dress. Imposition of symbols of authority function to permit street-level bureaucrats to test the general compliance of the client to the system. Thus the salute to the uniform, not the man; thus a policeman's concern that disrespect for him is disrespect for the law.

We suggest the following hypotheses about these mechanisms for threat reduction. The mechanisms will be employed more frequently than objective conditions might seem to warrant because for them to be effective they must be employed in all instances of possible threat. The consequences of failure to guard against physical threat are so severe that the tendency will develop to employ safety mechanisms as often, rather than as little, as possible. This pattern contrasts significantly with routines invoked for efficiency. Traffic law enforcement, for example, may be ensured by sporadic enforcement; occasional intervention serves as a sufficient deterrent for the police department. But in threatening circumstances, the risks are too great for *individual* bureaucrats to depend upon sporadic invocation.

Threat-reduction mechanisms also are more likely to be invoked in circumstances where the penalties for employing them are nonexistent, rarely imposed, or not severe. Penalties for using threat-reducing mechanisms are least likely to be invoked in street-level bureaucracies where employees are most exposed to threat, because for these bureaucracies ability to reduce threat and thus reduce personnel anxiety are organizational maintenance requisites.

Additionally, street-level bureaucrats may have a stake in exaggerating the potential for danger or job-oriented difficulties. The reasoning is similar. If the threat is exaggerated, then the threat-reduction mechanisms will be employed more often, presumably decreasing the likelihood of actual physical danger. However, as suggested below, increased invocation of threat-reducing routines may evoke the very actions that are feared.

Exaggerating the threat publicly will also reduce the likelihood of imposition of official sanctions, since bureaucrats' superiors will have greater confidence that knowledge of the dangers accompanying job performance will be widely disseminated. Thus street-level bureaucrats paradoxically have a stake in continuing to promote information about the difficulties of their jobs at the same time that they seek to publicize their professional competence. This is analogous to the paradox of police administrators who thrive simultaneously on public anxiety over crime waves and public recognition of victories over crime.

One function of professional associations of policemen and teachers has been to publicize information about the lack of adequate resources with which they must work. This public relations effort permits the street-level bureaucrat to say (to himself and publicly) with greater confidence that his position will be appreciated by others: "Any failures attributed to me can be understood as failures to give me the tools to do the job."

The psychological reality of the threat may bear little relationship to the statistical probabilities. One teacher knifed in a hallway will evoke concern among teachers for order, even though statistically the incident might be insignificant. Policemen may imagine an incipient assault and shoot to kill, not because of the probabilities that the putative assailant will have a knife, but perhaps because once, some years ago, a policeman failed to draw a gun on an assailant and was stabbed to death. Such incidents may also be affected by tendencies to perceive some sets of people as hostile and potentially dangerous. In such circumstances the threat would be heightened by the conjunction of both threatening event and actor.

Accommodations to Role Expectations

Role expectations that are ambiguous, contradictory, and in some ways unrealizable represent additional job difficulties with which street-level bureaucrats must cope. Here we will discuss two coping processes with which street-level bureaucrats may effectively reduce the pressures generated by lack of clarity and unattainability of role expectations.

Changing Role Expectations   Street-level bureaucrats may attempt to alter expectations about job performance. They may try to influence the expectations of people who help give their role definition. They may try to create a definition of their roles that includes a heroic component recognizing the quality of job performance as a function of the difficulties encountered. Teachers may see themselves and try to get others to see them as the unsung heroes of the city. They may seek an image of themselves as people who work without public recognition or reward, under terrific tension, and who, whatever their shortcomings, are making the greatest contribution to the education of minority groups. Similarly, policemen appear interested in projecting an image of themselves as soldiers of pacification, keeping the streets safe despite community hostility and general lack of recognition. Judges, too, rationalize their job performance by stressing the physical strain under which they work and the extraordinary caseloads they must process.

One of the implications of role redefining may be the disclaiming of responsibility over the results of work. It is surely difficult to demand improvement in job performance if workers are not responsible for the product. Furthermore, the claim of lack of responsibility is often not falsifiable unless illustrations are available of significantly more successful performances under similar constraints.

Another facet of role redefinition may be efforts to perform jobs *in some way* in accordance with perceived role expectations. Such efforts are manifested in greater teacher interest in some children who are considered bright ("If I can't teach them all, I can at least try to teach the few who have something on the ball"); in the extraordinary time some judges will take with a few cases while many people wait for their turn for a hearing; and in the time policemen spend investigating certain crimes. In these cases, street-level bureaucrats may be responding to role expectations that emphasize individual attention and personal concern for community welfare. The judge who takes the time to hear a case fully is hardly blameworthy. But these tendencies, which partially fulfill role expectations, deflect pressures for adequate routine treatment of clienteles. They also marginally divert resources from the large bulk of cases and clients, although not so many resources as to make a perceptible dent in public impressions of agency performance. Like the public agency that creates a staff to ensure a quick response to "crisis" cases, these developments may be described as routines to deal with public expectations on a selective case basis, reducing pressures to develop routines conforming to idealized role expectations on a *general* basis.

Changing Definition of the Clientele   A second set of strategies by which street-level bureaucrats can attempt to alter expectations about job performance is to alter assumptions about the clientele to be served. This approach may take the form either of attributing responsibility for all actions to the client or of perceiving the client as so victimized by social forces that he cannot really be helped by service. Goffman explains well the function of the first mode of perception:

> Although there is a psychiatric view of mental disorder and an environmental view of crime and counterrevolutionary activity, both freeing the offender from moral responsibility for his offense, total institutions can little afford this particular kind of determinism. Inmates must be caused to *self-direct* themselves in a manageable way, and, for this to be promoted, both desired and undesired conduct must be defined as springing from the personal will and character of the individual inmate himself, and defined as something he himself can do something about.

Police tendencies to attribute riots to the riffraff of the ghettos (criminals, transients, and agitators) may also be explained in this way. Instances of teachers beating children who clearly display signs of mental disturbance provide particularly brutal illustrations of the apparent need of at least some street-level bureaucrats to attribute self-direction to noncompliant clients.

The second perceptual mode also functions to absolve street-level bureaucrats from responsibility by attributing clients' performance difficulties to cultural or societal factors. If children are perceived to be primitive, racially inferior, or "culturally deprived," a teacher can hardly fault himself if his charges fail to progress. Just as policemen respond to calls in different ways depending on the victim's "legitimacy," teachers often respond to children in terms of their "moral acceptability." According to Howard Becker, children may be morally unacceptable to teachers in terms of values centered around health and cleanliness, sex and aggression, ambition and work, and age-group relations. These considerations are particularly related to class discrepancies between teacher and pupil.

Undeniably there are cultural and social factors that affect client performance. Similarly, there is a sense in which people are responsible for their actions and activities. What is important to note, however, is that these explanations function as cognitive shields between the client and street-level bureaucrat, reducing what responsibility and accountability may exist in the role expectations of street-level bureaucrats. These explanations may also contribue to hostility between clients and bureaucrats.

The street-level bureaucrat can conform to role expectations by redefining the clientele in terms of which expectations are framed. This may be called "segmenting the population to be served." In police work the tendency to segment the population may be manifested in justifications for differential rates of law enforcement between white and black communities. It is also noticeable in police harassment of "hippies," motorcycle gangs, and college students where long hair has come to symbolize the not-quite-human quality that a black skin has long played in some aspects of law enforcement. The police riots during the Democratic National Convention of 1968, and since then in various university communities, may be more explicable if one recognizes that long-haired white college students are considered by police in some respects to be "outside" of the community that can expect to be protected by norms of due process. Segmenting the population to be served reinforces police and judicial practices that condone failure to investigate crimes involving black against black or encourage particular vigilance in attempting to control black crime against whites. In New York City, the landlord orientations of public officials and judges concerned with landlord-tenant disputes are reinforced by diffuse but widely accepted assumptions that low-income blacks and Puerto Ricans are insensitive to property and property damage.

As coping behavior these strategies are similar to defense mechanisms, in that they involve reappraisal and distortion of the conditions of threat and work-related stresses. For street-level bureaucrats segmentation functions psychologically to permit bureaucrats to make some of their clienteles even more remote in their hierarchies of reference groups. At the same time, it allows bureaucrats to perform without the need to confront their manifest failure. They can think of themselves as having performed adequately in situations where raw materials were weak or the resources necessary to deploy their technical skills were insufficient.

We conclude this section by noting some of the institutional mechanisms developed in street-level bureaucracies that are conducive to greater bureaucratic control over the work environment and thus responsive to the needs of street-level bureaucrats. These relationships obtain regardless of the reasons for introducing the structural arrangements discussed here. The tracking system, whereby early in a pupil's career schools institutionally structure teacher expectations about him, represents one such institutional mechanism. Thus the educational "system" becomes responsible for pupils' progress and direction, and teachers are free to make only marginal decisions about their students (to decide in rare cases whether a student should leave a given track). In addition to reducing the decision-making burden, the tracking system, as many have argued, largely determines its own predicted stability.

Another institutional mechanism that results in reducing client-related difficulties in street-level bureaucracies is the development of procedures for effectively limiting clientele demands by making systems financially or psychologically costly or irritating to use. For lower courts this kind of development results in inducing people to plead guilty in exchange for lighter sentences. Welfare procedures and eligibility requirements have been credited with limiting the number of actual recipients. Ina-

bility to solve burglary cases results in peremptory investigations by police departments, resulting further in reduced citizen burglary reports. The Gothic quality of
civilian review board procedures effectively limits complaints. The unfathomable
procedures for filing housing violation complaints in New York City provides yet
another illustration of effective limitation of demand.

Still another institutional mechanism resulting in reduced pressures on the general system is the "special unit" designed to respond to particularly intense client
complaints. Illustrations may be found in the establishment of police review boards,
human relations units of public agencies, and public agency emergency services. The
establishment of such units, whether or not they perform their manifest functions,
also works to take bureaucracies off the hook by making it appear that something is
being done about problems. However, usually in these cases the problems about
which clients want something done (police brutality, equitable treatment for minority
groups, housing inspections and repairs) are related to *general* street-level bureaucratic behavior. Thus they can only be ameliorated through *general* attacks on
bureaucratic performance. These units permit street-level bureaucrats to allege that
problems are being handled and provide a "place" in the bureaucracy where particularly vociferous and persistent complainants can be referred. At the same time, the
existence of the units deflects pressures for general reorientations.

III. The Role of Stereotypes

Routines, simplifications, and other mechanisms utilized by street-level bureaucrats
in interactions with their nonvoluntary clients are not made in a social vacuum. The
ways in which these mechanisms are structured will be highly significant. Some simplifications will have a greater impact on people's lives than others, and the ways
they are structured will affect some groups more than others. The simplifications by
which park department employees choose which trees to trim will have much less
impact on people's lives than the simplifications in terms of which policemen make
judgments about potential suspects.

In urban bureaucracies, stereotyping and other forms of racial and class biases
significantly inform the ways in which simplifications and routines are structured.
This simple conclusion is inescapable for anyone familiar with studies of police,
teachers, and judges.

Stereotypes affect simplifications and routines, but they are not equivalent. In
the absence of stereotypes, simplifying and routinizing would go on anyhow. Cate-
gorization is a necessary part of the bureaucratic process. But in American urban
life, easily available stereotypes affect bureaucratic decision making in ways which
independently exacerbate urban conflict.

First, in a society that already stigmatizes certain racial and income groups the
bureaucratic needs to simplify and routinize become colored by the available stereotypes, resulting in *institutionalization* of the stereotyping tendencies.

Second, as will be discussed below, street-level bureaucratic behavior is perceived as bigoted and discriminatory, probably to a greater degree than the sum of
individual discriminatory actions.

Third, and perhaps most interesting, the results of the interaction between simplifications, routines, and biases are masked from both bureaucrats and clients. Clients primarily perceive bias, while street-level bureaucrats primarily perceive their own responses to bureaucratic necessities as neutral, fair, and rational (that is, based upon empirical probabilities). The bureaucratic mode becomes a defense against allegations of unfairness or lack of service. By stressing the need for simplifying and routinizing, street-level bureaucrats can effectively deflect confrontations concerning inadequate client servicing by the mechanisms mentioned earlier. And when confrontations do occur, street-level bureaucrats may effectively diminish the claims of organized client groups by insisting that clients are unappreciative of service, ignorant of bureaucratic necessity, and unfair in attributing racial motives to ordinary bureaucratic behavior.

The conflict over the tracking systems in Washington, D.C., and other cities illustrates this point. The school bureaucracy defended tracking as an inherently neutral mechanism for segregating students into ability groupings for more effective teaching. Rigidities in the system were denied; reports that tracking decisions were made on racial bases were ignored; and evidence of abuse of the tracking system was attributed to correctable malfunctioning of an otherwise useful instrument. Missing from the school bureaucracy's side of the debate was recognition that in the District school system, tracking would inevitably be permeated by stereotypic and biased decision making.

In addition to the interaction between stereotyping and simplifications, three developments may be mentioned briefly that tend to reinforce bureaucratic biases: (1) playing out of self-fulfilling prophecies; (2) street-level bureaucrats' acceptance of partial empirical validation, and (3) their acceptance of illustrative validation.

In categorizing students as low or high achievers, in a sense predicting their capacity to achieve, teachers appear to create validity for the very simplifications in which they engage. Evidence has been presented that suggests that on the whole students will perform better in class if teachers think pupils are bright, regardless of whether or not they are. Policemen ensure the validity of their suspicions in many ways. They provoke "symbolic assailants" through baiting them or through oversurveillance tactics. They also concentrate patrol among certain segments of the population, thereby ensuring that there will be more police confrontations with that group. In this context there is triple danger in being young, black, and noticed by the law. Not only may arrests be more frequent, but employers' concerns for clean arrest records and the ways in which American penal institutions function as schools for criminals rather than rehabilitative institutions increase the probabilities that the arrested alleged petty offender will become the hardened criminal that he was assumed to be turning into. Hospital staffs, to illustrate from somewhat different sets of bureaucrats, appear to "teach" people how to be mentally and physically ill by subtly rewarding conforming behavior. Value judgments may intrude into supposedly neutral contexts to ensure that the antipathies of some bureaucrats will be carried over in subsequent encounters, for instance, in the creating of client "records" that follow them throughout their dealings with bureaucracies.

Partial empirical validation of the legitimacy of simplifications informed by stereotypes may occur through selective attention to information. Statistics can be marshaled to demonstrate that black crime has increased. A policeman may screen out information that places the statistical increase in perspective, never recognizing that his own perceptions of the world have contributed to the very increases he deplores. He also "thinks" he knows that black crime is worse than it was, although some studies have suggested that he overestimates its extent. Similarly, it is unquestionable that children from minority groups with language difficulties have greater problems in school than those without difficulties. Obviously there is something about lack of facility in English in an English-speaking school system that will affect achievement, although it may not be related to potential.

Illustrative validation may confirm simplifications by illustration. The common practice of "proving" the legitimacy of stereotypes, and thus the legitimacy of biased simplifications, by example may be a logical horror but it is also a significant social fact that influences the behavior of street-level bureaucracies. Illustrative validity not only confirms the legitimacy of simplifications but also affects the extent to which simplifications are invoked. The policeman killed in the course of duty because he neglected to shoot his assailant provides the basis for illustrative validity not only about the group of which the assailant is a part but also about the importance of invoking simplifications in the first place.

IV. Street-Level Bureaucracy and Urban Conflict

To better understand the interaction between government and citizens at the "place" where government meets people, I have attempted to demonstrate common factors in the behavior of street-level bureaucrats. I have suggested that there are patterns to this interaction, that continuities may be observed that transcend individual bureaucracies, and that certain conditions in the work environment of these bureaucracies appear to be relatively salient in structuring the bureaucrat–citizen interaction.

This analysis may help to explain some aspects of citizen antagonism to contemporary urban bureaucracies. Clients may conclude that service is prejudiced, dehumanizing, and discriminatory in greater degree than is warranted by the incidence of such behavior. Just as it may take only one example of a policeman killed by an assailant to reinforce police tendencies to overreact to potential assailants, so it only takes a few examples of bigoted teachers or prejudiced policemen to reinforce widespread conviction on the part of clients that the system is prejudiced. As Herman Goldstein has put it in discussing police–client relations:

> A person who is unnecessarily aggrieved is not only critical of the procedure which was particularly offensive to him. He tends to broaden his interest and attack the whole range of police procedures which suddenly appear to him to be unusually oppressive.

To refer again to propositions concerning threat, citizen stereotyping of bureaucracies may be greater in direct relation to the extent of control and impact that these bureaucracies have on their lives. Thus these tendencies will be relatively salient in institutional settings with considerable impact on citizens, such as schools, in courts, and in police relations. And they will be relatively salient to low-income clients, whose resource alternatives are minimal. Furthermore, such clients may recognize the sense in which the bureaucracies "create" them and the circumstances in which they live.

Just as street-level bureaucrats develop conceptions of nonvoluntary clients that deflect responsibility away from themselves, so citizens may also respond to bureaucracies by attributing to bureaucracies qualities that deflect attention away from their own shortcomings. This may result in citizens' developing conceptions of bureaucrats and bureaucracies as more potent than they actually are. On the other hand, because of predicted neglect or negative experiences in the past, citizens may withdraw from bureaucratic interaction or act with hostility toward street-level bureaucrats, evoking the very reactions *they* have "predicted." Minority groups particularly may have negative experiences with these bureaucracies, since they may be the citizens most likely to be challenged by street-level bureaucrats and most likely to be unable to accept gracefully challenges to self-respect.

Citizens will also share to some extent the role expectations of street-level bureaucrats, although they may have had little influence in shaping them. This may be another source of tension, since citizens may expect personal, individualized consideration or may demand it in spite of bureaucratic needs to provide impersonal treatment in a routinized fashion.

This analysis may help place in perspective the apparent paradox that some community groups insist that street-level bureaucracies are biased and discriminatory, while at the same time members of these bureaucracies insist in good faith that their members do not engage in discriminatory and biased practices. Regardless of whatever dissemblance may be involved here, we can partially explain the paradox by noting: (1) the ways in which relatively little discriminatory behavior can result in client ascription of a great deal of bureaucratic behavior to discriminatory attitudes; (2) the ways in which mechanisms developed by street-level bureaucrats to cope with problems in job performance are informed and colored by discriminatory stereotypes; and (3) the ways in which street-level bureaucrats institutionalize bias without necessarily recognizing the implications of their actions.

If this analysis has been at all persuasive, it suggests that in significant respects street-level bureaucracies as currently structured may be inherently incapable of responding favorably to contemporary demands for improved and more sympathetic service to some clients. Street-level bureaucrats respond to work-related pressures in ways that, however understandable or well-intentioned, may have invidious effects on citizen impressions of governmental responsiveness and equity in performance. If, indeed, government may be most salient to citizens where there is frequent interaction with its "representatives" and where the interactions may have important consequences for their lives, then these conclusions should evoke sympathy for current proposals for urban decentralization of authority. Whatever their other merits or difficulties, these proposals commend themselves at least for their concentration on fundamental alterations of the work environment of street-level bureaucrats.

PART TWO

Police

From philosophical, historical, and administrative perspectives, the concept of "law and order" is not a simple one. It has wide implications for the preservation of civil rights and the rule of law. A key question in a democratic society is, "For what social purpose do police exist?" History gives us little help in providing an answer, because law-enforcement agencies have often played many different and contradictory roles. Are the police to be concerned primarily with peacekeeping or with crime fighting? Should they be social workers with guns or guntoters in social work? Should they be instruments of social change or defenders of the faith?

Law and order is not a new problem, but it has been a focus for discussion since the first police force was formed in metropolitan London in 1829. If society gives arrest and incarceration powers to the police, it must control the power it has delegated so that the civil liberties of citizens are not infringed. The potential for misuse of power by law-enforcement agencies led many thoughtful nineteenth-century Americans to contend that an organized police force is alien to democracy and would lead to an end of freedom. Looking even further back in history, to the Magna Carta, we can see that limits were placed upon the constables and bailiffs of thirteenth-century England. Reading between the lines of this ancient document, we can see that abuses by police, maintenance of order, and the rule of law were problems then, as they are today. What is surprising is that the same remedies—recruitment of better police officers, stiffening of the penalties for official malfeasance, creation of a civilian board of control—were suggested in that earlier time to ensure that order was kept according to the rule of law.

The 20,000 law-enforcement agencies that are today dispersed throughout the counties, cities, and towns of the United States have their origins in the second quarter of nineteenth-century England, during the early stages of the Industrial Revolution. Arguing for establishment of a police force in metropolitan London, Sir Robert Peel cited the need for public order, using statistics indicating that crime was increasing faster than the population and pointing out that slum residents were rioting and destroying property and life in the "respectable" sections. Yet even under these conditions, there was so much fear of centralizing power in a quasi-military body that it took Peel seven years to persuade Parliament to establish the Metropolitan Constabulary for London. Organized along military lines, this 1,000-man force was responsible to the home secretary. Because the home secretary was accountable to Parliament, the first regular police force was actually controlled by the democratically elected legislature. Opposition to the new force came mostly from people of goodwill of all classes who genuinely believed that police of any kind were destructive of liberty.

Three Eras of American Policing

As with so many other public institutions, the English example was quickly copied in the United States. Between 1830 and 1870 there was unprecedented civil disorder, caused by the social upheavals of massive immigration, hostility toward nonslave blacks and abolitionists, and mob actions against banks. The major cities of the United States created daytime police forces to supplement the night watchmen. Boston and Philadelphia became the first cities to augment their forces, and in 1844 the New York legislature authorized creation of city uniformed police forces under the command of a chief appointed by the mayor and the council. By the middle of the century, most principal U.S. cities had followed this pattern.

Much of the nineteenth century can be characterized as the political era of policing in the United States. During the period close ties were developed between the police and local political leaders. In many cities, especially in the Northeast, this link to neighborhoods and politicians was such that the police often appeared to be adjuncts to the local party machine. This relationship served both groups, since the political machines recruited and maintained the police while the police helped ward leaders to get out the vote for favorite candidates.

During the political era the police focused on crime prevention and order maintenance by foot patrol. The decentralization of authority meant that the officer on the beat dealt with crime, disorder, and other problems as they arose. In addition, the police carried out a number of service functions, such as caring for derelicts, operating soup kitchens, regulating public health, and handling medical and social emergencies. Because of their closeness to the community, the police enjoyed citizen support during the political era.

It was not until the early twentieth century that civic reformers pushed for the development of professional police forces. The professional era that dominated American policing from about 1920 to 1970 emphasized that the police had to be completely divorced from politics, that personnel should be recruited and promoted on the basis of merit, that the force should take advantage of technological developments, and that the crime-fighter role should be predominant. New law-enforcement techniques were inaugurated by such administrators as August Vollmer, police chief of Berkeley, California, and later by O. W. Wilson, who gained national attention as a result of innovations he made in Wichita, Kansas.

With the rise of urban crime in the 1960s and demands from minority communities that public services be delivered in a manner consistent with local values, questions about the exercise of discretion within the professional model began to arise. There was no consensus on whether the police officer's main role should be that of crime fighter, maintainer of order, or public service worker. Many argued that the professional model was too impersonal to be responsive to differences in the community and that crime fighting played a minor role in police work.

Since the beginning of the 1970s there have been calls to move the American police away from their law enforcement–crime-fighting orientation so as to place new emphasis on maintaining order and providing services to the community. Research studies published during the past quarter century have shown that the day-to-day operations of the police deviate from the professional model. Critics have argued that the crime-fighter role isolated the police from the community and seemed not to be accountable to it. This was particularly true with regard to motorized patrol in which officers are seemingly encapsulated in their squad cars, never being able to develop much personal contact with citizens.

The third era, emphasizing a model of community policing, is becoming the hallmark of contemporary America. Advocates of community policing urge a greater use of foot patrols so that officers will become known to the citizens they serve, who in turn will cooperate with and assist the police. They believe that through attention to "little problems" the police will not only reduce disorder and citizen fear of crime but also improve public attitudes toward policing. This shift means that the police must be prepared to handle the broad range of troublesome situations—for example, battered wives, runaway children, noisy teenagers, accidents, and persons in distress—that prompt citizens to call them. Time will tell if this new orientation will become as influential and widespread as was the focus on professionalism during the first half of this century.

Police Functions

Police decisions and practices are greatly shaped by the local community. Although statutes insist that all laws be fully implemented, they usually do not provide specific instructions for carrying out this policy. Even if the police were given the necessary resources, a policy of "enforcement" would make life intolerable and almost surely preclude the protection of civil rights. In reality, although laws are written as if full enforcement were expected, the police determine the outer limits of "actual enforcement." A number of factors lead them to enforce some laws but not others: the difficulty of making arrests, the resources needed to obtain evidence, disagreement in the community about whether certain acts should be unlawful, and pressure from influential people. These low-visibility choices by police administrators are among the political ingredients of the criminal justice system. Enforcement agencies must fulfill their obligations under the law, but they must do so in ways that will ensure community and organizational support.

The work of the police is more complex than most of us assume. Police officers are charged with maintaining order, enforcing the law, providing a variety of social services, and carrying out policies that specify the persons and offenses to be labeled deviant. If we agree with French sociologist Emile Durkheim that no society is free of crime, the determination of policies allocating resources and setting criteria for law-enforcement goals becomes an important variable. This consideration was well stated by the President's Crime Commission: "The police must make important judgments about what conduct is in fact criminal; about the allocation of scarce resources;

and about the gravity of each individual incident and the proper steps that should be taken."

In a heterogeneous society such as the United States, there are bound to be varying interpretations of deviance. Should emphasis be on "white-collar" crimes such as embezzlement, on "organized crime," or on "low-level" violations such as public drunkenness, shoplifting, and crimes without victims? Each of these categories involves different social classes, different perceptions of deviance, and different modes of enforcement. Each type of deviation embodies different threats and rewards for criminal justice agencies.

To help in conceptually organizing the functions of the police, three primary categories have been developed: order maintenance, law enforcement, and service. The order maintenance function is a broad mandate to prevent behavior that disturbs or threatens to disturb the public peace. Domestic quarrels, a noisy "drunk," a tavern brawl, a panhandler soliciting on the streets—these are examples of behavior that may require peacekeeping efforts of the police. Whereas most criminal laws specify acts that are illegal, laws regarding disorderly conduct define conditions that are ambiguous and that depend on the social environment and on the perceptions and norms of the actors. Law enforcement involves violations of the law in which only guilt must be assessed (murder, rape, burglary), whereas order maintenance involves violations of the law when interpretation of right conduct and assignment of blame may be in dispute. In modern society the police are increasingly called upon to perform a number of services for the populace. This service function—providing first aid, rescuing animals, finding missing persons, and helping the disabled—has become the dominant source of police activities. Although the public may depend on the order maintenance and service functions of the police, it acts as if law enforcement—catching lawbreakers—were the most important function.

In a democracy, efforts of police to carry out their functions are mainly reactive (citizen-invoked) rather than proactive (police-invoked). Only in the vice, narcotics, and traffic divisions of the modern police department does one find law officers activated by information gathered internally by the organization. Most criminal acts occur at times that are unpredictable and in a private rather than public place. The police respond to calls from persons who telephone, who signal a patrol car or an officer on foot, or who appear at the station to register a need or complaint. All these factors influence the way the police do their job. In addition, because the police usually arrive at the scene only after the crime has been committed and the perpetrator has fled, the job of finding the guilty party is hampered by the time lapse and the reliability of the information supplied by the victim. To a large extent, reports by victims define the boundaries of law enforcement.

The role of the police in U.S. society is indeed undergoing a critical rethinking. After many years of focusing on the law-enforcement–crime fighter role, we are now emphasizing the value of order maintenance and service as a primary focus of police resources. Parallel to this reorientation is an emphasis upon greater community response by the police and the importance of police accountability for police actions. If these trends become widespread, a restructuring of police organizations will probably follow.

In the justice system, the police stand as the gateway for the entrance of the raw materials to be processed. The cases sent to the prosecutor for charging, and thence to the courts for adjudication, begin with the decision of an individual police officer that probable cause exists to make an arrest. In the criminal justice system the ultimate fate of one group of clients rests with another group of clients. Decisions made by the police concerning offenders may be reversed by the prosecutor or the judge. Although the police may introduce clients into the system through their power of arrest, the outcome of each case is in the hands of others. The police have final power only in those cases filtered out of the system at the intake point.

Police Culture

The position of "police officer" is more than a cluster of formally prescribed duties and role expectations held jointly by criminal justice officials and members of the political community. In addition to the formal administrative language that specifies duties and responsibilities, there is a cultural dimension to the position that has a profound influence on the operational code of the police, both as a unit and as individuals behaving within a bureaucratic framework.

Social scientists have demonstrated that there is a definite relationship between one's occupational environment and the way one interprets events; an occupation may be seen as a major badge of identity that an individual acts to protect as a facet of his or her self-esteem and person. Thus, entry requirements, training, and professional socialization produce a homogeneity of attitudes that guides the police in their daily work.

National studies of occupational status have shown that the public ascribes more prestige to the police now than in prior decades, even though police officers do not believe the public regards their calling as honorable. Publications of police organizations repeatedly take up the theme that the public does not appreciate law-enforcement agents. In a Denver survey, 98 percent of police officers reported that they had experienced verbal or physical abuse and that these incidents tended to occur in neighborhoods of minority and underprivileged groups. Part of the burden of the police is that they have doubts about their professional status. Yet opinion polls consistently indicate that the overwhelming majority of citizens, even those in the ghetto, see the police as protectors of persons and property.

Discretion is a characteristic of bureaucracy. Unlike most organizations, however, the discretion the police have increases as one moves down the hierarchy. Thus the patrol officer, the most numerous and lowest-ranking of officers, has the greatest amount of discretion. He or she deals with clients alone and is almost solely in charge of enforcing the most ambiguous laws—conflicts among citizens where the definition of offensive behavior is most often open to dispute. The police officer's perception of the situation, as shaped by his or her personal values and norms, is crucial in determining what action the officer will take and what charges will be filed.

The police officer's world is circumscribed by the all-encompassing demands of the job. Not only are the police socialized to norms that accentuate loyalty to fellow officers, a professional esprit de corps, and the symbolism of authority, but the situational context of their position limits their freedom to isolate their vocational role from other aspects of their lives. From the time they are first given their badges and guns, they must always carry these reminders of their position—the tools of the trade—and be prepared to use them. Thus, the requirements that the police maintain vigilance against crime even when off duty and that they work at "odd hours," along with the limited opportunities for social contact with persons other than fellow officers, reinforce the values of the police subculture.

The "Impossible" Mandate

In a thoughtful essay Peter Manning wrote that the police agree with their audiences, their professional interpreters—the American family, criminals, and politicians—in at least one respect: they have an "impossible" mandate. In society, various occupational groups are given license to carry out certain activities that others are not. Indeed, groups achieving professional status have formal rules and codes of ethics that not only set their own standards but also define their occupational mandate. Medical doctors, for example, have the right to prescribe drugs and perform operations, but they are also able to set the boundaries of their mandate. Because over time the practice of medicine has become a secure profession, there is little disagreement in society about the tasks, attitudes, and values that set its practitioners apart.

The police in contemporary society are in trouble largely because they have been unable to define their mandate; it has been defined for them by those they serve. As a result, citizens have a distorted notion of police work. People are aware of the excitement of a small portion of police work, but then mistakenly broaden this notion to include all police activities. For much of the public, the police are viewed as always ready to respond to citizen demands—as highly organized crime fighters able to keep society from falling apart.

Sociopolitical changes in the United States have added to the tensions between the mandate of the police and their ability to fulfill it. In the past hundred years there have been massive shifts of population from rural areas to the cities. Criminal law has been called upon to serve a variety of purposes that are only tangentially related to law enforcement and order maintenance. Affluence has brought the criminal justice system new problems—such as the ease of communication and the abundance of property. Police have been assigned the tasks of crime prevention, crime detection, and the apprehension of criminals. Because they have a monopoly on legal violence, they have a mandate that claims to include efficient, apolitical, and professional enforcement of the law. All this is to be accomplished within the bounds dictated by a democratic society that values due process of law.

The mandate given the police is indeed "impossible." This will be true so long as there are misunderstandings, on the part of the police and the public, about the nature of law-enforcement work, the potential for success in controlling crime, and the role of law in a democratic society.

Suggestions for Further Reading

BAKER, MARK. *Cops.* New York: Simon & Schuster, 1985. A picture of police work based on interviews of officers in both rural and urban police departments throughout the United States.

BAYLEY, DAVID, AND JEROME SKOLNICK. *The New Blue Line: Police Innovation in Six American Cities.* New York: Free Press, 1986.

GELLER, WILLIAM A., ed. *Police Leadership in America.* New York: Praeger, 1985. Forty-one essays by leaders of police organizations and scholars concerned with law enforcement and order maintenance in the United States. The focus is on the questions "Who runs the police?" and "Who should?"

GOLDSTEIN, HERMAN. *Problem-Oriented Policing.* New York: McGraw-Hill, 1990. Examination of the move toward problem-oriented or community policing. Goldstein argues for a shift to this focus.

MAAS, PETER. *Serpico.* New York: Bantam Books, 1973. The experience of a New York City police officer's fight against corruption in his department.

MANNING, PETER K. *Police Work.* Cambridge, Mass.: M.I.T. Press, 1977. An analysis of police work and the dilemma of the police mandate. The author discusses the political means and strategies that police use in an attempt to live up to the ideal imposed by the public's expectations.

McCLURE, JAMES. *Cop World.* New York: Pantheon Books, 1984. A case study of the San Diego Police Department giving an in-depth account of police work.

MUIR, WILLIAM K., JR. *Police: Streetcorner Politicians.* Chicago: University of Chicago Press, 1977. A study of the attitudes and values of police officers.

MURANO, VINCENT. *Cop Hunter.* New York: Simon & Schuster, 1990. The story of an undercover cop who worked for ten years for the Internal Affairs Division of the New York City Police Department. Murano emphasizes the moral dilemmas of policing fellow officers.

WESTLEY, WILLIAM. *Violence and the Police.* Cambridge, Mass.: M.I.T. Press, 1971. Although somewhat dated, this is a seminal work on the sociological context that promotes secrecy among the police.

WILSON, JAMES Q. *Varieties of Police Behavior.* Cambridge, Mass.: Harvard University Press, 1968. An examination of the police function and the styles of policing in a variety of communities. It shows the links between culture, politics, and law enforcement policies.

4

Police Discretion Not to Invoke the Criminal Process: Low-Visibility Decisions in the Administration of Justice

Joseph Goldstein

Legislatures write the criminal laws as if they were commands to be enforced by the police, but officers have wide latitude in determining how the laws will be enforced. Professor Joseph Goldstein of the Yale Law School notes that decisions not to invoke the law are shielded from the public's view. Of particular interest is his development of the concepts of "total," "full," and "actual" enforcement. The extent to which the police pursue a policy approaching "full" enforcement for all offenses depends upon the values of the community.

Police decisions not to invoke the criminal process largely determine the outer limits of law enforcement. By such decisions, the police define the ambit of discretion throughout the process of other decision makers—prosecutor, grand and petit jury, judge, probation officer, correction authority, and parole and pardon boards. These police decisions, unlike their decisions to invoke the law, are generally of extremely low visibility and consequently are seldom the subject of review. Yet an opportunity for review and appraisal of nonenforcement decisions is essential to the functioning of the rule of law in our system of criminal justice. This article will therefore be an attempt to determine how the visibility of such police decisions may be increased and what procedures should be established to evaluate them on a continuing basis, in the light of the complex of objectives of the criminal law and of the paradoxes toward which the administration of criminal justice inclines.

I. The criminal law is one of many intertwined mechanisms for the social control of human behavior. It defines behavior which is deemed intolerably disturbing to or destructive of community values and prescribes sanctions which the state is authorized to impose upon persons convicted or suspected of engaging in prohibited conduct. Following a plea or verdict of guilty, the state deprives offenders of life,

Source: Reprinted by permission of the Yale Law Journal Company and Fred B. Rothman & Company from *The Yale Law Journal,* Vol. 69, pp. 543–594. Footnotes omitted.

liberty, dignity, or property through convictions, fines, imprisonments, killings, and supervised releases, and thus seeks to punish, restrain, and rehabilitate them, as well as to deter others from engaging in proscribed activity. Before a verdict, and despite the presumption of innocence which halos every person, the state deprives the suspect of life, liberty, dignity, or property through the imposition of deadly force, search and seizure of persons and possessions, accusation, imprisonment, and bail, and thus seeks to facilitate the enforcement of the criminal law.

These authorized sanctions reflect the multiple and often conflicting purposes which now surround and confuse criminal law administration at and between key decision points in the process. The stigma which accompanies conviction, for example, while serving a deterrent, and possibly retributive, function, becomes operative upon the offender's release and thus impedes the rehabilitation objective of probation and parole. Similarly, the restraint function of imprisonment involves the application of rules and procedures which, while minimizing escape opportunities, contributes to the deterioration of offenders confined for reformation. Since police decisions not to invoke the criminal process may likewise further some objectives while hindering others, or, indeed, run counter to all, any meaningful appraisal of these decisions should include an evaluation of their impact throughout the process on the various objectives reflected in authorized sanctions and in the decisions of other administrators of criminal justice.

Under the rule of law, the criminal law has both a fair-warning function for the public and a power-restricting function for officials. Both post- and preverdict sanctions, therefore, may be imposed only in accord with authorized procedures. No sanctions are to be inflicted other than those which have been prospectively prescribed by the Constitution, legislation, or judicial decision for a particular crime or a particular kind of offender. These concepts, of course, do not preclude differential disposition, within the authorized limits, of persons suspected or convicted of the same or similar offenses. In an ideal system differential handling, individualized justice, would result, but only from an equal application of officially approved criteria designed to implement officially approved objectives. And finally a system which presumes innocence requires that preconviction sanctions be kept at a minimum consistent with assuring an opportunity for the process to run its course.

A regularized system of review is a requisite for ensuring substantial compliance by the administrators of criminal justice with these rule-of-law principles. Implicit in the word "review" and obviously essential to the operation of any review procedure is the visibility of the decisions and conduct to be scrutinized. Pretrial hearings on motions, the trial, appeal, and the writ of habeas corpus constitute a formal system for evaluating the actions of officials invoking the criminal process. The public hearing, the record of proceedings, and the publication of court opinions—all features of the formal system—preserve and increase the visibility of official enforcement activity and facilitate and encourage the development of an informal system of appraisal. These proceedings and documents are widely reported and subjected to analysis and comment by legislative, professional, and other interested groups and individuals.

But police decisions not to invoke the criminal process, except when reflected in gross failures of service, are not visible to the community. Nor are they likely to be visible to official state reviewing agencies, even those within the police department. Failure to tag illegally parked cars is an example of gross failure of service, open to public view and recognized for what it is. An officer's decision, however, not to investigate or report adequately a disturbing event which he has reason to believe constitutes a violation of the criminal law does not ordinarily carry with it consequences sufficiently visible to make the community, the legislature, the prosecutor, or the courts aware of a possible failure of service. The police officer, the suspect, the police department, and frequently even the victim, when directly concerned with a decision not to invoke, unlike the same parties when responsible for or subject to a decision to invoke, generally have neither the incentive nor the opportunity to obtain review of that decision or the police conduct associated with it. Furthermore, official police records are usually too incomplete to permit evaluations of nonenforcement decisions in the light of the purposes of the criminal law. Consequently, such decisions, unlike decisions to enforce, are generally not subject to the control which would follow from administrative, judicial, legislative, or community review and appraisal.

Confidential reports detailing the day-to-day decisions and activities of a large municipal police force have been made available to the author by the American Bar Foundation. These reports give limited visibility to a wide variety of police decisions not to invoke the criminal process. Three groups of such decisions will be described and analyzed. Each constitutes a police "program" of nonenforcement either based on affirmative departmental policy or condoned by default. All of the decisions, to the extent that the officers concerned thought about them at all, represent well-intentioned, honest judgments, which seem to reflect the police officer's conception of his job. None of the decisions involve bribery or corruption, nor do they concern "obsolete," though unrepealed, criminal laws. Specifically, these programs involve police decisions (1) not to enforce the narcotics laws against certain violators, who inform against other "more serious" violators; (2) not to enforce the felonious assault laws against an assailant whose victim does not sign a complaint; and (3) not to enforce gambling laws against persons engaged in the numbers racket, but instead to harass them. Each of these decisions is made even though the police "know" a crime has been committed and even though they may "know" who the offender is and may, in fact, have apprehended him. But before describing and evaluating these nonenforcement programs, as an agency of review might do, it is necessary to determine what discretion, if any, the police, as invoking agents, have, and conceptually to locate the police in relation to other principal decision makers in the criminal law process.

II. The police have a duty not to enforce the substantive law of crimes unless invocation of the process can be achieved within bounds set by constitution, statute, court decision, and possibly official pronouncements of the prosecutor. *Total enforcement,* were it possible, is thus precluded, by generally applicable due process restrictions on such police procedures as arrest, search, seizure, and interrogation. *Total enforcement* is further precluded by such specific procedural restrictions as prohibitions on invoking an adultery statute unless the spouse of one of the parties complains, or an unlawful-possession-of-firearms statute if the offender surrenders his dangerous weapons during a statutory period of amnesty. Such restrictions of general and specific application mark the bounds, often ambiguously, of an area of *full enforcement* in which the police are not only authorized but expected to enforce fully the law of crimes. An area of *no enforcement* lies, therefore, between the perimeter of *total enforcement* and the outer limits of *full enforcement.* In this *no-enforcement* area, the police have no authority to invoke the criminal process.

Within the area of *full enforcement,* the police have not been delegated discretion not to invoke the criminal process. On the contrary, those state statutes providing for municipal police departments which define the responsibility of police provide:

> It shall be the duty of the police . . . under the direction of the mayor and chief of police and in conformity with the ordinances of the city, and the laws of the state, . . . to pursue and arrest any persons fleeing from justice . . . to apprehend any and all persons in the act of committing any offense against the laws of the state . . . and to take the offender forthwith before the proper court or magistrate, to be dealt with for the offense; to make complaints to the proper officers and magistrates of any person known or believed by them to be guilty of the violation of the ordinances of the city or the penal laws of the state; and at all times diligently and faithfully to enforce all such laws. . . .

Even in jurisdictions without such a specific statutory definition, declarations of the *full enforcement* mandate generally appear in municipal charters, ordinances, or police manuals. Police manuals, for example, commonly provide, in sections detailing the duties at each level of the police hierarchy, that the captain, superintendent, lieutenant, or patrolman shall be responsible, so far as is in his power, for the prevention and detection of crime and the enforcement of all criminal laws and ordinances. Illustrative of the spirit and policy of *full enforcement* is this protestation from the introduction to the Rules and Regulations of the Atlanta, Georgia, Police Department:

> Enforcement of all Criminal Laws and City Ordinances, is my obligation. There are no specialties under the Law. My eyes must be open to traffic problems and disorders, though I move on other assignments, to slinking vice in back streets and dives though I have been directed elsewhere, to the suspicious appearance of evil wherever it is encountered. . . . I must be impartial because the Law surrounds, protects, and applies to all alike, rich and poor, low and high, black and white. . . .

Minimally, then, *full enforcement,* so far as the police are concerned, means (1) the investigation of every disturbing event which is reported to or observed by them and which they have reason to suspect may be a violation of the criminal law; (2) following a determination that some crime has been committed, an effort to discover its perpetrators; and (3) the presentation of all information collected by them to the prosecutor for his determination of the appropriateness of further invoking the criminal process.

Full enforcement, however, is not a realistic expectation. In addition to ambiguities in the definitions of both substantive offenses and due process boundaries, countless limitations and pressures preclude the possibility of the police seeking or achieving *full enforcement.* Limitations of time, personnel, and investigative devices—all in part but not entirely functions of budget—force the development, by plan or default, of priorities of enforcement. Even if there were "enough police" adequately equipped and trained, pressures from within and without the department, which is after all a human institution, may force the police to invoke the criminal

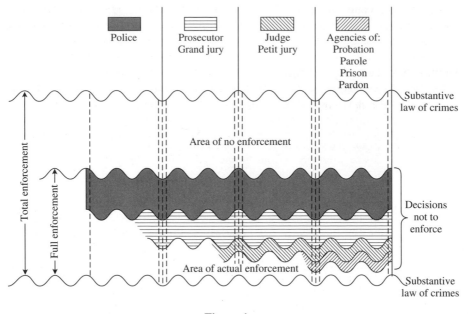

Figure 1

process selectively. By decisions not to invoke within the area of *full enforcement,* the police largely determine the outer limits of *actual enforcement* throughout the criminal process. This relationship of the police to the total administration of criminal justice can be seen in the diagram [Figure 1]. They may reinforce, or they may undermine, the legislature's objectives in designating certain conduct "criminal" and in authorizing the imposition of certain sanctions following conviction. A police decision to ignore a felonious assault "because the victim will not sign a complaint" usually precludes the prosecutor or grand jury from deciding whether to accuse, judge or jury from determining guilt or innocence, judge from imposing the most "appropriate" sentence, probation or correctional authorities from instituting the most "appropriate" restraint and rehabilitation programs, and finally parole or pardon authorities from determining the offender's readiness for release to the community. This example is drawn from one of the three programs of nonenforcement about to be discussed.

III. Trading enforcement against a narcotics suspect for information about another narcotics offense or offender may involve two types of police decisions not to invoke fully the criminal process. First, there may be a decision to ask for the dismissal or reduction of the charge for which the informant is held; second, there may be a decision to overlook future violations while the suspect serves as an informer. The second type is an example of a relatively pure police decision not to invoke the criminal process while the first requires, at a minimum, tacit approval by prosecutor or judge. But examination of only the pure types of decisions would oversimplify the problem. They fail to illustrate the extent to which police nonenforcement decisions may permeate the process as well as influence, and be influenced by, prosecutor and court action in settings which fail to prompt appraisal of such decisions in light of the purposes of the criminal law. Both types of decision, pure and conglomerate, are nonetheless primarily police decisions. They are distinguishable from a prosecutor's or court's decision to trade information for enforcement under an immunity statute, and from such parliamentary decisions as the now-repealed seventeenth- and eighteenth-century English statutes which gave a convicted offender who secured the conviction of his accomplice an absolute right to pardon. Such prosecutor and parliamentary decisions to trade information for enforcement, unlike the police decisions to be described, have not only been authorized by a legislative body but have also been made sufficiently visible to permit review.

In the municipality studied, regular uniformed officers, with general law enforcement duties on precinct assignments, and a special narcotics squad of detectives, with citywide jurisdiction, are responsible for enforcement of the state narcotics laws. The existence of the special squad acts as a pressure on the uniformed officer to be the first to discover any sale, possession, or use of narcotics in his precinct. Careful preparation of a case for prosecution may thus become secondary to this objective. Indeed, approximately 80 percent of those apprehended for narcotics violations during one year were discharged. In the opinion of the special squad, which processes each arrested narcotics suspect, either the search was illegal or the evidence obtained inadequate. The precinct officer's lack of interest in carefully developing a narcotics case for prosecution often amounts in effect to a police decision not to enforce but rather to harass.

But we are concerned here primarily with the decisions of the narcotics squad, which, like the Federal Narcotics Bureau, has established a policy of concentrating enforcement efforts against the "big supplier." The chief of the squad claimed that informers must be utilized to implement that policy, and that in order to get informants it is necessary to trade "little ones for big ones." Informers are used to arrange and make purchases of narcotics, to elicit information from suspects, including persons in custody, and to recruit additional informants.

Following arrest, a suspect will generally offer to serve as an informer to "do himself some good." If an arrestee fails to initiate such negotiations, the interrogating officer will suggest that something may be gained by disclosing sources of supply and by serving as an informer. A high mandatory minimum sentence for selling, a high maximum sentence for possession, and, where users are involved, a strong desire on their part to avoid the agonies of withdrawal, combine to place the police in an excellent bargaining position to recruit informers. To assure performance, each informer is charged with a narcotics violation, and final disposition is postponed until the defendant has fulfilled his part of the bargain. To protect the informer, the special squad seeks to camouflage him in the large body of releasees by not disclosing his identity even to the arresting precinct officer, who is given no explanation for release. Thus persons encountered on the street by a uniformed patrolman the day after their arrest may have been discharged, or they may have been officially charged and then released on bail or personal recognizance to await trial or to serve as informers.

While serving as informers, suspects are allowed to engage in illegal activity. Continued use of narcotics is condoned; the narcotics detective generally is not concerned with the problem of informants who make buys and use some of the evidence themselves. Though informers are usually warned that their status does not give them a "license to peddle," possession of a substantial amount of narcotics may be excused. In one case, a defendant found guilty of possession of marijuana argued that she was entitled to be placed on probation since she had cooperated with the police by testifying against three persons charged with the sale of narcotics. The sentencing judge denied her request because he discovered that her cooperation was related to the possession of a substantial amount of heroin, an offense for which she was arrested (but never charged) while on bail for the marijuana violation. A narcotics squad inspector, in response to an inquiry from the judge, revealed that the defendant had not been charged with possession of heroin because she had been cooperative with the police on that offense.

In addition to granting such outright immunity for some violations, the police will recommend to the prosecutor either that an informer's case be *nolle prossed* or, more frequently, that the charge be reduced to a lesser offense. And, if the latter course is followed, the police usually recommend to the judge, either in response to his request for information or in the presentence report, that informers be placed on probation or given relatively light sentences. Both the prosecutor and judge willingly respond to police requests for reducing a charge of sale to a lesser offense because they consider the mandatory minimum too severe. As a result, during a four-year period in this jurisdiction, less than 2.5 percent of all persons charged with the sale of narcotics were convicted of that offense.

The narcotics squad's policy of trading *full enforcement* for information is justified on the grounds that apprehension and prosecution of the "big supplier" is facilitated. The absence of any such individual is attributed to this policy. As one member of the squad said, "[The city] is too hot. There are too many informants." A basic, though untested, assumption of the policy is that ridding the city of the "big supplier" is the key to solving its narcotics problem. Even if this assumption were empirically validated, the desirability of continuing such a policy cannot be established without taking into account its total impact on the administration of criminal justice in the city, the state, and the nation. Yet no procedure has been designed to enable the police and other key administrators of criminal justice to obtain such an appraisal. The extent and nature of the need for such a procedure can be illustrated, despite the limitations of available data, by presenting in the form of a mock report some of the questions, some of the answers, and some of the proposals a policy appraisal and review board might consider.

Following a description of the informer program, a report might ask: *To what extent, if at all, has the legislature delegated to the police the authority to grant, or obtain a grant of, complete or partial immunity from prosecution, in exchange for information about narcotics suppliers?* No provisions of the general immunity or narcotics statutes authorize the police to exercise such discretion. The general immunity statute requires a high degree of visibility by providing that immunity be allowed only on a written motion by the prosecuting attorney to the court and that the information given be reduced to writing under the direction of the judge to preclude future prosecution for the traded offense or offenses. The narcotics statutes, unlike comparable legislation concerning other specific crimes, make no provision for obtaining information by awarding immunity from prosecution. Nor is there any indication, other than possibly in the maximum sentences authorized, that the legislature intended that certain narcotics offenses be given high priority or be enforced at the expense of other offenses. What evidence there is of legislative intent suggests the contrary; this fact is recognized by the local police manual. And nothing in the statute providing for the establishment of local police departments can be construed to authorize the policy of trading enforcement for information. That statute makes *full enforcement* a duty of the police. The narcotics squad has ignored this mandate and adopted an informer policy which appears to constitute a usurpation of legislative function. It does not follow that the police must discontinue employing informers, but they ought to discontinue trading enforcement for information until the legislature, the court, or the prosecutor explicitly initiates such a program. Whether the police policy of trading enforcement for information should be proposed for legislative consideration would depend upon the answers to some of the questions which follow.

Does trading enforcement for information fulfill the retributive, restraining, and reformative functions of the state's narcotics laws? By in effect licensing the user–informer to satisfy his addiction and assuring the peddler–informer, who may also be a user, that he will obtain dismissal or reduction of the pending charge to a lesser offense, the police undermine, if not negate, the retributive and restraining functions of the narcotics laws. In addition, the community is deprived of an opportunity to subject these offenders, particularly the addicts, to treatment aimed at reformation. In fact, the police ironically acknowledge the inconsistency of their program with the goal of treatment: "cured" addicts are not used as informers for fear that exposure to narcotics might cause their relapse. A comparison of the addict-release policies of the police, sentencing judge, and probation and parole authorities demonstrates the extent to which the administration of criminal justice can be set awry by a police nonenforcement program. At one point on the continuum, the police release the addict to informer status so that he can maintain his association with peddlers and users. The addict accepts such status on the tacit condition that continued use will be condoned. At other points on the continuum, the judge and probation and parole authorities make treatment a condition of an addict's release and continued use or even association with narcotics users the basis for revoking probation or parole. Thus the inherent conflict between basic purposes of the criminal law is compounded by conflicts among key decision points in the process.

Does trading enforcement for information implement the deterrent function of criminal law administration? If deterrence depends—and little if anything is really known about the deterrent impact of the criminal law—in part at least, upon the potential offender's perception of law enforcement, the informer policy can have only a negative effect. In addition to the chance of nondetection which accompanies the commission of all crimes in varying degrees, the narcotics suspect has four-to-one odds that he will not be charged following detection and arrest. And he has a high expectation, even if charged, of obtaining a reduction or dismissal of an accurate charge. These figures reflect and reinforce the offender's view of the administration of criminal justice as a bargaining process initiated either by offering information "to do himself some good" or by a member of the narcotics squad advising the uninformed suspect, the "new offender," of the advantages of disclosing his narcotics "connections." Such law enforcement can have little, if any, deterrent impact.

That the "big supplier," an undefined entity, has been discouraged from using the city as a headquarters was confirmed by a local federal agent and a U.S. attorney in testimony before a Senate committee investigating illicit narcotics traffic. They attributed the result, however, to the state's high mandatory minimum sentence for selling, not to the informer policy. In fact, that municipal police policy was not made visible at the hearings. It was mentioned neither in their testimony nor in the testimony of the chief of police and the head of the narcotics squad. These local authorities may have reasoned that since the mandatory sentence facilitates the recruitment of informers who, in turn, are essential to keeping the "big supplier" outside city limits, the legislature's sentencing policy could be credited with the "achievement."

Whether the police informer program, the legislature's sentencing policy, both, or neither, caused the "big supplier" to locate elsewhere is not too significant; the traffic and use of narcotics in the city remain major problems. Since user demand is maintained, if not increased, by trading enforcement for information, potential and actual peddlers are encouraged to supply the city's addicts. Testimony before the Senate committee indicates that although the "big suppliers" have moved their headquarters to other cities, there are now in the city a large number of small peddlers serving a minimum of 1,500 and in all probability a total of 2,500 users, and that the annual expenditure for illicit narcotics in the city is estimated at not lower than $10 million and probably as high as $18 million. Evaluated in terms of deterrent effect, the program of trading enforcement for information to reach the "big supplier" has failed to implement locally the ultimate objective of the narcotics laws— reducing addiction. Furthermore, the business of the "big supplier" has not been effectively deterred. At best suppliers have been discouraged from basing their operations in the city, which continues to be a lucrative market. Thus by maintaining the market, local policy, although a copy of national policy, may very well hinder the efforts of the Federal Narcotics Bureau.

A report of a policy appraisal and review board might find: "Trading little ones for big ones" is outside the ambit of municipal police discretion and should continue to remain so because it conflicts with the basic objectives of the criminal law. Retribution, restraint, and reformation are subverted by a policy which condones the use and possession of narcotics. And deterrence cannot be enhanced by a police program which provides potential and actual suppliers and users with more illustrations of nonenforcement than enforcement.

A report might conclude by exploring and suggesting alternative programs for coping with the narcotics problem. No attempt will be made here to exhaust or detail all possible alternatives. An obvious one would be a rigorous program of *full enforcement* designed to dry up, or at least drastically reduce, local consumer and peddler demand for illicit narcotics. If information currently obtained from suspects is essential and worth a price, compensation might be given to informers, with payments deferred until a suspect's final release. Such a program would neither undermine the retributive and restraining objectives of the criminal law nor deprive the community of an opportunity to impose rehabilitation regimes on the offender. Funds provided by deferred payments might enhance an offender's chances of getting off to a good start upon release. Moreover, changing the picture presently perceived by potential violators from nonenforcement to enforcement would at least not preclude the possibility of deterrence. Such a program might even facilitate the apprehension of "big suppliers" who, faced with decreasing demand, might either be forced to discontinue serving the city because sales would no longer be profitable or to adopt bolder sales methods which would expose them to easier detection.

Full enforcement will place the legislature in a position to evaluate its narcotics laws by providing a basis for answering such questions as: Will *full enforcement* increase the price of narcotics to the user? Will such inflation increase the frequency of crimes committed to finance narcotics purchases? Or will *full enforcement* reduce the number of users and the frequency of connected crimes? Will too great or too costly an administrative burden be placed on the prosecutor's office and the courts by *full enforcement?* Will correctional institutions be filled beyond "effective" capacity? The answers to these questions are now buried or obscured by decisions not to invoke the criminal process.

Failure of a *full enforcement* program might prompt a board recommendation to increase treatment or correctional personnel and facilities. Or a board, recognizing that *full enforcement* would be either too costly or inherently ineffective, might propose the repeal of statutes prohibiting the use and sale of narcotics and/or the enactment, as part of a treatment program, of legislation authorizing sales to users at a low price. Such legislative action would be designed to reduce use and connected offenses to a minimum. By taking profits out of sales it would lessen peddler incentive to create new addicts and eliminate the need to support the habit by the commission of crimes.

These then are the kinds of questions, answers, and proposals a policy appraisal and review board might explore in its report examining this particular type of police decision not to invoke the criminal process.

IV. Another low-visibility situation which an appraisal and review board might uncover in this municipality stems from police decisions not to invoke the felonious assault laws unless the victim signs a complaint. Like the addict–informer, the potential complainant in an assault case is both the victim of an offense and a key source of information. But unlike him, the complainant, who is not a suspect, and whose initial contact with the police is generally self-imposed, is not placed under pressure to bargain. And in contrast with the informer program, the police assault program was clearly not designed, if designed at all, to effectuate an identifiable policy.

During one month under the nonenforcement program of a single precinct, thirty-eight out of forty-three felonious assault cases, the great majority involving stabbings and cuttings, were cleared "because the victim refused to prosecute." This program, which is coupled with a practice of not encouraging victims to sign complaints, reduces the pressure of work by eliminating such tasks as apprehending and detaining suspects, writing detailed reports, applying for warrants to prefer charges, and appearing in court at inconvenient times for long periods without adequate compensation. As one officer explained, "run-of-the-mill" felonious assaults are so common in his precinct that prosecution of each case would force patrolmen to spend too much time in court and leave too little time for investigating other offenses. This rationalization exposes the private value system of individual officers as another policy-shaping factor. Some policemen feel, for example, that assault is an acceptable means of settling disputes among Negroes, and that when both assailant and victim are Negro, there is no immediate discernible harm to the public which justifies a decision to invoke the criminal process. Anticipation of dismissal by judge and district attorney of cases in which the victim is an uncooperative witness, the police claim, has been another operative factor in the development of the assault policy. A policy appraisal and review board, whose investigators had been specifically directed to examine the assault policy, should be able to identify these or other policy-shaping factors more precisely. Yet on the basis of the data available, a board could tentatively conclude that court and prosecutor responses do not explain why the police have failed to adopt a policy of encouraging assault victims to sign complaints, and, therefore, that the private value system of department members, as reflected in their attitude toward work load and in a stereotypical view of the Negro, is of primary significance.

Once some of the major policy-shaping factors have been identified, an appraisal and review board might formulate and attempt to answer the following or similar questions: Would it be consistent with any of the purposes of the criminal law to authorize police discretion in cases of felonious assaults as well as other specified offenses? Assuming that it would be consistent or at least more realistic to authorize police discretion in some cases, what limitations and guides, if any, should the legislature provide? Should legislation provide that factors such as work load, willingness of victims or certain victims to sign a complaint, the degree of violence, and attitude of prosecutor and judge be taken into account in the exercise of police discretion? If work load is to be recognized, should the legislature establish priorities of enforcement designed to assist the police in deciding which offenses among equally pressing ones are to be ignored or enforced? If assaults are made criminal in order to reduce threats to community peace and individual security, should a victim's willingness to prosecute, if he happens to live, be relevant to the exercise of police discretion? Does resting prosecution in the hands of the victim encourage him to "get even" with the assailant through retaliatory lawlessness? Or does such a policy place the decision in the hands of the assailant whose use of force has already demonstrated an ability and willingness to fulfill a threat?

Can the individual police officer, despite his own value system, sufficiently respond to officially articulated community values to be delegated broad powers of discretion? If not, can or should procedures be designed to enable the police department to translate these values into rules and regulations for individual policemen? Can police officers or the department be trained to evaluate the extent to which current practice undermines a major criminal law objective of imposing upon all persons officially recognized minimum standards of human behavior? For example, can the individual officer of the department be trained to evaluate the effect of decisions in cases of felonious assault among Negroes on local programs for implementing national or state policies of integration in school, employment, and housing, and to determine the extent to which current policy weakens or reinforces stereotypes which are used to justify not only police policy but, more importantly, opposition to desegregation programs? Or should legislation provide that the police invoke the process in all felonious assault cases unless the prosecutor or court publicly provides them in recorded documents with authority and guides for exercising discretion, and thus make visible both the policy of nonenforcement and the agency or agencies responsible for it?

Some of these issues were considered and resolved by the Oakland, California, Police Department in 1957 when, after consultation with prosecutors and judges, it decided to abandon a similar assault policy and seek *full enforcement.* Chief of Police W. W. Vernon, describing Oakland's new program, wrote:

> In our assault cases for years we had followed this policy of releasing the defendant if the complainant did not feel aggrieved to the point of being willing to testify. . . . [Since] World War II . . . our assault cases increased tremendously to the point where we decided to do something about the increase.

Training materials prepared by the Oakland Police Academy disclose that between 1952 and 1956, while the decision to prosecute was vested in the victim, the rate of reported felonious assaults rose from 93 to 161 per 100,000 population and the annual number of misdemeanor assaults rose from 618 to 2,630. The materials emphasize that these statistics mean a work load of "nearly ten assault reports a day every day of the year." But they stress:

> The important point about these figures is not so much that they represent a substantial police workload, which they do, but more important, that they indicate an increasing lack of respect for the laws of society by a measurable segment of our population, and a corresponding threat to the rest of the citizens of our city. The police have a clear responsibility to develop respect for the law among those who disregard it in order to ensure the physical safety and well-being of those who do. . . .
>
> We recognize that the problem exists mainly because the injured person has refused to sign a complaint against the perpetrator. The injured person has usually refused to sign for two reasons: first, because of threats of future bodily harm or other action by the perpetrator and, secondly, because it has been a way of life among some people to adjust grievances by physical assaults and not by the recognized laws of society which are available to them.
>
> We, the police, have condoned these practices to some extent by not taking advantage of the means at our disposal; that is, by not gathering sufficient evidence and signing complaints on information and belief in those cases where the complainant refuses to prosecute. The policy and procedure of gathering sufficient evidence and signing complaints on information and belief should instill in these groups the realization that the laws of society must be resorted to in settling disputes. When it is realized by many of these people that we will sign complaints ourselves and will not condone fighting and cuttings, many of them will stop such practices.

Following conferences with the police, the local prosecutors and judges pledged their support for the new assault program. The district attorney's office will deny a complainant's request that a case be dropped and suggest that it be addressed to the judge in open court. The judge, in turn, will advise the complainant that the case cannot be dismissed, and that a perjury, contempt, or false-report complaint will be issued in "appropriate cases" against the victim who denies facts originally alleged. The police have been advised that the court and prosecutor will actively cooperate in the implementation of the new program, but that every case will not result in a complaint since it is the "job [of the police] to turn in the evidence and it's the prosecuting attorney's job to determine when a complaint will be issued." Thus the

role of each of the key decision-making agencies with preconviction invoking authority is clearly delineated and integrated.

With the inauguration of a new assault policy, an appraisal and review board
might establish procedures for determining how effectively the objectives of the policy are fulfilled in practice. A board might design intelligence-retrieving devices
which would provide more complete data than the following termed by Chief Vernon
"the best evidence that our program is accomplishing the purpose for which it was
developed." Prior to the adoption of the new policy, 80 percent of the felonious
assault cases "cleared" were cleared because "complainant refuses to prosecute,"
while only 32.2 percent of the clearances made during the first three months in 1958
were for that reason, even though the overall clearance rate rose during that period.
And "during the first quarter of this year Felony Assaults dropped 11.1 percent
below the same period last year, and in March they were 35.6 percent below March
of last year. Battery cases were down 19.0 percent for the first three months of
1958." An appraisal and review board might attempt to determine the extent to
which the police in cases formerly dropped because "complainant refused to testify"
have consciously or otherwise substituted another reason for "case cleared." And it
might estimate the extent to which the decrease in assaults *reported* reflects, if it
does, a decrease in the *actual* number of assaults or only a decrease in the number
of victims willing to report assaults. Such follow-up investigations and what actually
took place in Oakland on an informal basis between police, prosecutor, and judge
illustrate some of the functions an appraisal and review board might regularly
perform.

V. Police decisions to harass, though generally perceived as overzealous
enforcement, constitute another body of nonenforcement activities meriting investigation by an appraisal and review board. Harassment is the imposition by the police,
acting under color of law, of sanctions prior to conviction as a means of ultimate
punishment, rather than as a device for the invocation of criminal proceedings. Characteristic of harassment are efforts to annoy certain "offenders" both by temporarily
detaining or arresting them without intention to seek prosecution and by destroying
or illegally seizing their property without any intention to use it as evidence. Like
other police decisions not to invoke the criminal process, harassment is generally of
extremely low visibility, probably because the police ordinarily restrict such activity
to persons who are unable to afford the costs of litigation, who would, or think they
would, command little respect even if they were to complain, or who wish to keep
themselves out of public view in order to continue their illicit activities. Like the
informer program, harassment is conducted by the police in an atmosphere of cooperation with other administrators of criminal justice. Since harassment, by definition,
is outside the rule of law, any benefits attributed to such police activity cannot justify
its continuation. An appraisal and review board, however, would not limit its investigations to making such a finding. It would be expected to identify and analyze
factors underlying harassment and to formulate proposals for replacing harassment—
lawless nonenforcement—with enforcement of the criminal law.

Investigators for an appraisal and review board in this jurisdiction would discover, for example, a mixture of enforcement and harassment in a police program
designed to regulate the gambling operations of mutual-numbers syndicates. The

enforcement phase is conducted by a highly trained unit of less than a dozen men who diligently gather evidence in order to prosecute and convict syndicate operators of conspiracy to violate the gambling laws. This specialized unit, which operates independently of and without the knowledge of other officers, conducts all its work within the due process boundaries of *full enforcement.* Consequently, the conviction rate is high for charges based upon its investigations. The harassment phase is conducted by approximately sixty officers who tour the city and search on sight, because of prior information, or such telltale actions as carrying a paper bag, a symbol of the trade, persons who they suspect are collecting bets. They question the "suspect" and proceed to search him, his car, or home without first making a valid arrest to legalize the search. If gambling paraphernalia are found, the police, fully aware that the exclusionary rule prohibits its use as evidence in this jurisdiction, confiscate the "contraband" and arrest the individual without any intention of seeking application of the criminal law.

Gambling operators treat the harassment program as a cost of doing business, "a risk of the trade." Each syndicate retains a bonding firm and an attorney to service members who are arrested. When a "runner" or "bagman" is absent from his scheduled rounds, routine release procedures are initiated. The bondsman, sometimes prematurely, checks with the police to determine if a syndicate man has been detained. If the missing man is in custody, the syndicate's attorney files an application for a writ of habeas corpus and appears before a magistrate who usually sets bail at a nominal amount and adjourns hearing the writ, at the request of the police, until the following day. Prior to the scheduled hearing, the police usually advise the court that they have no intention of proceeding, and the case is closed. Despite the harassee's release, the police retain the money and gambling paraphernalia. If the items seized are found in a car, the car is confiscated, with the cooperation of the prosecutor, under a nuisance abatement statute. Cars are returned, however, after the harassee signs a "consent decree" and pursuant to it, pays "court costs"—a fee which is based on the car's value and which the prosecutor calls "the real meat of the harassment program." The "decree," entered under a procedure devised by the court and prosecutor's office, enjoins the defendant from engaging in illegal activity and, on paper, frees the police from any tort liability by an acknowledgment that seizure of the vehicle was lawful and justified—even though one prosecutor has estimated that approximately 80 percent of the searches and seizures were illegal. A prosecuting attorney responsible for car confiscation initially felt that such procedures "in the ordinary practice of law would be unethical, revolting, and shameful," but explained that he now understands why he acted as he did:

> To begin with ... the laws in ... [this state] with respect to gambling are most inadequate. This is equally true of the punishment feature of the law. To illustrate ... a well-organized and productive gambling house or numbers racket would take in one-quarter of a million dollars each week. If, after a long and vigorous period of investigation and observation, the defendant was charged with violating the gambling laws and convicted therefor, the resulting punishment is so obviously weak and unprohibitive that the defendants are willing to shell out a relatively small fine or serve a relatively short time in prison. The ... [city's] gamblers and numbers men confidently feel that the odds are in their favor. If they operate for six months or a year, and accumulate untold thousands of dollars from the illegal activity, then

the meager punishment imposed upon them if they are caught is well worth it. Then, too, because of the search and seizure laws in . . . [this state], especially in regard to gambling and the numbers rackets, the hands of the police are tied. Unless a search can be made prior to an arrest so that the defendant can be caught in the act of violating the gambling laws, or a search warrant issued, there is no other earthly way of apprehending such people along with evidence sufficient to convict them that is admissible in court.

Because of these two inadequacies of the law (slight punishment and conservative search and seizure laws with regard to gambling) the prosecutor's office and the police department are forced to find other means of punishing, harassing, and generally making life uneasy for gamblers.

This position, fantastic as it is to be that of a law-trained official, a guardian of the rule of law, illustrates how extensively only one of many police harassment programs in this jurisdiction can permeate the process and be tolerated by other decision makers in a system of criminal administration where decisions not to enforce are of extremely low visibility.

Having uncovered such a gambling-control program, an appraisal and review board should recommend that the police abandon such harassment activities because they are antagonistic to the rule of law. In addition, the board might advance secondary reasons for eliminating harassment by exposing the inconsistencies between this program and departmental justifications for its narcotics and assault policies. While unnecessary to the condemnation of what is fundamentally lawless nonenforcement, such exposure might cause the police to question the wisdom of actions based on a personal or departmental belief that the legislature has authorized excessively lenient sanctions and restrictive enforcement procedures. The comparison might emphasize the inconsistencies of police policy toward organized crime by exposing the clash between an informer program designed to rid the city of the "big supplier" and a harassment program which tends to consolidate control of the numbers racket in a few syndicates "big" enough to sustain the legal, bonding, and other "business" costs of continued interruptions and the confiscation of property. More importantly, it should cause a reexamination and redefinition of "work load" which was so significant in the rationalization of the assault policy. A cost accounting would no doubt reveal that a significant part of "work load," as presently defined by the police, includes expenditures of public funds for personnel and equipment employed in unlawful activities. Once harassment is perceived by municipal officials concerned with budgets as an unauthorized expenditure of public funds, consideration for increased awards to the police department might be conditioned upon a showing that existing resources are now deployed for authorized purposes. Such action should stimulate police cooperation in implementing the board's proposal for curtailing harassment.

Further, to effectuate its recommendation, the board might attempt to clarify and redefine the duties of the police by a reclassification of crimes which would emphasize the mandate that no more than *full enforcement* of the existing criminal law as defined by the legislature is expected. For many crimes, this may mean little or no *actual enforcement* because the values protected by procedural limitations are more important than the values which may be infringed by a particular offense. A board might propose, for example, that crimes be classified not only as felonies and misdemeanors, but in terms of active and passive police enforcement. An *active enforcement* designation for an offense would mean that individual police officers or specialized squads are to be assigned the task of ferreting out and even triggering violations. *Passive enforcement* would mean that the police are to assume a sit-back-and-wait posture, that is, that they invoke the criminal process only when the disturbing event is brought to their attention by personal observation during a routine tour of duty or by someone outside the police force registering a complaint. Designation of gambling, for example, as a *passive enforcement* offense would officially apprise the police that substantial expenditures of personnel and equipment for enforcement are not contemplated unless the local community expresses a low tolerance for such disturbing events by constantly bringing them to police attention. The adoption of this or a similar classification scheme might not only aid in training the police to understand that harassment is unlawful, but it may also provide the legislature with a device for officially allowing local differences in attitude toward certain offenses to be reflected in police practice and for testing the desirability of removing criminal sanctions from certain kinds of currently proscribed behavior.

VI. The mandate of *full enforcement,* under circumstances which compel selective enforcement, has placed the municipal police in an intolerable position. As a result, nonenforcement programs have developed undercover, in a hit-or-miss fashion, and without regard to impact on the overall administration of justice or the basic objectives of the criminal law. Legislatures, therefore, ought to reconsider what discretion, if any, the police must or should have in invoking the criminal process, and what devices, if any, should be designed to increase visibility and hence reviewability of these police decisions.

The ultimate answer is that the police should not be delegated discretion not to invoke the criminal law. It is recognized, of course, that the exercise of discretion cannot be completely eliminated where human beings are involved. The frailties of human language and human perception will always admit of borderline cases (although none of the situations analyzed in this article are "borderline"). But nonetheless, outside this margin of ambiguity, the police should operate in an atmosphere which exhorts and commands them to invoke impartially all criminal laws within the bounds of *full enforcement.* If a criminal law is ill advised, poorly defined, or too costly to enforce, efforts by the police to achieve *full enforcement* should generate pressures for legislative action. Responsibility for the enactment, amendment, and repeal of the criminal laws will not, then, be abandoned to the whim of each police officer or department, but retained where it belongs in a democracy—with elected representatives.

Equating *actual enforcement* with *full enforcement,* however, would be neither workable nor humane nor humanly possible under present conditions in most, if not all, jurisdictions. Even if there were "enough police" (and there are not) to enforce all of the criminal laws, too many people have come to rely on the nonenforcement of too many "obsolete" laws to justify the embarrassment, discomfort, and misery which would follow implementation of *full enforcement* programs for every crime. *Full enforcement* is a program for the future, a program which could be initiated with the least hardship when the states, perhaps stimulated by the work of the American Law Institute, enact new criminal codes clearing the books of obsolete offenses.

In the interim, legislatures should establish policy appraisal and review boards not only to facilitate coordination of municipal police policies with those of other key criminal law administrators, but also to assist commissions drafting new codes in reappraising basic objectives of the criminal law and in identifying laws which have become obsolete. To ensure that board appraisals and recommendations facilitate the integration of police policies with overall state policies and to ensure the cooperation of local authorities, board membership might include the state's attorney general, the chief justice of the supreme court, the chairman of the department of correction, the chairman of the board of parole and the chief of parole supervision, the chairman of the department of probation, the chairman of the judiciary committees of the legislature, the chief of the state police, the local chief of police, the local prosecutor, and the chief judge of each of the local trial courts. In order regularly and systematically to cull and retrieve information, the board should be assisted by a full-time director who has a staff of investigators well trained in social science research techniques. It should be given power to subpoena persons and records and to assign investigators to observe all phases of police activity including routine patrols, bookings, raids, and contacts with both the courts and the prosecutor's office. To clarify its functions, develop procedures, determine personnel requirements, and test the idea itself, the board's jurisdiction should initially be restricted to one or two major municipalities in the state. The board would review, appraise, and make recommendations concerning municipal police nonenforcement policies as well as follow up and review the consequences of implemented proposals. In order to make its job both manageable and less subject to attack by those who cherish local autonomy and who may see the establishment of a board as a step toward centralization, it would have solely an advisory function and limit its investigations to the enforcement of state laws, not municipal ordinances. And to ensure that board activity will not compromise current enforcement campaigns or place offenders on notice of new techniques of detection or sources of information, boards should be authorized, with court approval, to withhold specified reports from general publication for a limited and fixed time.

Like other administrative agencies, a policy appraisal and review board will in time no doubt suffer from marasmus and outlive its usefulness. But while viable, such a board has an enormous potential for uncovering in a very dramatic fashion basic inadequacies in the administration of criminal justice and for prompting a thorough community reexamination of the why of a law of crimes.

5

Who Ya Gonna Call?
The Police as Problem-Busters

John E. Eck

William Spelman

After almost half a century dominated by the crime-fighter, professional model of law enforcement, the American police have begun to shift toward a focus on community policing. This new model, also referred to as problem-oriented policing, urges that greater emphasis be placed on maintaining order and providing services to the community. As discussed by John Eck and William Spelman, community policing seeks to solve problems that underlie crime and fear in neighborhoods.

Charlie Bedford couldn't sleep. Most nights, his residential Newport News street was quiet, marred only by the low rumble of an occasional truck on Jefferson Avenue two blocks away. But lately, Friday and Saturday nights had been different: groups of a dozen or more rowdy teenagers kept him awake, with their loud music and their horseplay. There had been no violence. But there had been some vandalism, and the kids seemed unpredictable. More disturbing, the kids came from another section of town, miles away. One sleepless Friday night it became too much. Charlie Bedford called the cops.[1]

Problems like Mr. Bedford's plague many urban neighborhoods. Disorderly behavior and other incivilities make life difficult for residents while creating fears of more serious harm. Wilson and Kelling (1982) have suggested that without intervention, citizens' fear may spark disinvestment in neighborhoods, leading to decay, more crime, and more fear. Because of concerns like these, incivilities have become a focus of researcher interest and police action.[2]

The increased interest in social order, fear, and community policing is the latest development of a continuing discussion about the role of the police in the community. The last two decades have seen a variety of proposals to bring the police closer to the community—community relations units, team policing, neighborhood watch, and foot patrol, among others. At the same time there has been equal interest in police operational effectiveness especially with regard to crime control; directed

Source: From John E. Eck and William Spelman, *Crime and Delinquency,* Vol. 33, No. 1 (1987), pp. 31–52. Reprinted by permission of Sage Publications, Inc.

patrol, case screening, crime analysis, and differential response were but a few of the ideas proposed and tested. For the most part, these two lines of thinking have developed independently. But we can help the Charlie Bedfords of our communities by combining the two areas. To see why, let us take a closer look at what might be called "community policing" and "crime control policing."

Community Policing

Largely as a result of the riots of the 1960s, police began to examine their ties to the communities they served. Black and Hispanic communities were concerned largely with controlling police use of force. The police were concerned with defusing the dissension, creating a more favorable image for themselves. Perhaps because these aims were so politically charged, these first attempts were formal, involving new bureaucratic structures such as community relations units and civilian review boards. Both were limited: community relations units had little effect on the behavior of street officers; line officers objected so strenuously to civilian review boards that most were dismantled or rendered impotent shortly after they were implemented (Goldstein, 1977).

Dissatisfied, some police administrators began efforts aimed at bringing police closer to people. The most ambitious of these efforts, team policing, typically involved a radical restructuring of the police bureaucracy. The hierarchical structure of policing was to be abandoned; decision making was to be decentralized; police officers were to be well-rounded generalists, rather than specialized technicians. These operational changes were to put police decision making closer to the communities served. In practice, team policing proved too hard to implement, and few efforts survive today. But three team-policing strategies survived: storefront police stations, foot patrol, and community crime watch.

Storefront police stations put police officers in the community at all times, forcing them to deal with the public constantly. And, presumably, members of the public would be more willing to walk into a station located in an unpretentious setting in their own neighborhood if they wished to provide information or make a complaint. Storefronts were often well accepted by the communities they served, and increased the amount of communication between police and citizens. There were indications that they helped to reduce fear of crime, too. But officers who did not staff the storefronts often regarded these jobs as "public relations," far removed from "real police work."[3]

Foot patrols cast police in the most traditional of roles. Because they are in direct contact with the public at almost all times, foot officers become informal authority figures wielding the (usually) discreet threat of force to get results (Kelling, 1987). The bulwark of policing at the turn of the century, foot patrols were enjoying a comeback as early as the mid-1960s. The trend has become more pronounced in the last few years. Evaluations of foot patrol programs conflict over whether they reduce serious crime (Trojanowicz, n.d.; Police Foundation, 1981; Williams and Pate, 1987). However, they agree that foot patrols lead to increased contact between police and citizens, often leaving the citizens feeling safer and more satisfied with their police services. Perhaps more important, foot patrol officers learned more about the neighborhood's problems; the best foot patrol officers tried to solve them.

Finally, community crime watches emerged as an important means of police–citizen communication in the 1970s. At first, police just provided citizens with crime prevention information. Later, police grew more ambitious and tried to organize communities. Organized communities were supposed to exert more control over rowdy youths and wayward adults, thus reducing illegal and threatening behavior. Despite some initial successes (for example, Cirel, et al., 1977), crime watch programs have led to few sustained crime reductions nor do they seem to make people feel much safer. Indeed, there are indications that the organizing tactics usually used by police leave people more afraid than before (Lavrakas, 1985; Rosenbaum, 1987).

Most evidence suggests that storefronts, foot patrols, and crime watches do little to control crime. But they are all successful in increasing communication between the police and the public, and sometimes they have made people feel safer. Surely this is a gain, particularly in light of research that suggests that citizens may be more harmed by fear of crime than by victimization itself (Taub, Taylor, and Dunham, 1984; Greenberg, Rohe, and Williams, 1984). To the degree that fear of crime is a vague and somewhat irrational sense of unease, sighting an officer on foot, in a local station, or standing before a neighborhood meeting can help to reduce it. But most research indicates that fear of crime is quite rational, grounded in reasonable perceptions of vulnerability (Fowler and Mangione, 1974). To the degree that fear of crime is rational, we can expect that fear will return to its prior levels, so long as the conditions that cause it do not change. Indeed, there are indications that fear-reduction strategies based on increased police–public communication are only effective in the short run (Fowler and Mangione, 1983).

The community policing projects also showed the disparity between the problems people face and the problems police attack. Most citizens' concerns are not directly related to crime. Trash on the streets, noise, abandoned and ill-maintained buildings, barking dogs, and the like form the bulk of calls for police service. In many areas, residents judge these problems to be more serious than street crime (Spelman, 1983). Still, police are oriented to crime control. Given the attention police have paid to crime over the years, one would expect that they would have learned to control it. In fact, the opposite is true.

Crime Control Policing

Also as a result of the riots of the 1960s, researchers began to examine the ability of the police to control crime. Over the next two decades, researchers steadily undermined five basic premises of police crime control practice.

First, the Kansas City Preventive Patrol Experiment questioned the usefulness of random patrol in cars (Kelling et al., 1974). Second, studies of response time undermined the premise that the police must rapidly send officers to all calls (Kansas City Police Department, 1980; Spelman and Brown, 1984). Third, research suggested, and experiments confirmed, that the public does not always expect fast response by police to nonemergency calls (Farmer, 1981; McEwen, Connors, and Cohen, 1984). Fourth, studies showed that officers and detectives are limited in their abilities to successfully investigate crimes (Greenwood, Petersilia, and Chaiken, 1977; Eck, 1982). And fifth, research showed that detectives need not follow up every reported unsolved crime (Greenberg, Yu, and Lang, 1973; Eck, 1979). In short, most serious crimes were unaffected by the standard police actions designed to control them. Further, the public did not notice reductions in patrol, response speed to nonemergencies, or lack of follow-up investigations.

Random, unmanaged patrol operations did not seem to work. Special units, although occasionally successful, were expensive and could not be used routinely. But, police administrators reasoned, perhaps the problem was not that patrol and investigation tactics did not work. Perhaps they just needed to be managed better.

Research was showing that patrol officers and detectives had time available that could be better used (Gay, Schell, and Schack, 1977; Greenwood, Petersilia, and Chaiken, 1977). And additional time could be created, since citizens did not notice changes in patrol or detective operations. To free up patrol officer time, differential police strategies were developed. Citizen calls that could be handled over the phone, through the mail, or by the caller appearing at a police station were diverted from patrol officers to civilians. Nonemergency calls requiring an officer received a scheduled response instead of an immediate dispatch (Farmer, 1981; McEwen, Connors, and Cohen, 1984). To free up detective time, crimes that had no leads, short of murder or rape, were no longer investigated once a patrol officer had completed the initial investigation. Managers would direct investigative efforts so that the free time could be used effectively in the fight against crime (Eck, 1982). To direct these efforts, information about crime and criminals was needed. Crime analysis seemed to be the answer.

Crime analysis units used police records describing initial and follow-up investigations, arrests of offenders, and police encounters with suspicious persons to analyze the nature of crime and criminals (Reinier, Greenlee, and Gibbens, 1976). The crimes that analysts reviewed were usually burglaries, robberies, and, in a few agencies, rapes and auto thefts. Crime analysts looked for patterns. They plotted the locations and times of burglaries to direct patrol officers to the most likely targets. They mapped robberies to deploy stakeouts by patrol officers and detectives. They collated offender descriptions to identify suspects for detectives. In some agencies, crime analysts even gave information about crime patterns to neighborhood watch groups.

These efforts showed that collecting and analyzing information about crimes may improve police operations. But it is doubtful whether they reduce crime (Gay, Beall, and Bowers, 1984). Crime analysis units have too many limitations to have more than a marginal influence on crime, or any other problem. One limitation is particularly critical: crime analysis is an attempt to find out where to apply established police responses. The responses are set before problems are understood; the same responses are used on widely differing problems. Instead the aim should be to understand a problem and then determine what is needed to solve it.

Street operations do need more and better management. In order to manage, police managers need better information about local problems. But they must understand the problem before designing a solution. They must look for solutions to such problems as vandalism, rowdy behavior, drug use, drunkenness, and noise.

Community policing has used the same responses—foot patrol, storefront stations, and neighborhood watch—to address a wide variety of community concerns.

Crime control policing has applied another standard set of procedures—patrol, investigation, surveillance, and stakeouts—to a wide variety of crime problems. In neither form of policing has there been a systematic attempt to tailor the responses to the characteristics of each particular problem.

> Sergeant Hogan was on duty when Mr. Bedford called. He assigned the problem to Officer Paul Summerfield. Summerfield suspected that the source of the problem might be a roller skating rink. The rink had been trying to increase business by offering reduced rates and transportation on Friday and Saturday nights. At two in the morning, as he drove north along Jefferson Avenue to the rink, Summerfield saw several large groups of youths walking south. Other kids were hanging around at the rink. Summerfield talked to several of them and found that they were waiting for a bus. The other kids, he was told, had become impatient and begun the three-mile walk home. Summerfield talked to the rink owner. The owner had leased the bus to pick up and drop off kids who lived far from the rink. But there were always more kids needing rides at the end of the night than the bus had picked up earlier.
>
> Officer Summerfield returned to the skating rink early the next evening. He saw fifty or so youngsters get out of the bus rented by the skating rink. But he saw others get out of the public transit buses that stopped running at midnight. And he saw parents in pajamas drop their kids off, then turn around and go home. Clearly the rink's bus would be unable to take home all the kids who would be stranded at closing time. Summerfield left, perplexed.

Problem-Oriented Policing

How could Officer Summerfield solve this problem? Herman Goldstein has described an approach that could help (Goldstein, 1979). According to Goldstein, police have lost sight of their objectives in their efforts to improve management. They must begin focusing on problems the public expects them to solve. Problems are "the incredibly broad range of troublesome situations that prompt citizens to turn to the police." Management improvements, though important, are only a means for improving police capacities to solve problems. Goldstein described three key elements of this problem-oriented approach.

First, problems must be defined more specifically. Broad legal definitions, such as burglary or robbery, should be replaced by descriptions that include such characteristics as location, time, participants' behaviors and motivation, and so on.

Second, information about problems must be collected from sources outside the police agency and not just from internal sources. The officers who have to deal with problems are a good source of information that is seldom exploited. But businesses, other government agencies, and private citizens can often provide data needed to understand problems fully.

Third, police agencies must engage in a broad search for solutions, including alternatives to the criminal justice process. The best solutions often involve public and private individuals and organizations who have a stake in seeing the problem resolved.

The Baltimore County Police Department and the Newport News Police Department have begun to implement problem-oriented policing. Let us look at how these agencies diagnose problems and try to resolve them.

Baltimore County   Two sensational murders within a week brought fear of violent crime among Baltimore County residents to a head in August 1981. The incidents were unrelated and unlikely to be repeated, and the murderers were soon caught and eventually imprisoned for their acts. Still, the public's concern did not subside. In response, the Baltimore County Council provided its police department with forty-five new officers.

Realizing that these officers would be spread very thin in a 1,700-officer department, Chief Cornelius Behan and his command staff decided to concentrate them into a special, forty-five-officer unit to combat fear of crime—the Citizen-Oriented Police Enforcement unit (COPE).

In 1981, no one knew much about fighting fear of crime. As a result, COPE officers confined their activities in target neighborhoods to directed patrol, motorcycle patrol, and community crime prevention. Despite some modest successes, COPE managers were dissatisfied with their efforts. Chief Behan had given them a charge to be innovative; so far, they had done little that had not been done many times before.

Gary Hayes, the late executive director of the Police Executive Research Forum and a friend of Chief Behan's, was asked to help. Hayes arranged for Herman Goldstein to train COPE supervisors in the theory and practice of problem solving. Almost immediately, COPE began to take on a sense of direction it had lacked in its first year of operation.

COPE's approach to problem solving relies heavily on a unique combination of creativity and standard procedures. A problem is usually referred to COPE by another unit of the police department, or by another county agency. An initial assessment of the nature of the problem is made, and one officer is assigned to lead the solution effort. COPE officers then conduct a door-to-door survey of residents and businesses in the problem neighborhood. The officers also solicit other opinions: patrol officers, detectives, and officials from other agencies are often important sources of information. The results are used to define the problem more specifically and to identify aspects of the problem the police never see.

The COPE officers assigned to solve the problem then meet to consider the data they have collected and to brainstorm possible solutions. Next they design an action plan, which details the solution to be attempted and a timetable for implementing them. Once the solutions are in place, COPE officers often conduct a second survey, to see whether they have been successful.

Three years after its inception, these procedures have become the COPE unit's primary approach to reducing fear. But this is not the only method of solving problems; in Newport News, a complementary approach was designed.

Newport News   In 1984 the National Institute of Justice funded the Police Executive Research Forum to develop and test a new approach to crime analysis. Darrel Stephens, then chief of the Newport News, Virginia, Police Department, was particularly interested in this approach and he invited the forum to test it in his agency. Like the COPE unit, this project relies heavily on Goldstein's problem-oriented approach, and Goldstein consulted with the project staff and officials of the Newport News Police.

There are several differences between the Newport News Police Department's project and the Baltimore County COPE project. First, problem-oriented policing is an agencywide strategy in Newport News. All department members, including supervisors, are responsible for identifying, analyzing, and solving problems. Second, any type of problem is fair game, whether it is crime, fear, or another disorder. Third, less emphasis is placed on procedures in Newport News. Instead, a department task force under the guidance of Chief Stephens developed a "problem analysis model," a set of guidelines for data collection and thinking.

But the Newport News approach has many similarities with Baltimore County's. Both departments emphasize careful definition and analysis of problems prior to developing solutions. Evaluating solutions is also stressed. In both departments, supervisors encourage officers analyzing problems to look beyond the police department for information. This means talking to residents, business people, offenders, city agency personnel, and anyone else who could know something about the problem. Similarly, supervisors encourage officers to work with people and organizations outside policing to develop solutions. Criminal justice responses, although not discouraged, are seen as only one option among many.

Problem-Oriented Policing at Work

Let us look at how these two agencies have handled several common problems. Much attention has been devoted to crime and fear in residential neighborhoods, so we will first look at two problems of this type. Problems occur in nonresidential areas, as well; we next describe an effort to solve a problem occurring in a downtown area with few residents and little commercial activity. Finally, some problems are not confined to a small geographic area but affect people everywhere. As our last case study shows, the problem-oriented approach can be applied equally well to problems like these.

Neighborhood Problems

Loch Raven Apartments (Baltimore County)   Residents of the Loch Raven Apartments were shocked and frightened when beset by a spate of street robberies in 1984. While patrol officers and detectives tried to solve the crimes, COPE was called in to deal with the problem of fear. Officer Wayne Lloyd was assigned to lead the effort.

Officer Lloyd first coordinated a door-to-door survey of Loch Raven residents. He found that most of the residents were elderly women who felt particularly vulnerable to street attacks. Most were unwilling to leave their apartments after dark. Their feelings were exacerbated by the conditions of the complex: many street and building lights were broken; unkempt trees and shrubs created many hiding places; rats, stray dogs, and unrepaired structural damage all contributed to the feeling— widespread among residents—that they were trapped.

Reasoning that many solutions were needed for so complex a problem, Lloyd and his colleagues found a way to get almost everyone involved. Representatives of two local neighborhood associations agreed to help Loch Raven Apartments residents form their own association. The police convinced a variety of organizations to assist the new neighborhood group: a local printer produced crime prevention information, free of charge; a local church donated its meeting facilities; a local baker contributed free donuts. Other agencies helped in other ways. Alerted to the poor lighting situation, Baltimore Gas and Electric repaired its streetlights and installed new ones. The walkways and hallways of Loch Raven Apartments were visited by representatives of numerous local agencies, including the Animal Control, Health, Fire, and Housing Departments. The apartment manager bowed to the accumulated pressures and began to refurbish the buildings.

Perhaps because of the deterrent effect of patrolling dog catchers, building inspectors, and the like, the string of robberies stopped completely. Burglaries in the complex, running at a rate of six per month prior to the COPE unit's intervention, dropped to one every two months; it has remained at that level ever since. Perhaps most important, COPE provided the residents with better living conditions and a new Community Association that can help them obtain further improvements.

As the Loch Raven case illustrates, the police can draw upon the resources of many other public and private agencies in their problem-solving efforts. These "hidden allies" may only need guidance as to where they can be most effective. In this case, a variety of agencies respected the COPE unit's opinion that Loch Raven was a trouble spot that deserved their attention.

The Belmont Treehouse (Baltimore County)   No one ever seemed to use the Belmont Community Park. Casual passersby would rarely see a child in its playground or a jogger on one of the park's tree-shaded walks. Had they looked closely, they might have seen the reason: rowdy youths frequented one corner of the park. They used drugs and drank, and resisted all attempts by patrol officers to remove them. Neighborhood residents kept their children—and themselves—far away, fearing intimidation and exposure to alcohol and drugs. Residents had complained to various local government agencies for years with no response. Finally, one of the residents read about COPE in his community newspaper and called the unit.

COPE Officers Sam Hannigan and James Chaconas were assigned to handle the Belmont problem. Their survey of neighborhood residents revealed that the problem did not focus on the park, after all; instead, it centered on a shed, dubbed the "treehouse," that older youths had constructed in the vacant, wooded lot next door. The treehouse was often used as a crash pad and drinking place by a few local teenagers.

Hannigan and Chaconas felt that the public nature of the drinking and drug abuse was mostly responsible for the residents' fears. So, at the suggestion of several neighborhood residents, they decided to make the drinking and drug abuse less visible by removing the treehouse.

Their first efforts went nowhere. The County Roads Department agreed that the treehouse posed a hazard and was in violation of city codes. They refused to take the problem seriously, however, since no one lived there. The Health and Fire Departments felt the same way. Even if they had been willing to condemn the shack, the formal process would have taken months.

Instead, the officers decided to work with the owner. They searched through tax records to find the owner of the vacant lot. When interviewed at his home, the owner readily admitted that the treehouse was a nuisance and a hazard, and that he had no use for it whatever. Still, he feared retaliation from the kids who had constructed it and was unable to pay the costs of demolishing the building.

Hannigan and Chaconas discussed the situation with Central COPE Lieutenant Veto Mentzell. They agreed that the two officers should demolish the treehouse themselves. Two employees of the County Roads Commission agreed to help out. Next Saturday morning, the four, armed with saws and sledgehammers, quickly reduced the treehouse to rubble. Then they carted the pieces to a waiting county truck and took them to the dump.

The kids still drink and use drugs, and most of them have stayed in the neighborhood. They now meet in private places, however, where they are not visible to their neighbors. Most important, residents are no longer subject to their unpredictable, loud, and threatening behavior. The Belmont Neighborhood Association reports that residents are less fearful. One tangible result of the fear reduction is that, for the first time in years, the park is filled with children.

The Belmont case shows that an apparently intractable problem—here, fear created by teenage drinking and drug abuse can be ameliorated with a little analysis and through some simple actions. The treehouse case took two weeks from start to finish. The key was to accept the neighborhood's definition of the problem (threatening public behavior) rather than the usual police definition (illegal drinking and drug abuse).

A Nonneighborhood Problem

Not all problems occur in areas used by people who have common concerns. Some parts of cities have no real community of interests. Our next example shows how the problem-oriented approach can be applied in this sort of area.

Thefts from vehicles (Newport News)   For years, thefts from vehicles parked near the Newport News Shipyards have constituted around 10 percent of all index crime reported in Newport News. In 1984, 738 such thefts were reported; dollar losses from the thefts—not including damage to the vehicles—totaled nearly $180,000. Patrol Officer Paul Swartz was assigned to analyze the issues involved and to recommend solutions. He reviewed offense and arrest reports for the parking lot area going back three years and began tracking current cases. Because of these efforts, he was able to identify several parking areas where large numbers of thefts had taken place. These theft-prone areas became the focus of patrol officers' efforts. Swartz also interviewed patrol officers and detectives familiar with the area and talked to members of the shipyard's security force. As a result, Swartz identified a couple of brothers who stole from vehicles in the northern lots and a few individual offenders who stole in the southern lots.

Swartz gave the descriptions of the known offenders to the officers patrolling the lots. These officers began to stop and talk to suspects when they were seen in the area. Meanwhile, Swartz interviewed several thieves already convicted and sentenced for breaking into vehicles in these parking lots. He promised the offenders that nothing said in the interviews would be used against them. Swartz learned that drugs were a prime target of the northern thieves, but stereo equipment and auto parts were also targets. They especially looked for "muscle" cars, cars with bumper stickers advertising local rock and roll stations, or cars with other evidence that the owner might be a marijuana smoker or cocaine user (for example, a roach clip or a feather hanging from the rearview mirror). The southern thieves did not focus on drugs but instead concentrated on car stereo equipment and auto parts. Swartz also learned the names, descriptions, and addresses of other thieves; he confirmed that a few were particularly frequent offenders. This information was passed on to other street officers, who made several in-progress arrests. The detectives and the prosecutor worked to ensure that the most frequent offenders were convicted and sentenced to several months in jail.

As of this writing, the department is still developing a long-term solution to this problem. It will probably include working with the shipyard and its workers to develop a theft prevention strategy. In the interim, there has been a 55 percent decrease in the number of these thefts since April 1985 (from 51 per month to 23 per month), when the field interrogations and arrests of the repeat offenders began.

This is an example of using previously untapped information. Some street officers had knowledge of who was involved in the thefts, but this information was never put to use until Swartz began his analysis. Offenders were another source of information that had not been used before. As with the community problems described above, collecting information about nonneighborhood problems gives the police the ability to design a response that has a good chance of solving the problems. In this case, the solution involved standard police practices, but they were the practices that fit the need.

A Jurisdictionwide Problem

In addition to problems occurring in small geographic areas, police must deal with problems that affect their entire jurisdictions. Among these problems are some of the most troublesome issues confronting the police: juvenile runaways, drunk driving, and spouse abuse, for example. The last example describes how an officer dealt with a jurisdictionwide problem.

Domestic violence (Newport News)   Marvin Evans was a Newport News homicide detective. He was also a member of the task force that designed the department's approach to problem-oriented policing. Frustrated with investigating murders after they had been committed, Evans decided to find a way to prevent them. His analysis of homicide data indicated that most occurred in the southern part of the city; but, more important, half were the direct result of domestic violence, and half of these cases involved couples who had come to police attention previously. When Evans reviewed national research on domestic violence he found that his findings were typical. This encouraged him to look into the handling of these cases locally. So he began interviewing counselors at the local woman's shelter, assistant state's attorneys, judges, ministers, and anyone else who had an interest in the problem.

Since his fellow officers had an important role in dealing with this issue, he sought their views. Evans used a survey to determine how officers handled domestic cases and their knowledge of the available options. He found that officers were unaware of the fact that they could file a complaint that could result in a warrant, even if the victim refused. He found that officers did not like handling domestic violence cases because those officers who did handle these cases spent many frustrating hours processing them.

So Evans decided to bring together a group of interested people who could design a better way of handling these cases. This group included representatives of the local woman's shelter, the state's attorney's office, the circuit court, churches, the local newspaper, the army, and other organizations, as well as the police.

The result of their efforts was a comprehensive plan for handling family violence in the city. The objective was to keep families together while showing both the abuser and the victim how to handle stressful situations without resorting to violence. Although a mandatory arrest policy was adopted for specific types of circumstances (incidents involving injuries, the presence of a weapon, or a prior history of violence, for example), arrest was not seen as an end in itself, but as a means to provide treatment that could preserve the valuable aspects of the families involved. To support this strategy, the state's attorney's office and the court agreed that they would not drop charges if the victim refused to prosecute. Instead they would use the threat of legal sanctions to get both parties into counseling.

The program was pretested in the fall of 1985 and officers were instructed as to its operation. In January the program was officially begun, and in February the local newspaper published a twenty-page, special section on domestic violence. Virtually all aspects were covered, from the causes of domestic violence as seen by victims, offenders, and researchers, to the responses to domestic violence by the police, courts, and counselors.

This example shows that line officers can identify problems, conduct an analysis, and organize a communitywide response. In this case the solution included the entire city. In addition to mobilizing many private and public organizations to help reduce domestic killings and assaults, Evans was able to convince the local newspaper to show the public what they could do to curb domestic violence.

Summary

As these cases illustrate, the problem oriented approach can be applied to a wide variety of problems. Problem solving can assist in the resolution of neighborhood problems, but it is equally applicable to problems that affect areas with no residential population or to citywide problems. Problem-oriented policing relies on and supports community policing, but it is not synonymous with community policing.

Moreover, the experience of Baltimore County and Newport News shows that police officers have the skill and interest needed to conduct thorough studies of problems and to develop creative solutions. Training and management direction can improve officers' problem diagnosis and analysis skills. And officers involved in problem solving seem to enjoy improving the quality of life of the citizens whom they serve. For many, problem solving is more satisfying than traditional police work, because they can see the results of their work more clearly (Cordner, 1985).

The case studies also demonstrate that police have the time available to handle their current work load and to solve problems as well. Differential patrol response, investigative case screening, and similar practices can free up time for nontraditional activities.

The additional free time can be structured in a variety of ways. Baltimore County adopted one approach—it created a special unit. Newport News adopted a different approach—it had all department members solve problems, part of the time. In Newport News, problem-solving time was structured in two ways. For a few problems, an officer was temporarily assigned to attack the problem full time. (For example, Officer Swartz was assigned full time to the parking lots problem.) For most others, an officer was assigned to handle the problem in addition to his or her other duties. (Detective Evans created a domestic violence program while investigating homicides, for instance.) Each of the three methods offers its own set of costs and benefits, and it is too soon to tell which methods are best. Most likely, different methods will work better for different problems and police agencies.

Finally, the case studies make it clear that problem-oriented policing is a state of mind, and not a program, technique, or procedure. The keys are clearheaded analysis of the problem and an uninhibited search for solutions. These can be achieved by applying standard operating procedures (as is typically the case in Baltimore County) or a looser analytic model (as in Newport News). There probably is no single best method for developing this state of mind. The best method for any given agency will depend on the characteristics of the agency.

Long-Run Considerations

As problem-oriented policing becomes standard practice in more and more departments, we can expect to see three other fundamental changes in the way police do business. The problem-oriented police department will probably have to change its internal management structure. The role of the police will change, and with it their relationship with the community and other parts of the city bureaucracy. Finally, although problem solving creates the opportunity for greatly increased benefits, it also brings with it the potential for increased risks. Let us consider these long-run considerations in more detail.

Management structure   As we have emphasized, the point of problem solving is to tailor the police response to the unique circumstances of each problem. Inevitably, this means that decision-making authority must be decentralized; the discretion of line officers and their supervisors—those members of the department who know most about each problem—must increase. As a result, we can expect that mid- and upper-level managers will need to develop new methods of structuring this increased discretion.

Decentralizing authority will affect all levels of the hierarchy, but it will probably affect line supervisors—sergeants—the most. As a result, agencies adopting a problem-oriented approach will have to provide much more extensive policy guidance and training to their sergeants. Problem solving puts a dual burden on these officials. On the one hand, they must make many of the tough, operational decisions. Line supervisors—those members of the department who know most about each of their officers—set priorities among different problems, facilitate work with other divisions of the police department and outside agencies, and make sure their officers solve the problems they are assigned. On the other hand, the sergeants must also provide leadership, encouraging creative analysis and response. So a first-line supervisor under problem solving might come to resemble the editor of a newspaper, or the manager of an R & D unit, more than an army sergeant.[4] Indeed, in Baltimore County there are indications that these changes are beginning to happen (Taft, 1986).

Police role   It is almost certain that problem solving will influence the police officers who undertake it to reconsider their role in society. As we have described above, identifying, studying, and solving problems requires that officers make more contacts with people and organizations outside the police agency. As they do this, they will become exposed to a wider variety of interests and perspectives. Many officers will discover that they can accomplish more by working with these individuals and groups. As a consequence, they will begin to take a broader, more informed view of the problems they must handle.

This is all to the good, but few improvements are without complications. A police agency taking on a complex problem may find itself in the midst of a contentious community power struggle. This could undermine the authority of the agency in other, less controversial areas. As a result, police agencies may avoid important but controversial problems. On the other hand, the problem-oriented police agency may find that it must get involved in controversial problems to avoid favoring one side over another.

Political problems will probably not be limited to police–community relations. Solving problems will require police agencies to work closely with a host of other public agencies, as well. This raises the issue of "turf." Other public agencies may view a problem-solving endeavor as encroachment, rather than collaboration. This is especially likely when the problem is largely due to the failure of another agency to do its job. Even if police are successful in avoiding conflict with other agencies and with the public, problem solving will almost certainly increase the political complexity of managing a police agency.

Increased risks and benefits   The case studies described above suggest that police agencies who take on a broader, problem-solving role can be more effective than before. But they may also do more harm than before, either through inadvertent mistakes or through outright abuses of authority.

Even creative responses based on careful analysis will sometimes fail. Some responses may even make matters worse. This has always been true of police work, or the work of any government agency. Currently, however, failures to handle calls adequately seldom result in difficulties for the public at large. Few people are involved in each incident, and the scope of police intervention is usually very limited. The consequences of a failure to solve a problem may be much more serious: problems involve many people; ill-advised responses may have far-reaching social implications.

Abuse of authority presents an even thornier issue. The police will be actively intervening in situations they had previously left alone, presenting more opportunities for abuse.

At the same time, however, the problem-oriented approach encourages police to analyze problems in detail and solicit the cooperation of outside organizations and individuals before responding. This will help to reduce the likelihood of both errors and abuses. In addition, because problem-oriented policing emphasizes noncoercive responses, inappropriate use of force and sanctions should become less likely. Mistakes and abuses will persist, of course; whether they are more or less benign than present mistakes and abuses remains to be seen.

In any case, it is clear that the limits of police authority will become more and more an issue as problem solving becomes standard practice. Who will set these limits? The short answer is, some combination of the same actors who already set and enforce police standards: informal pressure from private citizens in their contacts with individual officers; elected officials; the staff of other public and private agencies; and the police themselves. What limits will be established is an open question, considered at greater length elsewhere (Goldstein, 1987). One thing is certain: problem solving will require a new consensus on the role, authority, and limitations of the police in each jurisdiction that tries it.

Full implementation of problem solving will be a slow and sometimes difficult process. No agency will be able to "adopt" problem solving simply by making a few changes in standard operating procedures, or just by telling officers to go to it. If it becomes a fad—if police managers try to implement it too quickly, without doing the necessary spadework—problem-oriented policing will fail. As Charlie Bedford's case shows, however, careful planning can yield great benefits for an agency that works to solve its community's problems

> Officer Summerfield consulted Sergeant Hogan. They agreed that the skating rink owner should be asked to bus the kids home. Summerfield returned to the rink and spoke with the owner. The owner agreed to lease more buses. By the next weekend, the buses were in use and Summerfield and Hogan saw no kids disturbing Mr. Bedford's neighborhood.
>
> Sergeant Hogan summed it up: "Look, we can have the best of both worlds. People here can get their sleep and the kids can still have fun. But we can't do it by tying up officers and chasing kids every Friday and Saturday night. There has to be a way of getting rid of the problem once and for all."

Notes

1. This case study and those that follow are true. Names of citizens have been changed, but names of police officials and places have not been. The information on which these case studies are based came from two projects being conducted by the authors. The Newport News study was funded by the National Institute of Justice under grant 84-IJ-CX-0040. The Baltimore County project was funded in part by the Florence V. Burden Foundation.

   The opinions expressed in this article are those of the authors, and not necessarily those of the National Institute of Justice, the Burden Foundation, the police agencies described, or the Police Executive Research Forum.
2. See, for example, Skogan and Maxfield (1981); Police Foundation (1981); Williams and Pate, *Crime & Delinquency* 33 (1, 1987), Brown and Wycoff, *Crime & Delinquency* 33 (1, 1987).
3. For descriptions and evaluations of the effectiveness of storefronts in Detroit and Houston, see Holland (1985); and Brown and Wycoff, *Crime & Delinquency* 33 (1, 1987).
4. For examples of supervision in an R&D unit and a high-tech firm, see Kidder (1981) and Auletta (1984). For a broader discussion of this management style, see Drucker (1985) and Peters and Waterman (1982).

References

AULETTA, KEN (1984). *The Art of Corporate Success: The Story of Schlumberger.* New York: Penguin.

BROWN, LEE, AND MARY ANN WYCOFF (1987). "Policing Houston: Reducing Fear and Improving Service." *Crime and Delinquency* 33(1).

CIREL, PAUL, PATRICIA EVANS, DANIEL MCGILLIS, AND DEBRA WITCOMB (1977). *Community Crime Prevention Program, Seattle, Washington: An Exemplary Project.* Washington, D.C.: Department of Justice, National Institute of Justice.

CORDNER, GARY W. (1985). *The Baltimore County Citizen Oriented Police Enforcement (COPE) Project: Final Evaluation.* Final Report to the Florence V. Burden Foundation. Baltimore: Criminal Justice Department, University of Baltimore.

DRUCKER, PETER F. (1985). *Innovation and Entrepreneurship: Practice and Principles.* New York: Harper & Row.

ECK, JOHN E. (1979). *Managing Case Assignments: The Burglary Investigation Decision Model Replication.* Washington, D.C.: Police Executive Research Forum.

———— (1982). *Solving Crimes: The Investigation of Burglary and Robbery.* Washington, D.C.: Police Executive Research Forum.

FARMER, MICHAEL (ed.) (1981). *Differential Police Response Strategies.* Washington, D.C.: Police Executive Research Forum.

FOWLER, FLOYD J., JR., AND THOMAS W. MANGIONE (1974). "The Nature of Fear." Center for Survey Research Working Paper. Boston: Center for Survey Research, University of Massachusetts and Joint Center for Urban Studies, Massachusetts Institute of Technology and Harvard University.

———— (1983). *Neighborhood Crime, Fear and Social Control: A Second Look at the Hartford Program.* Washington, D.C.: Government Printing Office.

GAY, WILLIAM G., THOMAS M. BEALL, AND ROBERT A. BOWERS (1984). *A Four-Site Assessment of the Integrated Criminal Apprehension Program.* Washington, D.C.: University City Science Center.

GAY, WILLIAM G., THEODORE H. SCHELL, AND STEPHEN SCHACK (1977). *Prescriptive Package: Improving Patrol Productivity, Volume I, Routine Patrol.* Washington, D.C.: Government Printing Office.

GOLDSTEIN, HERMAN (1977). *Policing a Free Society.* Cambridge, Mass.: Ballinger.

———— (1979). "Improving Policing: A Problem-oriented Approach." *Crime & Delinquency* 25: 236–258.

———— (1987). "Toward Community-Oriented Policing: Potential Basic Requirements and Threshold Questions." *Crime & Delinquency* 33(1).

GREENBERG, BERNARD, OLIVER S. YU, AND KAREN LANG (1973). *Enhancement of the Investigative Function, Volume I, Analysis and Conclusions.* Final Report, Phase I. Springfield, Va.: National Technical Information Service.

GREENBERG, STEPHANIE W., WILLIAM M. ROHE, AND JAY R. WILLIAMS (1984). *Safe and Secure Neighborhoods: Physical Characteristics and Informal Territorial Control in High and Low Crime Neighborhoods.* Washington, D.C.: Government Printing Office.

GREENWOOD, PETER, JOAN PETERSILIA, AND JAN CHAIKEN (1977). *The Criminal Investigation Process.* Lexington, Mass.: D.C. Heath.

HOLLAND, LAWRENCE H. (1985). "Police and the Community: The Detroit Ministration Experience." *FBI Law Enforcement Bulletin* 54 (February): 1–6.

KANSAS CITY POLICE DEPARTMENT (1980). *Response Time Analysis: Volume II—Part I Crime Analysis.* Washington, D.C.: Government Printing Office.

KELLING, GEORGE L. (1987). "Acquiring A Taste For Order: The Community and Police." *Crime & Delinquency* 33(1).

KELLING, GEORGE, TONY PATE, DUANE DIECKMAN, AND CHARLES E. BROWN (1974). *The Kansas City Preventive Patrol Experiment: A Technical Report.* Washington, D.C.: Police Foundation.

KIDDER, TRACY. (1981). *Soul of a New Machine.* New York: Avon.

LAVRAKAS, PAUL J. (1985). "Citizen Self-Help and Neighborhood Crime Prevention Policy." In *American Violence and Public Policy,* edited by Lynn A. Curtis. New Haven: Yale University Press.

McEWEN, J. THOMAS, EDWARD F. CONNORS, AND MARCIA I. COHEN (1984). *Evaluation of the Differential Police Response Field Test.* Alexandria, Va.: Research Management Associates.

PETERS, THOMAS J., AND ROBERT H. WATERMAN (1982). *In Search of Excellence: Lessons from America's Best-Run Companies.* New York: Warner.

POLICE FOUNDATION (1981). *The Newark Foot Patrol Experiment.* Washington, D.C.: Author.

REINIER, G. HOBART, M.R. GREENLEE, AND M.H. GIBBENS (1976). *Crime Analysis in Support of Patrol.* National Evaluation Program: Phase I Report. Washington, D.C.: Government Printing Office.

ROSENBAUM, DENNIS P. (1987). "The Theory and Research Behind Neighborhood Watch: Is It a Sound Fear and Crime Reduction Strategy?" *Crime & Delinquency* 33(1).

SKOGAN, WESLEY G. (1987). "The Impact of Victimization on Fear." *Crime & Delinquency* 33(1).

SKOGAN, WESLEY G., AND MICHAEL G. MAXFIELD (1981). *Coping with Crime: Individuals and Neighborhood Reactions.* Beverly Hills, Calif.: Sage.

SPELMAN, WILLIAM (1983). *Reactions to Crime in Atlanta and Chicago: A Policy-Oriented Reanalysis.* Final report to the National Institute of Justice. Cambridge: Harvard Law School.

SPELMAN, WILLIAM, AND DALE K. BROWN (1984). *Calling the Police: Citizen Reporting of Serious Crime.* Washington, D.C.: Government Printing Office.

TAFT, PHILIP B., JR. (1986). *Fighting Fear: The Baltimore County C.O.P.E. Project.* Washington, D.C.: Police Executive Research Forum.

TAUB, RICHARD, D. GARTH TAYLOR, AND JAN DUNHAM (1984). *Patterns of Neighborhood Change: Race and Crime in Urban America.* Chicago: University of Chicago Press.

TROJANOWICZ, ROBERT C. (n.d.). *An Evaluation of the Neighborhood Foot Patrol Program in Flint, Michigan.* East Lansing: Neighborhood Foot Patrol Center, Michigan State University.

WILLIAMS, HUBERT, AND ANTONY M. PATE (1987). "Returning to First Principles: Reducing the Fear of Crime in Newark." *Crime & Delinquency* 33(1).

WILSON, JAMES Q., AND GEORGE L. KELLING (1982). "Broken Windows: The Police and Neighborhood Safety." *The Atlantic Monthly* (March): 29–38.

6

A Sketch of the Policeman's "Working Personality"

Jerome H. Skolnick

Each of us views the real world through cognitive lenses that influence our perception and interpretation of events. Because their role contains the two important variables of danger and authority, police officers develop a distinctive view of the world. Sociologist Jerome Skolnick explores this view and shows how the "working personality" affects the actions of the police.

A recurrent theme of the sociology of occupations is the effect of a man's work on his outlook on the world.[1] Doctors, janitors, lawyers, and industrial workers develop distinctive ways of perceiving and responding to their environment. Here we shall concentrate on analyzing certain outstanding elements in the police milieu, danger, authority, and efficiency, as they combine to generate distinctive cognitive and behavioral responses in police: a "working personality." Such an analysis does not suggest that all police are alike in "working personality," but that there are distinctive cognitive tendencies in police as an occupational grouping. Some of these may be found in other occupations sharing similar problems. So far as exposure to danger is concerned, the policeman may be likened to the soldier. His problems as an authority bear a certain similarity to those of the schoolteacher, and the pressures he feels to prove himself efficient are not unlike those felt by the industrial worker. The combination of these elements, however, is unique to the policeman. Thus, the police, as a result of combined features of their social situation, tend to develop ways of looking at the world distinctive to themselves, cognitive lenses through which to see situations and events. The strength of the lenses may be weaker or stronger depending on certain conditions, but they are ground on a similar axis.

Analysis of the policeman's cognitive propensities is necessary to understand the practical dilemma faced by police required to maintain order under a democratic rule of law. . . . A conception of order is [essential] to the resolution of this dilemma. [We

Source: From *Justice without Trial: Law Enforcement in a Democratic Society* by Jerome H. Skolnick (New York: John Wiley & Sons, 1966), pp. 42–62. Reprinted by permission of the author and publisher.

suggest] that the paramilitary character of police organization naturally leads to a high evaluation of similarity, routine, and predictability. Our intention is to emphasize features of the policeman's environment interacting with the paramilitary police organization to generate a "working personality." Such an intervening concept should aid in explaining how the social environment of police affects their capacity to respond to the rule of law.

[Emphasis] will be placed on the division of labor in the police department . . . ; "operational law enforcement" [cannot] be understood outside these special work assignments. It is therefore important to explain how the hypothesis emphasizing the generalizability of the policeman's "working personality" is compatible with the idea that police division of labor is an important analytic dimension for understanding "operational law enforcement." Compatibility is evident when one considers the different levels of analysis at which the hypotheses are being developed. Janowitz states, for example, that the military profession is more than an occupation; it is a "style of life" because the occupational claims over one's daily existence extend well beyond official duties. He is quick to point out that any profession performing a crucial "life and death" task, such as medicine, the ministry, or the police, develops such claims.[2] A conception like "working personality" of police should be understood to suggest an analytic breadth similar to that of "style of life." That is, just as the professional behavior of military officers with similar "styles of life" may differ drastically depending upon whether they command an infantry battalion or participate in the work of an intelligence unit, so too does the professional behavior of police officers with similar "working personalities" vary with their assignments.

The policeman's "working personality" is most highly developed in his constabulary role of the man on the beat. For analytical purposes that role is sometimes regarded as an enforcement specialty, but in this general discussion of policemen as they comport themselves while working, the uniformed "cop" is seen as the foundation for the policeman's "working personality." There is a sound organizational basis for making this assumption. The police, unlike the military, draw no caste distinction in socialization, even though their order of ranked titles approximates the military's. Thus, one cannot join a local police department as, for instance, a lieutenant, as a West Point graduate joins the army. Every officer of rank must serve an apprenticeship as a patrolman. This feature of police organization means that the constabulary role is the primary one for all police officers, and that whatever the special requirements of roles in enforcement specialties, they are carried out with a common background of constabulary experience.

The process by which this "personality" is developed may be summarized: the policeman's role contains two principal variables, danger and authority, which should be interpreted in the light of a "constant" pressure to appear efficient.[3] The element of danger seems to make the policeman especially attentive to signs indicating a potential for violence and lawbreaking. As a result, the policeman is generally a "suspicious" person. Furthermore, the character of the policeman's work makes him less desirable as a friend, since norms of friendship implicate others in his work. Accordingly, the element of danger isolates the policeman socially from that segment of the citizenry which he regards as symbolically dangerous and also from the conventional citizenry with whom he identifies.

The element of authority reinforces the element of danger in isolating the policeman. Typically, the policeman is required to enforce laws representing puritanical morality, such as those prohibiting drunkenness, and also laws regulating the flow of public activity, such as traffic laws. In these situations the policeman directs the citizenry, whose typical response denies recognition of his authority and stresses his obligation to respond to danger. The kind of man who responds well to danger, however, does not normally subscribe to codes of puritanical morality. As a result, the policeman is unusually liable to the charge of hypocrisy. That the whole civilian world is an audience for the policeman further promotes police isolation and, in consequence, solidarity. Finally, danger undermines the judicious use of authority. Where danger, as in Britain, is relatively less, the judicious application of authority is facilitated. Hence, British police may appear to be somewhat more attached to the rule of law, when, in fact, they may appear so because they face less danger, and they are as a rule better skilled than American police in creating the appearance of conformity to procedural regulations.

The Symbolic Assailant and Police Culture

In attempting to understand the policeman's view of the world, it is useful to raise a more general question: What are the conditions under which police, as authorities, may be threatened?[4] To answer this, we must look to the situation of the policeman in the community. One attribute of many characterizing the policeman's role stands out: the policeman is required to respond to assaults against persons and property. When a radio call reports an armed robbery and gives a description of the man involved, every policeman, regardless of assignment, is responsible for the criminal's apprehension. The raison d'être of the policeman and the criminal law, the underlying collectively held moral sentiments which justify penal sanctions, arises ultimately and most clearly from the threat of violence and the possibility of danger to the community. Police who "lobby" for severe narcotics laws, for instance, justify their position on grounds that the addict is a harbinger of danger since, it is maintained, he requires $100 a day to support his habit, and he must steal to get it. Even though the addict is not typically a violent criminal, criminal penalties for addiction are supported on grounds that he may become one.

The policeman, because his work requires him to be occupied continually with potential violence, develops a perceptual shorthand to identify certain kinds of people as symbolic assailants, that is, as persons who use gesture, language, and attire that the policeman has come to recognize as a prelude to violence. This does not mean that violence by the symbolic assailant is necessarily predictable. On the contrary, the policeman responds to the vague indication of danger suggested by appearance.[5] Like the animals of the experimental psychologist, the policeman finds the threat of random damage more compelling than a predetermined and inevitable punishment.

Nor, to qualify for the status of symbolic assailant, need an individual ever have used violence. A man backing out of a jewelry store with a gun in one hand and jewelry in the other would qualify even if the gun were a toy and he had never in his life fired a real pistol. To the policeman in the situation, the man's personal history is momentarily immaterial. There is only one relevant sign: a gun signifying danger. Similarly, a young man may suggest the threat of violence to the policeman by his manner of walking or "strutting," the insolence in the demeanor being registered by the policeman as a possible preamble to later attack.[6] Signs vary from area to area, but a youth dressed in a black leather jacket and motorcycle boots is sure to draw at least a suspicious glance from a policeman.

Policemen themselves do not necessarily emphasize the peril associated with their work when questioned directly, and may even have well-developed strategies of denial. The element of danger is so integral to the policeman's work that explicit recognition might induce emotional barriers to work performance. Thus, one patrol officer observed that more police have been killed and injured in automobile accidents in the past ten years than from gunfire. Although his assertion is true, he neglected to mention that the police are the only peacetime occupational group with a systematic record of death and injury from gunfire and other weaponry. Along these lines, it is interesting that of the 224 working Westville policemen (not including the sixteen juvenile policemen) responding to a question about which assignment they would like most to have in the police department,[7] 50 percent selected the job of detective, an assignment combining elements of apparent danger and initiative. The next category was adult street work, that is, patrol and traffic (37 percent). Eight percent selected the juvenile squad,[8] and only 4 percent selected administrative work. Not a single policeman chose the job of jail guard. Although these findings do not control for such factors as prestige, they suggest that confining and routine jobs are rated low on the hierarchy of police preferences, even though such jobs are least dangerous. Thus, the policeman may well, as a personality, enjoy the possibility of danger, especially its associated excitement, even though he may at the same time be fearful of it. Such "inconsistency" is easily understood. Freud has by now made it an axiom of personality theory that logical and emotional consistency are by no means the same phenomenon.

However complex the motives aroused by the element of danger, its consequences for sustaining police culture are unambiguous. This element requires him, like the combat soldier, the European Jew, the South African (white or black), to live in a world straining toward duality, and suggesting danger when "they" are perceived. Consequently, it is in the nature of the policeman's situation that his conception of order emphasize regularity and predictability. It is, therefore, a conception shaped by persistent *suspicion*. The English "copper," often portrayed as a courteous, easygoing, rather jolly sort of chap, on the one hand, or as a devil-may-care adventurer, on the other, is differently described by Colin MacInnes:

> The true copper's dominant characteristic, if the truth be known, is neither those daring nor vicious qualities that are sometimes attributed to him by friend or enemy, but an ingrained conservatism, and almost desperate love of the conventional. It is untidiness, disorder, the unusual, that a copper disapproves of most of all: far more, even than of crime which is merely a professional matter. Hence his profound dislike of people loitering in streets, dressing extravagantly, speaking with exotic accents, being strange, weak, eccentric, or simply any rare minority—of their doing, in fact, anything that cannot be safely predicted.[9]

Policemen are indeed specifically *trained* to be suspicious, to perceive events or changes in the physical surroundings that indicate the occurrence or probability of disorder. A former student who worked as a patrolman in a suburban New York police department describes this aspect of the policeman's assessment of the unusual:

> The time spent cruising one's sector or walking one's beat is not wasted time, though it can become quite routine. During this time, the most important thing for the officer to do is notice the *normal*. He must come to know the people in his area, their habits, their automobiles and their friends. He must learn what time the various shops close, how much money is kept on hand on different nights, what lights are usually left on, which houses are vacant . . . only then can he decide what persons or cars under what circumstances warrant the appellation "suspicious."[10]

The individual policeman's "suspiciousness" does not hang on whether he has personally undergone an experience that could objectively be described as hazardous. Personal experience of this sort is not the key to the psychological importance of exceptionality. Each, as he routinely carries out his work, will experience situations that threaten to become dangerous. Like the American Jew who contributes to the "defense" organizations such as the Anti-Defamation League in response to Nazi brutalities he has never experienced personally, the policeman identifies with his fellow cop who has been beaten, perhaps fatally, by a gang of young thugs.

Social Isolation

The patrolman in Westville, and probably in most communities, has come to identify the black man with danger. James Baldwin vividly expresses the isolation of the ghetto policeman:

> The only way to police a ghetto is to be oppressive. None of the police commissioner's men, even with the best will in the world, have any way of understanding the lives led by the people they swagger about in twos and threes controlling. Their very presence is an insult, and it would be, even if they spent their entire day feeding gumdrops to children. They represent the force of the white world, and that world's criminal profit and ease, to keep the black man corralled up here, in his place. The badge, the gun in the holster, and the swinging club make vivid what will happen should his rebellion become overt. . . .
>
> It is hard, on the other hand, to blame the policeman, blank, good-natured, thoughtless, and insuperably innocent, for being such a perfect representative of the people he serves. He, too, believes in good intentions and is astounded and offended when they are not taken for the deed. He has never, himself, done anything for which to be hated—which of us has?—and yet he is facing, daily and nightly, people who would gladly see him dead, and he knows it. There is no way for him not to know it; there are few things under heaven more unnerving than the silent, accumulating contempt and hatred of a people. He moves through Harlem, therefore, like an occupying soldier in a bitterly hostile country; which is precisely what, and where he is, and is the reason he walks in twos and threes.[11]

While Baldwin's observations on police–black relations cannot be disputed seriously, there is greater social distance between police and "civilians" in general regardless of their color than Baldwin considers. Thus, Colin MacInnes has his English hero, Mr. Justice, explaining:

> The story is all coppers are just civilians like anyone else, living among them not in barracks like on the Continent, but you and I know that's just a legend for mugs. We *are* cut off: we're *not* like everyone else. Some civilians fear us and play up to us, some dislike us and keep out of our way but no one—well, very few indeed— accepts us as just ordinary like them. In one sense, dear, we're just like hostile troops occupying an enemy country. And say what you like, at times that makes us lonely.[12]

MacInnes' observation suggests that by not introducing a white control group, Baldwin has failed to see that the policeman may not get on well with anybody regardless (to use the hackneyed phrase) of race, creed, or national origin. Policemen whom one knows well often express their sense of isolation from the public as a whole, not just from those who fail to share their color. Westville police were asked, for example, to rank the most serious problems police have. The category most frequently selected was not racial problems, but some form of public relations: lack of respect for the police, lack of cooperation in enforcement of law, lack of understanding of the requirements of police work.[13] One respondent answered:

> As a policeman my most serious problem is impressing on the general public just how difficult and necessary police service is to all. There seems to be an attitude of "law is important, but it applies to my neighbor—not to me."

Of the 282 Westville policemen who rated the prestige police work receives from others, 70 percent ranked it as only fair or poor, while less than 2 percent ranked it as "excellent" and another 29 percent as "good." Similarly, in Britain, two-thirds of a sample of policemen interviewed by a royal commission stated difficulties in making friends outside the force; of those interviewed 58 percent thought members of the public to be reserved, suspicious, and constrained in conversation; and 12 percent attributed such difficulties to the requirements that policemen be selective in associations and behave circumspectly.[14]

A Westville policeman related the following incident:

> Several months after I joined the force, my wife and I used to be socially active with a crowd of young people, mostly married, who gave a lot of parties where there was drinking and dancing, and we enjoyed it. I've never forgotten, though, an incident that happened on one Fourth of July party. Everybody had been drinking, there was a lot of talking, people were feeling boisterous, and some kid there—he must have been twenty or twenty-two—threw a firecracker that hit my wife in the leg and burned her. I didn't know exactly what to do—punch the guy in the nose, bawl him out, just forget it. Anyway, I couldn't let it pass, so I walked over to him and told him he ought to be careful. He began to rise up at me, and when he did, somebody yelled, "Better watch out, he's a cop." I saw everybody standing there, and I could feel they were all against me and for the kid, even though he had thrown the firecracker at my wife. I went over to the host and said it was probably better if my wife and I left because a fight would put a damper on the party. Actually, I'd hoped he would ask the kid to leave, since the kid had thrown the firecracker. But he didn't, so we left. After that incident, my wife and I stopped going around with that crowd,

and decided that if we were going to parties where there was to be drinking and boisterousness, we weren't going to be the only police people there.

Another reported that he seeks to overcome his feelings of isolation by concealing his police identity:

I try not to bring my work home with me, and that includes my social life. I like the men I work with, but I think it's better that my family doesn't become a police family. I try to put my police work into the background, and try not to let people know I'm a policeman. Once you do, you can't have normal relations with them.[15]

Although the policeman serves a people who are, as Baldwin says, the established society, the white society, these people do not make him feel accepted. As a result, he develops resources within his own world to combat social rejection.

Police Solidarity

All occupational groups share a measure of inclusiveness and identification. People are brought together simply by doing the same work and having similar career and salary problems. As several writers have noted, however, police show an unusually high degree of occupational solidarity.[16] It is true that the police have a common employer and wear a uniform at work, but so do doctors, milkmen, and bus drivers. Yet it is doubtful that these workers have so close knit an occupation or so similar an outlook on the world as do police. Set apart from the conventional world, the policeman experiences an exceptionally strong tendency to find his social identity within his occupational milieu.

Compare the police with another skilled craft. In a study of the International Typographical Union, the authors asked printers the first names and jobs of their three closest friends. Of the 1,236 friends named by the 412 men in their sample, 35 percent were printers.[17] Similarly, among the Westville police, of 700 friends listed by 250 respondents, 35 percent were policemen. The policemen, however, were far more active than printers in occupational social activities. Of the printers, more than half (54 percent) had never participated in any union clubs, benefit societies, teams, or organizations composed mostly of printers, or attended any printers' social affairs in the past five years. Of the Westville police, only 16 percent had failed to attend a single police banquet or dinner in the past *year* (as contrasted with the printers' *five years*); and of the 234 men answering this question, 54 percent had attended three or more such affairs *during the past year.*

These findings are striking in light of the interpretation made of the data on printers. Lipset, Trow, and Coleman do not, as a result of their findings, see printers as an unintegrated occupational group. On the contrary, they ascribe the democratic character of the union in good part to the active social and political participation of the membership. The point is not to question their interpretation, since it is doubtless correct when printers are held up against other manual workers. However, when seen in comparison to police, printers appear a minimally participating group; put positively, police emerge as an exceptionally socially active occupational group.

Police Solidarity and Danger

There is still a question, however, as to the process through which danger and authority influence police solidarity. The effect of danger on police solidarity is revealed
when we examine a chief complaint of police: lack of public support and public
apathy. The complaint may have several referents including police pay, police prestige, and support from the legislature. But the repeatedly voiced broader meaning of
the complaint is resentment at being taken for granted. The policeman does not
believe that his status as civil servant should relieve the public of responsibility for
law enforcement. He feels, however, that payment out of public coffers somehow
obscures his humanity and, therefore, his need for help.[18] As one put it:

> Jerry, a cop, can get into a fight with three or four tough kids, and there will be
> citizens passing by, and maybe they'll look, but they'll never lend a hand. It's their
> country too, but you'd never know it the way some of them act. They forget that
> we're made of flesh and blood too. They don't care what happens to the cop so long
> as they don't get a little dirty.

Although the policeman sees himself as a specialist in dealing with violence, he does
not want to fight alone. He does not believe that his specialization relieves the general public of citizenship duties. Indeed, if possible, he would prefer to be the foreman rather than the workingman in the battle against criminals.

The general public, of course, does withdraw from the workday world of the
policeman. The policeman's responsibility for controlling dangerous and sometimes
violent persons alienates the average citizen perhaps as much as does his authority
over the average citizen. If the policeman's job is to ensure that public order is maintained, the citizen's inclination is to shrink from the dangers of maintaining it. The
citizen prefers to see the policeman as an automaton, because once the policeman's
humanity is recognized, the citizen necessarily becomes implicated in the policeman's work, which is, after all, sometimes dirty and dangerous. What the policeman
typically fails to realize is the extent he becomes tainted by the character of the work
he performs. The dangers of their work not only draw policemen together as a group
but separate them from the rest of the population. Banton, for instance, comments:

> Patrolmen may support their fellows over what they regard as minor infractions in
> order to demonstrate to them that they will be loyal in situations that make the great-
> est demands upon their fidelity. . . .
>   In the American departments I visited it seemed as if the supervisors shared
> many of the patrolmen's sentiments about solidarity. They too wanted their col-
> leagues to back them up in an emergency, and they shared similar frustrations with
> the public.[19]

Thus, the element of danger contains seeds of isolation which may grow in two directions. In one, a stereotyping perceptual shorthand is formed through which the police
come to see certain signs as symbols of potential violence. The police probably differ
in this respect from the general middle-class white population only in degree. This
difference, however, may take on enormous significance in practice. Thus, the policeman works at identifying and possibly apprehending the symbolic assailant; the ordinary citizen does not. As a result, the ordinary citizen does not assume the respon-

sibility to implicate himself in the policeman's required response to danger. The element of danger in the policeman's role alienates him not only from populations with a potential for crime but also from the conventionally respectable (white) citizenry, in short, from that segment of the population from which friends would ordinarily be drawn. As Janowitz has noted in a paragraph suggesting similarities between the police and the military, ". . . any profession which is continually preoccupied with the threat of danger requires a strong sense of solidarity if it is to operate effectively. Detailed regulation of the military style of life is expected to enhance group cohesion, professional loyalty, and maintain the martial spirit."[20]

Social Isolation and Authority

The element of authority also helps to account for the policeman's social isolation. Policemen themselves are aware of their isolation from the community, and are apt to weight authority heavily as a causal factor. When considering how authority influences rejection, the policeman typically singles out his responsibility for enforcement of traffic violations.[21] Resentment, even hostility, is generated in those receiving citations, in part because such contact is often the only one citizens have with police, and in part because municipal administrations and courts have been known to utilize police authority primarily to meet budgetary requirements, rather than those of public order. Thus, when a municipality engages in "speed trapping" by changing limits so quickly that drivers cannot realistically slow down to the prescribed speed or, while keeping the limits reasonable, charging high fines primarily to generate revenue, the policeman carries the brunt of public resentment.

That the policeman dislikes writing traffic tickets is suggested by the quota system police departments typically employ. In Westville, each traffic policeman has what is euphemistically described as a working "norm." A motorcyclist is supposed to write two tickets an hour for moving violations. It is doubtful that "norms" are needed because policemen are lazy. Rather, employment of quotas most likely springs from the reluctance of policemen to expose themselves to what they know to be public hostility. As a result, as one traffic policeman said:

> You learn to sniff out the places where you can catch violators when you're running behind. Of course, the department gets to know that you hang around one place, and they sometimes try to repair the situation there. But a lot of the time it would be too expensive to fix up the engineering fault, so we keep making our norm.

When meeting "production" pressures, the policeman inadvertently gives a false impression of patrolling ability to the average citizen. The traffic cyclist waits in hiding for moving violators near a tricky intersection, and is reasonably sure that such violations will occur with regularity. The violator believes he has observed a policeman displaying exceptional detection capacities and may have two thoughts, each apt to generate hostility toward the policeman: "I have been trapped," or "They can catch me; why can't they catch crooks as easily?" The answer, of course, lies in the different behavior patterns of motorists and "crooks." The latter do not act with either the frequency or predictability of motorists at poorly engineered intersections.

While traffic patrol plays a major role in separating the policeman from the respectable community, other of his tasks also have this consequence. Traffic patrol is only the most obvious illustration of the policeman's general responsibility for maintaining public order, which also includes keeping order at public accidents, sporting events, and political rallies. These activities share one feature: the policeman is called upon to *direct* ordinary citizens and therefore to restrain their freedom of action. Resenting the restraint, the average citizen in such a situation typically thinks something along the lines of "He is supposed to catch crooks; why is he bothering me?" Thus, the citizen stresses the "dangerous" portion of the policeman's role while belittling his authority.

Closely related to the policeman's authority-based problems as *director* of the citizenry are difficulties associated with his injunction to *regulate public morality.* For instance, the policeman is obliged to investigate "lovers' lanes" and to enforce laws pertaining to gambling, prostitution, and drunkenness. His responsibility in these matters allows him much administrative discretion since he may not actually enforce the law by making an arrest, but instead merely interfere with continuation of the objectionable activity.[22] Thus, he may put the drunk in a taxi, tell the lovers to remove themselves from the backseat, and advise a man soliciting a prostitute to leave the area.

Such admonitions are in the interest of maintaining the proprieties of public order. At the same time, the policeman invites the hostility of the citizen so directed in two respects: he is likely to encourage the sort of response mentioned earlier (that is, an antagonistic reformulation of the policeman's role) and the policeman is apt to cause resentment because of the suspicion that policemen do not themselves strictly conform to the moral norms they are enforcing. Thus, the policeman, faced with enforcing a law against fornication, drunkenness, or gambling, is easily liable to a charge of hypocrisy. Even when the policeman is called on to enforce the laws relating to overt homosexuality, a form of sexual activity for which police are not especially noted, he may encounter the charge of hypocrisy on grounds that he does not adhere strictly to prescribed heterosexual codes. The policeman's difficulty in this respect is shared by all authorities responsible for maintenance of disciplined activity, including industrial foremen, political leaders, elementary schoolteachers, and college professors. All are expected to conform rigidly to the entire range of norms they espouse.[23] The policeman, however, as a result of the unique combination of the elements of danger and authority, experiences a special predicament. It is difficult to develop qualities enabling him to stand up to danger and to conform to standards of puritanical morality. The element of danger demands that the policeman be able to carry out efforts that are in their nature overtly masculine. Police work, like soldiering, requires an exceptional caliber of physical fitness, agility, toughness, and the like. The man who ranks high on these masculine characteristics is, again like the soldier, not usually disposed to be puritanical about sex, drinking, and gambling.

On the basis of observations, policemen do not subscribe to moralistic standards for conduct. For example, the morals squad of the police department, when questioned, was unanimously against the statutory rape age limit, on grounds that as late teenagers they themselves might not have refused an attractive offer from a seventeen-year-old girl.[24] Neither, from observations, are policemen by any means total abstainers from the use of alcoholic beverages. The policeman who is arresting a drunk has probably been drunk himself; he knows it and the drunk knows it.

More than that, a portion of the social isolation of the policeman can be attributed to the discrepancy between moral regulation and the norms and behavior of policemen in these areas. We have presented data indicating that police engage in a comparatively active occupational social life. One interpretation might attribute this attendance to a basic interest in such affairs; another might explain the policeman's occupational social activity as a measure of restraint in publicly violating norms he enforces. The interest in attending police affairs may grow as much out of security in "letting oneself go" in the presence of police, and a corresponding feeling of insecurity with civilians, as an authentic preference for police social affairs. Much alcohol is usually consumed at police banquets with all the melancholy and boisterousness accompanying such occasions. As Horace Cayton reports on his experience as a policeman:

> Deputy sheriffs and policemen don't know much about organized recreation; all they usually do when celebrating is get drunk and pound each other on the back, exchanging loud insults which under ordinary circumstances would result in a fight.[25]

To some degree the reason for the behavior exhibited on these occasions is the company, since the policeman would feel uncomfortable exhibiting insobriety before civilians. The policeman may be likened to other authorities who prefer to violate moralistic norms away from onlookers for whom they are routinely supposed to appear as normative models. College professors, for instance, also get drunk on occasion, but prefer to do so where students are not present. Unfortunately for the policeman, such settings are harder for him to come by than they are for the college professor. The whole civilian world watches the policeman. As a result, he tends to be limited to the company of other policemen for whom his police identity is not a stimulus to carping normative criticism.

Correlates of Social Isolation

The element of authority, like the element of danger, is thus seen to contribute to the solidarity of policemen. To the extent that policemen share the experience of receiving hostility from the public, they are also drawn together and become dependent upon one another. Trends in the degree to which police may exercise authority are also important considerations in understanding the dynamics of the relation between authority and solidarity. It is not simply a question of how much absolute authority police are given, but how much authority they have relative to what they had, or think they had, before. If, as Westley concludes, police violence is frequently a response to a challenge to the policeman's authority, so too may a perceived reduction in authority result in greater solidarity. Whitaker comments on the British police as follows:

> As they feel their authority decline, internal solidarity has become increasingly important to the police. Despite the individual responsibility of each police officer to pursue justice, there is sometimes a tendency to close ranks and to form a square when they themselves are concerned.[26]

These inclinations may have positive consequences for the effectiveness of police work, since notions of professional courtesy or colleagueship seem unusually high among police.[27] When the nature of the policing enterprise requires much joint activity, as in robbery and narcotics enforcement, the impression is received that cooperation is high and genuine. Policemen do not appear to cooperate with one another merely because such is the policy of the chief, but because they sincerely attach a high value to teamwork. For instance, there is a norm among detectives that two who work together will protect each other when a dangerous situation arises. During one investigation, a detective stepped out of a car to question a suspect who became belligerent. The second detective, who had remained overly long in the back-seat of the police car, apologized indirectly to his partner by explaining how wrong it had been of him to permit his partner to encounter a suspect alone on the street. He later repeated this explanation privately, in genuine consternation at having committed the breach (and possibly at having been culpable in the presence of an observer). Strong feelings of empathy and cooperation, indeed almost of "clannishness," a term several policemen themselves used to describe the attitude of police toward one another, may be seen in the daily activities of police. Analytically, these feelings can be traced to the elements of danger and shared experiences of hostility in the policeman's role.

Finally, to round out the sketch, policemen are notably conservative, emotionally and politically. If the element of danger in the policeman's role tends to make the policeman suspicious, and therefore emotionally attached to the status quo, a similar consequence may be attributed to the element of authority. The fact that a man is engaged in enforcing a set of rules implies that he also becomes implicated in *affirming* them. Labor disputes provide the commonest example of conditions inclining the policeman to support the status quo. In these situations, the police are necessarily pushed on the side of the defense of property. Their responsibilities thus lead them to see the striking and sometimes angry workers as their enemy and, therefore, to be cool, if not antagonistic, toward the whole conception of labor militancy.[28] If a policeman did not believe in the system of laws he was responsible for enforcing, he would have to go on living in a state of conflicting cognitions, a condition which a number of social psychologists agree is painful.[29]

This hypothetical issue of not believing in the laws they are enforcing simply does not arise for most policemen. In the course of the research, however, there was one example. A Negro civil rights advocate (member of CORE) became a policeman with the conviction that by so doing he would be aiding the cause of impartial administration of laws for Negroes. For him, however, this outside rationale was not enough to sustain him in administering a system of laws that depends for its impartiality upon a reasonable measure of social and economic equality among the citizenry. Because this recruit identified so much with the Negro community as to be unable to meet the enforcement requirements of the Westville Police Department, his efficiency was impaired, and he resigned in his rookie year.

Police are understandably reluctant to appear to be anything but impartial politically. The police are forbidden from publicly campaigning for political candidates. The London police are similarly prohibited, and before 1887 were not allowed to vote in parliamentary elections or in local ones until 1893.[30] It was not surprising that the Westville chief of police forbade questions on the questionnaire that would have measured political attitudes.[31] One policeman, however, explained the chief's refusal on grounds that "A couple of jerks here would probably cut up, and come out looking like Commies."

During the course of administering the questionnaire over a three-day period, I talked with approximately fifteen officers and sergeants in the Westville department, discussing political attitudes of police. In addition, during the course of the research itself, approximately fifty were interviewed for varying periods of time. Of these, at least twenty were interviewed more than once, some over time periods of several weeks. Furthermore, twenty police were interviewed in Eastville, several for periods ranging from several hours to several days. Most of the time was *not* spent on investigating political attitudes, but I made a point of raising the question, if possible, making it part of a discussion centered around the contents of a right-wing newsletter to which one of the detectives subscribed. One discussion included a group of eight detectives. From these observations, interviews, and discussions, it was clear that a Goldwater type of conservatism was the dominant political and emotional persuasion of police. I encountered only three policemen who claimed to be politically "liberal," at the same time asserting that they were decidedly exceptional.

Whether or not the policeman is an "authoritarian personality" is a related issue, beyond the scope of this discussion partly because of the many questions raised about this concept. Thus, in the course of discussing the concept of "normality" in mental health, two psychologists make the point that many conventional people were high scorers on the California F scale and similar tests. The great mass of the people, according to these authors, is not much further along the scale of ego development than the typical adolescent who, as they describe him, is "rigid, prone to think in stereotypes, intolerant of deviations, punitive and anti-psychological—in short, what has been called an authoritarian personality."[32] Therefore it is preferable to call the policeman's a conventional personality.

Writing about the New York police force, Thomas R. Brooks suggests a similar interpretation. He writes:

> Cops are conventional people. . . . All a cop can swing in a milieu of marijuana smokers, interracial dates, and homosexuals is the night stick. A policeman who passed a Lower East Side art gallery filled with paintings of what appeared to be female genitalia could think of doing only one thing—step in and make an arrest.[33]

Despite his fundamental identification with conservative conventionality, however, the policeman may be familiar, unlike most conventional people, with the argot of the hipster and the underworld. (The policeman tends to resent the quietly respectable liberal who comes to the defense of such people on principle but who has rarely met them in practice.) Indeed, the policeman will use his knowledge of the argot to advantage in talking to a suspect. In this manner, the policeman *puts on* the suspect by pretending to share his moral conception of the world through the use of "hip" expressions. The suspect may put on a parallel show for the policeman by using only conventional language to indicate his respectability. (In my opinion, neither fools the other.)

Notes

1. For previous contributions in this area, see the following: Ely Chinoy, *Automobile Workers and the American Dream* (Garden City: Doubleday and Company, Inc., 1955); Charles R.

Walker and Robert H. Guest, *The Man on the Assembly Line* (Cambridge: Harvard University Press, 1952); Everett C. Hughes, "Work and the Self," in his *Men and Their Work* (Glencoe, Ill.: The Free Press, 1958), pp. 42–55; Harold L. Wilensky, *Intellectuals in Labor Unions: Organizational Pressures on Professional Roles* (Glencoe, Ill.: The Free Press, 1956); Wilensky, "Varieties of Work Experience," in Henry Borow, ed., *Man in a World at Work* (Boston: Houghton Mifflin Company, 1964), pp. 125–154; Louis Kriesberg, "The Retail Furrier: Concepts of Security and Success," *American Journal of Sociology* 57 (March 1952): 478–485; Waldo Burchard, "Role Conflicts of Military Chaplains," *American Sociological Review* 19 (October 1954): 528–535; Howard S. Becker and Blanche Geer, "The Fate of Idealism in Medical School," *American Sociological Review* 23 (1958): 50–56; and Howard S. Becker and Anselm L. Strauss, "Careers, Personality, and Adult Socialization," *American Journal of Sociology* 62 (November 1956): 253–363.

2. Morris Janowitz, *The Professional Soldier: A Social and Political Portrait* (New York: The Free Press of Glencoe, 1964), p. 175.

3. By no means does such an analysis suggest there are no individual or group differences among police. On the contrary, most of this study emphasizes differences, endeavoring to relate these to occupational specialties in police departments. This [section], however, explores similarities rather than differences, attempting to account for the policeman's general disposition to perceive and to behave in certain ways.

4. William Westley was the first to raise such questions about the police, when he inquired into the conditions under which police are violent. Whatever merit this analysis has, it owes much to his prior insights, as all subsequent sociological studies of the police must. See his "Violence and the Police," *American Journal of Sociology* 59 (July 1953): 34–41; also his unpublished Ph.D. dissertation "The Police: A Sociological Study of Law, Custom, and Morality," University of Chicago, Department of Sociology, 1951.

5. Something of the flavor of the policeman's attitude toward the symbolic assailant comes across in a recent article by a police expert. In discussing the problem of selecting subjects for field interrogation, the author writes:

A. Be suspicious. This is a healthy police attitude, but it should be controlled and not too obvious.

B. Look for the unusual.
   1. Persons who do not "belong" where they are observed.
   2. Automobiles which do not "look right."
   3. Businesses opened at odd hours, or not according to routine or custom.

C. Subjects who should be subjected to field interrogations.
   1. Suspicious persons known to the officer from previous arrests, field interrogations, and observations.
   2. Emaciated appearing alcoholics and narcotics users who invariably turn to crime to pay for cost of habit.
   3. Person who fits description of wanted suspect as described by radio, teletype, daily bulletins.
   4. Any person observed in the immediate vicinity of a crime very recently committed or reported as "in progress."
   5. Known troublemakers near large gatherings.
   6. Persons who attempt to avoid or evade the officer.
   7. Exaggerated unconcern over contact with the officer.
   8. Visibly "rattled" when near the policeman.
   9. Unescorted women or young girls in public places, particularly at night in such places as cafés, bars, bus and train depots, or streetcorners.
   10. "Lovers" in an industrial area (make good lookouts).
   11. Persons who loiter about places where children play.
   12. Solicitors or peddlers in a residential neighborhood.
   13. Loiterers around public rest rooms.
   14. Lone male sitting in car adjacent to schoolground with newspaper or book in his lap.

15. Lone male sitting in car near shopping center who pays unusual amount of attention to women, sometimes continuously manipulating rearview mirror to avoid direct eye contact.
16. Hitchhikers.
17. Person wearing coat on hot days.
18. Car with mismatched hub caps, or dirty car with clean license plate (or vice versa).
19. Uniformed "deliverymen" with no merchandise or truck.
20. Many others. How about your own personal experiences?
From Thomas F. Adams, "Field Interrogation," *Police* (March–April 1963): 28.

6. See Irving Piliavin and Scott Briar, "Police Encounters with Juveniles," *American Journal of Sociology* 70 (September 1964): 206–214.

7. A questionnaire was given to all policemen in operating divisions of the police force: patrol, traffic, vice control, and all detectives. The questionnaire was administered at police lineups over a period of three days, mainly by the author but also by some of the police personnel themselves. Before the questionnaire was administered, it was circulated to and approved by the policemen's welfare association.

8. Indeed, the journalist Paul Jacobs, who has ridden with the Westville juvenile police as part of his own work in poverty, observed in a personal communication that juvenile police appear curiously drawn to seek out dangerous situations, as if juvenile work without danger is degrading.

9. Colin MacInnes, *Mister Love and Justice* (London: New English Library, 1962), p. 74.

10. Peter J. Connell, "Handling of Complaints by Police," unpublished paper for course in criminal procedure, Yale Law School, Fall 1961.

11. James Baldwin, *Nobody Knows My Name* (New York: Dell Publishing Company, 1962), pp. 65–67.

12. MacInnes, op. cit., p. 20.

13. Respondents were asked, "Anybody who knows anything about police work knows that police face a number of problems. Would you please state—in order —what you consider to be the most serious problems police have." On the basis of a number of answers, the writer and J. Richard Woodworth devised a set of categories. Then Woodworth classified each response into one of the categories (see table below). When a response did not seem clear, he consulted with the writer. No attempt was made to independently check Woodworth's classifications because the results are used impressionistically, and do not test a hypothesis. It may be, for instance, that "relations with public" is sometimes used to indicate racial problems, and vice versa. "Racial problems" include only those answers having specific reference to race. The categories and results were as follows:

Westville Police Ranking of Number-One Problem Faced by Police

	Number	Percent
Relations with public	74	26
Racial problems and demonstrations	66	23
Juvenile delinquents and delinquency	23	8
Unpleasant police tasks	23	8
Lack of cooperation from authorities (DA, legislature, courts)	20	7
Internal departmental problems	17	6
Irregular life of policeman	5	2
No answer or other answer	56	20
	284	100

14. Royal Commission on the Police, 1962, Appendix IV to *Minutes of Evidence,* cited in Michael Banton, *The Policeman in the Community* (London: Tavistock Publications, 1964), p. 198.

15. Similarly, Banton found Scottish police officers attempting to conceal their occupation when on holiday. He quotes one as saying: "If someone asks my wife 'What does your husband do?', I've told her to say, 'He's a clerk,' and that's the way it went because she found that being a policeman's wife—well, it wasn't quite a stigma, she didn't feel cut off, but that sort of invisible wall was up for conversation purposes when a policeman was there" (p. 198).
16. In addition to Banton, William Westley and James Q. Wilson have noted this characteristic of police. See Westley, op. cit., p. 294; Wilson, "The Police and Their Problems: A Theory," *Public Policy* 12 (1963): 189–216.
17. S. M. Lipset, Martin H. Trow, and James S. Coleman, *Union Democracy* (New York: Anchor Books, 1962), p. 123. A complete comparison is as follows:

Closest Friends of Printers and Police, by Occupation

	Printers N=1,236 (%)	Police N=700 (%)
Same occupation	35	35
Professionals, business executives, and independent business owners	21	30
White-collar or sales employees	20	12
Manual workers	25	22

18. On this issue there was no variation. The statement "the policeman feels" means that there was no instance of a negative opinion expressed by the police studies.
19. Banton, op. cit., p. 114.
20. Janowitz, op. cit.
21. O. W. Wilson, for example, mentions this factor as a primary source of antagonism toward police. See his "Police Authority in a Free Society," *Journal of Criminal Law, Criminology, and Police Science* 54 (June 1964): 175–177. In the current study, in addition to the police themselves, other people interviewed, such as attorneys in the system, also attribute the isolation of police to their authority. Similarly, Arthur L. Stinchcorabe, in "The Control of Citizen Resentment in Police Work," provides a stimulating analysis, to which I am indebted, of the ways police authority generates resentment.
22. See Wayne R. La Fave, "The Police and Nonenforcement of the Law," *Wisconsin Law Review* (1962): 104–137, 179–239.
23. For a theoretical discussion of the problems of leadership, see George Homans, *The Human Group* (New York: Harcourt, Brace and Company, 1950), especially the chapter on "The Job of the Leader," pp. 415–440.
24. The work of the Westville morals squad is analyzed in detail in an unpublished master's thesis by J. Richard Woodworth, "The Administration of Statutory Rape Complaints: A Sociological Study" (University of California, 1964).
25. Horace R. Cayton, *Long Old Road* (New York: Trident Press, 1965), p. 154.
26. Ben Whitaker, *The Police* (Middlesex, England: Penguin Books, 1964), p. 137.
27. It would be difficult to compare this factor across occupations, since the indicators could hardly be controlled. Nevertheless, I felt that the sense of responsibility to policemen in other departments was on the whole quite strong.
28. In light of this, the most carefully drawn lesson plan in the "professionalized" Westville police department, according to the officer in charge of training, is the one dealing with the policeman's demeanor in labor disputes. A comparable concern is now being evidenced in teaching policemen appropriate demeanor in civil rights demonstrations. See, e.g., Juby E. Towler, *The Police Role in Racial Conflicts* (Springfield, Ill.: Charles C Thomas, 1964).

29. Indeed, one school of social psychology asserts that there is a basic "drive," a fundamental tendency of human nature, to reduce the degree of discrepancy between conflicting cognitions. For the policeman, this tenet implies that he would have to do something to reduce the discrepancy between his beliefs and his behavior. He would have to modify his behavior, his beliefs, or introduce some outside factor to justify the discrepancy. If he were to modify his behavior, so as not to enforce the law in which he disbelieves, he would not hold his position for long. Practically, then, his alternatives are to introduce some outside factor, or to modify his beliefs. However, the outside factor would have to be compelling in order to reduce the pain resulting from the dissonance between his cognitions. For example, he would have to be able to convince himself that the only way he could possibly make a living was by being a policeman. Or he would have to modify his beliefs. See Leon Festinger, *A Theory of Cognitive Dissonance* (Evanston, Ill.: Row-Peterson, 1957). A brief explanation of Festinger's theory is reprinted in Edward E. Sampson, ed., *Approaches, Contexts, and Problems of Social Psychology* (Englewood Cliffs, N.J.: Prentice-Hall, 1964), pp. 9–15.
30. Whitaker, op. cit., p. 26.
31. The questions submitted to the chief of police were directly analogous to those asked of printers in the study of the I.T.U. See Lipset et al., op. cit., "Appendix 11–Interview Schedule," pp. 493–503.
32. Jane Loevinger and Abel Ossorio, "Evaluations of Therapy by Self-Report: A Paradox," *Journal of Abnormal and Social Psychology* 58 (May 1959): 392; see also Edward A. Shils, "Authoritarianism: 'Right' and 'Left'," in R. Christie and M. Jahoda, eds., *Studies in Scope and Method of "The Authoritarian Personality"* (Glencoe, Ill.: The Free Press, 1954), pp. 24–49.
33. Thomas R. Brooks, "New York's Finest," *Commentary* 40 (August 1965): 29–30.

7

Police Use of Deadly Force: Research and Reform

James J. Fyfe

Police use of deadly force first became a major public issue in the 1960s when many urban riots were precipitated by police killings of citizens. Since then, departments have made significant reforms in their policies regarding the use of deadly force, and the U.S. Supreme Court in Tennessee v. Garner *(1985) voided the rule existing in about half the states that allowed the use of deadly force to apprehend unarmed, nonviolent, fleeing felony suspects. James Fyfe examines the factors that seem to distinguish the extensive use of deadly force in some departments.*

When police officers fire their guns, the immediate consequences of their decisions are realized at the rate of 750 feet per second and are beyond reversal by any level of official review. As most police recruits learn in the academy, the cop on the street . . . carries in his holster more power than has been granted the Chief Justice of the Supreme Court. When used injudiciously, this power has led to riot and additional death, civil and criminal litigation against police and their employers, and the ousters of police chiefs, elected officials, and entire city administrations. Even when used with great restraint, police deadly force has created polarization, suspicion, and distrust on the part of those who need the police most.

· · ·

Legal and Administrative Controls on Deadly Force

. . . The President's Commission on Law Enforcement and Administration of Justice looked carefully at police–community relations. In the report of its Task Force on the Police—which, in my view, remains the single most significant and most influ-

Source: From James J. Fyfe, "Police Use of Deadly Force: Research and Reform," *Justice Quarterly* 5 (June 1988), pp. 165–166, 168–170, 171–174, 180–189, 199– 205. Some footnotes and references deleted. Reprinted with Permission of the Academy of Criminal Justice Sciences.

ential contribution to American police policy and practice to date—the commission made clear its dismay at the virtual absence of administrative policies to guide police officers' decisions to use deadly force (President's Commission 1967:189–190). In a report to the commission, Police Task Force chair Samuel Chapman cited the full text of one unnamed police department's policy on use of firearms as an illustration of the need for direction in this most critical matter of police discretion:

> Never take me out in anger; never put me back in disgrace (Chapman 1967).

Chapman also saw to it that the final report of the task force included a model administrative policy on use of firearms (President's Commission 1967:188–189). This was not the first time he had championed this cause; in 1963 he and Thompson Crockett reported on a 1961 survey of seventy-one Michigan police departments serving populations of 10,000 or more. They found that

> 54 percent (27 of 50) of the agencies furnishing information had no written policies in effect to govern the use of firearms. These twenty-seven departments, which relied upon "oral policy", were asked to indicate the main points of oral instructions given to their officers regarding when to use firearms. Of the twenty-seven, only five departments mentioned such basic situations as self-defense and fleeing felons where firearms may be used. Thus, based on the reported practice in these Michigan cities, it would appear reasonable to regard with grave reservation that suitability of relying singularly upon "oral policy" (Chapman and Crockett 1963:42).

Further:

> "[W]hen to fire" is frequently trusted to the "judgment" or "discretion" of officers as individuals . . . (1963:41).

· · ·

The Breadth of Law

In the absence of such policies, police shooting discretion generally was limited only by state criminal statutes or by case law defining justifiable homicide. These laws have several inadequacies. First, even the most restrictive state laws permit police to use their weapons in an extremely broad range of situations. Every state historically has permitted police officers to use deadly force to defend themselves or others against imminent death or serious physical harm, a provision that cannot be debated seriously. Indeed, except that generally they are obliged to attempt to retreat to safety before resorting to deadly force, American citizens enjoy the same justification for homicide. Because we ask the police to put their lives on the line in our behalf, it follows that they should enjoy this slight advantage over the rest of us.

Yet many states also have codified some variant of the common-law "fleeing felon" rule, which authorizes use of deadly force as a means of apprehending persons fleeing from suspected felonies. The Tennessee statute that eventually became the focus of *Tennessee* v. *Garner* (1985), illustrates the broadest category of such laws:

> *Resistance to Officer*—If after notice of the intention to arrest the [felony] defendant, he either flees or forcibly resists, the officer may use all the necessary means to effect the arrest (Tennessee Code Annotated sec. 40-7-108:55).

. . .

The manner in which felony suspects are pursued and apprehended has changed in important ways over the centuries. When the fleeing felon rule originated, those who typically pursued felons were ordinary male citizens who were obliged by law to respond to the *hue and cry* and to join in pursuit. Because they were usually armed only with clubs or knives, discharging their duty to arrest compelled them to overpower physically people who knew that arrest was likely to result in execution. These circumstances also are a far cry from more modern applications of the fleeing felon rule. The officer involved in *Garner*, for example, fired his fatal shot from the relative safety of 30 feet at the back of an unarmed, 5'4", 100-pound juvenile burglary suspect who, if apprehended alive, would likely have been sentenced to probation.

Debates about the merits of the *any* fleeing felon laws came to an abrupt end in 1985, when the Supreme Court ruled in *Garner* that the Tennessee statute, when applied against unarmed, nondangerous fleeing suspects, violated the Fourth Amendment's guarantees against unreasonable seizure. In his opinion for the majority, Justice White wrote that deadly force was a constitutional means of effecting arrest only when a felony "suspect threatens the officer with a weapon or there is probable cause to believe that he has committed a crime involving the infliction or threatened infliction of serious physical harm" (*Tennessee* v. *Garner,* 471 U.S. at 4). This decision affects the laws not only of the twenty-three states that followed the broad *any* fleeing felon rule; because Garner was a suspect in a nighttime residential burglary, it also affects the laws of several other states that included this offense under the limited category of offenses justifying deadly force for purposes of apprehension.

The Law as a Control on Professional Discretion

Although *Garner* moots some of the arguments about the great breadth of deadly force statutes, it does little to ameliorate a second and more general limitation of law in describing police shooting discretion: in no field of human endeavor does the criminal law alone define adequately the parameters of acceptable occupational behavior. In the course of their work, doctors, lawyers, psychologists, professors, soldiers, nursing home operators, truck drivers, government officials, and journalists can do many outrageous, unacceptable, and hurtful things without violating criminal law. In exchange for the monopolies on the activities performed by those in their crafts, the most highly developed of these professions keep their members' behavior in check by developing and enforcing codes of conduct that are both more specific and more restrictive than are criminal definitions. Who would submit to treatment by a surgeon whose choices in deciding how to deal with patients were limited only by the laws of homicide and assault?

Apply that logic to use of police firearms. Even post-*Garner,* no state law tells officers whether it is advisable to fire warning shots into the air on streets lined by high-rise buildings. The law provides no direction to officers who must decide quickly whether to shoot at people in moving vehicles and thereby risk turning them into speeding unguided missiles. The law related to police use of force, in short, is simply too vague to be regarded as a comprehensive set of operational guidelines.

Resistance to Rule Making Regarding Deadly Force

Even so, many police administrators did not act on policy recommendations like Chapman's until their officers had become involved in shootings that (although non-criminal) generated community outcries and crises (Sherman 1983). Their sometimes vigorous resistance to change was rooted in many considerations. First, police authority to restrict shooting discretion more tightly than state law was uncertain. In 1971, for example, the Florida Attorney General issued a written opinion that administrative policies overriding the state's any fleeing felon law were legally impermissible (Florida Attorney General 1971:68–75); this narrow view of the separation of powers has been cast aside since in favor of more realistic interpretations of police chiefs' administrative prerogatives. In addition, apparently on the theory that jurors were unlikely to find police behavior unreasonable unless officers had violated their own departments' formal rules and policies, some police officials refrained from committing deadly force policies to paper. Time also has shown that this rather self-serving attempt to avoid accountability and liability was counterproductive: jurors don't need a piece of paper to tell them whether an individual officer acted reasonably, but typically they do find that a police department's failure to provide officers with such paper is inexcusable. Finally, many police officers feared that restrictive deadly force policies would endanger the public and the police; by removing whatever deterrent value inhered in the fleeing felon rule, such policies would result in an increase in crime and a decrease in police ability to apprehend fleeing criminals. Indeed, even when research suggested that this was not the case (Fyfe 1979), many police chiefs continued to regard restrictive deadly force policies as invitations to public accusations that they were "weak on crime" or had "handcuffed the police."

By now, however, the question of whether police should promulgate restrictive deadly force policies has been answered in the affirmative; at least among larger agencies, it is the rare department whose manual does not include such a policy. Social science research has played some part in easing police resistance to formulation of deadly force policy, and in the Supreme Court's *Garner* decision as well.

·   ·   ·

Explanations of Variations in Police Homicide Rates

In attempts to explain why officers in some police departments are more likely than those in others to use deadly force and to kill, researchers generally have identified two sets of variables as salient. One is environmental and lies beyond the direct control of police administrators; the other is internal and is subject to control by police chiefs. The former category includes such variables as the level of violence among the constituencies of the police and the extent of lawful police authority to use deadly force. Included in the second category are such variables as general police operating philosophies and specific policies, both formal and unstated.

Environmental Explanations

Because police exposure to situations likely to precipitate shooting is presumably greatest where levels of general community violence are high, we would expect to find strong relationships between police homicide rates and measures of community violence and police contact with offenders. Perhaps the first researchers to explore such a hypothesis were Kania and Mackey (1977), who reported strong associations between the National Center for Health Statistics police homicide rates (however inaccurate) and rates of public homicide and violent crime across the states. In their intercity study, Sherman and Langworthy (1979) found the same kinds of associations between police homicide rates and such measures of potential police–citizen violence as gun density and rates of arrest for all offenses and for violent offenses. Finally, I (Fyfe 1980b) found strong associations between rates of shooting by onduty officers and rates of public homicide and arrests for violent crime across twenty police subjurisdictions within New York City.

There is a statistically significant association ($p=.002$) between the police homicide rates shown in Table 1 and the most easily derivable measure of public violence, the corresponding public homicide rates. As even a cursory examination of the table would suggest, however (is New Orleans really four times as violent as Washington, D.C., for example?), this measure accounts for only 13 percent of the variation in police homicide rates ($r=.37$; $r^2=.13$).

The table also suggests that the second environmental factor, the law of police deadly force, is of little help in explaining variation in police homicide rates. If the law were operative here, one would not expect to find (for example) that officers in Long Beach (rate=6.10) killed citizens twice as often as their colleagues across the city line in Los Angeles (rate=3.05), or that the police homicide rate in Jacksonville (7.17) was twice as high as in the more notorious Miami (3.50).

Internal Organizational Explanations

Certainly the police reflect the violence of the environments in which they work, and the police are duty-bound to operate within the law. Yet the limits of the law have been discussed already, and it is apparent that other things also are at work here. More specifically, as Uelman (1973) suggested in his research on variations in shooting rates among fifty police departments in Los Angeles County, it is clear that such internal organizational variables as the philosophies, policies, and practices of individual police chiefs and supervisors account for a considerable amount of variation in police homicide rates. Uelman's conclusion has been buttressed by studies (Fyfe 1979; Gain 1971; Meyer 1980; Milton, Halleck, Lardner, and Abrecht 1977; Scharf and Binder 1983) that report, with varying degrees of rigor and certainty, that reductions in police shooting frequency and changes in police shooting patterns have followed implementation of restrictive administrative policies on deadly force and weapons use.

T A B L E   1 / **Mean Annual Rate of Police Homicide per 1,000 Officers by Geographic Region and City, 1975–1983**

	Rate per 1,000	Number		Rate per 1,000	Number
Northeast	1.39	480	Memphis	3.75	42
Boston	1.19	22	Miami	3.50	25
Buffalo	0.50	5	Nashville	3.28	28
Newark	1.90	22	New Orleans	6.80	91
New York	1.36	295	Norfolk	1.68	9
Philadelphia	1.66	116	Tampa	3.14	17
Pittsburgh	0.81	10	Washington	1.55	56
Rochester	1.78	10	West	2.85	751
North Central	2.24	628	Albuquerque	1.94	9
Akron	0.97	4	Austin	0.87	4
Chicago	1.71	197	Dallas	4.32	78
Cincinnati	1.88	17	Denver	2.26	28
Cleveland	2.59	44	El Paso	1.88	11
Columbus	2.94	28	Fort Worth	1.91	12
Detroit	3.33	143	Honolulu	0.37	5
Indianapolis	3.75	34	Houston	4.73	130
Kansas City	2.71	29	Long Beach	6.10	34
Milwaukee	0.86	16	Los Angeles	3.05	192
Minneapolis	1.62	11	Oakland	5.22	30
Omaha	2.42	12	Oklahoma City	4.79	30
St. Louis	3.61	64	Phoenix	1.84	27
St. Paul	0.42	2	Portland, OR	0.81	5
Toledo	1.86	11	Sacramento	0.44	2
Wichita	4.33	16	San Antonio	2.74	28
South	3.10	447	San Diego	2.87	32
Atlanta	3.28	37	San Francisco	1.40	22
Baltimore	1.82	53	San Jose	2.62	19
Birmingham	5.19	31	Seattle	1.86	17
Charlotte	1.31	7	Tucson	3.08	15
Jacksonville	7.17	61	Tulsa	3.54	21
Louisville	3.11	20	Totals	2.24	2,236

SOURCE: Derived from Kenneth Matulia, *A Balance of Forces,* 2nd ed. (Gaithersburg, Md.: International Association of Chiefs of Police, 1985), pp. A–4, A–5.

A Case in Point

Without detailed analysis of the context and content of police officials' utterances and policy statements, it is impossible in an essay of this type to sort out their effects in a manner that would satisfy methodological purists. Even so, the effect of police operating philosophy and policy on police deadly force has been most striking in Philadelphia. There the police commissioner in 1970 and 1971 was Frank Rizzo, the flamboyant hard-liner[1] who went on to serve as mayor from 1972 through 1979. In 1973, when the Pennsylvania legislature modified its deadly force statute to prohibit shooting at fleeing persons who were not suspected of "forcible felonies" (Pennsylvania Statutes Annotates 1973), the Philadelphia Police Department (PPD) abol-

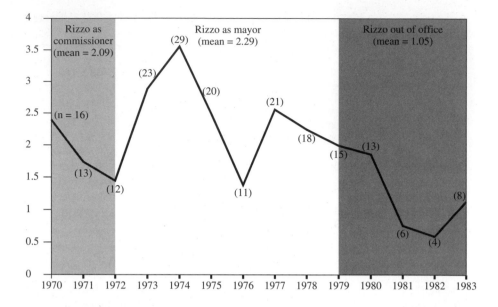

SOURCE: Data for 1970–1978 from Philadelpia Police Department, Homicide Division, *Shooting Files;* 1979–1983 from Matulia (1985), p. A.5.

Figure 1   Fatal shootings per 1,000 police officers, Philadelphia, 1970–1983

ished its former restrictive policy on deadly force on the grounds that the legislature had not defined "forcible felonies" adequately. From that point until Rizzo left office, PPD adopted an operating style in which police were effectively free to do anything with their guns, as long as they did not use them to resolve their own personal disputes.[2]

Figure 1 suggests that some PPD officers took great advantage of this freedom. During 1972, the last full year in which PPD operated under a restrictive deadly force policy, the PPD homicide rate per 1,000 officers was 1.47 (with twelve deaths resulting); the rate jumped to 2.87 (twenty-three deaths) in 1973 and peaked at 3.52 (twenty-nine deaths) in 1974. In 1976, when the city was cooperating in a federal court request to develop means of ending abuse of citizens, the police homicide rate dipped briefly to 1.35. In 1977, after the Supreme Court dismissed the case that had resulted in this agreement, the rate doubled (deaths rose from eleven to twenty-one). In 1981, the first full year of a new restrictive deadly force policy,[3] the rate decreased to 0.80 and remained relatively low during the next two years. Overall, the PPD police homicide rates were 2.09 while Rizzo was police commissioner, 2.29 while he was mayor, and 1.05 after he was out of office (as compared to the annual PPD homicide rate of 0.61 over 1950–1960; see Robin 1963).

These are powerful numbers. Indeed, when I attempted to quantify Rizzo's influence (R) over PPD operations . . . I found that the extent of his authority was a strong predictor of the annual PPD police homicide rate $(r=.72; p=.002)$, and that adding the public homicide rate to this equation added only marginally to predictive ability

($r=.26$; $R=.78$). In short—and except for the bizarre MOVE incident—knowing what Frank Rizzo was doing was far more valuable for estimating the PPD police homicide rate than were data on public homicides.

Elective and Nonelective Shootings

This analysis obviously suffers from the body count flaw; it includes only fatal shootings rather than all incidents of deadly force by PPD officers. Further, although I am convinced otherwise, many researchers will argue that my analysis of PPD homicides may have omitted some critical variable or set of variables. In addition, and if we assume for the moment that I am correct in asserting that Frank Rizzo was *the* critical variable in all Philadelphia police issues during the years in question, analysis of trends in police use of deadly force typically involves far more sophistication than when police or government administrators are as straightforward as Rizzo in espousing and executing their views.

In less extreme cases, examining in detail the circumstances of shootings is perhaps the most direct way to measure the relative effects of organizational and environmental variables on officers' use of deadly force. For these purposes it is useful to conceive of police shootings as incidents on a continuum that runs from *elective* situations, in which officers may decide to shoot or to refrain from shooting at no risk to themselves or of others, to *nonelective* situations, in which officers have no choice but to shoot or die (see Fyfe 1981c).

By these standards, Edward Garner's death—the shot at the back of the fleeing, unarmed, nonthreatening, property crime suspect who presents no apparent danger to anybody—was the prototypical elective shooting. Shootings such as this are influenced by internal police organizational variables; Garner and others in Memphis were shot in such circumstances because the police department encouraged or tolerated such action. Yet, as in the case of the Memphis Police Department in 1979, the police also can put an end to such shootings by simple administrative fiat (Memphis Police Department 1979). Shootings at the other end of the continuum are a different manner; no police department can direct officers to refrain from shooting when failure to do so may mean imminent death. Formal discretionary guidelines are of little relevance in such situations because, by any reasonable standard, the officers involved have only one choice.

Between these two extremes are more ambiguous police shootings that may be influenced to varying degrees by such variables as general organizational culture and the presence or absence of training in tactics. It is my experience, for example, that officers in some departments sometimes find themselves in harm's way because they respond to encouragement, both formal and from peers, to take charge of threatening situations quickly with as little assistance (and as little inconvenience to colleagues) as possible. In other departments, the operative norm encourages officers to use caution, to take cover, and to search for nonlethal means of resolving potential violence. These midrange shootings typically involve officers who, for whatever reasons, find themselves dangerously close to individuals who are armed with knives or other weapons, who attempt to run them down with vehicles, or who are determined to overpower them through mere physical force. Thus, in decreasing order of potential lethality, we can derive the following typology of police shootings, which will be useful in reexamining data already published elsewhere:

Gun assault: Citizen(s) armed with gun uses or attempts to use it against police.

Knife or other assault: Citizen(s) armed with cutting instrument or other weapon (for example, bat, chain, club, hammer, vehicle) uses or attempts to use it against police.

Physical assault: Citizen(s) attacks or attempts to attack police with fists, feet, or other purely physical means.

Unarmed, no assault: Unarmed citizen(s) makes no threat and attempts no attack on police or on any other person

As inexact as this typology may be, it does allow for some assessment of the relative extent to which police shootings are influenced by environmental and internal organizational forces. One would expect, for example, that shootings by officers whose discretion is limited carefully would tend toward the nonelective end of this continuum, and that a great percentage of shootings by officers in less stringently regulated departments would be elective.

This said, we move to Table 2, which demonstrates great variation in the nature of reported shootings across Chicago, New York, and Philadelphia ($p<.0001$). Even though the data included in the table are not absolutely compatible (my coding scheme for New York and Philadelphia includes accidental shootings and others that Geller and Karales [1981] treated separately, and that are described in note b of the table), it is clear that shootings occurred in significantly different circumstances in the places and times included in the table. About eight in ten of the shootings in Chicago and New York involved citizens who reportedly attacked officers with guns (Chicago=62.1%; New York=53.0%) or other weapons (Chicago=15.3%; New York=34.0%), but fewer than six in ten Philadelphia shootings (39.0% guns; 19.6% knives and other) fell into either of these two categories. At the other end of the continuum, the percentage of "unarmed, no-assault" incidents in New York City, which operated under an essentially "defense of life only" deadly force policy during much of the period studied (see Fyfe 1979), was considerably smaller than in either Chicago or Philadelphia (8.5% versus 20.9% and 24.9%, respectively), where police were given relatively more freedom to use their guns in elective situations. Therefore, not surprisingly, the rates presented on the table also indicate that the greatest discrepancies among these three police agencies' shooting experiences are found at the elective end of our continuum ("unarmed, no-assault" rates from New York, Philadelphia, and Chicago=0.52, 2.94, and 1.36, respectively).

The rates in this table also illustrate the dangers of attempting to describe deadly force in terms of body counts. The three departments included in Table 2 do not appear to differ much in regard to deadly force resulting in fatalities (1971–1975 police homicide rates per 1,000 officers=2.39 and 2.42 for New York and Philadelphia; 1974–1978 Chicago rate=1.97). When incidents resulting in nonfatal wounds are added to these figures, however, the differences among these cities grow and change direction (rates=6.09, 7.57, and 11.82 for New York, Chicago, and Philadelphia). In other words, Philadelphia police officers were only slightly more likely

T A B L E   2 / **Shooting Incident Types in New York City, Philadelphia, and Chicago**

Shooting Type	New York 1971–1975[a]	Philadelphia 1971–1975[a]	Chicago 1974–1978[b]
Gun assault	53.0%	39.0%	62.1%
	(n = 481)	(n = 185)	(n = 264)
Rate[c]	3.20	4.60	4.02
Knife/other assault	34.0%	19.6%	15.3%
	(n = 308)	(n = 93)	(n = 65)
Rate	2.07	2.32	0.99
Physical assault	4.5%	16.5%	1.7%
	(n = 41)	(n = 78)	(n = 7)
Rate	0.28	1.95	0.11
Unarmed, no assault	8.5%	24.9%	20.9%
	(n = 77)	(n = 118)	(n = 89)
Rate	0.52	2.94	1.36
Totals	100.0%	100.0%	100.0%
	(n = 907)	(n = 474)	(n = 497)[d]
Rate	6.09	11.82	7.57

Chi-square = 216.45
p < .0001

[a] *Source:* Fyfe (1988). Includes all reported incidents in which police officers shot and wounded or killed others.

[b] Derived from Geller and Karales (1981:103). Includes the number of persons shot rather than the number of incidents in which persons were shot. Excludes persons shot and wounded or killed for the following reasons:

Reason for shooting	n	Rate[c]
Not ascertained	6	0.09
Stray bullet	17	0.26
Mistaken identity	4	0.06
Accidental	52	0.79
Other intentional	7	0.11
Civilian appeared to display an unknown object without pointing it.	5	0.08
Civilian appeared to possess an unknown concealed object without pointing it.	7	0.11
Total	98	1.49

[c] Mean annual rate per 1,000 officers.

[d] Total number of incidents in which citizens were shot.

than New York or Chicago officers to shoot and kill citizens during the periods included in Table 2, but they were nearly twice as likely to shoot and kill *or wound* citizens. Further, because Chicago police apparently maintained records of missed shots only from 1975 through 1977 (Geller and Karales 1981: 162) and because PPD did not do so at all during the period studied, there is no way to determine with any precision how great these discrepancies might have been if we had been able to include incidents in which officers' bullets failed to hit their targets.

Even so, there is reason to believe that the differences among these cities would be even more striking if such data were available. First, police departments that permit shooting in elective situations are likely to experience high percentages of missed shots. Just as nonelective shootings are extremely dangerous for the officers involved, they are also very dangerous for their opponents. It is far easier to hit someone who is standing 8 or 10 feet away with a shotgun in his hands than someone who is running away in the dark (see, e.g., Horvath and Donahue 1982:87). Second, such departments also tend to experience high percentages of woundings in relation to fatalities. The four-to-one ratio of nonfatal to fatal wounds for Philadelphia did not result from any extraordinary humaneness on the part of PPD officers. It came about because an extraordinary percentage of the people shot at by the Philadelphia police were running targets; the officers fired at ranges so great that they were unable to hit the center body mass at which they were trained to shoot.

The data in my own work and in Geller and Karales's (1981) study support these assertions. The differences among police homicide rates for these cities are relatively small, but become more marked when nonfatal woundings are added to the equation. Finally, when the 1975–1977 data on all Chicago police shootings at citizens ($n=1,145$; Geller and Karales 1981:162) are compared to the corresponding 1971–1975 data ($n=2,234$; Fyfe 1978:390), the derived shooting rates per 1,000 officers differ greatly (Chicago=29.07; New York=14.09). It is difficult to imagine that inclusion of data from Philadelphia—where officers had by far the most liberal shooting license among these three cities—would not skew this contrast even further.

• • •

Conclusions

On balance, and even though the available data are skimpier than we would like, it appears that the frequency of police use of deadly force is influenced heavily by organizational philosophies, expectations, and policies; that levels of community violence are marginal predictors, useful chiefly when organizational variables may be held constant (as in studying a single police jurisdiction); and that variations in law play a role in determining frequency of deadly force only when administrators abdicate their responsibility to see that propriety is not limited only by statutory definitions of criminal assault and homicide.

For this last reason, *Tennessee* v. *Garner* probably is not as sweeping as many suspect. By the time this case was decided, virtually all major police departments had adopted their own administrative policies that were at least as restrictive as the *violent* felon rule propounded by the Supreme Court. In his decision for the majority, in fact, Justice White made repeated suggestions that the Court's holding was not a major intervention into police administrative prerogatives because most large police departments already were in compliance. Indeed, the fact that Memphis itself had abolished administratively the *any* fleeing felon rule five years before the case came to the Court weakened seriously the city attorney's oral argument that the *any* fleeing felon rule was a valuable adjunct to the effectiveness of law enforcement. Thus it is likely that the major effects of *Garner* will be (and have been) felt in smaller police jurisdictions where, as Neilsen (1983) suggests, administrative rule making related to deadly force has been less frequent.

Still, although *Garner* itself will not revolutionize American law enforcement, the process leading up to it has altered dramatically the police community's view of the whole deadly force issue. As recently as 1980, for example, attendees at the annual International Association of Chiefs of Police (IACP) meeting voted "by a 4-to-1 margin reaffirming [the association's] support of laws and policies permitting police to shoot fleeing felony suspects" (*St. Louis Post-Dispatch* 1980). In the same year, the International Union of Police Associations passed a resolution seeking to remove Patrick Murphy "as President of a private corporation known as the Police Foundation and to boycott any organization or foundation that supports the Police foundation" because Murphy had criticized "police officers' use of weapons," "notoriously accused our nation's police officers as the immediate cause of the riots that took place in the 60's," indicated that four police officers who had been acquitted in a Miami beating death (a verdict that sparked Miami's Liberty City riot) had committed the beating of which they were accused, and had "further stated that a restrictive shooting policy not only reduces police shootings of civilians but does not result in any increased danger to police officers or a rise in crime" (International Union of Police Associations 1980).

By 1982, however, IACP had promulgated a model policy on police use of force that would permit shooting at fleeing felony suspects only when "freedom is reasonably believed to represent an *imminent* threat of grave bodily harm or death to the officer or other person(s)" (Matulia 1982:164; emphasis in original). In 1983 IACP joined in recommending that the Commission on Accreditation for Law Enforcement Agencies adopt its present strict *defense of life only* standard for deadly force policies (1983:1–2). In 1984 the Police Foundation's *amici curiae* brief against Tennessee and the Memphis Police Department in *Garner* was joined by "nine national and international associations of police and criminal justice professionals, the chiefs of police associations of two states, and thirty-one law enforcement chief executives" (Police Foundation 1984). Equally significant, and contrary to past practice in cases of substantial constitutional issues involving the police, no *amicus* briefs were filed on the other side of the case. In 1985, when *Garner* was decided, IACP's executive director hailed it as a great step forward. This remarkable turnaround and disavowal of tradition and professional dogma was stimulated in large measure by research findings that suggested that the value of broad police shooting authority was overrated; rarely have researchers had such an effect on criminal justice policies and practices.[4]

Research regarding the people involved in incidents of deadly force by police generally shows that blacks and other minorities are overrepresented at both ends of police guns. Explanations for these disparities vary, but at least by my interpretation they typically involve embarrassing realities over which police have little control. Black citizens are overrepresented in the most violent and most criminogenic neighborhoods; individual black officers, who are still underrepresented in American policing generally, are far more likely than individual white officers to draw the most hazardous police duties in those same neighborhoods. Until these realities are altered, we can expect continuing minority disproportion in deadly force statistics no matter how stringently police officers' discretion is controlled.

This probability, I think, illustrates the central theme that may be drawn from all the research on deadly force reviewed in this essay. Police officers and the people at whom they shoot are simply actors in a much larger play. When police officers' roles in this play are defined carefully by their administrators and when the officers have been trained well to perform those roles, their individual characteristics mean little; the young cop, the old cop, the male cop, the female cop, the white cop, and the black cop all know what is expected of them, and they do it. When such clear expectations are not provided, officers improvise, and often we give their performances bad reviews. Yet because we put them on the stage in the first place, we also should criticize ourselves for failing to ensure that they have been directed adequately. When black children's roles are defined so clearly by the conditions in which so many are raised, we should expect that some will end their lives at the wrong end of police guns. We should not blame the police for that; we should blame ourselves for creating the stages on which so many black lives are played out.

Editor's Postscript

What has been the impact of the Supreme Court's ruling in *Tennessee* v. *Garner* that the police may not use deadly force against a suspected fleeing, unarmed felon? In a 1990 study Fyfe and Walker found that only four of the thirty-one states affected by the *Garner* decision had made statutory changes to bring their laws in line with the Court's interpretation of the Fourth Amendment, yet the authors argue that police officers now know the rules and that *Garner* types of shootings are a thing of the past. From their research the authors draw the following conclusions (Fyfe 1991):

1. Statutes relating to deadly force are irrelevant to officers on the street. Like other professionals or craftsmen, police behavior is most directly affected by organizational and professional guidelines that place limits on their discretion.
2. Most likely changes have not been made in state laws because legislators are reluctant to build political records indicating that they have voted for restrictions that would appear to "handcuff" the police.
3. The decline in fleeing felon shootings is apparently the result of modifications to guidelines made by police administrators.
4. The post-*Garner* impact thus reinforces the belief that control of police street-level decisions is in the chief's office rather than in the legislature's, prosecutor's, or attorney general's chambers.

Notes

1. Former Mayor Rizzo perhaps is best known for his advice that officers should "break their heads before they break yours." My favorite Rizzoism, however, dates from late 1979, when, in response to a question about a United States Justice Department suit against his administration and the Philadelphia Police Department, Rizzo commented on ABC-TV's *Nightline* that "when I became mayor, the Philadelphia Police Department had only one shotgun. Now we've got enough guns to invade Cuba and win."
2. Despite extensive review of PPD reports of all firearm discharges resulting in injury or death from 1970 through 1978, for example, I can find only two cases that resulted in departmental discipline against officers who had fired their guns while on duty. In one case an officer shot and killed his wife in a police station during an apparent argument over the disposition of his paycheck; the other resulted in the two-day suspension of an officer who had fired unnecessary shots into the air.

3. The policy (Philadelphia Police Department 1980) was promulgated on April 2, 1980. It authorizes officers to shoot in defense of life and, when no alternative exists, to apprehend fleeing suspects who officers know are in possession of deadly weapons that they have used or threatened to use, or who have committed forcible felonies. Of these last, PPD's position was as follows:

> Until forcible felony is defined by statute, the Police Department adopts the position that forcible felony includes the crimes of Murder, Voluntary Manslaughter, Rape, Robbery, Kidnapping, Involuntary Deviate Sexual Intercourse, Arson, Burglary of a Private Residence, Aggravated Assault Causing Serious Bodily Injury (Davis 1980).

4. This observation is tempered by the knowledge that increased governmental exposure to civil liability for failure to supervise police officers adequately has served also as a major stimulant to reform of deadly force policies and practices. Almost certainly, *Monell v. New York City Department of Social Services* (1978), in which the Supreme Court holds government entities liable when unreasonable policies and practices are proved to be the causes of constitutional violations suffered at the hands of individual agents, has had more effect on police operations than have any of the Court's more celebrated rulings related to criminal procedure.

References

CHAPMAN, S.G. (1967). *Police Firearms Use Policy.* Report to the President's Commission on Law Enforcement and Administration of Justice. Washington, D.C.: United States Government Printing Office.

CHAPMAN, S.G. AND T.S. CROCKETT (1963). "Gunsight Dilemma: Police Firearms Policy." *Police* 6:40–45.

DAVIS, A.J. (1980). Letter to Burton A. Rose of Peruto, Ryan, and Vitullo, counsel for the Philadelphia chapter of the Fraternal Order of Police, October 15.

FLORIDA ATTORNEY GENERAL (1971). *Annual Report.* In Herman Goldstein (ed.), *Policing a Free Society.* Cambridge, Mass.: Ballinger, p. 127.

FYFE, J.J. (1978). "Shots Fired: An Analysis of New York City Police Firearms Discharge." Ph.D. dissertation, State University of New York at Albany. Ann Arbor: University Microfilms.

———— (1979). "Administrative Interventions on Police Shooting Discretion: An Empirical Examination." *Journal of Criminal Justice* 7:309–324.

———— (1980a). "Always Prepared: Police Off-Duty Guns." *Annals of the American Academy of Political and Social Science* 452:72–81.

———— (1980b). "Geographic Correlates of Police Shooting: A Microanalysis." *Journal of Research in Crime and Delinquency* 17:101–113.

———— (1981a). "Observation on Police Deadly Force." *Crime and Delinquency* 27:376–389.

———— (1981b). "Race and Extreme Police-Citizen Violence." In R.L. McNeely and C.E. Pope (eds.), *Race, Crime, and Criminal Justice.* Beverly Hills: Sage, pp. 89–108.

———— (1981c). "Toward a Typology of Police Shootings." In J.J. Fyfe (ed.), *Contemporary Issues in Law Enforcement.* Beverly Hills: Sage, pp. 136–151.

———— (1981d). "Who Shoots? A Look at Officer Race and Police Shooting." *Journal of Police Science and Administration* 9:367–382.

———— (1982). "Blind Justice: Police Shootings in Memphis." *Journal of Criminal Law and Criminology* 73:707–722.

———— (1986). "Enforcement Workshop: The Supreme Court's New Rules for Police Use of Deadly Force." *Criminal Law Bulletin* 22:62–68.

———— (1988). "Police Shooting Environment and License." In J.E. Scott and T. Hirschi (eds.), *Controversial Issues in Crime and Justice.* Beverly Hills: Sage, pp. 79–94.

———— (1991). Communication to the editor.

FYFE, J.J., AND JEFFERY T. WALKER (1990). "*Garner* Plus Five Years: An Examination of Supreme Court Intervention into Police Discretion and Legislative Prerogatives." *American Journal of Criminal Justice* 14:167–188.

GAIN, C. (1971). "Discharge of Firearms Policy: Effecting Justice through Administrative Regulation." Unpublished statement, Oakland, Calif., December 23.

GELLER, W.A., AND K.J. KARALES (1981). *Split-Second Decisions: Shootings of and by Chicago Police.* Chicago: Chicago Law Enforcement Study Group.

HORVATH, F., AND M. DONAHUE (1982). *Deadly Force: An Analysis of Shootings by Police in Michigan, 1976–1981.* East Lansing: Michigan State University.

ILLINOIS REVISED STATUTES (1975). Chapter 38, Para. 2–8.

INTERNATIONAL UNION OF POLICE ASSOCIATIONS (1980). *Resolution of July 15, 1980.* Washington, D.C.: mimeo.

KANIA, R.R.E., AND W.C. MACKEY (1977). "Police Violence as a Function of Community Characteristics." *Criminology* 15:27–48.

MATULIA, K.R. (1982). *A Balance of Forces.* Gaithersburg, Md.: International Association of Chiefs of Police.

———— (1985). *A Balance of Forces.* Second edition. Gaithersburg, Md.: International Association of Chiefs of Police.

MEMPHIS POLICE DEPARTMENT (1979). *General Order 95-79, Deadly Force Policy,* July 16.

MEYER, M.W. (1980). *Report to the Los Angeles Board of Police Commissioners on Police Use of Deadly Force in Los Angeles: Officer-Involved Shootings, Part IV.* Los Angeles: Los Angeles Board of Police Commissioners.

MILTON, C., J.W. HALLECK, J. LARDNER, AND G.L. ABRECHT (1977). *Police Use of Deadly Force.* Washington, D.C.: Police Foundation.

MONELL V. NEW YORK CITY DEPARTMENT OF SOCIAL SERVICES. (1978). 436 U.S. 658.

NIELSEN, E. (1983). "Policy on the Police Use of Deadly Force: A Cross-National Analysis." *Journal of Police Science and Administration* 11:104–108.

PENNSYLVANIA STATUTES ANNOTATED (1973).

PHILADELPHIA POLICE DEPARTMENT (1980). *Directive* 10, April 2.

POLICE FOUNDATION, JOINED BY NINE NATIONAL AND INTERNATIONAL ASSOCIATIONS OF POLICE AND CRIMINAL JUSTICE PROFESSIONALS, THE CHIEFS OF POLICE ASSOCIATIONS OF TWO STATES, AND THIRTY-ONE LAW ENFORCEMENT CHIEF EXECUTIVES (1984). *Amici Curiae Brief in Tennessee v. Garner.* United States Supreme Court 83-1035, 83-1070. Washington, D.C.: August 6.

PRESIDENT'S COMMISSION ON LAW ENFORCEMENT AND ADMINISTRATION OF JUSTICE (1967). *Task Force Report: The Police.* Washington, D.C.: United States Government Printing Office.

ROBIN, G. (1963). "Justifiable Homicide by Police." *Journal of Criminal Law, Criminology and Police Science* (May/June): 225–231.

SCHARF, P., AND A. BINDER (1983). *The Badge and the Bullet.* New York: Praeger.

ST. LOUIS POST-DISPATCH (1980). "The Police Chiefs on Deadly Force." Editorial, September 21:16.

SHERMAN, L.W. (1980). "Execution without Trial: Police Homicide and the Constitution." *Vanderbilt Law Review* 33:71–110.

———— (1983). "Reducing Police Gun Use: Critical Events, Administrative Policy and Organizational Change." In Maurice Punch (ed.), *The Management and Control of Police Organizations.* Cambridge, Mass.: M.I.T. Press, pp. 98–125.

————, AND R. LANGWORTHY (1979). "Measuring Homicide by Police Officers." *Journal of Criminal Law and Criminology* 70:546–560.

TENNESSEE CODE ANNOTATED (1977).

TENNESSEE V. GARNER, (1985). 471 U.S. 1, 105 S. Ct. 1694, 85 L. Ed. 1.

UELMAN, G. (1973). "Varieties of Public Policy: A Study of Police Policy Regarding the Use of Deadly Force in Los Angeles County." *Loyola of Los Angeles Law Review* 6:1–65.

PART THREE

Prosecution

For many years the radio serial "Mr. District Attorney" held audiences spellbound as its namesake sought "not only to prosecute to the limit of the law all persons accused of crime within this county, but to defend with equal vigor the rights and privileges of all its citizens." In real life, there are counterparts to the crusading fictional prosecutors. Over the years a number of political leaders at the national and state levels have come to prominence as fighting prosecutors, and many have based campaigns for higher political office on reputations gained from widely publicized investigations or trials. The influence prosecutors have flows directly from their legal duties, but must be understood within the context of the administrative and political environment of the system.

It seems natural that the prosecutor's office should serve as a stepping-stone to advancement. Because they deal with dramatic and sensational situations, prosecutors can use the communications media to create a favorable climate of opinion. They can also use discretionary powers to impress voters with their prosecuting ability. To avoid difficult cases, prosecutors can just drop charges. They can also initiate investigations at politically opportune times and disclose suspected wrongdoing by members of the opposition. Because they have a staff that they can use for campaign work, and hold offices that make it easy to gather political contributions, prosecutors may be formidable opponents in politics.

Although the partisan advantages of the prosecutor's office are great, they tend to overshadow the real political importance of daily decisions the office makes. These decisions exert a tremendous influence on the values in the community. Of the many positions within the legal process, the position of prosecuting attorney is distinctive because it is concerned with all aspects of the criminal justice system. Not only do prosecutors have the formal power to determine which cases will be prosecuted, what charges will be made, and what bargains there will be with defendants, but what prosecutors do also influences the operations of the police, the coroner, the grand jury, and the judge. Accordingly, if we were to place prosecutors' activities on a scale, we would see that at one end they perform many tasks concurrently and in cooperation with the police. They may, for instance, investigate areas of suspected wrongdoing, directing the police in the actual apprehension of law violators. At the other end of the scale, we would recognize prosecutors as officers of the court, concerned in the role of adjudicator that justice be accorded defendants. In the United States, where public prosecution is the only means by which defendants are brought to trial, the prosecuting attorney is the vital link between the police and the courts. In each role, prosecutors are able to make decisions that vitally affect the administration of justice without strictly adhering to legal rules, relying rather on their personal judgment. This faculty is often influenced by their exchange relationships with other actors in the judicial and political system.

The powers of prosecutors are enhanced by the circumstances under which they may make decisions. Prosecutors are usually elected on a partisan basis for a four-year term; there are few other public checks on their actions. In most states, the prosecutor is responsible either to no one other than the voters, or to the governor—and then only for aggravated nonfeasance or misfeasance. In addition, the prosecutor generally makes decisions out of the glare of publicity. For example, a deputy prosecutor and a defense attorney may reach a verbal agreement over a cup of coffee or in the hall outside the courtroom. This agreement may result in a reduced charge in exchange for a guilty plea, or dismissal of the charge if the defendant is willing to seek psychiatric help.

As the nexus of the adjudicative and enforcement functions, the prosecutor has been called the most powerful single individual in local government. If the prosecutor does not act, the judge and the jury are helpless and the police officer's word is meaningless. In this position, the prosecutor plays many roles: crusader, administrator, counselor to other government officials, advocate. Each person occupying the position interprets the roles differently, depending on the others in the relationship, the environment within which he or she operates, and his or her own personality. The power of the prosecuting attorney was well stated by the Wickersham Commission in 1931.

> The prosecutor [is] the real arbiter of what laws shall be enforced and against whom, while the attention of the public is drawn rather to the small percentage of offenders who go through the courts.

Decision Making

At each stage of prosecution there are a number of ways to deal with each case. The closer a case is to coming to trial, the less latitude is available to decision makers. A sieve effect operates, so that a case is handled in an increasingly finite manner as it goes from the police to a preliminary hearing and trial. At each succeeding step the number of judicial personnel associated with the case increases and the formal requirements of the system become more intricate. As a case moves toward the courtroom, the visibility of decision making increases and the exchange relationships of participants become more complex. Under these circumstances, the prosecutor, the accused, and the court have less freedom in their attempts to find a solution beneficial to all.

To the layperson it might appear that there is little discretion in determining what charge should be made against a lawbreaker. But because of the nature of the charging process, prosecutors actually have a great deal of discretion as they define cases and file information or indictments.

Suppose that Smith—carrying a gun—breaks into a grocery store, assaults the proprietor, and robs the cash drawer. What charges can the prosecutor file? The accused can be charged with at least four violations: breaking and entering, assault, armed robbery, and carrying a dangerous weapon. Other charges might be added, depending on the circumstances—whether it was day or night, for instance.

David Sudnow has distinguished between "necessarily included offenses" and "situationally included offenses." He asks, "Could Smith have committed crime A and not crime B?" If the answer is yes, B is not a necessarily included offense. In the example of the grocery store, Smith has committed the necessarily included crime of carrying a dangerous weapon in the course of the armed robbery. The prosecutor may either charge Smith solely with the armed robbery or include any number of other charges or combination of charges in the information. With multiple charges, the prosecutor increases his or her bargaining power in plea negotiations.

It is difficult to determine the exact motives of decision makers in selecting one alternative over another. As the exchange model emphasizes, decision making is a product of the needs and goals of the system as affected by the environment in which it exists. The factors that influence the decision to prosecute seem to fall into three categories: evidential, humanitarian, and organizational.

Evidential

"Is there a case?" "Does the evidence warrant the arrest of an individual and the expense of a trial?" These are two major questions prosecutors ask when deciding whether to prosecute. The prosecutor must determine whether a violation of the criminal law, as seen within the context of the local political system, has been committed. There are many borderline offenses, particularly those concerned with morality, that will not result in prosecution. The nature of the case may require presentation of evidence that can prove such broadly defined terms as *neglect* or *intent*. The prosecutor must be certain that the evidence will coincide with the court's interpretation of these terms. In many cases, the facts may be clear but the ambiguity of the law makes application of these facts difficult.

Evidence is considered weak when it is difficult to use in proving the charges, when the value of a stolen article is questionable, when the case results from a brawl, or when there is lack of corroboration. Prosecution of cases involving victimless crimes is especially difficult for these reasons. In prostitution and narcotics cases, evidence is usually produced by plainclothesmen or stool pigeons, whose effectiveness is lost once they appear in court. Judicial strictures against "entrapment" may make the evidence inadmissible. Community standards may not support prosecution efforts in all cases.

The prosecutor's position in the judicial process requires that the evidence be considered before a decision to file is made. At the initial stage, the amount and type of evidence reflected by the police report appears to be a dominant factor. As one deputy prosecutor told the author, "If you have the evidence, you file, then bring the other considerations in during the bargaining phase."

Humanitarian

The prosecutor can individualize justice in ways that will benefit the accused, the victim, and society. Especially when the offense involves conduct arising from mental illness, the prosecutor may believe that some form of psychiatric treatment is needed, rather than imprisonment. Protection of the victim can also be a reason for deciding against prosecution. In cases involving sexual molestation of a child, prosecution may not be sought if conviction hinges on the testimony of the victim and there is a possibility that the courtroom experience would hurt the child. The character of the accused, his or her status in the community, and the impact of prosecution on the family may be factors influencing the charge filed.

Prosecutors seem to believe that punishments stipulated in criminal laws affect the guilty in different ways, depending upon their socioeconomic background and status. Often one hears the remark that a year in jail will hurt an upper-status person much more than it will hurt someone from the ghetto. Charges are often filed with this in mind. Perhaps a felony charge will be changed to a misdemeanor if the defendant is a lawyer, because conviction on a felony would mean disbarment. Such actions are rationalized on humanitarian grounds—the desire to use the law to see justice accomplished.

Organizational

The exchange relationships among units of the judicial system, the political environment of the community, and the resource demands placed upon the system figure in the decision to prosecute. In this context, public reaction is often important. The nature of the crime, the pressure of publicity, and the influence of complaining victims circumscribe the prosecutor's discretion. Another consideration affecting the prosecutor's actions is the cost of expending organization resources when the matter is trivial, when extradition from another state is required, or when caseload pressures on the system are great. In these contexts, the attitudes and potential actions of the police, defense attorneys, and judges—actors whose cooperation makes the prosecutor's job easier—may influence the decision.

Plea Bargaining

As a case moves toward trial, it is often assumed that the court acquires the power to determine the fate of the defendant because the prosecutor takes on the role of advocate. However, the prosecuting attorney and defense counsel may negotiate a reduction of the charges in exchange for a guilty plea, thus limiting the sentencing decision of the judge. Plea bargaining has the obvious advantage of helping with processing a large number of cases, but it also assures conviction of the guilty, all for a minimal expenditure of resources. From the perspective of the organization, the guilty plea performs the latent function of helping to maintain the equilibrium and viability of the system. Not only does it help achieve the efficient use of the organization's resources, it also allows the system to operate in a more predictable environment. Because actors do not have to expose themselves to the unpredictable results of a jury trial, the cooperative (some might say "symbiotic") relationships necessary for operation of the system are maintained.

This emphasis on the role of negotiation within the criminal justice process seems to be at variance with our theory and customs, which have emphasized the adversary nature of the system. According to the traditional concept, criminal cases are not "settled" as in civil law; the outcome is determined through the symbolic combat of the state against the accused. Yet it has been estimated that up to 90 percent of all defendants charged with crimes before the state and federal courts plead guilty rather than exercise their right to trial. When a case does go to trial, it is usually won by the prosecutor. Prosecutors seek to avoid trials through compromise; there are incentives for them to take to court only those cases that seem winnable.

The prosecutor and defense attorney both bring certain objectives to a bargaining session. Each has attempted to structure the situation to personal advantage and comes armed with tactics designed to improve his or her position. It is common for prosecutors to draw up multiple-offense indictments; defense counsel may threaten to ask for a jury trial if concessions are not made. Another tactic is to seek pretrial continuances in hopes that witnesses will become unavailable, that public interest will die, and that memories of the incident will fade. Neither partner in the exchange is a free agent. Each depends on the cooperation of the defendant and the judge. In addition, the partners recognize that they will probably face their adversaries again in the future. Concessions extracted at a high cost may prove to be a disadvantage in the long run.

Plea bargaining is often criticized on the ground that it is hidden from judicial scrutiny. Because the bargain is generally made at an early stage of the proceedings, the judge has little information about the crime or the defendant and is not able to review prosecutorial judgment. As a result, there is no judicial review of the propriety of the bargain—no check on the amount of pressure applied to the defendant to plead guilty. Unconstitutional behavior may contribute to successful prosecution. The police may engage in illegal searches, neglect the procedural rights of the defendant, and carry out station house punishment because they know the case will never come to trial.

Until public attention became focused on crime and the administration of justice in the 1970s, plea bargaining was one of the secrets of the legal profession. It was rarely mentioned, and the scholarly literature took little note of it until the 1960s. Journalists' exposés of the extent of plea bargaining increased public awareness of the practice, and decisions by the U.S. Supreme Court granted it legitimacy. In the case *North Carolina* v. *Alford* (1970), the Court ruled that a trial court could accept a guilty plea even though the defendant maintained innocence, providing there was evidence of guilt and no indication of coercion in securing the plea. In *Santobello* v. *New York* (1971) the justices indirectly approved the practice by holding that the parties were required to keep the agreed-upon bargain. The Supreme Court in *Blackledge* v. *Allison* (1976) clearly acknowledged the legitimacy of plea bargaining, saying, "Whatever might be the situation in an ideal world, the fact is that the guilty plea and the often concomitant plea bargain are important components of this country's criminal justice system. Properly administered, they can benefit all concerned."

Intercity Variations

The criminal justice system clearly responds to the values of the local community. The prosecutor's office in a major metropolitan area such as Los Angeles, which has more than 400 deputies, operates quite differently from the one- or two-person offices found in most counties in the United States. One might also assume that cities where political parties are weak and the civil-service ethos is strong would have prosecution offices that function quite differently from those where traditional political considerations such as patronage hold sway. More important, the crucial functions of filtering, charging, and plea bargaining are made at different points in the real criminal justice continuum and by different actors.

Recent research has documented the many variations in the felony disposition process. Although the formal organization of decision making from arrest to conviction is similar throughout the United States, informal practices may shift the point of filtering from one part of the process to another. Therefore, to focus, for example, on the conviction rate of an individual prosecutor's office may obscure what is actually the situation: the police in that jurisdiction forward only the cases that they believe are "solid." In some cities, case screening is accomplished primarily by the police; in others, this is done by the prosecutor's office; in still others, by judges. Comparisons of felony dispositions in a number of cities show that great numbers of cases are dropped at some juncture but that local customs and policies have a lot to do with which agency is the major filter.

Feeney, Dill, and Weir describe the procedural and policy differences in the prosecutors' offices in two cities. Prosecutors in both offices eliminate weak cases through rigorous early screening, but in Jacksonville cases are organized vertically (the attorney who files a case is responsible for its disposition), while in San Diego they are organized horizontally (cases are assigned to specialists for charging and to a separate group of attorneys for trial). Even though there are many procedural differences between the systems, the outcomes for robbery, burglary, and felony assault cases appear to be about the same. The study found that arrest and prosecutorial screening policies determine the attrition rate. In both systems, many cases are weeded out (in San Diego the police do most of this, in Jacksonville the district attorney does it), plea bargaining is used extensively, and convictions at trial are proportionately the same.

Variations in the role of the prosecutor in the cities examined seem to reflect divergent responses by the various parts of the criminal justice system. These responses are shaped by the power of the exchange relations, the influence of particular actors, and the political environment of the community. More important, *somewhere* in the system cases are screened or removed, or the charges are altered. Under pressures caused by limited resources, political and social forces, and the desire to remove uncertainty, administrative decision making replaces adjudication of offenses through the adversarial process.

Suggestions for Further Reading

FEENEY, FLOYD, FORREST DILL, AND ADRIANNE WEIR. *Arrests without Convictions: How Often They Occur and Why.* Washington, D.C.: National Institute of Justice, 1983. A study of felony case processing in two cities, showing how arrest and prosecutorial screening policies determine the attrition rate.

HEILBRONER, DAVID. *Rough Justice: Days and Nights of a Young D.A.* New York: Pantheon, 1990. The experience of an assistant district attorney learning the ropes in New York's criminal courts.

HEUMANN, MILTON. *Plea Bargaining: The Experiences of Prosecutors, Judges, and Defense Attorneys.* Chicago: University of Chicago Press, 1978. A study of the adaptation of prosecutors, judges, and defense attorneys to plea bargaining. Heumann presents a challenge to the belief that the criminal court bureaucracy forces plea bargaining on its participants.

JACOBY, JOAN. *The American Prosecutor: Search for Identity.* Lexington, Mass.: Lexington Books, 1980. An overview of the development and role of the prosecutor in the U.S. criminal justice system.

McDONALD, WILLIAM F., ed. *The Prosecutor.* Newbury Park, Calif.: Sage Publications, 1979. Ten essays discussing various aspects of the prosecutor's role.

MOLEY, RAYMOND. *Politics and Criminal Prosecution.* New York: Minton, Balch & Company, 1929. Written by one of the major participants in the crime commission studies of the 1920s, this book shows the direct relationship of politics to the prosecutor's office in urban areas in the United States.

NAIFEH, STEVEN, AND GREGORY SMITH. *The Mormon Murders.* New York: New American Library, 1989. Prosecution for murder in the context of a scandal within the Morman Church and its political ramifications.

NEUBAUER, DAVID W. *Criminal Justice in Middle America.* Morristown, N.J.: General Learning Press, 1974. Much of the criminal justice literature focuses on big-city crime, but Neubauer examines the criminal justice system of Prairie City, a medium sized industrial city in Illinois.

ROWLAND, JUDITH. *The Ultimate Violation.* New York: Doubleday, 1985. A former San Diego district attorney describes her pioneering legal strategy to prosecute rapists.

8

The Decision to Prosecute

George F. Cole

The prosecuting attorney works within the context of an exchange system of clientele relationships that influence decision making. In this case study I explore the nature of these relationships and link politics to the allocation of justice.

This paper is based on an exploratory study of the Office of Prosecuting Attorney, King County (Seattle), Washington. The lack of social-scientific knowledge about the prosecutor dictated the choice of this approach. An open-ended interview was administered to one-third of the former deputy prosecutors who had worked in the office during the ten-year period 1955–1965. In addition, interviews were conducted with court employees, members of the bench, law-enforcement officials, and others having reputations for participation in legal decision making. Over fifty respondents were contacted during this phase. A final portion of the research placed the author in the role of observer in the prosecutor's office. This experience allowed for direct observation of all phases of the decision to prosecute so that the informal processes of the office could be noted. Discussions with the prosecutor's staff, judges, defendants' attorneys, and the police were held so that the interview data could be placed within an organizational context.

The primary goal of this investigation was to examine the role of the prosecuting attorney as an officer of the legal process within the context of the local political system. The analysis is therefore based on two assumptions. First, that the legal process is best understood as a subsystem of the larger political system. Because of this choice, emphasis is placed upon the interaction and goals of the individuals involved in decision making. Second, and closely related to the first point, it is assumed that broadly conceived political considerations explained to a large extent "who gets or does not get—in what amount—and how, the good (justice) that is hopefully produced by the legal system."[1] By focusing upon the political and social linkages

Source: From *Law and Society Review* 4 (February 1970): 313–343. Reprinted by permission of the Law and Society Association.

between these systems, it is expected that decision making in the prosecutor's office will be viewed as a principal ingredient in the authoritative allocation of values.

The Prosecutor's Office in an Exchange System

While observing the interrelated activities of the organizations in the legal process, one might ask, "Why do these agencies cooperate?" If the police refuse to transfer information to the prosecutor concerning the commission of a crime, what are the rewards or sanctions that might be brought against them? Is it possible that organizations maintain a form of "bureaucratic accounting" that, in a sense, keeps track of the resources allocated to an agency and the support returned? How are cues transmitted from one agency to another to influence decision making? These are some of the questions that must be asked when decisions are viewed as an output of an exchange system.

The major findings of this study are placed within the context of an exchange system.[2] This serves the heuristic purpose of focusing attention upon the linkages found between actors in the decision-making process. In place of the traditional assumptions that the agency is supported solely by statutory authority, this view recognizes that an organization has many clients with which it interacts and upon whom it is dependent for certain resources. As interdependent subunits of a system, then, the organization and its clients are engaged in a set of exchanges across their boundaries. These will involve a transfer of resources between the organizations that will affect the mutual achievement of goals.

The legal system may be viewed as a set of interorganizational exchange relationships analogous to what Long has called a community game.[3] The participants in the legal system (game) share a common territorial field and collaborate for different and particular ends. They interact on a continuing basis as their responsibilities demand contact with other participants in the process. Thus, the need for cooperation of other participants can have a bearing on the decision to prosecute. A decision not to prosecute a narcotics offender may be a move to pressure the U.S. Attorney's Office to cooperate on another case. It is obvious that bargaining occurs not only between the major actors in a case—the prosecutor and the defense attorney—but also between the clientele groups that are influential in structuring the actions of the prosecuting attorney.

Exchanges do not simply "sail" from one system to another but take place in an institutionalized setting that may be compared to a market. In the market, decisions are made between individuals who occupy boundary-spanning roles and who set the conditions under which the exchange will occur. In the legal system, this may merely mean that a representative of the parole board agrees to forward a recommendation to the prosecutor, or it could mean that there is extended bargaining between a deputy prosecutor and a defense attorney. In the study of the King County prosecutor's office, it was found that most decisions resulted from some type of exchange relationship. The deputies interacted almost constantly with the police and criminal lawyers; the prosecutor was more closely linked to exchange relations with the courts, community leaders, and the county commissioners.

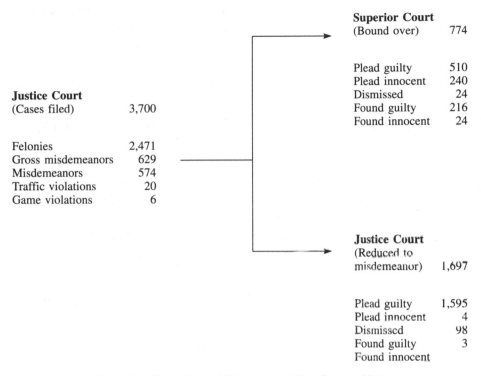

Justice Court
(Cases filed)   3,700

Felonies   2,471
Gross misdemeanors   629
Misdemeanors   574
Traffic violations   20
Game violations   6

Superior Court
(Bound over)   774

Plead guilty   510
Plead innocent   240
Dismissed   24
Found guilty   216
Found innocent   24

Justice Court
(Reduced to
misdemeanor)   1,697

Plead guilty   1,595
Plead innocent   4
Dismissed   98
Found guilty   3
Found innocent

Figure 1   Disposition of felony cases, King County, 1964

The Prosecutor's Clientele

In an exchange system, power is largely dependent upon the ability of an organization to create clientele relationships that will support and enhance the needs of the agency. For, although interdependence is characteristic of the legal system, competition with other public agencies for support also exists. Because organizations operate in an economy of scarcity, the organization must exist in a favorable power position in relation to its clientele. Reciprocal and unique claims are made by the organization and its clients. Thus, rather than being oriented toward only one public, an organization is beholden to several publics, some visible and others seen clearly only from the pinnacle of leadership. As Gore notes when these claims are "firmly anchored inside the organization and the lines drawn taut, the tensions between conflicting claims form a net serving as the institutional base for the organization."[4]

An indication of the stresses within the judicial system may be obtained by analyzing its outputs. It has been suggested that the administration of justice is a selective process in which only those cases that do not create strains in the organization will ultimately reach the courtroom.[5] As noted in Figure 1, the system operates so that only a small number of cases arrive for trial, the rest being disposed of through reduced charges, *nolle prosequi,* and guilty pleas.[6] Not indicated are those cases removed by the police and prosecutor prior to the filing of charges. As the focal organization in an exchange system, the office of the prosecuting attorney makes

decisions that reflect the influence of its clientele. Because of the scarcity of resources, marketlike relationships, and the organizational needs of the system, prosecutorial decision making emphasizes the accommodations made to the needs of participants in the process.

Police

Although the prosecuting attorney has discretionary power to determine the disposition of cases, this power is limited by the fact that usually he is dependent upon the police for inputs to the system of cases and evidence. The prosecutor does not have the investigative resources necessary to exercise the kind of affirmative control over the types of cases that are brought to him. In this relationship, the prosecutor is not without countervailing power. His main check on the police is his ability to return cases to them for further investigation and to refuse to approve arrest warrants. By maintaining cordial relations with the press, a prosecutor is often able to focus attention on the police when the public becomes aroused by incidents of crime. As the King County prosecutor emphasized, "That [investigation] is the job for the sheriff and police. It's their job to bring me the charges." As noted by many respondents, the police, in turn, are dependent upon the prosecutor to accept the output of their system; rejection of too many cases can have serious repercussions affecting the morale, discipline, and work load of the force.

A request for prosecution may be rejected for a number of reasons relating to questions of evidence. Not only must the prosecutor believe that the evidence will secure a conviction, but he must also be aware of community norms relating to the type of acts that should be prosecuted. King County deputy prosecutors noted that charges were never filed when a case involved attempted suicide or fornication. In other actions, the heinous nature of the crime, together with the expected public reaction, may force both the police and prosecutor to press for conviction when evidence is less than satisfactory. As one deputy noted, "In that case [murder and molestation of a six-year-old girl] there was nothing that we could do. As you know the press was on our back and every parent was concerned. Politically, the prosecutor had to seek information."

Factors other than those relating to evidence may require that the prosecutor refuse to accept a case from the police. First, the prosecuting attorney serves as a regulator of caseloads not only for his own office, but for the rest of the legal system. Constitutional and statutory time limits prevent him and the courts from building a backlog of untried cases. In King County, when the system reached the "overload point," there was a tendency to be more selective in choosing the cases to be accepted. A second reason for rejecting prosecution requests may stem from the fact that the prosecutor is thinking of his public exposure in the courtroom. He does not want to take forward cases that will place him in an embarrassing position. Finally, the prosecutor may return cases to check the quality of police work. As a former chief criminal deputy said, "You have to keep them on their toes, otherwise they get lazy. If they aren't doing their job, send the case back and then leak the situation to the newspapers." Rather than spend the resources necessary to find additional evidence, the police may dispose of a case by sending it back to the prosecutor on a lesser charge, implement the "copping out" machinery leading to a guilty plea, drop the case, or in some instances send it to the city prosecutor for action in municipal court.

In most instances, a deputy prosecutor and the police officer assigned to the case occupy the boundary-spanning roles in this exchange relationship. Prosecutors reported that after repeated contacts they got to know the policemen whom they could trust. As one female deputy commented, "There are some you can trust, others you have to watch because they are trying to get rid of cases on you." Deputies may be influenced by the police officer's attitude on a case. One officer noted to a prosecutor that he knew he had a weak case, but mumbled, "I didn't want to bring it up here, but that's what they [his superiors] wanted." As might be expected, the deputy turned down prosecution.

Sometimes the police perform the ritual of "shopping around," seeking to find a deputy prosecutor who, on the basis of past experience, is liable to be sympathetic to their view on a case. At one time, deputies were given complete authority to make the crucial decisions without coordinating their activities with other staff members. In this way the arresting officer would search the prosecutor's office to find a deputy he thought would be sympathetic to the police attitude. As a former deputy noted, "This meant that there were no departmental policies concerning the treatment to be accorded various types of cases. It pretty much depended upon the police and their luck in finding the deputy they wanted." Prosecutors are now instructed to ascertain from the police officer if he has seen another deputy on the case. Even under this more centralized system, it is still possible for the police to request a specific deputy or delay presentation of the case until the "correct" prosecutor is available. Often a prosecutor will gain a reputation for specializing in one type of case. This may mean that the police will assume he will get the case anyway, so they skirt the formal procedure and bring it to him directly.

An exchange relationship between a deputy prosecutor and a police officer may be influenced by the type of crime committed by the defendant. The prototype of a criminal is one who violates person and property. However, a large number of cases involve "crimes without victims." This term refers to those crimes generally involving violations of moral codes, where the general public is theoretically the complainant. In violations of laws against bookmaking, prostitution, and narcotics, neither actor in the transaction is interested in having an arrest made. Hence, vice control men must drum up their own business. Without a civilian complainant, victimless crimes give the police and prosecutor greater leeway in determining the charges to be filed.

One area of exchange involving a victimless crime is that of narcotics control. As Skolnick notes, "The major organizational requirement of narcotics policing is the presence of an informational system."[7] Without a network of informers, it is impossible to capture addicts and peddlers with evidence that can bring about convictions. One source of informers is among those arrested for narcotics violations. Through promises to reduce charges or even to *nolle pros.,* arrangements can be made so that the accused will return to the narcotics community and gather information for the police. Bargaining observed between the head of the narcotics squad of the Seattle police and the deputy prosecutor who specialized in drug cases involved the question of charges, promises, and the release of an arrested narcotics pusher.

In the course of postarrest questioning by the police, a well-known drug peddler intimated that he could provide evidence against a pharmacist suspected by the police of illegally selling narcotics. Not only did the police representative want to transfer the case to the friendlier hands of this deputy, but he also wanted to arrange for a reduction of charges and bail. The police officer believed that it was important that the accused be let out in such a way that the narcotics community would not realize that he had become an informer. He also wanted to be sure that the reduced charges would be processed so that the informer could be kept on the string, thus allowing the narcotics squad to maintain control over him. The deputy prosecutor, on the other hand, said that he wanted to make sure that procedures were followed so that the action would not bring discredit on his office. He also suggested that the narcotics squad "work a little harder" on a pending case as a means of returning the favor.

Courts

The ways used by the court to dispose of cases is a vital influence in the system. The court's actions affect pressures upon the prison, the conviction rate of the prosecutor, and the work of probation agencies. The judge's decisions act as clues to other parts of the system, indicating the type of action likely to be taken in future cases. As noted by a King County judge, "When the number of prisoners gets to the 'riot point,' the warden puts pressure on us to slow down the flow. This often means that men are let out on parole and the number of people given probation and suspended sentences increases." Under such conditions, it would be expected that the prosecutor would respond to the judge's actions by reducing the inputs to the court either by not preferring charges or by increasing the pressure for guilty pleas through bargaining. The adjustments of other parts of the system could be expected to follow. For instance, the police might sense the lack of interest of the prosecutor in accepting charges; hence they will send only airtight cases to him for indictment.

The influence of the court on the decision to prosecute is very real. The sentencing history of each judge gives the prosecutor, as well as other law-enforcement officials, an indication of the treatment a case may receive in a courtroom. The prosecutor's expectation as to whether the court will convict may limit his discretion over the decisions on whether to prosecute. "There is great concern as to whose court a case will be assigned. After Judge ———— threw out three cases in a row in which entrapment was involved, the police did not want us to take any cases to him." Since the prosecutor depends upon the plea-bargaining machinery to maintain the flow of cases from his office, the sentencing actions of judges must be predictable. If the defendant and his lawyer are to be influenced to accept a lesser charge or the promise of a lighter sentence in exchange for a plea of guilty, there must be some basis for belief that the judge will fulfill his part of the arrangement. Because judges are unable formally to announce their agreement with the details of the bargain, their past performance acts as a guide.

Within the limits imposed by law and the demands of the system, the prosecutor is able to regulate the flow of cases to the court. He may control the length of time between accusation and trial; hence he may hold cases until he has the evidence that will convict. Alternatively, he may seek repeated adjournment and continuances until the public's interest dies; problems such as witnesses becoming unavailable and similar difficulties make his request for dismissal of prosecution more justifiable. Further, he may determine the type of court to receive the case and the judge who will hear it. Many misdemeanors covered by state law are also violations of a city ordinance. It is a common practice for the prosecutor to send a misdemeanor case to the city prosecutor for processing in the municipal court when it is believed that a conviction may not be secured in justice court. As a deputy said, "If there is no case—send it over to the city court. Things are speedier, less formal, over there."

In the state of Washington, a person arrested on a felony charge must be given a preliminary hearing in a justice court within ten days. For the prosecutor, the preliminary hearing is an opportunity to evaluate the testimony of witnesses, assess the strength of the evidence, and try to predict the outcome of the case if it is sent to trial. On the basis of this evaluation, the prosecutor has several options: he may bind over the case for trial in superior court; he may reduce the charges to those of a misdemeanor for trial in justice court; or he may conclude that he has no case and drop the charges. The presiding judge of the Justice Courts of King County estimated that about 70 percent of the felonies are reduced to misdemeanors after the preliminary hearing.

Besides having some leeway in determining the type of court in which to file a case, the prosecutor also has some flexibility in selecting the judge to receive the case. Until recently the prosecutor could file a case with a specific judge. "The trouble was that Judge ———— was erratic and independent, [so] no one would file with him. The other judges objected that they were handling the entire work load, so a central filing system was devised." Under this procedure cases are assigned to the judges in rotation. However, as the chief criminal deputy noted, "The prosecutor can hold a case until the 'correct' judge comes up."

Defense Attorneys

With the increased specialization and institutionalization of the bar, it would seem that those individuals engaged in the practice of criminal law have been relegated, both by their profession and by the community, to a low status. The urban bar appears to be divided into three parts. First there is an inner circle, which handles the work of banks, utilities, and commercial concerns; second, another circle includes plaintiffs' lawyers representing interests opposed to those of the inner circle; and finally, an outer group scrapes out an existence by "haunting the courts in hope of picking up crumbs from the judicial table."[8] With the exception of a few highly proficient lawyers who have made a reputation by winning acquittal for their clients in difficult, highly publicized cases, most of the lawyers dealing with the King County prosecutor's office belong to this outer ring.

In this study, respondents were asked to identify those attorneys considered to be specialists in criminal law. Of the nearly 1,600 lawyers practicing in King County, only 8 can be placed in this category. Of this group, 6 were reported to enjoy the respect of the legal community, while the others were accused by many respondents of being involved in shady deals. A larger group of King County attorneys will accept criminal cases, but these lawyers do not consider themselves specialists. Several respondents noted that many lawyers, because of inexperience or age, were required to hang around the courthouse searching for clients. One Seattle attorney described the quality of legal talent available for criminal cases as "a few good criminal lawyers and a lot of young kids and old men. The good lawyers I can count on my fingers."

In a legal system where bargaining is a primary method of decision making, it is not surprising that criminal lawyers find it essential to maintain close personal ties with the prosecutor and his staff. Respondents were quite open in revealing their dependence upon this close relationship to pursue their careers successfully. The nature of the criminal lawyer's work is such that his saleable product or service appears to be influence rather than technical proficiency in the law. Respondents hold the belief that clients are attracted partially on the basis of the attorney's reputation as a fixer, or as a shrewd bargainer.

There is a tendency for ex-deputy prosecutors in King County to enter the practice of criminal law. Because of his inside knowledge of the prosecutor's office and friendships made with court officials, the former deputy feels that he has an advantage over other criminal law practitioners. All of the former deputies interviewed said that they took criminal cases. Of the eight criminal law specialists, seven previously served as deputy prosecutors in King County and the other was once prosecuting attorney in a rural county.

Because of the financial problems of the criminal lawyer's practice, it is necessary that he handle cases on an assembly-line basis, hoping to make a living from a large number of small fees. Referring to a fellow lawyer, one attorney said, "You should see ————. He goes up there to Carroll's office with a whole fistful of cases. He trades on some, bargains on others, and never goes to court. It's amazing but it's the way he makes his living." There are incentives, therefore, to bargaining with the prosecutor and other decision makers. The primary aim of the attorney in such circumstances is to reach an accommodation so that the time-consuming formal proceedings need not be implemented. As a Seattle attorney noted, "I can't make money if I spend my time in a courtroom. I make mine on the telephone or in the prosecutor's office." One of the disturbing results of this arrangement is that instances were reported in which a bargain was reached between the attorney and deputy prosecutor on a "package deal." In this situation, an attorney's clients are treated as a group; the outcome of the bargaining is often an agreement whereby reduced charges will be achieved for some, in exchange for the unspoken assent by the lawyer that the prosecutor may proceed as he desires with the other cases. One member of the King County bar had developed this practice to such a fine art that a deputy prosecutor said, "When you saw him coming into the office, you knew that he would be pleading guilty." At one time this situation was so widespread that the "prisoners up in the jail had a rating list which graded the attorneys as either 'good guys' or 'sellouts.' "

The exchange relationship between the defense attorney and the prosecutor is based on their need for cooperation in the discharge of their responsibilities. Most criminal lawyers are interested primarily in the speedy solution of cases because of their precarious financial situation. Because they must protect their professional reputations with their colleagues, judicial personnel, and potential clientele, however, they are not completely free to bargain solely with this objective. As one attorney noted, "You can't afford to let it get out that you are selling out your cases."

The prosecutor is also interested in the speedy processing of cases. This can only be achieved if the formal processes are not implemented. Not only does the pressure of his caseload influence bargaining, but also the legal process, with its potential for delay and appeal, creates a degree of uncertainty that is not present in an exchange relationship with an attorney with whom you have dealt for a number of years. As the presiding judge of the Seattle District Court said, "Lawyers are helpful to the system. They are able to pull things together, work out a deal, keep the system moving."

Community Influentials

As part of the political system, the judicial process responds to the community environment. The King County study indicated that there are different levels of influence within the community and that some people had a greater interest in the politics of prosecution than others. First, the general public is able to have its values translated into policies followed by law-enforcement officers. The public's influence is particularly acute in those gray areas of the law where full enforcement is not expected. Statutes may be enacted by legislatures defining the outer limits of criminal conduct, but they do not necessarily mean that laws are to be fully enforced to these limits. There are some laws defining behavior that the community no longer considers criminal. It can be expected that a prosecutor's charging policies will reflect this attitude. He may not prosecute violations of laws regulating some forms of gambling, certain sexual practices, or violations of Sunday Blue Laws.

Because the general public is a potential threat to the prosecutor, staff members take measures to protect him from criticism. Respondents agreed that decision making occurs with the public in mind—"Will a course of action arouse antipathy toward the prosecutor rather than the accused?" Several deputies mentioned what they called the "aggravation level" of a crime. This is a recognition that the commission of certain crimes, within a specific context, will bring about a vocal public reaction. "If a little girl, walking home from the grocery store, is pulled into the bushes and indecent liberties taken, this is more disturbing to the public's conscience than a case where the father of the girl takes indecent liberties with her at home." The office of the King County prosecuting attorney has a policy requiring that deputies file all cases involving sexual molestation in which the police believe the girl's story is credible. The office also prefers charges in all negligent homicide cases where there is the least possibility of guilt. In such types of cases the public may respond to the emotional context of the case and demand prosecution. To cover the prosecutor from criticism, it is believed that the safest measure is to prosecute.

The bail system is also used to protect the prosecutor from criticism. Thus it is the policy to set bail at a high level with the expectation that the court will reduce the amount. "This looks good for Prosecutor Carroll. Takes the heat off of him, especially in morals cases. If the accused doesn't appear in court the prosecutor can't be blamed. The public gets upset when they know these types are out free." This is an example of exchange where one actor is shifting the responsibility and potential onus onto another. In turn, the court is under pressure from county jail officials to keep the prison population down.

A second community group having contact with the prosecutor is composed of those leaders who have a continuing or potential interest in the politics of prosecution. This group, analogous to the players in one of Long's community games, is linked to the prosecutor because his actions affect their success in playing another game. Hence community boosters want either a crackdown or a hands-off policy toward gambling, political leaders want the prosecutor to remember the interests of the party, and business leaders want policies that will not interfere with their own game.

Community leaders may receive special treatment by the prosecutor if they run afoul of the law. A policy of the King County office requires that cases involving prominent members of the community be referred immediately to the chief criminal deputy and the prosecutor for their disposition. As one deputy noted, "These cases can be pretty touchy. It's important that the boss knows immediately about this type of case so that he is not caught 'flat-footed' when asked about it by the press."

Pressure by an interest group was evidenced during a strike by drugstore employees in 1964. The striking unions urged Prosecutor Carroll to invoke a state law that requires the presence of a licensed pharmacist if the drugstore is open. Not only did union representatives meet with Carroll, but picket lines were set up outside the courthouse protesting his refusal to act. The prosecutor resisted the union's pressure tactics.

In recent years, the prosecutor's tolerance policy toward minor forms of gambling led to a number of conflicts with Seattle's mayor, the sheriff, and church organizations. After a decision was made to prohibit all forms of public gaming, the prosecutor was criticized by groups representing the tourist industry and such affected groups as the bartenders' union, which thought the decision would have an adverse economic effect. As Prosecutor Carroll said, "I am always getting pressures from different interests — business, the Chamber of Commerce, and labor. I have to try and maintain a balance between them." In exchange for these considerations, the prosecutor may gain prestige, political support, and admission into the leadership groups of the community.

Summary

By viewing the King County Office of Prosecuting Attorney as the focal organization in an exchange system, data from this exploratory study suggests the marketlike relationships that exist between actors in the system. Because prosecution operates in an environment of scarce resources and because the decisions have potential political ramifications, a variety of officials influence the allocation of justice. The decision to prosecute is not made at one point, but rather the prosecuting attorney has a number of options he may employ during various stages of the proceedings. But the prosecutor is able to exercise his discretionary powers only within the network of exchange relationships. The police, court congestion, organizational strains, and community pressures are among the factors that influence prosecutorial behavior.

Notes

1. James R. Klonoski and Robert I. Medelsohn, "The Allocation of Justice: A Political Analysis," *Journal of Public Law* 14 (May 1965): 323–342.
2. William M. Evan, "Towards a Theory of Inter-Organizational Relations," *Management Science* 11 (August 1965): 218–230.

3. Norton Long, *The Polity* (Chicago: Rand McNally, 1962), p. 142.
4. William J. Gore, *Administrative Decision-Making* (New York: John Wiley, 1964), p. 23.
5. William J. Chambliss, *Crime and the Legal Process* (New York: McGraw-Hill, 1969), p. 84.
6. The lack of reliable criminal statistics is well known. These data were gathered from a number of sources, including King County, "Annual Report of the Prosecuting Attorney," State of Washington, 1964.
7. Jerome L. Skolnick, *Justice Without Trial* (New York: John Wiley, 1966), p. 120.
8. Jack Ladinsky, "The Impact of Social Backgrounds of Lawyers on Law Practice and the Law," *Journal of Legal Education* 16 (1963): 128.

9

Prosecutorial Discretion in Filing Charges in Domestic Violence Cases

Janell Schmidt
Ellen Hochstedler Steury

What factors influence a prosecutor's decisions? This study of the prosecution of domestic violence cases provides us with an opportunity to better understand the role of discretion in determining which cases will lead to an indictment, which will be dropped, and which will be diverted. What are some of the troubling factors associated with the domestic violence offense?

Considerable scholarly attention has been directed to the exercise of police discretion in response to incidents of domestic violence, but little empirical research has analyzed the exercise of legal and extralegal considerations prosecutors take into account then screening domestic violence cases for prosecution. Data on case, victim, and defendant characteristics were gathered in order to examine variables associated with a decision to charge.

The discretion of the prosecutor to issue charges or decline to issue charges may be exercised in either a positive or negative manner. Such discretion has a "reversible nature" and may be used to "prosecute someone based on little, if any, evidence [or] not prosecute someone, despite the fact that he [or she] is clearly guilty of a crime" (Friedman, 1982:70). Selective prosecution of the latter type, quite often fully justified by legal and organizational considerations, has inflamed critics and nurtured accusations that the criminal justice system fails female victims of abuse. In light of such accusations, prosecutorial decision making in domestic violence cases bears further scrutiny. The few empirical studies of prosecutorial dispositions of domestic violence cases, supplemented by studies of prosecutorial decision making in general, provide a context for the research reported here.

Source: From Janell Schmidt and Ellen Hochstedler Steury, "Prosecutorial Discretion in Filing Charges in Domestic Violence Cases," *Criminology* 27 (1989):487–510. Some footnotes and references deleted. Reprinted by permission of The American Society of Criminology.

Literature Review

In a study of domestic violence cases, Ellis (1984) exposed a legal tradition that encourages the use of prosecutorial discretion to keep such cases out of the formal legal system. Limited resources, the questionable wisdom of state intervention in family, affairs, the motivation and potential culpability of the victim, and the perceived reluctance of the victim to complete the court process are four extralegal variables routinely considered by prosecutors when screening domestic violence cases for prosecution. Stanko (1982) provided a further description of how prosecutors rely on gender stereotypes to determine victim credibility and of how the goal of successful prosecution takes precedence over the needs of an aggrieved victim. Although this literature, along with the negative appraisal of prosecutorial policies by the U.S. Commission of Civil Rights (1982), paints a bleak picture for victims, analysis of the actual application of prosecutorial discretion in domestic violence cases is scarce.

Some empirical studies of prosecutorial screening, not limited to domestic violence cases, have identified factors that affect felony case processing. Spohn and associates (1987) found gender and ethnic differences in felony case processing. Particularly with respect to weak cases, these researchers found that prosecutors were more lenient with female offenders and more severe with Hispanic males. Brosi (1979) and Boland and associates (1983) cite problems of evidence and witnesses as the primary reasons for decisions to decline prosecution or to dismiss a case later. Brosi (1979) notes that a higher proportion of felony assault cases are rejected at screening. While evidence and witness problems at first appear to be legally relevant, these factors may well be confounded by extralegal factors, such as gender, race, and relationship between victim and defendant. A victim with a history of sexual intimacy with the offender, for example, may be viewed as a less credible or less reliable witness.

Cole's (1970) examination of prosecutorial decision making on an organizational level revealed the difficulty in determining what motivates prosecutors to select one prosecutorial alternative over another. Aside from the prosecutor's personal perception of the evidence and his or her humanitarian role, Cole (1970) found the needs of the organization to be a salient factor in decision making. The necessity for cooperation between police and prosecutors, for example, results in an exchange of information and effort. Prosecutors need viable cases to pursue; officers need arrest practices legitimized through the issuance of charges. Should prosecutors fail to respond to police-supported cases, the number and quality of complaints will decline. This finding has important implications for the processing of domestic violence cases because in some jurisdictions many such complaints are initiated by citizens rather than police. Cole's findings suggest that domestic violence cases brought to the prosecutor's attention by the police would be screened with an a priori standard of legitimacy because of the shared language and territorial field of police and prosecutors. Citizen-initiated complaints, on the other hand, would be scrutinized more critically because citizens/victims do not know the language, expectations, or shortcomings of the system, and more important, they have little to offer in exchange for prosecution.

Jacoby's (1980) study of citizen complaint procedures in prosecutors' offices depicted their operation as revolving doors, shunting victims from one social service agency to another, reinforcing Cole's (1970) implied prediction. Although initially designed to provide citizens access to the criminal justice system in situations given short shrift by the police, the citizen complaint process is not necessarily geared to bringing such complaints into the system. Jacoby (1980:131) alleges that the process is particularly fraught with abuse because there is little opportunity to fix responsibility for decision making or to establish accountability for decisions or actions. This conclusion suggests that citizen-invoked complaints of domestic violence stand a slim chance of producing criminal charges because of their lower legal visibility and because, as critics claim, prosecutors view such cases as more appropriate for social service agencies. More lenient responses, such as diversion, hold-open, and *nolle prosequi* dispositions, are less energetic but traditional responses to domestic abuse. Indeed, even victims who initiate complaints often appear to prefer more lenient dispositions to full prosecution. In a recent study of citizen-initiated complaints of domestic violence, Ford and Burke (1987) found little concordance between a request for prosecution and the result the victim really wanted.

In an effort to provide some preliminary answers to questions left unanswered by other research, this article presents findings from a study of the exercise of prosecutorial discretion in domestic violence cases. The following issues are addressed:

1. How do legal variables (for example, seriousness of injury, defendant's record, legal sufficiency of the evidence) influence the prosecutor's decision to charge as opposed to pursuing more lenient dispositions (diversion, hold-open, *nolle prosequi*)? Do the findings suggest that reverse discretion, as described by Friedman (1982:70) is practiced in these cases? Do the findings support those who claim that certain combination of variables must exist before prosecutors issue charges?

2. What is the influence of extralegal variables on prosecutorial decision making with respect to choosing punitive/lenient dispositions? To what extent does the relationship of the parties influence the prosecutor's response and what is the nature of that response?

3. To what extent does the initiator of the complaint, police or citizen, account for the variability of decision making in domestic abuse cases, as suggested by Cole's (1970) exchange paradigm and Jacoby's (1980) critique of citizen complaint procedures?

In short, the study seeks to distinguish whether any variable or group of variables is associated with the normal exercise of discretion by prosecutors in misdemeanor domestic abuse cases.

The Sample

The data for the study were gathered from the official files, records, and police reports of misdemeanor cases reviewed by staff attorneys of the Milwaukee County district attorney's office between January 1, 1983 and June 30, 1984. Operationally, a domestic abuse victim was defined as a female, over age sixteen, who was harmed by a male with whom she was or had been sexually intimate. Harm was defined as an intentionally inflicted physical injury of a misdemeanor level or the threat of such injury. This definition included cases involving the reckless use of a weapon, infraction of domestic violence restraining orders, violation of bail conditions on pending battery cases, disorderly conduct, threat, and property damage.

The sample was selected by using two distinct sampling frames: the total population of charged domestic violence cases during the period under study and a random sample of noncharged cases. Charged cases were drawn from two sources: (1) police-supported cases falling within the operational definition that were charged during the study period and closed by May 1, 1985 ($n = 106$), and (2) all cases originating from a complaint filed in the Citizen Complaint Unit (CCU) that fell within the operational definition and were charged during the period under study ($n = 103$).[1] To provide a point of comparison, two random samples of 100 cases each were gathered from the official files of noncharged police complaints and noncharged CCU complaints screened during the period under study.

Case files and police reports contain demographic information as well as legal data. Admittedly, written reports and notations present the researcher with a less complete picture of the case than was available to the prosecutor at the time of review. Nonetheless, the primary legal criteria supporting a charging decision—extent of injury, defendant's record, and evidentiary strength of the case—are factors that were recorded and were available for this analysis.

In noncharged cases, notations in the records reflect whether the decision was based primarily on the victim's wishes or the prosecutor's assessment of the evidence, regardless of the victim's wishes. Variation existed in the extent of documentation prosecutors provided in noting their decision not to charge. Some simply used official codes to explain the decision not to charge; others went to greater lengths to provide written summaries of why or how they reached a particular decision. Such notations reflect what a prosecutor thinks is important to justify the action taken as well as a familiarity with the difficulties of domestic violence cases can present. Beyond that, the motivation of a victim, any pressures placed on her by either the abuser of the prosecutor, and the reasoning of a prosecutor are unknown to the researcher collecting recorded data.

Research Setting

This study focuses on the screening decisions of thirty-eight prosecutors employed in the office of the Milwaukee County district attorney. The screening decisions were made by both newly hired attorneys with little or no prosecutorial experience and veteran assistant district attorneys (ADAs).

Milwaukee prosecutors are not obligated to commence prosecution in every case involving allegations of domestic abuse, nor are they required to issue assault charges in the cases selected for prosecution. The charge might be disorderly conduct or some other charge supported by the evidence available. For every complaint a charging conference is conducted to evaluate and select cases that may lead to successful criminal prosecution and cases that best serve the interest of the state through noncriminal resolution. Prosecutors exercise relatively unchecked discretion in choosing one of three dispositions short of formal issuance of charges. Cases simply may be not processed and the defendant sent away with a verbal admonishment, warned of the consequences of repetitive behavior, or advised to seek counseling. Prosecutors may decline to process the complaint if the guilt of the defendant is doubtful or the evidence insufficient, if the fact situation does not meet the level required for criminal prosecution, or if the victim declines to cooperate with the charging process.

A second disposition, informal hold open, occurs when the prosecutor agrees not to issue charge if the defendant agrees to meet certain conditions, such as counseling, restitution, or no further contact with the victim. This option may be employed if the victim declines charges or the ADA believes the merits of the case dictate leniency.

Another choice involves diversion of the defendant from the legal system. Eligibility for diversion is primarily reserved for first-time perpetrators of nonviolent crimes. Formal charges and a diversion agreement are initiated, with the victim's approval, but the charges are held in abeyance so long as the defendant meets the conditions of the agreement.

Because all victims in the study voluntarily appeared in the district attorney's office, their willingness to proceed with some type of official legal action was presumed. No cases were found in which prosecution was commenced without the victim's concurrence. Victims may not have considered the ramifications of a formal charge or distinguished the differences between hold-open and diversion options, but the fact that they followed procedures implies their desire to obtain some sort of official legal response.

Research Findings
Victim Characteristics

As expected, the demographic data on victims in this study comform to the now familiar profile researchers have etched of the quintessential battered woman. Women filing domestic abuse complaints were young; 62 percent ($n = 247$) were under twenty-nine years and the range was between sixteen and seventy-one years. They were disproportionately minority (66 percent were nonwhite; $n = 259$), victims of prior abuse (88 percent; $n = 260$), and unmarried (59 percent [$n = 243$] were never married and 4 percent [$n = 16$] were divorced from the abuser). Although 100 cases were missing data on this variable, it appears that most of the victims were mothers of children; only 10 percent reported having no dependents under eighteen years of age ($n = 31$).

Perhaps because the study was composed of victims who voluntarily sought assistance from the criminal justice system to remedy or alleviate the abuse, the sample differed in an important respect from characteristics often associated with abused women: situational and financial dependence. While 64 percent ($n = 251$) reported current sexual intimacy with the abuser, over half (54 percent; $n = 219$) the victims lived apart from him. Only 18 percent ($n = 55$) of all victims were considered financially dependent on the abuser for support; nearly one-third ($n = 97$) were primarily self-supporting, and 52 percent ($n = 163$) were unemployed or dependent on government support.

Defendant Characteristics

Defendants in the study also presented characteristics familiar to researchers. Not unlike abusers in the Sherman and Berk (1984) study of police response to domestic incidents in Minneapolis, the defendants were disproportionately minority (75 percent; $n = 295$), primarily unemployed (61 percent; $n = 168$), and had been previously involved with the criminal justice system (52 percent had prior convictions; $n = 173$); a substantial minority had been previously convicted of assaultive behavior (30 percent $n = 100$). The men ranged in age from eighteen to seventy-one years and the majority (57 percent; $n = 229$) were under twenty-nine years. The mean age was twenty-seven years, slightly younger than their counterparts in Minneapolis, where the mean age was thirty-two years.

Incident Characteristics

The great majority of injuries (coded according to the most severe injury sustained by the victim) in these cases were bruises and blackened eyes. Nine percent ($n = 38$) of the cases did not involve physical attack but rather some other threat or menace to the victim (for example, verbal threats, waving or pointing a weapon, violation of bail conditions on a pending battery case, breach of a domestic violence restraining order, or property damage to the victim's home, usually occurring when the defendant entered without the victim's consent). An equal number of incidents resulted in more serious injuries, such as broken bones and cuts requiring stitches.

The primary weapon of attack, used in 52 percent ($n = 209$) of the cases, was a closed fist, which denote a certain amount of force. The open hand, used in more than one-quarter (27 percent; $n = 111$) of the cases, does not so clearly depict the amount of force because an open hand may be used to slap, choke, or push the victim into an object.

Twenty-eight percent ($n = 74$) of the cases involved the use of a weapon other than the defendant's body to harm or intimidate the victim. A wide variety of objects, posing a broad range of potential harm, were used to inflict pain on the victim. Among the objects were common household items, perhaps chosen because of their proximity: brooms, vases, shoes, scissors, belts, ashtrays, weight-lifting bars, hot irons, hot food, and telephones. Knives were rarely used (3 percent; $n = 11$) and guns were used even more rarely (2 percent; $n = 9$).

The data support the conclusions from other research that these acts of violence occur primarily in private and in the home (Gelles, 1982; Wolfgang, 1958). Three-fourths ($n = 304$) of the incidents occurred in the privacy of the victim's and defendant's shared home or in the victim's home. Forty of the forty-nine incidents occurring in public involved victims who did not live with the abuser.

Information about the use of alcohol or drugs, a characteristic often associated with domestic violence, was not available for the majority of cases. Its existence was noted primarily in the files of charged cases. The available information indicates that 25 percent ($n = 54$) of the victims and 67 percent ($n = 114$) of the defendants were under the influence of drugs or alcohol at the time of the offense.

Decision-Making Criteria

Of the 200 noncharged cases sampled, slightly more than two-thirds were simply not processed (70 percent), 24 percent were held open, and 6 percent were diverted. Prosecutors in the Milwaukee County district attorney's office are required to record

their reasons for not issuing charges in any case screened. Given that the ADAs were required to provide a reason for not prosecuting, it was not possible to discover any cases in which prosecution was denied "despite the fact the defendant was clearly guilty of a crime," that is, could be proven guilty of a crime (Friedman, 1982:70), if in fact such cases existed.

Acceding to the victim's wishes is one justification for not charging a defendant in a case, and a common one found in these data. In nearly half (45 percent; n = 92) of the noncharged cases sampled, "victim wishes" was the primary reason given for not prosecuting. Conversely, more than 50 percent of the cases in which the victim sought to have the abuser officially sanctioned resulted in a disposition other than a formal charge. As a matter of practice, victim cooperation with the decision to charge is necessary for the prosecutor to go forward in misdemeanor cases. Thus, victim wishes fall far short of explaining the prosecutor's decision. Victim attrition in domestic violence cases at the trial stage is well documented. Less is known about their cooperation at the screening stage. Victims may be willing to proceed upon arrival at the charging conference, but may change their mind during the proceeding. There is no way of knowing if the change of heart reflects their true desires, a possibility suggested by Ford and Burke's (1987) finding, or whether the influence of the defendant or the prosecutor is responsible. Threats, promises, or deception by the defendant or interaction with the prosecutor, through the application of pressure or the giving of information, may cause victims to lose their nerve.

Other justifications for not charging cases include legal problems with the cases (30 percent; $n = 60$), a problem of victim provocation (7 percent; $n = 13$), a judgment that the case is *de minimus* (14 percent; $n = 27$), or a probation or parole hold on the defendant (4 percent; $n = 8$). The discussion below examines legal, extralegal, and organizational variables associated with these justifications for not charging a defendant.

In examining which variables best distinguish between cases that are charged and those that are not charged, we turn first to so-called legal variables and then extralegal ones. Finally, we examine organizational variables that might influence the prosecutor's disposition. In doing so, we look, first, at which variables are more strongly associated with charged cases and, second, at those factors associated with the reason for not filing charges with the court.

Legal Variables

Seriousness of the offense The seriousness of the offense is measured by the degree of injury and the instrument used to inflict the injury, either a part of the body or some object or weapon. These variables are often used to infer malice or the intent of the accused to cause the victim bodily harm. They also embody an element of potential harm, aside from the harm actually inflicted.

Considering only cases in which an actual injury was sustained by the victim, we found a strong correlation between injury and a decision to charge ($G = .48$). (See Table 1.) Victims who suffered severe injuries (broken bones, cuts requiring stitches, or internal injuries) were more likely to see the case result in a charge against the abuser. Only four of the most severely injured victims saw the case not processed due to the prosecutor's perception of victim or legal problems; victim

T A B L E   1 / **Charging Decision, by Legal Variables**

Variable	N	Percent Not Charged	Charged	Gamma[a]
Injury				
Minor[b] or none	363	51	49	.48
Moderate or severe[c]	45	27	73	
Instrument				
Open hand only	106	65	34	.42
Other[d]	302	43	57	
Medical treatment				
None sought	228	50	50	.12
Received	172	44	56	
Missing data[e]	8	100	0	
Witness availability				
None available	242	51	49	.16
Available	141	43	57	
Missing data[e]	25	54	46	
Defendant at charging conference				
Present	234	66	34	.71
Absent[f]	159	20	80	
Missing data[e]	15	80	20	
Prior convictions				
None	159	53	47	
Nonassaultive	73	38	62	.36
Assaultive	100	32	68	
Missing data[e]	76	71	29	
Current legal status				
Free	291	45	55	.12
Probation/parole	49	39	61	
Missing data[e]	68	71	29	

[a] Gamma is a PRE measure reflecting strength and direction of association between two ordinal-level variables.

[b] Minor injuries include bruises, blackened eyes, scratches.

[c] Moderate or severe injuries include cuts requiring stitches, broken bones, teeth knocked out, internal injuries, loss of consciousness.

[d] "Other" includes teeth, fist, feet, and objects such as knife, gun, vase, pan, lit cigarette, scissors.

[e] Category not employed in calculating gamma.

[f] Includes those not notified and therefore, perhaps, not expected to attend.

wishes accounted for the majority (*n* = 9) of the cases involving severely injured victims that resulted in a disposition other than a charge. Charges were issued in almost three-quarters of the cases involving more that minor injuries, but only 44 percent of the victims with bruises or blackened eyes saw their complaint result in charges.

In thirty-eight cases no injuries were sustained, but most (90 percent; *n* = 34) of those resulted in charges being issued. The high charging rate may be explained as a "get-tough" response of the prosecutor in cases in which a preexisting no-contact court order had been imposed as a condition of bail or through an injunction,

or in which a prosecutor had already issued an informal warning to stay away from the victim. The decision to issue charges in the absence of injury may also reflect cases in which dangerous weapons were used to threaten victims.

Charges were more often than not issued when a gun was used to harm or threaten a victim ($n = 9$; the small number of cases requires caution in interpretation here, however). The use of some other object, such as a knife, vase, ashtray, scissors, or broom, is not strongly related to a decision to charge the defendant.

Charges were least frequently issued in cases in which the only instrument of attack was an open hand; 35 percent of such cases resulted in charges. In contrast, 57 percent of all other cases were charged ($G = .42$). Unfortunately, an open hand is not a straightforward indicator of either potential or actual harm, because it may be used to hold, slap, smother, or choke.

Strength of the evidence) Three variables were used to measure the evidentiary strength of the case: the existence of medical records, the availability of witnesses, and the defendant's appearance at the charging conference. Because medical treatment is often the sole bit of corroborative evidence in what is usually a one-to-one incident of criminal behavior, the availability of medical records was expected to show a substantial association with case disposition, but in fact its impact appeared negligible. Slightly more than one-half of the victims ($n = 228$), however, had not sought medical treatment by the time of the charging conference. Prosecutors, nonetheless, chose to prosecute in 50 percent of the cases in which medical corroboration was not available. One possible explanation for the positive action in such cases is the availability of a camera to prosecutorial staff. Prosecutors and/or CCU staff routinely photographed the victim's injuries. These photographs of blackened eyes, scratches, or lacerations may speak louder than written medical descriptions and are of perhaps greater value to prosecutors in negotiations and jury presentations.

Witnesses for either the complainant or defendant were noted in 37 percent ($n = 141$) of the cases, but their availability made little apparent difference in the decision to charge ($G = .16$). About 40 percent of both the charged and not-charged cases had witnesses. Little can be interpreted from this finding except that prosecutors apparently did not think it necessary to have an independent witness to charge the case. In fact, the slight majority ($n = 118$) of the charged cases did not have any witnesses other than the victim.

The defendant's presence at the charging conference is not a direct measure of the strength of the evidence, but it indicates whether the ADA has heard "the other side of the story." Given that the charging conference is the forum for rebuttal of the victim's accusations, it is not surprising that the defendant's presence has a pronounced influence on prosecutorial discretion ($G = .71$). In fact, it seems to have a more pronounced effect on the charging decision than does the presence of an attorney. As shown in Table 1, the prosecutor charged the defendant in four-fifths of the cases for which the defendant did not attend the charging conference.

Of 234 defendants interviewed by prosecutors at the charging conference, including 67 who had been arrested, leniency was shown to 67 percent ($n = 157$) through *nolle prosequi*, hold-open, and diversion dispositions. This leniency was attributed to victim wishes in less than half of those cases (46 percent; $n = 72$). Other reasons for decisions to decline issuing charges in cases in which defendants were interviewed included perceived legal problems (28 percent; $n = 45$), victim problems (7 percent; $n = 12$), and *de minimus* rationale (15 percent; $n = 23$).

Defendant's prior convictions   A record of convictions shows a moderate association with the screening decision ($G = .36$). Defendants with prior convictions were more likely to be charged, whether the prior conviction was for an assaultive offense (68 percent) or a nonassaultive offense (62 percent), than were those with no prior conviction (47 percent).

Current legal status, however, is only negligibly related to charging disposition ($G = .12$). Legally free defendants were nearly as likely to be charged as were defendants already on probation or parole for some other offense. This finding may be explained by the powers vested in the probation or parole officer. During the period of study, state agents were mandated to take clients into custody if violent behavior was alleged and reported to them. Agents had the power to commence revocation proceedings or to order no-contact or counseling provisions as part of probation or parole conditions. Thus, it may have been unnecessary from both a prosecutor's and a victim's perspective to invoke prosecution because control could be exercised in other ways.

Summary   The bivariate analysis of legally relevant variables indicated that degree of injury to the victim, instrument of attack, defendant's failure to appear at the charging conference, and defendant's record are clearly related to the prosecutor's decision to charge the case. Victims who sustained relatively severe injuries or who were harmed or threatened with some sort of object or weapon more menacing than an open hand were more likely than other victims to see the complaint against the defendant proceed to court. Defendants were less likely to be given lenient dispositions if they failed to appear at the charging conference or had a prior conviction. Discretionary practices with respect to legal variables, therefore, appear to operate only partially as described by Friedman (1982). Prosecutors in domestic abuse cases chose to proceed against some defendants even when scant corroborative evidence was available. Sometimes, this decision appeared to be based on the defendant's record. On the other hand, prosecutors sometimes elected not to proceed when they perceived problems establishing proof beyond a reasonable doubt. Decisions short of formal charging were also made in cases in which the burden of proof could conceivably be met, but the victim expressed a desire for the prosecutor to be lenient.

Extralegal Variables

Bivariate analysis showed that five commonly cited extralegal variables are associated with the screening decision in domestic abuse cases: sexual intimacy with the defendant, cohabitation with the defendant, the couple's history of domestic violence, the defendant's source of support, and incident-related use of drugs or alchol (see Table 2). Victims claiming to have no sexual intimacy with the abuser at the time of the incident were more likely to have their complaint charged ($G = .22$). The legal dwelling of the victim also appeared to have a modest impact on the decision to charge ($G = .20$). Cases were more often charged when the victim did not live with the abuser, but this finding can be interpreted in divergent ways. Prosecutors

T A B L E   2 / **Charging Decision, by Extralegal Variables**

Variable	N	Percent Not Charged	Charged	Gamma[a]
Current relationship				
Sexually intimate	251	53	47	.22
Not sexually intimate	141	42	58	
Missing data[b]	16	50	50	
Dwelling				
With defendant	187	54	46	.20
Apart from defendant	218	44	56	
Missing data[b]	3	100	0	
Couple's history of abuse				
No prior abuse	34	53	47	.22
Prior abuse	260	42	58	
Missing data[b]	114	62	38	
Defendant's source of support				
Self	109	60	40	.49
Other[d]	167	34	66	
Missing data[b]	132	59	41	
Defendant's use of intoxicants[c]				
None	57	79	21	.61
Drugs or alcohol	114	47	53	
Missing data[b]	237	42	58	

[a]Gamma is a PRE measure reflecting strength and direction of association between two ordinal-level variables.
[b]Category not employed in calculating gamma.
[c]Use of intoxicants at time of assault.
[d]"Other" includes no apparent means of support, public and private charity.

may believe a victim is more likely to cooperate with the goal of prosecution if she is not exposed to the continual presence or pressure of the defendant. Prosecutors may also be unwilling to put a victim at further risk until she establishes a safer living arrangement or obtains a civil restraining order banning the defendant from the home. On the other hand, despite the widely held view that prosecutors refrain from intervening in family affairs, this study shows that marital status alone appeared to exert little influence on prosecutorial leniency (47 percent of the decisions to not prosecute in each group were based on victim's wishes).

Conventional wisdom maintains that prosecutors are reluctant to use the coercive power of the law against defendants whose victims have repeatedly tolerated abuse. To the extent that our data address this issue, our findings contradict that belief. Our data do not reveal the extent of prior abuse or the response of the victim to it, only whether the defendant had assaulted the victim at some earlier time. Data are missing in slightly more than one-quarter of the cases (28 percent), but for those cases for which information is available, we found a modest association ($G = .22$) between the incidence of prior abuse and the prosecutor's decision to issue a charge. These data suggest that the prosecutorial response to repeated abuse is not to hold the victim responsible but rather to hold the defendant responsible.

T A B L E   3 / **Reason Given for No-Charge Decision, by Source of Complaint**

Reason	Citizen Unit				Police Unit			
	NP	HO	DV	N	NP	HO	DV	N
De minimus	75%	25%	—	4	52%	48%	—	23
Victim provocation	75	25	—	4	89	11	—	9
Legal problems	90	7	2%	41	74	21	5%	19
Probation parole hold	67	33	—	3	60	40	—	5
Victim wishes	63	29	8	48	64	25	11	44
Total N	75	20	5	103	65	29	6	106

NOTE: NP = *nolle prosequi;* HO = hold open; DV = diversion; N = number.

Data on the defendant's source of support were available in only 68 percent of the cases. As expected, employed defendants received more leniency than their unemployed counterparts ($G = .49$). Prosecutors more often selected *nolle prosequi,* hold-open, or diversion dispositions rather than prosecution for employed defendants.

Family violence researchers have often linked the use of drugs and intoxicants to violence, but the legal community has often viewed its involvement as mitigating evidence. Although data were available for only two-thirds of the accused, in this study the absence of alchol or drugs is clearly linked to a lenient disposition ($G = .61$), which contradicts the notion that prosecutors discount domestic violence committed under the influence of drugs or alcohol. Prosecutors were not inclined to defer charges or order treatment in these cases, either. One explanation is that prosecutors may have interpreted their role as gaining control over the defendant and that referral for treatment may be considered at a later stage.

Organizational Variables

If Cole's (1970) exchange paradigm and Jacoby's (1980) critique of citizen complaint procedures is applied to these data, the entry point of the complaint, police or citizen, may be interpreted as accounting for some of the variability in prosecutorial decision making. In addition, Cole's exchange model would suggest that prosecutors might be more inclined to show less leniency in cases in which police arrested defendants than in cases in which the suspect was gone when the police arrived or the police were not even called. Because of the manner in which the sample was drawn, the number of noncharged cases originating in the police unit and the Citizen Complaint Unit is fixed and equal. (No significant differences were found with respect to incident characteristics of cases belonging to the two groups.) Although the research design controlled the variation in charged cases originating in the police unit and Citizen Complaint Unit, the dispositions of noncharged cases originating in each unit did vary. As can be seen from Table 3, the police unit produced fewer cases that were simply not processed. Instead, the police unit cases had slightly greater numbers of hold-open and diversion decisions.

As shown in Table 3, victims contacting the Citizen Complaint Unit were about as likely as victims in the police unit cases to want to resolve the case short of prosecution; victim wished accounted for less than 50 percent of the recorded major reasons for not charging a case in each of the groups. Legal problems were a reason offered far more often in the CCU cases (41 percent) than in the police unit (19 percent) cases. On the other hand, police unit cases were far more likely to be declared *de minimus* (23 percent) than were CCU cases (4 percent). One explanation of the variation in reasons is that ADAs were simply more reluctant to tell a victim that her case was *de minimus* than to deliver that message to a police officer, who has less personal investment in the case. On reflection, it becomes fairly obvious that the difference between *de minimus* and legal problems as justifications for declining prosecution is very subtle, and it is easy to imagine that a prosecutor could cite a legal problem with a *de minimus* case. Further, a prosecutor may be more comfortable disposing of a case as *de minimus* in the presence of a police officer, who then has the option of immediately issuing a municipal citation for the same misconduct. Prosecutors in CCU cases did not have to explain their decision to a uniformed police officer, which eliminates one layer accountability, a factor noted by Jacoby. Perhaps this accounts for why more of the police unit cases resulted in hold-open and diversion decisions. Or perhaps Cole's notion of reinforcement of police effort explains this difference. In any event, because the Citizen Complaint Unit was structured to assist victims of domestic abuse, it is a bit surprising to find fewer hold-open and diversion for complaints originating in this unit.

Arrest can be analyzed as an organizational variable in addressing the question of prosecutorial review of police practices. Police officers learn what is acceptable to prosecutors (and judges) from the feedback they glean from the charging decision or, more directly, from what they learn in a charging conference. Prosecutors, conversely, can influence police efforts and improve case quality by rewarding police practices. Police were called in 85 percent ($n = 348$) of the cases in the sample and made an arrest in 19 percent ($n = 67$) of those cases. Nearly two-thirds (61 percent; $n = 41$) of the defendants arrested were charged, a finding that suggest prosecutorial reinforcement of police discretion. In the majority (61 percent; $n = 16$) of cases in which arrestees were not charged, the major reason was the victim's wish to decline pressing charges. Of the other cases involving arrestees who were not charged, half ($n = 5$) had cases deemed legally insufficient for charging. Again, the data indicate that the prosecutor's decision approves and reinforces police discretion.

Data on organizational variables may be interpreted to support Cole's (1970) model and Jacoby's (1980) critique in their application to incidents of domestic abuse. Research by Black (1971), Berk and Loseke (1981), and Worden and Pollitz (1984) indicates that factors that lead police to an arrest disposition are not necessarily legally relevant. In this study, the majority of arrests were followed by a charge, a finding that suggests that actions by prosecutors assigned to review police-supported cases tend to reaffirm police efforts. At the same time, defendants who are brought to the prosecutor's attention by the police and whose cases are not charged are more likely to be sanctioned, particularly informally, for their behavior than similarly situated defendants whose cases are screened by prosecutors assigned to handle citizen complaints. Prosecutors in CCU cases are not accountable to anyone but the victim in their decision making. One result may be that victims supported by the police receive more response from the prosecutor's office than do victims who appeal directly to the prosecutor.

. . .

Summary and Conclusion

Previous literature has identified several salient factors that appeared to influence prosecutorial discretion in this study as well, in particular, legal variables associated with seriousness of the offense and the defendant's arrest record. Screening decisions were also influenced by the prosecutor's interpretation of legal and extralegal variables, by organizational variables, and by the wishes of the victim.

Victims and defendants in this study presented profiles very similar to those etched in previous research. The majority of victims were young, nonwhite, poor, and parents of minor children. Typically, victims in these cases were currently sexually intimate with the abuser and had been previously abused. Defendants commonly had prior convictions, although not necessarily for offenses of an assaultive nature.

The findings in this study show that the severity of injury and the defendant's arrest record appear to influence the prosecutor's decision more than the evidentiary strength of the case. (It is possible that the evidentiary strength of the case operated as a threshold criterion and that most cases meet a minimum standard.) Prosecutors were strongly inclined to take legal action against the abuser when the defendant failed to appear at the charging conference. Criticism attributing prosecutorial reticence to charge in the absence of serious injury, corroborating medical records, or witness availability is not justified by these findings. Prosecutors for the most part were not reluctant to proceed in cases in which corroborative evidence was unavailable.

The extralegal considerations found in this study to be associated with the decision to charge were the incident-related use of drugs or alcohol by the defendant, the defendant's source of financial support, and the couple's history of abuse. Two variables that showed a modest bivariate association with the charging decision—sexual intimacy and shared dwelling—did not have strong effects when considered simultaneously with other independent variables in the logit analysis.

The analysis also supports claims that the screening disposition is used to reinforce organizational goals and police efforts. Although not any less serious as measured by incident characteristics, noncharged citizen complaints less often resulted in decisions to divert or hold open the case compared with police-supported complaints. One can only speculate as to the meaning of this finding. An obvious explanation may be the small number of prosecutors assigned to the Citizen Complaint Unit. Nevertheless, the attenuation of cases by CCU prosecutors, while reminiscent of the often-criticized prosecutorial approach to domestic abuse, does not necessarily imply that those screening decisions represent less effective resolutions than those meted out by police unit prosecutors. One finding of this research was a greater tendency among prosecutors to apply some formal sanction to police-supported complaints, through the imposition of hold-open or diversion conditions. The lack of uniformity in charging decisions between police-supported and citizen-initiated complaints may be more a matter of style than of substance, because the conditions of hold-open dispositions are not systematically monitored and enforced.

Because the data do not fully reconstruct the fact situation presented to the prosecutor at the time of case review, our conclusions concerning the application of discretion to charging decisions must be viewed as limited. Inferential clues provided by the data point to a handful of salient factors that apparently affect the prosecutor's decision and indicate that, for the most part, prosecutors strive to balance victim needs, conviction goals, and the interest of justice in their screening deliberations. There is little to suggest that victims are blamed or denied equal protection of the law; there is much to suggest that the decision to prosecute is largely based on the defendant's past and current actions and choices.

Note

1. Established in 1976, the CCU had evolved into a primary resource for victims of intrafamily disputes by the time of this study. Victims often go to the CCU on their own accord, and referrals typically originate from hospital personnel, social service agencies, and police officers. One of the authors, Ms. Schmidt, was formerly a CCU complaint specialist.

References

BERK, SARAH F., AND DONILEEN LOSEKE (1981). "Handling Family Violence: Situational Determinants of Police Arrest in Domestic Disturbances." *Law and Society Review* 15:317–346.

BLACK, DONALD J. (1971). "The Social Organization of Arrest." *Stanford Law Review* 23:1087–1111.

BOLAND, BARBARA, ELIZABETH BREADY, HERBERT TYSON, AND JOHN BASSLER (1983). *The Prosecution of Felony Arrests, 1979.* INSLAW, Inc. NCJ-86482. Washington, D.C.: Bureau of Justice Statistics.

BROSI, KATHLEEN (1979). *A Cross-City Comparison of Felony Case Processing.* Washington, D.C.: INSLAW, Inc.

COLE, GEORGE F. (1970). "The Decision to Prosecute" *Law and Society Review* 4:313–343.

ELLIS, JANE E. (1984). "Prosecutorial Discretion to Charge in Cases of Spousal Assault: A Dialogue." *Journal of Criminal Law and Criminology* 75:56–102.

FORD, DAVID A., AND MARY JANE BURKE (1987). Victim-Initiated Criminal Complaints for Wife-Battery: An Assessment of Motives." Paper presented at 3rd Annual Conference for Family Violence, Durham, N.H.

FRIEDMAN, LEON (1982). "Discretion and Public Prosecution." In Burton Adkins and Mark Pogrebin (eds.), *The Invisible Justice System: Discretion and the Law.* 2nd. ed. Cincinnati, Ohio: Anderson.

GELLES, RICHARD J. (1982). "Domestic Criminal Violence." In Marvin E. Wolfgang and Neil A. Weiner (eds.), *Criminal Violence.* Beverly Hills, Calif.: Sage.

JACOBY, JOAN (1980). *The American Prosecutor: A Search for Identity.* Lexington, Mass.: Lexington Books.

SHERMAN, LAWRENCE W., AND RICHARD A. BERK (1984). The Specific Deterrent Effects of Arrest for Domestic Assault." *American Sociological Review* 49:261–272.

SPOHN, CASSIA, JOHN GRUHL, AND SUSAN WELCH (1987). "The Impact of Ethnicity and Gender of Defendants on the Decision to Reject or Dismiss Felony Charges." *Criminology* 25:175–191.

STANKO, ELIZABETH ANNE (1982). "Would You Believe This Women?" In Nicole Hahn Rafter and Elizabeth A. Stanko (eds.), *Judge, Lawyer, Victim, Thief.* Boston: Northeastern University Press.

U.S. COMMISSION ON CIVIL RIGHTS (1982). *Under the Ruling of Thumb: Battered Women and the Administration of Justice.* Washington, D.C.: Government Printing Office.

WOLFGANG, MARVIN E. (1958). *Patterns of Criminal Homicide.* Philadelphia: University of Pennsylvania Press.

WORDEN, ROBERT E., AND ALISSA A. POLLITZ (1984). "Police Arrests in Domestic Disturbances: A Further Look." *Law and Society Review* 18:105–119.

10

Adapting to Plea Bargaining: Prosecutors

Milton Heumann

Plea bargaining has been openly discussed only since the late 1960s. Before then, it was a widespread practice that was one of the secrets of criminal justice officials. In this analysis of the way new prosecutors adapt to plea bargaining, Milton Heumann shows how negotiated justice serves the needs of all participants in the process.

The new prosecutor shares many of the general expectations that his counterpart for the defense brings to the court. He expects factually and legally disputable issues, and the preliminary hearings and trials associated with these. If his expectations differ at all from the naive "Perry Mason" orientation, it is only to the extent that he anticipates greater success than the hapless Hamilton Burger of Perry Mason fame.

The new prosecutor's views about plea bargaining parallel those of the defense attorney. He views plea bargaining as an expedient employed in crowded urban courts by harried and/or poorly motivated prosecutors. He views the trial as "what the system is really about" and plea bargaining as a necessary evil dictated by case volume. The following exchange with a newly appointed prosecutor is illustrative.

Q: Let's say they removed the effects of case pressure, provided you with more manpower. You wouldn't have that many cases. . . .

A: Then everybody should go to trial.

Q: Everybody should go to trial?

A: Yeah.

Source: Reprinted from *Plea Bargaining* by Milton Heumann by permission of The University of Chicago Press and the author. © 1978 by The University of Chicago Press.

Editor's note: This study is based on data from Connecticut, where, until a reorganization of the court system in July 1978, prosecution was conducted by state's attorney's in the supreme court and by prosecutors in the circuit court. Readers should understand that the powers of each office are essentially the same; only the workplace is different.

Q: Why?

A: Because supposedly if they're guilty they'll be found guilty. If they're not guilty they'll be found not guilty. That's the fairest way . . . judged by a group of your peers, supposedly.

Q: So you think that plea bargaining is a necessary evil?

A: Yeah.

Q: Would justice be better served if all cases went to trial?

A: That's the way it's supposed to be set up. Sure. Why wouldn't it?

Q: Would prosecutors be more satisfied?

A: Probably.

Q: If cases went to trial?

A: Sure.

Q: Why?

A: Because they could talk in front of twelve people and act like a lawyer. Right. Play the role.

It should be emphasized that these expectations and preferences of the new prosecutor are founded on the minimal law school preparation. . . . The newcomers simply do not know very much about the criminal justice system.

Unlike defense attorneys, however, the new prosecutor is likely to receive some form of structured assistance when he begins his job. The chief prosecutor or chief state's attorney may provide this aid, if the prosecutor's office is staffed by a number of prosecutors or state's attorneys—that is, if the newcomer is not the only assistant prosecutor—it is more common for the chief prosecutor to assign to one or more of his experienced assistants the responsibility for helping the newcomer adjust. Since the newcomer's actions reflect on the office as a whole, it is not surprising that this effort is made.

The assistance the newcomer receives can be described as a form of structured observation. For roughly two weeks, he accompanies an experienced prosecutor to court and to plea-bargaining sessions and observes him in action. The proximity of the veteran prosecutor—and his designation as the newcomer's mentor—facilitates communication between the two. The experienced prosecutor can readily explain or justify his actions, and the newcomer can ask any and all relevant questions. Certainly, this is a more structured form of assistance than defense attorneys receive.

However, new prosecutors still feel confused and overwhelmed during this initial period. Notwithstanding the assistance they receive, they are disoriented by the multitude of tasks performed by the prosecutor and by the environment in which he operates. This is particularly true in the circuit court, where the seemingly endless shuffling of files, the parade of defendants before the court and around the courtroom, the hurried, early-morning plea-bargaining sessions all come as a surprise to the new prosecutor.

Q: What were your initial impressions of the court during this "orientation period?"

A: The first time I came down here was a Monday morning at the arraignments. Let's face it, the majority of people here, you don't expect courts to be as crowded as they are. You don't expect thirty to thirty-five people to come out of the cell block who have been arrested over the weekend. It was . . . you sit in court the first few days, you didn't realize the court was run like this. All you see, you see Perry Mason on TV, or pictures of the Supreme Court, or you see six judges up there in a spotless courtroom, everyone well dressed, well manicured, and you come to court and find people coming in their everyday clothes, coming up drunk, some are high on drugs, it's . . . it's an experience to say the least.

Q: Could you describe your first days when you came down here? What are your recollections? Anything strike you as strange?

A: Just the volume of business and all the stuff the prosecutor had to do. For the first week or two, I went to court with guys who had been here. Just sat there and watched. What struck me was the amount of things he [the prosecutor] has to do in the courtroom. The prosecutor runs the courtroom. Although the judge is theoretically in charge, we're standing there plea bargaining and calling the cases at the same time and chewing gum and telling people to quiet down and setting bonds, and that's what amazed me. I never thought I would learn all the terms. What bothered me also was the paperwork. Not the Supreme Court decisions, not the *mens rea* or any of this other stuff, but the amount of junk that's in those files that you have to know. We never heard about this crap in law school.

As suggested in the second excerpt, the new prosecutor is also surprised by the relative insignificance of the judge. He observes that the prosecutor assumes—through plea bargaining—responsibility for the disposition of many cases. Contrary to his expectations of being an adversary in a dispute moderated by the judge, he finds that often the prosecutor performs the judge's function.

It is precisely this responsibility for resolving disputes that is most vexing to the new superior court state's attorney. Unlike his circuit court counterpart, he does not generally find hurried conferences, crowded courts, and so on. But he observes that, as in the circuit court, the state's attorney negotiates cases, and in the superior court far more serious issues and periods of incarceration are involved in these negotiations. For the novice state's attorney, the notion that he will in short order be responsible for resolving these disputes is particularly disturbing.

Q: What were your initial impressions of your job here [as a state's attorney]?

A: Well, I was frightened of the increased responsibility. I knew the stakes were high here. . . . I didn't really know what to expect, and I would say it took me a good deal of time to adapt here.

Q: Adapt in which way?

A: To the higher responsibilities. Here you're dealing with felonies, serious felonies all the way up to homicides, and I had never been involved in that particular type of situation. . . . I didn't believe that I was prepared to handle the type of job that I'd been hired to do. I looked around me and I saw the serious charges, the types of cases, and the experienced defense counsel on the one hand and the inexperience on my part on the other, and I was, well. . . .

Q: Did you study up on your own?

A: No more than. . . . Before I came over here I had done some research and made a few notes, et cetera, about the procedures. I think I was prepared from the book end of things to take the job, but, again, it was the practical aspects that you're not taught in law school and that you can only learn from experience that I didn't have, and that's what I was apprehensive about.

These first weeks in the court, then, serve to familiarize the newcomer with the general patterns of case resolution. He is not immediately thrust into the court but is able to spend some time simply observing the way matters are handled. The result, though, is to increase his anxiety. The confusion of the circuit court and the responsibilities of a state's attorney in the superior court were not anticipated. The newcomer expects to be able to prepare cases leisurely and to rely on the skills learned in law school. Yet he finds that his colleagues seem to have neither the time nor the inclination to operate in this fashion. As the informal period of orientation draws to a close, the newcomer has a better perspective on the way the system operates, but still is on very uneasy footing about how to proceed when the responsibility for the case is his alone. In short, he is somewhat disoriented by his orientation.

The Prosecutor on His Own:
Initial Firmness and Resistance to Plea Bargaining

Within a few weeks after starting his job, the prosecutor and the state's attorney are expected to handle cases on their own. Experienced personnel are still available for advice, and the newcomer is told that he can turn to them with his problems. But the cases are now the newcomer's, and, with one exception, he is under no obligation to ask anyone for anything.

The new prosecutor is confronted by a stream of defense attorneys asking for a particular plea bargain in a case. If the prosecutor agrees, his decision is irreversible. It would be a violation of all the unwritten folkways of the criminal court for either a defense attorney or a prosecutor to break his word. On the other hand, if the prosecutor does not plea bargain, offers nothing in exchange for a plea, he at least does not commit himself to an outcome that may eventually prove to be a poor decision on his part. However, a refusal to plea bargain also places him "out of step" with his colleagues and with the general expectation of experienced defense attorneys.

Like the new attorney, the new prosecutor is in no hurry to dispose of the case. He is (1) inclined toward an adversary resolution of the case through formal hearings and trial, (2) disinclined to plea bargain in general, and (3) unsure about what constitutes an appropriate plea bargain for a particular case. Yet he is faced with demands by defense attorneys to resolve the case through plea bargaining. The new defense attorney has the luxury of postponing his decision for any given case. He can seek the advice of others before committing himself to a particular plea bargain in a particular case. For the new prosecutor, this is more difficult, since he is immediately faced with the demands of a number of attorneys in a number of different cases.

When the new prosecutor begins to handle his own cases, then, he lacks confidence about how to proceed in his dealings with defense attorneys. He often masks his insecurity in this period with an outward air of firmness. He is convinced that he must appear confident and tough, lest experienced attorneys think they can take advantage of him.

Q: What happened during your first few days of handling cases on your own?

A: Well, as a prosecutor, first of all, people try to cater to you because they want you to do favors for them. If you let a lawyer run all over you, you are dead. I had criminal the first day, on a Monday, and I'm in there [in the room where cases are negotiated], and a guy comes in, and I was talking to some lawyer on his file, and he's just standing there. Then I was talking to a second guy, and he was about fourth or fifth. So he looked at me and says: "When the hell you going to get to me?" So I says: "You wait your fucking turn. I'll get to you when I'm ready. If you don't like it, get out." It's sad that you have to swear at people, but it's the only language they understand—especially lawyers. Lawyers are the most obstinate, arrogant, belligerent bastards you will ever meet. Believe me. They come into this court—first of all—and we are really the asshole of the judicial system [circuit court], and they come in here and don't really have any respect for you. They'll come in here and be nice to you, because they feel you'll give them a *nolle*. That's all. Lawyers do not respect this court. I don't know if I can blame them or not blame them. You can come in here and see the facilities here; you see how things are handled; you see how it's like a zoo pushing people in and out. . . . When they do come here, lawyers have two approaches. One, they try to soft-soap and kiss your ass if you give them a *nolle*. Two, they'll come in here and try to ride roughshod over you and try to push you to a corner. Like that lawyer that first day. I had to swear at him and show him I wasn't going to take shit, and that's that. The problem of dealing with lawyers is that you can't let them bullshit you. So, when I first started out I tried to be. . . . It's like the new kid on the block. He comes to a new neighborhood, and you've got to prove yourself. If you're a patsy, you're going to live with that as long as you're in court. If you let a couple of lawyers run over you, word will get around to go to _____ , he's a pushover. Before you know it, they're running all over you. So you have to draw a line so they will respect you.

At first I was very tough because I didn't know what I was doing. In other words, you have to be very wary. These guys, some of them, have been practicing in this court for forty years. And they'll take you to the cleaners. You have to be pretty damn careful.

The new prosecutor couples this outward show of firmness toward attorneys with a fairly rigid plea-bargaining posture. His reluctance to offer incentives to the defendant for a plea or to reward the defendant who chooses to plead is, at this point in the prosecutor's career, as much a function of his lack of confidence as it is a reflection of his antipathy toward plea bargaining. During this very early stage he is simply afraid to make concessions. Experienced court personnel are well aware that new prosecutors adopt this rigid stance.

Q: Have you noticed any differences between new prosecutors and prosecutors that have been around awhile?

A: Oh, yes. First of all, a new prosecutor is more likely to be less flexible in changing charges. He's afraid. He's cautious. He doesn't know his business. He doesn't know the liars. He can't tell when he's lying or exaggerating. He doesn't know all the ramifications. He doesn't know how tough it is sometimes to prove the case to juries. He hasn't got the experience, so that more likely than not he will be less flexible. He is also more easily fooled. [Circuit court judge]

I can only answer that question in a general way. It does seem to me that the old workhorses [experienced prosecutors] are more flexible than the young stallions. [Superior court judge]

Q: You were saying about the kids, the new prosecutors, the new state's attorneys. Are they kind of more hard-assed?

A: They tend to be more nervous. They tend to have a less well defined idea of what they can do and what they can't do without being criticized. So, to the extent that they are more nervous, they tend to be more hard-assed. [Private criminal attorney]

Q: What about new prosecutors? Do they differ significantly from prosecutors who have been around awhile?

A: Initially a new prosecutor is going to be reluctant to *nolle,* reluctant to give too good a deal because he is scared. He is afraid of being taken advantage of. And if you are talking about the circuit court, they've got the problem that they can't even talk it over with anybody. They've got a hundred fifty cases or whatever, and they make an offer or don't make an offer, that's it. Maybe at the end of the day they may get a chance to talk it over and say: "Gee, did I do the right thing?" The defense attorney, when the offer is made, has the opportunity to talk to somebody plus his client before making a decision. So I think it takes the prosecutor a longer time to come around and work under the system. [Legal aid attorney]

It is not difficult to understand why the new prosecutor is reluctant to plea bargain and why he appears rigid to court veterans. Set aside for the moment the prosecutor's personal preference for an adversary resolution and consider only the nature of the demands being made on him. Experienced attorneys want charges dropped, sentence recommendations, and *nolles.* They approach him with the standard argument about the wonderful personal traits of the defendant, the minor nature of the crime, the futility of incarceration, and so on. When the new prosecutor picks up the file, he finds that the defendant probably has an extensive prior criminal record and, often, that he has committed a crime that does not sound minor at all. Under the statute for the crime involved, it is likely that the defendant faces a substantial period of incarceration, yet in almost all circuit court cases and in many superior court cases, the attorneys are talking about a no-time disposition. What to the new prosecutor frequently seems like a serious matter is treated as a relatively inconsequential offense by defense attorneys. And, because the newcomer views the matter as serious, his resolve to remain firm—or, conversely, his insecurity about reducing charges—is reinforced.

Illustrations of this propensity for the new prosecutor or state's attorney to be "outraged" by the facts of the case, and to be disinclined to offer "sweet" deals, are plentiful. The following comments by two circuit court prosecutors and a superior court state's attorney, respectively, illustrate the extent to which the newcomer's appraisal of a case differed from that of the defense attorney and from that of his own colleagues.

Q: You used to go to _____ [chief prosecutor] for help on early cases. Were his recommendations out of line with what you thought should be done with the case?

A: Let's say a guy came in with a serious crime . . . a crime that I thought was serious at one time, anyway. Take fighting on _____ Avenue [a depressed area of Arborville]. He got twenty-five stitches in the head and is charged with aggravated assault. One guy got twenty-five stitches, the other fifteen. And the attorneys would want me to reduce it. I'd go and talk to _____ [chief prosecutor]. He'd say: "They both are drunk, they both got head wounds. Let them plead to breach of peace, and the judge will give them a money fine." Things like that I didn't feel right about doing, since, to me, right out of law school, middle class, you figure twenty-five stitches in the head, Jesus Christ.

Q: How did you learn what a case was worth?

A: What do you mean, what it's worth?

Q: In terms of plea bargaining. What the going rate. . . .

A: From the prosecutors and defense attorneys who would look at me dumbfounded when I would tell them that I would not reduce this charge. And then they would go running to my boss and he'd say, "Well, it's up to him." Some would even go running to the judge, screaming. One guy claimed surprise when I intended to go to trial for assault in second, which is a Class D felony. Two counts of that and two misdemeanor counts. It was set for jury trial. His witnesses were there. His experience in this court, he said, having handled two or three hundred cases, was that none has ever gone to trial. So he claimed surprise the day of trial. He just couldn't believe it.

Q: Were you in any way out of step with the way things were done here when you first began handling cases on your own?

A: In one respect I was. I evaluated a case by what I felt a proper recommendation should be, and my recommendations were almost always in terms of longer time. I found that the other guys in the office were breaking things down more than I expected. As a citizen, I couldn't be too complacent about an old lady getting knocked down, stuff like that. I thought more time should be recommended. I might think five to ten, six to twelve, while the other guys felt that three to seven was enough

Implicit in these remarks are the seeds of an explanation for a prosecutor's gradually becoming more willing to plea bargain. One can hypothesize that as his experience with handling cases increases, he will feel less outraged by the crime, and thus will be more willing to work out a negotiated settlement. One assistant state's attorney likened his change in attitude to that of a nurse in an emergency room.

> It's like nurses in emergency rooms. You get so used to armed robbery that you treat it as routine, not as morally upsetting. In the emergency room, the biggest emergency is treated as routine. And it's happening to me. The nature of the offense

doesn't cause the reaction in me that it would cause in the average citizen. Maybe this is a good thing; maybe it isn't.

Though there is merit in this argument—prosecutors do become accustomed to crime—it is hardly a sufficient explanation of prosecutorial adaptation to plea bargaining. Other factors, often far more subtle, must be considered if we are to understand how and why the novice prosecutor becomes a seasoned plea bargainer.

Learning about Plea Bargaining

In the preceding sections I have portrayed the new prosecutor as being predisposed toward an adversary resolution of a case, uncertain about his responsibilities, rigid in his relations with defense attorneys, reluctant to drop charges and to plea bargain in cases that he considers serious, and anxious to try out the skills he learned in law school. This characterization of the newcomer contrasts sharply with that of the veteran prosecutor. [The veteran prosecutor takes] an active role in plea bargaining— urging, cajoling, and threatening the defense attorney to share in the benefits of a negotiated disposition. How is the veteran prosecutor to be reconciled with the new prosecutor . . . ?

The answer lies in what the prosecutor learns and is taught about plea bargaining. His education, like the defense attorney's, is not structured and systematic. Instead, he works his way through cases, testing the adversary and plea-bargaining approaches. He learns piecemeal the costs and benefits of these approaches, and only over a period of time does he develop an appreciation for the relative benefits of a negotiated disposition.

Rather than proceed with a sequential discussion of the newcomer's experience, I think it more profitable at this point to distill from his experiences those central concerns that best explain his adaptation to the plea-bargaining system. Some of the "flavor" of the adaptation process is sacrificed by proceeding in this fashion, but in terms of clarity of presentation, I think it is a justifiable. Thus, I will discuss separately the considerations that move the prosecutor in the plea-bargaining direction, and later tie these together into an overall perspective on prosecutorial adaptation.

The Defendant's Factual and Legal Guilt

Prosecutors and state's attorneys learn that their roles primarily entail the processing of factually guilty defendants. Contrary to their expectations that problems of establishing factual guilt would be central to their job, they find that in most cases the evidence in the file is sufficient to conclude (and prove) that the defendant is factually guilty. For those cases where there is a substantial question as to factual guilt, the prosecutor has the power—and is inclined to exercise it—to *nolle* or dismiss the case. If he himself does not believe the defendant to be factually guilty, it is part of his formal responsibilities to filter the case out. But of the cases that remain after the initial screening, the prosecutor believes the majority of defendants to be factually guilty.

Furthermore, he finds that defense attorneys only infrequently contest the prosecutor's own conclusion that the defendant is guilty. In their initial approach to the prosecutor they may raise the possibility that the defendant is factually innocent, but in most subsequent discussions their advances focus on disposition and not on the problem of factual guilt. Thus, from the prosecutor's own reading of the file (after screening) and from the comments of his "adversary," he learns that he begins with the upper hand; more often than not, the factual guilt of the defendant is not really disputable.

Q: Are most of the defendants who come to this court guilty?

A: Yeah, or else we wouldn't have charged them. You know, that's something that people don't understand. Basically the people that are brought here are believed very definitely to be guilty or we wouldn't go on with the prosecution. We would *nolle* the case, and, you know, that is something, when people say, "Well, do you really believe. . . ." Yeah. I do. I really do, and if I didn't and we can clear them, then we *nolle* it, there's no question about it.

But most cases are good, solid cases, and in most of them the defendant is guilty. We have them cold-cocked. And they plead guilty because they are guilty . . . a guy might have been caught in a package store with bottles. Now, he wasn't there to warm his hands. The defendant may try some excuse, but they are guilty and they know they are guilty. And we'll give them a break when they plead guilty. I don't think we should throw away the key on the guy just because we got him cold-cocked. We've got good cases, we give them what we think the case is worth from our point of view, allowing the defendant's mitigating circumstances to enter.

Q: The fact that you're willing to offer a pretty good bargain in negotiations might lead a person to plead guilty even if he had a chance to beat it at trial. But if he was found guilty at the trial he might not get the same result?

A: That's possible. I mean, only the accused person knows whether or not he's committed the crime, and. . . . It's an amazing thing, where, on any number of occasions, you will sit down to negotiate with an accused's attorney . . . and you know [he will say]: "No, no, he's not guilty, he wants his trial." But then if he develops a weakness in the case, or points out a weakness to you, and then you come back and say: "Well, we'll take a suspended sentence and probation," suddenly he says, "Yes, I'm guilty." So it leads you to conclude that, well, all these people who are proclaiming innocence are really not innocent. They're just looking for the right disposition. Now, from my point of view, the ideal situation might be if the person is not guilty, that he pleads not guilty, and we'll give him his trial and let the jury decide. But most people who are in court don't want a trial. I'm not the person who seeks them out and says, "I will drop this charge" or "I will reduce this charge, I will reduce the amount of time you have to do." They come to us, so, you know, the conclusion I think is there that any reasonable person could draw, that these people are guilty, that they are just looking for the best disposition possible. Very few people ask for a speedy trial.

In addition to learning of the factual culpability of most defendants, the prosecutor also learns that defendants would be hard-pressed to raise legal challenges to the state's case. As was discussed earlier, most cases are simply barren of any contestable legal issue, and nothing in the prosecutor's file or the defense attorney's arguments leads the prosecutor to conclude otherwise.

The new prosecutor or state's attorney, then, learns that in most cases the problem of establishing the defendant's factual and legal guilt is nonexistent. Typically, he begins with a very solid case, and, contrary to his expectations, he finds that few issues are in need of resolution at an adversary hearing or trial. The defendant's guilt is not generally problematic; it is conceded by the defense attorney. What remains problematic is the sentence the defendant will receive.

Distinguishing among the Guilty Defendants

Formally, the prosecutor has some powers that bear directly on sentence. He has the option to reduce or eliminate charges leveled against the defendant; the responsibility for the indictment is his, and his alone. Thus, if he *nolles* some of the charges against the defendant, he can reduce the maximum exposure the defendant faces or ensure that the defendant is sentenced only on a misdemeanor (if he *nolles* a felony), and so forth. Beyond these actions on charges, the formal powers of the prosecutor cease. The judge is responsible for sentencing. He is supposed to decide the conditions of probation, the length of incarceration, and so on. Notwithstanding this formal dichotomy of responsibility, prosecutors find that defense attorneys approach them about both charge and sentence reduction.

Since charge reduction bears on sentence reduction, it is only a small step for defense attorneys to inquire specifically about sentence; and, because there is often an interdependence between charge and sentence, prosecutors are compelled at least to listen to the attorney's arguments. Thus, the prosecutor finds attorneys parading before him asking for charge and sentence reduction, and, in a sense, he is obligated to hear them out.

It is one thing to say that prosecutors and state's attorneys must listen to defense attorneys' requests about disposition and another to say that they must cooperate with these attorneys. As already indicated, new prosecutors feel acutely uneasy about charge and sentence reduction. They have neither the confidence nor the inclination to usurp what they view as primarily the judge's responsibility. Furthermore, one would think that their resolve not to become involved in this area would be strengthened by their learning that most defendants are factually and legally guilty. Why should they discuss dispositions in cases in which they "hold all the cards?"

This query presupposes that prosecutors continue to conceive of themselves as adversaries, whose exclusive task is to establish the defendant's guilt or innocence. But what happens is that as prosecutors gain greater experience handling cases, they gradually develop certain standards for evaluating cases, standards that bear not just on the defendant's guilt or innocence but, more importantly, on the disposition of the defendant's case. These standards better explain prosecutorial behavior in negotiating dispositions than does the simple notion of establishing guilt or innocence.

Specifically prosecutors come to distinguish between serious and nonserious cases, and between cases in which they are looking for time and cases in which they are not looking for time. These standards or distinctions evolve after the prosecutor has processed a substantial number of factually and legally guilty defendants. They provide a means of sorting the raw material—the guilty defendants. Indeed, one can argue that the adversary component of the prosecutor's job is shifted from establishing guilt or innocence to determining the seriousness of the defendant's guilt and whether he should receive time. The guilt of the defendant is assumed, but the problem of disposition remains to be informally argued.

Prosecutors and state's attorneys draw sharp distinctions between serious and nonserious cases. In both instances, they assume the defendant guilty, but they are looking for different types of dispositions, dependent upon their classification of the case. If it is a nonserious matter, they are amenable to defense requests for a small fine in the circuit court, some short, suspended sentence, or some brief period of probation; similarly, in a nonserious superior court matter the state's attorney is willing to work out a combination suspended sentence and probation. The central concern with these nonserious cases is to dispose of them quickly. If the defense attorney requests some sort of no-time disposition that is dependent upon either a prosecutorial reduction of charges or a sentence recommendation, the prosecutor and state's attorney are likely to agree. They have no incentive to refuse the attorney's request, since the attorney's desire comports with what they are "looking for." The case is simply not worth the effort to press for greater penalty.

On the other hand, if the case is serious, the prosecutor and state's attorney are likely to be looking for time. The serious case cannot be quickly disposed of by a no-time alternative. These are cases in which we would expect more involved and lengthy plea-bargaining negotiations.

Whether the case is viewed as serious or nonserious depends on factors other than the formal charges the defendant faces. For example, these nonformal considerations might include the degree of harm done the victim, the amount of violence employed by the defendant, the defendant's prior record, the characteristics of the victim and defendant, the defendant's motive; all are somewhat independent of formal charge, and yet all weigh heavily in the prosecutor's judgment of the seriousness of the case. Defendants facing the same formal charges, then, may find that prosecutors sort their cases into different categories. Two defendants charged with robbery with violence may find that in one instance the state's attorney is willing to reduce the charge and recommend probation, while in the second case he is looking for a substantial period of incarceration. In the former case, the defendant may have simply brushed against the victim (still technically robbery with violence), whereas in the second, he may have dealt the victim a severe blow. Or possibly, the first defendant was a junkie supporting his habit, whereas the second was operating on the profit motive. These are, of course, imperfect illustrations, but the point is that the determination as to whether a case is serious or not serious only partially reflects the charges against the defendant. Often the determination is based on a standard that develops with experience in the court and operates, for the most part, independently of formal statutory penalties.

The following excerpts convey a sense of the serious/nonserious dichotomy and also support the argument that charge does not necessarily indicate seriousness.

Q: How did you learn what cases were worth?

A: You mean sentences.

Q: Yeah.

A: Well, that's a hit-or-miss kind of an experience. You take a first offender; any first offender in a nonviolent crime certainly is not going to jail for a nonviolent crime. And a second offender, well, it depends again on the type of crime, and maybe there should be some supervision, some probation. And a third time, you say, well now this is a guy who maybe you should treat a little more strictly. Now, a violent crime, I would treat differently. How did I learn to? I learned because there were a few other guys around with experience, and I got experience, and they had good judgments, workable approaches, and you pick it up like that. In other words, you watch others, you talk to others, you handle a lot of cases yourself.

Q: Does anybody, the public, put pressure on you to be tougher?

A: Not really.

Q: Wouldn't these sentences be pretty difficult for the public to understand?

A: Yeah, somewhat. . . . Sure, we are pretty easy on a lot of these cases except that. . . . We are tough on mugging and crimes by violence. Say an old lady is grabbed by a kid and knocked to the ground and her pocketbook taken as she is waiting for the bus. We'd be as tough as anybody on that one, whether you call it a breach of peace or a robbery. We'd be very tough. And in this case there would be a good likelihood of the first offender going to jail, whatever the charge we give him. The name of the charge isn't important. We'd have the facts regardless.

Q: So you think you have changed? You give away more than you used to?

A: I don't give away more. I think that I have reached the point where. . . . When I started I was trying to be too fair, if you want to say that, you know, to see that justice was done, and I was severe. But, you know, like _____ [head prosecutor] says, you need to look for justice tempered with mercy, you know, substantial justice, and that's what I do now. When I was new, a guy cut [knifed] someone he had to go to jail. But now I look for substantial justice—if two guys have been drinking and one guy got cut, I'm not giving anything away, but a fine, that's enough there.

Q: But you are easier now? I mean, you could look for time?

A: Look, if I get a guy that I feel belongs in jail, I try to sentence bargain and get him in jail. We had this one guy, _____. He was charged with breach of peace. We knew he had been selling drugs but we couldn't prove anything. He hits this girl in _____'s parking lot [large department store], and tried to take her purse. She screams and he runs. This was a real son-of-a-bitch, been pimping for his own wife. On breach of peace I wanted the full year, and eventually got nine months. Cases like that I won't give an inch on. And the lawyer first wanted him to plead to suspended sentence and a money fine. I said this guy is a goddamned animal. Anybody who lets his wife screw and then gets proceeds from it, and deals in drugs . . . well, if you can catch the bastard on it, he belongs behind bars.

· · ·

The second standard used by prosecutors and state's attorneys in processing factually and legally guilty defendants is the time/no-time distinction. There is an obvious relationship between the serious/nonserious standard and this one: in the serious case time is generally the goal; whereas in the nonserious case, a no-time disposition is satisfactory to the prosecutor. But this simple relationship does not always hold, and it is important for us to consider the exceptions.

In some serious cases, the prosecutor or state's attorney may not be looking for time. Generally, these are cases in which the prosecutor has a problem establishing either the factual or legal guilt of the defendant, and thus is willing to settle for a plea to the charge and offer a recommendation of a suspended sentence. The logic is simple: the prosecutor feels the defendant is guilty of the offense but fears that if he insists on time, the defense attorney will go to trial and uncover the factual or legal defects of the state's case. Thus, the prosecutor "sweetens the deal" to extract a guilty plea and to decrease the likelihood that the attorney will gamble on complete vindication.

Of the prosecutors I interviewed, a handful expressed disenchantment with plea bargaining. They felt that their associates were being too lenient, giving away too much in return for the defendant's plea. They argued that the prosecutor's office should stay firm and go to trial if necessary in order to obtain higher sentences. They were personally inclined to act this way: they "didn't like plea bargaining." But when pushed a bit, it became clear that their antipathy to plea bargaining was not without its exceptions. In the serious case with factual or legal defects they felt very strongly that plea bargaining was appropriate. The sentiments of such an "opponent" to plea bargaining are presented below.

Q: So you are saying that you only like some kinds of plea bargaining?

A: I like to negotiate cases where I have a problem with the case. I know the guy is guilty, but I have some legal problem, or unavailability of a witness that the defendant doesn't know about that will make it difficult for us to put the case on. I would have trouble with the case. Then it is in my interest to bargain; even in serious cases with these problems, it is in the best interests of the state to get the guy to plead, even if it's to a felony with suspended sentence.

Q: If there was no plea bargaining, then the state would lose out?

A: Yes, in cases like these. These would be cases that without plea bargaining we would have trouble convicting the defendant. But this has nothing to do with the defendant's guilt or innocence. Yet we might have to let him go. It is just to plea bargain in cases like this. It is fair to get the plea from the defendant, since he is guilty. Now, there is another situation; whereas in the first situation, I have no philosophical problems with plea bargaining. We may have a weak case factually. Maybe the case depends on one witness, and I have talked to the witness and realized how the witness would appear in court. Maybe the witness would be a flop when he testifies. If I feel the defendant is guilty, but the witness is really bad, then I know that we won't win the case at trial, that we won't win a big concession in plea bargaining. So I will evaluate the case, and I will be predisposed to talking about a more lenient disposition.

• • •

The other unexpected cross between the standards—nonserious case/looking for time—occurs in several types of situations. First, there is the case in which the defendant has a long history of nonserious offenses, and it is felt that a short period of incarceration will "teach him a lesson," or at least indicate that there are limits beyond which prosecutors cannot be pushed. Second, there is the situation where the prosecutor holds the defense attorney in disdain and is determined to teach the attorney a lesson. Thus, though the defendant's offense is nonserious, the prosecutor would generally be amenable to a no-time disposition, the prosecutor chooses to hold firm. It is precisely in those borderline cases that the prosecutor can be most successful in exercising sanctions against the uncooperative defense attorney. The formal penalties associated with the charges against the defendant give him ample sentencing range, and by refusing to agree to a no-time disposition, the costs to the defense attorney become great. The attorney is not able to meet his client's demands for no time, and yet he must be leery about trial, given the even greater exposure the defendant faces. These borderline decisions by prosecutors, then, are fertile grounds for exploring sanctions against defense attorneys. It is here that we can expect the cooperative defense attorney to benefit most, and the recalcitrant defense attorney to suffer the most. Relatedly, one can also expect prosecutors to be looking for time in nonserious offenses in which the defendant or his counsel insists on raising motions and going to trial. These adversary activities may be just enough to tip the prosecutor into looking for time.

In addition to its relationship to the serious/nonserious standard, the time/no-time standard bears on prosecutorial plea-bargaining behavior in another way. As prosecutors gain experience in the plea-bargaining system, they tend to stress "certainty of time" rather than "amount of time." This is to say that they become less concerned about extracting maximum penalties from defendants and more concerned with ensuring that in cases in which they are looking for time, the defendant actually receives some time. Obviously, there are limits to the prosecutor's largesse—in a serious case thirty days will not be considered sufficient time. But prosecutors are willing to consider periods of incarceration substantially shorter than the maximum sentence allowable for a particular crime. In return, though, prosecutors want a guarantee of sorts that the defendant will receive time. They want to decrease the likelihood that the defendant, by some means or other, will obtain a suspended sentence. Thus, they will "take" a fixed amount of time if the defendant agrees not to try to "pitch" for a lower sentence, or if the defendant pleads to a charge in which all participants know some time will be meted out by the judge. In the latter instance, the attorney may be free to "pitch," but court personnel know his effort is more a charade for the defendant than a realistic effort to obtain a no-time disposition. The following excerpts illustrate prosecutorial willingness to trade off years of time for certainty of time.

> I don't believe in giving away things. In fact _____ [a public defender] approached me; there's this kid _____, he has two robberies, one first degree, one second, and three minor cases. Now, this kid, I made out an affidavit myself for tampering with a witness. This kid is just n.g. _____ came to me and said, "We'll plead out, two to five." He'll go to state's prison. I agreed to that—both these offenses are bindovers. These kids belong in jail. I'd rather take two to five here than bind them over to superior court and take a chance on what will happen there. At least my two to five will be a year and three-quarters in state's prison. The thing is, if I want to get a guy in jail for a year, I'll plea bargain with him, and I'll

take six months if I can get it, because the guy belongs in jail, and if I can get him to jail for six months why should I fool around with that case, and maybe get a year if I am lucky? If I can put a guy away for six months I might be cheated out of six months, but at least the guy is doing six months in jail.

What is a proper time? It never bothers me if we could have gotten seven years and instead we got five. In this case, there was no violence; minor stuff was stolen. We got time out of him. That is the important thing.

A: It makes no difference to me really if a man does five to ten or four to eight. The important thing is he's off the street, not a menace to society for a period of time, and the year or two less is not going to make that great a difference. If you do get time, I think it's . . . you know, many prosecutors I know feel this way. They have achieved confinement, that's what they're here for.

Q: Let's take another example. Yesterday an attorney walked in here when I was present on that gambling case. He asked you if it could be settled without time?

A: And I said no. That ended the discussion.

Q: What will he do now?

A: He'll file certain motions that he really doesn't have to file. All the facts of our case were spelled out; he knows as much about our cases as he'll ever know. So his motions will just delay things. There'll come a point, though, when he'll have to face trial; and he'll come in to speak with us, and ask if we still have the same position. We'll have the same position. We'll still be looking for one to three. His record goes back to 1923, he's served two or three terms for narcotics, and he's been fined five times for gambling. So we'd be looking for one to three and a fine. Even though he's in his sixties, he's been a criminal all his life, since 1923. . . .

Q: But if the attorney pushes and says, "Now look. He's an old guy. He's sixty two years old, how about six months?"

A: I might be inclined to accept it because, again, confinement would be involved. I think our ends would be met. It would show his compadres that there's no longer any immunity for gambling, that there is confinement involved. So the end result would be achieved.

Justice Holmes, who is supposed to be the big sage in American jurisprudence, said it isn't the extent of the punishment but the certainty of it. This is my basic philosophy. If the guy faces twelve years in state's prison, I'm satisfied if on a plea of guilty he'll go to state's prison for two or three years.

The experienced prosecutor, then, looks beyond the defendant's guilt when evaluating a case. He learns—from a reading of the file and from the defense attorney's entreaties—that most defendants are factually and legally guilty and that he generally holds the upper hand. As he gains experience in processing these cases, he gradually begins to draw distinctions within this pool of guilty defendants. Some of the cases appear not to be serious, and the prosecutor becomes willing to go along with the defense attorney's request for no-time dispositions. The cases simply do not warrant a firmer prosecutorial posture. In serious cases, when he feels time is in order, he often finds defense attorneys in agreement on the need for some incarceration.

In a sense, the prosecutor redefines his professional goals. He learns that the statutes fail to distinguish adequately among guilty defendants, that they "sweep too broadly," and give short shrift to the specific facts of the offense, to the defendant's prior record, to the degree of contributory culpability of the victim, and so on. Possessing more information about the defendant than the judge does, the prosecutor— probably unconsciously—comes to believe that it is his professional responsibility to develop standards that distinguish among defendants and lead to "equitable" dispositions. Over time, the prosecutor comes to feel that if he does not develop these standards, if he does not make these professional judgments, no one else will.

The prosecutor seems almost to drift into plea bargaining. When he begins his job he observes that his colleagues plea bargain routinely and quickly finds that defense attorneys expect him to do the same. Independent of any rewards, sanctions, or pressures, he learns the strengths of his cases, and learns to distinguish the serious from the nonserious ones. After an initial period of reluctance to plea bargain at all (he is fearful of being taken advantage of by defense attorneys), the prosecutor finds that he is engaged almost unwittingly in daily decisions concerning the disposition of cases. His obligation to consider alternative charges paves the way for the defense attorney's advances; it is only a small jump to move to sentence discussions. And as he plea bargains more and more cases, the serious/nonserious and time/no-time standards begin to hold sway in his judgments. He feels confident about the disposition he is looking for, and if a satisfactory plea bargain in line with his goals can be negotiated, he comes to feel that there is little point to following a more formal adversary process. . . .

Case Pressure and Potential Backlog

Though they may do so during the first few weeks, the newcomer's peers and superiors do not generally pressure him to move cases because of volume. Instead, he is thrust in the fray largely on his own and is allowed to work out his own style of case disposition. Contrary to the "conspiratorial perspective" of the adaptation process, he is not coerced to cooperate in processing "onerously large caseloads."

The newcomer's plea-bargaining behavior is conditioned by his reactions to particular cases he handles or learns about and not by caseload problems of the office. The chief prosecutor within the jurisdiction may worry about his court's volume and the speed with which cases are disposed, but he does not generally interfere with his assistant's decision about how to proceed in a case. The newcomer is left to learn about plea bargaining on his own, and for the reason already discussed, he learns and is taught the value of negotiating many of his cases. The absence of a direct relationship between prosecutor plea bargaining and case pressure is suggested in the following remarks.

Q: Is it case pressure that leads you to negotiate?

A: I don't believe it's the case pressure at all. In every court, whether there are five cases or one hundred cases, we should try to settle it. It's good for both sides. If I were a public defender I'd try to settle all the cases for my guilty clients. By negotiating you are bound to do better. Now take this case. [He reviewed the facts of a case in which an elderly man was charged with raping a seven-year-old girl. The defendant claimed he could not remember what happened, that he was drunk, and that, though the girl might have been in the bed with him, he did not think he raped her.] I think I gave the defense attorney a fair deal. The relatives say she was raped, but the doctor couldn't conclusively establish that. I offered him a plea to a lesser charge, one dealing with advances toward minors, but excluding the sex act. If he takes it, he'll be able to walk away with time served [the defendant had not posted bail and had spent several months in jail]. It's the defendant's option though. He can go through trial if he wants, but if he makes that choice, the kid and her relatives will have to be dragged through the agonies of trial also. Then I would be disposed to look for a higher sentence for the defendant. So I think my offer is fair, and the offer has nothing to do with the volume of this court. It's the way I think the case—all things considered—should be resolved.

Q: You say the docket wasn't as crowded in 1966, and yet there was plea bargaining. If I had begun this interview by saying why is there plea bargaining here. . . .

A: I couldn't use the reason there's plea bargaining because there are a lot of cases. That's not so; that's not so at all. If we had only ten cases down for tomorrow and an attorney walked in and wanted to discuss a case with me, I'd sit down and discuss it with him. In effect, that's plea bargaining. Whether it's for the charge or for an agreed recommendation or reduction of the charge or what have you, it's still plea bargaining. It's part of the process that has been going on for quite a long time.

Q: And you say it's not because of the crowded docket, but if I gave you a list of reasons for why there was plea bargaining and asked you to pick the most important. . . .

A: I never really thought about the. . . . You talk about the necessity for plea bargaining, and you say, well, it's necessary, and one of the reasons is because we have a crowded docket, but even if we didn't we still would plea bargain.

Q: Why?

A: Well, it has been working throughout the years, and the way I look at it, it's beneficial to the defendant, it's beneficial to the court, and not just in saving time but in avoiding police officers coming to court, witnesses being subpoenaed in, and usually things can be discussed between prosecutors and defense counsel which won't be said in the open court and on the record. There are many times that the defense counsel will speak confidentially with the prosecutor about his client or about the facts or about the complainant or a number of things. So I don't know if I can justify plea bargaining other than by speaking of the necessity of plea bargaining. If there were only ten cases down for one day, it still would be something that would be done.

Maybe in places like New York they plea bargain because of case pressure. I don't know. But here it is different. We dispose of cases on the basis of what is fair to both sides. You can get a fair settlement by plea bargaining. If you don't try to settle a case quickly, it gets stale. In New York the volume probably is so bad that it becomes a matter of "getting rid of cases." In Connecticut, we have some pretty big dockets in some cities, but in other areas—here, for example—we don't have that kind of pressure. Sure, I feel some pressure, but you can't say that we negotiate our cases out to clear the docket. And you probably can't say that even about the big cities in Connecticut either.

Prosecutors, then, do not view their propensity to plea bargain as a direct outcome of case pressure. Instead, they speak of "mutually satisfactory outcomes," "fair dispositions," "reducing police overcharging," and so on. We need not here evaluate their claims in detail; what is important is that collectively their arguments militate against according case pressure the "top billing" it so often receives in the literature.

Another way to conceptualize the relationship between case pressure and plea bargaining is to introduce the notion of a "potential backlog." Some prosecutors maintain that if fewer cases were plea bargained, or if plea bargaining were eliminated, a backlog of cases to be disposed of would quickly clog their calendars. A potential backlog, then, lurks as a possibility in every jurisdiction. Even in a low-volume jurisdiction, one complex trial could back up cases for weeks, or even months. If all those delayed cases also had to be tried, the prosecutor feels he would face two not-so-enviable options. He could become further backlogged by trying as many of them as was feasible, or he could reduce his backlog by outright dismissal of cases. The following comments are typical of the potential backlog argument.

Q: Some people have suggested that plea bargaining not be allowed in the court. All cases would go to trial before a judge or jury and. . . .

A: Something like that would double, triple, and quadruple the backlog. Reduce that 90 percent of people pleading guilty, and even if you were to try a bare minimum of those cases, you quadruple your backlog. It's feasible.

Well, right now we don't have a backlog. But if we were to try even 10 percent of our cases, take them to a jury, we'd be so backed up that we couldn't even move. We'd be very much in the position of. . . . Some traffic director in New York once said that there will come a time that there will be one car too many coming into New York and nobody will be able to move. Well, we can get ourselves into that kind of situation if we are going to go ahead and refuse to plea bargain even in the serious cases.

Though a potential backlog is an ever-present possibility, it should be stressed that most prosecutors develop this argument more as a prediction as to the outcome of a rule decreasing or eliminating plea bargaining than as an explanation for why they engage in plea bargaining. If plea bargaining were eliminated, a backlog would develop; but awareness of this outcome does not explain why they plea bargain.

Furthermore, prosecutors tend to view the very notion of eliminating plea bargaining as a fake issue, a straw-man proposition. It is simply inconceivable to them that plea bargaining could or would be eliminated. They maintain that no court system could try all of its cases, even if huge increases in personnel levels were made; trials consume more time than any realistic increase in personnel levels could manage. They were willing to speculate on the outcome of a rule proscribing plea bargaining, but the argument based on court backlog that they evoked was not a salient consideration in understanding their day-in, day-out plea-bargaining behavior.

It is, of course, impossible to refute with complete certainty an argument that prosecutors plea bargain because failure to do so would cause a backlog of unmanageable proportions to develop. However, the interviews indicate other more compelling ways to conceptualize prosecutorial adaptation to plea bargaining, and these do not depend on a potential backlog that always can be conjured up. Though the backlog may loom as a conquence of a failure to plea bargain, it—like its case pressure cousin—is neither a necessary nor sufficient explanatory vehicle for understanding the core aspects of prosecutorial plea-bargaining behavior.

A Perspective on Prosecutorial Adaptation

Perhaps the most important outcome of the prosecutor's adaptation is that he evidences a major shift in his own presumption about how to proceed with a case. As a newcomer, he feels it to be his responsibility to establish the defendant's guilt at trial, and he sees no need to justify a decision to go to trial. However, as he processes more and more cases, as he drifts into plea bargaining, and as he is taught the risks associated with trials, his own assumption about how to proceed with a case changes. He approaches every case with plea bargaining in mind, that is, he presumes that the case will be plea bargained. If it is a "nonserious" matter, he expects it to be quickly resolved; if it is "serious" he generally expects to negotiate time as part of the disposition. In both instances, he anticipates that the case will eventually be resolved by a negotiated disposition and not by a trial. When a plea bargain does not materialize, and the case goes to trial, the prosecutor feels compelled to justify his failure to reach an accord. He no longer is content to simply assert that it is the role of the prosecutor to establish the defendant's guilt at trial. This adversary component of the prosecutor's role has been replaced by a self-imposed burden to justify why he chose to go to trial, particularly if a certain conviction—and, for serious cases, a period of incarceration—could have been obtained by means of a negotiated disposition.

Relatedly, the prosecutor grows accustomed to the power he exercises in these plea-bargaining negotiations. As a newcomer, he argued that his job was to be an advocate for the state and that it was the judge's responsibility to sentence defendants. But, having in fact "sentenced" most of the defendants whose files he plea bargained, the distinction between prosecutor and judge becomes blurred in his own mind. Though he did not set out to usurp judicial prerogatives—indeed, he resisted efforts to engage him in the plea-bargaining process—he gradually comes to expect that he will exercise sentencing powers. There is no fixed point in time when he makes a calculated choice to become adjudicator as well as adversary. In a sense, it simply "happens"; the more cases he resolves (either by charge reduction or sentence recommendations), the greater the likelihood that he will lose sight of the distinction between the roles of judge and prosecutor.

11

Plea Bargaining and the Structure of the Criminal Process

Malcolm M. Feeley

Do plea bargaining and other accommodations in the system occur because of heavy caseloads, organizational influences, or limited resources? Malcolm Feeley views the criminal justice system at a higher level of analysis, pointing to historical, structural, and legal factors that he believes are the cause of increased plea bargaining. His thesis is that negotiation has increased in direct proportion to adversariness— precisely the opposite of what people think.

As a society we have high expectations for our courts, and when they are not met, as inevitably they will not be, we are disappointed. No doubt disappointment serves as an important stimulus for change, but it can also lead to exaggeration and misdiagnosis. An exaggerated sense of urgency can easily lead to misunderstanding and superficial analysis, lacking in perspective and context. In the concern with the practice of plea bargaining, something of this distortion has taken place. The result has been, I think, a misunderstanding of both the origins and nature of plea bargaining. This in turn has contributed to an inaccurate analysis of the operations of the courts and a downgrading of the magnitude and significance of changes in the adversary process in recent years. In general many so-called improvements, and indeed some of their seeming shortcomings, can also be seen as signs of strength. Plea bargaining is one such change.

We have been told time and time again within recent years that plea bargaining has reached epidemic proportions, that reliance on the guilty plea has all but displaced the traditional trial as the means for handling criminal cases. In a widely read book, Abraham Blumberg concludes that the defense attorney has shifted from being a fighter in behalf of his client to a "confidence man," whose primary function is to "manipulate the client and stage manage the case so that help and service at least appear to be rendered" (Blumberg 1967: 111). Blumberg sees in this shift the "twi-

Source: From *Justice System Journal* 7 (Winter 1982): 338–355. Reprinted by permission.

light of the adversary system" and the emergence of bureaucratic justice, where nominal adversaries—the prosecutor and the defense attorney—are bound together in a
common desire to maintain a smooth-functioning system. Organizational maintenance and financial self-interest, he argues, have replaced a concern with justice.
Hence the demise of the adversary process and the rise of plea bargaining, a device
which can *appear* to operate in the interests of the accused but in fact serves other
more salient organizational interests.

Blumberg is not alone in ascribing the demise of the adversary system to the
rise of plea bargaining. In what have quickly become classics, University of Colorado
law professor Albert Alschuler has examined plea bargaining from the perspectives
of the prosecutor, judge, and defense attorney (Alschuler 1968, 1975, 1976, 1979).
He concludes that from each of these views the prevailing incentive is one of institutional convenience and organizational maintenance rather than in the interests of
the accused and the concern with justice. What disturbs Alschuler most is the threat
(implicit or explicit) that the accused who exercises his right to trial and is convicted
will be sentenced more severely than one who pleads guilty. That such practices are
common few would seriously deny. Systematic studies of a number of courts all
indicate that the practice of offering "discounts" for guilty pleas—or conversely
penalties for trials—is common, although it is not always explicitly acknowledged
by court officials. Even where such penalties do not occur, court officials, defense
attorneys, and defendants clearly believe they do and act accordingly (Feeley 1979).

Prosecutors and judges agree with the scholars that plea bargaining has become
the primary means of securing conviction, but tend to be less critical of the practice.
Some see it as a necessary evil, a practical response to rising crime and limited
resources. Others view plea bargaining more positively, arguing that it introduces
flexibility into an otherwise rigid system. Despite some dramatic pronouncements
and much rhetoric, few practitioners seriously work to abolish the practice of plea
bargaining. Indeed, there seems to be a growing belief that plea bargaining is
inevitable.

My intention here is neither to defend the institution of plea bargaining nor to
challenge its critics. Rather it is to examine its antecedents, origins, practices, and
functions in light of the charge that it signifies a decline of the adversary process
and the rise of bureaucratic justice. Put bluntly, the charge against plea bargaining
is that it is a cooperative practice that has come to replace the combative trial, and
as such has reduced the vigor of the adversary process. This charge, if that is what
it is, is false. It is a charge unduly fettered by the constraints of organizational theory;
it lacks historical perspective and fails to place plea bargaining in broader structural
and social context.

My thesis here is that adversariness and negotiation are directly related. Plea
bargaining is not a cooperative practice that undermines or compromises the adversary process; rather, the opportunity for adversariness has expanded in direct proportion to, and perhaps as a result of, the growth of plea bargaining. As the requirements of due process have expanded, as resources have become more accessible to
both the prosecution and the criminally accused, as the substantive criminal law has
developed, and as the availability and role of defense counsel have expanded, the
opportunity for both adversariness and negotiations has increased. At first glance,
this thesis runs counter to most of the theoretical and practical discussions of the

criminal process. But when examined in historical perspective and seen in comparative context, the argument can be sustained.

This thesis does not so much purport to refute the findings of contemporary studies on or critics of plea bargaining as its means to build on them and place the process of plea bargaining in broader perspective and context. By identifying the importance of hitherto unrecognized or underrecognized factors shaping the institution of plea bargaining (and negotiation in the criminal process generally), I hope to broaden and correct the conventional understanding of plea bargaining that has risen in recent years.

Organizational Analysis and Plea Bargaining

One concern for students of formal organizations is the process by which the formal goals of an organization are displaced as a consequence of pressures to adapt to the larger environment, to serve the personal interests of its members, and to cope with scarce resources. This approach, which by now has become the conventional approach to studying criminal courts, accounts for plea bargaining in terms of goal displacement and adaptation (Nardulli 1979a). The frequent contact between defense attorneys and prosecutors fosters a tendency to replace formal adversarial roles with cooperative relationships. Others emphasize that the pressure to "produce" within the constraints of severely limited resources leads to the replacement of slow and deliberate formal practices with more expeditious forms of decision making. Thus plea bargaining comes to be understood as a consequence of these and related extralegal organizational factors.

This approach is not without considerable merit and insight. It has successfully challenged long-standing myths about the causes and consequences of plea bargaining. For instance, it has revealed dynamics that foster cooperation in a system that many feel should be conflictual (Skolnick 1967). It has challenged heavy caseloads and limited resources as the primary causes for plea bargaining. For instance, Heumann (1975, 1978), Feeley (1975, 1979), Nardulli (1979b), Rosett and Cressey (1976), and the Vera Institute (1981) have marshaled evidence suggesting that heavy caseloads are not necessarily the important causes of plea bargaining so many practitioners assert they are. Other studies anchored in organizational theory examine the incentive structures of the primary participants, and in doing so have shed considerable light on the ways courts operate, and on the functions of plea bargaining (Eisenstein and Jacob 1977; Nardulli 1978; Mather 1979; Utz 1978; Cole 1970). Some of these studies examined the important policy issue about the extent to which a defendant who exercises a right to trial is or is not penalized for exercising this right. Although the results of these investigations are mixed, and indeed different jurisdictions may follow different policies (Miller et al. 1978), these studies have provided useful theoretical insights into the operations of courts and contributed important data for the policy issues about the desirability and nature of plea bargaining. Above all, what these studies have shown is that factors fostering plea bargaining are not confined to a few unskilled lawyers, overworked prosecutors, or uncaring judges, but are part and parcel of the *structure* of the criminal court system itself. Both individual case studies (for example, Nardulli 1978; Mather 1979; Feeley 1979; Utz 1978) and ambitious comparative analyses (Miller et al. 1978) show that plea bargaining must be seen in a larger context, as only one facet of an elaborate structure of negotiation in the criminal courts. These insights go a long way to explain the findings of Church (1976), Heumann and Loftin (1979), Rubenstein and White (1979), and others who have found that when plea bargaining is "abolished" it usually reappears in slightly different forms elsewhere within the court system.

Although these and other related studies have made significant contributions in clarifying the nature and function of plea bargaining and the operations of the criminal courts in general, they have been most successful in debunking myths and cataloging the functions of plea bargaining. *But what the organizational approach does not and cannot easily explain is why the practice of plea bargaining grew up in the first place, and what legal, theoretical, and structural factors (as opposed to organizational functions) gave birth to and help sustain it.* The exigencies of the pressures on organizations with limited resources may help to explain the contemporary practice of plea bargaining in America, but these same factors cannot easily account for its rise in the first place. Nor do they account for the limitations of resources that in turn encourage such practices as plea bargaining. To pursue the full explanation for plea bargaining a historical and comparative perspective, examining practices in light of a host of social, doctrinal, and structural factors, is required.

A Broader Framework for Understanding Plea Bargaining

Below I sketch out a broader framework for understanding plea bargaining. This approach identifies the historical origins of plea bargaining in terms of the influence of legal doctrine and the formal legal process. My argument is that plea bargaining has become the standard method for securing convictions for a complex set of reasons that go well beyond limitations of resources. Indeed, I argue that it has been the increase in resources and opportunities that has in fact fostered the rise of plea bargaining. To sustain this thesis, I will first demonstrate the shortcoming of conventional discussions of the origins of plea bargaining by reviewing its history, and then I will turn to comment on five factors that together have fostered the rise and helped sustain the practice of plea bargaining. These factors are:

1. Plea bargaining in relation to the operative assumptions of the criminal process as it developed from a tradition of private prosecution
2. Plea bargaining in relation to changes in the substantive criminal law
3. Plea bargaining in relation to changes in criminal procedure
4. Plea bargaining in relation to the rise of full-time criminal court "professionals," specialists who replaced "amateur" officials who once staffed the court system
5. Plea bargaining in relation to the expansion of the availability of defense attorneys

Plea Bargaining in Historical Perspective

A cursory look at court records reveals that disposition by means of guilty pleas is a phenomenon of the late nineteenth and twentieth centuries. What little readily available evidence there is all points in the same direction. In 1928 Raymond Moley (1928) reported on his survey of dispositional practices of American criminal courts in the early part of this century. In the 1920s in New York City, guilty pleas accounted for 88 percent of all convictions, in Cleveland 86 percent, in Chicago 85 percent, in Des Moines 79 percent, and in Dallas 70 percent. Moley presented additional figures to show that these high rates of guilty pleas were not restricted to large or rapidly growing urban centers, but were found in less populated areas with less crowded courts as well. For instance, guilty pleas accounted for 91 percent of all convictions in rural upstate New York in the 1920s, a figure even higher than that for New York City during the same period (Moley 1928: 163–164). Similarly high figures were presented for other rural and less congested courts. Two recent studies of Connecticut reveal that while trial rates have fluctuated over the past ninety years, they have hovered around 10 percent throughout this period (Feeley 1975; Heumann 1975). These data suggest that plea bargaining—or at least the guilty plea—has a long history that predates the reported dramatic increase in crime and arrests of the past two or three decades.

Was there a time when trials were much more common? In a word, yes. Albert Alschuler reports that in the United States the guilty plea began to replace the trial as the dominant mode of disposition at around the time of the Civil War (Alschuler 1979). My own work with court records in New Haven, Connecticut, New York, and London's Old Bailey reinforces this impression. Analysis of these records is still under way, but the broad trends they reveal are instructive. In London's Central Criminal Court in the 1830s, trials accounted for over 95 percent of all dispositions. This figure steadily declined throughout the nineteenth and into the twentieth century. An even more pronounced pattern of decline is found in the United States. For instance, in Superior Court in New York City in 1846 only 28 percent of dispositions were by confessions; by 1860 this figure had risen to 47 percent; in 1890, it was 61 percent; and by 1919 it was 88 percent. A sample of criminal court records from New Haven, Connecticut, during roughly the same period reveals a similar shift: in 1837, 21 percent of my sample cases were disposed of by guilty pleas; in 1860, the figure was 50 percent; in 1888, it was 73 percent; in 1914, it was 91 percent; in 1934, it was 97 percent. There has been little room for increase since then. Furthermore, another pattern emerged in the late 1800s: the practice of changing initial pleas of not guilty to guilty, which were accompanied by the prosecutor's decision to drop one charge or more in a multiple-charge case. In 1873, this practice accounted for roughly one-half of all guilty pleas; by 1934 two-thirds of all guilty pleas involved switches of this nature, and of those who switched almost half involved pleas to lesser or fewer charges than they had originally faced. The only striking difference in disposition patterns since the 1930s has been the increased tendency to plead guilty to lesser or only some charges, a practice that clearly indicates *plea bargaining*.

What can we make of all this? Certainly these figures support Raymond Moley's 1928 argument, lamenting "our vanishing jury" (1928). And they appear to support the more recent contention that we are witnessing the "twilight of the adversary process," which is being replaced by a cooperative bureaucratic process that relies upon the guilty plea.

But let us penetrate the surface of these data and consider the *substance* of these processes. Once we do, the "decline" thesis loses much of its power. Indeed, it can be stood on its head.

Recall my original thesis. It was not that things have remained relatively constant, but that in fact the adversary process has become more vigorous in recent years and that plea bargaining is in fact an indicator of this vigor. To examine this argument we must go beyond rates of trial and inspect the *process* of court decision making more closely. Two issues concern us here. What were trials like in this earlier era when they were most frequent? And what is entailed in the modern process of pleading guilty?

First the trials. Lawrence Friedman and Robert Percival have sifted through the court files in Florida and California for the period around the turn of the century. While they found that there was an appreciably higher rate of trials at that time than there is today (although trials still constituted a distinct minority of dispositions), they proceeded to inquire into the nature of these trials. Let them describe what they found (Friedman and Percival 1981: 194).

> We have to ask, however, what kind of trial? Trial to most of us conjures up a definite image: a real courtroom battle, with two sides struggling like young stags and the judge acting as umpire, applying fair and honorable rules. Reality was quite different. In many places, the normal case was nasty and short. We examined the minute books of a Florida county from the 1890s. Here "trials" lasted a very short time, half an hour at most. A jury was hurriedly thrown together. Case after case paraded before them. The complaining witness told his story; sometimes another witness or two appeared; the defendant told his story, with or without witnesses; the lawyers (if any) spoke; the judge charged the jury. The jury retired, voted, and returned. Then the court went immediately into the next case on its list.

My own inspection of contemporary accounts on the trial process in London and New Haven, Connecticut, is equally revealing. Transcripts of the trial court proceedings in mid-nineteenth-century London reveal practices that are at odds with our image of the trial. Defendants were *not* represented by counsel; they did not confront hostile witnesses in any meaningful way; they rarely challenged evidence or offered defenses of any kind. Typically when they or occasionally someone in their behalf did take the witness stand, they requested mercy or offered only perfunctory excuses or defenses. Similar practices appear to have characterized trials in Connecticut during this same period as well.

Perhaps what is most revealing about their substance is the speed at which these early trials were conducted. The record of proceedings in London reveals that the same judge *and* jury would hear several cases per day with hardly a pause between them. Similarly, the New Haven court register indicates that the same judge and jury might handle several cases in a one- or two-day period; trial, deliberation, and sentencing could all occur within the span of an hour or two. It should be emphasized that these cases usually involved felonies and that substantial sentences were often involved.

Contemporary accounts flesh out still more the nature of the nineteenth-century trial. In all but the occasional celebrated cases, preparation was negligible. For all practical purposes, the courtroom and trial were the location and the event at which evidence and witnesses were gathered and examined *for the first time* by both the prosecutor and (when there was one) the defense attorney. Trials during this period must be understood as events where those centrally involved met for the first (and usually only) time to "muck about" with the available evidence in order to arrive at an immediate judgment.

This brief examination points to an inescapable conclusion: there was no golden era or "high noon" of the adversary process. To speak of the "twilight" of the adversary process is to foster a myth of a nonexistent past. When trials were once extensively relied upon, they were perfunctory affairs that bear but scant resemblance to contemporary trials, which while few and far between are often deliberate and painstaking affairs, at least as compared to what they once were. In a real sense, the very nature of what a trial is has undergone revolutionary changes to such an extent that comparisons across lengthy periods are not even meaningful.

Indeed it is my contention that when it was used with great frequency, the criminal trial was one of the very few devices available to the accused to try to protect his interests. That is, the trial was relied on extensively when criminal justice was administered in a rough way, often by "amateurs." During this time it served to protect the interests of a largely dependent accused. But as other institutions emerged to protect these interests, the significance and frequency of the trial declined. In brief, as the criminal process became more professionalized, as other opportunities for the defense expanded, the need to rely on the trial to protect the interests of the accused declined.

From this historical perspective, the ability to negotiate and bargain must be seen as an extension of or increase in adversariness. The very terms "negotiation" and "bargaining" imply some degree of parity between prosecution and defense, something that was often lacking in an earlier era when trials were more prevalent but an unrepresented defendant was more likely to be at the mercy of the court. While I do not want to argue that the process has shifted from a position of complete dependency to one of full equivalency, I do mean to argue that some movement in this direction has taken place and that this change can go a long way to accounting for the vanishing jury and the rise of plea bargaining. Several components of this thesis are examined below.

1. *Plea bargaining in relation to the operating assumptions and structure of the criminal process.* Criminal law has its roots in the law of torts, private wrongs pursued at the initiative of the aggrieved party. Although crimes are now offenses against the public, the criminal process retains residual practices of this earlier era. For instance, even today in England, the fiction remains that prosecutors are private parties acting in behalf of private complainants.

Even more important is another vestige of private prosecution. In the United States and England, the prosecutor in "public" criminal law has inherited the private complainant's discretion to bring or drop charges. Under both common and statutory law in the United States, the prosecutor's power to *nolle prosequi,* that is, to suspend prosecution, has remained intact and complete. Although there is some move toward judicial supervision of this function, legal controls are generally weak and American judges remain quite passive (Davis 1971; Goldstein 1981). The residue of this practice under the common law goes a long way toward explaining a *structure* that permits, if not encourages, plea bargaining.

The authority and discretion of the prosecutor has fostered a passivity on the part of the judiciary. Historically this has led to heavy reliance on confessions as sufficient to prove guilt. While confessions in capital cases and obtained under coercion have long been prohibited, freely made confessions in lesser cases have long been recognized if not encouraged by law and by the very structure of Anglo-American criminal process. For instance, a bifurcated court structure, which provides limited sentencing authority in lower courts, has long functioned on an inducement for the accused, if given the opportunity, to plead guilty in order to avoid exposure to harsher penalties that could be meted by a higher court (Langbein 1974; Vera Institute 1981; Feeley 1979).

In the United States, we find a long tradition of prosecutorial discretion, judicial passivity, and court structures with overlapping jurisdictions. While these factors alone do not explain plea bargaining, they do foster the practice by creating and legitimizing structures that invite it. It is interesting to note that in Germany, where plea bargaining is largely unknown, prosecutors do not have such discretionary authority and judges are much more active than their Anglo-American counterparts (Langbein 1974, 1979; Langbein and Weinreb 1978). More generally, see Damaska (1973), Weinreb (1977), Goldstein and Marcus (1977).

2. *Plea bargaining in relation to changes in the substantive law.* This century has witnessed a mushrooming of new criminal offenses and redefinitions of old ones. Not long ago criminal laws were brief statements written in broad language.

Today they are long; types of crimes are defined in minute detail and distinguished in several degrees. Plea bargaining can in part be accounted for by this change. Rather than falling under a single broad definition, any given incident of criminal conduct may now easily be defined as illegal in any of several ways or degrees. In short, we have an overdetermined system of law that invites the exercise of discretion and negotiation. Indeed, much of what is characterized as "plea bargaining" involves assessment or reassessment of the facts as they fit under various definitions or categories of offenses (Feeley 1979; Utz 1978). Because many of these fine-lined distinctions involve exposure to sentences of quite different lengths, the incentive to clarify them is obvious and important in a way and to a degree that it was not when there were simpler and more sweeping definitions of criminal offenses.

3. *Plea bargaining in relation to changes in criminal procedure.* Changes in the law of evidence and criminal procedure have paralleled developments in the substantive criminal law. The criminal trial is governed by more carefully constructed rules than its counterpart in the nineteenth century, and the criminally accused are today surrounded by many more procedural protections than they once were when trials were more common. Many of these new or newly enforced provisions come into play at the early stages of the criminal process. Probable cause hearings, bills of particulars, motions to suppress evidence, and the like, all shape the criminal process prior to trial and formal adjudication of guilt or innocence. In many cases, pre-

trial hearings—or for that matter negotiations in the shadow of the law—can become minitrials. Whether the early review of the evidence reveals a strong or weak case or whether the testimony of a particular witness or the introduction of a specific piece of evidence will or will not be admitted into the record can make or break a case, and depending on the conclusion reached, charges may be dropped, reduced, or the accused may plead guilty or take his case to trial. So, while we have witnessed the demise of the trial, we have at the same time experienced an increase in pretrial opportunities to review in adversarial context some of the same types of issues that once were *less* carefully considered by the jury at trial.

Similarly the rules for introducing evidence into trial have been refined and tightened since the mid-nineteenth century. While once the jury was expected to weigh the value of a vast amount of evidence, the modern tendency has been to screen out problematic information from the jury (presumably on the theory that it cannot recognize the possible weaknesses in the evidence). The objective has been to improve the trial process, to ensure fairness in decision making. But one consequence is that these refinements have placed increased importance on pretrial decision making and have made the trial more costly, more time-consuming, and perhaps more unpredictable. Although there are many other differences between American and European criminal justice systems, it is perhaps not surprising that on the Continent, where a larger proportion of cases are taken to trial, trial procedure and the rules of evidence are much simpler—as they once were in the United States when, here too, trials were more common. Thus, ironically, as the price for this quest for perfect justice has increased, so too has the incentive to avoid it. Plea bargaining is one such alternative.

4. *Plea bargaining in relation to the rise of full-time professionals.* Reports on the operations of the criminal justice system in the United States and England at the turn of the century and earlier reveal a time when trials were much more frequent than they are today. But they also describe practices that by today's standards are wanting. Frequently courts were staffed with part-time officers; often prosecutors and judges were not trained in the law (as most magistrates in England still are not). Typically, the accused was not represented by counsel of any sort. Police officers often acting as prosecutors in court were unfamiliar with the rudiments of the law and cared even less (Haller 1970, 1979). Admissibility of evidence was capricious; points of law were treated with casualness.

Historically, the modern trial by jury emerged when the criminal justice system was staffed by untrained amateurs who were charged with the task of trying to cope with the problem of accusing, trying and convicting, or acquitting someone. Presumably the public and collective nature of the proceedings and often the personal knowledge of the judge and jury compensated for the lack of training of officials and the simplicity of the proceedings.

Although trained professionals—judges, prosecutors, defense attorneys—have over the years assumed increasing importance in handling criminal cases in the courts, especially with major felony charges, it is only in a relatively recent past that courtrooms have routinely been staffed by law-trained specialists who devote substantial portions of their time to criminal matters. Universal representation by counsel of those accused of criminal charges and who cannot afford their own attorney has not yet been fully realized.

What we have witnessed in recent years is—in the most basic and obvious sense of the term—the professionalization of the court system. Part-time lay officials have been replaced by full-time officials, and in many instances lay officials have been replaced by law-trained specialists. The demise of the trial and the rise of plea bargaining has paralleled this development, and I am suggesting there is a connection.

Why? The modern trial by jury, as I have suggested, originated at a time when laypeople administered many of the positions in the criminal justice system and at a time when few resources were available and few rules governed pretrial and trial practices. The trial was the major focus and institution in this simplified process. It was usually the first time that the evidence was collectively considered. But as reliance on professionals with staffs has expanded, opportunities for considering issues, other than at trial, have also emerged. Ironically, the expanded use of defense counsel may have sounded the death knell for the trial. A defendant who might have once sat passively through a perfunctory trial without an attorney is now likely to be represented by counsel, who has an opportunity for early review of evidence and who may prefer to bargain under the shadow of the law than go to trial. Similarly, full-time prosecutors with staffs have replaced part-time and untrained police prosecutors, who earlier had replaced private prosecutors. They have the opportunity to scrutinize cases prior to trial in ways that once were largely unavailable. Thus, as trials have decreased, pretrial activities have assumed many of the functions that were once performed at trials themselves. And as professionals have replaced untrained laypeople, some of the benefits provided by trials have declined.

Let me summarize the essence of my argument about the impact of professionalism. The trial declined in the latter part of the nineteenth century (in both England and the United States) at roughly the same time the criminal process was undergoing a transformation from a lay-administered process to one dominated by legally trained, full-time professionals. (It should be noted also that in the United States this transformation took place during the same period that the modern university-associated law school was rapidly expanding, and more generally during a period when the modern professions were gaining in strength and prestige [Larson 1977].) During this same period both pretrial procedures and the rules of evidence expanded in number and complexity. These various rules were designed in large to structure and restrict the power to lay decision makers, but they had the effect of giving greater authority to lawyers who could then exercise their expertise prior to trial. And as resources earmarked for criminal justice expanded, these professional decision makers had increased opportunity and incentive to use the pretrial process. Ironically, if I am correct, if resources for prosecutors and defense attorneys are further increased, one might expect an increase in negotiations and a further decrease in trials—precisely the opposite of what is often assumed!

Still, there is a troublesome problem. If, as I contend, plea bargaining is the result of an expansion of adversariness, why is plea bargaining so often perceived as a sign of decline, decay, or demise of the adversary system? Why do the old days of frequent trials appear to be preferable to the bargained justice of today? Let me suggest two reasons. The first I have already alluded to—the romantic yearning for a nonexistent yesterday. But in fact trials of, say, the nineteenth century were perfunctory affairs, where meaningful defenses were rarely offered and the accused was often dependent on the court.

Second, discontent is inherent and is a by-product of the rise of professionalism in general (Freidson 1970). Even as it fosters valuable talents that serve useful functions, professionalism brings with it a distinctive set of problems. Because of his or her own monopoly on information, training, access, and language, there is the danger that the (professional) agent becomes the master. Professionals foster client dependence, which in turn breeds discontent and suspicion. Furthermore, the technical language of professionals fosters rapid communication among themselves that is not easily understood by their clients, and as such links them together in a way that alienates professionals from clients. This tension is common in all walks of professional life. Patients are suspicious of doctors, homeowners of architects, students of teachers, and the like, but it creates special strains in an adversarial setting.

The evils of plea bargaining are asserted more frequently than they are documented (although undoubtedly a great many of them are real and deplorable), and the explanation, in part, is due to a suspicion and discontent with professionals in general. Ironically much of the discontent with the rapid and seemingly perfunctory decision making in the criminal courts may be an inevitable by-product of the *increased* resources available to the accused rather than any decrease in standards, practices, or capacity.

5. *Plea bargaining and the rise of public defense services.* There is one particular feature of the rise of professionalism that merits special attention. It is the expanded role and availability of defense counsel. Until well into the nineteenth century in England, defense counsel had only a limited role in felony trials. They could help prepare a defense but could not appear at trial (Langbein and Weinreb 1978). Thus throughout much of the period during which the criminal trial emerged in its modern form, counsel for the accused was not allowed to take part. Although the theory on which this exclusion rested was relaxed and eventually rejected in the nineteenth century, the actual impact of these changes was evolutionary, because most criminally accused could not afford counsel. In the United States the first legal-aid societies were formed in the late nineteenth century as services provided by ethnic organizations to help newly arrived immigrants. During the twentieth century, provision of defense counsel for the poor has expanded, first on a volunteer basis, then in many jurisdictions by legislation, and finally as a matter of constitutional right. I think there is a link between the expansion of this resource for the defense and the decline of the trial.

A perusal of accounts of criminal court proceedings when trials were common reveals a process that is difficult for the contemporary observer to recognize: those accused of criminal offenses—misdemeanor or felony alike—were typically rushed through crowded and noisy courts [and] either subjected to a perfunctory trial lasting an hour or two or pressured to plead guilty by overbearing prosecutors whose practices were condoned by judges. All this took place without benefit of counsel. While expansion of the right to counsel has not provided all the benefits many had hoped for, the change has made a substantial difference in the ways criminal courts now operate. Current observers of American courts would be hard-pressed to find many of the practices that were commonplace when trials were more common. Seen from this perspective, the presence of an attorney who is able to *bargain* with the prosecutor constitutes something of a substantial increase in adversariness. The attorney's presence replaces intimidation with negotiation, domination with exchange. The very terms *negotiation* and *bargaining* imply that both the prosecutor and defense possess resources, a relationship that did not hold in a great many criminal cases when trials were more prevalent but the accused was more dependent. Even if defense attorneys do not pursue their tasks as vigorously as we would like, their collective presence and their familiarity with the courthouse all go a long way toward preventing the types of problems of dependence that once were commonplace. In this respect, whatever one thinks about plea bargaining, it is difficult to characterize it as ushering in the "twilight" of the adversary process. On the contrary, it appears to be a step toward a more evenly balanced relationship between the state and the accused, and as such it represents an increase not a decrease in adversariness.

Conclusion

My objective in this discussion is to demonstrate that plea bargaining has its roots in a host of often overlooked factors that are part and parcel of generally acknowledged improvements in the modern criminal process. That is, plea bargaining is a product of the very nature and structure of the modern criminal process rather than a result of extralegal factors or organizational pressures that have caused the criminal process to deviate from its true purposes. In elaborating this thesis, I do not mean to give the impression that I think plea bargaining is either inevitable or desirable. Indeed, I think it is neither. But I do want to emphasize that the factors that give rise to plea bargaining are intertwined with a host of factors that are generally regarded as highly desirable. In our quest for perfect justice, we have constructed an elaborate and costly criminal process. When this reality confronts the long-standing discretion granted to prosecutors, plea bargaining emerges. I do not believe that plea bargaining can be eliminated or even substantially reduced over the long run, without either significantly restricting prosecutors' discretion or relaxing the rigorous standards that currently infuse the criminal process. Despite a great deal of opposition to the practice of plea bargaining, I see little support for either type of these fundamental changes. More generally, the policy debate over plea bargaining has all too often taken place in a vacuum, neither placing bargaining in a broad perspective nor seriously contemplating the nature and implications of a criminal process that could handle cases expeditiously in the absence of plea bargaining. Nor, as I suggested at the outset, has plea bargaining been treated as part of a broader process of negotiation that permeates the entire criminal process. This no doubt goes a long way in explaining why so many policies banning plea bargaining have had such short lives.

References

ALSCHULER, ALBERT W. (1968). "The Prosecutor's Role in Plea Bargaining." 36 *University of Chicago Law Review* 50.

———— (1975). "The Defense Attorney's Role in Plea Bargaining." 84 *Yale Law Journal* 1179.

———— (1976). "The Trial Judge's Role in Plea Bargaining." 76 *Columbia Law Review* 1059.

———— (1979). "Plea Bargaining and Its History." 13 *Law and Society Review* 211.

BLUMBERG, ABRAHAM (1967). *Criminal Justice.* New York: Quadrangle.

CHURCH, THOMAS, JR. (1976). "Plea Bargains, Concessions and the Courts: Analysis of a Quasi-Experiment." 10 *Law and Society Review* 377.

COLE, GEORGE (1970). "The Decision to Prosecute." 4 *Law and Society Review* 331.

DAMASKA, MIRJAN (1973). "Evidentiary Barriers to Conviction and Two Models of Criminal Procedure: A Contemporary Study." 121 *University of Pennsylvania Law Review* 506.

DAVIS, KENNETH CULP (1971). *Discretionary Justice: A Preliminary Inquiry.* Urbana: University of Illinois Press.

DAVIS, WILLIAM, II (1974). "*Nolle Prosequi* in the Sixth Circuit Court: Prosecutor Discretion to Dispense with Charge." Paper on file at the Yale Law Library.

EISENBERG, MELVIN A. (1976). "Private Ordering Through Negotiation: Dispute Settlement and Rule Making." 89 *Harvard Law Review* 376.

EISENSTEIN, JAMES, AND HERBERT JACOB (1977). *Felony Justice.* Boston: Little, Brown.

FEELEY, MALCOLM M. (1975). "The Effects of Heavy Caseloads." Paper presented at the annual conference of the American Political Science Association.

———— (1979). *The Process Is the Punishment: Handling Cases in a Lower Criminal Court.* New York: Russell Sage Foundation.

FLEMING, MACKLIN (1974). *The Price of Perfect Justice.* New York: Basic Books.

FRIEDMAN, LAWRENCE (1979). "Plea Bargaining in Historical Perspective." 13 *Law and Society Review* 247.

FRIEDMAN, LAWRENCE M., AND ROBERT V. PERCIVAL (1981). *The Roots of Justice: Crime and Punishment in Alameda County, California 1870–1910.* Chapel Hill: University of North Carolina Press.

FRIEDSON, ELIOT (1970). *Professional Dominance.* Chicago: Aldine Publishing Co.

GOLDSTEIN, ABRAHAM S. (1981). *The Passive Judiciary.* Baton Rouge: Louisiana State University Press.

————, AND MARTIN MARCUS (1977). "The Myth of Judicial Supervision in Three 'Inquisitorial' Systems: France, Italy and Germany." 87 *Yale Law Journal* 240.

HALLER, MARK (1970). "Urban Crime and Criminal Justice: The Chicago Case." 57 *Journal of American History* 619.

———— (1978). *Plea Bargaining: The Experiences of Prosecutors, Judges, and Defense Attorneys.* Chicago: University of Chicago Press.

———— (1979). "Comment: Urban Courts." 13 *Law and Society Review* 273.

HEUMANN, MILTON (1975). "A Note on Plea Bargaining and Case Pressure." 9 *Law and Society Review* 515.

————, AND COLIN LOFTIN (1979). "Mandatory Sentencing and Abolition of Plea Bargaining: The Michigan Felony Firearms Statute." 13 *Law and Society Review* 373.

LANGBEIN, JOHN H. (1974a). "Controlling Prosecutorial Discretion in Germany." 41 *University of Chicago Law Review* 445.

———— (1974b). *Prosecuting Crime in the Renaissance: England, Germany, and France.* Cambridge, Mass.: Harvard University Press.

———— (1978). "The Criminal Trial before the Lawyers." 45 *University of Chicago Law Review* 263.

———— (1979). "Land without Plea Bargaining: How the Germans Do It." 78 *Michigan Law Review* 204.

————, AND LLOYD WEINREB (1978). "Continental Criminal Procedure: Myth and Reality." 87 *Yale Law Journal* 1549.

LARSON, MAGALI S. (1977). *The Rise of Professionalism: A Sociological Analysis.* Berkeley: University of California Press.

MATHER, LYNN (1979). *Plea Bargaining or Trial.* Lexington, Mass.: Lexington Books.

MILLER, HERBERT S., WILLIAM F. McDONALD, AND JAMES A. CRAMER (1978). *Plea Bargaining in the United States.* Washington, D.C.: National Institute of Justice.

MOLEY, RAYMOND (1928). "The Vanishing Trial Jury." 2 *Southern California Law Review* 97.

NARDULLI, PETER (1978). *The Courtroom Elite.* Cambridge, Mass.: Ballinger Publishing Co.

———— (ed.) (1979a). *The Study of Criminal Courts: Political Perspectives.* Cambridge, Mass.: Ballinger Publishing Co.

———— (1979b). "The Caseload Controversy and the Study of Criminal Courts." 70 *Journal of Criminal Law and Criminology* 125.

ROSETT, ARTHUR, AND DONALD CRESSEY (1976). *Justice by Consent.* Philadelphia: Lippincott.

RUBENSTEIN, MICHAEL, AND TERRESSA WHITE (1979). "Plea Bargaining: The Alaska Experience." 13 *Law and Society Review* 367.

SKOLNICK, JEROME (1967). "Social Control in the Adversary System." 11 *Journal of Conflict Resolution* 52.

UTZ, PAMELA (1978). *Settling the Facts.* Lexington, Mass.: Lexington Books.

VERA INSTITUTE (1981). *Felony Arrests: Their Prosecution and Disposition in New York City.* Rev. ed. New York: Longman.

WEINREB, LLOYD (1977). *Denial of Justice.* New York: Free Press.

PART FOUR

Defense Attorneys

Criminal lawyers have traditionally been caught between divergent conceptions of their position. On the one hand, defense attorneys are viewed as "Perry Masons," involved in a constant searching and creative questioning of official decisions at all stages of the justice process. On the other hand, they are seen as somehow "soiled" by their clients, engaged in shady practices to free clients who have committed crimes from the rightful demands of the law. Although Perry Mason remains a hero, the public retains the more tarnished image.

The public's assumption probably accurately reflects the lifestyles of many lawyers engaged in criminal practice in large urban areas. In the vicinity of many metropolitan courthouses, one can find the offices of those who are called the "Fifth Streeters" in the District of Columbia and the "Clinton Street Bar" in Detroit. These terms refer to attorneys who prowl criminal courts in search of clients who can pay a modest fee. Some have referral arrangements with police officers, bondsmen, and other minor officials. Rather than prepare cases for disposition through the adversary process, these lawyers negotiate guilty pleas and try to convince their clients that they received exceptional treatment. Such lawyers are not true professionals; they act as fixers for a fee. They exist in a relatively closed system where there are great pressures to process large numbers of cases for small fees, and they are dependent on the cooperation of judicial officials. This small group of practitioners is usually less well educated, works harder, and is in a more precarious financial situation than peers in corporate practice.

A number of nationally known attorneys, such as Melvin Belli, F. Lee Bailey, and Gerry Spence, have built reputations by adhering to the Perry Mason model, but these counselors are few and expensive. They usually take only dramatic, widely publicized cases; they are rarely found at the county courthouse. Between the polar types of a Melvin Belli and a "Fifth Streeter" are many general practitioners who sometimes take criminal cases but have little experience in trial work and do not have well-developed relationships with actors in the criminal justice system. Lacking inside knowledge, they may find that a client would be better served if a courtroom regular took the case.

With increased specialization and institutionalization of the bar, individuals engaged in the practice of criminal law seem to have been assigned a lower status, both by other lawyers and by the community at large. In addition, the unpleasant aspects of criminal law practice are not offset by monetary inducements. Criminal cases, as well as those concerned with matrimonial problems, tend to involve lawyers in emotional situations. Most services they render involve preparing defendants and their relatives for the possible outcome. The lawyer must share the client's troubles. Even exposure to "guilty knowledge" may be a psychological burden. Criminal lawyers are also called on to interact continuously with a lower class of clients and with police officials and minor political appointees. They may have to visit such depressing places as the local jail at all hours of the day or night. After winning a case, they may be unable to collect their fee. Research shows that the financial aspect is the key variable, influencing most other aspects of criminal practice. The vast majority of criminal defendants are poor and plead guilty.

Defense of Indigents

Most criminal defendants come to court without lawyers of their own. Because the U.S. Supreme Court has ruled that a defendant may not be sent to prison unless he or she has been represented by counsel, the court usually appoints a public defender or private attorney in cases of indigency. Research has shown that more than 50 percent of defendants in rural areas and up to 92 percent of defendants in urban areas are provided with counsel by government.

In the United States there are three basic ways of providing indigent defendants with counsel: (1) through assigned counsel, in which the attorney is appointed by the court to represent a particular defendant; (2) through the contract system, under which the government has an arrangement with an individual law firm or private attorney to handle cases on a fixed-price basis; and (3) through a defender system, in which a salaried public attorney is counsel for indigents. Although the defender system is growing rapidly, 1,833 counties (60 percent) still use the assigned counsel system, and 6 percent contract for defender services. The public defender system is the dominant form in forty-three of the fifty most populous counties, however, and such programs serve 70 percent of the U.S. population.

Defense Counsel in the Exchange Process

In a judicial system where bargaining within an administrative context is a primary decision-making method, it is not surprising that defense attorneys find it essential to have close personal ties with the police, prosecutor, and other court officials. Their own professional survival and the opportunity to serve clients' needs may depend on establishing and maintaining relations with these actors. At each point in the criminal process, from the first contact with the accused until the final disposition of the case, the defense attorney is dependent on decisions made by other judicial actors. Even such seemingly minor activities as visiting the defendant in jail, learning from the prosecutor what the case against the defendant is, and setting bail can be made difficult by the officials involved unless there is cooperation from the defense attorney. Concern with preserving these relationships within the criminal justice system may have greater weight for defense attorneys than any short-term interest in particular clients.

Counsel is not completely at the mercy of judicial actors. At any phase, the defense has the ability to invoke the adversary model, with its formal rules and public battles. The potential for an expensive, time-consuming, and disputatious trial can be used by the effective counsel as a bargaining tool with the police, prosecutor, and judge. A well-known tactic of defense attorneys, certain to raise the ante in the bargaining process, is to ask for a trial and to proceed as if they meant it. However, because judicial personnel must interact on a continuing basis, they try to make sure that personal relationships are cordial. The introduction of adversary tactics is disruptive, so potential animosities are tempered for the benefit of the participants. The defendant passes through the system; the others involved in the case must meet again.

Suggestions for Further Reading

BAILEY, F. LEE. *The Defense Never Rests.* New York: Stein & Day, 1971. One of the best-known criminal defense specialists in the United States describes his work, featuring some of the famous cases he has won.

LEWIS, ANTHONY. *Gideon's Trumpet.* New York: Vintage, 1964. A vivid account of the case of Clarence Gideon and the opinion of the U.S. Supreme Court requiring appointment of counsel for indigents in criminal prosecutions.

MCDONALD, WILLIAM R., ed. *The Defense Counsel.* Newbury Park, Calif.: Sage Publications, 1983. A collection of outstanding articles by social scientists and lawyers on the role of defense counsel in criminal cases.

WICE, PAUL. *Criminal Lawyers: An Endangered Species.* Newbury Park, Calif.: Sage Publications, 1978. Of 400,000 lawyers in the United States, only about 15,000 accept criminal cases on more than an occasional basis. Some 4,000 of these are public defenders. Wice's national study of the private criminal bar found that the quality of these attorneys varied from city to city, with legal, institutional, and political factors accounting for much of the variation.

WISHMAN, SEYMOUR. *Confessions of a Criminal Lawyer.* New York: Times Books, 1981. As the title indicates, the author describes his life as a criminal lawyer and raises questions about the ethics of some tactics he used to secure acquittals.

12

The Practice of Law as a Confidence Game: Organization Co-Optation of a Profession

Abraham S. Blumberg

Central to the adversary system is the defense attorney, who will engage the pros-ecution in a "fight" to ensure that the defendant's rights are protected and that the case is presented to the judge and jury in the best possible light. What happens when the professional environment of the criminal lawyer moderates the adversarial stance? Bargain justice occurs when it is believed to be in the best interests of both the prosecutor and the defense attorney to avoid the courtroom confrontation. Abra-ham Blumberg argues that the defense attorney acts as a double agent, to get the defendant to plead guilty.

A recurring theme in the growing dialogue between sociology and law has been the great need for a joint effort of the two disciplines to illuminate urgent social and legal issues. Having uttered fervent public pronouncements in this vein, however, the respective practitioners often go their separate ways. Academic spokesmen for the legal profession are somewhat critical of sociologists of law because of what they perceive as the sociologist's preoccupation with the application of theory and meth-odology to the examination of legal phenomena, without regard to the solution of legal problems. Further, it is felt that "contemporary writing in the sociology of law ... betrays the existence of painfully unsophisticated notions about the day-to-day operations of courts, legislatures, and law offices." Regardless of the merit of such criticism, scant attention—apart from explorations of the legal profession itself— has been given to the sociological examination of legal institutions, or their sup-porting ideological assumptions. Thus, for example, very little sociological effort is expended to ascertain the validity and viability of important court decisions, which may rest on wholly erroneous assumptions about the contextual realities of social structure. A particular decision may rest upon a legally impeccable rationale; at the same time it may be rendered nugatory or self-defeating by contingencies imposed by aspects of social reality of which the lawmakers are themselves unaware.

Source: From *Law and Society Review* 1 (June 1967): 15–39. Reprinted by per-mission of the Law and Society Association.

Within this context, I wish to question the impact of three recent landmark decisions of the United States Supreme Court, each hailed as destined to effect profound changes in the future of criminal law administration and enforcement in America. The first of these, *Gideon* v. *Wainwright,* 372 U.S. 335 (1963), required states and localities henceforth to furnish counsel in the case of indigent persons charged with a felony. The *Gideon* ruling left several major issues unsettled, among them the vital question: What is the precise point in time at which a suspect is entitled to counsel? The answer came relatively quickly in *Escobedo* v. *Illinois,* 378 U.S. 478 (1964), which has aroused a storm of controversy. Danny Escobedo confessed to the murder of his brother-in-law after the police had refused to permit retained counsel to see him, although his lawyer was present in the station house and asked to confer with his client. In a 5 to 4 decision, the court asserted that counsel must be permitted when the process of police investigative effort shifts from merely investigatory to that of accusatory: "when its focus is on the accused and its purpose is to elicit a confession—our adversary system begins to operate, and, under the circumstances here, the accused must be permitted to consult with his lawyer."

As a consequence, Escobedo's confession was rendered inadmissible. The decision triggered a national debate among police, district attorneys, judges, lawyers, and other law-enforcement officials, which continues unabated, as to the value and propriety of confessions in criminal cases. On June 13, 1966, the Supreme Court in a 5 to 4 decision underscored the principle enunciated in *Escobedo* in the case of *Miranda* v. *Arizona.* Police interrogation of any suspect in custody, without his consent, unless a defense attorney is present, is prohibited by the self-incrimination provision of the Fifth Amendment. Regardless of the relative merit of the various shades of opinion about the role of counsel in criminal cases, the issues generated thereby will be in part resolved as additional cases move toward decision in the Supreme Court in the near future. They are of peripheral interest and not of immediate concern in this paper. However, the *Gideon, Escobedo,* and *Miranda* cases pose interesting general questions. In all three decisions, the Supreme Court reiterates the traditional legal conception of a defense lawyer based on the ideological perception of a criminal case as an *adversary, combative* proceeding, in which counsel for the defense assiduously musters all the admittedly limited resources at his command to *defend* the accused. The fundamental question remains to be answered: Does the Supreme Court's conception of the role of counsel in a criminal case square with social reality?

The task of this paper is to furnish some preliminary evidence toward the illumination of that question. Little empirical understanding of the function of defense counsel exists; only some ideologically oriented generalizations and commitments. This paper is based upon observations made by the writer during many years of legal practice in the criminal courts of a large metropolitan area. No claim is made as to its methodological rigor, although it does reflect a conscious and sustained effort for participant observation.

• • •

Court Structure Defines Role of Defense Lawyer

The overwhelming majority of convictions in criminal cases (usually over 90 percent) are not the product of a combative, trial-by-jury process at all, but instead merely involve the sentencing of the individual after a negotiated, bargained-for plea of guilty has been entered. Although more recently the overzealous role of police and prosecutors in producing pretrial confessions and admissions has achieved a good deal of notoriety, scant attention has been paid to the organizational structure and personnel of the criminal court itself. Indeed, the extremely high conviction rate produced without the features of an adversary trial in our courts would tend to suggest that the "trial" becomes a perfunctory reiteration and validation of the pretrial interrogation and investigation.

The institutional setting of the court defines a role for the defense counsel in a criminal case radically different from the one traditionally depicted. Sociologists and others have focused their attention on the deprivations and social disabilities of such variables as race, ethnicity, and social class as being the source of an accused person's defeat in a criminal court. Largely overlooked is the variable of the court organization itself, which possesses a thrust, purpose, and direction of its own. It is grounded in pragmatic values, bureaucratic priorities, and administrative instruments. These exalt maximum production and the particularistic career designs of organizational incumbents, whose occupational and career commitments tend to generate a set of priorities. These priorities exert a higher claim than the stated ideological goals of "due process of law," and are often inconsistent with them.

Organizational goals and discipline impose a set of demands and conditions of practice on the respective professions in the criminal court to which they respond by abandoning their ideological and professional commitments to the accused client, in the service of these higher claims of the court organization. All court personnel, including the accused's own lawyer, tend to be co-opted to become agent-mediators who help the accused redefine his situation and restructure his perceptions concomitant with a plea of guilty.

Of all the occupational roles in the court, the only private individual who is officially recognized as having a special status and concomitant obligations is the lawyer. His legal status is that of "an officer of the court" and he is held to a standard of ethical performance and duty to his client as well as to the court. This obligation is thought to be far higher than that expected of ordinary individuals occupying the various occupational statuses in the court community. However, lawyers, whether privately retained or of the legal-aid, public defender variety, have close and continuing relations with the prosecuting office and the court itself through discreet relations with the judges via their law secretaries or "confidential" assistants. Indeed, lines of communication, influence, and contact with those offices, as well as with the Office of the Clerk of the Court, the Probation Division, and the press, are essential to present and prospective requirements of criminal law practice. Similarly, the subtle involvement of the press and other mass media in the court's organizational network is not readily discernible to the casual observer. Accused persons come and go in the court system schema, but the structure and its occupational incumbents remain to carry on their respective career, occupational, and organizational enterprises. The individual stridencies, tensions, and conflicts a given accused person's case may present to all the participants are overcome, because the formal and informal relations of all the groups in the court setting require it. The probability of continued future relations and interaction must be preserved at all costs.

This is particularly true of the "lawyer regulars"—that is, those defense lawyers, who by virtue of their continuous appearances in behalf of defendants, tend to represent the bulk of a criminal court's nonindigent case work load, and those law-yers who are not "regulars," who appear almost casually in behalf of an occasional client. Some of the lawyer "regulars" are highly visible as one moves about the major urban centers of the nation; their offices line the back streets of the court-houses, at times sharing space with bondsmen. Their political "visibility" in terms of local clubhouse ties, reaching into the judge's chambers and the prosecutor's office, is also deemed essential to successful practitioners. Previous research has indi-cated that the "lawyer regulars" make no effort to conceal their dependence upon police, bondsmen, and jail personnel. Nor do they conceal the necessity for main-taining intimate relations with all levels of personnel in the court setting as a means of obtaining, maintaining, and building their practice. These informal relations are the *sine qua non* not only of retaining a practice but also in the negotiation of pleas and sentences.

The client, then, is a secondary figure in the court system as in certain other bureaucratic settings. He becomes a means to other ends of the organization's incum-bents. He may present doubts, contingencies, and pressures which challenge existing informal arrangements or disrupt them; but these tend to be resolved in favor of the continuance of the organization and its relations as before. There is a greater com-munity of interest among all the principal organizational structures and their incum-bents than exists elsewhere in other settings. The accused's lawyer has far greater professional, economic, intellectual, and other ties to the various elements of the court system than he does to his own client. In short, the court is a closed community.

This is more than just the case of the usual "secrets" of bureaucracy which are fanatically defended from an outside view. Even all elements of the press are zeal-ously determined to report on that which will not offend the board of judges, the prosecutor, and probation, legal-aid, or other officials, in return for privileges and courtesies granted in the past and to be granted in the future. Rather than any view of the matter in terms of some variation of a "conspiracy" hypothesis, the simple explanation is one of an ongoing system handling delicate tensions, managing the trauma produced by law enforcement and administration, and requiring almost path-ological distrust of "outsiders" bordering on group paranoia.

The hostile attitude toward "outsiders" is in large measure engendered by a defensiveness itself produced by the inherent deficiencies of assembly-line justice, so characteristic of our major criminal courts. Intolerably large caseloads of defen-dants, which must be disposed of in an organizational context of limited resources and personnel, potentially subject the participants in the court community to harsh scrutiny from appellate courts and other public and private sources of condemnation. As a consequence, an almost irreconcilable conflict is posed in terms of intense pres-sures to process large numbers of cases, on the one hand, and the stringent ideolog-ical and legal requirements of "due process of law," on the other hand. A rather tenuous resolution of the dilemma has emerged in the shape of a large variety of bureaucratically ordained and controlled "work crimes," shortcuts, deviations, and outright rule violations adopted as court practice in order to meet production norms. Fearfully anticipating criticism on ethical as well as legal grounds, all the significant participants in the court's social structure are bound into an organized system of complicity. This consists of a work arrangement in which the patterned, covert, infor-mal breaches and evasions of "due process" are institutionalized but are, neverthe-less, denied to exist.

These institutionalized evasions will be found to occur to some degree in all criminal courts. Their nature, scope, and complexity are largely determined by the size of the court and the character of the community in which it is located—for example, whether it is a large, urban institution or a relatively small rural county court. In addition, idiosyncratic, local conditions may contribute to a unique flavor in the character and quality of the criminal law's administration in a particular community. However, in most instances a variety of stratagems are employed—some subtle, some crude, ineffectively disposing of what are often too-large caseloads. A wide variety of coercive devices are employed against an accused client, couched in a depersonalized, instrumental, bureaucratic version of due process of law, and which are in reality a perfunctory obeisance to the ideology of due process. These include some very explicit pressures which are exerted in some measure by all court personnel, including judges, to plead guilty and avoid trial. In many instances the sanction of a potentially harsh sentence is utilized as the visible alternative to pleading guilty, in the case of recalcitrants. Probation and psychiatric reports are "tailored" to organizational needs, or are at least responsive to the court organization's requirements for the refurbishment of a defendant's social biography, consonant with his new status. A resourceful judge can, through his subtle domination of the proceedings, impose his will on the final outcome of a trial. Stenographers and clerks, in their function as record keepers, are on occasion pressed into service in support of a judicial need to "rewrite" the record of a courtroom event. Bail practices are usually employed for purposes other than simply assuring a defendant's presence on the date of a hearing in connection with his case. Too often, the discretionary power as to bail is part of the arsenal of weapons available to collapse the resistance of an accused person. The foregoing is a most cursory examination of some of the more prominent "shortcuts" available to any court organization. There are numerous other procedural strategies constituting due process deviations, which tend to become the work-style artifacts of a court's personnel. Thus, only court "regulars" who are "bound in" are really accepted; others are treated routinely and in almost a coldly correct manner.

The defense attorneys, therefore, whether of the legal-aid, public defender variety or privately retained, although operating in terms of pressures specific to their respective role and organizational obligations, ultimately are concerned with strategies which tend to lead to a plea. It is the rational, impersonal elements involving economies of time, labor, expense, and a superior commitment of the defense counsel to these rationalistic values of maximum production of court organization that prevail in his relationship with a client. The lawyer "regulars" are frequently former staff members of the prosecutor's office and utilize the prestige, know-how, and contacts of their former affiliation as part of their stock-in-trade. Close and continuing relations between the lawyer "regular" and his former colleagues in the prosecutor's office generally overshadow the relationship between the regular and his client. The continuing colleagueship of supposedly adversary counsel rests on real professional and organizational needs of a *quid pro quo,* which goes beyond the limits of an accommodation or *modus vivendi* one might ordinarily expect under the circumstances of an otherwise seemingly adversary relationship. Indeed, the adversary features which are manifest are for the most part muted and exist even in their attenuated form largely for external consumption. The principals, lawyer and assistant district attorney, rely upon one another's cooperation for their continued professional existence, and so the bargaining between them tends usually to be "reasonable" rather than fierce.

Fee Collection and Fixing

The real key to understanding the role of defense counsel in a criminal case is to be found in the area of the fixing of the fee to be charged and its collection. The problem of fixing and collecting the fee tends to influence to a significant degree the criminal court process itself, and not just the relationship of the lawyer and his client. In essence, a lawyer–client "confidence game" is played. A true confidence game is unlike the case of the emperor's new clothes wherein that monarch's nakedness was a result of inordinate gullibility and credulity. In a genuine confidence game, the perpetrator manipulates the basic dishonesty of his partner, the victim or mark, toward his own (the confidence operator's) ends. Thus, "the victim of a con scheme must have some larceny in his heart."

Legal service lends itself particularly well to confidence games. Usually, a plumber will be able to demonstrate empirically that he has performed a service by clearing up the stuffed drain, repairing the leaky faucet or pipe—and therefore merits his fee. He has rendered, when summoned, a visible, tangible boon for his client in return for the requested fee. A physician, who has not performed some visible surgery or otherwise engaged in some readily discernible procedure in connection with a patient, may be deemed by the patient to have "done nothing" for him. As a consequence, medical practitioners may simply prescribe or administer by injection a placebo to overcome a patient's potential reluctance or dissatisfaction in paying a requested fee, "for nothing."

In the practice of law there is a special problem in this regard, no matter what the level of the practitioner or his place in the hierarchy of prestige. Much legal work is intangible either because it is simply a few words of advice, some preventive action, a telephone call, negotiation of some kind, a form filled out and filed, a hurried conference with another attorney or an official of a government agency, a letter or opinion written, or a countless variety of seemingly innocuous and even prosaic procedures and actions. These are the basic activities, apart from any possible court appearance, of almost all lawyers, at all levels of practice. Much of the activity is not in the nature of the exercise of the traditional, precise professional skills of the attorney such as library research and oral argument in connection with appellate briefs, court motions, trial work, drafting of opinions, memoranda, contracts, and other complex documents and agreements. Instead, much legal activity, whether it is at the lowest or highest "white shoe" law firm levels, is of the brokerage, agent, sales representative, lobbyist type of activity, in which the lawyer acts for someone else in pursuing the latter's interests and designs. The service is intangible.

The large-scale law firm may not speak as openly of their "contacts," their "fixing" abilities, as does the lower-level lawyer. They trade instead upon a facade of thick carpeting, walnut paneling, genteel low pressure, and superficialities of traditional legal professionalism. There are occasions when even the large firm is on the defensive in connection with the fees they charge because the services rendered or results obtained do not appear to merit the fee asked. Therefore, there is a recurrent problem in the legal profession in fixing the amount of fee and in justifying the basis for the requested fee.

Although the fee at times amounts to what the traffic and the conscience of the lawyer will bear, one further observation must be made with regard to the size of the fee and its collection. The defendant in a criminal case and the material gain he may have acquired during the course of his illicit activities are soon parted. Not infrequently the ill-gotten fruits of the various modes of larceny are sequestered by a defense lawyer in payment of his fee. Inexorably, the amount of the fee is a function of the dollar value of the crime committed and is frequently set with meticulous precision at a sum which bears an uncanny relationship to that of the net proceeds of the particular offense involved. On occasion, defendants have been known to commit additional offenses while at liberty on bail, in order to secure the requisite funds with which to meet their obligations for payment of legal fees. Defense lawyers condition even the most obtuse clients to recognize that there is a firm interconnection between fee payment and the zealous exercise of professional expertise, secret knowledge, and organizational "connections" in their behalf. Lawyers, therefore, seek to keep their clients in a proper state of tension, and to arouse in them the precise edge of anxiety which is calculated to encourage prompt fee payment. Consequently, the client attitude in the relationship between defense counsel and an accused is in many instances a precarious admixture of hostility, mistrust, dependence, and sycophancy. By keeping his client's anxieties aroused to the proper pitch, and establishing a seemingly causal relationship between a requested fee and the accused's ultimate extrication from his onerous difficulties, the lawyer will have established the necessary preliminary groundwork to assure a minimum of haggling over the fee and its eventual payment.

In varying degrees, as a consequence, all law practice involves a manipulation of the client and a stage management of the lawyer-client relationship so that at least an *appearance* of help and service will be forthcoming. This is accomplished in a variety of ways, often exercised in combination with each other. At the outset, the lawyer-professional employs with suitable variation a measure of sales puff which may range from an air of unbounding self-confidence, adequacy, and dominion over events, to that of complete arrogance. This will be supplemented by the affectation of a studied, faultless mode of personal attire. In the larger firms, the furnishings and office trappings will serve as the backdrop to help in impression management and client intimidation. In all firms, solo or large-scale, an access to secret knowledge and to the seats of power and influences is inferred, or presumed to a varying degree as the basic vendable commodity of the practitioners.

The lack of visible end product offers a special complication in the course of the professional life of the criminal court lawyer with respect to his fee and in his relations with his client. The plain fact is that an accused in a criminal case always "loses" even when he has been exonerated by an acquittal, discharge, or dismissal of his case. The hostility of an accused which follows as a consequence of his arrest, incarceration, possible loss of job, expense, and other traumas connected with his case is directed, by means of displacement, toward his lawyer. It is in this sense that it may be said that a criminal lawyer never really "wins" a case. The really satisfied client is rare, since in the very nature of the situation even an accused's vindication leaves him with some degree of dissatisfaction and hostility. It is this state of affairs that makes for a lawyer–client relationship in the criminal court which tends to be a somewhat exaggerated version of the usual lawyer-client confidence game.

At the outset, because there are great risks of nonpayment of the fee, due to the impecuniousness of his clients, and the fact that a man who is sentenced to jail may be a singularly unappreciative client, the criminal lawyer collects his fee *in advance*. Often, because the lawyer and the accused both have questionable designs of their own upon each other, the confidence game can be played. The criminal lawyer must serve three major functions, or stated another way, he must solve three problems. First, he must arrange for his fee; second, he must prepare and then, if necessary, "cool out" his client in case of defeat (a highly likely contingency); third, he must satisfy the court organization that he has performed adequately in the process of negotiating the plea, so as to preclude the possibility of any sort of embarrassing incident which may serve to invite "outside" scrutiny.

In assuring the attainment of one of his primary objectives, his fee, the criminal lawyer will very often enter into negotiations with the accused's kin, including collateral relatives. In many instances, the accused himself is unable to pay any sort of fee or anything more than a token fee. It then becomes important to involve as many of the accused's kin as possible in the situation. This is especially so if the attorney hopes to collect a significant part of a proposed substantial fee. It is not uncommon for several relatives to contribute toward the fee. The larger the group, the greater the possibility that the lawyer will collect a sizeable fee by getting contributions from each.

A fee for a felony case which ultimately results in a plea, rather than a trial, may ordinarily range anywhere from $550 to $1,500. Should the case go to trial, the fee will be proportionately larger, depending upon the length of the trial. But the larger the fee the lawyer wishes to exact, the more impressive his performance must be, in terms of his stage-managed image as personage of great influence and power in the court organization. Court personnel are keenly aware of the extent to which a lawyer's stock-in-trade involves the precarious stage management of an image which goes beyond the usual professional flamboyance, and for this reason alone the lawyer is "bound in" to the authority system of the court's organizational discipline. Therefore, to some extent, court personnel will aid the lawyer in the creation and maintenance of that impression. There is a tacit commitment to the lawyer by the court organization, apart from formal etiquette, to aid him in this. Such augmentation of the lawyer's stage-managed image as this affords is the partial basis for the *quid pro quo* which exists between the lawyer and the court organization. It tends to serve as the continuing basis for the higher loyalty of the lawyer to the organization; his relationship with his client, in contrast, is transient, ephemeral, and often superficial.

Defense Lawyer as Double Agent

The lawyer has often been accused of stirring up unnecessary litigation, especially in the field of negligence. He is said to acquire a vested interest in a cause of action or claim which was initially his client's. The strong incentive of possible fee motivates the lawyer to promote litigation which would otherwise never have developed.

However, the criminal lawyer develops a vested interest of an entirely different nature in his client's case: to limit its scope and duration rather than do battle. Only in this way can a case be "profitable." Thus, he enlists the aid of relatives not only to assure payment of his fee, but he will also rely on these persons to help him in his agent-mediator role of convincing the accused to plead guilty, and ultimately to help in "cooling out" the accused if necessary.

It is at this point that an accused-defendant may experience his first sense of "betrayal." While he had perhaps perceived the police and prosecutor to be adversaries, or possibly even the judge, the accused is wholly unprepared for his counsel's role performance as an agent-mediator. In the same vein, it is even less likely to occur to an accused that members of his own family or other kin may become agents, albeit at the behest and urging of other agents or mediators, acting on the principle that they are in reality helping an accused negotiate the best possible plea arrangement under the circumstances. Usually, it will be the lawyer who will activate next of kin in this role, his ostensible motive being to arrange for his fee. But soon latent and unstated motives will assert themselves with entreaties by counsel to the accused's next of kin to appeal to the accused to "help himself" by pleading. *Gemeinschaft* sentiments are to this extent exploited by a defense lawyer (or even at times by a district attorney) to achieve specific secular ends, that is, of concluding a particular matter with all possible dispatch.

The fee is often collected in stages, each installment usually payable prior to a necessary court appearance required during the course of an accused's career journey. At each stage, in his interviews and communications with the accused, or in addition, with members of his family, if they are helping with the fee payment, the lawyer employs an air of professional confidence and "inside-dopesterism" in order to assuage anxieties on all sides. He makes the necessary bland assurances, and in effect manipulates his client, who is usually willing to do and say the things, true or not, which will help his attorney extricate him. Since the dimensions of what he is essentially selling, organizational influence and expertise, are not technically and precisely measurable, the lawyer can make extravagant claims of influence and secret knowledge with impunity. Thus, lawyers frequently claim to have inside knowledge in connection with information in the hands of the district attorney, police, or probation officials or to have access to these functionaries. Factually, they often do, and need only to exaggerate the nature of their relationships with them to obtain the desired effective impression upon the client. But, as in the genuine confidence game, the victim who has participated is loath to do anything which will upset the lesser plea which his lawyer has "conned" him into accepting.

In effect, in his role as double agent, the criminal lawyer performs an extremely vital and delicate mission for the court organization and the accused. Both principals are anxious to terminate the litigation with a minimum of expense and damage to each other. There is no other personage or role incumbent in the total court structure more strategically located, who by training and in terms of his own requirements, is more ideally suited to do so than the lawyer. In recognition of this, judges will cooperate with attorneys in many important ways. For example, they will adjourn the case of an accused in jail awaiting plea or sentence if the attorney requests such action. While explicitly this may be done for some innocuous and seemingly valid reason, the tacit purpose is that pressure is being applied by the attorney for the collection of his fee, which he knows will probably not be forthcoming if the case is concluded. Judges are aware of this tactic on the part of lawyers, who, by requesting an adjournment, keep an accused incarcerated awhile longer as a not too subtle method of dunning a client for payment. However, the judges will go along with this, on the ground that important ends are being served. Often, the only end served is to protect a lawyer's fee.

The judge will help an accused's lawyer in still another way. He will lend the official aura of his office and courtroom so that a lawyer can stage-manage an impression of an "all-out" performance for the accused in justification of his fee. The judge and other court personnel will serve as a backdrop for a scene charged with dramatic fire, in which the accused's lawyer makes a stirring appeal in his behalf. With a show of restrained passion, the lawyer will intone the virtues of the accused and recite the social deprivations which have reduced him to his present stage. The speech varies somewhat, depending on whether the accused has been convicted after trial or has pleaded guilty. In the main, however, the incongruity, superficiality, and ritualistic character of the total performance is underscored by a visibly impassive, almost bored reaction on the part of the judge and other members of the court retinue.

Afterward, there is a hearty exchange of pleasantries between the lawyer and district attorney, wholly out of context in terms of the supposed adversary nature of the preceding events. The fiery passion in defense of his client is gone, and the lawyers for both sides resume their offstage relations, chatting amiably and perhaps including the judge in their restrained banter. No other aspect of their visible conduct so effectively serves to put even a casual observer on notice that these individuals have claims upon each other. These seemingly innocuous actions are indicative of continuing organizational and informal relations, which, in their intricacy and depth, range far beyond any priorities or claims a particular defendant may have.

Criminal law practice is a unique form of private law practice since it really only appears to be private practice. Actually it is bureaucratic practice, because of the legal practitioner's enmeshment in the authority, discipline, and perspectives of the court organization. Private practice, supposedly, in a professional sense, involves the maintenance of an organized, disciplined body of knowledge and learning; the individual practitioners are imbued with a spirit of autonomy and service, the earning of a livelihood being incidental. In the sense that the lawyer in the criminal court serves as a double agent, serving higher organizational rather than professional ends, he may be deemed to be engaged in bureaucratic rather than private practice. To some extent the lawyer–client "confidence game," in addition to its other functions, serves to conceal this fact.

The Client's Perception

The "cop-out" ceremony, in which the court process culminates, is not only invaluable for redefining the accused's perspectives of himself, but also in reiterating publicly in a formally structured ritual the accused person's guilt for the benefit of significant "others" who are observing. The accused not only is made to assert publicly his guilt of a specific crime, but also a complete recital of its details. He is further made to indicate that he is entering his plea of guilt freely, willingly, and voluntarily, and that he is not doing so because of any promises or in consideration of any commitments that may have been made to him by anyone. This last is intended as a blanket statement to shield the participants from any possible charges of "coercion" or undue influence that may have been exerted in violation of due process requirements. Its function is to preclude any later review by an appellate court on these grounds, and also to obviate any second thoughts an accused may develop in connection with his plea.

However, for the accused, the conception of self as a guilty person is in large measure a temporary role adaptation. His career socialization as an accused, if it is successful, eventuates in his acceptance and redefinition of himself as a guilty person. However, the transformation is ephemeral, in that he will, in private, quickly reassert his innocence. Of importance is that he accept his defeat, publicly proclaim it, and find some measure of pacification in it. Almost immediately after his plea, a defendant will generally be interviewed by a representative of the probation division in connection with a presentence report which is to be prepared. The very first question to be asked of him by the probation officer is: "Are you guilty of the crime to which you pleaded?" This is by way of double affirmation of the defendant's guilt. Should the defendant now begin to make bold assertions of his innocence, despite his plea of guilty, he will be asked to withdraw his plea and stand trial on the original charges. Such a threatened possibility is, in most instances, sufficient to cause an accused to let the plea stand and to request the probation officer to overlook his exclamations of innocence. Table 1 is a breakdown of the categorized responses of a random sample of male defendants in Metropolitan Court during 1962, 1963, and 1964 in connection with their statements during presentence probation interviews following their plea of guilty.

It would be well to observe at the outset that of the 724 defendants who pleaded guilty before trial, only 43 (5.94 percent) of the total group had confessed prior to their indictment. Thus, the ultimate judicial process was predicated upon evidence independent of any confession of the accused.

As the data indicate, only a relatively small number (95) out of the total number of defendants actually will even admit their guilt following the cop-out ceremony. However, even though they have affirmed their guilt, many of these defendants felt that they should have been able to negotiate a more favorable plea. The largest aggregate of defendants (373) were those who reasserted their "innocence" following their public profession of guilt during the cop-out ceremony. These defendants employed differential degrees of fervor, solemnity, and credibility, ranging from really mild, wavering assertions of innocence which were embroidered with a variety of stock explanations and rationalizations, to those of an adamant, "framed" nature. Thus, the "innocent" group, for the most part, were largely concerned with underscoring for their probation interviewer their essential "goodness" and "worthiness," despite their formal plea of guilty. Assertion of innocence at the postplea stage resurrects a more respectable and acceptable self-concept for the accused defendant who has pleaded guilty. A recital of the structural exigencies which precipitated his plea of guilt serves to embellish a newly proferred claim of innocence, which many defendants mistakenly feel will stand them in good stead at the time of sentence, or ultimately with probation or parole authorities.

TABLE 1 / **Defendant Responses as to Guilt or Innocence After Pleading Guilty (Years: 1962, 1963, 1964; $N = 724$)**

Nature of response		Number of defendants
Innocent (manipulated)	"The lawyer, judge, police, or D.A. 'conned me'"	86
Innocent (pragmatic)	"Wanted to get it over with" "You can't beat the system" "They have you over a barrel when you have a record"	147
Innocent (advice of counsel)	"Followed my lawyer's advice"	92
Innocent (defiant)	"Framed"—Betrayed by "complainant," "police," "squealers," "lawyer," "friends," "wife," "girlfriend"	33
Innocent (adverse social data)	Blames probation officer or psychiatrist for "bad report," in cases where there was prepleading investigation	15
Guilty	"But I should have gotten a better deal" Blames lawyer, D.A., police, judge	74
Guilty	Won't say anything further	21
Fatalistic (doesn't press his "innocence," won't admit "guilt")	"I did it for convenience" "My lawyer told me it was only thing I could do" "I did it because it was the best way out"	248
No response		8
Total		724

Relatively few (33) maintained their innocence in terms of having been "framed" by some person or agent-mediator, although a larger number (86) indicated that they had been manipulated or conned by an agent-mediator to plead guilty, but as indicated, their assertions of innocence were relatively mild.

A rather substantial group (147) preferred to stress the pragmatic aspects of their plea of guilty. They would only perfunctorily assert their innocence and would in general refer to some adverse aspect of their situation which they believed tended to negatively affect their bargaining leverage, including in some instances a prior criminal record.

One group of defendants (92), while maintaining their innocence, simply employed some variation of a theme of following "the advice of counsel" as a covering response to explain their guilty plea in the light of their new affirmation of innocence.

The largest single group of defendants (248) were basically fatalistic. They often verbalized weak suggestions of their innocence in rather halting terms, wholly without conviction. By the same token, they would not admit guilt readily and were generally evasive as to guilt or innocence, preferring to stress aspects of their stoic submission in their decision to plead. This sizeable group of defendants appeared to

T A B L E   2 /   **Role of Agent-Mediators in Defendant's Guilty Plea**

Person or official	First suggested plea of guilty	Influenced the accused most in his final decision to plead
Judge	4	26
District attorney	67	116
Defense counsel	407	411
Probation officer	14	3
Psychiatrist	8	1
Wife	34	120
Friends and kin	21	14
Police	14	4
Fellow inmates	119	14
Others	28	5
No response	8	10
Total	724	724

perceive the total court process as being caught up in a monstrous organizational apparatus, in which the defendant's role expectancies were not clearly defined. Reluctant to offend anyone in authority, fearful that clear-cut statements on their part as to their guilt or innocence would be negatively construed, they adopted a stance of passivity, resignation, and acceptance. Interestingly, they would in most instances invoke their lawyer as being the one who crystallized the available alternatives for them and who was therefore the critical element in their decision-making process.

In order to determine which agent-mediator was most influential in altering the accused's perspectives as to his decision to plead or go to trial (regardless of the proposed basis of the plea), the same sample of defendants were asked to indicate the person who first suggested to them that they plead guilty. They were also asked to indicate which of the persons or officials who made such a suggestion was most influential in affecting their final decision to plead.

Table 2 indicates the breakdown of the responses to the two questions.

It is popularly assumed that the police, through forced confessions, and the district attorney, employing still other pressures, are most instrumental in the inducement of an accused to plead guilty. As Table 2 indicates, it is actually the defendant's own counsel who is most effective in this role. Further, this phenomenon tends to reinforce the extremely rational nature of criminal law administration, for an organization could not rely upon the sort of idiosyncratic measures employed by the police to induce confessions and maintain its efficiency, high production, and overall rational-legal character. The defense counsel becomes the ideal agent-mediator since, as "officer of the court" and confidant of the accused and his kin, he lives astride both worlds and can serve the ends of the two as well as his own.

While an accused's wife, for example, may be influential in making him more amenable to a plea, her agent-mediator role has, nevertheless, usually been sparked and initiated by defense counsel. Further, although a number of first suggestions of a plea came from an accused's fellow jail inmates, he tended to rely largely on his counsel as an ultimate source of influence in his final decision. The defense counsel being a crucial figure in the total organizational scheme for constituting a new set of perspectives for the accused, the same sample of defendants was asked to indicate at which stage of their contact with counsel the suggestion of a plea was made. There are three basic kinds of defense counsel available in Metropolitan Court: legal-aid, privately retained counsel, and counsel assigned by the court (but may eventually be privately retained by the accused).

The overwhelming majority of accused persons, regardless of type of counsel, related a specific incident which indicated an urging or suggestion, either during the course of the first or second contact, that they plead guilty to a lesser charge if this could be arranged. Of all the agent-mediators, it is the lawyer who is most effective in manipulating an accused's perspectives, notwithstanding pressures that may have been previously applied by police, district attorney, judge, or any of the agent-mediators that may have been activated by them. Legal-aid and assigned counsel would apparently be more likely to suggest a possible plea at the point of initial interview as response to pressures of time. In the case of the assigned counsel, the strong possibility that there is no fee involved may be an added impetus to such a suggestion at the first contact.

In addition, there is some further evidence in Table 3 of the perfunctory, ministerial character of the system in Metropolitan Court and similar criminal courts. There is little real effort to individualize, and the lawyer's role as agent-mediator may be seen as unique in that he is in effect a double agent. Although, as "officer of the court" he mediates between the court organization and the defendant, his roles with respect to each are rent by conflicts of interest. Too often these must be resolved in favor of the organization which provides him with the means for his professional existence. Consequently, in order to reduce the strains and conflicts imposed in what is ultimately an overdemanding role obligation for him, the lawyer engages in the lawyer–client "confidence game" so as to structure more favorably an otherwise onerous role system.

Conclusion

Recent decisions of the Supreme Court, in the area of criminal law administration and defendants' rights, fail to take into account three crucial aspects of social structure which may tend to render the more libertarian rules as nugatory. The decisions overlook (1) the nature of courts as formal organization, (2) the relationship that the lawyer "regular" *actually* has with the court organization, and (3) the character of the lawyer–client relationship in the criminal court (the routine relationships, not those unusual ones that are described in "heroic" terms in novels, movies, and television).

Courts, like many other modern large-scale organizations, possess a monstrous appetite for the co-optation of entire professional groups as well as individuals. Almost all those who come within the ambit of organization authority find that their definitions, perceptions, and values have been refurbished, largely in terms favorable to the particular organization and its goals. As a result, recent Supreme Court decisions may have a long-range effect which is radically different from that intended or

T A B L E   3 /   **Stage (Contact) at Which Each Type of Counsel Suggests That Defendant Plead Guilty (N = 724)**

Contact	Privately retained		Legal-aid		Assigned		Total	
	N	%	N	%	N	%	N	%
First	66	35	237	49	28	60	331	46
Second	83	44	142	29	8	17	233	32
Third	29	15	63	13	4	9	96	13
Fourth or more	12	6	31	7	5	11	48	7
No response	0	0	14	3	2	4	16	2
Total	190	100	487	100[a]	47	101[a]	724	100

[a]Rounded percentage.

anticipated. The more libertarian rules will tend to produce the rather ironic end result of augmenting the *existing* organizational arrangements, enriching court organizations with more personnel and elaborate structure, which in turn will maximize organizational goals of "efficiency" and production. Thus, many defendants will find that courts will possess an even more sophisticated apparatus for processing them toward a guilty plea!

13

Client Games: Defense Attorney Perspectives on Their Relations with Criminal Clients

Roy B. Flemming

Is the attorney–client relationship different when the services are being paid for by the public rather than by the individual defendant? The 155 defense attorneys from nine felony trial courts interviewed in this study by Roy Flemming assert that public clients are more skeptical and less willing to accept their professional authority than are private clients, and that they need to take extra steps to gain the cooperation of public clients. The problem of "client control" is addressed.

Lawyer–client relations substantially define the reality of law in society. It is through these interactions and encounters that the legal system takes on form and substance for both parties. What clients learn of the reality of their rights, the operation of courts, and the inner workings of the law, and whether they feel they are treated fairly or justly, are all colored by their experiences with attorneys. By the same token, the satisfactions and disappointments, financial rewards, and social returns of law-yering strongly reflect the kinds of clients attorneys represent. Moreover, as professionals, lawyers presumably have considerable latitude in choosing how to relate to clients, raising concerns over their accountability to clients and equal treatment of them.

The social preconditions for traditional lawyer–client relationships that puta-tively foster accountability are often missing in the practice of criminal law, however. Criminal clients express deep misgivings about attorneys assigned to them by courts, reactions to a policy reform not anticipated at the time of its adoption. While atten-tion to the client's or defendant's perspective on attorneys has not languished for this reason, the attorney's view of clients has been neglected. And yet a fuller under-standing of this relationship obviously demands an exploration of the attorney's side. This study takes this tack and looks at how attorneys feel they are seen by their clients and the implications of client reactions for how they practice criminal law. In this sense it adds another dimension toward a more complete view of the professional

Source: American Bar Foundation Research Journal (Spring 1986): 253–277.
Reprinted by permission of the publisher.

behavior of criminal attorneys, a dimension that stresses the difference between public and private clients in affecting the accountability or, at least, responsiveness of attorneys to their clients.

Skepticism about the accountability of criminal defense attorneys is not a new concern. Some twenty years ago Blumberg described the private practice of criminal law as a "confidence game."[1] The intangible quality of the attorney's work, the concern over fees, and the need to prepare clients for guilty pleas or trial convictions while satisfying the interests of the court system all came together as ingredients in this game. A few years later, however, it became clear that clients distrust their public defenders and court-appointed attorneys and hold them in low esteem. Casper neatly captured their views and caught the tone of subsequent studies with the title of his seminal article "Did You Have a Lawyer When You Went to Court? No, I Had a Public Defender."[2] A rather substantial body of research agrees that in contrast with their attitudes toward privately retained attorneys, criminal defendants see publicly paid and assigned counsel as part of the "system"—overly eager to plead them guilty, disinclined to give them much time, and little concerned about their welfare.[3]

Doubts about a lawyer's professional skills and fears of not being faithfully represented raise questions about the attorney's role as described in Blumberg's "confidence game." For what kind of game is it if clients do not trust their attorneys? And how do lawyers cope with this problem? Without the aura of professional legitimacy, do they dominate their clients to the degree found in civil cases? And how do they gain control of them?[4] When faced with these problems, plus the social, racial, and economic differences that usually separate them from criminal defendants, how can they function as "translators" of their needs as they apparently do in civil matters, where the social gap between lawyer and client is often narrower?[5]

This study offers answers to these questions. Specifically, it reports how attorneys feel they are viewed by their clients, how they try to develop working relationships with them, and what roles they think are most useful in dealing with criminal clients. Interviews with 155 defense attorneys provide the data for this study, and excerpts are presented to establish their concerns and views. The study concludes by placing the defense attorneys' relations with criminal clients in a perspective that extends and revises Blumberg's notion of a "confidence game" between attorneys and their clients to show how attorney accountability arises in a situation characterized by mistrust.

The interviews were conducted as part of a larger research project on felony justice in nine medium-sized counties located in three states.[6] The attorneys, almost all of whom were white males, were "regulars": they generally handled substantial portions of the local circuit court felony caseload in the period centering around 1980–1981 as public defenders, assigned counsel, or private attorneys. Because of their pivotal positions in the courts, sizeable caseloads, and usually long tenure in the jurisdictions, they were well-versed, knowledgeable informants. The interviews were semistructured, recorded, and covered a variety of topics; this study draws on those segments dealing with their encounters with clients.

Overall, twenty-nine full-time public defenders, thirty-four part-time defenders, forty-four court-appointed or -assigned attorneys, and forty-eight private attorneys were interviewed. The value of including the latter three groups of attorneys is that they had experience with both public and private clients. Table 1 indicates the num-

T A B L E   1 / Characteristics of Interviewed Attorneys and Trial Court Caseloads

Type of Lawyer	Illinois			Michigan			Pennsylvania		
	DuPage	Peoria	St. Clair	Oakland	Kalamazoo	Saginaw	Montgomery	Dauphin	Erie
Public defender									
Full-time	6	—	6	—	—	—	2	10	5
Part-time	2	6	3	—	—	—	15	—	8
Court-appointed or private attorney	14	8	10	19	12	13	4	6	6
Total	22	14	19	19	12	13	21	16	19
Proportion of cases handled by interviewed attorneys	76.1%	66.6%	55.7%	18.5%	74.3%	26.8%	24.5%	59.1%	47.6%
Proportion of all sampled cases with public clients	71.6%	70.0%	51.6%	56.2%	79.0%	73.1%	26.5%	47.0%	43.8%
Number of sampled felony cases	649	930	996	900	681	650	673	1,063	588

ber of attorneys interviewed, their practice type, and the proportion of the sampled felony cases they handled in each court. This table also shows the proportions of the sampled cases in the nine courts in which defendants were assigned to an attorney by the court or through a public defender's office. As these proportions indicate, public clients often constitute a large proportion of the local felony caseloads in the courts.

Problematical Authority and Public Clients

Attorneys with public clients labor in the shadow of the "public defender" stereotype. Whether they actually work as public defenders makes no difference; their clients give them little respect and distrust them. A sampling of the attorneys' comments illustrates their problem.[7]

> The standard joke around this country is "Do you want a public defender or a real attorney?" (1303)
> Well, I think the general impression is "I don't have the money to hire a real attorney, so I have you." We get a lot of that. (3303)
> A lot of times they don't respect you as an attorney because you accepted this court appointment, and that creates a problem. (6437)
> It's very tough being an appointed defense attorney. I think a lot of the clients . . . really don't trust you. (5419)
> They think because you're free, you're no good. (2306)
> Because you're part of the system, your indigent client doesn't trust you. (6451)

Public clients have doubts about the status of their lawyers, are skeptical about their skills as advocates, and are worried about whose side the lawyers are on. These attitudes complicate the attorneys' work. They cannot assume their clients respect them professionally, and they do not presume that they have their trust or confidence. Thus, perhaps even before procedural or substantive issues can be thrashed out, attorneys need to establish relationships with public clients that will quiet their qualms. Attorneys with private clients run into these problems less often.

> Private clients accept that you are going to do a good job or you know what you're doing. Public defender clients have no idea where you come from; no idea of your background, no idea of whether you've ever done another criminal case in your life. (2303)
> A guy that comes in here and pays $5,000 in cash wants to believe you're good, I guess. He handles you with a lot of respect and is less likely to call you every day with some bullshit question. He's more likely to treat you as you want to be treated as an attorney, that you're representing him as best as you can, and you have his interests in mind always. (6437)

A third attorney explained why he refused to take any further public defender cases after a client questioned his professional judgment:

> Well, I like to be my own man, and I was assigned to represent this black man who was caught stone cold in a robbery. I filed a habeas corpus petition, and I took it over to him to show him.

He said, "Not good enough, man." It was fine. It was enough to get me where I wanted to go. It was fine. So I said, "Well, why don't you do this? Why don't you go to law school and learn? And then take my petition and stick it up your ass." I quit. That was the end of it.

I certainly believe you should take your client's interest to heart and do the best job you possibly can, but I'm not going to have some idiot tell me that my paperwork is wrong when it's not. (9427)

Client disrespect dismays and irritates attorneys; it sours associations with clients and makes the job less pleasant. A public defender (1303) complained, "It's frustrating to have to constantly sell yourself" to clients. Moreover, the etiquette of normal client–professional relations seems weaker to public attorneys who find that their clients or family and friends freely criticize them and treat them cavalierly. When asked what makes their work unsatisfying, attorneys often point to their public clients.

Sometimes we aren't treated the best by our clients. . . . I had someone this morning whose father was yelling about how bad the public defender was right when I was appointed. That wasn't exactly thrilling. (1302)

I think my dissatisfaction with being a public defender is that the people don't appreciate you. They figure they have a right to an attorney, and you can't really say, "Hey, look. Take a hike. Just get out of here. I don't want to talk to you anymore." There really is a lot of personal abuse, a lot of stuff that gets on my nerves. (3310)

They tend to feel that since they're getting a lawyer for free that they sometimes can be abusive if that's their personality. (2306)

Mistrust compounds these problems. According to an attorney (6451) who represented both kinds of clients, public clients see him as part of the courthouse machinery: "They just figure that if the prosecutor is part of the system, the judge is part of the system; then, as an attorney, you're part of the system too." Another also said his public clients think he would work more diligently if he were retained. Allaying their suspicions took time and patience: "In three-quarters of the cases, there is an immediate skepticism where they say, 'Well, I suppose if I were paying, you wouldn't hesitate to go dig these witnesses up.' Overcoming their skepticism is a very slow process" (4410). Such anxieties, a public defender (3310) stated, "just put that much more pressure on you when you can't get along with the person." They also stymie communication between attorneys and their clients.

I had one guy who told me, "I don't like public defenders. All they do is plea bargain. They don't protect your interests." And it was obvious to me that no matter what I said to this guy, he wasn't gonna listen to me. And he was stuck with me, and I was stuck with him. (9307)

One guy wouldn't even talk to me when I went into the jail. He wouldn't tell me his name or his birth date. "Because you're the public defender, I'm not talking to you." So, we do have problems with that. (3303)

Distrust undermines the chances for cooperation. "Because they think you're part of the system, you end up doing all the worrying, you end up doing all the scrambling around, and your client could really care less," an attorney (6451) quoted earlier concluded. Another (2303) said a "prime frustration" in representing public clients was the feeling that "basically you're out there by yourself because you don't have a client along with you." Finally, trust matters because disgruntled clients can make trouble for attorneys later on. The prospects of facing grievances or appeals loom too large for an attorney to shrug off a client's distrust.

> Doing so much appointed work, you've got to really cover your rear end. These guys, if they're gonna turn on anybody when nothing else is left, they're gonna turn on you. (5519)
> I have to watch myself more with a public defender case because I can't kick the guy out. And if I am nasty to him, he'll complain and make my life miserable later. So I swallow my pride a lot more with a public defender case. (9324)

Attorneys see client disrespect and mistrust as inherent to indigent defense systems. Few mentioned that racial or class differences impede empathy or communication. Still, one attorney (2303) confided, "I don't really identify with my clients. I'm not from that level of society." Three others also commented on this problem.

> I'm an attorney, live in a nice neighborhood. I'm white. I don't know whether the black defendant in particular trusts me as much as he would a black lawyer. (5406)
> In a lot of ways our clientele is our worst enemy. . . . We get quite a few poverty cases in here. Guys come in, they're on welfare. You sit down and work with them. You say, "You're going to trial. I want you dressed like you're going to church." Because I've had guys come in for trial dressed in T-shirts. I say, "Hey, are you crazy?" It's really difficult for me to comprehend. (9304)
> It seems that most attorneys, a lot of them, are dealing with appointed cases. . . . The defendants maybe are repulsive people. They may not even like these guys, but they're representing them. And it's difficult for them. (6437)

Attorneys' perceptions of public clients do not rest on vague, unsubstantiated notions that the grass is greener on the private side of the legal fence; many handled both kinds of clients, and their perceptions corresponded with those of attorneys who had never practiced privately. Attorneys' experience of day-to-day defense work, then, divides sharply according to this public–private dimension and may be underlined by racial or class differences. Attorneys find publicly assigned clients to be more skeptical, less deferential, and less trusting. These perceived qualities are more than mere irritations or inconveniences for attorneys, however, because when they perceive an absence of client respect and trust, they feel that their professional authority is weakened. Consequently, as long as clients question or reject this authority, "client control" remains problematical.

Client Control: Gaining the Client's Respect and Trust

The attorney's craft rests on knowing how to persuade clients who have the most to lose from tactical miscues or strategic errors to listen to them. When considering the stakes involved, an attorney (1310) admitted, "I suppose it's natural to feel like you want to be in control of your own destiny." Nonetheless, attorneys try to disabuse clients of this desire as well as of other misconceptions of their role. As one attorney (4412) put it, "I'm not gonna let any guy [client] tell me how to try my case. . . . So I think client control is a key." In addition, they drive home to them that they are neither novices in the courthouse nor naive about criminal defendants.

A lot of these defendants are very streetwise, and they will try to manipulate the system and their lawyer. And they look at the lawyer as someone who is going to get them off, as opposed to protect their rights. And that's a problem. You have got to establish yourself from the outset with them, so that they don't take advantage of you. (3401)

The problem most often is that they want to control their own case. . . . They have a hard time because most are incarcerated on felony cases, and they get a lot of jailhouse talk. I think the biggest problem is that they think they know all the answers. (1310)

I've been through the system ten damn years, and I know the ins and outs. . . . And this schmuck doesn't know from nothing. He wants to run some bullshit by you. He didn't do it. Well, maybe he didn't. But in my experience there's damn few of them like that. When a dude just says, "I didn't do it," white or black, because they're too smart to admit to anything, you got problems. (4415)

If you're slipshod from the beginning, he's not gonna trust you, he's not gonna do what you say. You've gotta develop trust as soon as possible, get control of the client as much as you can. It's still their decision to make, but they gotta trust you. And once they trust you then they'll work with you, and they'll tell you the truth. (8301)

Client control requires respect and trust for the lawyer. Without respect from the client, the attorney's advice or suggestions may be ignored. Without the client's trust, the attorney may not be believed; in turn, attorneys are not always sure if they can trust their clients. Once attorneys secure their clients' confidence, they can exercise their judgment and satisfy a desire for professional autonomy.

Spending time with clients, attorneys claim, can help win their confidence. Yet time, a limited resource, also carries opportunity costs. Time spent with clients favorably influences their reactions to attorneys, but its effects on case outcomes are questionable.[8] Moreover, client demands are not always reasonable and, because attorneys have no way of knowing in advance which ones deserve attention, time spent with clients may be wasted. Attorneys grow weary of listening to clients if what they say has little bearing on their case; moreover, indigent clients are often detained, which means visiting the jail—an unpleasant chore. Finally, because actions usually speak louder than words, the exchange value of time when purchasing a client's confidence is weak compared with what is gained when the client actually sees the attorney at work in the courtroom.

The most common complaint of prisoners is that they don't see their attorney enough. The problem frankly is that a lot of the things they want to tell us are irrelevant. It depends on the client. But a lot of times they want to tell you things that are totally irrelevant to your presentation of the case. (1310)

I don't know how it works in other public defender's offices, but you won't find people here running out to the jail to calm a guy down because he might have a question. More times than not you'll just say, "Ah, shit, let him stew." The only time you see your client is either at arraignment or just before trial. Most of the time you have, maybe, one or two visits of no more than 15 or 20 minutes with your client. And they have to be wondering, "What the fuck is that guy doing?" (9321)

There are cases where the stigma [of being an assigned attorney] is really strong and where they [the clients] think they're gonna get railroaded. I literally go out of my way to do things. I'll go out there and see them at the jail once a week if that's what it takes. And to be honest with you, I found that it's not all that successful. I think, if they distrust you, you can be out there every week, and, until they see you do something, you can sit there and talk with them every night for three months and it makes no difference to them. (4210)

"Being honest" also can settle client misgivings because, according to one attorney (4417), "The biggest problem with court-appointed counsel is the credibility factor. . . . So you go out to the jail, and you try to be up front and candid with him right off the bat." By extending candor, attorneys hope to purchase their clients' trust, honesty, and cooperation. This overture counters their suspicions that they will not be dealt with squarely. Moreover, by telling them what they think of their stories, what their chances look like, and how the case will be handled in court, attorneys flourish their insider's knowledge, which bolsters efforts to win the clients' respect as well. During these encounters, attorneys who are skilled at impression management take the opportunity to portray themselves as competent, concerned, and not easily fooled or buffaloed. As one attorney (5423) pointed out:

> You can waste a lot of time with criminal defendants unless they have enough confidence in you to skip all the baloney right from the beginning. I think that one of the ways to develop that kind of confidence is to present yourself in a manner so that they think that this time their court-appointed attorney may really know what he or she is doing.

Once again, however, client reactions reflect whether or not the lawyer is privately retained; attorneys believe that deference and honesty are inherent in relations with private clients but not with public ones. Still, regardless of the type of client, attorneys first feel them out so that they can adopt the right manner to elicit the respect, cooperation, and frankness they need.

Respondent: When I'm retained, there is a certain rapport immediately. That means the person paid me for my experience and my judgment. When I'm appointed to a case, generally there is no rapport whatsoever. So in an appointed case, the first thing I have to do is establish that rapport and convince my client (1) I'm being truthful with him, and (2) I'm a good lawyer.

Interviewer: How do you do it?

Respondent: Well, sometimes you don't. It's difficult. A valuable way of doing it is by going to the jail to see your client ahead of time. But that's not always easily done, since you've got a law practice, and time and economics don't allow you to go to the jail and sit down with your client. . . .

I find it absolutely invaluable to be honest. I will not tell my client a fib. These people are far more intelligent than we generally give them credit for. Plus, they have a disbelief in what you're telling them; so if you're honest, you at least don't have anything to worry about. They check out everything you tell them. So you'd better tell them the truth.

And later on when I have to say to him, "Now, look. You make the decision, but here are your alternatives, and you know I've never lied to you." He at least will say, "Well, I don't like Mr. Smith, and I don't like what he's telling me, but the guy's always been honest with me." (5431)

Respondent: It's difficult to establish yourself with the client.

Interviewer: So how do you do that?

Respondent: Well, I think what you do is wait and see what the client is like. You look at the case before you go over and see him. Then you just start to feel the client out. Find out what his thoughts are. Review what his prior record is. And feel him out. If he's the kind of person who, because you're an attorney, is gonna listen to you right off the bat, then you have no problem. You can sit there and say, "Okay. Now this is what I think we should do." Boom, boom, boom.

But if you sit down and the guy starts throwing all kinds of things at you right away, then you just have to sit back and, again, it's hard to give a concrete method of procedure, but you have to determine whether or not this guy is being uncooperative, or is he just concerned with his case? . . . If he's just being plain uncooperative, well, then you've got another problem. Then you have to maybe speak a little louder, you know. Speak with a little bit more authority.

Interviewer: In well-modulated, middle-class tones, or what?

Respondent: I've been able to modify my vocabulary to the point where I can usually get the point across no matter who I'm speaking to. I know how to talk to them so that they know I'm not just some clown out of law school who doesn't know anything about what's going on. (9317)

"Client control" too bluntly describes the complex, often-subtle relationships attorneys try to arrange to gain their clients' confidence. Once it is established, they feel they are less likely to be surprised by a sudden balkiness or by unexpected revelations of something the client concealed from them. Again, this task is harder in public cases than in private ones, and it affects the manner in which attorneys approach clients when making decisions about the dispositions and handling of their cases.

Styles of Client Control: Advising and Recommending

If attorneys prepare the ground well enough by giving clients time, frank assessments of their situations, and the impression they can be trusted, and if the clients respond by listening and offering to cooperate, the attorneys' authority takes root in the nascent relationship. This social exchange nurtures and, in effect, legitimates their status with public clients, while with private clients, professional legitimacy generally accompanies the retainer or fee. In either instance, legitimation forms the basis for client control and allows attorneys to moderate their clients' demands and adjust their expectations to courthouse realities. The styles they use, however, range from a soft "advising" approach to a more forceful "recommending" posture,[9] with finer gradations in between. Advising can consist of simply listing the options facing clients and leaving the decision in their hands, or it can mean providing much blunter appraisals that, even without explicit recommendations, make the attorneys' preferences clear. Similarly, recommendations can be made in ways that give clients room to disagree or that present little more than a "take it or leave it" proposition.

A public defender described a situation that approximates the latter extreme of the recommending approach. With the plea conditions set beforehand, the lawyer relies on four factors to convince the client to take the plea offer: a lenient sentence

(11½ to 23 months in the local jail), the favorable reactions and support of his client's detained colleagues, the client's doubts about the fairness of the court, and the odds against getting a better sentence.

> Most times I've struck a deal before I even talk to my client. You know pretty well what the hell went on without talking to your guy. I think I've run across three people who I believe to be innocent since I've been here, and that's five years.
>
> If I get a good deal, then I'll go over to the guy, and I'll say, "Look, here's the way it is. That's the best I could get from the D.A. I think you ought to take it." And then I go over the case, you know, what the strong points are, what the weak points are, etc., etc. . . . And then I say, "11½ to 23." The guy says, "No, man, I'm not going to do any time. I want to go to court." You know, "I'm gonna take this up to the Supreme Court."
>
> So, you say, "Fine, are you prepared to spend 10 months in jail asserting your rights?" They aren't completely stupid, you know. They come around. I'll say, "Okay, I'll see you tomorrow. Talk to your guys in the joint because they know what's good and what isn't."
>
> I never really pressure them per se, but I guess you could say that I use some influence upon them. Most of our people are black, and I think they realize they just really aren't going to get that great a shake out here. Either with the jury or with the judge. And most of our guys have street sense. They know what the hell is going on. (9321)

In contrast with this attorney, who exerts "some influence" and orchestrates his client's decision, others adopt a softer, more indirect "advising" style for reasons of effectiveness and professional ethics. As one of these lawyers explained,

> I find that if they are actively involved at all points in the proceedings, they'll give you more help, you'll find out things about the case that you wouldn't have known. And it isn't so much that when they get into court that they're gonna balk at what happened or say "I didn't expect this to happen," it's just keeping them involved at all times is vitally important to your own role as a defense attorney. Also, I don't think it's ethically proper for an attorney to make decisions for his client, especially in a criminal defense situation. (5404)

Attorneys generally prefer this lawyer's advising approach when representing public clients. An emphatic stance and urgent recommendations strain fragile relationships with wary clients and raise the possibility of problems farther down the road. As two lawyers quoted earlier mentioned, attorneys must "cover" their "rear end" and perhaps "swallow" their pride to avoid having public clients "turn on" them. Another attorney underscored the need for caution and the importance of letting public clients make the key decisions in their cases:

> Certainly I'm not gonna twist an arm. If anything, I'm very, very cautious with these guys. I was warned about that when I first took it over. Be very specific that any decision is their decision. Because a lot of times they'll plead, they'll go through it, they'll get sentenced. And they'll immediately say, "My attorney forced me into it." So you try to be very cautious. It puts the burden on them. (4411)

Some attorneys learn the hard way about advising public clients: they discover that even though recommending a course of action may seem more professional, clients may react strongly against what they see as overbearing attitudes. A headstrong style can provoke a client's anger, reawaken suspicions, and undermine an attorney's tentative authority. In private cases, where clients are more accepting of professional authority, attorneys feel freer to recommend what their clients should do, and they push more vigorously those dispositions they see as in their clients' interests. Being privately retained also means that if significant or unresolvable differences arise, clients can go elsewhere for an attorney. The odds, however, of clients switching attorneys after paying nonrefundable fees or retainers undoubtedly are slim, and perhaps these "sunk costs" add to the clients' willingness to listen to and follow their attorneys' recommendations. Nevertheless, for attorneys, the ability of their clients to go elsewhere for service (however chimerical it may be for private clients) represents a psychological escape hatch their public clients do not have at all. As a public defender concluded, the "psychology of representation" in private cases was "totally different" from that of private cases.

> The longer you're [in the public defender's office], the more you get into the psychology of representation. It's totally different than private representation. In private you always have the threat of, "Look, if you don't want to follow my advice, go down the road." Here you don't have that luxury. . . . I think we've learned to deal with the type of client that we're dealing with. But, you know, if we're not dealing with a client who is willing to listen to us, we're not like the private bar. If the guy says, "I want you to file an X, Y, Z motion," you're gonna have to file it. (9318) When I started, I found myself getting upset with my clients because they wouldn't settle, and I was just determined I was going to eliminate that. Now I don't force them to do anything. And I find if you put that burden on them and don't give them any reason to get pissed off at you, then they have to start thinking about this thing and making their own decisions. A lot of them turn pretty reasonable the morning of the trial. And, you know, I don't have that many problems with my clients anymore. (2203)
> It used to be I would argue with a client on why he should take the plea. Now, somewhat to his disadvantage, I have said, "Screw him." I just thought, "Why get in an argument with this guy and really lean on him because I know he's gonna be convicted?" . . .
> I'm not gonna fight with him and tell him he's gonna plead. Because over and over again you see cases in which the defendant is appealing. And one of the grounds is—"I told the lawyer I wasn't guilty, but all he ever wanted to talk about was how I should plead guilty to this charge." That's on appointed.
> Now in private cases, I will lean on him. That is the difference that comes out in a private case. If he doesn't like the advice, it's sure easy enough to hire somebody else. But on an appointed case it doesn't work that way. (5406)
> If you walk in and say, "Mr. Jones, I want you to handle my case," then I will talk to you about the facts, I will consider all the alternatives. I will see what it's gonna take in time and money, and I will quote you a fee. And I will decide ahead of time whether or not I'm gonna be able to call the shots with you and if you're gonna listen to me. . . . On an indigent case, I'm assigned by the court. I'm out of the blue, he doesn't trust me, he's not paying me, there's no rapport between us. I may have to try that case, even though it's absolutely deadly. (5431)

As a matter of style, if not substance, attorneys who "advise" public clients seek to impress on them that they sit in the driver's seat, that they are the arbiters of strategy in their cases. Two purposes lie behind this approach. First, advising invites

client participation, or at least a *feeling* of participation that counteracts client apprehensions about being railroaded by an attorney. Second, by placing the burden for
decisions on their clients' shoulders, attorneys hope to extract a measure of personal
commitment to their decisions that will facilitate the handling of cases and forestall
later complaints about their performance.

It is not easy to measure the effects of these two styles on case outcomes. Indeed,
it may be preferable to view the quality or nature of relationships between attorneys
and clients as dependent on "procedural" rather than "substantive" justice. Both
Casper and Tyler, for example, offer evidence that perceptions of fairness—and not
just the outcomes of their cases—matter greatly to defendants in appraising their
treatment in court.[10] The larger study from which this study derived its data did not
have information regarding the nature of attorney–client relations and client reactions to their attorneys on a case-by-case basis. Nonetheless, a useful purpose can
be served by looking at three selected facets of how public and private cases were
handled by attorneys in each of the nine courts. Table 2 compares the proportions
of preliminary hearings held, mean or average number of due process–related
motions (for example, suppression of statements or exclusion of evidence) filed per
case, and the proportion of trials in public and private cases.

In general, the data suggest that public and private clients were treated rather
similarly by attorneys in these courts. With respect to preliminary examinations, statistically significant differences existed between the two types of cases in four of the
nine courts. But after taking into account the severity of trial court charges lodged
against defendants and their prior criminal records, the type of attorney mattered only
in DuPage, where public defenders requested preliminary hearings more often than
private attorneys, and in Oakland and Kalamazoo, where the pattern reversed itself
and attorneys in private cases held these examinations more frequently than when
they were appointed by the courts.[11]

A mixed pattern also exists for the mean number of motions. In five of the
courts, no statistically significant differences emerged. However, in two (DuPage and
Kalamazoo) private attorneys filed more motions than did attorneys with public clients; in two others (St. Clair and Montgomery), motion activity in public cases
exceeded that in private cases after controlling for charge and record. In Erie, these
control variables erased an apparent difference between types of attorneys. This also
happened in the comparison of Erie's trial rates, so that no significant differences
were found in eight of the nine trial courts. Only in Dauphin were public defenders
significantly more likely to go to trial than were private attorneys.

To the extent overall patterns can be found in this table, Kalamazoo is one court
where public cases apparently were handled differently from private ones: in public
cases preliminary hearings were less frequent, fewer motions were filed, and while
not statistically significant, trial rates were lower than in private cases. However, St.
Clair and Erie displayed reverse images of Kalamazoo, with higher, but statistically
insignificant, preliminary hearing and trial rates in public cases along with significantly greater motion activity. For the remaining six courts, no consistent patterns
emerged.

This short analysis is not definitive. Yet, when viewed in light of systematic,
comparative analyses of the impact of defense attorneys on other measures of case
outcomes such as sentencing, the evidence indicates that public clients do not fare

TABLE 2 / Preliminary Hearings, Motions, and Trials by Type of Attorney

	Illinois			Michigan			Pennsylvania		
	DuPage	Peoria	St. Clair	Oakland	Kalamazoo	Saginaw	Montgomery	Dauphin	Erie
Preliminary hearings held									
Public cases	90.4%	34.1%	98.0%	58.3%	34.6%	73.1%[a]	95.4%	71.0%	68.6%
Private cases	85.3%	41.8%	96.5%	69.8%[b]	48.1%[b]	64.3%	95.4%	70.2%	66.5%
Attorney effect	−.09[a]	.05	−.04	.13[c]	.13[c]	−.08	.00	.01	.03
Mean no. of motions per case									
Public cases	0.64	0.77	2.36[c]	0.43	0.20	0.46	1.16[c]	0.15	0.65[c]
Private cases	1.08[c]	0.69	1.56	0.43	0.52[c]	0.41	0.63	0.16	0.36
Attorney effect	.22[c]	−.04	−.23[c]	−.01	.19[c]	.00	−.09[a]	.02	−.07
Bench or jury trials									
Public cases	4.1%	5.4%	9.7%	4.1%	5.0%	4.4%	5.1%	8.6%[b]	8.5%[b]
Private cases	4.1%	4.1%	7.3%	4.5%	7.5%	7.1%	5.2%	4.0%	4.2%
Attorney effect	.02	−.02	−.03	.02	.06	.05	.04	−.09[b]	−.02

NOTE: Attorney effect is the standardized regression coefficient for the dummy variable "type of attorney," where 0 = public defender or assigned counsel and 1 = privately retained attorney, in a multiple regression equation using severity of the trial charge and criminal record of the defendant as control variables.
[a] $p < .05$. [b] $p < .01$. [c] $p < .001$.

more poorly in court than their peers who retain private counsel.[12] Although the sampling of attorney complaints about public clients clearly shows that their dealings with these clients are often contentious and at times disagreeable, with few notable exceptions in the nine counties, public clients are not treated in significantly different ways than are private clients. In this sense, attorney–client relations may be best viewed as part of procedural justice, in which style, approach, rapport, attitudes, and perception define "fairness." Thus, in games between attorneys and clients, clients perceive fairness if they trust their attorneys and believe they have a say or voice in the handling of their cases.

Client Games: Concluding Thoughts, a Paradox, and Policy Questions

This exploration of attorney–client relations in criminal cases relied on the comments of "regular" attorneys. The picture that emerges reflects their particular angle of vision and exposes only certain aspects of lawyer relationships with criminal clients.[13] For example, in their eyes, public clients were skeptical and uncooperative, but by the same token, some frankly admitted they did not give these clients much of their time. Thus, they stressed the resistance of public clients while downplaying their own actions or inactions that may have played a part in their clients' negative responses.[14]

Most also felt their difficulties with public clients were institutionally rooted in the fact that indigent defense systems rarely allow criminal defendants to choose their lawyers. This fact, when combined with the commonly held precept that "you get what you pay for," suggests that the public client's lack of trust and respect is neither peculiar to certain programs nor characteristic of particular kinds of clients. Instead, these responses are intrinsic to an involuntary relationship in which the client holds no readily available, easily employed, and culturally sanctioned lever to assure professional accountability.

The attorneys quoted in this study worked in a wide variety of settings. The indigent defense systems differed considerably from each other, for instance. Only Dauphin County had a traditional, full-time public defender office in which the attorneys could not practice privately on the side; Peoria used a part-time public defender staff; and the others had mixes of full-time and part-time defenders with different rules regarding private practices. As for the Michigan counties, Oakland and Saginaw used assigned counsel programs of different designs, but Kalamazoo had a contract attorney system that closely resembled Peoria's program. These systems also followed varying operating practices; some, for example, had horizontal or "zone" representation, in which clients had different attorneys at each stage of the disposition process; others provided vertical representation, in which clients had the same attorney from beginning to end. Finally, without going into further detail, plea negotiation policies and customs as well as sentencing practices varied widely across these nine courts.[15]

The point here is that attorneys' comments about their relations with public and private clients revealed the same basic themes despite the many dissimilarities of policy and politics in the courts in which they worked. Casper found the same thing to be true for Baltimore, Detroit, and Phoenix, where relationships between client views and type of attorney held across the three different cities.[16]

A few attorneys felt that race and class affected their relations with public clients. According to the case data for the nine counties, 43.6 percent of the public clients were black, whereas the proportion of private clients who were black was 26.8 percent. It is also worth mentioning that public clients were more likely to have prior criminal records (59.0 percent) than were private clients (38.6 percent). Finally, 35.3 percent of the public clients were detained prior to trial, while only 10.7 percent of the private clients were in jail, a reflection of their different economic statuses as well as their criminal histories.

According to Casper, a prior criminal record, but not a defendant's race, has a consistent, eroding effect on defendants' views of public attorneys.[17] Incarceration also diminishes their trust. With the data available for this study, it is not possible to compare the effect of these factors on client behavior with the effect of the institutional factors that most attorneys offered as explanations for client behavior. Undoubtedly these factors combine and possibly interact with one another to exacerbate attorneys' problems with public clients. Although sorting out their relative impacts remains an unresolved problem, the literature provides little evidence that differences between public and private clients can totally replace the fundamental institutional reasons for client mistrust and lack of confidence.

Attorneys in this study say they generally "advised" their public clients, while they "recommended" what their private clients should do. Casper, however, found that most criminal defendants felt public defenders told them what to do instead of offering advice, giving information, or making suggestions. Defendants with private attorneys, in contrast, did not think their lawyers "muscled" them even when they insisted on something. Casper suggests these different views rested on more than just the attorney's behavior:

> The nature of the transaction between attorney and client provides a context for *interpreting* the behavior of the attorney. In part because the defendant (or his family) was paying the attorney, the whole tone of the relationship was altered. For example, insistence upon a particular course of action by a street [private] lawyer (e.g., pleading guilty, commitment for observation to a hospital) is interpreted differently by his client. Similar "advice" from a public defender might well be interpreted as giving orders, as telling the client what to do rather than discussing it with him. With a street lawyer insistent advice is only the lawyer's "proper" role and the exercise of the expertise that he is supposed to possess.[18]

Defense attorneys work in a social setting where expectations and interpretations of their behavior count as much as what they actually do. Their role, then, is symbolic as well as substantive because they need the respect and trust of clients before they enter the courtroom or do anything on a case. When combined with its intangible qualities, this inherently political side of lawyering produces, as Blumberg argued, a "confidence game" with clients. But it is a confidence game in the literal

sense, since attorneys must win the confidence of clients who do not initially recognize or accept their professional authority before they can gain their cooperation.
Client control, therefore, is a confidence game in which cooperation between lawyers
and mistrustful clients is at stake.

Clients refuse to cooperate in various ways. Some have mild consequences for
attorneys, others do not. For instance, attorneys said that public clients were dis-
courteous or that they refused to talk to them, which made their work unpleasant
and more arduous. An attorney lamented earlier that some clients were so alienated
that "You don't have a client along with you," while another complained that attorneys "end up doing all the worrying" and "doing all the scrambling around"
because "your client could really care less." Clients may also spurn advice or balk
at suggestions, which not only increases the lawyers' work but threatens their reputation for client control within the courthouse community.

Deception, dishonesty, and a lack of candor are equally serious problems. Clients, especially public ones, were described as "streetwise," often manipulative,
sometimes "too smart to admit anything," less than candid "at least 50 percent of
the time," and reluctant to talk openly with their lawyer, according to one attorney
(5425) whose remarks echoed those made by others.[19] The attorneys' difficulty is
that evasion and deception can affect tactical and strategic decisions.[20] Mather
describes a case in which a public defender went to trial at the request of a client
who claimed she had no prior record. Expecting a sentence of no more than probation
if she were found guilty, the defender went through a five-day jury trial that ended
in a conviction. To his surprise the defendant's presentence report revealed that she
had a five-year history of similar crimes. She was sentenced to the state prison. The
public defender said his client "fooled everyone."[21]

By the same token public clients hold serious reservations as to how vigorously
attorneys will represent client interests if it means sacrificing their own longer-term
interests within the court system—and the attorneys know the clients are thinking
this. As one attorney (3310) put it, "You know, the scuttlebutt goes around in jail,
'Hey, the public defenders, they get along well with the state's attorney. They're
gonna send you down the river.' " And, as another (5406) explained, "If you say to
an indigent client, 'I think you should plead,' and he doesn't want to plead, he'll
say, 'See, that proves it. They appointed him to lean on me.' "

By substantial margins, defendants interviewed by Casper and others think public attorneys are less likely to fight hard for them and are more concerned about
wrapping up their cases quickly than in getting justice; defendants also doubt whether
public attorneys will be honest with them. Overwhelmingly, they believe private
attorneys work for their clients, but that public attorneys do not.[22] Indeed, concern
that defense attorneys are co-opted by the court system has been a staple of contemporary research on defense attorneys. As "repeat players" with "one-shotter" clients, defense attorneys presumably rely on cooperative relations within the courthouse that would be jeopardized by aggressive advocacy.[23] More generally, Carlin
suggested some time ago that "clients are expendable" whenever their lawyers do
not depend on them for their fees or future business.[24]

Attorneys acknowledge how they are perceived. Thus, in their relations with
clients, they are enmeshed in perceptions and expectations running along the lines
of "If he thinks I am thinking of selling him out, he will not trust me even though

I am not thinking of that, and if he knew this, he would go along with what I say." Attorneys fear their clients will not cooperate because they think they will be deceived. They fear deceit by clients just as much. Attorneys consequently fret over what kind of game their clients may be playing and whether they will find out soon enough to know if they should try to change their minds or take other precautions. As their comments amply suggested, however, attorneys make important distinctions between public and private clients.

Attorneys claim that because private clients pick them and pay them a fee, these clients respect and trust them, believe they are good, have faith in what they are doing, and are willing to accept a "certain rapport" so that matters can be discussed frankly. One attorney (5406) summed it up by saying, "There is a difference, I think, in the relationship—as far as openness and working together for the same goal—between being an appointed attorney and a retained attorney." Attorneys perceive private clients as generally more cooperative. Even if they encounter fee problems later on or discover a private client is less candid than they thought at first, they nevertheless see private clients as generally more trusting than public clients, largely because of the nature of their contractually based relationship. Private clients choose their attorneys, pay them a fee and, however remote the chance, can replace them. Similarly, attorneys can nip problems in the bud by declining to accept cases.[25] As a private attorney (9427) said, "I blow them out of here" if potential clients refused to heed his directions. In public cases, where this option is usually missing for both parties, a lawyer (3310) described the relationship as a "shotgun wedding."

The ambivalence in attorney–client relationships is cleared away in private criminal cases because the retainer or fee reflects the attorneys' assessment of cases and how they should be handled. Consequently, clients have both an idea and a commitment from their attorneys about their intentions; at the same time, attorneys assume that the fees signal the clients' good faith. Neither expects deception by the other. In public cases, clients have no immediate leverage at hand to assure themselves that their attorneys will serve their interests and, indeed, see them as having long-term commitments to the courts, not to them. Attorneys sense this mistrust and wonder if their clients will cooperate with them. With no easy way of ascertaining, measuring, or purchasing each other's commitment, proclamations of honesty and dependability may be viewed as trying to pull the wool over one another's eyes. From the attorneys' perspective, public clients often act as if they need to avoid being taken advantage of by their attorneys or try to exert misguided efforts to take control of their cases. Their immediate problem focuses on changing these perceptions. Their task with private clients is much easier; the attorneys only have to keep their clients' confidence while making sure that they are not gulled by the appearance of client comity.

Because private clients come to attorneys in an apparently cooperative frame of mind, the attorneys' goal in this client game boils down to simply keeping their trust.[26] Because attorneys first must win the confidence of public clients, the game changes and is more involved. "You've really got to earn their trust," an attorney (5419) declared, but "sometimes you do, sometimes you don't." In attorneys' eyes, clients are the chief losers if they refuse to cooperate; but they also know from personal experience what clients suspect they might do to them under the guise of representing them before the court. Consequently, they face the critical, interrelated problems of not only gaining their confidence but dispelling thoughts that they will desert them.

In this situation, where each side is skeptical of the other's intentions but mutual cooperation is required, attorneys can take the first step by "being honest" and by trying to assure clients that mutual trust is necessary. As an attorney (9307) warned, "If you get to a point where the two of you really can't talk with each other, you're both losing." In addition to being honest, visiting with clients and engaging in court-room activities are "moves" in this confidence game. These moves give clients a chance to assess their attorneys' preferences and commitments. In turn, through these moves, attorneys try to rid themselves of the public defender stereotype so their clients can see that "this time their court attorney may really know what he or she is doing," as another lawyer quoted earlier said. This helps to counteract the effects of self-confirming labels that impede cooperation. The advising style also reinforces these moves, since it encourages clients to feel they have a say in the handling of their cases.

The decision to cooperate depends lastly on its rewards and costs. If clients believe that confiding in their lawyers will not penalize them, they will be more likely to cooperate. Sentencing weighs heavily in this equation. Client concerns and uncertainties over this issue offer attorneys another opening to persuade them to cooperate, since they are the ones with knowledge of what is likely to occur and the ability to do something about it. The attorney's chore is lightened especially if the client is faced with a lenient sentence on the one hand and the specter of more severe punishment for going to trial on the other. For the nine courts taken as a whole, nearly two-thirds (65.8 percent) of the 4,100 sampled cases that ended in guilty pleas received probation.[27] Defendants who went to trial and were convicted, however, fared worse—even after controlling for relevant sentencing variables.[28] First offenders less often received probation after a jury trial, and repeat offenders were sentenced more severely than comparable defendants who pled guilty.[29]

The mere threat of trial penalties probably eases the attorney's efforts. The prospect of more severe punishment, for whatever reason, usually chills a client's desire to go to trial rather than to plead guilty. Similarly, the price for deceiving an attorney may be a stiffer sentence if the client miscalculates and the deception is uncovered, as in the case Mather described.[30] The upshot is that if attorneys succeed in convincing their public clients to trust them and persuade them to listen to them, they successfully convert the public client confidence game into something more like the cooperative game attorneys perceive to exist with private clients.

A paradox may exist in this confidence game between suspicious public clients and wary attorneys who are involuntarily joined in an association from which they generally cannot exit until the case is over. Rosenthal distinguished between "traditional" and "participatory" models of lawyer-client relations. In the traditional model, "the client who is passive, follows instructions, and trusts the professional without criticism, with few questions or requests, is preferable, and will do better than the difficult client who is critical and questioning."[31] Conversely, the participatory model stresses an active, skeptical client who shares the responsibility for making choices with an attorney who must be patient and earn the client's cooperation. Many criminal attorneys who handle public cases may prefer the traditional model, particularly younger or less experienced ones who are insecure about their professional status and react to questioning clients as though their self-esteem and pride were threatened; but with practice, others learn to adopt more participatory styles because of the suspiciousness of their public clients. The need to win their confidence means attorneys must persuade their clients that they can be trusted or else they may fail to gain control of them.

The paradox here is twofold. First, the mistrust public clients hold for their attorneys may force them to bow more to their clients' wishes than one might expect from folk wisdom or from arguments like Carlin's about "client expendability." Because of their clients' qualms, attorneys may find the advisory role more palatable, with the result that clients participate more actively in the progress of their cases. By including clients in decisions and restraining their own urge to make them alone, attorneys hope to prove that they are not trying to stampede their clients into decisions contrary to their interests. The second aspect involves the involuntary nature of their relationship. The public client's reluctance to recognize an attorney's professional authority denies the lawyer a major resource in gaining the client's compliance and acquiescence, yet the attorney cannot refuse to handle the case as easily as one who is privately retained. The lawyer's overtures and advice also can be shunned, which threatens his or her reputation for "client control," and unless matters between them get totally out of hand, little can be done but to try again. This involuntary relationship means the client gains a measure of power in dealings with the attorney, a certain equalization of positions buttressed further by the client's ability to file grievances or appeal cases. Together these add yet other incentives to adopt the participatory mode—advising public clients about their options and letting them bear the responsibility for making decisions. The paradox, then, is that those things that irritate attorneys about public clients foster what many observers consider a more appropriate professional role, though clients evidently do not see it this way. They still prefer fee arrangements with private lawyers where, ironically, according to the lawyers in this study, more traditional lawyer–client relationships prevail because they have their clients' confidence.

The institutional basis of client estrangement from court-appointed counsel and public defenders calls into question the design of indigent defense policies. In all nine courts, felony defendants deemed to be indigent and eligible for publicly paid counsel had no say in the selection of their attorneys. In one court (Oakland), the judges appointed specific lawyers to handle these cases; in seven of the others (the Illinois and Pennsylvania courts plus Kalamazoo), the public defenders or contract attorneys allocated the cases among themselves, while in the ninth (Saginaw), a court official chose counsel to represent indigent defendants. In each instance, criminal defendants were expected to live with the lawyer assigned to them.

In the eyes of criminal clients, professional accountability hinges on a market conception and fee-for-service definition of lawyer responsibility. They place little faith in the notion that ethical concerns and feelings of professional obligation by themselves are sufficient guarantees that a lawyer picked seemingly "out of the hat" will adequately represent their interests. Postconviction proceedings offer them something of a retributive stick, but by that time they already have paid a price for what they feel was mistakenly listening to their lawyers; moreover, the prevalence of guilty pleas removes many grounds for appeal and grievances. Stuck with their attorneys, and their attorneys stuck with them, they are caught up in a confidence game in which competing interests and the need for accommodation are resolved in ways that are not as self-evidently effective as choosing and paying a lawyer to represent them.

Given the finding of this and other studies that public clients fare no worse but are treated no better than private clients, the policy implications of client mistrust and disrespect reported by attorneys depend on (1) whether an equivalence of outcomes and attorney behavior is a satisfactory standard for evaluating attorney performance and (2) what weight is given to "procedural justice" in designing indigent defense policies. Comparisons of how attorneys treat public and private clients are necessary but limited indicators of substantive fairness because, while feasible, they also leave the criteria of accountability undefined. Equivalence in and by itself necessarily adopts the outcome of either private or public cases as a benchmark to gauge the other, without stating explicitly whether this benchmark might itself be too high or too low; indeed, it is likely that both are inadequate and that some other criterion is required.

Without alternative evaluation standards, and in the absence of readily apparent, substantive differences in the treatment of publicly and privately represented criminal defendants, changes in the provision of indigent defense counsel may seem unwarranted. Public client mistrust and the problems attendant on the assignment of attorneys may be viewed as the inevitable but nonetheless harmless consequence of an otherwise beneficial policy that, thus, can be safely ignored. A concern for procedural justice, however, suggests that the perceptions, reactions, and feelings of clients regarding policy and institutional arrangements ought to matter as much as substantive effects in prompting reform or change.

From this perspective, it can be asked whether indigent defense systems might be designed to allow criminal defendants to select their own attorneys. If organized along the lines of a voucher system, attorney fees and costs would still be paid publicly, but defendants could, if they wished, select an attorney from among those who wanted to represent indigent criminal clients. Indigent defendants with the freedom to choose might express fewer apprehensions about their attorneys. The disappearance, or at least amelioration, of these fears as public policy is brought into line with client conceptions may, however, weaken the apparent paradox that client mistrust fosters attorney accountability and client participation in public cases.

notes

1. Abraham Blumberg, "The Practice of Law as a Confidence Game: Organizational Cooptation of a Profession," 1 *Law and Society Review* 15 (1967).
2. Jonathan D. Casper, "Did You Have a Lawyer When You Went to Court? No, I Had a Public Defender," 1 *Yale Review of Law and Social Action* 4 (1971).
3. Jonathan D. Casper, *American Criminal Justice: The Defendant's Perspective* (Englewood Cliffs, N.J.: Prentice-Hall, 1972); idem, *Criminal Courts: The Defendant's Perspective* (Washington, D.C.: U. S. Government Printing Office, 1979); Glen Wilkerson, "Public Defenders as Their Clients See Them," *American Journal of Criminal Law* 141 (1972); Antoinette N. Hetzler and Charles H. Kanter, "Informality and the Court: A Study of the Behavior of Court Officials in the Processing of Defendants," in Sawyer P. Sylvester, Jr., and Edward Sagarin, eds., *Politics and Crime* (New York: Praeger, 1974); F. Arcuri, "Lawyers, Judges, and Plea Bargaining," 4 *International Journal of Criminology and Penology* 177 (1976); Burton M. Atkins and E. W. Boyle, "Prisoner's Satisfaction with

Defense Counsel," 12 *Criminal Law Bulletin* 427 (1976); Geoffrey P. Alpert and Donald A. Hicks, "Prisoners' Attitudes Toward Components of the Legal System," 14 *Criminology* 461 (1977); Stewart O'Brien, Steven Pheterson, Michael Wright, and Carl Hosticka, "The Criminal Lawyer: The Defendant's Perspective," 5 *American Journal of Criminal Law* 283 (1977); Geoffrey P. Alpert and C. Ronald Hutt, "Defending the Accused: Counsel Effectiveness and Strategies," in William F. McDonald, ed., *The Defense Counsel* (Beverly Hills, Calif.: Sage Publications, 1983).

4. Carl Hosticka, "We Don't Care about What Happened, We Only Care about What Is Going to Happen," 26 *Social Problems* 599 (1979); Douglas E. Rosenthal, *Lawyer and Client: Who's in Charge?* (New York: Russell Sage Foundation, 1974).

5. Maureen Cain, "The General Practice Lawyer and the Client," *International Journal of Society and Law* 331 (1979).

6. The counties were chosen on the basis of social, economic, and political criteria that produced diverse triplets of counties within each state while forming roughly comparable triplets of matched counties across states. There were three suburban "ring" counties that were primarily middle class and Republican, three "autonomous" counties, and three declining industrial, Democratic counties. More detailed information on the methods and scope of the larger project can be found in Peter F. Nardulli, Roy B. Flemming, and James Eisenstein, *The Tenor of Justice: Criminal Courts and the Guilty Plea Process* (Champaign: University of Illinois Press, 1988).

7. The numbers shown in parentheses after each interview excerpt are codes assigned to assure anonymity to each attorney.

8. Casper, *Criminal Courts*, p. 83.

9. This distinction parallels the two meanings of "representation" identified by Skolnick: in one, an attorney accepts a client's view of how the case should be handled and provides counsel as to how to implement the strategy; in the other, the attorney takes the responsibility for both strategy and tactics. Jerome Skolnick, "Social Control in the Adversary System," 11 *Journal of Conflict Resolution* 52, 65 (1967).

10. Jonathan D. Casper, "Having Their Day in Court: Defendant Evaluations of the Fairness of Their Treatment," 12 *Law and Society Review* 237 (1978); Tom R. Tyler, "The Role of Perceived Injustice in Defendants' Evaluations of Their Courtroom Experience," 18 *Law and Society Review* 51 (1984).

11. For a more detailed examination of the preliminary hearing decision in these nine courts, see Roy B. Flemming, "Elements of the Defense Attorney's Craft: An Adaptive Expectations Model of the Preliminary Hearing Decision," 8 *Law and Policy* 33 (1986).

12. R. Hermann, E. Single, and J. Boston, *Counsel for the Poor: Criminal Defense in Urban America* (Lexington, Mass.: Lexington Books, 1977). An analysis of "regular" defense attorneys, their "styles," and their negligible impact on case outcomes and sentencing in these nine courts can be found in Peter F. Nardulli, "Insider's Justice: Defense Attorneys and the Handling of Felony Cases" (paper presented at the annual meeting of the Law and Society Association, San Diego, California, June 6–9, 1985).

13. For a discussion of the problems in more direct observation of lawyer–client interaction, see Brenda Danet, Kenneth B. Hoffman, and Nicole C. Kermish, "Obstacles in the Study of Lawyer–Client Interaction: The Biography of a Failure," 14 *Law and Society Review* 905 (1980); Douglas E. Rosenthal, "Comment on 'Obstacles to the Study of Lawyer–Client Interaction: The Biography of a Failure,' " 14 *Law and Society Review* 923 (1980); Stewart Macaulay, "Law and Behavioral Sciences: Is There Any There There?" 6 *Law and Policy* 149 (1984). These problems may not be insurmountable, however; for example, see Hosticka (note 4) and Cain (note 5).

14. Casper found that privately retained lawyers spent dramatically different, more extensive periods with their clients; 47 percent of 132 defendants with private lawyers said they saw their attorneys for more than three hours. In contrast, 59 percent of the 463 defendants with public attorneys reported that their attorneys spent a half hour or less with them. Casper, *Criminal Courts* (note 3), p. 35.

15. See Nardulli et al. (note 6) for further descriptions of the nine courts.

16. Casper, *Criminal Courts*, p. 12.

17. Ibid., pp. 22–23.

18. Casper, *American Criminal Justice* (note 3), pp. 117–118 (emphasis in original).

19. In autobiographies of their work and careers, defense attorneys frequently bemoan their clients' lack of veracity. For example, Moldovsky states, "I know that clients lie to me . . . I just don't know which ones are the liars" (Joel Moldovsky and Rose DeWolf, *The Best Defense* [New York: Macmillan Publishing Co., 1975], p. 76). Wishman also recalls, "It didn't take me long to realize that nearly every client had lied to me" (Seymour Wishman, *Confessions of a Criminal Lawyer* [New York: Times Books, 1981], p. 84). Finally, Kunen describes the awkward situation a new client created for him when he asked, "Do you believe me?" "I didn't want to say I didn't believe him, because then it would seem I wasn't on his side. But I didn't want to say I did believe him, because then he'd think I was a fool" (James S. Kunen, *How Can You Defend Those People? The Making of a Criminal Lawyer* [New York: Random House, 1983], p. 187).

20. Alan M. Dershowitz, *The Best Defense* (New York: Vintage Books, 1983), recounts his shock at discovering his client was a stool pigeon for the prosecution: "After all, when I agreed to become his lawyer I had taken his case to defend a *landsman*, a fellow Boro Parker, a kid from the old neighborhood—not a stool pigeon. How could I ever trust Seigel again? For months he had tricked me and my colleagues into believing that he was a murder suspect, when all the while he was working for the other side, probably reporting every detail of our strategy right back to the prosecutor" (p. 21).

21. Lynn Mather, "The Outsider in the Courtroom: An Alternative Role for Defense," in Herbert Jacob, ed., *The Potential for Reform of Criminal Justice* (Newbury Park, Calif.: Sage Publications, 1974), p. 283.

22. Casper, *Criminal Court*, p. 16.

23. Marc Galanter, "Why the 'Haves' Come Out Ahead: Speculations on the Limits of Change," 9 *Law and Society Review* 95 (1974).

24. Jerome E. Carlin, *Lawyers on Their Own* (New Brunswick, N.J.: Rutgers University Press, 1962), pp. 161–162.

25. In an early study, Arthur Lewis Wood, *Criminal Lawyer* (New Haven, Conn.: College and University Press, 1967), p. 101, found that of ninety-three criminal lawyers, all of whom were private practitioners, twenty-one said they refused to accept clients who would not follow their advice.

26. This means that attorneys who are successful in this respect can play the kind of "confidence game" Blumberg describes. Blumberg (above, note 1).

27. See Nardulli et al. (note 6) for an analysis of the guilty plea process in the nine courts.

28. See ibid., regarding trial penalties in these courts. For other analyses, see Thomas M. Uhlman and N. Darlene Walker, "He Takes Some of My Time: I Take Some of His: An Analysis of Sentencing Patterns in Jury Cases," 14 *Law and Society Review* 323 (1980); David Brereton and Jonathan D. Casper, "Does It Pay to Plead Guilty? Differential Sentencing and the Functioning of Criminal Courts," 16 *Law and Society Review* 45 (1981–1982).

29. While sentences are important components of the client's decision, grievances and appeals are part of the attorney's choice and concerns. Between 1973 and 1983, criminal appeals more than doubled in Michigan and rose by 80 percent in Illinois (U.S. Department of Justice, Bureau of Justice Statistics, *The Growth of Appeals: 1973–1983 Trends* [Feb. 1985]). However, all appeals do not center on the attorney's performance, and success rates for defendants are not high. Thomas Y. Davies, "Affirmed: A Study of Criminal Appeals and Decision-Making Norms in a California Court of Appeals," 1982 *American Bar Foundation Research Journal* 543.

30. See text accompanying note 21.

31. Rosenthal (note 4), p. 13.

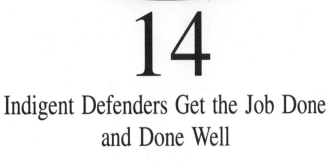

Indigent Defenders Get the Job Done and Done Well

Roger A. Hanson

Brian J. Ostrom

Data from a nine-state trial court study show that the methods of providing counsel to indigents does not conform to the usual division of public defender, assigned counsel, and contract systems. The article also challenges the common assumption that attorneys for indigents are less successful in representing their clients than privately retained defense attorneys.

Introduction

It has been nearly thirty years since the U.S. Supreme Court in the case of *Gideon v. Wainwright* required that the states provide counsel for indigent defendants in criminal cases. Since that time the debate over whether indigent defenders are effective advocates or merely functionaries has continued unabated. Do attorneys paid by the state have the same skill, autonomy, and freedom to represent their clients as privately retained attorneys? Serious doubts were expressed shortly after *Gideon* and continue to be echoed today. Moreover, current skeptics do not limit their judgments to backwater areas, as evidenced by the following view of McConville and Mirsky concerning New York City's appointed counsel arrangement:

> Against this background, the creation of an indigent defense system whose object is the mass disposal of criminal cases through guilty pleas, lesser pleas, and other non-trial dispositions should not be viewed as a heroic response to the needs of poor people by public-spirited individuals. Nor should it be viewed as a rational response

Source: This is the first publication of "Indigent Defenders Get the Job Done and Done Well" by Roger A. Hanson and Brian J. Ostrom. The article was developed under a grant from the State Justice Institute (SJI-89-05X-B-045) to the National Center for State Courts. Points of view are those of the authors and do not necessarily represent the official position of the State Justice Institute. Reprinted by permission.

to modern case pressure, as a product of the individual, or collective behavior of courtroom actors, or as the logical result of procedural and evidential complexity attendant upon a trial. Instead, the routine processing of defendants is exactly what the indigent defense system was designed to accomplish.[1]

The assertions that indigent defenders are inferior in training, limited advocates for their clients, and without sufficient resources accentuate the importance of understanding this area of legal policy. Are the critics correct or incorrect in their generalizations? Unfortunately, the answer is not obvious. There are several reasons for taking another look at this topic due to the inherent limitations in past research.

Prior studies have three deficiencies. First, many of the studies fail to go beyond the boundaries of a single court and thereby lack comparative perspective.[2] Second, cross-court studies tend not to incorporate large-, medium-, and small-sized communities.[3] This omission fails to control for the effects of population size, which generally are regarded as influential in shaping the delivery of public policy services. Third, none of the prior studies compare all of the basic types of defenders (for example, public defender, assigned counsel, and contract attorneys) to privately retained counsel.[4] As a result, available evaluations of indigent defense performance are incomplete.

The objective of this article is to describe the knowledge gained from an examination of felony case processing in nine state general jurisdiction trial courts and the role that indigent defenders play in their respective systems. The research was aimed at addressing a series of interrelated issues that are central to understanding the positive and negative effects that indigent defenders have both on court operations and on defendants. Do indigent defenders frustrate or promote the court's desire to dispose of cases expeditiously? How well do indigent defenders serve their clients? Do indigent defenders rush their clients to guilty pleas? When they go to trial, how frequently do they win?

The answers to these questions are drawn from the examination of felony case processing in the following nine diverse courts: (1) Wayne County (Detroit, Michigan) Circuit Court; (2) King County (Seattle, Washington) Superior Court; (3) Denver County (Colorado) District Court; (4) Norfolk (Virginia) Circuit Court; (5) Monterey County (Salinas, California) Superior Court; (6) Oxford County (South Paris, Maine) Superior Court; (7) Gila County (Globe, Arizona) Superior Court; (8) Island County (Coupeville, Washington) Superior Court; and (9) San Juan County (Friday Harbor, Washington) Superior Court.[5] These courts were selected in order to gain a mixture of the basic categories of indigent defenders (public defender, assigned counsel, contract attorney) in large-, and small-sized communities located in different parts of the country. They are not necessarily representative of all courts, but they do represent a broad spectrum along which many courts in the country are found.

Information was obtained from an examination of random samples of felony cases disposed of in 1987. As a result, this article provides a description of the courts in 1987 except where explicit references are made to other years. The analysis of case-level data was augmented with interviews with over 125 defense attorneys, prosecutors, judges, and court staff.

What Do the Indigent Defense Systems Look Like?

Legal representation of indigent defendants is viewed commonly as fitting into one of three basic categories: (1) public defender, (2) assigned counsel, and (3) contract attorneys. Each category is assumed to have a particular organizational structure and a particular method of financing, and each is oriented toward achieving one or more of several different goals, such as efficiency, accountability, or effectiveness. Moreover, systems in each category are presumed to be alike (for example, all public defender offices are similar).

One or more of these three basic categories is represented in each of the nine courts. If the courts are classified according to the major provider of services, as shown in Table 1, then Seattle, Denver, and Monterey are public defender systems; Detroit, Norfolk, Oxford, and Island are assigned counsel systems; and Globe and San Juan are contract systems.

This configuration corresponds to the expected pattern of public defender offices existing primarily in large-sized communities and rarely, if at all, in small communities. The occurrence of assigned counsel systems in four of the nine courts is consistent with the national pattern of assigned counsel systems' being the most frequent type of system. And the two contract systems in Globe and in San Juan fit the national estimate that this type of system exists in a minority of, usually small-sized, courts.[6]

Table 2 indicates the percent of felony dispositions in 1987 drawn from random samples of case files involving indigent defendants (represented by public defenders, assigned counsel, contract attorneys) and nonindigent defendants (represented by privately retained counsel) in each of the nine courts. Privately retained counsel represent 20 percent or more in five of the courts (Denver, Norfolk, Oxford, Island, and San Juan), and nearly that many in Globe (18 percent) and in Detroit (17.1 percent). Despite assertions to the contrary by some observers,[7] the evidence from the nine courts indicates that the private bar is not an endangered species, unless privately retained counsel are expected to handle a majority of the cases in order to be deemed viable.[8]

These data also provide a background against which to reconsider the conventional wisdom that indigent defenders fall into three mutually exclusive categories (public defender, assigned counsel, and contract attorney). The experiences of the nine courts suggest that there is considerable flexibility in constructing indigent defense systems. For example, it is neither necessary nor true that the public defender's office must be the major provider of legal services, if it is to be used. Detroit's Legal Aid and Defender Association, which handles 25 percent of the appointments, is a counterexample to that proposition. Additionally, the types of indigent defense structures may be complementary rather than competitive, as commonly supposed. Monterey's use of all three types of indigent defenders illustrates this situation. Finally, the data from the nine courts do not support the inexorable law that says that a particular type of structure must exist in a particular size of community (for example, public defenders in a large-sized community). Again, Detroit, where the

TABLE 1 / Defense Representation–Structure and Institutional Issues

	Detroit	Seattle	Denver	Norfolk	Monterey	Globe	Oxford	San Juan and Island
Percent of all felony dispositions handled by indigent defenders	83%	88%	80%	71%	90%	82%	53%	SJ: 61% I: 66%
Type(s) of indigent defense structures	Assigned counsel, public defender	Three public defender firms on contract, assigned counsel	Public defender, assigned counsel, contract attorneys	Assigned counsel	Public defenders, contract attorneys, assigned counsel	Contract attorneys, assigned counsel	Assigned counsel	Contract attorneys, assigned counsel
Level of funding	County	County	State	State	County	County	State	County
Eligibility of attorneys for appointment	Certification by court; judge appoints to case at first appearance	Private assignment rare and handled informally	Pre-1990, no formal requirements and handled informally by judge at first appearance	Attorney requests to be added to list; no formal requirements	No formal requirements on rare occasions when individual attorney assigned	Not applicable	Informal by judge or clerk	SJ: N/A I: Must be approved by defender association
Average attorney tenure	3–6 years (LADA)	3–5 years	6–7 years	Not available	5–8 years	15–18 years	10–12 years	SJ: 3 Years (1989) I: 3–8 Years

TABLE 2 / Percent of Felony Dispositions Handled by the Different Types of Defense Attorneys in the Courts

Types of Defense Attorneys	Detroit	Seattle	Denver	Norfolk	Monterey	Globe	Oxford	Island	San Juan
Public defender	18.4% (84)	86.8% (526)	74.6% (276)	0.0 (0)	72.8% (297)	0.0 (0)	0.0 (0)	0.0 (0)	0.0 (0)
Assigned counsel	64.6% (295)	1.2% (7)	5.4% (20)	71.1% (329)	3.7% (15)	0.0 (0)	52.9% (118)	65.6% (82)	0.0 (0)
Contract attorneys	0.0 (0)	0.0 (0)	0.0 (0)	0.0 (0)	13.5% (55)	82.4% (140)	0.0 (0)	0.0 (0)	61.3% (19)
Private counsel	17.1% (78)	12.0% (73)	20.0% (74)	28.9% (134)	10.0% (41)	17.6% (30)	47.1% (105)	34.4% (43)	38.7% (12)
Totals	100.1% (457)	100% (606)	100% (370)	100% (463)	100% (408)	100% (170)	100% (223)	100% (125)	100% (31)

dominant category is assigned counsel, is a strong counterexample to that notion. The only linkage between the categories of indigent defenders and size is the absence of public defenders in the four small-sized communities. But even this remnant of the conventional wisdom unravels on closer examination. As noted below, Island County's system of assigned counsel exhibits several characteristics of a public defender office. A closer examination of the nine systems reveals interesting similarities and differences in the defense structures in greater detail.

Detroit's Indigent Defense System[9]

Detroit uses primarily assigned counsel for indigent defense. The assignments, however, are distributed between two major groups. Approximately 75 percent of the caseload is assigned by judges to individual private attorneys, with the remaining 25 percent going to the Legal Aid and Defender Association (LADA). LADA is essentially a public defender's office but without the usual publicly provided budget and management. It is a private, nonprofit defender organization that was established in 1968. The caseload division is the result of a 1972 Michigan Supreme Court ruling that mandated 25 percent of all criminal cases go to LADA. The director of LADA monitors this allocation very closely and ensures that it is met.

All indigent defenders, both assigned counsel and LADA attorneys, operate under the voucher system. The Wayne County payment system for assigned counsel underwent substantial change in 1988. Prior to July 1, 1988, attorneys were paid on an event-based schedule. They were paid separately for every court event (for example, each hearing, motion, trial day, and so forth) based upon the seriousness of the offense. Now attorneys are paid a fixed fee based on the statutory maximum penalty for the offense (ranging from a low of $475 for a twenty-four month maximum case to $1,400 for first-degree murder).

There are currently about 653 individual private attorneys on the assigned counsel list, with about ten new attorneys being added each month and an indeterminate number (less than ten) dropping off the roll or moving to a more occasional status. This total is composed of approximately 200 hard-core "regulars," who depend on the assigned counsel system for a substantial share of their clients and income, and about 450 "irregulars," who use the assigned counsel system to supplement their private (criminal and/or civil) practice.

There are nineteen defense attorneys (in addition to the director and deputy director) who work for the Legal Aid and Defender Association. Although LADA is often referred to as a public defender organization, its structure is closer to an assigned counsel/public defender hybrid. As with a public defender, the operation of LADA is overseen by an independent board, with no formal government connection, that chooses the office head and sets general policy. However, LADA attorneys generate fees in the same way as private assigned counsel (vouchers are submitted to the administrative office of the court and payments are calculated on the same scale), and this accounts for the vast majority of office funding. Finally, LADA attorneys have no overhead to pay and have access to good secretarial support and experienced in-house investigators. The average tenure of attorneys at LADA is three to six years.

Seattle's Indigent Defense System[10]

The provision of indigent defense services is overseen by the King County Office of Public Defense (OPD). The OPD contracts with three nonprofit public defender firms to provide the majority of defense representation for persons charged with felony offenses.[11] Each of the defender firms has its own board of directors and internal management structure. The oldest and largest of the three firms is The Defender Association (TDA). In 1990–1991, TDA was scheduled to handle approximately 41 percent of the felonies, 25 percent of the misdemeanors, 33 percent of the juvenile offender cases, 40 percent of the juvenile dependency cases, 100 percent of the involuntary commitments, and 43 percent of the cases in the Seattle municipal court.[12] The second largest firm is the Associated Counsel for the Accused (ACA), which was assigned 37 percent of the felonies, 50 percent of the misdemeanors, 22 percent of the juvenile offender cases, and 34 percent of the cases in the Seattle municipal court.[13] The third firm, the Society of Counsel Representing Accused Persons (SCRAP), was allocated 22 percent of the felonies, 25 percent of the misdemeanors, 33 percent of the juvenile offender cases, and 60 percent of the juvenile dependency cases.[14]

OPD is a division within the County Department of Human Services that provides management oversight of the indigent defense budget and services, and it assigns all indigent clients to the contracting public defender firms. OPD staff complete a two-page form during a defendant interview. It covers various aspects of the charged offense, whether an interpreter is needed, and the defendant's financial situation. Individuals are determined to be indigent if their total resources are less than 125 percent of the poverty line or if they are on public assistance.

OPD assigns each case to a particular defender firm the same day as indigency is determined. Notice of the case (defendant name, charge, and bail status) is delivered to the defender firm the following day. All payments to each defender firm are specified in the contract, except payments for aggravated homicide and complex fraud cases and conflicts appointments. The payment in these cases is based upon negotiation between OPD and the defender firm. The defense firms are paid monthly through OPD.[15]

Denver's Indigent Defense System[16]

A statewide public defender system has been in place in Colorado since the early 1970s. Organizationally, it is part of the judicial branch. It is responsible for all indigent representation except in conflict cases (in every court, an attorney may decline to accept appointment because it would conflict with the representation of defendants that were already being represented). There are eighteen regional trial offices with attorneys, two regional offices staffed only with support staff (paralegals and investigators), and an appellate division. The system is administered by a state public defender, a chief trial deputy, a chief deputy, and an administrative unit of five (three professionals). The public defender is appointed by an independent public defender commission established by the supreme court.

The Colorado public defender in Denver handles representation for the city and county of Denver. In 1987, the office had twenty-seven staff attorneys and eight contract attorneys. There were twenty-six staff attorneys in 1990. The appointment of counsel in felony cases generally takes place in the Denver County Court. Colorado uses federal guidelines for determining indigency, but the information that defendants give is not verified. Eligibility determination is done by the public defender.

The Denver office is unique in several ways. First, many public defenders begin their employment doing misdemeanor and juvenile casework there and then move to other locations in the state. Denver proper (as opposed to the surrounding counties) is decreasing in caseload, so the office is not expanding. Because it is easy to find private attorneys to do contract work, contract attorneys are used in Denver for county court work on misdemeanors at the rate of $2,025 per month. A similar use of contract attorneys elsewhere in the state is not typical.

The average tenure of public defenders in Denver was six to seven years, with the statewide average estimated at five years. Salaries of public defenders statewide are higher than those of prosecuting attorneys, but in Denver, the salaries start off even, with the public defenders losing ground as they go up. Attorneys who leave tend to go into solo practice, although some have gone to private firms, judgeships, and so forth.

Counsel are appointed by the court when the public defender must decline the representation of an indigent defendant. The assigned counsel attorneys indicate their areas of interest and expertise (for example, misdemeanors, lesser felonies, more serious felonies), and appointments are taken from the appropriate lists. The amount of reimbursement is determined by the judge, but since 1985, the state public defender administers the funds appropriated. Control over the conflict budget by the state public defender has created an incentive to minimize conflicts and to scrutinize requests by assigned counsel for payments. The state public defender is said to earn credit with the state legislature by returning unspent funds at the end of the year.

Norfolk's Indigent Defense System[17]

Representation of indigent defendants in the upper (circuit) court is provided by private attorneys who are appointed to individual cases. Appointments generally are made in lower (district) court; however, the circuit court appoints counsel for indigent defendants when the cases do not originate in the lower court.

Appointment of counsel is made from a list of attorneys that is maintained by the circuit court but is also used by the general district court. The list contains seventy-eight names. There is apparently no formal process for getting on the list: an individual writes to the court and sets forth whatever information is deemed relevant (for example, experience and references).

Compensation is by voucher. At the conclusion of the representation the attorney completes a form indicating the total of in-court (compensated at the rate of $60 per hour) and out-of-court ($40 per hour) time.

There were recent changes in how individuals received appointments. At one time, appointments were made from the list at the first appearance in the district court, with the attorney then being notified by mail that he or she had been appointed to a case. The approach had two shortcomings. First, the attorney was not present at the first appearance, thus missing an early opportunity to speak with the client. The attorney then had to arrange to see the client in jail or try to locate the individual in the community. Second, some attorneys contended that appointments were not being equitably made from the list.

To address both issues, the district court now assigns attorneys to specific court days. The designated attorney will be appointed to all new indigent cases that come before the court for first appearance on that day. With seventy-eight people on the list, an attorney will have a "duty day" about once every two and a half months. This system equalizes the number of appointments, or at least eliminates biased use of the list. A disadvantage, however, is that it treats the attorneys as fungible commodities and can result in inappropriate appointments when it is applied inflexibly by the court.

Monterey's Indigent Defense System[18]

Monterey's indigent defense services are provided primarily by the county public defender's office. Conflict cases are farmed out to a "consortium," which consists of six attorneys who contract with the county. Each consortium attorney handles a narrow range of cases and negotiates his own contract to provide those services. When neither the public defender's office nor a consortium attorney can be appointed, the court has a list of local attorneys on whom it can call.

The public defender's office has a staff of thirty-three individuals structured as follows: chief public defender, two assistant public defenders, eighteen deputy public defenders, seven secretaries, and five investigators. The office handles most of the indigent felony defendants. Felony cases are assigned to individual attorneys by the criminal division supervisor, taking work load and experience into account. Most of the new attorneys have worked in another public defender's office, usually in a metropolitan area. There is a low turnover rate, and those who have left have gone on to be judges or defenders in other jurisdictions or have gone into private practice. Training is primarily informal, by interoffice discussion, California Public Defender Association Briefs, bar courses, and communication with the bench.

The county contracts with six attorneys to provide indigent representation in conflict cases. Each attorney submits a monthly claim with a list of her or his active caseload in order to receive a monthly check from the county. The attorney must cover all expenses out of the contract (with the exception of investigative costs). The consortium attorneys tend to be experienced practitioners. All of them have been in practice for at least fifteen years. They include attorneys with prior experience in the public defender's office, including one of the former heads of the office.

When consortium attorneys are not able to take appointments, private attorneys are assigned. In 1987, there was no clear indication of what attorneys were eligible for these appointments, the process of how attorneys could be placed on the list was unspecified, and attorneys were not graded in a systematic way to handle different types of cases. More recently, the court has taken steps to formalize the assignment system by clarifying the criteria for appointment and what attorneys satisfy the criteria.

Globe's Indigent Defense System[19]

Gila County contracts with private lawyers for indigent services. From 1986 through 1989 three lawyers held contracts. A fourth attorney was added in 1990 to handle lesser felonies and juvenile dependency cases exclusively. Attorneys contract with the County Board of Supervisors, who fund indigent defense services. The system is not merely "low-bid," however, and the court plays a meaningful role in the process of awarding the contracts. Although the County Board of Supervisors issues a request for proposals, bids are returned to the judges of the court. Thereafter, applicants negotiate with the court before contracts are finalized. The system for assigning cases to each of the contract attorneys blends work load and geographic considerations. In theory, each contract attorney receives an equal number of new cases each year. One of the indigent defense attorneys practices almost exclusively in a remote community within the county (Payson-Pine), and the other attorneys occasionally practice there.

All of the attorneys have a private practice in addition to the Gila County contract. One attorney estimates that 60 percent of his work was indigent defense and 40 percent private practice. Another attorney supplements his Gila County practice with additional contract indigent defense work in an adjacent county, which compensates him on an hourly rather than flat-fee basis. All of the attorneys maintain an office in Gila County, except for the recently hired contract attorney who handles the misdemeanors and less serious felony work.

The three attorneys who handle felony cases are veteran lawyers with more than fifteen years of experience in criminal practice, which includes forty to sixty felony cases each year. In Globe, the superiority of experience by indigent defense counsel over the deputy prosecuting attorneys is apparent and generally acknowledged. They go to trial infrequently, but they usually win when they do go.

Oxford's Indigent Defense System[20]

The state funds indigent defense in Maine, and Oxford County uses an assigned counsel system. Attorneys are appointed to a case by a judge from a list of available attorneys, with the assistance of the superior court clerk (in the instance of a direct indictment) and the chief deputy district court clerk (in the instance of a felony bind over). Attorneys who wish to be considered for assigned criminal cases inform the clerks of the respective courts who maintain the appointment lists. About twelve Oxford County lawyers accepted indigent criminal cases during the study period, with six of them receiving the majority of the appointments.

Although the state office manages the fiscal elements of the program, the local clerk of court processes the vouchers to get them approved by the judge and forwards them to the administrator in Portland. The state office reviews them and forwards them to Augusta for payment. Checks are written from the state capital in Augusta and mailed to the attorneys. Attorneys receive their checks four to ten weeks after submitting a voucher. The judges must approve vouchers submitted by counsel, and they may adjust the approved amount. The fee structure is set by the supreme court. No ceilings have been legislated for permissible attorney's fees, although the judge must approve the voucher. The judges have discretion to pay less than the full hourly rate.

Island's Indigent Defense System[21]

Island delivers indigent defense services through an assigned counsel system. In the 1970s an association of lawyers—Island County Defender's Association—was formed to certify lawyers for the service, to manage referrals and appointments, and to negotiate with the board of commissioners over fee schedules. The association maintained a governing board and employed a secretary to provide administrative services. The same secretary was hired later by the county commissioners as the full-time administrator of the indigent defense system. Through the association, the consortium of attorneys continued to speak to the county as a group, set standards for eligibility, and, in effect, controlled admission to the indigent defense practice. Thus, even though Island is classified as an assigned system, it has important elements characteristic of a public defender system.

The indigent defense administrator for the Island County Defender's Association runs a tight ship with lots of statistics, careful scrutiny of appointment documentation and the fees charged, review of defendant eligibility, and determination of partial ability to pay. She is responsible for quality control of services, fiscal control, and arrangement for promissory notes when clients have some ability to pay. There is an expectation that attorneys will meet with clients within forty-eight hours of admission to jail.

The assigned counsel system matches attorneys to case severity, with the more experienced attorneys getting the more serious cases. There are approximately twelve attorneys on the assigned counsel roster, all of whom have had several years of experience. Judges and other court personnel state that Island County's system appears to represent the values that should be present in a system of criminal defense—access to experienced attorneys who specialize in trial practice and criminal law and the opportunity for a "personal" relationship.

San Juan's Indigent Defense System

San Juan is an island community with no bridges to the mainland. Indigent defense service has been provided there since 1980 through a contract system. Before that time, defense was provided by an assigned counsel system, similar to Oxford County's. Most attorneys accepted appointments reluctantly, however. From 1979 to 1980, some local lawyers lobbied the county to revise the fee schedule upward; instead, a contract system was initiated by the county commissioners. Until recently, the contract was strictly on a low-bid criterion. The contract attorney assumed responsibility for all criminal, juvenile, and mental health cases, including all overhead. The court at the time was passive, under the theory that so long as there was a vehicle for appointment of counsel, the commissioners were free to fund the service in whatever manner they saw fit.

During the first year of the contract program, the contract attorney moved from the island to a mainland community, three hours distant by automobile and ferry. Thereafter, until 1990, a succession of three attorneys who did not live in the county held the contracts. One of these attorneys had previously been the deputy prosecutor responsible for criminal cases. Throughout this period there was general dissatisfaction with the contract service among the bar and criminal justice community, but no organized attempts to intervene with the commissioners were undertaken. Complaints generally had to do with the unavailability of the lawyer at critical times. Not only was the lawyer rarely available to clients immediately following arrest, but he also often would be late for, or entirely miss, scheduled court appearances. These proceedings would have to be rescheduled.

Comparative Perspective

Indigent defense should be thought of in terms of a flexible system of interrelated elements rather than three mutually exclusive structures. There is no doubt that there are public defenders, assigned counsel, and contract attorneys and that the methods by which they receive appointments tend to be different. Looking at these systems in the nine courts, however, the following three lessons emerge.

First, there is no single organizational model of public defenders, assigned counsel, or contract attorneys. There are important variants within each of these three categories. Second, virtually all possible combinations of public defenders, assigned counsel, and contract attorneys are feasible. Courts have the opportunity to design the arrangements that meet their particular needs and circumstances. Third, indigent defense systems should not be assessed simply in terms of organizational structure and the assumed advantages of the preferred structure. Instead, the performance of a given structure should be measured in terms of how well the indigent defenders actually handle their cases. That topic is the subject of the next two sections.

Timeliness

The expeditious resolution of criminal cases is both a right guaranteed under the U.S. Constitution and a standard to which courts are held accountable. According to the Sixth Amendment, defendants are entitled to a speedy trial as well as the assistance of counsel. Consequently, indigent defenders have a fiduciary obligation to avoid unnecessary delays.

Timeliness is also a goal that the courts are expected to achieve. Both the American Bar Association (ABA) and the Conference of State Court Administrators (COSCA) have stipulated standards for courts. Specifically, the ABA states that all felony cases should take no longer than one year from the date of the arrest to be adjudicated. It is expected, moreover, that most cases should take considerably less than one year to reach final disposition. According to the ABA, 90 percent of all felony cases should be adjudicated within 120 days from the date of arrest and 98 percent should be adjudicated within 180 days from the date of arrest.

Length of Time from Arrest to Disposition

The indigent defenders consistently process the typical case in less time than privately retained attorneys, except in Island County. As shown in Table 3, the median number of days from the date of arrest to the date of adjudication for indigent defenders is less than it is for privately retained counsel in each of the eight other courts

TABLE 3 / Typical Length of Time That Indigent Defenders and Privately Retained Counsel Take to Resolve Cases (Median Number of Days from Date of Arrest to Adjudication,[a] Felony Dispositions)

	Detroit	Seattle[b]	Denver	Norfolk	Monterey	Globe	Oxford	Island	San Juan
Public defender	79	75	151	—	56	—	—	—	—
Contract attorney	—	—	—	—	78	125	—	—	79
Assigned counsel	62	—	162	114	115	—	134	156	—
Privately retained counsel	102	101	167	184	89	141	215	131	88
All cases	71	85	156	126	63	129	161	146	83

[a] Adjudication is the entry of a dismissal, guilty plea, deferred adjudication, or diversion, or verdict.

[b] In Seattle, the indigent defense attorneys represented are from three public defender firms (The Defender Association [TDA]; Associated Counsel for the Accused [ACA]; Society of Counsel Representing Accused Persons [SCRAP]). The typical case-processing time for each firm is as follows: TDA, 89 days; ACA, 77 days; SCRAP, 59 days.

for all types of indigent defenders except for the small group of assigned counsel in Monterey. In Monterey, assigned counsel have a median number of days (115) that is longer than the time associated with privately retained counsel (eighty-nine days). However, both the public defenders (fifty-six days) and the contract attorneys (seventy-eight days), which are the primary and secondary providers of indigent defense in Monterey, are more timely than privately retained counsel (eighty-nine days).

Meeting the ABA Standard

The same pattern of positive performance by indigent defenders emerges when the ABA's standard of resolving 98 percent of felony cases within 180 days of the arrest data is used. Only San Juan meets the standard; in the other eight courts more than 2 percent of the felony cases are still open at 180 days. However, as shown in Table 4, the percentage of cases remaining open after 180 days is consistently less for the indigent defenders in all the courts except Globe. In Globe, 28.6 percent of the cases represented by contract attorneys remain open after 180 days, and 27.2 percent of the cases represented by privately retained attorneys remain open after 180 days from the date of arrest. Additionally, in Monterey, relatively more of the cases with privately retained counsel meet the ABA standard than do the cases with assigned counsel. However, the two larger groups of indigent defenders in Monterey (public defender and contract attorneys) approximate the standard more closely than do the privately retained attorneys.

The quantitative results, which indicate that indigent defenders do well in terms of timeliness, have profound implications. One implication is that the expeditious adjudication of cases reduces the demand for additional court appearances and the length of time that defendants spend in jail awaiting disposition of their cases. The assembling of all the participants in the legal process for court proceedings and the pretrial detention of defendants are undeniably costly. Hence, indigent defenders contribute to cost savings by their timeliness.

Second, the closer approximation by indigent defenders to established time standards presents a picture that diverges from the popular image. A common view of indigent defenders is that they are engaging in dilatory tactics in one case in order to meet deadlines in other cases. Simply stated, they are viewed as unable to schedule their work, to satisfy time requirements, and to live within budgetary constraints. That point of view is not supported by the data from the nine courts under study. In terms of approximating time standards, indigent defenders perform better than privately retained attorneys. What other public institutions can make the claim that they perform as well as (or better than) the private sector?

Third, the achievement of timeliness frames the issue of effective representation in a new light. Instead of engaging in a philosophical debate over whether timeliness is inherently good or bad, one can ask the empirical question, Are the gains in efficiency made at the expense of the defendants? Are the rights or interests of defendants sacrificed in some way? The achievement of timeliness needs to be viewed side by side with information on the outcomes for defendants. The tasks of presenting and interpreting the necessary information are the subject of the next section.

TABLE 4 / Percent of Felony Cases Unresolved after 180 Days from the Date of Arrest for Indigent Defenders and Privately Retained Counsel (ABA Standards Stipulate That 2 Percent or Less of the Cases Should Be Unresolved)

	Detroit	Seattle[a]	Denver	Norfolk	Monterey	Globe	Oxford	Island	San Juan
Public defender	16.7%	19.0%	43.8%	—	8.3%	—	—	—	—
Contract attorney	—	—	—	—	3.9%	23.5%	—	—	0%
Assigned counsel	11.9%	—	45.5%	20.9%	20.0%	—	42.4%	44.6%	—
Privately retained attorneys	21.8%	26.4%	45.6%	51.1%	11.5%	27.2%	60.0%	47.2%	9.1%
All cases	14.4%	21.1%	44.2%	29.7%	8.0%	28.3%	49.1%	45.6%	3.4%

[a]In Seattle, the indigent defense attorneys represented are from three public defender agencies (The Defender Association [TDA]; Associated Counsel for the Accused [ACA]; Society of Counsel Representing Accused Persons [SCRAP]). The percentages of unresolved cases after 180 days for the three firms are as follows: TDA, 23.0%; ACA, 17.6%; SCRAP, 16.3%.

Performance and Indigent Defense

There are two basic approaches to assessing indigent defenders in the literature. The first approach has what may be called an input orientation. Indigent defenders are expected to represent their clients by being adequately prepared—meeting with clients, contacting witnesses, conducting research, reviewing presentence investigation reports, and so forth. Hence, a body of guidelines has been formulated that identifies how effective representation is to be conducted and the resources required to facilitate advocacy.[22]

The second approach has what may be called an output orientation.[23] Indigent defenders are expected to represent their clients by achieving favorable outcomes, such as acquittals and dismissals, charge reductions, noncustodial sentences, and the shortest possible periods of incarceration in prison. In this approach, the performance of indigent defenders is determined by comparing them with privately retained counsel. Do indigent defenders achieve the same percentage of favorable outcomes for their clients as privately retained counsel? This comparison sets a very high standard of evaluation for indigent defenders. There are several factors that have very little to do with the relative capabilities of attorneys that make it more difficult for indigent than nonindigent defendants to gain favorable outcomes. First, indigent defendants are more likely to be detained than defendants who can afford an attorney. Second, indigent defendants are more likely to have prior records that will be influential at sentencing. Third, indigent defendants are thought to be less assertive of their rights than defendants who can afford to pay for attorneys.[24]

Both of these approaches have their role to play in assessing indigent defense counsel. The first approach is appropriate for examining work that individual attorneys put into specific cases, but it provides no assessment of what the attorney accomplishes. Certainly, an attorney may meet with the client, interview witnesses, research the law, but do none of these activities effectively. Because the second approach draws conclusions concerning the performance of attorneys, it is the preferred orientation.

Conviction Rates

A fundamental concern to criminal defendants is gaining an acquittal or a dismissal. With a conviction comes the imposition of penalties. One basic goal of the defense attorney is to minimize the possibility of criminal penalties. In terms of measuring this goal, the standard is that the lower the conviction rate for a given set of attorneys, the more successful they are in gaining favorable outcomes for their clients.

The data indicate that indigent defenders perform as well as privately retained counsel in meeting this standard under a wide range of conditions. The conviction rates of defendants represented by public defenders, contract attorneys, assigned counsel, and privately retained counsel, when all nine courts are combined, are strikingly similar. Public defenders have a rate of 84.4 percent, contract attorneys have a rate of 83.6 percent, assigned counsel have a rate of 85.3 percent, and privately retained counsel have a rate of 83.4 percent. There is no statistically significant difference (chi-square = 1.26, significance level = .77) among these rates.[25] Defendants are no worse off with one type of defense attorney than another, which means that defendants with privately retained counsel do no better, on average, than do indigent defendants with a publicly appointed attorney.

The similarity in the conviction rates among the different types of defense attorneys extends to cases that go to trial. Public defenders secured acquittal or dismissal in 23.2 percent of cases; contract attorneys, 28.6 percent; assigned counsel, 33.3 percent; and privately retained counsel, 25.6 percent. Thus indigent defenders are no less successful in gaining acquittals or dismissals for their clients than are privately retained counsel. There is no statistically significant relationship (chi-square = 2.74, significance level = .43) between the types of attorneys and the likelihood of conviction at trial.

These results raise an additional question. Are the conviction rates similar for different types of attorneys in both the large- and small-sized courts? This more refined question outstrips the available data to some extent. There are too few contract attorneys in either the large-sized or the small-sized courts to permit valid statistical testing. However, if all the indigent defenders are collapsed into one category, then this question can be addressed in terms of the conviction rates of publicly appointed attorneys versus privately retained counsel.

The data indicate that there is no linkage between the type of attorney and the likelihood of conviction either in the large-sized or in the small-sized courts. The conviction rates for publicly appointed and privately retained attorneys in the large courts (Detroit, Seattle, Denver, Norfolk, and Monterey) are 84.8 percent and 82 percent, respectively. In the small-sized courts (Oxford, Globe Island, and San Juan), the parallel percentages are 84.1 and 86.3.[26] These are not statistically significant differences. Hence, within the limitations of the available data, the evidence indicates that indigent defenders do as well as privately retained counsel in terms of a fundamental criterion of performance. The likelihood of an indigent defendant being convicted is not influenced significantly by the fact that the defense attorney is publicly appointed.

Charge Reductions

From the perspective of the defendant and the defense attorney, any success is a victory. Given the fact that most defendants are convicted, one of the best outcomes that most defendants can realistically strive for is a reduction in the seriousness of charge. If the offense at conviction is a less serious offense than the offense with which the defendant was initially charged, this outcome is favorable to the defendant. The empirical question is, Do privately retained counsel have significantly different charge reduction rates from those of indigent defenders?

For the four types of defense attorneys, this question can be addressed only for the cases disposed of by guilty pleas, because the number of trials is limited for some categories of attorneys. The data reveal that there are significant differences in charge reduction rates among the categories of defense attorneys. The charge reduction rates for public defenders, contract attorneys, assigned counsel, and privately retained counsel are 25.7, 50.9, 26.4, and 31.9 percent, respectively. Contract attorneys do considerably better than the privately retained counsel, who do slightly better than the public defenders or the assigned counsel.[27] Hence, for cases involving guilty pleas, there are mixed results concerning the performance of indigent defenders. Some indigent defenders perform quite well whereas others perform less well than privately retained counsel.

If all indigent defenders are combined into one category, then the question of the linkage between type of attorney and charge reductions also can be examined for different-sized courts. From this perspective the size of the court produces opposite effects. In the large courts, privately retained attorneys gain more reductions (32 percent) than do publicly appointed counsel (26.3 percent). In the small-sized courts, privately retained counsel gain fewer reductions (28.7 percent) than do publicly appointed counsel (37.4 percent). Both sets of results are weak statistically, however.[28] In the large courts the correlation between the type of attorney and the likelihood of a charge reduction in very low (phi-square $= .05$). For the small-sized courts, the relationship is not statistically significant.[29] Hence, while the type of defense attorney may have some effect on charge reductions, the effect is negligible.

On the basis of these data, the performance of indigent defenders in gaining charge reductions is somewhat mixed. Contract attorneys do better than privately retained counsel, while public defenders and assigned counsel do less well. This connection, however, is weak statistically (Cramer's $V = .15$). Similarly, publicly appointed counsel gain more charge reductions in small-sized courts and fewer charge reductions in large-sized courts than do privately retained counsel. These connections, while demonstrating opposite effects, are weak. Thus, overall, indigent defenders perform about as well as privately retained counsel in obtaining charge reductions.

Incarceration Rates

The potential advantage that privately retained counsel have over indigent defenders should be the greatest in determining whether a convicted defendant is incarcerated in jail or prison, sentenced to probation, given community service, or fined. The prior record of the defendant is likely to play a major role in this decision. Unfortunately, the collection of data on the defendant's prior record was beyond the scope of this research. If it is true that indigent defendants are more likely to have prior records than nonindigent defendants, this missing information means that the examination of incarceration rates, without controlling for the effects of prior record, is tipped somewhat in favor of privately retained counsel. Yet, despite this potential advantage, privately retained counsel are only slightly more successful in keeping their clients out of jail or prison.

The incarceration rates are lower for cases represented by privately retained counsel. Assigned counsel and privately retained counsel have approximately the same incarceration rates (60.3 versus 57.1). Public defenders (78.2) and contract attorneys (74.6) are less successful in keeping their clients out of penal institutions. However, the association between the four types of defense attorneys and the corresponding incarceration rates is only moderate (Cramer's $V = .20$).[30] This correlation means that privately retained attorneys are more likely to gain favorable outcomes for their clients, but this advantage is limited. A majority of the convicted defendants represented by every type of defense attorney are incarcerated. The size of the majority is greater for indigent defense attorneys, but nearly six of every ten defendants represented by privately retained counsel are incarcerated.

How indigent defenders and privately retained counsel compare is seen more clearly when all indigent defenders are grouped together. Felony defendants with publicly appointed counsel are incarcerated 72.4 percent of the time, while those who privately retain their attorneys end up in prison or jail 58.2 percent of the time. The correlation between these two types of defense attorneys and the in/out decision is a very weak one (phi-square = .12).[31] The slightly better performance by privately retained counsel, moreover, appears to be due to the effect of public defenders on the population of all indigent defenders. The use of a public defender appears to influence the higher incarceration rate among publicly appointed attorneys. The question thus arises, If public defenders are excluded from the analysis, then what do the results look like? The absence of public defenders occurs naturally when the courts are separated according to size. Whereas public defenders work in four of the five large courts, they are not present in any of the four small courts. The results of this analysis show that privately retained attorneys perform better than publicly appointed attorneys in both the large courts and the small courts.

In the large courts, privately retained attorneys perform better (50.5 percent of clients incarcerated) than publicly appointed counsel (71.5 percent of clients incarcerated). The difference in incarceration rates is statistically significant, but it is limited, as indicated by a weak correlation coefficient (phi-square = .17).[32] The underlying reason why the connection is weak rests on the fact that indigent defenders represented 83 percent of defendants and obtained 74 percent of the sentences involving some penalty other than incarceration. Privately retained counsel represented 17 percent of the defendants and obtained 26 percent of the sentences involving nonincarceration. Given that indigent defenders cannot choose their clients, and privately retained counsel do have some control over whom they represent, these differences are much smaller than expected. Moreover, in the small-sized courts, the differences are in favor of publicly appointed counsel, although the incarceration rates are not statistically different. The incarceration rate is 77.4 percent for privately retained counsel and 75.2 percent for publicly appointed counsel, which is in the opposite direction of the advantage that privately retained counsel are expected to enjoy.[33]

Thus, privately retained counsel perform somewhat better than indigent defenders on the basic in/out dimension. However, the greater likelihood that privately retained counsel keep their clients out of jail or prison is limited both in magnitude and in the scope of the effects. In the small-sized courts, privately retained counsel and publicly appointed attorneys perform at the same level. Given the assumption that indigent defendants are much less likely to win favorable outcomes because of their prior records, limited ties to the community, and other social circumstances, the limited degree of success by privately retained counsel falls short of that expectation. The results suggest that indigent defenders are able to overcome the potential liabilities of their clients to a very great extent.

Conclusion

How frequently do indigent defenders gain favorable outcomes for their clients? Are they more successful than, less successful than, or equally as successful as privately retained counsel in gaining favorable outcomes? The evidence gained from an examination of felony dispositions in the nine courts is that indigent defenders generally are as successful as privately retained counsel. The conviction rates, the charge reduction rates, and the incarceration rates for their clients are similar to the outcomes associated with privately retained counsel. These results raise a couple of issues for future consideration.

First, the results are helpful in identifying what aspects of performance are translatable into management information systems and what aspects warrant further research and development. The measurement of case outcomes seems sufficiently feasible and the results seem sufficiently meaningful to merit inclusion into the monitoring of indigent defense systems. Consequently, judges, policy makers, and others concerned with the quality of indigent defense representation should take the necessary steps to gather information on how well indigent defenders do in gaining favorable outcomes for their clients.

However, the measures of performance in this article do not speak to the issue of lawyer–client relations, especially the time that indigent defenders give to individual defendants. How frequently do they meet with clients? What is the average amount of time spent with clients? Previous research has indicated that the amount of time that indigent defenders spend with their clients makes a difference in client satisfaction. The more time that is spent, the more defendants are satisfied with their attorneys.

Satisfaction should not be confused with productive work. Indigent defenders know how to husband resources and to gain the most favorable outcomes for their clients expeditiously. However, satisfaction is part of performance and deserves further examination. Future research needs to be conducted on this topic in order to establish more precisely what amount and what kind of time indigent defenders should be expected to devote to meeting with their clients, within the constraints of their caseloads.[34]

Second, the results suggest that judges, policy makers, attorneys, and others are not required to choose between timeliness and performance. Evidence from the nine courts in this study indicate that both goals are possible to achieve. The fact that these goals are not necessarily in conflict means that the task confronting the courts is to organize an indigent defense system responsible to community needs and circumstances that achieves both goals. That task, which is neither easy nor obvious, is possible. However, the lesson to be learned is that courts have the opportunity to design a system where both timeliness and performance are attained.

Notes

1. Michael McConville and Chester L. Mirsky, "Criminal Defense of the Poor in New York City," 15 *New York University Review of Law and Social Change* 881 (1986–1987). An underlying theme to McConville and Mirsky's work is that indigent defenders are co-opted by the courthouse community. This theme is a traditional one in the literature. See, for example, David Sudnow, "Normal Crimes: A Sociological Feature of the Penal Code in a Public Defender Office," 12 *Social Problems* 253 (1965); Abraham S. Blumberg, "The Practice of Law Is a Confidence Game: Organizational Co-optation of a Profession," 1 *Law and Society Review* 15 (1967); Dennis R. Eckart and Robert V. Stover, "Public Defenders and Routinized Criminal Defense Processes," 51 *Journal of Urban Law,* 665 (May 1974); J. P. Levine, "The Impact of 'Gideon': The Performance of Public

and Private Defense Lawyers," 8 *Polity* 215 (1975); Suzzane E. Mounts and Richard Wilson, "Systems for Providing Indigent Defense: An Introduction," 14 *New York University Review of Law and Social Change* 193 (1986).

2. See, for example, Lisa J. McIntyre, *The Public Defender: The Practice of Law in the Shadows of Repute* (Chicago: University of Chicago Press, 1987).

3. Some studies focus on very large communities. See, for example, Robert Hermann, Eric Single, and John Boston's study of New York, Los Angeles, and Washington, D.C., in *Counsel for the Poor: Criminal Defense in Urban America* (Lexington, Mass.: D.C. Heath, 1977). See also James Eisenstein and Herbert Jacob's study of Baltimore, Detroit, and Chicago in *Felony Justice: An Organizational Analysis of Criminal Courts* (Boston: Little, Brown, 1977). On the other hand, Peter Nardulli focuses exclusively on nine medium-sized communities (DuPage, Peoria, and St. Clair counties in Illinois; Kalamazoo, Oakland, and Saginaw counties in Michigan; Dauphin, Erie, and Montgomery counties in Pennsylvania) in "Insider's Justice: Defense Attorneys and the Handling of Felony Cases," 77 *Journal of Criminal Law and Criminology* 379 (1986). Prior research with the broadest scope is a study of eight medium-sized and small-sized communities all located in Virginia by Larry J. Cohen, Patricia P. Semple, Robert and E. Crew, Jr., "Assigned Counsel versus Public Defender Systems in Virginia: A Comparison of Relative Benefits," in *The Defense Counsel*, edited by William F. McDonald (Newbury Park, Calif.: Sage Publications, 1983).

4. Some of the studies, in fact, do not compare indigent defenders with privately retained counsel. See, for example, McConville and Mirsky, "Criminal Defense of the Poor in New York City," (note 1). The lack of a comparison group poses severe methodological problems because evaluations require some form of comparison.

5. Hereafter the courts will be referred to by the names that they commonly are called in order to facilitate exposition. The names are: Detroit, Seattle, Denver, Norfolk, Monterey, Oxford, Globe, Island, and San Juan.

6. Robert L. Spangenberg, Beverely Lee, Michael Battaglia, Patricia Smith, and A. David Davis, *National Criminal Defense System Study: Final Report* (Washington, D.C.: U.S. Department of Justice, 1986).

7. Paul B. Wice, *Criminal Lawyers: An Endangered Species* (Newbury Park, Calif.: Sage Publications, 1978).

8. There are minor differences in the caseload composition of defense attorneys. All three basic categories of indigent defenders tend to have the same distribution of felony cases. Most of their cases involve burglary and theft offenses, followed by, in descending order of frequency, crimes against the person, drug sale and possession, and other types of felonies. The only difference between their caseloads and those of privately retained counsel lies in the fact that privately retained counsel have more crimes against the person than burglary and theft cases. However, this difference is not sharp.

9. The population of Wayne County was 2,164,300 in 1986. The city of Detroit accounted for just over one-half of the total county population (1,086,220), making it the sixth-largest city in the United States. The total population living within the city, however, has been in decline since the 1950s. Approximately 39 percent of the Wayne County population is identified as nonwhite. Per capita income is $10,681, with just over 14 percent of the population living below the poverty level. Wayne County's crime rate was 9,864 serious crimes per 100,000 population.

10. In 1988, the Seattle primary metropolitan area had a population of 1,862,000, with the city of Seattle accounting for just under one-third of the total (502,000). Seattle, the twenty-fourth-largest city in the country, experienced a growth in population of 1.7 percent from 1980 to 1988; just over 12 percent of its population is identified as nonwhite. Of the nine communities under examination, Seattle had the second-highest per capita income ($13,192) and the lowest percentage of individuals living below the poverty line (7.7 percent).

11. Several years ago, the Seattle City Council, members of the bar, and some indigent defendants questioned whether there was insufficient minority representation on the board of directors and in management positions at TDA, ACA, and SCRAP. The response, in addi-

tion to increasing the awareness of affirmative action in the three agencies, was to create a fourth firm with management by minority-group members, Northwest Defenders Association (NDA). NDA, which did not represent felony cases in 1990–1991, is not investigated in this study.

12. The Defender Association, an outgrowth of Seattle's Model City Program, was created in 1969 with a staff of five. In 1987, 166 individuals were employed at TDA, seventy-one of whom were attorneys. It was the only agency that provided indigent defense services for all case types: felony, misdemeanor, juvenile offender, juvenile dependency, and municipal court cases.

13. In 1987, ACA employed eighty-three individuals, fifty-five of whom were professional staff. The types of cases handled by ACA are felony, misdemeanor, juvenile offender, and Seattle municipal court cases. The director of ACA values having a core of experienced attorneys (that is, four to six years), but he has reservations about "lifers." About 20 percent of the attorneys have five to seven years of experience, and most attorneys have about three years of experience.

14. In 1987, SCRAP employed 29.5 full-time equivalents, 18 of whom were professionals. Most attorneys are recent law school graduates. New attorneys start in juvenile offender or dependency and may work into felonies if they are interested. Most felony attorneys gain experience within the firm in other divisions, but there are some lateral hires of experienced felony lawyers. Felony attorneys are hired by an ad hoc, two-member hiring committee consisting of the felony supervisor and another felony lawyer. Tenure in the felony division was difficult to assess because the firm had been handling these cases for only about the last five years.

15. The defender firms have no funding in their own budgets for expert witnesses. Funds for experts are found in the superior court budget, and defenders obtain them through an order from the judge. The judge is able to sign off for up to $350. If a higher amount is requested, it goes to an audit committee for acceptance or rejection. Some of the attorneys who were interviewed were not aware of the procedure for obtaining an amount in excess of $350.

16. Denver is the largest city in the Rocky Mountain region. Its population of 505,000 in 1986 tended to be divided between a relatively affluent majority and a very poor minority. A most striking feature of Denver is its crime rate of 10,557 serious crimes per 100,000 population.

17. Norfolk, Virginia, is a core city declining in population, with limited growth due to the out-migration of both middle-income residents and some poor residents (through the demolition of housing projects). Racial minorities constitute 38.4 percent of the population, and about 21 percent live below the poverty level. Norfolk had a violent crime rate in 1985 of 6,561 per 100,000.

18. The population of Monterey County was 340,000 in 1986. Approximately 15 percent of the county's population is Hispanic. In 1985, the per capita income was $10,420, with 11.4 percent of the population below the poverty level. Monterey County's crime rate was 5,419 serious crimes per 100,000 population.

19. Gila County is a large geographic area (4,752 square miles), approximately half the size of Rhode Island. It is located approximately 90 miles east of Phoenix in the state's copper mining region. It also includes a growing recreational and retirement community (Payson-Pine), although the Miami-Globe community is larger. Demographically, Gila County is a community of 37,000 persons, with 15 percent of the population identified as nonwhite (primarily Hispanic and American Indian, since the county is bordered on the east by two Indian reservations). The per capita income in 1985 was $7,399.

20. The population of Oxford County was 50,200 in 1986, approximately 4 percent of Maine's total population of 1,250,000. Oxford County is located in the southwestern mountain region of Maine. The basic industries in this area center around lumbering and paper production. The per capita income is $8,379, with just under 13 percent of the population living below the poverty level. Less than one-half of 1 percent of Oxford County is identified as nonwhite. The serious crime rate for Oxford was 1,781 index crimes per 100,000 population in 1985.

21. Island and San Juan counties are adjacent counties that consist only of islands. By Western United States standards they are very small in area (212 square miles for Island; 179 square miles for San Juan). Both counties are rural in character; however, a Naval Air Station in Island County gives Island a somewhat different flavor. Both counties have a low to virtually nonexistent minority population and high real estate values. The median value of homes in San Juan county is $87,300—the highest in the state and nearly one-third higher than the state median—and the median real estate value in Island County is nearly identical to the state median of $60,700. Crime rates are 2,278 and 2,843 per 100,000 population for Island and San Juan, respectively.

22. Roberta Rovner-Pieczenik, Alan Rapoport, and Martha Lane, *How Does Your Defender Office Rate? Self-Evaluation Manual for Public Defender Offices* (Washington, D.C.: Government Publications Office, 1977), especially pages 38–43 concerning measures of "attorney competence." American Bar Association Project on Standards for Criminal Justice, *Standards Relating to the Prosecution Function and the Defense Function* (Washington, D.C.: American Bar Association, 1971), especially pages 225–228 concerning the "duty to investigate." William Genego, "Future of Effective Assistance of Counsel: Performance Standards and Complete Representation," 22 *American Criminal Law Review* 181 (Fall 1984). National Study Commission on Defense Services, *Guidelines for Legal Defense System in the United States* (Washington, D.C.: National Legal Aid and Defender Association, 1976), especially pages 428–447 on "ensuring effectiveness."

23. See, for example, Hermann, Single and Boston, *Counsel for the Poor* (note 3); Joyce Sterling, "Retained Counsel Versus the Public Defender," in William F. McDonald, ed., *The Defense Council* (Newbury Park, Calif.: Sage Publications, 1983), pp. 68–76; David Willison, "The Effects of Counsel on the Severity of Criminal Sentences: A Statistical Assessment," 9 *Justice System Journal* 87 (1984).

24. Some scholars suggest that it is utopian to expect that indigent defenders will perform as well as privately retained counsel. Willison "The Effects of the Severity of Criminal Sentences" (note 23) writes that indigent defenders will "fail to perform as successfully as privately retained counsel even if they are adequately funded and have workable caseloads so long as they continue to represent disadvantaged defendants facing serious criminal charges and possessing extensive criminal records" (88).

25. In this section, two basic statistical tests are applied to determine whether there is a connection between the different types of defense attorneys and performance and the strength of the connection. The first test is a test of significance. The test of significance indicates whether there is a systematic connection as opposed to a coincidental connection. The chi-square test is the particular test that is applied. This technique generates a number and a corresponding level of significance. The smaller the significance level, the less likely it is that the observed pattern could have happened by chance alone. In this article, the benchmark of .01 is used to determine when there are statistically significant differences (that is, results could have happened by chance alone only one time out of a hundred). In all of the tables, the chi-square value and the level at which it is significant are reported.

   The second test is a test of association. If there is a systematic connection, how close is it? The test of association measures the strength of connection in terms of a correlation coefficient. The coefficient ranges in value from zero to one. Basically, the larger the value of the coefficient, the tighter the connection is between the different types of attorneys and various case outcomes. The phi-square and the Cramer's V correlations are the tests of association that are applied. Phi-square is appropriate for all two-by-two tables, and Cramer's V is appropriate for all the others. Finally, the rule of thumb is that coefficients below .20 are considered to be indications of weak connections between the types of attorneys and case outcomes, those from .21 to .40 are considered to indicate moderate connections, and coefficients from .41 to 1.0 are considered to indicate strong connections.

26. Large courts: chi-square = 1.91, significance level = .17, phi-square = .03. Small courts: chi-square = .46, significance level = .49, chi-square = .46.

27. The relatively high level of success among contract attorneys may be due to the unusually high level of experience, especially among the contract attorneys in Monterey and Globe.

28. Chi-square = 48.12, significance level = .0001, Cramer's V = .15.

29. Large courts: chi-square = 4.43, significance level = .04, phi-square = .05. Small courts: chi-square = .46, significance level = .49, phi-square = .03.
30. Chi-square = 87.79, significance level = .0001, Cramer's V = .20.
31. Chi-square = 36.00, significance level = .0001, phi-square = .12.
32. Chi-square = 55.00, significance level = .0001, phi-square = .17.
33. Chi-square = .261, significance level = .01, phi-square = .03.
34. Jonathan D. Casper, "Did You Have a Lawyer When You Went to Court? No. I Had a Public Defender," *Yale Review of Law and Social Action* 4–9 (Spring 1971). More generally, researchers have found that the felony defendant's degree of satisfaction with the outcome of the case is shaped by the procedural fairness of the process. Procedural fairness includes measures of the defendant's views of the defense attorney's, prosecutor's, and judge's behavior (for example, Did your lawyer listen to you? Did the prosecutor pay careful attention to your case? Did the judge try hard to find out if you were guilty or innocent?). See also Jonathan D. Casper, Tom Tyler, and Bonnie Fisher, "Procedural Justice in Felony Cases," 22 *Law and Society Review* 483 (1988).

PART FIVE

Courts

Conditions in the lower criminal courts are shocking to observers. Most city courtrooms have little of the quiet dignity one expects to see when decisions concerning individual freedom and justice are being made. The scene is usually one of noise and confusion as attorneys, police, and prosecutors mill around conversing with one another and making bargains to keep the assembly line of the criminal justice process in operation. One might see a judge accepting guilty pleas and imposing sentences at a rapid pace, going through the litany of procedure like a bored priest. It is not surprising that visitors are shocked and that first offenders are confused by what they see.

The courts, like other parts of the justice system, function under conditions of mass production, congestion, and limited resources. Even in the courts, the interests of the organization and of the principal actors often take precedence over the claims of justice. The mass production of judicial decisions is accomplished because the street-level bureaucrats in the system work on the basis of three assumptions. The first is that only people for whom there is a high probability of guilt will be brought before the courts; doubtful cases will be filtered out of the system by the police and the prosecution. Second, the vast majority of defendants will plead guilty. In most urban courts less than 10 percent of defendants plead not guilty. Third, those charged with minor offenses will be processed quickly. This usually means that all the defendants will be called together before the bench, the citation will be read by the clerk, individual pleas will be taken by the judge, and sentences quickly pronounced.

It is tempting to believe that adding more judges and constructing new facilities will relieve courtroom overload, but other factors contribute to the situation—for example, poor management, the rise in the amount of crime, and the presence of lawyers. Some argue that the procedural requirements laid down by the U.S. Supreme Court have lengthened the processing time, yet observers point out that defendants are typically informed en masse of their rights by a droning bailiff. In addition, most defendants actually waive their right to a trial, and many do not even want the services of an attorney.

The problem of court congestion has become widely recognized during the past decade. Observers both inside and outside of government have deplored the fact that defendants in criminal cases often wait in jail for months before they come to trial. More important than conditions in the criminal courts are the filtering effect, the administrative determination of guilt, and the exchange relationships that characterize the system. As long as the system is able to function in accordance with the needs of the players, the additional judges and courtrooms demanded by reformers will not bring about a shift to due process values.

Judging

Of the many actors in the criminal justice process, judges are perceived as having the greatest amount of leverage and influence. Decisions made by the police, defense attorneys, and prosecutors are greatly affected by the rulings and sentencing practices of judges. Although we tend to think of judges primarily in connection with trials, their work is much more varied; they are a continuous presence throughout the range of activities leading to disposition of a case. Signing warrants, fixing bail, arraigning defendants, accepting guilty pleas, scheduling cases—all are portions of the judge's work outside the formal trial.

More than any other actor in the system, the judge is expected to embody justice, making sure that due process rights are respected and that the defendant is treated fairly. The judge is expected to act inside and outside the courthouse according to well-defined role prescriptions that are designed to prevent involvement in activities that could bring the judicial office into disrepute. Yet the pressures of today's justice system often relegate the ideals associated with the judge's position to secondary status. The need for speedy disposition of cases takes priority.

In most cities the criminal court judge occupies the lowest rank in the judicial hierarchy. Neither lawyers nor laypersons accord these judges the prestige that is part of the mystique usually surrounding the bench. Perhaps their status is tarnished by the defendants with whom they have to deal. Studies have shown that criminal judges tend to come from backgrounds that have lower socioeconomic characteristics than those of civil judges. Often, the jurist has assumed the bench directly from a criminal law practice before the same court and has come to the position through influence in party politics. Yet the lower-court judge is able to exercise discretion in the disposition of summary offenses without the constant supervision of higher courts. This is especially noticeable in courts of first instance, where sentencing is carried out in a hurried manner, usually without any record of the session being kept.

Popular election of judges occurs in more than half the states, with thirteen states using the partisan approach. This method has probably received the most criticism because of the belief that judgeships go only to those who have earned their robes through duty to a political party. Yet this criticism is not universal. The reformist American Judicature Society claims that political parties usually provide competent candidates and that the worst judges emerge from nonpartisan elections where the voter is not guided by the party emblem.

In many states, judgeships furnish much of the fuel for party engines. Because of the honorific and material rewards of the position, political parties can secure the energy and money of attorneys who view a judgeship as the capstone of a legal career. In addition, a certain amount of courthouse patronage may adhere to the position. Clerks, bailiffs, and secretaries—all positions that may be filled with active party workers—are appointed by the judge. Because of the hegemony of the Democratic party in such cities as New York and Chicago, selections for judicial posts are solely in the hands of political leaders. There usually are many interested candidates, and it is often charged that money is a prime factor in selecting one. In some cities a contribution to the party equal to two years' salary is the going price. More common are such approaches as making contributions to fund-raising benefits or "loans" to the party.

The nature of the road to a judgeship greatly determines the type of person who will handle the gavel and wear the robes. The political and social milieu encourages the advancement of individuals with certain attitudes and leaves others by the wayside. These factors, in turn, influence the decisions made from the bench. In most communities, the selection of judges is of minor interest to the general public. Good persons must be recruited to the bench, but the definition of *good* remains in dispute.

Decision Making

What factors influence the making of decisions by prosecutors, defense attorneys, and judges during the adjudication process? Although the traditional picture of the courtroom emphasizes the adversarial posture, in reality interactions among the major actors take place within the context of the local legal culture—norms shared by members of a particular criminal court community (judges, attorneys, clerks, bailiffs, and so forth) as to case handling and participants' behavior in the judicial process. The local legal culture influences court operations since the norms work as follows:

1. They help participants distinguish between "our" court and other jurisdictions.
2. They stipulate how members should treat one another.
3. They describe how cases *should* be processed—what is often referred to as the "going rate," that is, the local view of the appropriate sentence given the offense and the defendant's prior record and other characteristics.

Established informal rules and practices arise within particular settings, and "the way things are done" differs from place to place. Differences between legal cultures can often explain why court processes and decisions vary even though the formal rules of criminal procedures are similar throughout the United States.

Adjudication takes place in the local legal setting, but decisions are also influenced by the fact that courtroom participants are organized as work groups. From this perspective, the reciprocal relationships of the judge, prosecutor, and defense attorney, along with those of the support cast (clerk, reporter, and bailiff), are necessary to complete the group's basic task—the disposition of cases.

Although sharing norms and goals, each member of the courtroom group occupies a specialized position and is expected to fit into the socially accepted definition of that status. Because each member has specific rights and duties, there is no exchange of roles. When the career of a lawyer takes him or her from the public defender's office to the prosecutor's office, or ultimately to the bench, he or she lives out each status as a different role in the courtroom group. Because actors are expected to conform to the role prescriptions for the positions they occupy in the group, there can be a high degree of stability in the interpersonal relations among group members. This stability allows members of the courtroom work group to become proficient at the routines associated with their roles and allows the group to develop reliable expectations about the actions of its members. In this way, the business of the courtroom proceeds in a regularized, informal manner. Members rely on many "understandings" that are never recorded but ease much of the work of the court.

In addition to these interrelationships there are ties that bind each actor to a "sponsoring organization"—units that provide the staff and the resources for the court. Thus, although the judges are the formal leaders of their own work groups, they have their own organizations that assign members to various courtrooms and enact policies that each is expected to follow. Likewise, the individual prosecutor has links to the office of the prosecuting attorney, and the defense attorney is associated with either the public defender's office or the private bar. Because of the influence of the sponsoring organizations, courtroom participants are expected to adhere to the norms and policies of these "outside" groups when they are on the courtroom stage. Judges must keep in mind the reaction of their associates to particular sentences; prosecutors may feel peer pressure to reduce charges only under specific circumstances; and public defenders may believe they are expected to ensure that a certain number of cases are processed each day. These constraints from outside the workshop influence the activities in the courtroom and may even serve to bolster the shared norms of the work group, with the effect that cohesion is increased—that is, the secrets of the proceedings must be shielded from the view of the audience.

To a significant degree, the same prosecutors, judges, and defense attorneys find themselves in contact face to face, handling similar cases month after month, with only the defendant changed. Accused persons pass through the system while the court personnel remain, carrying on their careers and organizational enterprises. Individual cases may cause tensions, but these are generally overcome because of the larger need to preserve relationships so that work-group interaction may continue in the future. The officers of the court have more in common, both in cultural values and in goals, than any one of them shares with the defendant. The major actors have been socialized by law school to the norms of the legal profession, values that have been learned "on the job" by the supporting cast. They share the technical language of the law and can use it to distinguish their roles from those of others. All share a social status with corresponding cultural values that may be different from those of the predominantly lower-class defendants being processed.

The arrangement of the actors on the courtroom stage further illustrates the close relationship of the group. Although the judge's bench is usually elevated, symbolizing authority, it faces the lawyer's table. Persons in the audience, and sometimes even the defendant, are unable to observe all the verbal and nonverbal exchanges. In some courts the attorneys for both sides sit at either end of a long table—the furniture does not define them as adversaries. Throughout the proceedings, lawyers from both sides periodically engage in muffled conversations with the judge, out of the hearing of defendant and spectators. When the judge calls the principals into the judicial chamber for private discussion, the defendant remains in the courtroom. In most settings the role of the accused is defined physically: isolated, sitting either in the "dock" or in a chair behind defense counsel. To observers, defendants are silent onlookers, persons unable to negotiate their own fate.

Jury

Although only 8 percent of criminal cases are disposed of through jury trial, the benefit of "trial by jury" is one of the most ingrained features of the American ideology. Like the exposed tip of an iceberg, the jury exerts a greater influence than the case volume might suggest. As we have noted, the potential call for a jury trial weighs in decisions to prosecute, plea bargaining, and the sentencing behavior of judges. The jury thus affects not only the formal resolution of controversies but also the informal disposition of cases that never get to trial.

Although every member of the community should have an equal chance to be chosen for jury duty, selection methods stipulate various qualifications that exclude citizens with certain characteristics. For example, in most states jurors must be registered voters. In addition, particular occupational categories, such as doctors, lawyers, teachers, and police officers, are excluded because their professional services are needed or because of their connection to the court. Even if chosen for jury duty, a citizen may be dropped during the process of *voir dire* ("to speak the truth"). This questioning of potential jurors is designed to ensure a fair trial by excluding those who may be biased toward the issues of a specific case. If it appears that a person will be unable to be fair, he or she may be challenged for *cause* by one of the attorneys. If the judge agrees, the person will be excused from service. When an attorney is unable to give a reason that a potential juror should not sit, a *peremptory challenge* may be issued. This is often done when an attorney has a hunch that the person will be unsympathetic. The number of peremptory challenges available to defense and prosecution is limited by law, but challenges for cause depend only upon the ruling of the judge.

The value of the jury system has long been debated. Jerome Frank noted in the 1930s that "jury-made law" was a prime example of capricious and arbitrary decision making. From time to time, public interest has been aroused by this controversy. When juries in highly publicized trials reach verdicts that are in accord with community sentiment, great praise is heaped on the system; when the outcome is unpopular, the public raises questions about the value of this method of fact-finding. It must be kept in mind that juries are a factor in only a small number of the decisions in the administration of criminal justice. Our due process ideals may have obscured this fact.

The Sentencing Wilderness

Among judges in Western nations, only U.S. trial judges have the power to decide absolutely within the framework of the penal code the nature of the sentence. In other countries, the power belongs to a panel of judges, or a panel of judges and laypersons, and the panel's decision is often subject to review. In Europe becoming a judge is a distinct career objective, and special training is required for the post. Judges in the United States are chosen from the bar, and there is nothing in the law curriculum or their experience as lawyers that prepares them to assume the extensive power they receive when they don the robes. Further, they may be trained in the rules of evidence and courtroom procedure but know nothing about correctional theories.

In the administrative context of the criminal courts, judges often do not have time to consider all the crucial elements of the offense and the special characteristics of the offender before imposing a sentence. Especially when the violation is minor, there is a tendency for judges to routinize decision making, announcing sentences to fit certain categories of crimes without paying much attention to the particular offender. Individuals convicted of minor offenses, and therefore possibly the most likely to be reformed, are frequently sentenced immediately after being found guilty or when they enter a guilty plea. If counsel requests a presentence report before imposition of sentence, the necessary delay may require that the defendant remain in jail—a price many are unwilling to pay.

Individual differences in the sentencing tendencies of judges have fascinated social scientists. These disparities can be attributed to a number of factors: the conflicting goals of criminal justice; the differing backgrounds and social values of judges; administrative pressures on judges; and the influence of community values on the system. Each of these factors influences a judge's exercise of discretion in sentencing offenders. In addition, a judge's perception of these factors can be dependent on his or her own attitudes toward the law, toward a particular crime, or toward a type of offender.

Who receives unfavorable treatment as a result of sentencing decisions? At first we might suspect that out-groups (such as minorities, the poor, substance abusers, and mental patients) would receive the longest prison terms, pay the highest fines, and be placed on probation the fewest times. Although some investigations have sustained these assumptions, the evidence is not totally conclusive. In most states the racial composition of the prisons shows a higher percentage of blacks to whites than in the general population. Is this a result of biased attitudes on the part of judges, police officers, and prosecutors? Are poor people more liable to commit violations that elicit a greater response from society? Are enforcement resources distributed in such a way that certain groups are subject to closer scrutiny than other groups? These are but a few of the questions that must be answered if we are to correct present inequities in the criminal justice system and find our way out of the "sentencing wilderness."

Suggestions for Further Reading

EISENSTEIN, JAMES, ROY FLEMMING, AND PETER NARDULLI. *The Contours of Justice: Communities and Their Courts.* Boston: Little, Brown, 1988. A study of nine felony courts in three states. The study emphasizes the impact of the local legal culture on court operations.

EISENSTEIN, JAMES, AND HERBERT JACOB. *Felony Justice.* Boston: Little, Brown, 1977. An analysis of the processing of felony cases in Baltimore, Chicago, and Detroit. The analysis develops the concept of the courtroom work group.

FEELEY, MALCOLM. *The Process Is the Punishment.* New York: Russell Sage Foundation, 1979. An analysis of a misdemeanor court and the finding that it is not the sentence handed out by the judge but rather the costs, both monetary and emotional, associated with the pretrial process, that constitute the real punishment.

FRANKEL, MARVIN E. *Criminal Sentences: Law Without Order.* New York: Hill & Wang, 1972. What factors should a judge consider when imposing sanctions? Judge Frankel explores the "sentencing wilderness" and finds that there are a few standards to guide this important decision. This results in a disparity among the sentences given to offenders.

GAYLIN, WILLARD. *The Killing of Bonnie Garland.* New York: Simon & Schuster, 1982. This account of the murder of a Yale student and the conviction of her lover raises disturbing questions about the goals of the criminal sanction by viewing the process and the punishment from the perspectives of Christianity, law, and psychiatry.

HASTIE, REID, STEVEN PENROD, AND NANCY PENNINGTON. *Inside the Jury.* Cambridge: Harvard University Press, 1983. A study of the jury process and the elements of decision making.

RYAN, JOHN PAUL, ALLAN ASHMAN, BRUCE D. SALES, AND SANDRA SHANE-DU BOW. *American Trial Judges.* New York: Free Press, 1980. The results of a national survey of trial judges, describing their work patterns, recruitment, attitudes, and performance.

SATTER, ROBERT. *Doing Justice: A Trial Judge at Work.* New York: Simon & Schuster, 1990. A judge's view of the cases he faces daily and the factors influencing the decisions.

ARTICLE 15

Discretion, Exchange, and Social Control: Bail Bondsmen in Criminal Courts

Forrest Dill

Bail bondsmen are private entrepreneurs who perform many important functions within the criminal justice system. As Forrest Dill shows, bondsmen supply the money that allows defendants to be free awaiting trial and shepherd them through the procedural maze. Throughout the system, they engage in exchange relationships with officials so that both their tasks are eased.

Business Imperatives and Illegitimate Practices in Bail Bonding

The bail system is at once an important legal procedure and a lucrative business enterprise. By allowing commercial intermediaries to post bail for the release of arrested persons prior to trial, the state has created a business operation within the criminal courts. The bondsman's role cannot be easily catalogued. Freed and Wald (1964: 30) assigned the institution of bail "a hybrid status, somewhere between a free enterprise and a public utility." Bail bondsmen are private businessmen who render a service to individuals in return for remuneration at levels fixed by the state. In one sense, then, bondsmen are government subcontractors. But their work injects them into direct participation in the business of criminal courts, where their actions can and do affect the outcomes of criminal cases. Their behavior must be examined from two different and somewhat conflicting perspectives, the first emphasizing business concerns and the second stressing legal responsibilities.

The Business Setting

Bail may be looked upon as a specialized insurance system. It is designed to reconcile the conflicting interests between defendants, who desire to be at liberty before

Source: Law and Society Review 9 (1975): 644–674. Notes omitted. Reprinted by permission of the Law and Society Association.

trial, and the state, which insists that defendants be present for court proceedings. Bail bondsmen are the visible commercial operatives of this system. In principle, these conflicting interests will be held in balance by the operation of a set of positive and negative incentives. There must be, on the one hand, sufficient financial gain to induce bondsmen to invest in defendants to relieve pressures on custodial facilities. Bondsmen, then, are legally permitted to collect nonrefundable premiums or interest charges (usually 10 percent of the amount of bail) from defendants for whom they post bail. Bondsmen regain the bail amounts posted when they have satisfied their promises that defendants will appear in court as required. On the other hand, the state needs to protect itself against the inconvenience and public outrage likely to arise when bailed defendants fail to appear for trial. Thus, the law requires that amounts pledged as security for defendants released on bail will be forfeited to the state in the event of nonappearance.

At one time, bondsmen were marginal, independent entrepreneurs operating with scant resources (Beeley 1927). Today, major insurance companies stand behind the individual bondsmen who operate the bail-bonding business. A dozen companies are said (Sutherland and Cressey 1970: 404) to control nearly all the corporate bail bonds written in this country. The policies of these companies affect the administration of criminal law. Bail bondsmen are located at the bottom of this business described by Goldfarb (1965: 95–96) as

> a straight line beginning with the large national insurance companies and running down through the regional subadministrators and eventually to local agents (the bondsmen) who camp around the local courthouses and actually hustle the business. ... There is little real business interplay between these three levels. The business functions begin at the top; and the responsibilities and risks increase on the way down, while inversely the profit risks also increase on the way down. The insurance company on top sets the public image of a respectable business and within the working scheme of its bail setup takes no risk with its agents. The agents go about their business in their own fashion, and for this privilege agree to retain only a small percentage of the profit.

This surety company dominance of the bail bond business is found in most states and in all large metropolitan areas—wherever criminal court activity is sizeable enough to attract and support corporate investment.

A key feature of the business is the low degree of risk for the surety companies. To protect themselves against loss, companies which sell bail bonds require bondsmen to deposit with the companies reserve funds, built up through assessments on fees or premiums bondsmen collect from customers. For each corporate bond used, the bondsman must contribute 10 percent of the premium he collects from the customer to reserve funds. In addition, the surety company levies a 20 percent charge on each premium the bondsman collects for posting a corporate bond. This leaves the bondsman with a gross profit of 70 percent of each premium collected on a corporate surety bond. In theory, the amount of bonds that the bondsman can write is determined by the amount in his reserve fund. Any forfeitures declared against bonds he has written are paid with the reserve fund. If forfeitures exceed the total amount of reserves, the company may take the remaining amount from future premiums the bondsman receives.

The sale of bail bonds is thus an immensely profitable, low-risk arena of enterprise within the insurance industry. Individual bondsmen supply nearly all the labor necessary for corporate profit from the sale of bail bonds and are sometimes said to work for the companies. Bondsmen in fact are not employees of these companies; they are independent businessmen who, by serving as agents of the surety companies, obtain financial backing necessary to satisfy solvency standards set by the state. Bondsmen are not salaried; rather, they receive their earnings on something nearer to a sales commission basis. They pay their own business expenses, set their own hours, and work out their own local arrangements for conducting their affairs. For example, a bondsman who has developed a large business may employ additional persons on various terms—hourly wages, salaries, or commissions. Moreover, instead of using corporate bonds, they may post their own assets (for example, treasury bonds or cash) as bail and reap a higher rate of profit. In this respect, their business arrangement is quite different from that of other insurance salesmen.

Surety companies have little direct control over the activities of individual bondsmen despite—or possibly because of—the pattern of corporate authority. Corporate policy may make itself felt in a very general way by placing broad limits on the amount of bonds that particular bondsmen may write at any period of time. Where bondsmen represent several surety companies, corporate influence is weakened. The ability of surety companies to insure themselves against loss reduces their need to exercise continuous supervision and control over bondsmen.

Competition for Business

Within the local court system, the bondsman's interactions with defendants, attorneys, and law-enforcement and court officials are permeated by a multitude of legal and illegal commercial possibilities. For this reason the bondsman's business affairs are subject to comprehensive legal regulation, and his work therefore has some unusual restraints. He must maintain detailed accounts of all his transactions and submit them to state insurance commission officials as matters of public record. He may not legally enter into any special agreements with government officials about when or on what terms he is to supply his services. Moreover, he is forbidden to offer as incentives to potential clients or as advantages to actual customers any extra services such as legal advice, attorney referral information, or assistance with court cases. Finally, he may bargain with potential clients over fees, but must sell his services at rates set by the state.

The bondsman's primary occupational difficulties stem from the fact that legal restrictions compel him to meet business imperatives without the use of many standard business techniques. Like many small businessmen, the bondsman operates in an environment offering neither steady demand for his services nor reliable means for guarding against incursions by competitors. In other business settings such conditions foster highly competitive modes of behavior. Legal regulations drastically narrow the initiative the bondsman can legitimately exercise, theoretically closing off all but a few forms of competition as illegal practices. Beyond rendering "prompt, courteous service twenty-four hours a day," the only legitimate business technique that the bondsman can use is advertising. In practice, however, only marginal returns are expected from this source.

The principal competitive devices employed by bondsmen are illegal. Reciprocal referrals are a common business arrangement among bondsmen and criminal lawyers. All the bondsmen I talked to have client-sharing agreements with lawyers and assume that the practice is universal. Many bondsmen seek to develop illegal ways of gaining access to potential clients and transforming them into paying customers. They also attempt to cultivate informal exchange relationships with police, judges, and other officials for the information, protection, and administrative influence—in short, the business advantages—that such relationships can provide.

Bondsmen devote considerable effort to developing and expanding illegitimate sources of business within the legal system. One means of illegal recruitment of customers is the "jailhouse lawyer." Typically this role is filled by a person who spends a great deal of time in jail on minor charges like intoxication, begging, or loitering. His job is to steer defendants from inside the jail to a particular bondsman on the outside. These services may come quite cheaply, and the relationship is likely to be very casual. The arrangement is not capable of much formalization owing to the irregular habits of the destitute alcoholics available as personnel; for the same reason it is not very productive for bondsmen. Only a few customers are likely to be recruited in this way and they tend to be first offenders facing minor charges. Experienced defendants are more likely to know bondsmen from past encounters with the law or by reputation, and defendants arrested on serious charges are likely to make contact with bondsmen through other channels, usually lawyers.

Practicing attorneys offer a much more important opportunity through which the bondsman recruits business. The bondsman can count on criminal lawyers for a certain proportion of his clientele, since even attorneys not wishing to deal with bondsmen must occasionally enlist their services for defendants. Attorneys may legitimately refer cases to bondsmen, but reciprocal client-referral agreements between lawyers and bondsmen are forbidden. When questioned during field observations, some bondsmen expressed apprehension about this subject and offered insistent denials that any such arrangements existed. In several instances, the subject of bondsman–attorney arrangements had not even arisen in conversation before bondsmen began making unsolicited denials. The phenomenon is so widespread and so much a part of bail-bonding and criminal law practice, however, that it is impossible to conceal for long.

The following event occurred after one week of steady observation with a bondsman in Mountain City. The case was instructive because the relationship between the bondsman and the attorney was still being defined at the time of the meeting.

> Late one morning, Walt told me that he would be meeting a young lawyer named Dave Redding for lunch. Walt explained that he had sent some cases to this attorney in the past. Opening his desk drawer to show me the business cards of several attorneys, he said, "It's against the law to refer attorneys, so I usually show the people these cards and allow them to choose which lawyer they want."
>
> When Redding arrived, Walt suggested that I join them for lunch, but qualified his invitation by saying to Redding, "If you have any private business to talk over, then we of course won't consider this." Redding's immediate reply was: "What do

you mean, private business? We have nothing to hide. Our contacts are well regulated by the state insurance commission. Sure he can come along."

On the way to the restaurant, Walt asked: "Well, Dave, what's the purpose of today's meeting, and what can I do for you?" Redding responded: "Oh, there's no special purpose. I just wanted to thank you for the business. This is a courtesy lunch, a social visit, if you will."

After lunch, the two kidded each other about the $200 fee that Redding had collected from Martinez, a young Mexican-American whom Walt had bailed out two weeks earlier on charges of narcotics possession and suspicion of burglary. They also discussed another case involving a defendant's hit-and-run accident. Walt had referred this case to Redding, who had taken it without hesitation. Now some question had arisen about the defendant's ability or willingness to pay Redding's fee. Walt assured him that the defendant had money and counseled Redding to "work on him."

Then Redding said, "I certainly appreciate the business you've sent me. I'm trying to build up a practice and this helps a great deal. I knew this wasn't a get-rich-quick business, but I had no idea it would be this hard." Walt assured him that the future held great promise for a fine young attorney like himself, and then added: "Sure, I'll send you some more cases. And let me ask that in return you refer your cases to me. Now if you ever have anybody who needs to get out and you know he's a good risk, just call me and tell me that he's good as gold and I'll take him right out without collateral. Understand?"

As this case illustrates, the bondsman may have vital knowledge of the defendant's financial situation. First-time defendants in particular may unwittingly reveal financial information to the bondsman during "routine" questioning. Such defendants frequently do not understand the nature of the bondsman's role and may see him as yet another official whose powers must be respected. Inexperienced defendants are more vulnerable to the attorney-referral arrangement. Bondsmen in some other cities are said to exploit defendants by requiring them to take their cases to certain attorneys as a condition of posting bail for their release (Goldfarb 1965: 114). No evidence of this practice could be found in Westville or Mountain City, where the bondsman–attorney referral system may have been working in favor of defendants. One lawyer speculated that attorneys needed to exercise caution with cases referred from bondsmen. "They have to give these clients a fair deal," he said, "or the defendants might resent the attorney and mess up the system. It's too risky for the attorney working with a bondsman not to give good representation."

Collusion with jail personnel may be another valuable means of customer recruitment for the bondsman. During the period of field observation, it became apparent to me that certain jail police in Mountain City were assisting certain bondsmen in getting customers. The simplest and most reliable method was one that required only a moment's effort by an individual jail staff member. "All he has to do," an attorney explained, "is find out if the defendant has a bondsman lined up. If not, he points to a particular bondsman's number in the telephone directory and pushes a dime into the guy's hand." Even this simple arrangement can result in unexpected complications, as the following account reveals:

I was present with Walt in his office when he received a call from a woman requesting that bail be posted for one of her employees. The defendant had been arrested the night before for driving on a suspended license. Walt told the woman that he

would call the jail to determine the amount of bail and then call her back. Bail had been set at $296, making the premium charge $39.60—ten percent of the amount of bail plus an additional $10 charge which bondsmen are allowed to collect on all bails under $500. Walt called the woman back advising her that she would need to submit the premium as well as her signature to a deed promising to pay the full amount of bail if the defendant failed to appear in court. The woman said that she would send another of her employees with the money to Walt's office.

When the second employee arrived, Walt and I went to jail across the street "to get the body." At the jail another bondsman was waiting to post bail for the defendant Walt had come to get. Walt immediately sensed what was happening and informed one of the jailors that he wanted to talk to the defendant. A jail policeman stepped forward and said, "No, Alvarez wants to go with the other guy." There was some discussion, and eventually it was decided that the defendant would determine which bondsman would "get the bail."

Alvarez (a black) was brought out, and he turned to the other bondsman (also a black). The two spoke briefly in hushed tones. Then Walt (not black) approached Alvarez and said, "Mrs. McGee called me to help you. Your friend Smith is over in my office right now waiting for you." Alvarez turned to the other bondsman, shrugged apologetically, and said, "I guess I'll have to go with him," indicating Walt. As we rode down in the elevator, the other bondsman mumbled that he had also received a telephone call. Walt remained silent. Alvarez said, "Well, that's the way it goes."

After Alvarez and Smith left, I asked Walt how the other bondsman had become involved. Walt speculated that someone in the jail had persuaded Alvarez to call the other bondsman. Smith, Alvarez's co-worker, knew nothing about the other bondsman. I asked whether one of the jail police we had just seen had been responsible for the other bondsman's appearance. Walt replied, "Well, you saw the way he wanted Alvarez to be taken out by the other guy, didn't you?"

The same bondsman related an incident illustrating another variation of this method:

A man entered Walt's office and presented a slip of paper on which had been written the name of the defendant, the charge in exact penal code section terminology, the date of the next court appearance, and the amount of bail. The man was a supervisor in a public utility company where the defendant, a woman, was employed. The slip of paper, Walt was convinced, was prima facie evidence that one of the police had recommended a bondsman. Apparently the man had come to the wrong address.

Walt gladly cooperated with the man, however, and immediately went to the jail to take the woman out. When one of the jailors asked about the slip of paper, Walt "played dumb," saying that he never got any slips of paper from the jail. With great reluctance, the jailor released the defendant to Walt, who patiently explained several times that the woman's supervisor was waiting over in his office. "That guy was pretty unhappy, because he'd lost some sure money in the mixup."

Other methods requiring collective efforts by jail police may sometimes be employed. These are more complicated and carry greater risks of discovery and failure. A Westville bondsman recounted an experience of his at the Mountain City jail:

I got a call from the relative of a guy who had been put in jail over there. It was a pretty good bail, so I decided to drive over and take him out myself. When I got there I found a police hold on him. Now that hold wasn't on him when I left West-

ville only a half an hour before, so whoever put it on him should have still been around. But I couldn't find anybody who knew anything about it. They passed the buck and I went from one office to another trying to find out whose hold it was. Nobody knew, and finally they said they were going to let him go. Next thing I knew another bondsman came walking out with the defendant. Then they told me that they had taken the hold off him, but actually they were keeping him for this other bondsman.

In general, collective agreements among jail officials appear necessary to protect the system of collusion. Since this system functions as a means of restricting competition, its value depends on excluding some bondsmen so that business can be channeled to other bondsmen. But competition among bondsmen may result in some degree of participation in the system by nearly all local bondsmen.

There was no evidence to indicate the existence of collusion between jail police and bondsmen in Westville at the time of my study. With a smaller population, a more professionally disciplined police force, and a different political complexion, Westville presented relatively poor opportunities for collusive relations to develop between police and bondsmen. All of my informants claimed that defendants selected bondsmen on their own from inside the jail. If the Westville police were collaborating with particular bondsmen, the arrangement was either very well concealed or quite minor in scale.

In some cities, bondsmen reportedly refuse to extend services to defendants accused of minor offenses which require "nominal"—that is, low—bail, because they view the modest premiums in such cases as not worth the trouble and risk of posting bond (Freed and Wald 1964: 33). It seems likely that this practice would be found only where bail bonding had fallen under monopoly control by a small number of bondsmen. By assuring privileged bondsmen a guaranteed share of the profits, monopoly conditions would make it possible for bondsmen to neglect defendants in minor cases.

Aside from some petty collusion in Mountain City bail practices, bail bonding in the two cities seemed to offer relatively undisturbed market conditions. For most bondsmen operating there, defendants in minor cases appeared to constitute the bulk of business and the most reliable source of income. Such cases were especially attractive because the bondsman could post his own assets and thereby avoid the costs of using corporate surety bonds. Although minor cases yield small premiums, they may be attractive to bondsmen as business opportunities precisely because of the low bail amounts on which the premiums are based. Also, by permitting bondsmen to charge defendants an extra $10 for posting bail in amounts less than $500—as done in the state where this research was carried out—the legal system increases the attractiveness of such cases.

Profit Maximization and Case Management by Bondsmen

Shortly after bondsmen enter the criminal justice process, some defendants are granted pretrial liberty and others are ordered held in detention to await further action in their cases. The timing of these events has created the impression that bondsmen

are "purveyors of freedom" who play a key role in determining whether defendants will obtain release before trial (Wice 1974). This view greatly exaggerates the influence that bondsmen have in such determinations, however.

Although bail procedures in different parts of the country are far from uniform (Silverstein 1966), it is clear that bail administration everywhere belongs primarily to law-enforcement and court officials. The most critical decisions—the bail amounts set in particular cases—are entirely controlled by local criminal justice officials, with prosecuting attorneys taking the dominant role. Bondsmen do not participate at all in these decisions for cases making up the largest volume of criminal court business. This is because of the widespread use of the bail schedule, a form approved by local judges listing uniform bail amounts for the most common misdemeanor violations (for example, disorderly conduct, petty theft, simple assault, and certain vehicle offenses). It is true that bondsmen can and sometimes do refuse to post bail for defendants in such cases, but decisions as to the amounts required in particular cases are determined more or less automatically as a matter of clerical routine, usually by station house police.

For cases involving charges of serious misdemeanor and felony offenses, bail setting typically takes place in court at the time of arraignment. This process involves negotiation between the judge, prosecutor, and defense attorney; the prosecutor's recommendations usually determine the final decision (Suffet 1966). The bondsman plays no formal part in this process either. In many cases of this kind, the defendant or his attorney may contact a bondsman before the bail hearing, and the bondsman may supply informal advice to the judge or the prosecutor concerning his willingness to post bail for the defendant. This may help the defendant by inducing the judge to set bail at a level which the defendant can afford. It can hardly work to the defendant's disadvantage.

Unlike the standardized bail amounts required in the most common misdemeanor cases, amounts set in cases involving serious offenses often vary a good deal, even when the charges are identical. Defendants who are unable to secure release at amounts initially set may request that bail be lowered. The frequency of bail reduction probably provides a rough measure of the extent of excessive bail in various jurisdictions, although in general bail reduction does not occur with much frequency in most places (Silverstein 1966: 634–637). Both the bail schedule and the bail hearing lead to decisions that discriminate against sizeable proportions of the defendant population (Foote 1954, 1958; Ares and Sturz 1962; Silverstein 1966). But it is mistaken to attribute these discriminatory results to bail bondsmen, given the economics of the situation in general and the bondsmen's inclinations to seek profits in particular.

The Bondsman's Interest in Court Efficiency

If bondsmen play only a minor role in determining defendants' chances for release, the same cannot be said of their role in handling defendants who are released on bail. Bondsmen actively employ a number of different techniques of case management. These practices are aimed at protecting investments and maximizing profits, but they also have positive functions for the court system. Nominally, bondsmen are private businessmen situated outside the criminal courts. Examination of their routine activities, however, indicates that they serve as agents of the court system responding to many of the problems that concern those who occupy official positions within it.

The strategies bondsmen use in managing cases reveal many generic similarities to the practices of lawyers, probation officers, and other agent-mediators within the court system (Blumberg 1970). An important first step is often to establish a good relationship with the defendant. The bondsman usually extends a cordial, business-like manner to each customer, seeking to convey a willingness to separate the defendant's specific dereliction from his or her general moral character. He therefore treats in a routine or "professional" way matters that his customers may regard as emergencies, but his mode of dealing with particular customers may vary depending on his perception of situational demands. A bondsman explained, "Each one of these people is different, and you've gotta handle them in different ways." Thus when the customer is a first-time defendant charged with a relatively minor offense, the bondsman's strategy may be to play down the seriousness of the defendant's plight by reciting such homilies as "We get cases like this every day. Don't worry, it'll come out all right." In other minor cases, where the customer is an experienced defendant and perhaps an old customer behind in payments for previous bail bond services, the bondsman may act in a slightly patronizing and officious manner, counseling the defendant to "be a good boy, don't get into any more trouble, and bring that money in next Friday." In cases involving more serious charges, the bondsman may deal calmly and quietly with the customer, emphasizing his neutrality by carefully avoiding any mention of the alleged offense.

Another and more important element of case management involves giving various forms of legal assistance and advice. Bondsmen always remind their customers of future court dates and instruct them about how to find the room in the court building where their cases will be heard, what time to show up, and what to expect during the proceeding. An indirect form of advice is sometimes employed if the defendant has already retained an attorney or has a particular attorney in mind. In this situation, the bondsman may issue a reassuring comment to the defendant, as, for example, "Oh, I know Bart will give you all the help he can. He's a fine lawyer." In another instance, I observed a bondsman attempting vigorously to persuade a defendant whom he had just bailed out to call an attorney whose name the defendant had mentioned as we walked from the jail to the bondsman's nearby office. The defendant was allowed to leave the office only after promising that he would go directly to look up the attorney. Bondsmen may also refer unrepresented defendants to attorneys. Here, the practice of recommending attorneys appears in a different light, for it has the same purpose as is intended by congratulating the legally sophisticated defendant on his choice of attorney. Both of these techniques serve to increase the customer's feeling of personal competence and to reinforce his self-definition as a "defendant"—a person who is going through the court process and who will accept its judgment. The chances of panic and flight are thereby reduced.

In other cases, the bondsman gives direct legal advice. The following observed instances, both involving the same bondsman, suggest typical possibilities. In the first case, the bondsman counseled against retaining an attorney:

At about one o'clock one afternoon, one of Al's customers came into his office. The man had been arrested for drunk driving many weeks before. His court date was for two o'clock that day. Al told him that he had two alternatives: either he could demand a jury trial and hope that the complaint would be withdrawn, or he could plead guilty and ask the judge for probation and some time "to put a few beans aside and pay the fine."

Al explained: "If you ask for a jury trial, you'll need a lawyer and that can run into money. It might easily run you $250, and then you have no guarantee that you'll be acquitted. Of course, if you get a jury trial and an attorney, you will have a better judge. But with no priors the fine's only $296, so you might as well plead guilty, ask the judge for probation, and then get the money together over a period of time."

The customer contemplated Al's advice, then gave a resigned shrug and said, "Well, I guess I'll plead guilty. See you later."

The second case also involved a motor vehicle code violation:

Shortly after lunch on another afternoon, a young man who had been charged with littering and possessing open containers of beer in his car stopped by to see Al about his case. He was apprehensive about the outcome because the girl who had been arrested with him had already "copped out as charged." He asked: "What will happen if I change my earlier plea to guilty?"

Al answered: "It won't make any difference. They got the girl and all they want are guilty pleas. The judge will fine you $25, and that will be the end of it."

Al was correct. Later that afternoon the client returned and jubilantly told Al, "It's all over. I got out for $29."

Two features of these incidents deserve attention. First, each involved a minor offense. The bondsman's ability to offer sound legal advice depends on the degree to which court processing of the kind of case involved is routinized and therefore predictable. His legal expertise thus seems to be confined to traffic violations, public order offenses such as drunkenness and disturbing the peace, and minor property crimes. For the bondsman this may be a happy coincidence, since the typically small penalties facing defendants in such cases may take much of the risk out of the prospect of confronting the court without legal representation.

Second, the examples suggest that bondsmen share the interests of court officials in guilty pleas. More generally, both groups are interested in efficiency. The bondsman's liability for each bond he posts does not end until the defendant's case is cleared from the court docket. Every new customer represents a case that will remain open and a bond that will remain "out" for an indeterminate but roughly predictable amount of time. For example, after posting bail for a woman charged with welfare fraud, a Westville bondsman explained why this had been a good business decision: "She'll plead guilty and be put on probation. The case will be over in about two and a half months." The strength of the bondsman's business position depends on the volume of cases he handles: the amount of bonds in use is inversely related to the amount of new bonds that he can post. Therefore, his interests lie in efficient, routinized court procedures and compliant defendants. Anything that lengthens the duration of criminal cases—disorderly judicial administration, militant defense attorneys, nonappearance by defendants, new and unfamiliar legal procedures—weakens the bondsman's position.

The Quasi-Bureaucratic Role of the Bondsman

An important consideration for understanding the bondsman's activities is that coop- eration from defendants may be contingent on the administrative practices of courts. Some defendants may fail to make required court appearances because they get lost in the system. For example, they may have separate appearances scheduled in two different court departments at exactly the same time, or they may be uninformed or confused about the court dates. In other cases, defendants may be unable to comply with required court appearances because of employment obligations or family emergencies.

Such problems are less likely to arise for defendants who have private legal representation. One of the key functions performed by attorneys in the criminal pro- cess is to direct the passage of cases through the procedural and bureaucratic mazes of the court system (Blumberg 1967). For unrepresented defendants, however, the bondsman may perform the crucial institutional task of helping to negotiate court routines. In order to protect his investment, the bondsman may find it not merely desirable but necessary to guide defendants through the court process. By providing legal advice to his customers, arranging more convenient court dates for them, and negotiating their passage through the court process, the bondsman increases his chances of collecting fees and reduces the amount of time that his assets are encum- bered. At the same time, these methods of case management promote orderly and efficient court administration. They also implicate bondsmen in the unauthorized practice of law.

Efforts by bondsmen to organize the actions of individual customers in relation to the actions of court officials deepen the involvement of bondsmen in the criminal justice process. Not only do these efforts require frequent visits to courtrooms, but they may also require informal assistance from court personnel. The experienced bondsman knows each of the bailiffs, court clerks, and accounting office members on a first-name basis and how much and what kinds of assistance each is willing to provide. The bondsman typically takes advantage of mutualized exchange opportu- nities at Christmas and New Year's to reciprocate favors received through court "connections." If it is consistent with his personal style, he may seek to improve his relations with court clerks, bailiffs, and other court participants by "buttering them up" through flattery and other forms of interpersonal artifice. He may also supplement his day-to-day dealing with officials by occasionally dispensing gifts (such as free passes to professional sports events) and supplying drinks at nearby bars in after-hours gatherings.

One measure of the degree of cooperativeness of court officials is whether they will comply with the bondsman's request to bring a case forward on a particular day's court calendar. This small but nonetheless significant service, which can be easily rendered by the court clerk, is a favor that the bondsman may seek in order to keep track of his cases or to accelerate release of a new customer for whom bail has just been posted. Without this assistance, the bondsman cannot "move" cases in court. Where such influence is available, however, the bondsman can sometimes negotiate convenient court dates, coordinate multiple appearances, and forestall issuance of bench warrants.

A more important form of assistance that the bondsman may wish to arrange is for certain of his customers to be released on recognizance—that is, without being required to make financial bail. If a defendant is returned to jail because of new difficulties with the law before he has paid his debt to the bondsman, the bondsman's fee may be jeopardized. When this happens, the bondsman may face two unsatisfactory options: either lose the balance of the money owed by the defendant or assume a greater risk by posting another bail bond in hopes of collecting the fees owed on the original bond. If a judge or prosecutor can be persuaded to grant release without requirement of financial bail on the new charges, however, the need for deciding between the two options is eliminated.

By now it has become evident that the court clerk is a figure of major importance to the bondsman. In high-volume urban courts, there are many persons with this designation—one, in fact, for every separate court "part" or "department" to which each of the judges of a given court district is assigned. The administrative position of the court clerk makes him an object of continuous attention from other participants seeking information about or access to the court calendar. The resources he holds may be an important means for the bondsman's efforts to protect his investments. One bondsman stated:

> The court clerk is probably one of the most important people I have to deal with. He moves cases, he can get information to the judge, and he has control over various calendar matters. When he's not willing to help you out, he can make life very difficult. He know's he's important, and he acts like it.

Observations confirmed the value of cooperation from the court clerk for case management strategies employed by bondsmen. Two examples are given below:

> A bondsman and a court clerk were chatting amiably during a recess in one of the Westville courtrooms. They kidded each other for a short time, each complaining about the "easy life" of the other. Then the court clerk asked the bondsman: "Hey, what about O'Hanlon? Isn't he your case? He didn't show this morning and I've got a bench warrant on him sitting on my desk right now. You'd better get in touch with Sheldon [an attorney] and have him call the judge for a continuance right away or that warrant is gonna be on its way."
>
> On another occasion, a Westville bondsman was summoned to a nearby city by a prospective customer. After obtaining a verbal promise from the defendant's brother that the premium would be paid, the bondsman went to that city to post bail. When we arrived there at mid-morning, the bondsman's first contact was with the court clerk:

Al: You've got Mallen scheduled to come up this afternoon, don't you?

(The clerk checked his records and nodded affirmatively.)

Al: Look, this guy was picked up last night on plain drunk and he's still got a george heat on. I don't think he's fit to appear in anybody's court. He's still so stiff I swear I could smell it over the phone.

Clerk: Hmmm.

Al: I'm going over to the jail and take him out. How's about putting the guy on for tomorrow? He's gotta get himself cleaned up.

(After momentary hesitation, the clerk agreed.)

Clerk: Okay, I'll set him up for nine tomorrow.

As we walked to the jail, the bondsman told me that he had done a favor for the defendant. The postponement would give the defendant an extra day to sober up and would enable him to appear in court freshly shaved and wearing clean clothes. "Makes a much better impression on the judge if the guy looks decent." A short time later the defendant appeared at the jail booking desk. A middle-aged man, he had spent the night and most of the morning in jail. He was now completely sober, and although he presented a shabby appearance there seemed little doubt that he could have stood trial that afternoon. After posting bail, Al counseled the man: "Go home and get some rest, and then come back tomorrow morning at nine and put on your best manners. I don't think you've got anything to worry about. Judge Gardner is one of the best in the country."

In later conversation, the bondsman said that he regarded the man as "an alcoholic obviously beyond the point of being helped." He revealed that the reason for arranging postponement of the man's case was to increase the likelihood that the man would make his court appearance. "I've seen hundreds of cases like this guy — just simple drunks. In that condition, they're likely to wander off somewhere and fall asleep for a whole day. This way the guy doesn't have to worry about it. He can go home, sack out, and his chances of being able to make a court appearance in the morning are much better than if he has to hang around the court building for a couple of long, dry hours until his case is called."

Court "connections" are primarily useful to the bondsman for managing minor cases. One bondsman reported that a high proportion of his clientele consisted of persons arrested for traffic warrant violations. When asked about the business consequences of this fact, he replied:

Great! [Laughter] What I mean by great is that these cases make up a lot of the bread and butter in this business. But they're much more work than the big cases. Felony cases can't be moved around in the courts, but chicken-shit cases can. With traffic cases, you sometimes find yourself doing a lot of extra work in getting postponements and that kind of thing. You know, like when a guy is afraid he'll lose his job if he has to appear in court on a working day without permission from his boss.

This parallels the situation described above in which dispensation of legal advice appears to be confined to relatively trivial, although statistically frequent, criminal matters. Thus, minor cases provide a more reliable basis of income, higher returns on investments, and greater opportunity to exercise influence in the process of criminal justice.

Bail Administration and Control of Arrestees

Bail administration does not come to an abrupt end with the release of some defendants and the detention of others. On the contrary, it extends throughout the entire period between arrest and disposition. Official actions in this process have been described in several empirical studies (Foote 1954, 1958). This section shows how

the bondsman's decisions to post bail are linked to considerations of subsequent decisions by court officials. Through collaborative exercise of their respective discretionary powers, bondsmen and court officials exchange outcomes which strengthen legal control over arrested persons in the period before disposition.

Decisions to Post Bail

Compared with its importance for official decisions, the factor of offense appears to play a very minor role in the bondsman's assessment of defendants as possible customers. More serious crimes involve high bails, of course, and bondsmen have greater reason to be concerned over the possibility that defendants in these cases will "skip." At the same time, higher bails mean higher premiums. Some bondsmen believe that drug addicts and certain kinds of violent offenders tend to be less reliable than other criminals, and in such cases the bondsman may exercise special care in deciding to post bail. In general, however, bondsmen do not make categorical judgments about defendants based upon the offenses with which they are charged.

Similarly, bondsmen are not concerned about the possibility that released defendants might be rearrested on new charges while at liberty. Bondsmen believe, just as do criminal justice officials, that chances of rearrest may be quite high among certain classes of defendants, especially those accused of minor offenses like prostitution and shoplifting. Indeed, bondsmen share the view of many law-enforcement and court officials that for some defendants release on bail and return to "the streets" signals a period of intensified criminal activity in order to earn money to pay fees owed to bondsmen and attorneys. But bondsmen cannot afford to base their decisions on the probability of recidivism by released defendants. One bondsman revealed the tough-minded outlook required by his business:

> I don't care what any bondsmen's association says on this score. We don't care and we can't care about protecting society. We have means and methods of making these people pay, so we take the risks and the gambles. That's what we're in business for. There is almost nobody I won't take out, including people I'm certain will repeat their crimes.

The most important question is whether the defendant is likely to pay the premium for his bail. Ideally, full payment of the premium is demanded before the bondsman agrees to post bail. Depending on his assessment of the defendant's background, character, and financial capacity, however, the bondsman may decide to post bail on credit—that is, to allow the defendant to pay the premium in installments. The financial qualifications of family members and friends may become an important consideration at this point. Surety companies seem to discourage installment agreements, but bondsmen generally operate on the assumption that it is better to extend credit broadly, accepting the risks of nonpayment and partial payment that this method implies. Therefore, bondsmen usually have collection problems.

Bondsmen sometimes appear to make attempts at estimating the probability of defaults or "skips" by prospective customers before posting bonds, but not primarily because they entertain any special concern for the efficiency or integrity of court operations. The dominant question is rather the defendant's reliability as a paying customer. One bondsman said that he regarded the family life of defendants as being

particularly important in this respect. "If a man is happily married and loves his kids, he's not going to leave town." Another bondsman attempted to sum up the problem by stating, "The good people are gonna cooperate and the bad people are gonna run." Later, however, he qualified this by explaining that he, like other bondsmen, looks into each defendant's criminal record, employment history, residence, and family situation before deciding to post bail. A third bondsman commented, "Good actors have roots in the community."

Having determined that a defendant has the ability to pay the premium, however, the bondsman is extremely likely to accept the defendant as a customer. He may refuse to post bail on a defendant who already owes him a considerable amount of money for past services. Similarly, he will probably refuse to extend credit to a defendant whom he knows—either from his own past experience or occasionally on the advice of another bondsman—to be a "wise guy" or a "bad actor," that is, a person likely to withhold payments or to go into hiding. Hesitancy on the bondsman's part is also likely when police records indicate outstanding warrants, for in such cases the defendant may be rearrested and returned to custody before the bondsman has collected his fee. The police follow the business dealings of bondsmen with special interest and can sometimes use this knowledge to advantage when they wish to prevent particular defendants from gaining release.

Indemnification Agreements

Of course, if he chooses to do so, the bondsman can insure himself against all losses from forfeited bonds by requiring each customer to complete a collateral agreement. To accomplish this, the defendant signs a collateral form or persuades another person to act as a guarantor. This step would eliminate all uncertainty in client selection, since such an agreement guarantees complete indemnification of the surety for any losses he may incur. But bondsmen usually do not require indemnification contracts from their customers, for most criminal defendants are extremely poor and are unable to find guarantors to co-sign indemnification agreements on bail bonds posted for defendants. Although the guarantor may not fully understand the legal significance of his role, he generally recognizes that he is being asked to pledge an amount of money or perhaps his property for the defendant's good conduct. The guarantor must place great trust in the defendant, which for most defendants narrows the field of potential guarantors to a small circle of persons.

It is difficult to determine the frequency with which bondsmen post bail unaccompanied by collateral agreements. No official figures are collected to indicate how often this happens, but some reasonable estimates can be made. During field interviews, bondsmen stated that they received "hard" collateral—indemnification contracts backed up by specific assets such as bank accounts or property deeds—in 5 to 10 percent of their cases. These are probably cases involving more serious offenses and thus higher bail amounts. Estimates of the frequency of "hard" collateral were all within this range (see National Conference on Bail and Criminal Justice 1965: 234). Similarly, another study of bail practices (Hoskins 1968: 1141) concluded that "complete indemnification is seldom achieved" by bail bondsmen. However, in a fairly large proportion of cases, written promises of indemnification are obtained.

In these cases, the bondsman accepts from defendants or guarantors the pledge of such possessions as automobiles, jewelry, or household furnishings and appliances as collateral. Estimates by bondsmen of the frequency of such agreements ranged from 40 to 60 percent. The realizable market value of these items is often considerably less than the personal value they have for the guarantors who offer them. Thus it appears that most of the indemnification agreements obtained by bondsmen have relatively little value as collateral.

This impression is strengthened by bondsmen's reports concerning the difficulties of enforcing collateral agreements. "Unless you hold the collateral in your hand, it isn't worth anything," stated one bondsman. In five years of writing bail bonds, this informant claimed, three guarantors had reimbursed him for forfeited bonds without protesting. Another bondsmen said that he had received voluntary compensation from a co-signer only once in fifteen years. Legal remedies are available to the bondsman, and when enforcement of collateral agreements becomes necessary the bondsman can turn to these. In many states, for example, co-signers are legally liable to pay costs incurred by bondsmen in attempting to recapture fugitive defendants up to the limit of the outstanding bond. Given the inevitable costs and uncertainties of litigation, however, bondsmen are more likely to resort to informal means of enforcing indemnification agreements with defendants and co-signers. The overriding purpose of indemnification agreements appears to be their presumed "psychological" value for protecting investments by underlining the obligations of defendants and co-signers to the bondsman.

In practice, therefore, whether to post bail on a defendant without obtaining collateral is the most important decision facing the bondsman. Because most defendants are unable to provide adequate collateral, the bondsman confronts this decision often. It is in exercising discretion not to impose "hard" collateral conditions on defendants and guarantors that the bondsman runs his largest risks and stands to make his highest profits. The bondsman must summon all of his business acumen and skill in "human relations" to make this decision. It is here that the bondsman's greatest impact on the justice system occurs, and it is here also that cooperative relations with court officials become most important.

Nonenforcement of Bail Forfeitures

The key factor in this aspect of bail bonding is the discretionary power of judges to exonerate outstanding bonds and to set aside bail forfeitures. When a bailed defendant fails to appear in court, the bondsman may have to forfeit the bail he has posted if he is unable to produce the defendant within the legal "grace" period (six months in the state where this study was done). Whether forfeiture is actually imposed is decided by the judge who presides in the case. Remission procedures, which permit this decision to be made, set out the conditions under which judges may authorize the return of forfeited bonds to sureties.

The law gives judges wide latitude in these procedures, creating the suspicion that such decisions may sometimes reflect judicial improprieties. The opportunity for official misconduct would, of course, be present even if judges were not directly involved in approving requests for exoneration of forfeited bonds. But from another standpoint, the existence of these procedures is fortunate, for without them officials

would be compelled to carry out a policy of strict and uniform enforcement of forfeited bail bonds. This would probably lead to a considerable increase in the number
of persons unable to gain release on bail. Bondsmen ordinarily obtain complete
indemnification on only a small percentage of all defendants for whom they post
bonds, and insistence of bondsmen on full collateral would be a very likely adjustment to a policy of strict enforcement. Many defendants would thus fail to qualify
for the services of bondsmen due to inability to raise collateral. This might be compounded by another effect of a policy of strict enforcement of bail forfeitures: such
a policy quickly drives noncorporate sources of bail, including friends and relatives
of defendants, out of the system (see Foote 1954: 1060–1066).

   Virtually every study of bail administration ever conducted has found that a large
proportion of forfeitures are set aside by judges. This generous use of judicial discretion stems from one or more of several possible sources. As already suggested,
one possibility is that forfeitures are routinely set aside because judges recognize the
dependence of the court on the willingness of bondsmen to post bail for defendants
who cannot provide full collateral. That bondsmen accept many defendants as customers without securing legally enforceable indemnification agreements not only
increases the overall profitability of writing bail bonds, but it also enables large numbers of defendants to obtain release who would otherwise face pretrial detention,
thereby preventing intolerable pressures on detention facilities. The stake of the criminal justice system in the willingness of bail bondsmen to depart from norms of conservative business practice is considerable.

   A second reason that judges so often exercise their power to remit bail forfeitures in favor of bondsmen is that they sometimes need reciprocity from bondsmen
to prevent defendants from obtaining release. When court officials desire that a particular defendant not be released, they may pass the word on to local bondsmen
(National Conference on Bail and Criminal Justice 1966: 118). I learned of no such
instance during my study, but it is fairly common knowledge that bondsmen in various cities were subject to severe pressures against writing bonds for persons arrested
during civil rights protests during the last decade (Goldfarb 1965: 84–85). Because
bondsmen need the court's cooperation for a variety of reasons, they are unlikely to
offend court officials by posting bail in such instances. In this way, judges can prevent release without actually denying bail or setting bail in an amount that the legally
competent defendant might challenge as "excessive." The effective discretion exercised by court officials is therefore augmented by informal relationships with
bondsmen.

   These relationships also help explain why it is that bondsmen ordinarily make
no efforts to supervise defendants for whom they post bail. Bondsmen require only
those defendants who owe money to make regular reports, and then the purpose is
not to remind the defendant that his behavior is under scrutiny but to enable the
bondsman to collect his fee. Even when a defendant fails to make a required court
appearance the bondsman is likely to make only minimal efforts to locate the defendant—for example, by placing a few telephone calls to persons whom the defendant
has named as references or by sending a telegram to an address given by the defendant. Only once during field observations did I learn of a case in which a bondsman
was actively attempting to locate a defendant for reasons other than payment.

Despite the extensive protection afforded, bail bondsmen cannot place complete reliance on court officials to return all forfeited bonds. In some instances, particularly when large bail amounts are at stake, bondsmen may need to attempt to locate fugitive defendants. Bondsmen have extraordinary powers of arrest and extradition over bailed defendants who have fled. No criminal justice official possesses the degree of legal authority over citizens that the bondsman holds and occasionally wields over his customers. Under powers vested in him by law, the bondsman can compel a defendant for whom he has posted bail to return with him to court at the point of a gun. The bondsman does not need to obtain a warrant for this purpose, and the defendant legally cannot offer resistance. The frequency with which bondsmen exercise their powers to retrieve fugitive defendants is not readily ascertainable and officials hold divergent views. Some law-enforcement officials claim that the most important service the bondsman renders to the state is in retrieving defendants who have absconded (Hoskins 1968: 1144; National Conference on Bail and Criminal Justice 1965: 237). But others assert that bondsmen rarely make special efforts to locate defaulting defendants for whom they have assumed bail obligations and that fugitive defendants are returned only when they later commit crimes for which they are rearrested (U.S. Senate 1964: 131). Of course, both of these views may be correct.

Even when bondsmen make use of their powers to capture and return fugitive defendants to court, they rarely engage directly in efforts to locate defendants. During field observations, several Westville bondsmen mentioned a legendary case in which one of their colleagues had spent considerable time and money "chasing a $14,000 skip all over the country" without result. But the more common practice involves indirect search operations whereby the bondsman seeks to purchase information about the location of a fugitive defendant for whom he is financially responsible. A Westville bondsman described one possibility:

> I have a case right now of a $1,100 skip. The guy is down in Valley City somewhere, I know that much. I've got a pimp down there working on it for me. There's no way anybody could find out that this pimp works for me, because he's cool and I'm cool. He's going to ask around to see if he can locate this guy. Then I'll go down there with another guy and we'll bring him back to Westville. It'll cost me about $150 to catch the guy, so I'll just about break even on this one. [The bondsman had already collected the $110 premium.]

Other bondsmen indicated that they contract with specialists—either professional detectives ("skip tracers") or underworld figures—to locate defaulting defendants. Such persons receive a certain proportion of the bail amount for information leading to successful capture of the defendant.

The bondsman's legal powers of arrest and extradition, like his discretion in posting bail, may occasionally be put to the advantage of criminal justice officials. Bondsmen "own" defendants for whom they post bail. Therefore, law-enforcement officials can informally borrow the bondsman's legal authority to avoid having to comply with expensive and cumbersome procedures necessary for interstate extradition of fugitive defendants. Under this arrangement, defendants who have been arrested in another state are turned over to bondsmen for return to face original charges in the state where they jumped bail. It is not known how widespread this practice is, but the use of bail bondsmen to circumvent formal extradition procedures is thought to be quite common in some states (see U.S. Senate 1966: 23–24; *Yale Law Journal*, 1964).

Summary and Discussion of Findings

The presence of bail bondsmen in American criminal courts rests upon the right of bail to which all persons accused of noncapital crimes are said to be entitled. The basis of this familiar legal concept is embedded in a tersely ambiguous clause of the United States Constitution. Most state constitutions, and particularly those adopted after ratification of the U.S. Constitution, contain similar provisions. But the Eighth Amendment clause in question simply states that "excessive bail shall not be required of defendants" in criminal cases. It says nothing about bail bondsmen, the surety companies which stand behind them, forfeitures of bail, and so on. These and other details of bail administration are spelled out in statutes and case law at both the federal and state levels (see Foote 1965; Paulsen 1966).

The bail system has come in for much criticism in the past decade and a half, mostly directed at the excessive reliance placed on money as a means of securing the presence of defendants for hearings and—on the rare occasions when they are held—trials. The problem, however, is not only that the bail system makes release before trial hinge on the defendant's financial situation. It is also that American law refuses to entrust officials with formal power to detain citizens who are only accused of crime.

Two comparative law scholars (Mueller and Le Poole-Griffiths 1969: 23–24) highlight the problem in the following way:

> Continental law has faced this issue with great candor. Pretrial detention, despite the probable guilt of the defendant, is always an exceptional measure and can be imposed only when . . . extremely high standards for issuance of a warrant can be met. But when, thus, the guilt of the perpetrator is highly probable, when the offense is major, when there is danger that he will flee, tamper with the evidence and repeat his offense, why then bother with an insurance contract insuring the defendant's next appearance? To release a suspect under those circumstances would be more than a gambler's folly, or the premium should have to be so high that nobody could meet it. Realizing this, continental law rarely insists on preliminary detention when we do, and, while nearly all codes have provisions on bail, there is rarely any occasion to apply them. When the risk of release is worth taking, release is ordered. Any other system is nonutilitarian and would only discriminate against the poor, a reason which led Sweden to abandon this institution.

In contrast, American law forbids criminal court officials from detaining a defendant who may appear dangerous or likely to flee if released. Our procedures, by defining pretrial release decisions as questions of judicial and prosecutorial responsibility, are also unique in the extent to which they aim at excluding the police from such decisions (Goldfarb 1965: 213). American law's institutionalized suspicion of official discretion is apparent in the case of bail. Admittedly, the bail system fails to guarantee pretrial freedom to every defendant claiming it as a right. But even if such claims often go unrecognized, it is clear that officials are not absolutely free to ignore them.

Bail bondsmen serve several functions in the criminal court system. First, they facilitate pretrial release of large numbers of arrested persons. Of course, the defendant must pay for this "service." However, in deciding whether to post bail for a defendant's release, the only question in which the bondsman has any real interest is whether the defendant will pay the fee for what is in effect a loan of money. This means that monetary considerations override other concerns, such as the offense with which the defendant is charged, the likelihood of guilt, the probability of rearrest, or even the risk of flight.

Bondsmen can afford to ignore these matters because of their intimate knowledge of court operations and the personalized relationships they cultivate with court officials. In large part, their work consists of drawing upon these resources to manage cases and protect investments. This is related to a second function performed by bondsmen, which is to help move defendants through the courts. Because their earnings depend directly upon the number of customers they handle, bondsmen gear their activities toward promoting rapid disposition of cases.

Third, bondsmen aid officials in dealing selectively with difficult cases. In one such arrangement, for example, the bondsman acts upon his legitimate business prerogatives by refusing to bond a certain defendant for pretrial release, thereby tacitly carrying out official wishes. In another, the bondsman exercises his legal power of interstate extradition in order to help officials avoid the problems and expense of securing the return for prosecution of a fugitive defendant who has been apprehended in another state. Both of these arrangements work on the same principle. They require bondsmen to carry out informal and extralegal directives issued by court officials. In turn, officials cooperate with bondsmen because of the organizational benefits that bondsmen confer on the legal system. Official reciprocity takes several forms, the most important of which is judicial nonenforcement of forfeited bail bonds.

The bail system, then, links the personal interests of bondsmen with the organizational requirements of criminal court operations. This linkage is accomplished by means of discretionary exchanges of outcomes which augment the effective authority of law-enforcement and judicial personnel and which also take much of the risk out of bondsmen's business transactions. This system of interlocking obligations strengthens official control over arrested persons at the same time that it increases the profitability of selling bail bonds.

Conclusion

The last twenty years of appellate court rulings on criminal procedure have had profound effects on local court operations. For example, one articulate judge, viewing the scene from an intermediate appellate court, maintains that the cumulative impact on criminal courts has been literally devastating.

The mood of alarm expressed by contemporary observers of American criminal courts can be more readily understood by recalling that at no time since the beginning of this century has anything but the roughest kind of justice been available for the majority of the cases in these courts. As the appellate judiciary over the last two

decades has attempted to raise the standards of treatment accorded criminal defendants by local criminal justice officials, the resulting improvements have been slight
by comparison with expectations for change which have been generated by these
decisions.

In addition to the tensions generated by the politics of local justice, criminal
courts now face a qualitatively different set of problems arising from the fact that
their activities have been drawn into the politics of constitutional law.

In this vastly changed situation, the practical achievements of criminal court
administration seem always to be lagging farther behind the evolving constitutional
criteria of fair treatment. One should not imagine that this growing divergence has
gone unrecognized by criminal justice officials or that it has caused them only minor
inconveniences. In fact, as gaps between written law and official practice have wid-
ened, the exact role that trial courts are to play in the criminal justice system has
become increasingly unclear.

Ambiguity is reflected in many ways. For instance, one innovation which has
received great acclaim from judges and prosecutors in recent years is the idea that
some individuals accused of crime can usefully be channeled away from the coercive
context of court proceedings and toward the beneficent environment of informal
"treatment" (Vorenberg and Vorenberg 1973). In point of fact, every program based
on the concept of "diversion" uses "the threat or possibility of conviction of a criminal offense to encourage an accused to do something," and the agreement thus
obtained "may not be entirely voluntary, as the accused often agrees to participate
in a diversion program only because he fears formal criminal prosecution" (National
Advisory Commission 1973: 27). There can be little doubt that the growing appeal
of this concept among local criminal justice officials has an intimate and paradoxical
connection with developments in constitutional law over the past two decades (Balch
1974).

At the same time, a controversy has arisen over the question of whether and to
what extent it falls to criminal courts to supervise the police in order to assure their
compliance with changed procedural requirements (Milner 1971). For it can be
argued that the changes in police practices which have been mandated by appellate
decisions over the last two decades are so sweeping, and the lack of any alternative
enforcement mechanism so patent, as to presuppose a substantially new function for
local-level judicial officials. Many of these decisions, indeed, seem aimed precisely
at extending the political doctrine of separation of powers, and the companion doctrine of judicial supremacy, to the administration of local criminal justice. The core
assumption in nearly all of them has been that criminal courts must counterbalance
the activities of police agencies in order to prevent mistreatment of citizens accused
of crime. In this view, it becomes the responsibility of trial courts to monitor the
actions of law-enforcement officials and, using the remedy of dismissal as a sanction,
check any tendencies toward official lawlessness (LaFave and Remington 1965).

The period between arrest and disposition has special importance in American
criminal law, for it is during this period that defendants are supposed to begin taking
advantage of the procedural protections to which appellate courts hold them entitled
(Karlen 1967: 135–166). In practice, however, relatively few defendants get any
opportunity to do so. In most cases the period after arrest involves perfunctory official acknowledgment of the defendant's rights, followed by out-of-court negotiations

aimed at rapid disposition. In lower criminal courts, the defendant's first appearance tends to be his only appearance (Mileski 1971). The disposition process is somewhat less abbreviated in higher-level trial courts, but the same tendency toward truncated procedure can be observed there (Blumberg 1970).

The conception of the criminal court as a supervisor of police activities and the essentially hierarchical model of the criminal justice system implied in this conception have been criticized before (Bittner 1970: 22–30; Feeley 1973). The present article casts further doubt on these assumptions. It focuses on the stage of the criminal justice process that begins when law-enforcement functions give way, in principle at least, to judicial functions. The findings indicate that the business of court administration virtually merges with the enterprise of law enforcement at this period and strengthen the argument that the criminal court actually serves as an agency of law enforcement (Skolnick 1969: 236–243). Thanks to the growing interest in criminal courts among social scientists, we now have some idea of why this merger takes place and how it affects the treatment of defendants. We are also coming to realize that the problems of criminal courts are both causes and effects of the chronic crisis in American criminal justice.

References

ARES, CHARLES, AND HERBERT STURZ (1962). "Bail and the Indigent Accused." 8 *Crime and Delinquency* 12.

BALCH, ROBERT W. (1974). "Deferred Prosecution: The Juvenilization of the Criminal Justice System." 38 *Federal Probation* 46.

BEELEY, ARTHUR L. (1927). *The Bail System in Chicago.* Chicago: University of Chicago Press (reissued 1966).

BITTNER, EGON (1970). *The Functions of the Police in Modern Society.* Washington, D.C.: U.S. Government Printing Office.

BLUMBERG, ABRAHAM S. (1967). "The Practice of Law as a Confidence Game." 1 *Law and Society Review* 15.

——— (1970). *Criminal Justice.* Chicago: Quadrangle Books.

CHAMBLISS, WILLIAM J. (1971). "Vice, Corruption, Bureaucracy, and Power." *Wisconsin Law Review* 1150.

COX, ARCHIBALD (1968). *The Warren Court.* Cambridge, Mass.: Harvard University Press.

DOWNIE, LEONARD (1971). *Justice Denied.* Baltimore: Penguin Books.

FEELEY, MALCOLM M. (1973). "Two Models of the Criminal Justice System: An Organizational Perspective." 7 *Law and Society Review* 407.

FLEMING, MACKLIN (1974). *The Price of Perfect Justice.* New York: Basic Books.

FOOTE, CALEB (1954). "Compelling Appearance in Court: Administration of Bail in Philadelphia." 102 *University of Pennsylvania Law Review* 1031.

——— (1958). "A Study of the Administration of Bail in New York City." 106 *University of Pennsylvania Law Review* 693.

——— (1965). "The Coming Constitutional Crisis in Bail." 113 *University of Pennsylvania Law Review* 959.

FREED, DANIEL J., AND PATRICIA M. WALD (1964). *Bail in the United States: 1964.* Washington, D.C.: National Conference on Bail and Criminal Justice.

FRIEDMAN, LAWRENCE M. (1973). *A History of American Law.* New York: Simon & Schuster.

GOLDFARB, RONALD (1965). *Ransom: A Critique of the American Bail System.* New York: Harper & Row.

HOSKINS, JOHN (1968). "Tinkering with the California Bail System." 56 *California Law Review* 1134.

INGRAHAM, BARTON L. (1974). "The Impact of Argersinger—One Year Later." 8 *Law and Society Review* 615.

JACKSON, DONALD DALE (1975). *Judges.* New York: Atheneum.

JAMES, HOWARD (1971). *Crisis in the Courts.* New York: David McKay.

KARLEN, DELMAR (1967). *Anglo-American Criminal Justice.* New York: Oxford University Press.

LAFAVE, WAYNE R., AND FRANK J. REMINGTON (1965). "Controlling the Police: The Judge's Role in Making and Reviewing Law Enforcement Decisions." 63 *Michigan Law Review* 987.

LEFSTEIN, N., ET AL. (1969). "In Search of Juvenile Justice." 5 *Law and Society Review* 491.

LEMERT, EDWIN M. (1970). *Social Action and Legal Change.* Chicago: Aldine.

LEVIN, MARTIN (1972). "Urban Politics and Judicial Behavior." 1 *Journal of Legal Studies* 193.

LEVY, LEONARD W. (1974). *Against the Law.* New York: Harper & Row.

MATHER, LYNN M. (1973). "Some Determinants of the Method of Case Disposition: Decision-Making by Public Defenders in Los Angeles." 8 *Law and Society Review* 187.

MILESKI, MAUREEN (1971). "Courtroom Encounters: An Observation Study of a Lower Criminal Court." 5 *Law and Society Review* 473.

MILNER, NEAL A. (1971). *The Court and Local Law Enforcement.* Newbury Park, Calif.: Sage Publications.

MOLEY, RAYMOND (1930). *Our Criminal Courts.* New York: Minton, Balch & Co.

MUELLER, GERHARD O. W., AND FRE LE POOLE-GRIFFITHS (1969). *Comparative Criminal Procedure.* New York: New York University Press.

NATIONAL ADVISORY COMMISSION (1973). *National Advisory Commission on Criminal Justice Standards and Goals Report on Courts.* Washington, D.C.: U.S. Government Printing Office.

NATIONAL CONFERENCE ON BAIL AND CRIMINAL JUSTICE (1965). *Proceedings and Interim Report.* Washington, D.C.

—— (1966). *Bail and Summons: 1965.* Washington, D.C.

OHLIN, LLOYD E., ED. (1973). *Prisoners in America.* Englewood Cliffs, N.J.: Prentice-Hall.

PAULSEN, MONRAD (1966). "Pre-Trial Release in the United States." 66 *Columbia Law Review* 109.

POUND, ROSCOE (1945). *Criminal Justice in America.* Cambridge, Mass.: Harvard University Press.

PRESIDENT'S COMMISSION (1967). *The President's Commission on Law Enforcement and Administration of Justice Task Force Report: Courts.* Washington, D.C.: U.S. Government Printing Office.

ROTHMAN, DAVID (1972). "Of Prisons, Asylums, and Other Decaying Institutions." 26 *The Public Interest* 3.

SCHUBERT, GLENDON (1970). *The Constitutional Polity.* Boston: Boston University Press.

SILVERSTEIN, LEE (1966). "Bail in the State Courts—A Field Study and Report." 50 *Minnesota Law Review* 621.

SKOLNICK, JEROME H. (1967). "Social Control in the Adversary System." 11 *Journal of Conflict Resolution* 52.

—— (1969). *The Politics of Protest.* Washington, D.C.: U.S. Government Printing Office.

SUFFET, FREDERICK (1966). "Bail Setting: A Study of Courtroom Interaction." 12 *Crime and Delinquency* 318.

SUTHERLAND, EDWIN H., AND DONALD R. CRESSEY (1970). *Principles of Criminology.* Philadelphia: J. B. Lippincott Company.

U.S. SENATE (1964). Hearings, Bills to Improve Federal Bail Procedures. 88th Cong., 2nd Sess.

—— (1966). Hearings, A Proposal to Modify Existing Procedures Governing the Interstate Rendition of Fugitive Bailees. 89th Cong., 2nd Sess.

VIRTUE, MAXINE BOORD (1962). *Survey of Metropolitan Courts.* Ann Arbor: University of Michigan Press.

VORENBERG, ELIZABETH W., AND JAMES VORENBERG (1973). "Early Diversion from the Criminal Justice System." In Lloyd E. Ohlin, ed., *Prisoners in America.* Englewood Cliffs, N.J.: Prentice-Hall.

WASBY, STEPHEN L. (1970). *The Impact of the United States Supreme Court: Some Perspectives.* Homewood, Ill.: Dorsey Press.

WICE, PAUL (1974). "Purveyors of Freedom: The Professional Bondsmen." 11 *Society* 34.

WICE, PAUL, AND RITA JAMES SIMON (1970). "Pretrial Release: A Survey of Alternative Practices." 34 *Federal Probation* 60.

WOOD, ARTHUR L. (1967). *Criminal Lawyer.* New Haven: College and University Press.

YALE LAW JOURNAL (1961). "Bail: An Ancient Practice Reexamined." 70 *Yale Law Journal* 966.

———— (1964). "Bailbondsmen and the Fugitive Accused—The Need for Formal Removal Procedures." 73 *Yale Law Journal* 1098.

16

The Criminal Court Community in Erie County, Pennsylvania

James Eisenstein

Roy B. Flemming

Peter F. Nardulli

The traditional picture of the courtroom emphasizes adversarial attitudes, but a more realistic picture might emphasize the interaction among the major actors within the normative context of the work group and the local legal culture. As you read about the criminal court community in Erie County, Pennsylvania, think about the impact of the local legal culture and the interpersonal relationships among the principal actors on decision making. How might the court in Erie County differ from that in your home community?

Size, Composition, and Communication in the Court Community

Erie's criminal court community displayed several features that reflected the characteristics of the county it served. We begin our description of the court community by looking at these characteristics.

People tended to stay in Erie County. In 1980, 90 percent of its population had lived there at least since 1975, the highest proportion among our nine counties.[1] Among the five "standard metropolitan statistical areas" (SMSAs) in our nine counties, the Erie SMSA showed the lowest rate of migration into the area (10 percent) from 1975 to 1980. The low influx of newcomers meant that people tended to know each other. Despite its population of 280,000, the county, and especially the city and its suburbs, exhibited the familiarity and extensive network of social ties usually associated with small towns. One person told us:

> Erie's an interesting community in that there are a lot of people in this community who are related to one another. I mean with strings, and cousins and distant cous-

Source: From *The Contours of Justice: Communities and Their Courts,* by James Eisenstein, et al., pp. 74–103. Copyright © 1988 by James Eisenstein, Roy B. Flemming and Peter F. Nardulli. Reprinted by permission of HarperCollins Publishers. Some footnotes deleted.

ins—that's the problem. A lot of the marriages—I can think of several older Republican families, and their families have married. There are a lot of small (100 to 200) industrial firms that have been run by older Erie families. It's in the school board; it's in the government; it's just everywhere.

These patterns facilitated the development of another feature of small towns, a highly effective and extensive community grapevine. An attorney who had lived in Pittsburgh commented that

you could go over into another segment of Pittsburgh and nobody would know you. Here, someone once said, if you break a window at 10th and State, by the time you hit 6th and State, it's in the morning newspaper. There are grapevines all over the place.

Like many newspapers serving smaller towns, Erie's morning and evening papers combined a conservative editorial policy with "community boosterism." Published by the same company, both papers' editorials called for harsher sentences, and the morning paper's managing editor was described as a "hard-line criminal justice man." Nevertheless, because the papers wanted to project an image of Erie as a nice community with few serious problems, they did not sensationalize crime, single out individuals for criticism, or engage in in-depth investigative reporting on the courts. A content analysis of the papers' coverage of crime found fewer and shorter articles about crime and the courts than in the other two Pennsylvania counties. Furthermore, the papers deliberately refrained from reporting an important feature of sentencing policy. One attorney told us that

[E]verybody knows that prostitutes get six months or a year, and get out in ten days because the press doesn't follow it up. The press is there when the judge sentences them, but the press doesn't follow up, and the judge cuts them loose.

In fact, a prosecutor claimed that a reporter had written a story describing this practice, only to have it killed by his editors.

The newspapers' treatment of the courts probably also reflected the effects of social and business ties common in small communities. The head public defender's law firm and several of the judges had served as legal counsel to editors or publishers. Another attorney told us of his friendship with the editor: "We do things in charitable organizations together. It's a small town . . . everybody knows everybody."

The criminal court community reflected many of the characteristics of the larger community just described. Lawyers referred to the Erie County bar as "small," even though more than 300 lawyers practiced there. As one stated, "It's an easy place to get to know everybody." Furthermore, a relatively small group of people formed the core of the criminal court community. Three of the five judges heard most of the cases. Nine attorneys staffed the district attorney's office and fourteen the public defender's. Together, these twenty-eight people handled half the cases. A group of about fifty private attorneys joined the prosecutors and judges to handle the other half of the caseload. But just five of them represented about 40 percent of defendants with private counsel. Thus a core group of thirty-three people disposed of about 70 percent of the caseload.

Familiarity extended to other participants as well. One attorney summarized the results of his analysis of about 700 of his case files: "The same names appeared over and over again. . . . You see family names. . . . You'll get the father, the older brother, the younger brother, the sister, the mother." Another lawyer said that the judges, being political creatures, also knew many of the defendants. A third told us, "Basically, you see the same [police] officers. . . . There are a lot of detectives but there are only a few that do any work."

The Erie court community's small size and the familiarity of its members with one another undoubtedly contributed to the effectiveness of its grapevine.[2] . . . A public defender confirmed our suspicion about its effectiveness when we asked if there were *any* secrets in the county: "I'll tell you. Probably not very many. Because if you get around and know the people, you'll find out."

The grapevine, the court community's small size, and the familiarity of its members together provided the conditions for developing strong social ties that went beyond the courthouse. The description of an experienced defense attorney's ties to people in the district attorney's office illustrates these relationships:

> [One] is a personal friend of mine. He's over at my house; I'm over at his. A lot of those guys are personal friends. I have a corporation with another prosecutor. That's the thing that's unique about this county. Most of the lawyers—there's a couple of cliques—where everybody knows everybody else. After trial we go out and have dinner. . . . That's just the way we are.

Of course, criticism and conflict usually gave way to moderation and cooperation under such circumstances. One attorney explained, "Sometimes you have to be very careful whom you criticize in this town just because you never know who you're talking to." Mutual accommodation and working things out provided the principal formula for dealing with each other. A prosecutor explained,

> Detectives get along pretty well with defense attorneys, too. There's not a great deal of animosity. . . . The police get along with the DAs; the DAs get along with the defense attorneys.

A significant feature of Erie's court community was the ability to talk things over. This same prosecutor said that he shared a goal with public defenders, that if their client needed a break, they should "come see me." The ability to "talk about it" extended to judges: "I don't really have a problem walking in and seeing them at just about any time subject to their schedule," observed a prosecutor. A former public defender explained why Erie was a nice county in which to practice:

> It's a little bit looser than a lot of counties in Pennsylvania where the judges don't even want to talk to the lawyers. We have easy access to our judges.

And a full-time prosecutor, when asked what one needed to know to understand Erie's court, replied:

> My experience here has been that it's—I don't want to say that it's a family operation necessarily—but it's a fairly close interpersonal sort of operation, with some notable exceptions, like the public defender's office . . . in terms of the relationships, most of them are based on individual relationships with each other. Like given lawyers in this office and given probation officers on the third floor, or even given lawyers and judges.

He continued his description later:

The judges' secretaries make a big difference too. . . . It's all part of the wheels, the wheels of the system. The court administrator is the same as you. You have to know how to handle him . . . he's our age, he worked on our campaign right along with us, he's a hell of a nice guy.

Thus, cooperating, "going along," and adhering to established ways of treating others and doing things received powerful support in Erie.

If social relationships encouraged cooperation, they also provided the means for punishing those who refused. A prosecutor explained how he would get a postponement in a trial's starting date if key witnesses were unavailable when the 180-day deadline was about to expire:

So I'm gonna have to lean on the defense counsel to get a waiver of the 180-day rule. The judge will do it for me if necessary. He'll just lean on the defense counsel. This is a small town.

And a nonlawyer familiar with the court's operations explained that attorneys who violated widely accepted informal rules of behavior "suffered in some way down the line" in their dealings with the judges. Thus, the high degree of familiarity and interdependency characteristic of Erie's criminal court community heightened communication among its members and facilitated adherence to implicit rules. Personal rivalries and conflicts were there too, especially among the heads of the principal offices, but not extensively enough to threaten the prevailing mood of cooperation and accommodation.

Geography of Erie's Criminal Court Community

Where people worked subtly shaped the structure and dynamics of Erie's criminal court community. Here we explore the effects of the layout of the courthouse.

Public officials liked the façade of the old courthouse (built in 1852) so much that they built a new wing duplicating it in 1929. Behind these two buildings, traditional in appearance with marble columns and staircases, sat the newest addition, built in the 1970s. Here were housed county officials on the first floor, four of the five judges and the district attorney's office on the second, the public defender, probation department, and coffee room on the third, and the jail on the fourth.

These arrangements facilitated communication. A few steps led judges from their chambers to their courtroom or their brethren's quarters. The district attorney's cramped quarters forced frequent encounters among its staff, a pattern reinforced by the practice of gathering to work, meet, and shoot the breeze in the centrally located conference room. Any judge's chambers could be reached in thirty seconds. . . . The courthouse coffee room [was] a center for socializing, gossiping, and nourishing the grapevine. The presence of other county offices on the first floor guaranteed that the grapevine would carry information about everybody's activities. It was also a convenient shorthand in discussing relations between the court (the "second floor") and its source of funds (the "first floor").

•   •   •

The Judges

Unlike other enforcers of rules such as baseball umpires, judges find that their prestige, formal authority, and active participation place them at center stage in criminal courts. What kind of people are they? What attitudes, personality quirks, and decision patterns describe them? How do they get along with one another and with other members of the court community? These questions are a never-ending source of fascination and worry to other members of the court community. Though we can provide only brief answers, they will contribute much to understanding the criminal court community.

Five older, experienced "home-town boys" formed Erie's judiciary in 1980. One handled the juvenile docket; another devoted himself to probate. Only during trial terms did these two judges handle adult criminal cases, and then only by presiding over cases sent to them for trial. Our discussion consequently is focused on the three men who handled most of the criminal work load.

These three judges had served a total of thirty-five years. The youngest had already passed his sixtieth birthday and seventh year on the bench. The other two were sixty-four and sixty-seven, with thirteen and fifteen years' experience. Each indicated they were Republicans, though one of the other two was a Democrat, and the last an independent. Born and raised in Erie County, all three won election as district attorney between 1964 and 1970. Their election campaigns for DA and judge familiarized them with the county and its people. Commenting on his experience in campaigning for judge, one concluded that:

> I think it is an advantage because you tend to have a better feeling for people, and I think you've got a better feeling for problems, people's problems, practical problems. . . . I think it's easier to understand how people get into a situation that has led to some difficulty that ended up in court.

Their attitudes toward criminal law were distinctly conservative. In an article in *Pennsylvania Law Journal,* one publicly criticized the Warren Court's criminal law decisions, especially those such as *Miranda* dealing with confessions, as tipping the balance too far in favor of defendants; he went on to chastise the Pennsylvania Supreme Court for adhering too strictly to such decisions. In an interview with us, an Erie judge expressed views that reflected the tone of the entire court on such issues:

> The criminal law has become so much more detailed and complex, and in my opinion a little nauseous, and I'm losing interest. I really am opposed to a lot of criminal law decisions in Pennsylvania. . . . Frankly, I think they're basically absurd. . . .

All three scored low on our measure of the extent to which they believed in the due process guarantees for criminal defendants (the "due process" scale). When the attitudes of all five judges as a group were compared to those of judges in the other counties, only one other county's judges (Dauphin) scored lower. Questions measuring "belief in punishment" showed Erie judges ranked fourth.

Long service together and ideological compatibility facilitated good relations and a sense of comradery among the judges, one of them saying,

> Three of us have been district attorneys . . . all of us have been defense attorneys for a longer period of time, so we're pretty familiar with criminal law. I mean, I think we think alike without even talking. . . . I could tell you what the president judge thinks about criminal law without even talking to him.

Personal relations among four of the five judges appeared congenial, even close. Referring to the president judge, one commented that "He's over here every day talking to me and we're very close friends." The four normally gathered for morning coffee in the coffee room, engaged in social banter, shared opinions, and discussed common problems. The fifth judge, however, did not share in this fellowship. Younger, stern and aloof in personality, and strong in his views, his operating style differed sharply from that of his colleagues. We heard stories of his conflicts with the president judge, praise for his willingness to work hard, and descriptions of his distant manner. Prosecutors and defense attorneys ranked him as the least responsive to them and least involved in trying to encourage guilty pleas in order to avoid a trial.

The chief judge, called the president judge in Pennsylvania, exercised strong leadership, though his influence varied from one area to another. One judge described these differences:

> I assure you, when he expresses an opinion about my schedule I take that as something more than just an expression of opinion. But if he tells me that he disagrees with a sentence I may have imposed, or a particular finding that I made, I don't pay much attention to it.

The president judge sought to control sentencing in one area by prohibiting acceptance of "Accelerated Rehabilitative Disposition" (ARD) in retail theft cases.[3] He failed, however, to achieve complete adherence. We witnessed his close friend grant ARD in a retail theft; the other criminal judge expressed to us his willingness to do so if a good argument for it were made out to him.

His sway in matters of scheduling was great. A court official familiar with the judges' interactions concluded:

> As far as a unified judicial policy, as far as judges affixing their signature to a particular document or scheduling or something like that, the president judge dominates that. He's pretty much autonomous from the rest of the judges. . . . They can offer comments and suggestions. . . . But he has the ultimate say. All the other judges recognize that whatever the president judge wants, the president judge usually gets.

The president judge's descriptions of his duties conformed to this view. Asked if he facilitated joint decisions or bore the responsibility for running the court and exerting strong leadership, he replied:

> I think we have a little bit of both. I think like the saying, "The buck stops here." Somebody has to make the ultimate decision. That's the way it is. In other words,

you receive all the input you can or should get or need. But eventually you're gonna have to make the decision.

He backed up his position with expressed willingness to meet direct challenges to his authority. What would you do, we asked, if a judge consistently violated the prohibition against granting ARD in retail theft cases. "I talk to him and try to understand," he replied. But what if the judge persisted? "You'd have to report to the judicial review board . . . if there is an established policy, I think the judge should adhere to it."

Thus, the chief judge in Erie acted much like the president of the United States—exercising strong executive leadership. But like the president, his ability to get his way by persuasion surpassed his ability to command and order. Even in matters of scheduling, his control sometimes failed. When the juvenile court judge refused to hear adult trials because of a backlog in his own docket, the president judge backed down.

This description fails to convey adequately the personalities of the judges or the substantial differences among them. One judge earned a reputation, a prosecutor mentioned, as

notorious for settling the case . . . leaning on the case or requiring a plea . . . in the conference before the trial, in the recesses during the trial, all the way through.

Prosecutors and defense attorneys ranked him very high in his "involvement" in determining how cases would be disposed and low in his "responsiveness" to the problems of attorneys. Another judge presented the opposite profile: reluctant to be directive in settling a case and highly responsive to attorneys' requests and needs. Nearly everyone commented on his reluctance to make decisions.

If the Erie criminal court system benefited from its judges' experience, it also paid a price in interest and vigor. Some lawyers in the community believed that time had begun to pass the judges by. Our interviews picked up the loss of vigor. "I'm sort of winding down," one judge told us. "I'm getting closer to when I think I'll retire." Asked what he found satisfying and unsatisfying about his work, another replied:

Well, I read a lot and I enjoy studying, and I did originally enjoy studying and writing opinions. I'll admit it's getting a little tedious now, but at first I did. And I liked trial work at first. I liked all those things. Now I'm getting to the point where I'm thinking about retirement, to be frank with you.

The relations of Erie's judges with other significant figures in the courthouse presented a mixed picture. . . . The judges relied heavily on the probation department, routinely requiring a presentence report on convicted defendants from it before they imposed sentences. The chief probation officer enjoyed the judges' confidence, and had a crucial role in recommending which inmates in the overcrowded jail could be paroled to make room for a fresh recruit. But relations with the county executive and county council were strained. Products of Erie's old political system, the judges got on well with the old system's governing board, the three county commissioners. An individual who dealt with the new regime on behalf of the judges described the changes that came with the adoption of home rule in 1977:

We're not dealing with three people any more. We're dealing with many more. . . . not only the county executive, but his director of finance, his personnel director, and his director of administration. . . . Not only that, but we have to deal with seven county councilmen, because everything has to go before them.

A judge lamented, "They don't understand the operations of the courts, and I think there is a sort of resentment there. They think the judges are high and mighty. . . ." The resentment was mutual. "They always try to cut us once they have satisfied the needs of the other people," observed a court administrator. A showdown over the judges' hiring of additional courtroom personnel and probation officers nearly occurred, and tension lingered. But the court's operations did not appear to be greatly threatened, and self-restraint avoided an all-out public battle. One judge, reminded that in Pennsylvania the court had the power to issue an order to the county for needed funds, remarked: "But you don't like to be dogmatic. You have to be a little bit politician to get along with people."

The "home-town," "old-style politician" character of the judges produced strong links between the judges and the larger community. They knew the county and its people well. Though they were somewhat isolated once on the bench, we got the impression that old ties and lines of communication did not disappear. A prosecutor intriguingly depicted the judges' informal contacts:

> **R:** There is an awful lot of hearsay about it. But my understanding of it is that it will break itself down generally into a contact from someone along the way. That's a contact in terms of "We'll take a look at this," or "Judge, what can you do about this?" or "Judge, what can you do about that?"
>
> **I:** Are these attorneys or political figures?
>
> **R:** Oh, anybody. Anybody. Political figures, people who you might not want to call political figures, people who worked in campaigns, that kind of thing.
>
> **I:** So the telephone lines are open?
>
> **R:** Yeah.
>
> **I:** And they pay attention to it?
>
> **R:** Oh sure. The chambers are open, and that's a very difficult thing to have to deal with.

However you interpret phrases like "the chambers are open" and "people who you might not want to call political figures," it is clear that major participants in the criminal process believed that the judges responded to outside influences on cases for reasons that went beyond facts and law.

Prosecutor's Office

Erie's prosecutors contrasted sharply with the judges in almost every characteristic. When the judges themselves were at equivalent stages in their careers, most members of the office had not been born. Five of its nine-member staff were thirty-one or younger, the oldest only forty-one, and the DA himself but thirty-two. As a group, these eight men and one woman had spent less than half their lives in Erie County; in fact, five indicated that they had moved to Erie for professional reasons. The judges counted three Republicans, one Democrat, and one independent; the prosecutors had two Republicans, six Democrats, and an independent. The DA, elected just a few months before our field research began, displayed a vigor, enthusiasm, and vision in his work that the judges did not. And if the judges stood as remnants of the old political order with strong ties to the community, the prosecutor came to office as an insurgent.

The story of the new DA's route to office illustrates how events and human values shape the life of a criminal court community. The highly regarded Democratic DA who hired him as a young assistant died suddenly in 1974. The judges appointed an experienced trial attorney in the office to replace him, and this individual, running as a Democrat, narrowly won a new term in 1975. Soon nearly everyone on the deceased DA's staff left, citing a litany of complaints about the new DA ("not giving a damn," "not bothering to delegate," "no organization," "no leadership"). The young assistant, who became a defense attorney after he quit, was increasingly dismayed at the deterioration of an office he felt had been a fine one. A combination of nostalgia and anger led him to challenge the incumbent's reelection in 1979.

Because both were Democrats, it meant a fight in the primary for the nomination. Anyone wise in the way of politics knows that challenging incumbents, especially in their own party's primary, usually results in failure. Established politicians counseled him to keep out; labor leaders refused to support him. Then the politically powerful mayor of Erie announced his support for a third candidate. But he stubbornly persisted, assembling a brain trust of politically experienced advisers, several of whom had also served with him in the deceased DA's office. They waged an aggressive campaign in the primary, criticizing the incumbent's loss of thirty-five cases for violating the speedy-trial rule, and hammering on the theme, "It's time to get tough." The incumbent suffered an astonishing defeat, receiving a paltry 10 percent of the vote. The results demonstrated how effective Erie's grapevine was in informing the community of the low regard in which he was allegedly held in the courthouse. Equally unusual was the insurgent's 20 percent margin of victory over the mayor's candidate.

The Republicans had a strong prospective candidate, the man who barely lost the DA's race in 1975. Personal problems, however, caused him to surprise everyone by declining to run, leaving the GOP with no candidate. The Democrats' insurgent candidate faced no opposition in the general election. Rebuffed by Democratic party and labor union leaders in the early stages of his campaign, bucked by the mayor of Erie, and not requiring anyone's assistance in the uncontested general election, he came to office with very few political obligations. Ironically, the new DA did face his potential GOP challenger, but in a different capacity. The Republican county executive fired the longtime incumbent Republican public defender and appointed him to the vacancy. The absence of organized, politically effective groups such as the American Civil Liberties Union, civil rights organizations, and even business groups capable of pressuring the office also contributed to the freedom enjoyed by the new DA. In fact, when asked what organizations or groups impinged on the office, office officials identified only the local rape crisis center.

Motivated by the desire to restore the office to what he believed to be its former competence and performance, and unencumbered by political debts, the new Erie district attorney came to office eager to make big changes. He began with a clear view of the potential his office offered, a view expressed when he was asked if the criminal court administrator could change the way in which cases were scheduled:

He's not able to pull it off by himself. No. But the person who is, the guy who's got to be out on the point . . . is the district attorney—the combination lawyer, politician, administrator, social worker.

He started his initiatives before taking office, utilizing the general election campaign period to prepare an elaborate justification for increasing his budget. Initially rebuffed by the county executive, he finally prevailed by lobbying the county council to override the executive's veto of the increase. He consequently gained both an enhanced reputation for effectiveness and an additional $40,000.

The extra funds permitted basic restructuring of the office. Instead of five full-time assistants, he switched to three full-time and five half-time assistants. Only one attorney from the defeated incumbent's staff remained. His new full-time first assistant knew the criminal process well, because he had served as second assistant public defender. Two of the half-time assistants had also worked for the deceased DA, and a third had engaged in defense work for some time. The added half-timers gave the office some experienced "big guns" to handle the difficult cases and to help train the younger members of the staff who had never tried a case. The half-timers joined because of the new DA's leadership, not for the $12,000 salary. As one explained,

> I haven't been doing it for the money. It's a loss leader. It's a disaster. But it's fun. That's why you do it. That's why he has the staff that he has. It's an economic disaster, but you don't do everything for economic reasons in this world.

Several large changes in policy accompanied inauguration of the reinvigorated DA's office. And several of these flowed directly from the theme of the campaign, "It's time to get tough." The slogan reflected sentiment widely shared in the office, not merely campaign rhetoric. The office sought higher bail, especially in crimes of violence. "They oppose everything you do now," an experienced public defender complained. "You go in for a bond reduction and they oppose it, automatically." It became stingier in recommending lenient dispositions in less serious cases, including Accelerated Rehabilitative Disposition (ARD). The office's leadership felt the previous DA had agreed to plea bargains that reduced the seriousness of the charges "just for the sake of reduction." The new regime claimed it had stopped this practice, reducing charges only when the case was weak, a witness was missing, or the facts justified a lower charge. Finally, the office began writing what some referred to as "hate letters" to the probation department urging that its presentence reports to the judges recommend stiff sentences. Assistants also began appearing at sentencing to make their views known. A militant tenor about this practice arose from the interviews, as one assistant demonstrated:

> That's another thing that's happening that didn't happen before. The judges, under the old regime, were not asking the district attorney to comment at the time of sentence. They are now. We have a right to comment.

Despite widespread agreement among the staff on the need to "get tough," Erie's prosecutors did not appear from the interviews to be vindictive, "grind defendants into the dust" individuals. One administrator volunteered that he retained his belief in due process, and admitted he would find it difficult to sentence some defendants. As a group, Erie's prosecutors held less strong "belief in punishment" views and less negative attitudes toward "due process" than their counterparts in the other two Pennsylvania counties. They ranked seventh among the nine counties in "belief in punishment" and third in "regard for due process."

The leadership style of Erie's new district attorney flowed naturally from the composition of the office. Seven of the eight staff attorneys owed their appointments to the DA. Several part-timers helped plan election strategy, shared memories of the old office, and considered themselves close friends of his. The staff strongly approved of the changes in policy instituted. Its members also socialized in the evening. Both attorneys and secretaries, for instance, attended performances by a band in which one of the lawyers played. A spirit of comradery and pride seemed to prevail. One assistant enthusiastically remarked, "He's assembled a hell of a staff. And that's fun. It's always fun to be associated with competent people. It's interesting." Despite the youth of the office, it had much experience in the criminal process and a high degree of self-assurance, as one administrator's boast showed: "We know all the angles, we know the ropes, we know the way the system works."

These factors encouraged an informal, loose management style. No written rules or manual of office policies existed. No formal procedures for checking staff performance, such as auditing monthly disposition statistics for each attorney, were employed. The DA and the first assistant spent much time in the conference room; the proximity of the courtrooms made it easy to drop in on the inexperienced assistants' performances; the grapevine filled in any gaps. The DA gained familiarity with the cases by reviewing all new matters as they came into the office.

The half-timers were former colleagues older than the DA, precluding a traditional "boss–employee" relationship. The degree of supervision thus varied depending on the assistant's experience. The half-timers felt free to exercise discretion consistent with the DA's views, as the comments of one suggest:

> He knows me and I know him. If there is a question of policy, I would go and ask him. But generally, if a deal is to be made, I in my own discretion would make the deal, and I know he would accept it, just because I've been around. . . . I think we think alike, we act alike, and we have probably very similar attitudes on what law and order is and what justice is. . . . So consequently we really don't have any problems.

In fact, the DA did not always insist cases be handled as he would handle them, even when he became aware of such differences. An experienced assistant told us what happened when he discussed with his boss a plea bargain he had reached:

> He told me he disagreed with it. And I said, "Well, I think I have some pretty good reasons for doing it. . . ." He said, "Well, okay, I'm not going to overrule you. It's your decision."

Rookie assistants received closer scrutiny and direction, but typically through informal means. One, asked if his plea bargains were reviewed by the DA, explained:

> He does monitor that. Probably not on a formal basis as far as keeping a list. He very much stays in the conference room and just sort of sits here and sees what's going on, and asks, like, "Why did you do this?"

They often assisted veteran attorneys on difficult and important cases as part of their training. "Postmortems" in the conference room after trial were another way to give rookies feedback.

If internal office management and relations presented few problems and challenges, the same could not be said of external relations. The successful effort to obtain a budget increase was a significant though difficult victory in dealing with the county government. Like most members of criminal court communities everywhere, however, Erie's prosecutors felt county officials had little knowledge of or real interest in the operations of the criminal courts. The DA did not enjoy a close relationship with the Republican county executive, a political ally of the public defender. But he got on extremely well with the criminal court administrator, an employee of the judges who oversaw scheduling and other administrative matters pertaining to the criminal docket. In fact, everyone knew that the administrator participated actively in the DA's campaign. Good relations with the probation department also developed.

Interaction with several other organizations deserves brief mention. Relations with the news media seemed important to the office. One key office member, assessing the newspaper, strongly implied it favored the judges and the head public defender: "I've sensed that certain things will get printed and certain things won't get printed, and certain people get treated better in the media." The DA received better coverage from the broadcast media, appearing frequently on local television news programs. The office appreciated the cooperation the district justices showed, promptly forwarding copies of case documents after the preliminary hearing, but felt less happy about their refusal to toss out weak cases. Attitudes toward the police . . . varied from respect to disdain depending on the department.

Our description of the Erie DA's office would be incomplete without mentioning its desire to bring about a number of changes. It sought to enhance the office's investigative capabilities beyond the one county detective available, to institute a career criminal prosecution program, and to create a special unit to focus on consumer fraud, drug cases, and white-collar crime. The office's ambitious long-run agenda clashed with the bench's preferences. The judges engaged in almost no long-range planning. Major changes in the way things worked, indeed any changes, failed to excite them.

Our field research ended after the DA's first nine months, and so we could not assess his success in overcoming judicial apathy. His failure, however, to win the president judge's approval of a change in the structure of the criminal calendar demonstrated the need for judicial cooperation, and suggested the formidable obstacles to success that he faced.

Public Defender's Office

If Erie's judges contrasted sharply with its prosecutors, the public defenders displayed many superficial similarities. The public defender himself had also assumed control recently. Though slightly larger, with thirteen attorneys (counting the head) handling adult criminal cases, the officer's average age of thirty-three nearly matched that of the prosecutors. The staff also had three full-timers, including the first and second assistants, with the rest, including the head, part-timers. The new leader felt extensive changes needed to be made, and took steps to bring them about. He fired several people and encouraged others considered "deadwood" to retire. By June 1980, only two part-timers with the office when he took over in 1979 remained.

Despite these obvious similarities, however, major differences could be seen. All but three of the attorneys had lived in Erie County almost all their lives. Despite the head's status as a partisan Republican, the office had four Republicans, four Democrats, and five independents. Three women and two blacks worked there. The DA had one woman and no blacks. The PD's staff had much less experience in criminal law. The first assistant and the two holdover part-timers knew their way around criminal courts, though the first assistant won his knowledge in another state. But the other two full-timers were new both to the office and to criminal law, and five of the six other part-timers had served a year or less. The head PD owed his appointment to his political rather than legal activities. He practiced civil, not criminal, law, and had worked as a Washington lobbyist. Prominent in GOP politics, and narrowly defeated for DA in 1975, he played a central role in the county executive's campaign.

The office failed to achieve the esprit and social cohesion found in the prosecutor's office. The cramped third-floor offices provided space only for the full-timers. The others worked primarily from their private offices, appearing in the main office sporadically during trial terms. The PD called few staff meetings gathering everyone together. An assistant bothered by the lack of communication described several unsuccessful efforts to generate informal social get-togethers.

The head PD identified several long-range goals, including moving the main office out of the courthouse, establishing a student-intern program, and transforming the operation into a private corporation. Like the DA, he demonstrated considerable sophistication and political savvy in devising strategies to realize them. But he classified himself as a "short-run implementer" rather than a "long-range goal man."

Like nearly all supervisors we talked to in public defenders' offices, Erie's head PD believed his staff should be allowed wide autonomy in handling individual clients' cases.

> I am dealing with professionals and if they are good public defenders or good lawyers they have big egos. So that, to some extent, to get the best out of them, I have to take an equal or even a subordinate role in an individual case.

Some staff attorneys agreed that their discretion was not unduly limited. Asked what office policies influenced how he handled cases, one assistant public defender replied there were none. "And it's just like that person is a private client. I have complete latitude on the cases to do what I feel is in his best interest."

Several features of the office's relations outside the court community deserve mention. The head PD's relations with the county executive were very good, though no surprise given their close political ties. Like many aspects of life in other human communities, the effect of their ties on events, though powerful, was often quite subtle. For example, in January 1980, several assistant public defenders were, for various reasons, unavailable. Consistent with his desire to provide defendants with "continuous" representation by the same attorney, the head PD refused to reassign cases to other members of the office. The resulting disruption of the docket angered the rest of the court community, especially the judges. When we asked the public defender if his defiance of the judges might not lead to later trouble in the form of complaints from the judges to the county executive, he replied it would not be a problem due to the "independence" of the county executive from the president judge. Left unsaid was the fact that in such a dispute the public defender would win the county executive's support.

Like the prosecutor, the public defender received little pressure from the community. The private bar voiced few complaints about the office taking paying clients away from struggling attorneys, a situation the office attributed to its strict application of eligibility standards. The PD's law firm represented the newspapers, leading the prosecutors to claim that it received favorable coverage.

The office recognized the importance of district justices and probation officers, and sought to cultivate good relations with both. One policy the head PD pursued required cooperation by the district justices: disposition of minor charges at the preliminary-hearing stage. Erie's public defenders sounded a frequent refrain in discussing lower judges: "Some of the district judges are excellent; some are just dumb."

The lack of the same social cohesion and esprit found in the DA's office led to a less coherent "office view" among Erie's public defenders. The relative inexperience among its attorneys also made it difficult to summarize their attitudes neatly. We can, however, draw two useful conclusions. First, the office felt it did a very good job. An experienced assistant boasted:

> I think we give our clientele excellent service. I think we give the taxpayers a lot for their money. I think our services are really very effective, and are just as much— if not more—effective than private counsel.

The management orientation produced an emphasis on statistical measures of success. An office supervisor rattled off figures on performance in jury trials as proof of effectiveness:

> The public defender's staff had nine guilties, seven splits, nine not guilties, one hung, for twenty-six jury trials. The private bar had eleven guilties, five guilty of lesser offenses, seven not guilties. So we beat them in every category . . . we compare favorably with the private bar.

Several aspects of the head public defender's management style contrasted, though, with his expressed belief in autonomy. He believed strongly in "overmotioning," filing a whole series of pretrial motions as standard practice. Unlike the DA, he sought to implement and enforce this and other policies with formal written memos to the staff and a case file folder with places for the attorney to record every action taken. The data recorded there could then be used as a management tool. "I am not above evaluating lawyers and individual cases. That's one of the reasons I got this file-folder system," he informed us. He also differed from the DA in avoiding informal socializing with the staff: "It's fine when you're one or two years out of law school. But when you start fraternizing with people that you have to tell how to do things, it doesn't work." He used salary-increase allocations to reward some assistants, and gave no raises to others. Everyone knew he had fired several assistants. An individual who had served under the previous public defender summarized the changes as "a more formal and standardized basis now." Holdovers disliked his management style and some of the policies. One who quit complained: "Now it's kind of they're looking over your shoulder all the time. And when I've tried as many cases as I have, I don't need somebody looking over my shoulder."

Other stated policies contributed to the new regime's formal, strict tone. The office prohibited part-time assistants from representing paying criminal clients in their private practices, a common occurrence among part-time defenders in Montgomery County. It became stricter in applying criteria to determine eligibility of poor defendants for representation, and began keeping records of those turned down. It encouraged assistants to talk to defendants before preliminary hearings, tried to assign repeat clients to the attorney who handled the earlier case, and sought to provide a "continuous" or "vertical" defense (that is, have the same attorney represent the defendant from the initial stages to final disposition or sentencing). High turnover in the months just before our field research began, however, made such continuous assignment extremely difficult.

The head PD's management style thus contrasted with the DA's in his desire to establish and monitor compliance with formal policies, in his willingness to reward and punish assistants, in his rigidity, and in his lack of informality.

Did the PD succeed in running a tight ship and achieving conformity to his policies? The answer is complicated somewhat because assistants differed in their reaction to office policies. Acts that rankled old-timers as unnecessary interference were a perfectly acceptable and normal way of doing things for newcomers. A further complication arose from the head's spending relatively little time directly supervising the office. He remained uninvolved in day-to-day operations, and delegated much of the task of direct administration to the first assistant.

The first assistant employed a more informal and looser management style. He announced an open-door policy to assistants, especially the less experienced ones, and encouraged them to consult with him as equals in an atmosphere of low tension. He inserted memos in case files making suggestions to the trial attorney. "But," he told us, "I don't ever follow up to see if they do or not. It's none of my business." And he apparently failed to ensure that the head's wishes regarding "over-motioning" were met. One attorney said, "Each guy does as he sees fit—what he wants to do." The result was a public defender's office somewhat less tightly and formally run than the head sought, but also more formal and controlled than those in other counties.

Second, the office lacked a strong "defendant orientation" in the attitudes of its staff and its policies. Several assistants remarked that they could just as easily work for the prosecutor; one recent departee wanted to join the DA's staff. An assistant's answer to a question about his job's frustrations illustrated this attitude:

> Well, the frustration with being a public defender goes back to the fact that just basically our client is not what society is going to consider as an upstanding citizen by and large. . . . They don't really consider what they've done as wrong.

A recently departed assistant complained sentences were not harsh enough; another said he just got fed up with clients charged repeatedly with serious crimes lying each time about what happened. Public defenders in only one other county produced a higher mean on the "belief of punishment" measure, though they scored relatively high in "regard for due process." Finally, the office acquiesced in permitting defendants to accept a disposition entered in the records as "NPCOD," which stood for

"Noll Pros (that is, dismissal by the prosecutor), Costs on Defendant." The office did not challenge the practice. And even though some defenders thought it was unfair for defendants to pay court costs when charges were dropped, they felt it was up to the defendant to accept or reject such a disposition.

Erie's Private Defense Bar

In the first half of 1980, fifty different attorneys represented the 220 defendants who appeared on the arraignment docket in Erie's trial court. . . . Thirty-eight attorneys handled only one or two defendants. . . . Five men . . . handled the cases of ninety-one defendants, more than 40 percent of those privately represented. . . .

We found a few general characteristics of the defense bar. In the years just before our research began, several of the high-volume, established private defense attorneys began to cut back. Four of the five white male attorneys we spoke with had yet to reach their thirty-fifth birthdays. The gap in age between them and the fading group of old-timers interfered with the development of a cohesive defense bar, despite their familiarity with one another. One interviewee conveyed the tenor of relations among defense attorneys when he told us: "I'm not very active in the bar. I'm not crazy about most of them." . . . In 1980, only ten women practiced among the 300 lawyers in Erie, only the three assistant public defenders and an assistant prosecutor among them dealt with criminal matters. Except for several of the less active veteran specialists, the private defense bar enjoyed little status. Several had the reputation of benefiting their clients through, one prosecutor said, their "inexplicable access before certain judges" rather than through their legal ability. According to one judge, the top civil attorneys avoided criminal law.

Of course, the private defense bar had some communication and structure. As described earlier, a group of attorneys, including several currently handling criminal cases, joined in the effort to elect the new DA. They shared a common fate and interest. Several told us, for example, of widespread grumbling at the public defender's "slam" at the private bar when he hired an attorney from Pittsburgh to fill a vacancy.

· · ·

Social and Working Relationships in Erie's Court Community

For the most part, encounters between the people who formed Erie's criminal court community on the surface displayed courtesy, cordiality, and cooperation. This pattern seemed especially prevalent in personal relations between rank and file members of the DA's and the PD's office. Referring to assistant prosecutors, a PD said:

> The average "belief in punishment" for prosecutors was higher than for public defenders. Erie's judges, in keeping with their conservative views, expressed attitudes closer to those of the prosecutors than the public defenders. Public defenders'

> "regard for due process" was positive, and the difference exceeded that seen for belief in punishment.
>
> They're nice guys, you know. They're professionally enjoyable and you can get them aside over a cup of coffee and quite frankly tell them that they're just full of crap and they'll just laugh about it.

A former assistant defender expressed a similar view.

> If you don't normally give the DA's office a rough time—by rough I mean by being unavailable or not around—you say, "Listen, I've got a real important civil matter this morning. Can I start it this afternoon?" They're going to accommodate you.

The stereotyped image of the friendly way of life in small communities, the avoidance of conflict in favor of cooperation, and the unwillingness to offend, held true much of the time.

Under the surface in most small towns, college faculties, workers in fast-food restaurants, and most other places where people gather, we find another pattern, with personality clashes, disagreements, grudges, and lack of cooperation. Erie's criminal court was no exception. Relationships between a few prosecutors and public defenders were less friendly. But more significantly, relations between the principal personalities in the community displayed considerable tension, criticism, and dislike. It would be impossible (and tedious) to describe these conflicts in full detail, but we will briefly summarize the crucial characteristics of relations among the leading members of the criminal court community to convey this feature of Erie's court community.

The judges' cohesiveness, mutual friendship, long joint service, and strong leadership from the president judge produced a common outlook toward the DA and PD. They mentioned improvement in prosecutors' performances since the new DA took office, describing them as "better prepared," "more on the ball," "aggressive," "intelligent and scholarly." Nevertheless, all opposed his call for a change in the calendar, blaming the office for its failure to use the full two weeks of existing trial terms.

The judges expressed very different opinions about the public defender's office. "I'm not satisfied with the public defender," one judge revealed. "I think it's pathetic." He regarded its attorneys as "very inexperienced" and "incompetent." Resentment lingered over the office's failure to reassign the cases of PDs unable to work during the January trial term. The president judge demonstrated his lack of confidence by taking over himself the job of deciding which private attorneys would represent homicide defendants, a task formerly delegated to the PD. The PD wanted to reacquire this power, but the president judge refused.

Members of the prosecutor's office shared the judges' assessment of the public defender's office. Said one:

> It's really a sin what's happened up there in the last year.... They don't have a single experienced trial attorney on the staff.... He's picking real bad people. In consequence of doing that he's really destroying the reputation of the office that was good for a long time.

Another reported the common belief that the PD's appointment resulted from the return of a political debt.

There may be some merit to it because he doesn't have any trial experience, doesn't have any criminal law experience, and doesn't have any administrative experience.

An experienced assistant summarized the office's view:

As a generalization, by and large we don't particularly care for the public defender's office. We don't like the way they handle their office. We don't think it's administered well and we just don't think too much of how they handle their clients.

Part of the explanation for this tension and dislike can be attributed to the relationship between the heads of the two offices. Though they professed mutual friendship, their assertions lacked credibility. In fact, one complained to us that the other had lied a lot to him. The opinions expressed by their staffs reflected the tension between them. A member of the PD's staff observed that the "political stuff" between them was both messy and petty, and that they were "at each other all the time." A counterpart in the DA's office expressed views that revealed their rivalry. "There is bad blood between [the DA] and [the PD]. The [PD] is a political creature." Relations between assistants in administrative positions in the two offices showed similar tension. Prosecutors voiced other criticisms, such as, "they wait too long, or wait till the last minute to do much of their work."

The PD's office mirrored the DA's views in its assessment. An administrator charged the DA's office with lack of respect, failure to do its homework, and poor performance in trials. The public defenders considered a supervisor in the DA's office to be a poor trial attorney and a rigid, unreasonable administrator. They felt the DA's office had "gone overboard" in getting tough, refusing to plea bargain when it should have, backing out on tentative agreements, and generally being "inflexible," "unyielding," and "unbending."

We alluded to the attitudes of the prosecutor's office toward the judges. They blamed the early end of trial terms not on themselves, but on the pressures exerted by the judges to settle cases in order to avoid trials. Seven of the prosecutors we interviewed indicated in one way or another that they regarded the bench as a whole, and the two judges close to retirement in particular, as lazy. Immediately after stating that the aloof judge was "the only worker on the court," a prosecutor interjected:

while the other ones are—classic example—today: President judge is out to lunch at 11:15, back at 2:00, gone at 3:30, a month's vacation right during the middle of a court term.

They resented the president judge's refusal to alter the calendar. The one judge labeled "the only worker" received praise for his sentences. But the others' sentences appeared "very lenient" to the DA's office, especially the standard 11.5- to 23-month county jail sentences that frequently resulted in the defendant's release in a few days.

The public defenders said little about the judges. They neglected to complain about the harshness of sentences, an indirect expression of their apparent satisfaction. They shared the prosecutor's judgment that only one judge worked hard, that another was slow in making decisions, and that a third lacked much knowledge of criminal law. But administrators knew the judges did not think well of the office, telling us they got the idea the judges were displeased. This recognition, however, brought forth no efforts to modify the practices that aroused criticism.

Age and Generations in Erie's Court Community

Differences in the ages of judges, prosecutors, and public defenders in Erie and the prominence of "cohorts" were striking. . . . Data on the average age of judges (60.4 years) compared to those of prosecutors and public defenders (33.1 years and 32.9 years, respectively) confirms the size of Erie's generation gap. Only Kalamazoo's judges had a higher average age. Only Saginaw's judges had a higher average of years of service on the bench (12.8 versus Erie's 12.0). The ages of prosecutors and public defenders differed little from those in other counties. . . . Erie's prosecutors were a little older than the average for all nine counties, and its public defenders about a year younger.

Comparing the differences in age of the judge, prosecutor, and either the PD or private counsel who handled each defendant's case provides a clearer picture of Erie's generation gap. Judges averaged more than 30 years older than prosecutors and 28.6 years older than defense attorneys, a larger gap than in seven of the eight other counties. In fact, the gap in three counties was only about half as great, about 15 years.

Structure of Influence

In Erie, the judges set the tone and rhythm of the criminal court. The president judge believed in exercising strong leadership, and he enjoyed the support and friendship of a cohesive group of three of the four other judges. The general policies of Erie's newspapers, and their relationship with the president judge in particular, insulated the judges from criticism. The county's long tradition of strong president judges reinforced his status. One important attorney in the community minced no words in describing his control: "This is a county, historically, that has had under-the-thumb kind of rule from the president judge, from the incumbent as well as his predecessors." One subtle indication of his stature appeared in a prosecutor's response to a question about how the county officials on the first floor reacted when the judges came down from the second to request their budget:

> Well, the judges don't come down for their budget. I think that's a classic illustration of how it works. The second floor doesn't go down to see the first floor. The first floor comes up.

It was clear that his power had entered its final stages as retirement loomed. But his ability to prevail on issues like the structure of the calendar remained. Though the prosecutor began making speeches calling for change, he acknowledged that if the president judge were to call him in and ask him to stop, he would have to comply.

The public defender exerted little influence within the court community. He lost the duty of assigning attorneys to homicide cases, had an inexperienced staff, and was regarded by judges, prosecutors, and the private bar as inexperienced in criminal work and highly political. Only his strong ties to the county executive provided him with significant support. The new district attorney enjoyed a good reputation among the private bar and the judges. Though he established an ambitious agenda for change, only the initiatives that could be implemented within his own office succeeded in the early months of his tenure. The impending retirement of two judges, his vigor, and his access to the broadcast media augured well for a rise in the DA's influence. At the time of our research, however, the president judge still dominated Erie's criminal court community. As one important community member said, "It's a one-horse county. It always has been."

Summary

... The small size and extensive familiarity of the [Erie criminal] court community, which reflected characteristics of the county generally, contributed to the development of an effective grapevine, and to a tradition of informality and accommodation in interpersonal relations. The proximity of major participants in the courthouse facilitated informal interaction and exchange of information.

The principal characteristics of each of the three major sponsoring organizations—the judges, prosecutors, and public defenders—are described in some detail. For each, we look at the age and experience of its members, the content of policies and internal management styles, the degree of cohesion, the structure of attitudes, and the nature of relations with the newspapers, lower-court judges, and others. Comparing attitudes, we found both judges and prosecutors adhering more strongly to a belief in punishment than public defenders did; the judges were surprisingly negative in their regard for due process.

We found tension in relations between the public defender's office on the one hand, and judges and prosecutors on the other. The prosecutors criticized the judges for their lack of hard work, their leniency, and their unwillingness to change the calendar. Continuing a long tradition in Erie county, the judges, and the president judge in particular, exerted most influence over the operations of the court community.

Notes

1. *Editor's note:* The nine counties studied by the authors were Erie, Dauphin, and Montgomery counties, Pennsylvania; Kalamazoo, Oakland, and Saginaw counties, Michigan; and DuPage, Peoria, and St. Clair counties, Illinois.
2. *Editor's note:* The "grapevine" is the informal social and communication network found in organizations. It serves the function of providing court community members with information useful in the performance of their jobs. A public defender in Erie told the authors:
   I don't know how it is in other counties, but in this county the courthouse is just the fastest grapevine I've ever seen. If I fire a secretary at 9 o'clock, the whole courthouse knows about it by 9:30.
3. Prosecutors could propose to the court that offenders without a serious prior criminal record arrested for a minor offense could be placed on ARD. Prosecution was deferred, and if the defendant fulfilled the conditions set forth, such as attending classes and avoiding subsequent arrest, the case was dropped and the defendant had no conviction added to his or her record.

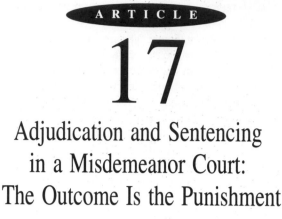

ARTICLE

17

Adjudication and Sentencing in a Misdemeanor Court: The Outcome Is the Punishment

John Paul Ryan

In a study of the New Haven lower court, Malcolm Feeley concluded that the "process is the punishment" because, although sentences were light, the additional costs borne by the people who were arrested and prosecuted were significant. John Paul Ryan's study of the Columbus (Ohio) Municipal Court showed that criminal sanctions imposed upon convicted defendants were much more severe. Ryan attributes these differences to the contrasting local political cultures, whose influence upon the courts is mediated by police department orientations, relationships between the police and prosecutors, and methods of judicial assignment.

A . . . published work on misdemeanor courts concludes that the major punishment of defendants occurs during the processing of their cases (Feeley 1979). Feeley contends that the pretrial costs associated with arrests on misdemeanor charges typically outweigh any punishments imposed after conviction. The need to make bail, hire an attorney, be present at court appearances, and even help prepare one's defense drain the economic and psychological resources of many defendants, whether they are ultimately adjudicated guilty or innocent. By contrast, the punishments meted out to defendants upon conviction appear insubstantial. Few are incarcerated, and fines rarely exceed $50.

These findings and arguments have a distinct appeal. They provide a new and creative interpretation to case processing in the lower criminal courts, one at variance with our understanding of felony courts. Yet as Feeley himself acknowledges, his work is a case study. His data are drawn exclusively from the New Haven (Connecticut) Court of Common Pleas. What about other misdemeanor courts? Is it reasonable to believe that most lower courts are like New Haven's? Studies of criminal justice and political culture might suggest otherwise. Levin's (1977) study of the felony courts of Pittsburgh and Minneapolis indicates substantial differences in sentencing severity, attributable in part to the political culture or values of the two com-

Source: Law and Society Review 15 (1980–1981): 79–108. Reprinted by permission of the Law and Society Association.

munities. Levin found that sentences were typically less severe in the highly partisan, ethnically diverse, working-class city (Pittsburgh) than in the reform-minded, socially homogeneous city (Minneapolis). Eisenstein and Jacob (1977) found sentencing practices in Baltimore to be much more harsh than in either Detroit or Chicago, and they attributed the greater harshness to a heritage of conservatism and racism in that southern border city. Likewise, the working environments of courts differ. Church and colleagues (1978) found that the pace at which cases are processed differs markedly from one large city to another, in part because of intangible factors which they termed "local legal culture." And Ryan and colleagues (1980) found that various administrative procedures, relationships among courtroom work-group members, and judicial perceptions are sensitive to the partisan climate of the local political environment. In short, the character of a community—its history, politics, and lifestyle—affects what takes place in its courts, both in terms of process and outcomes.

If the relationships between political culture and trial courts are viewed at all seriously (see Kritzer 1979), one must question not only the generalizability of Feeley's data but also his primary argument. More data from different communities would help to show whether the process actually constitutes a substantial punishment in the lower courts. These data should speak to the processing of cases and defendants, because it can be expected that some courts minimize pretrial costs by expediting cases, liberalizing indigency requirements for counsel, and utilizing cash bonds infrequently. Perhaps even more important, additional data should be collected on case outcomes, for likewise it can be expected that lower courts vary in the severity of sanctions imposed upon convicted defendants.

Data relating to process and outcomes in the Franklin County, Ohio, Municipal Court (Columbus) are reported below. This inquiry, like Feeley's, is a case study, but one that serves as a counterpoint. The findings suggest that New Haven may be among the least punitive lower courts in the nation. The Columbus court is sufficiently more severe in its sanctions—and less demanding in its process costs—that the outcome is the primary punishment. Throughout the article, comparative reference is made with an eye toward dramatizing the very real differences between the two courts. In the conclusion, some explanation as to why the courts differ is provided. As background for that analysis, an overview of the two cities and their courts follows.

Columbus and New Haven:
Contrasting Local Political Cultures

Columbus is a medium-sized American city, more populous and more sprawling than New Haven. Over half a million people live in the city of Columbus, a figure sharply on the rise in the 1960s and early 1970s, compared with a steadily declining population in New Haven of only 125,000. The citizenry of Columbus is better educated, more affluent, and of different ethnic origins than that of New Haven. Feeley (1979: 37–38) aptly characterizes New Haven as a town "beset with the standard ills of many old urban areas—shrinking population, declining tax base, deteriorating housing, smog, poor schools, encroaching superhighways, and an increasing underemployed minority population." In a comparative vein, Feeley goes on to say:

> It [New Haven] represents neither the worst nor the best of American urban centers. It does not convey the sense of hopelessness and decay that observers report in such urban centers as Newark or Gary, nor . . . the same sense of optimism as do new and more culturally homogeneous and prosperous cities as Des Moines or Minneapolis . . . [or, one might add, Columbus].

These differences in the physical and cultural characteristics of the two cities predictably presage differences of political culture. New Haven is predominantly Democratic in partisanship; Columbus is heavily Republican—an "urban Republican stronghold" (Barone et al. 1980: 694). Differences in partisan orientation are evident in presidential votes, mayoralty elections, and congressional representation. Columbus has not had a Democratic mayor in the last decade; New Haven has not had a Republican mayor in two decades. Two conservative Republicans represent portions of Columbus and its surrounding suburbs in Washington; one liberal Democrat represents New Haven. The political affiliation of judges, too, parallels community orientations, though judges are formally appointed on a statewide basis in Connecticut and elected locally in Ohio. Feeley (1979: 63) reported four Democratic and three Republican judges in the New Haven lower court. At the time of the study in Columbus, twelve Republican judges sat with a lone Democratic judge in that municipal court. Equally important, the significance of partisanship in the delivery of public services is much greater in New Haven than in the "good government" atmosphere of Columbus.

The political structure of the two communities also differs. Though both claim mayor–council forms of government, the similarity ends there. New Haven has been described as having a pluralistic leadership structure (Dahl 1961; Feeley 1979: 37). More impressionistically, Columbus has been described as relatively monolithic, dominated economically by big banks and insurance companies and ideologically by the Wolfe family and their newspaper (Barone et al. 1980: 694–695), and lacking New Haven's "vigorous group of residents involved in actively trying to cope with problems" (Feeley 1979: 38).

The courts also look quite different in their personnel, operations, and informal relationships. These differences are often traceable to the local political culture. Feeley (1979: 53–61) reports a substantial patronage system surrounding the New Haven courthouse, even after reforms intended to alleviate political influence in the courts were enacted. For example, judgeships are viewed as rewards for faithful party service. Prosecutors and public defenders are likely to be drawn from families active in the local political organizations. Lower-level personnel (deputies, clerks, and so on) are likely to come from the ranks of "ward leaders and vote mobilizers." Columbus, by contrast, reflects little political influence of this kind in its courts. Judgeships come either from association with the governor or a popular local campaign, possibly aided by bar endorsement. Prosecutors and public defenders need not have political sponsors. Lower-level court personnel are recruited through an elaborate system of checks and balances designed to remove partisan politics and judicial whim.

The orientation of the police department and its relations with the prosecutor's office are also quite distinctive in the two communities. Feeley (1979: 45–47) describes the New Haven police department as oriented to dispute resolution or, in Wilson's (1968) terminology, "order maintenance." Accordingly, it is not surprising that the police appear to play a small role in the development of prosecution cases, having little communication with the prosecutor and rarely appearing as witnesses in court. Prosecutors seem dominant vis-à-vis the police in the New Haven court, albeit both share dispute-processing views of the role of the lower court. In Columbus, the police department is much better characterized as "law-enforcement"-oriented, accounting for the importance which police officers attach to successful prosecution of minor cases. Officers regularly appear as witnesses in brief trials and are ready to appear on other occasions when a plea is entered. Indeed, when police officers "hang around" the Columbus court waiting for their cases to be called, they often sit in other courtrooms watching outcomes (with occasional astonishment at the perceived leniency of some judges). In short, by custom the police in Columbus have been an important, perhaps dominant, force in the lower court, much to the chagrin of the local defense bar.

Finally, there are differences of court structure, rooted in political history, that affect relationships among courtroom actors, notably between judges and others. Connecticut, unlike Ohio, does statewide assignment of judges (Feeley 1979; Ryan et al. 1980), which in practice means that lower-court judges are frequently rotated. Feeley (1979: 67) argues that one important consequence of rotation is the gravitation of judicial responsibility toward prosecutors and others permanently assigned to one court. Judges in New Haven have been heard to ask prosecutors about the "going rate" for particular offenses, suggesting a desire to adhere to work-group norms. In Columbus, the judges—who are elected or appointed to that municipal court—are much more individualistic and autonomous in their approach to sentencing.

New Haven, in sum, is a criminal court system that reflects the "particularistic values of ethnic, religious, political, and family associations" in its rendering of "swift, substantive justice" (Feeley 1979: 61). Columbus, by contrast, is a system that reflects the universalistic values of professional competence and technical efficiency in its rendering of swift but formal justice through the mechanisms of an adversary system as applied to a misdemeanor court.

Methods of Data Collection

Data were collected on 2,764 cases in the Franklin County (Columbus) Municipal Court. These represent the universe of cases scheduled for a "pretrial" during March, April, and May of 1978. Sampling from pretrials was necessitated by the court's assignment and scheduling systems: only cases which are *not* disposed of at arraignment can be scheduled for a pretrial hearing.[1] Nevertheless, cases scheduled for a pretrial are not an unrepresentative sample of all cases. Pretrials are routinely scheduled for nearly *all* cases which proceed beyond arraignment,[2] including a wide variety of criminal and traffic cases.

All available information was collected for each of these cases, including type and seriousness of offense, number of charges, type of defense counsel, judge at pretrial and disposition,[3] mode of disposition, and sentence or sanctions imposed. Because of the court's effective computerized system, there were virtually no missing

T A B L E   1 / **Distribution of the Court's Misdemeanor Caseload**

	Percent	*Number*
Traffic		
OMVI	30.2	834
Other traffic	17.8	492
Criminal		
Assault	17.1	472
Theft	10.8	300
Bad checks	7.1	196
Other criminal	17.0	470
	100.0	2,764

NOTE: Limited to cases scheduled for a pretrial

data on these items. Additionally, prior record information was collected from prosecutor files for OMVI (drunk-driving) cases.

Formal, semistructured interviews were conducted with the supervisor of the municipal unit of the prosecutor's office (hereafter, Prosecutor), two assistant prosecutors, and an administrative assistant. Also interviewed were the supervisor of the municipal unit of the public defender's office (hereafter, Defender), supervisors in the Probation Department and the Pre-Trial Release Program, and six of the thirteen municipal court judges. These interviews focused variably upon modes of case disposition, judicial styles in plea bargaining and sentencing, the treatment of OMVI cases, the operations of arraignment court, and the role of the pretrial stage. In addition, ten of the thirteen municipal court judges were observed, typically for several hours at a time, usually in pretrial sessions[4] but also at arraignments, in trials, and in the entry of guilty pleas. The observations focused upon judicial behaviors such as sentencing philosophy, involvement in plea negotiations, and relationships with prosecuting and defense attorneys.

The Columbus Court's Caseload: An Overview

The Franklin County (Columbus) Municipal Court has jurisdiction over a variety of matters, including small claims, civil cases up to $10,000, and preliminary hearings in felony cases. As Table 1 indicates, the court's misdemeanor caseload is composed of almost equal proportions of traffic and criminal cases. Operating a motor vehicle under the influence of alcohol (OMVI) is the most frequent type of case, and it accounts for nearly two-thirds of all traffic cases. Other traffic cases include reckless operation of a motor vehicle (ROMV), driving without a valid license or with a suspended license, hit-and-run, speeding, and lesser violations. The dominance of OMVI cases is not unique to Columbus. Although arrests for drunk driving are more frequent in Columbus than elsewhere in Ohio (Ohio Courts 1978), other municipal courts also report a large percentage of drunk-driving cases (see Neubauer 1974).

Assault is the most frequent type of criminal case, followed by theft and passing bad checks. Other criminal cases include trespass, carrying a concealed weapon,

obstructing justice, disorderly conduct, soliciting, drug use, public indecency, housing code violations, fleeing from a police officer, and resisting arrest. The Columbus
court's criminal caseload is presumably lightened by the operation of a night prosecutor program which screens all citizen-initiated complaints and diverts interpersonal disputes and bad-check cases, in substantial numbers, from the court (see
Palmer 1975).

The majority (58 percent) of cases involve a single charge against a defendant,
but a substantial proportion (42 percent) involve more than one charge (typically two
or three). Multiple-charge cases most often occur with the OMVI offense, where
another more visible violation brings the intoxication of the driver to the attention
of the police officer. Only 23 percent of OMVI cases involve a single charge; other
violations, especially driving on the wrong side of the road, out of control, across
lanes, or speeding, are likely to accompany a charge of drunk driving. Similarly,
certain other traffic offenses, such as driving without a valid license, are likely to
involve multiple charges, as a result of more visible traffic violations. By contrast,
most criminal cases involve only a single charge against a defendant.

Modes of Case Disposition

The court utilizes a number of ways to dispose of cases that proceed beyond arraignment. These include guilty plea to the original charge, guilty plea to a reduced
charge, court trial, jury trial, bond forfeiture, dismissal, and—in multiple-charge
cases—combinations of these. In addition, some defendants fail to appear, and these
"no-shows" are treated, for statistical purposes, as case terminations.

Almost half of the sample of cases in Columbus were disposed through a guilty
plea, similar to the percentage in New Haven (Feeley 1979: 127). The majority of
these represent pleas to *reduced* charges, indicating a form of charge bargaining. Case
type is the most important factor in determining whether a reduction of charges will
occur (see Table 2). In OMVI cases in particular, a charge reduction is common.
This reflects some uneasiness in imposing the required incarceration where a defendant is convicted of drunk driving.[5]

Three other factors, not readily available in case files, were cited by the prosecutor as influencing his decision to reduce charges: prior record of the defendant,
strength of the evidence, and actions of the defendant vis-à-vis the arresting officer.
Where the arresting police officer takes offense at the actions or attitude of the suspect, a charge reduction will not usually occur. This reflects the police dominance
of the lower court described earlier. Only recently have public defenders fostered the
idea that the prosecutor, not the police, should run the courtroom. The public defender's office still feels that prosecutors defer "too much" to police officers. Strength
of evidence, on the other hand, may be the kind of nebulous factor which operates
more in the minds of prosecutors than in their actual behavior. Individual prosecutors,
in this and other misdemeanor courts, rarely have the time or inclination to gauge
evidentiary matters precisely.

Prosecutors and defense counsel are the primary actors in the forging of guilty
pleas, particularly in charge bargaining. But what about the role of the trial judge?
Trial judges in misdemeanor courts do not always restrict their role to ratifying bargains struck by other parties (Ryan and Alfini 1979). Observations in Columbus sug-

T A B L E   2 / **Distribution of Case Disposition Modes, by Case Type**

	All cases	OMVI	Other traffic	Assault	Theft	Bad checks	Other criminal
Conviction at trial	1.9%	2.2%	2.3%	1.9%	1.3%	1.0%	1.5%
Guilty plea—original charge	17.3	19.5	35.0	5.1	7.3	9.2	17.1
Guilty plea—reduced charge	28.0	64.1	18.1	4.7	27.0	1.0	11.2
Bond forfeiture	6.3	.7	6.4	3.2	13.7	18.9	9.0
Dismissal	34.0	4.7	26.1	75.9	36.7	43.4	45.0
Acquittal at trial	1.0	.4	.8	3.0	.3	0	1.1
No show	11.5	8.4	11.3	6.2	13.7	26.5	15.1
	100.0%	100.0%	100.0%	100.0%	100.0%	100.0%	100.0%
N =	(2,715)	(807)	(486)	(469)	(300)	(196)	(457)

NOTE: Disposition for multiple-charge cases has been coded as follows. Dismissals have been disregarded in the presence of guilty pleas or bond forfeitures. Where there were guilty pleas to original and reduced charges, the disposition was treated as a guilty plea to a reduced charge. These coding decisions flow from discussions of multiple-charge cases in the text.

gest that at least a few judges do actively engage in sentence bargaining from the bench. For example, Judge H,[6] who has the reputation for making sentence commitments in advance as his normal practice, remarked to defense counsel in one case that was observed: "If the defendant wants to plead, I'll put on a fine and wrap it up today" (assault case). Judge D also encouraged guilty pleas, through a mixture of occasional sentence leniency and frequent gratuitous comments to defendants about the "break" they were getting. Furthermore, Judge D sometimes intimated that he would find a defendant guilty were the case to go to trial ("you gotta keep your eyes open" to a defendant charged with jaywalking, or "a driver has a responsibility, even under icy road conditions" to a defendant ticketed in an auto accident).

Determining exactly how much negotiating actually precedes the guilty pleas entered in this court is not simple. Charge bargaining may involve little more than the application of standard discounts, unless there are unusual circumstances. Sentence bargaining occurs in some guilty pleas, but its frequency varies from judge to judge. Nevertheless, the amount of bargaining accompanying guilty pleas in Columbus is almost certainly higher than, say, in Neubauer's Prairie City or even Feeley's New Haven. Unlike Prairie City in 1970 or New Haven more recently, many more cases in Columbus involve defendants represented by counsel. Defense attorney presence seems to lead inexorably toward increased bargaining in the guilty pleas entered in misdemeanor cases (see Alfini and Doan 1977: 431; Neubauer 1974: 209).

Trials are very infrequent in Columbus, but they are by no means the extinct species which Feeley reports in New Haven (1979: 127). In the sample of 2,764 cases, 32 (1.1 percent) were resolved by jury trial and 46 (1.6 percent) by court trial.[7] One gained the distinct impression from interviews and observations that trials are welcomed by many judges and attorneys, as an occasional relief from the monotony of calendar calls. Judge G remarked, "I enjoy trials when I get two good lawyers." The defender noted of Judge G, "He gives you a good trial." Not surprisingly, then, trials proceeded in a thorough and unharried manner.

Comparatively serious cases are more likely to go to a *jury* trial. For example, OMVI cases account for 30 percent of the sample of cases but 41 percent of all jury trials, and assault cases represent 17 percent of the sample of cases but 34 percent of all jury trials. By contrast, less serious cases more frequently go to a *court* trial. For court trials, OMVI cases are significantly underrepresented, whereas other traffic cases comprise a substantial share.

Conviction at trial is likely, but far from certain. Defendants fared better at jury trials, where the conviction rate was 56.3 percent (18 of 32 cases). In court trials, the conviction rate was 71.7 percent (33 of 46 cases). Likelihood of conviction varies by case type. Combining jury and court trials, the conviction rate was 5.5:1 in OMVI cases, 4:1 in theft cases, 3:1 in other traffic cases, 3:2 in other criminal cases, and a mere 2:3 in assault cases. The individual judge also makes some difference. Consider that two of the court's most active plea-bargaining judges, D and H, did not acquit a single defendant in the seven court trials which they heard. Their "inducements" to defendants to plead guilty, then, were reinforced by a reluctance to find for a defendant in a court trial.

Bond forfeitures are not convictions in a legal sense. In the words of one prosecutor, they represent a "hybrid between conviction and dismissal . . . a sentencing alternative occasionally used to dispose of cases expeditiously."[8] In Columbus, cases are sometimes disposed by bond forfeiture upon agreement of both sides. There may be evidentiary problems for the prosecutor, or uncertainty by the defense as to the outcome of a trial or plea negotiations. The court receives some money, and the defendant escapes the stigma of conviction. Bond forfeitures occur most often in minor cases.

Dismissals are a frequent occurrence in Columbus. One-third of the cases in the sample were dismissed (*nolle prosequi*). According to both the prosecutor and the defender, the most frequent cause of dismissal is the failure of the complaining witness to prosecute. These perceptions are supported by data collected and analyzed in the prosecutor's office. An examination of dismissals in January 1979 revealed the lack of a prosecuting witness to be the most frequently noted reason. Most often it was a civilian witness, but occasionally it was the failure of a police witness to appear.[9]

Other reasons cited for dismissals were "at the request of the prosecutor," correction of code violations, and restitution. Some prosecutor requests for dismissal probably do result from lack of preparation (as one person in the prosecutor's office charged),[10] but primarily it is a screening decision. Because police-filed complaints are not screened before the pretrial session, this court appearance offers the first opportunity to weed out weak cases. Given the power of the police in municipal court, it may be easier for prosecutors to request dismissals in the "full view," and occasional scrutiny, of the judge rather than in the "secrecy" of an aggressive screening unit in the prosecutor's office.

The role of the judge in the decision to dismiss appears to be little more than ratification of attorney requests. According to the prosecutor, judges play a significant role only "very occasionally." The defender cited the instance of prosecutorial objection to a defense motion for dismissal as the only occasion for judicial scrutiny. In interviews, judges themselves typically indicated a minimal role in the decision to dismiss. In the words of Judge G, "prosecutors should know." Thus, just as prosecutors defer to police in the charging decision, judges defer to the prosecutor in the screening decision at the pretrial.[11]

Cases with more than one charge may be disposed in more than one way. For example, one charge may be dismissed if there is a guilty plea to a second charge. This is, in fact, the most common pattern of multiple disposition in Columbus. It is also common in New Haven, where Feeley refers to this apparent give-and-take as "splitting the difference" (1979: 134). There may, however, be less bargaining in these dispositions than Feeley implies. It is hard to believe that many defendants feel a sense of victory when they are convicted on one charge rather than two. This must especially be the feeling among defendants who face conviction in drunk driving cases, the very defendants most likely to receive a "splitting-the-difference" disposition.

Defendants in Columbus who fail to appear for a pretrial session in the courtroom are not as lucky as some of the "no-shows" in New Haven. It is one thing not to appear at arraignment in a petty case; these cases in Columbus typically result in a bond forfeiture and termination. Failure to appear at a pretrial invariably results in the issuing of a bench warrant by the judge, often with a substantial bond.[12] No precise data are available on the percentage of these defendants who return to court for disposition, but court participants think the figure is quite high. For the sample period, 12 percent of all defendants scheduled to appear at a pretrial session failed to appear.

Table 2 illustrates that the variation in disposition across types of cases is enormous. At one extreme, most assault cases (76 percent) are dismissed. This is partly because the civilian complainant often has a change of mind regarding prosecution, but partly reflects the poor conviction ratio (only 2:3) of assault cases actually tried. At the other extreme, OMVI cases are rarely dismissed (only 5 percent). The charge is a serious one and is typically accompanied by other traffic violations. Furthermore, acquittal at trial in OMVI cases is rare (1 in 5.5). Between these two extremes, variations are modest.

A Multivariate Analysis of Case Disposition

We have a limited range of variables with which to explain case disposition. Some of these variables are characteristics of the case (or what Feeley calls "legal factors"); others bear upon individual courtroom actors; one reflects the court's processing of a case. No information about the characteristics of defendants—for example, race or age—was available.

A stepwise regression model was used to analyze data, in order to facilitate the disentanglement of joint effects among these variables. Type of case was operationalized as a series of dummy variables; also included were seriousness of charge (Ohio has five classifications of misdemeanor offenses ranging from six months incarceration to a $100 fine), the number of charges, the number of court appearances, the type of defense counsel, and the identity of the disposition judge. For the distribution of these variables, refer to Table A-1 [at the end of this article].

Case disposition, a categorical variable, has been collapsed into two categories: adjudicated guilty or not guilty. Included in the "guilty" category are pleas to original or reduced charges, convictions at trial, and bond forfeitures. Included in the "not-guilty" category are dismissals and acquittals at trial. (No-shows have been excluded from the analysis.) Treating bond forfeitures as guilty dispositions stretches the legal meaning of the disposition, but not their functional meaning. In Columbus, bond forfeitures are little more than a variant of the guilty plea.[13] Based upon this dichotomy, 61 percent of defendants were found guilty, and the remaining 39 percent were found not guilty.[14]

Table 3 illustrates that most of the explanatory variables entered in the regression equation are predictive of case disposition. The two most important variables are assault and OMVI cases. Assault cases are very likely to be dismissed, whereas OMVI cases are very likely *not* to be dismissed. Other case and structural characteristics are of some predictive value. By contrast, the identity of courtroom actors bears little upon disposition. The judge appears to make no difference once other factors are controlled. Presence of counsel also makes no difference. Type of counsel shows a very small effect: public defender cases are slightly more likely to result in not-guilty dispositions, when other factors are controlled, than are private counsel cases.

The six variables listed in Table 3 account for fully 36 percent of the variation in case dispositions ($R = .60$). This is a large amount when one considers the nature of the variables available in the court files and, correspondingly, other variables which are surely important but not available. The identity of the prosecutor, for example, may be important, especially in a court like Columbus where "prosecutor shopping" has been facilitated by the office's horizontal assignment system.

These findings parallel Feeley (1979) in some respects and contrast in other ways. The most important discrepancy occurs in the impact of counsel, where Feeley found that unrepresented defendants fare significantly less well (see also Katz 1968). One explanation may be the different proportions of unrepresented defendants in

T A B L E 3 / **A Multivariate Model of Case Disposition: Stepwise Regression**[a]

	Beta weights[b]
Assault case	.31
OMVI case	−.24
Number of charges	−.16
Number of court appearances[c]	−.13
Seriousness of case[d]	−.09
Public defender counsel	.05

$$R_2 = .60$$
$$R = 36\%$$
$$(N = 2,279)$$

[a]Case disposition is coded: not guilty (high), guilty (low).
[b]Each of the beta weights is statistically significant at .05; in no instance does the standard error approach beta.
[c]Number of court appearances is dichotomized, based upon the nonlinear relationship present in bivariate analysis: one appearance versus two or more appearances.
[d]Seriousness of case is dichotomized, based upon a curvilinear relationship present in bivariate analysis: most and least serious coded high; in-between coded low.

New Haven and Columbus. The large number of defendants without counsel in New Haven suggests a reluctance to implement fully the spirit of *Argersinger* v. *Hamlin* (1972). Columbus is not such a court. Most defendants have counsel (or access to counsel at arraignment), but those without fare equally well in case disposition. Limited courtroom observations support these interpretations. Indeed, in arraignment court, one judge consistently encouraged unrepresented defendants to consult with the public defender available in the courtroom before entering any plea.

Forms of Sentence or Sanction

Misdemeanor courts inflict upon their convicted defendants a wider variety of less severe sanctions than do felony courts. The Columbus misdemeanor court is no exception. Fines, bond forfeitures, terms in the county jail or municipal workhouse, suspensions of a driver's license, attendance at programs for alcoholics and drunk drivers, and probation are among the primary sanctions available and employed by the court. Sometimes convicted defendants receive only one form of sentence, but quite often they face several sanctions.

Fines are routinely imposed upon convicted defendants in Columbus. Some judges frequently hand out stiff fines, then suspend a portion of the fine. The practice may be designed to enhance a judge's popularity, as a skeptical Judge G remarked, declaring that "a heavy fine makes the police happy . . . suspending part of it makes the defense happy." Alternatively, the suspension may help to "keep in line" a defendant placed on probation, as Judge E noted. Both of these judges occasionally

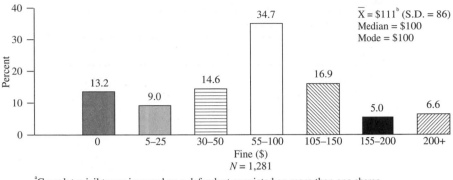

$\bar{X} = \$111^{b}$ (S.D. = 86)
Median = $100
Mode = $100

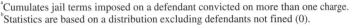

Fine ($)
N = 1,281

[a]Cumulates jail terms imposed on a defendant convicted on more than one charge.
[b]Statistics are based on a distribution excluding defendants not fined (0).

Figure 1 Distribution of net fines[a]

suspend portions of fines. The motives of judges who frequently suspend large portions of stiff fines, like Judges C and M, are not always clear.[15]

Figure 1 displays the net fines imposed, once suspensions are taken into account. Only 13 percent of defendants in Columbus escape a fine entirely. Of the remainder, fines range from a mere $5 to $1,750. The mean fine is $111, and the median and mode are both $100. Not unexpectedly, OMVI cases draw the heaviest fines $(\bar{X})$ = 128.

These fines represent a significant amount of money to most defendants, even in our presently inflated economy. This is particularly true for indigent defendants represented by the public defender's office. The severity of fines in Columbus is all the more striking when compared with New Haven (see Table 4). The two courts differ substantially in the amount of the fines they impose. In Columbus, nearly three-fourths of the net fines exceeded $50, whereas only a handful of fines (4 percent) in New Haven were greater than $50. Furthermore, in Columbus 87 percent of all convicted defendants paid some fine, compared with only 45 percent in New Haven (Feeley 1979: 138).

Several caveats should be applied to this comparison. The New Haven data were collected for three months in 1974, compared with three months in 1978 in Columbus. Nevertheless, according to Judge G, a veteran on the court, "fines are less today than ten years ago," a diminution which he attributed to the "more lenient judges now on the bench." Also, the range of cases heard in the New Haven court is different from Columbus. No traffic cases are heard in New Haven, and these cases in Columbus (notably OMVI) draw consistently the heavier fines. Still, the New Haven court had felony cases (about 20 percent of the docket), indicating that in some respects the Columbus court hears more petty cases. Thus, neither the different range of cases nor the different time periods studied appear to account for the variation in fines between the two courts.

Bond forfeitures are tantamount to fines, particularly in view of *when* the bond amount is set. The decision is made at the time of case disposition, and the defendant agrees to pay the fine. The modal amount of bond forfeitures is $50, and the mean is only slightly higher $(\bar{X}$ = 57). Again, in comparison with New Haven (where

TABLE   4 / **Comparison of Fines in the
Columbus and New Haven Lower Courts**

	Columbus	New Haven
$50 or less	27.2%	96.0%
More than $50	72.8	4.0%
N	(1,112)[a]	(377)[a]

[a]For comparative purposes, only convicted defendants receiving some fine have been included.

Feeley reports most bond forfeitures to be between $5 and $25), the sanction is greater in Columbus.[16]

Jail terms are announced to a majority (52 percent) of convicted defendants. However, one-third of these terms are entirely suspended, and many others are suspended in part. The use of suspended sentences for *jail terms* is much more widespread among the court's judges; nine judges suspend, in part or whole, more than half of their jail terms. Figure 2 reveals that 35 percent of convicted defendants serve some jail time, most often in the city workhouse. About half of these defendants serve three or four days; most of the others serve either thirty days or a longer sentence. Defendants convicted in OMVI cases are most likely to be incarcerated (44 percent), but typically serve a short sentence (three or four days).

Comparisons with New Haven again are striking. Only 4.9 percent of convicted defendants in New Haven served a jail term (Feeley 1979: 138), whereas almost *six times* as many defendants received a jail term in Columbus. Some mitigating factors should be considered in this comparison. Many defendants who do serve time in Columbus do not have their lives totally disrupted (for example, by loss of job). It is common for shorter sentences, and even some longer sentences, to be served on weekends, a phenomenon growing in popularity elsewhere (see Parisi 1980). Also, drunk driving cases contribute a moderately disproportionate number of jail terms in the Columbus court. Nevertheless, it appears that across a similar range of criminal cases (for example, assault, theft) a defendant in Columbus stands a much higher likelihood of incarceration, if convicted.

In traffic cases the court acts as an administrative entity in monitoring the driver's licenses of individual citizens. In sprawling and decentralized Columbus, the license is a valuable—often necessary—commodity. For a variety of offenses, the court is authorized, or even required, to suspend licenses. The Columbus lower court uses its authority selectively, but not infrequently. Fully one-third (36 percent) of defendants convicted in OMVI or other traffic cases have their license suspended for a period of time. The standard suspension is thirty days, but in a few instances the term may be for sixty or ninety days, or even one year. Defendants convicted in OMVI cases are much more likely to have their license suspended than those convicted of other traffic offenses.

The Columbus court also frequently requires attendance at drunk driver schools and alcohol-control programs upon conviction in traffic cases. At the least, this constrains defendants in time and transportation, no matter how "therapeutic" the program may be. Fully one-third of defendants convicted in OMVI cases are required to attend one or another local program as part of their sentence.

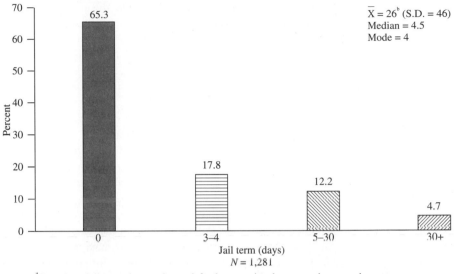

$\overline{X} = 26^{b}$ (S.D. = 46)
Median = 4.5
Mode = 4

[a]Cumulates jail terms imposed on a defendant convicted on more than one charge.
[b]Statistics are based on a distribution excluding defendants not incarcerated (0).

Figure 2   Distribution of net jail terms[a]

Probation is extensively used as a sanction in this court. A supervising officer in the probation department reported that more than 2,000 defendants convicted on misdemeanor charges are currently on probation, and he noted that probation is more frequently used now than ever before. The bulk of the department's caseload stems from theft, bad-check, and alcohol-related cases—areas where recidivism is high. Judges themselves vary in how often they use probation, some imposing it frequently, others selectively ("taking into account our caseload problems"), and one judge not at all. We have no further data on the use of probation, because the case files do not contain such information.

Finally, more than one type of sanction is often imposed. In criminal cases, about one defendant in five is incarcerated and fined. In traffic cases, fully half of all defendants face multiple sanctions involving some combination of fines, incarceration, suspension of the driver's license, and attendance at drunk driver programs. Furthermore, the use of multiple sanctions is seemingly not considered in determining the severity of each sanction. For example, leniency in fines is generally *not* granted to defendants who are sentenced to serve time in jail. Indeed, defendants who are sentenced to serve jail time are fined *more* heavily ($121 on average) than those not incarcerated ($83 on average), differences mostly attributable to traffic cases. Similarly, defendants do not typically attend a drunk driver's program in lieu of a (heavier) fine; it is usually in addition to the fine. The heaviest fines in OMVI and other traffic cases are levied against defendants who are incarcerated, lose their license for a period of time, and must attend an alcohol-control program.

In sum, the Columbus misdemeanor court views the variety of sanctions available in a relatively punitive, rather than ameliorative, light. Instead of choosing which one sanction to employ against convicted defendants, this court often chooses *how much* of several sanctions. In this regard, the court is quite different from New Haven, where fines are used much less frequently and where combinations of probation and suspended sentence often serve as punishment. No wonder, perhaps, that Feeley viewed the process to be the primary punishment. In Columbus, the outcome is the punishment.

A Multivariate Analysis of Sanctions

No single measure of sanction severity could adequately represent the variations described above. Thus, the correlates of two sanctions—fines and incarceration—are examined separately. All of the predictor variables earlier utilized were included here, as were two additional variables relevant for sentencing decisions: prior record and case disposition mode.

Defendant's prior record has been viewed by courtroom participants to be of the utmost importance in sentencing decisions. Previous research has cautiously, if not convincingly, demonstrated its predictive value (see Farrell and Swigert 1978; Gibson 1978; Rhodes 1978; but also, Eisenstein and Jacob 1977). In Columbus, prosecutors usually possess this information about a defendant. Based upon observations and interviews, prior record influences both plea-bargaining practices and the sentencing decision of the judge.[17]

It has long been suspected that a defendant's pursuit of the right to trial—particularly a jury trial—triggers a penalty upon conviction. Evidence was marshaled by early studies (see, for example, American Friends Service Committee 1971), but recent studies utilizing more sophisticated statistical techniques have reached varying conclusions (see Eisenstein and Jacob 1977; Rhodes 1978; Nardulli 1978; Uhlman and Walker 1979). Nevertheless, even Eisenstein and Jacob, who find no statistical effect, assert that the *perception* of a penalty for going to trial is still widely held by "court officials and defendants alike," one that is "instrumental in promoting a steady flow of guilty pleas" (1977: 271).

The regression equation for fines yielded a weak explanatory model. Only 14 percent of the variation was explained by the predictor variables ($R = .38$); the most important of these was whether the case was OMVI or not (beta $= .30$). Analysis of variations in fines by different types of cases proved more fruitful. Table 5 presents these data.

In OMVI cases, several variables are about equally important in explaining a small amount of variation (11 percent). Judge G, who has the reputation of being the toughest sentencer on the court,[18] contributes to the likelihood of receiving a heavier fine. So do multiple charges, being convicted upon a trial, and having a relevant prior record. In traffic cases, a similarly small amount of variation is explained (10 percent). The key variable is the number of charges; in traffic cases other than OMVI, the amount of the fine rises dramatically as the number of charges increases. In theft cases, a much larger proportion (41 percent) of variation is explained. Three of the four predictor variables are individual judges. Again, being in the courtroom of Judge G contributes to the likelihood of a more severe fine; so does conviction upon trial.

TABLE   5 / A Multivariate Model of Severity of Fines by Type of
Case: Stepwise Regression[a]

OMVI		Traffic		Theft	
	Beta[b]		Beta[b]		Beta[b]
Judge G	.17	Number of charges	.27	Judge M	.36
Number of charges	.15	Judge J	−.12	Judge G	.32
Disposition mode[c]	.13			Judge J	−.25
Prior record	.12			Disposition mode[c]	.23
$R = .33$		$R = .32$		$R = .64$	
$R^2 = 11\%$		$R^2 = 10\%$		$R^2 = 41\%$	
$(N = 313)$		$(N = 269)$		$(N = 107)$	

[a] Equations for the other three case types did not reach standard levels of statistical significance.

[b] Each of the beta weights is statistically significant at .05; in no instance does the standard error approach beta.

[c] Disposition mode: guilty at trial coded high; guilty upon plea coded low.

Two points bear further comment. First, the contrast in predictors between OMVI and theft cases highlights the degree to which the court has routinized the handling of drunk driving cases. Judicial sentencing philosophies are muted; variation across judges in fines levied is small. Only the court's tough sentencer, Judge G, is far from the court's norm. This routinization is facilitated by the comparative frequency of OMVI cases and by the unquestioned seriousness with which all courtroom actors view this type of case. In the words of Judge E, a self-characterized middle-of-the-road sentencer, "Judges are swayed by the community in which they live . . . people don't want to see rapists, thieves or *drunk drivers* go free" (emphasis added). Petty theft or larceny, on the other hand, may present value conflicts for judges sympathetic to poor people, accounting for the wide variation in sanction severity among the court's judges.

The second point to be emphasized is the effect on fines resulting from conviction at trial. Although not significant in the ordinary range of traffic cases where most trials are highly abbreviated, going to trial in OMVI or theft cases is a different matter. In these cases, there is a distinguishable penalty attached to pursuing full constitutional rights. Or in the words of several Columbus courtroom actors, "Rent is charged for the use of the courtroom."

Analysis of incarceration directs attention to two questions: (1) Should the defendant serve any time in jail? and (2) if so, how much time? Accordingly, separate regressions were performed for the use of the sanction and for its severity where used. In the former instance, the dependent variable is a dichotomy wherein 65 percent of defendants were not incarcerated and 35 percent were incarcerated. In the latter case, the dependent variable is interval, ranging from three days to one year. Table 6 presents the results of both regressions.

The decision to incarcerate is poorly explained by the model (only 11 percent of the variance). Six variables are statistically significant predictors, but the effect of each is small. The most important of these is OMVI; such cases are the most likely

TABLE   6 /   **A Multivariate Model of the Use and Severity of Incarceration: Stepwise Regression**

	Use of incarceration	Severity of incarceration
	Beta[a]	Beta[a]
OMVI case	.19	−.37
Disposition mode[b]	.12	.11
Judge M	.11	ns
Judge G	.10	.28
Number of charges	.10	.13
Judge A	−.07	ns
	$R = .33$	$R = .44$
	$R^2 = 11\%$	$R^2 = 19\%$
	$(N = 1,271)$	$(N = 439)$

[a]Each of the beta weights is statistically significant at .05; in no instance does the standard error approach beta.

[b]Disposition mode: guilty at trial coded high; guilty upon plea coded low.

to result in incarceration. Four of the six predictor variables for incarceration also appeared in the model for case fine severity. Thus, many of the same forces at work in one kind of sentencing decision are at work in another.

The severity of incarceration is somewhat better explained (19 percent of the variance). Again, OMVI is the most important variable, but in a negative direction. Most drunk driving cases receive very short sentences, usually the three days mandated by statute as the minimum. The court's reputed tough sentencer lives up to that reputation. As most defendants seem acutely aware, being in the courtroom of Judge G will result in a much longer sentence.

Attempts to improve explanation of incarceration by analyzing within types of cases were generally unsuccessful, probably because of skewed distributions and small numbers. In OMVI cases, however, a substantial 26 percent of the variance in the use of incarceration was explained ($R = .51$). The most important predictor was the type of plea, whether to the original or reduced charge (beta = .36). This is to be expected, since conviction on the original charge in OMVI cases requires some type of confinement. Prior record also showed a significant effect (beta = .16), suggesting the importance of tapping this difficult-to-collect variable.

Summary and Conclusions

The Columbus lower court yields a quite different picture from that of New Haven. Outcomes are costly to convicted defendants. Fines are substantial, incarceration is not infrequent, and in traffic cases one's license is in jeopardy. In many cases, more than one type of sanction is imposed. Furthermore, courtroom actors including defendants behave as if the outcome is important. Defendants hope to avoid Judge G. Seemingly minor cases appear on the pretrial docket, indicative of a decision not to plead guilty at first appearance. Defense counsel stall at pretrial hoping for a more sympathetic prosecutor or bargain on the day of trial. Prosecutors operate under strict guidelines for charge reduction in OMVI cases. The outcome *is* important to defendants and courtroom actors alike.

By contrast, the process of having one's case adjudicated is not very costly in Columbus. Indigency requirements are liberally interpreted by the public defender's office and by judges in arraignment court. Few defendants await the outcome of their case in custody. Many receive personal recognizance release or supervised release without bond; others pay a 10 percent appearance bond directly to the court (90 percent of which is returned upon appearance). Finally, the court requires few appearances of its defendants. Cases are not routinely continued. In all, the median elapsed time from initial arraignment to disposition is approximately thirty days. Process costs may seem high to unconvicted defendants, but for convicted defendants the outcome is unmistakably the more important punishment.

Why outcomes are more punishing in Columbus than in New Haven cannot be answered definitively. But differences in the political culture and structure of the two communities, described earlier, clearly play a key role. The political culture of Columbus breeds a climate of severity. This is manifested in the institutional domination of the police in the lower court, in the Columbus police department's orientation to law enforcement rather than order maintenance, and in the community's expectations that traffic laws will be enforced. Moreover, judges in Columbus may be more responsive to community expectations of full enforcement and meaningful sanctions[19] because they are elected locally and attached permanently to Columbus, unlike the rotating judges who serve the New Haven lower court. More precise linkages of the nexus between political culture and lower court outcomes must necessarily await comparative research.

The data from Columbus suggest several additional themes. First, the type of case structures the substance of the decision-making process (see also Feeley 1979: xv). Throughout the analysis, this is the most significant predictor of whether defendants are found guilty or go free, and which defendants go to jail if convicted. In particular, assault and drunk driving cases are handled in highly distinctive ways. This apparent "pigeonholing" of cases in lower courts contrasts, at least in degree, with felony courts.

Secondly, the adjudication and sentence decisions are often indistinct. In this respect the Columbus lower court is like many felony courts where the determination of guilt and negotiations over sentence run together. In Columbus, the two decision stages merge in the use of bond forfeitures where money is appropriated without any formal decision on guilt or innocence. The two stages also merge in plea bargaining in multiple-charge cases, where a decision to dismiss one charge occurs in exchange for submission of a guilty plea on other charges. And the two stages merge in the overlapping uses of prior record. Decisions to dismiss or to dispose of cases by way of bond forfeiture are often made in light of a defendant's prior record, a piece of data ordinarily, and legally, reserved for the sentence decision alone.

Finally, the perceptions of courtroom work-group members conform quite closely to the realities of case disposition in Columbus. For example, attorneys perceive that "rent is charged for the courtroom" (in trials), and the case data indicate a clear penalty for going to trial in more serious cases. Prior record is perceived by attorneys and judges to be significant in bargaining and sentencing, and likewise the case data indicate (in drunk driving cases) that a relevant prior conviction reduces the likelihood of severe fine and a jail term. Furthermore, personalities are perceived accurately. Everyone agrees that Judge G is a much tougher sentencer than any other judge on the court; Judge G himself says he is "likely to give the maximum," and the case data unmistakably paint Judge G as the dispenser of the heaviest fines and the longest jail terms. Such convergences of perception and behavior indicate the *rationality* of the court, a theme insufficiently highlighted either in misdemeanor or felony courts. Courtroom actors may have an excellent sense of how their own court operates, even if their world view is limited (Heumann 1977) or they are unable to articulate theories of criminal courts.

T A B L E   A – 1 / **Frequency Distribution of Selected Case Characteristics**[a]

	Percent	*Number*
Seriousness of offense		
M1	82.4	2,273
M2	3.7	103
M3	3.5	97
M4	6.4	173
MM (minor misdemeanor)	4.0	111
Number of charges		
1	57.6	1,586
2	28.3	780
3	10.3	284
4	2.5	70
5	.8	22
6 or more	.5	13
Type of defense counsel		
Private	59.6	1,626
Public defender	32.2	880
Pro se	8.2	225
Number of court appearances		
1 (disposed at arraignment)	—[b]	—[b]
2 (disposed at pretrial)	59.7	1,577
3	30.4	801
4	8.0	211
5	1.6	43
6	.3	7
Prior record[c]		
None	62.8	206
1 conviction	23.5	77
2 or more convictions	13.7	45

[a] For the distribution of case type, refer to Table 1; for disposition mode, refer to Table 2.

[b] Cases disposed at arraignment, due to their unavailability, were not included in this study.

[c] Refer to note 17 for operationalization of prior record; includes only OMVI cases.

Notes

1. The percentage of cases disposed at arraignment is not available.
2. Cases in which there is no jury demand can be scheduled directly for a court trial, without the scheduling of a pretrial. These constitute a small percentage of all cases, perhaps 100 in the three-month sampling period.
3. Although there is a central scheduling office, the court operates under an individual case assignment system (after arraignment), in which the same judge hears a case from the pretrial through final disposition. The individual assignment system is mandated by Ohio Rules of Superintendence promulgated for the lower trial courts in 1974 by the state supreme court (Ohio Sup R.4).
4. Pretrial hearings in this court are always conducted in the courtroom, in full view and hearing of all. Chambers are rarely used for plea-negotiation discussions.
5. Conviction of drunk driving carries a statutory minimum incarceration of three days. Judges may substitute for the jail term a confinement of a similar period in a drunk driving program. For a theory of penalty mitigation in OMVI cases, see Ross (1976).
6. All judges will be referenced by alphabetic letters selected at random in order to preserve anonymity. Though such a promise was not required to conduct observations, it was needed to gain access to case data.
7. But see note 2 above.
8. Bond forfeiture is also used to dispose of petty cases (for example, disorderly conduct) where the defendant fails to appear at arraignment, after having made bond with the court. Feeley (1979: 138) found that 16.6 percent of his sample was disposed in this way.
9. To alleviate this problem, a Police Liaison Program was recently instituted, whereby a small number of police officers are assigned on a regular basis to the courtroom for pretrial sessions.
10. Until 1980, prosecutors were assigned cases on a master calendar principle, from one to two weeks in advance of a court date. Thus, the prosecutor assigned for the pretrial was not necessarily the prosecutor on the day scheduled for trial, in the event it was not resolved at the pretrial.
11. Interestingly, though most dismissals did occur at the pretrial session, a significant percentage of all dismissals (22 percent) occurred on the scheduled trial date.
12. The median amount is $300, with a few bonds set as high as $1,000 or even $2,500.
13. In Columbus, "no-contest" pleas are counted as guilty pleas for the purpose of statistical record keeping. Some judges like to encourage defendants to plead "no contest" if that will facilitate a disposition, notably Judge D.
14. The use of a dichotomous dependent variable in multiple regression analysis is less than ideal (see Goodman 1972). Nevertheless, the distribution of case disposition is insufficiently skewed to warrant such statistical transformations as Goodman's log linear technique.
15. Judge C suspended some portion of a fine in 69 percent of his cases; the amount suspended averaged $150. Judge M suspended part of a fine in 63 percent of his cases, on the average for $135. Together, these two judges accounted for 56 percent of all cases in which a fine was suspended in whole or in part.
16. It is more difficult to compare accurately bond forfeitures in the two courts, since Columbus also utilizes bond forfeitures in cases where defendants do not skip.
17. Due to difficulties in finding (in the prosecutor's basement) prior record information, collection efforts were restricted to OMVI cases. For these cases, prior record was operationalized as *relevant prior convictions,* defining "relevant" as OMVI, ROMV (reckless; the charge to which most OMVI cases are reduced), physical control (of an automobile), and intoxication. These were the types of cases cited by members of the prosecutor's and public defender's offices as bearing upon a sentence decision in OMVI cases.
18. According to the Defender, defendants initially ask two questions: (1) Can I get a personal recognizance bond and (2) is Judge G assigned to the case? In the interview with Judge G, he confirmed his tough sentencing philosophy ("I'm likely to give them the maxi-

mum"), noting that his association with crimes has primarily been with the *victims* of crimes (through his stint as a prosecutor).
19. It seems clear that judges in Columbus perceive the community to be basically conservative and expecting of tough sentences. A major newspaper article about this study appeared in the *Columbus Dispatch* on June 22, 1980, in which the municipal court was characterized as "tough" and "efficient." The administrative judge was quoted in the article as being delighted that "somebody thinks that we're doing a good job." The author of the newspaper article inferred from my comparisons that, because Columbus was tougher, it was a better court.

References

ALFINI, JAMES J., AND RACHEL DOAN (1977). "A New Perspective on Misdemeanor Justice." 60 *Judicature* 425.

AMERICAN FRIENDS SERVICE COMMITTEE (1971). *Struggle for Justice: A Report on Crime and Punishment in America.* New York: Hill & Wang.

BARONE, MICHAEL, GRANT UJIFUSA, AND DOUGLAS MATTHEWS (1980). *Almanac of American Politics.* New York: E. P. Dutton.

CHURCH, THOMAS W., JR., ALAN CARLSON, JO-LYNNE LEE, AND THERESA TAN (1978). *Justice Delayed: The Pace of Litigation in Urban Trial Courts.* Williamsburg, Va.: National Center for State Courts.

DAHL, ROBERT (1961). *Who Governs? Democracy and Power in an American City.* New Haven: Yale University Press.

EISENSTEIN, JAMES, AND HERBERT JACOB (1977). *Felony Justice: An Organizational Analysis of Criminal Courts.* Boston: Little, Brown.

FARRELL, RONALD A., AND VICTORIA LYNN SWIGERT (1978). "Prior Offense Record as a Self-Fulfilling Prophecy." 12 *Law and Society Review* 437.

FEELEY, MALCOLM M. (1979). *The Process Is the Punishment: Handling Cases in a Lower Criminal Court.* New York: Russell Sage Foundation.

GIBSON, JAMES L. (1978). "Race as a Determinant of Criminal Sentences: A Methodological Critique and a Case Study." 12 *Law and Society Review* 455.

GOODMAN, LEO A. (1972). "A Modified Multiple Regression Approach to the Analysis of Dichotomous Variables." 37 *American Sociological Review* 28.

HEUMANN, MILTON (1977). *Plea Bargaining: The Experiences of Prosecutors, Judges, and Defense Attorneys.* Chicago: University of Chicago Press.

KATZ, LEWIS R. (1968). "Municipal Courts—Another Urban Ill." 20 *Case Western Reserve Law Review* 87.

KRITZER, HERBERT M. (1979). "Political Cultures, Trial Courts, and Criminal Cases." In Peter F. Nardulli, ed., *The Study of Criminal Courts: Political Perspectives.* Cambridge, Mass.: Ballinger.

LEVIN, MARTIN (1977). *Urban Politics and the Criminal Courts.* Chicago: University of Chicago Press.

NARDULLI, PETER F. (1978). *The Courtroom Elite: An Organizational Perspective on Criminal Justice.* Cambridge, Mass.: Ballinger.

NEUBAUER, DAVID W. (1974). *Criminal Justice in Middle America.* Morristown, N.J.: General Learning Press.

OHIO COURTS (1978). Columbus: Supreme Court, Office of the Administrative Director.

PALMER, JOHN W. (1975). "The Night Prosecutor." 59 *Judicature* 22.

PARISI, NICOLETTE (1980). "Part-Time Imprisonment: The Legal and Practical Issues of Periodic Confinement." 63 *Judicature* 385.

RHODES, WILLIAM M. (1978). *Plea Bargaining: Who Gains, Who Loses?* Washington, D.C.: Institute for Law and Social Research.

ROSS, H. LAURENCE (1976). "The Neutralization of Severe Penalties: Some Traffic Law Studies." 10 *Law and Society Review* 403.

RYAN, JOHN PAUL, AND JAMES J. ALFINI (1979). "Trial Judges' Participation in Plea Bargaining: An Empirical Perspective." 13 *Law and Society Review* 479.

RYAN, JOHN PAUL, ALLAN ASHMAN, BRUCE D. SALES, AND SANDRA SHANE-DU BOW (1980). *American Trial Judges: Their Work Styles and Performance.* New York: Free Press.

UHLMAN, THOMAS M., AND N. DARLENE WALKER (1979). "A Plea Is No Bargain: The Impact of Case Disposition on Sentencing." 60 *Social Science Quarterly* 218.

WILSON, JAMES Q. (1968). *Varieties of Police Behavior.* Cambridge, Mass.: Harvard University Press.

18

Urban Politics and Policy Outcomes:
The Criminal Courts

Martin A. Levin

Martin A. Levin compares the sentencing behavior of judges in two cities to deter-mine the impact of a traditional partisan system and that of a system subscribing to the nonpartisan, reform ethos. Social background, recruitment, and political cul-ture all seem to exert an influence on the judges' treatment of defendants.

In recent years students of urban government have analyzed the ways in which con-flict is managed in various cities. Some large cities (of over 300,000 in population) have a "traditional" political system with (typically) a formally partisan city gov-ernment, with, to a varying degree, strong parties that (1) rely on material rewards rather than issues to attract members, (2) have a generally working-class orientation toward politics, (3) emphasize conferring material benefits upon individuals, (4) identify with local areas of the city, rather than the city "as a whole," and (5) cen-tralize influence. Other large cities have a "good government" or reform political system with (typically) a formally nonpartisan city government and weak parties that (1) rely on nonmaterial rewards (primarily issues or personalities), (2) have a gen-erally middle-class orientation toward politics, (3) emphasize maximizing such val-ues as efficiency, honesty, impartiality, professionalism, and an identification with the city "as a whole," and (4) decentralize influence.

In short, these studies sought to answer the question "Who governs?" However, even more recently students of urban government have attempted to raise and answer a second and probably more important question: "What difference does it make who governs?" What difference does it make to *average citizens* whether they live in a city with a "traditional" political system or a "good-government" political system? It is very likely, as James Q. Wilson has argued, that the struggle for power in a city has little direct effect on the life of average citizens, but that the services provided by the government once in power (such as the administration of criminal justice,

Source: First published in the first edition of *Criminal Justice: Law and Politics,* by George F. Cole. Copyright © 1972 by Wadsworth Publishing Company, Inc. Reprinted by permission. Some footnotes omitted; others renumbered.

education, and welfare) are very likely to affect them directly and significantly. Moreover, it is possible that the policies followed in providing these services are closely related to, and indeed perhaps the product of, the city's political system. Thus these policies can be viewed as the outputs of the city's political system, and the political processes of the city can be viewed as the inputs.

This paper attempts to ascertain what consequences different political systems have for the sentencing decisions of the criminal court judges in Minneapolis and Pittsburgh and thus for the individuals that come into the courts. It also attempts to discover what happens when the selection of judges is taken "out of politics."

Judicial and Political Reform, Evaluation, and the Approach of this Study

For many years attorneys, their professional associations, many (but by no means all) judges, and reform-minded laypersons have advocated taking the selection process of judges out of politics. The proposals for this vary but are typically variations of the "Missouri Plan" or the "merit selection plan" in which the governor appoints the judges from a list of nominees selected by a nonpartisan nominating commission composed of lawyers and laypersons (and in some instances judges). Another selection method, which is also designed to remove judges from politics, but which reformers feel is less ideal, is the selection of judges in truly nonpartisan elections. The advocates of reform argue that judges are experts and should be selected by fellow experts in a nonpolitical manner and that expert, nonpolitical selection procedures will produce higher-quality, more efficient, more independent, and, therefore, more impartial and just judges. None of the reform advocates support their assertions with systematic evidence indicating that taking the selection of judges out of politics does in fact produce such judges, or indeed that it has any consequences for judicial behavior. Opponents of taking the selection of judges "out of politics" premise their argument on democratic values, but also fail to support their assertions with evidence that a political selection procedure would help attain such values.

To empirically evaluate the consequences of differing political systems and differing judicial selection systems, comparative research was undertaken on the criminal courts and political systems of Pittsburgh and Minneapolis. These cities represent two more or less opposed types of political systems (the "traditional" and the "good government," respectively) and both types of judicial selection systems (the political and the reform, respectively).

Pittsburgh has a formally partisan and highly centralized city government. In 1966, when this research was begun, the Democratic party organization was strong, hierarchical, disciplined, highly cohesive, and attracted workers with material incentives. It has dominated city politics since the early 1930s and has been influential in state and national politics. Public and party offices are filled by party professionals whose career patterns are hierarchical and regularized. They patiently "wait in line" because of the party's need to maintain ethnic and religious balance, even on a judicial ticket. There is a high degree of centralization of influence, and the citizens tend to accept pro-union and liberal social welfare policies. There is wide acceptance of partisanship and party activity in almost every sphere of Pittsburgh local government. Indeed, there has been little public enthusiasm for efforts to take the selection of judges out of politics, and parties view positions on the courts and their related agencies as primary sources of rewards for their workers.

There are nineteen judges on the Pittsburgh (Allegheny County) common pleas court (the trial court for both criminal and civil jurisdictions), and they are elected on a partisan basis for ten-year terms. Party designation appears on the ballot. In practice the political parties, especially the Democratic party, dominate primaries and the general elections for judicial positions in Pittsburgh, and the local bar association usually plays a very limited role.

When a court vacancy occurs, the governor appoints a successor who must stand for reelection at the next general election. Ten of the nineteen incumbent judges in 1965 initially reached the bench in this manner. These interim appointments have also been controlled by the local parties.[1] The Pittsburgh judges' career patterns also reflect the dominance of the parties and the limited role of the bar association in judicial selection. Almost all of the judges held a government position such as city solicitor, assistant prosecutor, city council member, state legislator, or even congressional representative, prior to coming to the bench (all are partisan offices and are controlled by the parties). They were also active members of the party organization.

Minneapolis has a formally nonpartisan and structurally fragmented city government. The Democratic-Farmer-Labor (DFL) party and the Republican party play a significant but limited role in city politics. They are both formally (because of nonpartisan elections) and informally (because of the wide acceptance of nonpartisanship) limited. The parties are moderately weak, loosely organized, highly democratic and undisciplined. They attract workers through nonmaterial incentives. Thus the parties do not overcome the formal decentralization of authority in the city. Individuals, including "amateur" politicians, with the ability and willingness to work, but with little seniority in the party, can and do rise rapidly in the party and in city government. The citizens tend to be disposed toward conservative policies for city government. Nonpartisanship in city politics is accepted by the people, and even by many party workers and some party leaders. Indeed, the electorate has had a strong negative response to candidates or incumbents who violate, or seem to violate, this ideal. This is especially true of the courts and their related agencies, and thus party leaders and workers tend not to regard them as a source of party rewards.

There are sixteen judges on the Minneapolis (Hennepin County) district court (the trial court for both criminal and civil jurisdictions), and they are formally elected for six-year terms on a nonpartisan basis. In practice the political parties have almost no role in the selection of judges in Minneapolis, while the local bar association generally plays a major role. Prior to a judicial election, the Minneapolis Bar Association polls its members and publicizes the results. The "winner" of the poll (or the second- or third-highest candidate) almost always wins the election. The governor makes appointments to interim vacancies, and fourteen of the sixteen incumbent judges in 1965 initially reached the bench in this manner. When vacancies occur, the Minneapolis Bar Association conducts a poll, and the Minnesota governors have closely adhered to the bar's preferences. The two DFL governors who have served in the last ten years have been significant exceptions to this pattern, but they were strongly criticized for this (even by some of their own party members) and had to work carefully around the bar association. Moreover, during the administrations of these DFL governors, the party played almost no role in judicial selections because the governor's decisions were, at the most, influenced by "political" rather than "party" considerations (for example, the appointees' relationships to these governors were personal rather than organizational).

The Minneapolis judges' career patterns also reflect the minor role of the parties and the major role of the bar association in judicial selection. Prior to coming to the bench, fourteen of the eighteen Minneapolis judges in this study had been exclusively or predominantly in private legal practice (usually business-oriented, and often corporate, practices). Those who held public positions before coming to the bench did not hold elective positions (with one exception) and were generally not active in either party.

This paper focuses on the criminal division of the courts in these two cities, in part because judges typically have a very high degree of discretion in criminal-sentencing decisions. Criminal statutes in Pennsylvania and Minnesota, as in most states, allow judges the choice of incarcerating a convicted defendant or of granting probation, in most felony cases. If they choose the former, the statutes also allow them, within prescribed limits, to fix the term of imprisonment. The high degree of discretion in sentencing decisions presents an opportunity to study judicial behavior that is shaped by the fewest external variables, such as the actual degree of the defendant's guilt and the quality of police investigation and prosecution. In contrast, conviction rates are not simply the product of the judges' discretion and are greatly affected by these three factors.

To understand typical judicial behavior patterns in each city, sentencing decisions were compared statistically for the nine most common felony offenses. To understand the judges' attitudes, decision-making processes, and courtroom behavior, interviews were conducted with all but one of the judges in both cities, and courtroom trial proceedings were observed over a period of several months in 1966. The judges' interview statements were crossvalidated on the basis of their actual sentencing decisions, observation of their courtroom behavior, and interviews with more than twenty criminal court participants in each city.

The Judges' Sentencing Decisions

There are significant differences in the sentencing decisions of the judges in each city. On the whole, the decisions are more lenient in Pittsburgh than in Minneapolis. White and black defendants receive both a greater percentage of probation and a shorter length of incarceration in Pittsburgh. This pattern persists when the defendant's previous record, plea, and age are also controlled, and it is rather consistent among all nine of the offenses compared. Table 1 indicates this pattern in summary terms. For probation, when the sentencing decisions are controlled for type of prior record and race, there is a sufficient number of cases to compare the nine offenses in each city for twenty-five categories. In twenty-two categories there is a greater percentage of probation in Pittsburgh, in two categories there is a greater percentage of probation in Minneapolis, and in one there is no significant difference between the cities. For incarceration, when type of prior record and race are controlled, there

T A B L E   1 / **Percentage of Probation in Pittsburgh and Minneapolis**

	Pittsburgh	(Percent "acquitted plus costs")[a]	Minneapolis	Ratio[b]
WHITES, NO PRIOR RECORD				
Burglary	58.4	7.9	56.0	1.04
	(60)	(6)	(275)	
Grand larceny	87.5	24.2	62.7	1.40
	(32)	(15)	(188)	
Aggravated assault	87.5	28.5	37.5	2.33
	(8)	(4)	(24)	
Aggravated robbery	0.0	0.0	5.9	NR
	(8)		(68)	
Indecent assault	50.0	36.9	50.0	1.0
	(6)	(7)	(70)	
Aggravated forgery	50.0	9.1	55.6	−1.11
	(8)	(1)	(117)	
Nonsufficient funds	81.8	23.8	67.3	1.22
	(11)	(5)	(101)	
BLACKS, NO PRIOR RECORD				
Burglary	47.5	3.8	38.2	1.24
	(40)	(2)	(34)	
Grand larceny	68.0	7.5	45.4	1.50
	(25)	(3)	(22)	
Aggravated assault	60.0	27.2	28.0	2.14
	(10)	(6)	(25)	
Aggravated robbery	25.0	10.0	12.0	2.08
	(8)	(1)	(25)	
Possession of narcotics	50.0	0	33.3	1.5
	(6)		(15)	
WHITES, PRIOR RECORD				
Burglary	59.4	6.8	22.0	2.7
	(227)	(21)	(159)	
Grand larceny	62.1	8.4	34.8	1.78
	(103)	(12)	(69)	
Aggravated assault	47.4	21.4	15.4	3.08
	(19)	(6)	(13)	
Aggravated robbery	26.1	3.6	2.8	9.32
	(23)	(1)	(36)	
Simple robbery	33.3	24.3	27.8	1.20
	(21)	(9)	(18)	
Indecent assault	72.4	16.9	28.6	2.53
	(47)	(13)	(28)	
Aggravated forgery	54.6	0	25.5	2.14
	(11)		(106)	
Nonsufficient funds	56.2	20.9	35.7	1.57
	(16)	(5)	(70)	
Possession of narcotics	77.8	7.7	55.6	1.40
	(9)	(1)	(9)	
BLACKS, PRIOR RECORD				
Burglary	32.6	3.7	28.6	1.14
	(291)	(14)	(28)	

(continued)

TABLE   1 / *(continued)*

	Pittsburgh	*(Percent "acquitted plus costs")*[a]	Minneapolis	Ratio[b]
Grand larceny	38.2	5.8	15.8	2.42
	(115)	(9)	(19)	
Aggravated robbery	8.3	4.4	0	NR
	(36)	(2)	(10)	
Aggravated forgery	50.0	5.6	28.6	1.75
	(16)	(1)	(7)	
Possession of narcotics	48.0	2.6	12.5	3.84
	(25)	(1)	(8)	

[a]This verdict is used in Pittsburgh but not in Minneapolis. Therefore, in comparing the sentencing decisions between cities, the percentage of defendants who receive this verdict is treated as an added increment of freedom resulting from the judges' discretion, which is comparable to an increment of probation. (By contrast, the proportion of defendants acquitted outright [that is, without being ordered to pay court costs] is an increment of freedom, but it is not comparable to an increment of probation because it is not the product of the judge's discretionary decision. His decision whether to convict or acquit is the product of many factors over which he has only minor control, such as the facts of the case as presented in the trial, and the quality of the police investigation and prosecution.) However, in making these comparisons, the percentage of defendants who are "acquitted plus costs" and the percentage who receive probation are reported separately because their sum is not the precise percentage of the total number of defendants who receive freedom as the result of the judge's discretionary decision. Their sum would slightly overstate the size of this total group because each percentage has a different base point. (The percentage of defendants who are "acquitted plus costs" is a proportion of the *total* number of *defendants*, whereas the percentage of defendants who receive probation is a proportion of the total number of *convicted* defendants.)

[b]The ratio is calculated by dividing the greater percentage of probation in the two cities by the lesser percentage of probation in the cities. When the percentage of probation is greater in Pittsburgh, the ratio is a positive number; when it is greater in Minneapolis, the ratio is a negative number. When the percentage of probation is zero in the one city, it is impossible to calculate the ratio, and the term "NR" (signifying no ratio) is used.

SOURCE: From Martin A. Levin, *Urban Politics and the Criminal Courts* (Chicago: University of Chicago Press, 1977), pp. 271–272. By permission of the University of Chicago Press, © the University of Chicago and by permission of the author. This table is a substitute for the tables appearing in Martin A. Levin, "Urban Politics and Policy Outcomes: The Criminal Courts," in George F. Cole, ed., *Criminal Justice: Law and Politics,* 1st ed. (North Scituate, Mass.: Duxbury Press, 1976).

is a sufficient number of cases to compare the nine offenses for sixteen categories. In thirteen categories there is a shorter length of incarceration in Pittsburgh, in two categories there is a shorter length of incarceration in Minneapolis, and in one there is no significant difference between the cities. Throughout every aspect of the data the pattern runs almost entirely in one direction—greater leniency in Pittsburgh— and there are only some marginal variations in the degree of this greater leniency.

Although both white and black defendants receive more lenient sentences in Pittsburgh, in both cities whites receive a greater percentage of probation than blacks in most categories, and in Minneapolis whites receive a shorter length of incarceration than blacks in most categories. In Pittsburgh blacks receive a shorter length of incarceration than whites in almost all offenses. On the whole, sentencing decisions are more favorable for blacks in Pittsburgh than in Minneapolis, both in absolute terms and relative to whites.

In the comparison of sentencing decisions by type of plea, the Minneapolis judges penalize defendants who plead not guilty by giving them more severe sentences more frequently than do the Pittsburgh judges. On the whole, in Pittsburgh, decisions for such defendants are only slightly more severe than those for defendants who plead guilty; in Minneapolis they are much more severe.

There is also much more consistency in the length of the terms of incarceration in Minneapolis than in Pittsburgh. In Minneapolis, white and black defendants with the same type of prior record received the identical or nearly identical median term of incarceration in five of the seven offenses in which there is a sufficient number of cases for comparison. By contrast, there is almost none of this consistency in Pittsburgh. White and black defendants with the same type of prior record receive a nearly identical median term of incarceration in two of the nine offenses in which there are sufficient cases.

The Judges' Views and Decision-Making Processes

The Minneapolis judges typically tend to be more oriented toward "society" and its needs and protection than toward the defendant. They are also more oriented toward the goals of their professional peers. Their decision making is legalistic and universalistic. The Pittsburgh judges typically are oriented toward the defendant, and they tend to lack orientation toward punishment or deterrence. Their decision making is nonlegalistic in that it tends to be particularistic, pragmatic, and based on policy considerations.

There are also significant differences in the judges' courtroom behavior prior to sentencing. Most nonjury trials in Pittsburgh are informal (for example, witnesses stand at the front bar) and abbreviated, and most of the judges prefer this arrangement. Most of the Pittsburgh judges also prefer informal procedures for obtaining information concerning defendants (the defense attorney's trial presentation, individuals intervening with the judge outside of court, the court staff's knowledge about the defendant) rather than the presentence investigations of the probation department. Trials in Minneapolis are formal, deliberate, and unabbreviated, and all of the judges prefer this arrangement. They also use presentence investigations in almost every case, and most of them dislike utilizing any informal sources of information concerning the defendant. In both cities plea bargaining is infrequent.[2]

The Minneapolis and Pittsburgh judges' views, decision-making processes, and sentencing behavior very closely approximate two general models of decision making. The Minneapolis judges' views and behavior approximate a judicial decision-making model, and the Pittsburgh judges' approximate an administrative decision-making model. The judicial model has the following characteristics: (1) Decisions are made on the basis of the "best" evidence as defined under the laws of evidence. (2) Decisions are made on the basis of complete evidence as developed by the adversary system. (3) Judges feel that they must maintain an image of detached objectivity, because it is as important to appear just as to be just. (4) A judge's decisions have a dichotomous specificity (yes–no), and they must assign legal wrong to one of the two parties. (5) Judges deduce their decision by a formal line of reasoning from legal principles that exist independent of policy considerations. (6) Judges evaluate their success by the degree to which their decisions have followed these procedures and by their satisfaction of abstract notions of justice and law. They generally have greater concern for procedure than for substantive issues, and thus are more concerned with satisfying "the law" as an abstract doctrine than arriving at "just" settlements of individual cases. (7) Judges base their decisions on what they feel is best in objective terms—their criteria usually come from "the law"—rather than what might be considered best from the perspective of the individual's self-interest, and they reach their decisions regardless of considerations of person.

The administrative model of decision making has the following characteristics: (1) Decisions are made on the basis of the kind of evidence on which reasonable people customarily make day-to-day decisions. (2) Decisions are made on the basis of sufficient evidence gathered by the administrator's own investigation, and the length and depth of the investigation is determined by the resources available. (3) Administrators feel that they must seek intimate contact with the real world to be able to administer effectively. They feel that this is more important than maintaining an image of detached objectivity (that is, appearing just). (4) Administrators may adopt dichotomous (yes–no) or intermediate decisions (for example, compromise decisions or delayed enforcement of a decision). (5) Administrators deduce their decisions by pragmatic methods from the policy goals incorporated in the programs they administer. They have greater concern for arriving at "just" settlements based on the particular merits of individual cases than for adherence to abstract notions of justice and the law. They seek to give their clients what they feel they "deserve," and they base their decisions in large part on the needs of their individual clients. (In some instances administrators may perceive that one of their client needs is exemption from the treatment involved in their program.) (6) Administrators have greater concern for substantive issues than for procedure, and thus they evaluate their success by the way the programs they administer "fit" real-world demands and supports. Thirteen of the seventeen Minneapolis judges seem to have little empathy for the defendants whom they describe as "coming from low intelligence groups," "crummy people," "congenital criminals," "not learning from their mistakes," or "not able to consider the consequences before they act." They tend to be resigned to the "criminality" of most defendants and often seem inclined to "give up" on them.[3] The Minneapolis judges' tendency to penalize with more severe sentences defendants who plead not guilty seems to be an indication of their greater concern for the needs of society than for the defendants.[4]

Thirteen of the seventeen judges are also oriented toward their professional peers (for example, correction authorities and law-enforcement officials) and their goals. Thus though in general they want to exercise discretion, they are willing to sacrifice some of it to achieve both greater consistency in their own sentencing and the goals of some of these peers (for example, "professional expertise" and "better law enforcement"). In almost all instances in recent years, the effect of pursuing these goals has been more severe sentences.[5]

In short, these judges tend to be enlightened in terms of professional doctrine rather than benevolent toward the defendant. Indeed, many Minneapolis judges explain that one reason they dislike and discourage informal sources of information about the defendant (which tend to convey personal and mitigating information) and prefer the probation department's formal presentence investigations (which tend to be professional and objective) is that they "don't want to become emotionally involved in individual cases."

Twelve of the seventeen Minneapolis judges believe in the effectiveness of institutional rehabilitation and penal deterrence, and thus are not reluctant to punish defendants by incarcerating them. For example, Judge Rasmussen told an interviewer, "I know I am considered a tough judge here, but that doesn't bother me because punishment works. You won't sit on a hot stove if you have been burned." Few of these judges are critical of the quality of prisons, but several complain about "the failure rate of the people we put on probation." Many of the judges spoke of the therapeutic effect of the "shock" of incarceration.[6]

The decision making of thirteen of the seventeen Minneapolis judges is legalistic and universalistic, and this seems to reinforce the effect of their greater orientation toward society. They feel little "closeness" to the defendant and thus, instead of acting as a buffer between them and the law, they act as if they *are* the law. The nature of the offense dominates these judges' considerations ("the offense itself is an indication of the man and his motives"), especially when the offense is a crime against person.[7] Thus, for example, though sentences in all offenses are more severe in Minneapolis than in Pittsburgh, this differential is much greater for armed robbery than for crimes against property. Moreover, ten of the seventeen Minneapolis judges even consider most crimes against property as "serious crimes."[8]

Universal criteria dominate these judges' decision making. They rarely regard individual characteristics (age, whether only property is involved in the crime, a black defendant's environment, a favorable family or employment situation, or addiction to alcohol or narcotics) as legitimate bases for making exceptions. They tend to follow a doctrine of equity rather formalistically: their consideration of individual and personal characteristics tends to be limited to highly unusual situations. Judge Slovack described such a situation:

> There are only a few situations in which I will give a fellow extra consideration. I had one in here on burglary and his attorney made a very emotional plea about the fellow's wife going blind and that he had to raise some money to help her. So I gave him probation.

In short their legalistic decision making is based on attributes of behavior rather than attributes of person. It tends to be based on the legal view of the act with little consideration of the context of the act—especially the personal context—or distinctions that might be made on this basis.

Many of these Minneapolis judges seem to be aware of nonlegalistic factors that they might consider, but they do not seem to feel that they are proper or relevant. For example, they feel that the stability of lower-income families is the proper concern of public agencies other than the criminal court.

Sixteen of the eighteen Pittsburgh judges seem to be oriented toward the defendant. Their view of most defendants is benevolent, and they describe their decision making as usually "giving the benefit of the doubt" to the defendant, "taking a chance on the defendant," or "err[ing] in the direction of being too soft." They feel that these "chances" are worth taking despite getting "taken in sometimes" because "some are rehabilitated." They explicitly seek to "help" them especially by "emphasiz[ing] probation and parole." Moreover, they tend to feel that they have a "closeness" and "kinship with the people that come into criminal court," that they are "more human" than the judges of the past, and that they have a "greater empathy and awareness of the [defendant's] problems" and "more insight into the different types of people" that come before them. Several judges explain this empathy and closeness as part of a general attachment to the "underdog," others explain it as a product of experience in their previous careers in political parties and government,[9] and some say it stems from their own minority-ethnic and lower-income backgrounds.[10]

The Pittsburgh judges' sentencing decisions for defendants who plead not guilty seem to be a manifestation of their greater orientation toward the defendant and his needs than toward "society."[11] The Pittsburgh judges' preference for using informal sources for information concerning the defendant—individual's intervention with the judge, the defense attorney's trial presentation, and the court staff—also seems to be a manifestation of this orientation.[12]

The Pittsburgh judges' closeness to and empathy with the defendant cause them to stand apart from the law and to act as a buffer between it and the people upon whom it is enforced. Most of them act as if they view the law primarily as a constraint within which they have to operate to achieve substantive justice for the defendant. Sixteen of the eighteen Pittsburgh judges tend to eschew a literal application of the law and prefer to exercise their discretion. They are critical of the law's inflexibilities, and they resist standardization of any of their sentencing decisions (even in offenses such as drunken driving and gambling).[13]

Most of the Pittsburgh judges tend to base their decisions on policy considerations rather than legalistic ones—especially policy considerations derived from criteria of "realism," "practicality," and pragmatism. Specifically, fourteen of the eighteen judges do not seem to be oriented toward institutional rehabilitation, punishment, or deterrence in their sentencing decisions because of their pragmatic and "realistic" attitudes concerning deterrence and the actual quality and effectiveness of prisons. For example, they feel that prisons today usually are ineffective in achieving rehabilitation or even deterrence because of their low quality ("not much is done for [defendants] in jail," "it's not helpful," the jails do "more damage" and defendants leave "worse off"). Moreover, they feel that this policy consideration is relevant to their decision making.

The judges' views on the gravity of offenses also seem to be based on "realistic" criteria. Twelve of the eighteen judges often tend to view criminal behavior as a manifestation of a dispute between two private parties rather than a conflict between an individual and society. Thus they often act as if they view this behavior less as a criminal act than as a civil act or a tort. From this perspective many acts appear less serious to the judges, especially when there is a special relationship between the defendant and the victim.[14] Similarly, thirteen of the eighteen Pittsburgh judges believe that many crimes against property that do not involve violence are "minor," involve "only money," and are "less serious than [harm to] a human being."

Thirteen of the eighteen judges feel that they should consider "realistic" and "practical" factors such as "how the defendants live," the heterogeneity of the city's population, and particularly the "mill town" character of the population in ascertaining the standards of proper conduct. Thus they often seem to base their sentencing decisions on extralegal standards—the standards of the group in which the offense occurred (for example, youths, blacks, lower-income persons, homosexuals, sex offenders and their "victims"). For example, several of the judges feel that many blacks often deserve "breaks" because of their "different code of morality." These judges seem to act as if they feel that in the context of a city with a heterogeneous population whose standards and values usually differ from those of the law, the frequent use of these extralegal standards is both more realistic and equitable than the "rule of law" (that is, the assumption that there is a single standard of conduct— the standard prescribed by law—to which all individuals are subjected). The use of these extralegal standards tends to reduce the gravity of these acts in their view because, according to these standards, these acts seem less inappropriate and less repugnant. Also, most of the Pittsburgh judges justify their use of informal courtroom procedures—which can potentially endanger a defendant's rights to due process, such as the verdict "acquitted plus costs"—on grounds that they introduce "compromise" and "practical considerations" into the law.

In addition to most of the judges' emphasis on policy, their decision making is nonlegalistic in that it tends to be particularistic. Sixteen of the eighteen judges base their sentencing decisions on a very wide range of individualistic and personal characteristics. The major criterion in their sentencing is the *individual defendant* rather than the *offense* that the defendant committed. Moreover, they feel that "everything counts"; it is the "whole system" and the "complete picture" that must be considered. They describe their decision making as "intuitive," "impressionistic," "unscientific," and "without rules of thumb." Thus their decision making seems to focus beyond individualistic differences in behavior. In addition, they make distinctions on the basis of differences in the defendants' personal attributes and characteristics (for example, the "type of person" he is and his relationship with his family); they attempt to establish an "idea of the 'person'" distinct from his conduct.

In part, they seem to base their sentencing decisions on the general criteria of the defendant's offense and the "type of person" he is, but they tend to act as if no general norm covers all individuals that fit one of these criteria. Within these general criteria they make numerous fine distinctions based on very diffuse and particularistic considerations (for example, "how the defendant conducted himself" during the commission of the offense, how "cooperative" he was when arrested, or the culpability and background of the victim, such as the degree of actual consent or female provocation and the past "purity" of a victim in a rape case).[15]

Thus these judges' decision making is characterized by numerous exceptions, which tend to be made in the direction of lenient decisions. Sixteen of the eighteen judges describe their decision making as being exceptional and expedient. They speak of seeking a basis for making an exception, giving defendants "breaks," and "helping" them. For example, Judge Guggliemi explained,

> If I can find a way—if the evidence ameliorates in some way—I'll give (the defendant) a "break." I suppose that it's unfair, but I try to help as many as I can. . . .
> I'm not constrained in sentencing by viewing defendants in set categories; I'm just trying to help them out.

The bases of these exceptions are not distinctions defined by the law as being relevant; they are distinctions based on the policy considerations that the judges feel are relevant to their decision making. These judges seem to consider one of the following characteristics as bases for making exceptions and giving "breaks": the absence of a prior record, youthfulness, the commission of "only" a crime against property, the defendant's "nonprofessional criminal" status, the environmental background of a black defendant, or the defendant's "favorable" employment or family situation.

The Explanation of the Judges' Views and Behavior

The behavior of the Pittsburgh and Minneapolis judges appears to be the indirect product of the cities' political systems. These systems influence judicial selection, leading to differential patterns of socialization and recruitment that in turn influence the judges' views and decision-making processes. The pre-judicial careers of most of the Pittsburgh judges in political parties and government and their minority-ethnic and lower-income backgrounds[16] seem to contribute to the development of the characteristic that many successful, local professional politicians possess—the ability to empathize and to grasp the motives of others by entering imaginatively into their feelings.

This pre-judicial experience (reinforced by the lack of highly legalistic experience) seems to have contributed to the nonlegalistic, particularistic character of the judges' decision making, their focus on police considerations, and their use of pragmatic criteria. In this experience in party- and policy-oriented government positions general rules usually seem to have been subordinated to achieve more immediate ends (for example, those of a constituent). In the milieu of the party organization, personal relationships were emphasized (especially with their constituents), and the judges seem to have focused on particular and tangible entities. Their successes in this milieu depended largely on their ability to operate within personal relationships. It depended on *whom* they knew, rather than what they knew. Abstractions such as "the good of society as a whole" seem to have been of little concern to them.

Thus their client relationships were usually characterized by expedient, exceptional, benevolent, and affirmative decisions that were the antithesis of legalistic behavior. Their decisions focused on interpersonal relationships and involved a great deal of discretion with little attention given to general rules. Indeed, a primary task of local party workers is to view a situation in personal terms, to dispense favors, and to make exceptions rather than to apply legal rules. It is usually their job to say "yes," particularly to an individual who has a problem or who is in trouble. The Pittsburgh judges seem to have brought many of these patterns to the bench with them.

The predominantly legalistic pre-judicial careers of most of the Minneapolis judges and their predominantly middle-class northern-European–Protestant backgrounds seem to have contributed to the development of their greater orientation toward "society" than toward the defendant. In their careers few had contact with individuals from lower-income backgrounds. Their experience in predominantly business-oriented private practice typically involved major societal institutions such as the "law," corporations, and commercial transactions.

This pre-judicial experience (reinforced by their lack of party policy-oriented experiences) seems to have contributed to the legalistic and universalistic character of their decision making and their eschewal of policy considerations. In this milieu, rules are generally emphasized, especially legalistic ones; these rules were used to maintain and protect these societal institutions. Learning to "get around" involved skill in operating in a context of rules. Their success seems to have depended more on their objective achievements and skills than on personal relationships. Furthermore, the predominantly middle-class background of these judges may in itself have contributed directly to the development of their universalistic decision making and their emphasis on the importance of laws.

Both the judges' social backgrounds and pre-judicial career experiences seem to have influenced their decision making. However, in both cities the decision making of the judges with cross-cutting backgrounds and experiences in effect serves as a control, and it seems to indicate that pre-judicial career experiences have been the more important influence. The decision making of the few Pittsburgh judges with middle-class Protestant backgrounds who also had careers in party and government positions tends to be oriented toward the defendant, particularistic, and based on policy considerations. Unfortunately all of the Pittsburgh judges with minority-ethnic and lower-class backgrounds also had party and government careers, and thus this conclusion cannot be tested with both variables independently controlled, but it can be in Minneapolis. The decision making of the few Minneapolis judges with middle-class northern-European–Protestant backgrounds who had less legalistic careers tends to be less oriented toward "society" and less legalistic and universalistic than that of most of the other Minneapolis judges.

The covariation of the dominant socialization and recruitment patterns of the judges in each city and their decision-making process suggests a causal linkage as the best available explanation. This is especially suggested by the deviant socialization and recruitment patterns, which in effect serve as controls; in each city, interview and sentencing data indicate that the decision making of the judges whose socialization and recruitment patterns deviate from the dominant pattern also tends to deviate significantly from that of most of the city's judges. In Pittsburgh the few judges with little party or policy experience tend to be less oriented toward the defendant, less particularistic, less pragmatic, and less policy-oriented than most of the other Pittsburgh judges. In Minneapolis the few judges with less legal experience and more political experience than most of their colleagues tend to be less oriented toward society and their professional peers, less legalistic, and less universalistic than most of the other Minneapolis judges.

We have seen how the judges' views and decision-making processes, influenced by their socialization and recruitment patterns, structure sentencing decisions. The Pittsburgh judges' predominant orientation toward the defendant, their tendency to "empathize" with many of the defendants, to act as a buffer between the law and the people upon whom it is enforced, seem to make leniency "natural." Their tendency to base decisions on "realistic" policy considerations (the defendant's background, the effect of the crime, the standards of proper conduct of the group in which the offense occurred) reduces the gravity of many of the defendant's acts in the judges' minds. Their emphasis on individualistic and personal characteristics leads them to view many defendants as "exceptional" and thus deserving of a "break."

In contrast, the various elements of the Minneapolis judges' views and decision-making processes seem to cumulatively contribute to severe sentencing decisions. Their predominant orientation toward "society," which leads them to emphasize its protection, their view of both crimes against person and crimes against property as very serious, and their tendency to be critical of defendants who plead not guilty seem to shape their severe sentencing decisions. This is reinforced by their low degree of empathy for most defendants and their belief in the effectiveness of institutional rehabilitation and penal deterrence. Mitigating exceptions are infrequent because judges' formalistic decision making rarely allows for consideration of personal characteristics, and because of their belief in the standards of conduct prescribed by law. The judges' orientation toward the goals of their professional peers (such as maximum indeterminate terms of incarceration and uniform severe sentencing for prostitution) contribute to severe decisions, as does their reliance on formal sources of information concerning defendants, which, unlike informal sources, provide them with both mitigating and aggravating information.

The covariation in both cities of the judges' views and decision-making processes and the ultimate substance of these decisions suggests this linkage, but it does not demonstrate it. Nevertheless, the evidence presented in this section and above seems to suggest this linkage as the best available explanation. Also, there are several additional pieces of evidence that seem to further suggest the existence of linkage between the cities' political and judicial selection systems, the judges' socialization and recruitment patterns, the judges' views and decision-making processes, and finally their sentencing decisions. Some of this evidence in effect allows us to partially test this conclusion by controlling for other possible explanatory variables. First, in each city there is a dominant pattern in the judges' attitudes and decision-making processes, which seems to represent a "system." This seems to indicate that the judges' attitudes and decisions are the product of structural factors, such as the influence of the cities' political system on judicial selection and judicial socialization and recruitment, rather than simply the product of the individual personal characteristics of the eighteen judges in each city.

Second, the characteristics and the sentencing decisions of the Pittsburgh "visiting" judges seem to further suggest the existence of linkage between a city's political and judicial selection system, socialization and recruitment, and judicial decisions. In addition to the three Pittsburgh judges regularly assigned to the criminal bench on a rotating basis, three or four "visiting" judges from rural counties in western Pennsylvania usually hear criminal cases in Pittsburgh. These are the same type of cases heard by the Pittsburgh judges and are tried by the same group of prosecutors and defense lawyers. Therefore the "visiting" judges' sentencing decisions in effect can serve as a limited control to test the validity of the suggested linkage between political systems and sentencing decisions.

The political systems of the rural areas from which the visiting judges come are very different from Pittsburgh's. The visiting judges' social backgrounds and pre-judicial careers are also different. Conservative and business-oriented Republican party organizations dominate these areas. A high proportion of both the population and political leadership in these areas is Protestant and of northern European background. In comparison with the Pittsburgh judges, a smaller proportion of the "visiting" judges had pre-judicial experience in public positions and a smaller proportion were active in a political party. Most were predominantly in private legal practice, and they were selected more *by* the Republican party than *from* the party. The visiting judges' sentencing decisions are less lenient than those of the Pittsburgh judges. There is no direct evidence that these different political systems and different social

backgrounds and career experiences are the primary factors accounting for the visiting judges' different sentencing decisions, but it is the explanation most often
offered by attorneys and other participants in the Pittsburgh courts and by the Pittsburgh judges themselves.[17]

Third, an additional piece of evidence of the linkage suggested here is the findings of studies of the way a city's political system affects such services as police,
education, welfare, and urban renewal. These studies indicate that while there is usually little day-to-day political direction of these services, many of the policies of
those administering the services reflect the values of the city's political system. Often
this seems to be a result of the selection by the political system of the top administrators of these services. For example, the mayor or city council's criteria and goals
in selecting a police chief (the "most professional" person, an "outsider," an
"insider" who gets along with the people in the department, or a person "close to
the party") are likely to affect the subsequent policies that the chief pursues. This
also seems to be true of the school board's or mayor's choice of a school superintendent. Similarly, the influence of the Pittsburgh and Minneapolis political systems
on judicial behavior has been indirect and through their effect on judicial selection.
Indeed, the specific outcomes of their effect probably have been largely unintended.
As already stated, Pittsburgh citizens tend to accept pro-union and liberal, social welfare policies, but Minneapolitans do not. However, no elements of either city's political system have consciously sought to develop the judicial decision making that
exists in each city. For example, the Pittsburgh political parties have not sought to
develop a criminal court bench that follows informal procedures and particularistic
and pragmatic decision making producing lenient sentencing decisions. They view
these positions on common court pleas primarily as sources of rewards for leading
party members. Only secondarily do they hope that the judges will decide the rare
policy-related civil cases favorably for the party or city administration. Similarly,
neither the Minneapolis parties (which play almost no role in judicial selection) nor
the bar association have sought to develop a criminal court bench that follows formal
procedures and formalistic decision making producing severe sentencing decisions.
The bar association is primarily concerned with keeping judicial selection out of partisan politics and within its own control, and with the selection of lawyers with the
preferred party affiliation and social, career, and bar association backgrounds.

Fourth, several similarities in the political systems of Pittsburgh and Minneapolis
and their judges' behavior are indirectly and tentatively suggestive of the linkage
between the two factors. The formal trial procedures and formal sources of information concerning the defendant that the Minneapolis judges use are generally advocated by professional and reform judicial organizations. By contrast, the informal
trial procedures and informal sources of information concerning the defendant that
the Pittsburgh judges use are generally criticized by professional and reform judicial
organizations. Patterns somewhat similar to these forms of judicial behavior seem to
exist in each city's political system. Minneapolis' political system is characterized
by procedures advocated by professional and reform organizations in city government (nonpartisan elections, widespread popular participation in governmental and
party decision making, frequent referenda and grass roots party nomination procedures, merit recruitment and appointments, and an emphasis on procedures as important ends in themselves). In contrast, Pittsburgh's political system is characterized by

procedures that are generally criticized by most of these professional and reform organizations (partisan elections, hierarchical control of government and party decision making, and party recruitment and appointments).

Some alternative explanations also should be noted. Recent studies have indicated the importance of political factors in judicial decision making. However, political influence does not seem to shape the behavior of the Pittsburgh and Minneapolis judges in criminal court. Almost all common-felony defendants have no influence because they are literally on the bottom rung of society. Typically they are young lower-income males, often from a minority group. In other cases in which defendants do have political influence, these judges' decisions may be shaped by it (though it seems less likely to occur in Minneapolis). For example, organized labor is quite influential in Pittsburgh, and almost all of the judges are reluctant to preside over a case involving a union (especially strike injunction requests) because they are wary of taking the "wrong" position.

Studies have also suggested that judges' social backgrounds significantly shape their decisions. Thus it is possible that the Pittsburgh judges are lenient primarily because of their predominant minority-ethnic backgrounds and the Minneapolis judges are more severe primarily because of their northern-European–Protestant backgrounds. However, two other explanations regarding the effect of the judges' ethnicity on their sentencing decisions are suggested by some control data and by data on the ethnicity of the courts and the cities as a whole and seem more persuasive. First, as the data above—and especially the controls provided by the deviant instances—seem to suggest, both the judges' pre-judicial career experiences and their social background seem to have influenced their decision making, but in both cities the former seems to have been the more important influence. Second, any relationship between the judges' background characteristics and their decision making seems to be indirect. The crucial intervening variable seems to be the city's political system and its influence on judicial selection, recruitment, and socialization. Judges with these social and career backgrounds are recruited by the city's political and judicial selection systems. The ethnic composition of the bench in each city can serve as a partial test of the intervening impact of these political and judicial selection systems on judicial decision making. This composition is more reflective of the influence of particular groups in the city's political system than it is of the precise ethnic composition of the city's population.[18]

Evaluating the Courts and Some Policy Implications

This analysis of the Pittsburgh and Minneapolis judges' decision making in criminal court indicates some of the consequences of these cities' political systems and methods of judicial selection. However, to more fully understand these consequences, some evaluation of these judges' decisions in themselves is necessary. To what degree and in what manner does each pattern of decisions (more lenient in Pittsburgh and more severe in Minneapolis) affect the defendants in crime in the community, all other factors being equal? Which type of sentencing has the greatest tendency to rehabilitate the defendant; which is most likely to reduce recidivism and deter future criminals?

My analysis elsewhere of the factors affecting recidivism indicated that both nonexperimental and experimental studies found that offenders who have received probation generally have significantly lower rates of recidivism than those who have been incarcerated.[19] They also found that of those incarcerated, the offenders who have received a shorter term of incarceration generally have a somewhat lower recidivism rate than those who receive longer terms. With a few exceptions, these differences persist when one controls for factors such as type of offense, type of community, the offender's age, race, and number of previous convictions. However, for those with certain characteristics there are some significant variations in the overall recidivism rates when type of treatment is controlled (for example, for all those who receive probation the recidivism rates are highest for the youngest and for those with the greatest prior record).

On this basis one might conclude that the Pittsburgh judges' decisions on the whole tend to contribute more effectively to reduced recidivism because they grant probation more frequently. However, their frequent grants of probation for individuals with a high probability of recidivating (for example, those with a prior record and blacks) probably does not effectively contribute to reduced recidivism. By contrast, the Minneapolis judges' decisions for these specific individuals may contribute to reduced recidivism more effectively. Moreover, there are other goals of the criminal court in addition to reduced recidivism, and there is considerable tension among them.

Thus recidivism data do not present a complete means of evaluating criminal courts. Ultimately the Pittsburgh and Minneapolis criminal court judges also must be evaluated directly in terms of their behavior—lenient decisions and informal procedures in Pittsburgh and more severe decisions and formal procedures in Minneapolis. It is possible to make a persuasive case for the Minneapolis criminal court in terms of the goals of equality and the "rule of law," all other things being equal. In actual policy situations, however, "all other things" are rarely equal. Realistic policy choices are never made in an ideal context, but in a real, and therefore imperfect, context. Most big-city criminal courts, including those in this study, operate in a context of a heterogeneous population that includes a large proportion of lower-class and minority-group individuals.

In this context, it is possible to make a persuasive case for the Pittsburgh criminal court whose judges often tend to base their decisions on the standards of conduct of the group in which the offense occurred. Indeed, the assumptions of the "rule of law" (that all men are equal or similar) seldom square with the realities of our urban context. Nevertheless, despite the benevolence of intention, criminal court decisions based on these extralegal standards may tend to have serious unintended consequences. John Dollard suggests this with respect to criminal justice in the South. He concludes that among the institutional features of southern life that sustain the high level of aggression among poor blacks is the double standard of justice—viewing "black crime" as less serious than "white crime."

This tension between the style of criminal court that may be preferable in an ideal context and that which may be necessary because of the actual context and the difficulties inherent in the latter style seems to be a product of a more general tension in the larger cities of our society and in our theory of democracy. According to the "rule of law" and democratic theory, we ought to ignore class differences, but urban realities are such that it is difficult. "Two cultures" exist in our large cities—a large lower-class as well as the dominant middle-class culture—but our theory of democracy assumes that we will be a society with one culture. It assumes that we will be able and willing to live together under a single set of rules or standards. The idea that two sets of rules may be necessary—one for the middle class and the other for the lower class—cannot be reconciled to our theory.

This tension indicates that any evaluation or policy prescription concerning the criminal courts in our large cities must consider the existence of these "two cultures." The Minneapolis judges tend to adhere to the "rule of law," but they fail to consider these "two cultures." On the other hand, the Pittsburgh judges, in part, often tend to base their decisions on the existence of these "two cultures," but they usually fail to adhere to the "rule of law." These shortcomings in both courts are thus largely a function of these "two cultures"—a factor *external* to these court systems. Any prescription for remedying these inadequacies should be primarily directed at this external factor and more basic cause. As long as these "two cultures" exist, there will be a tension in our theory of democracy, and the criminal courts will have to ignore either the "rule of law" or the realities of urban life.

Notes

1. The only names that Democratic governors have considered for a judicial appointment are those that came from the Pittsburgh organization. Some Republican governors have requested, and sometimes followed, the Pittsburgh Bar Association's recommendations, but its influence has been limited even during Republican state administrations (including reform-oriented administrations). Its recommendations have first been cleared (and sometimes modified) by the Pittsburgh Republican organization, and then often they were ultimately blocked by the Democratic organization, which has successfully opposed interim Republican judicial appointments at the next election several times since 1950.
2. Informal discussions between the judge and attorneys occur in Minneapolis, but they are infrequent in Pittsburgh. Moreover, in both cities these discussions concern the defendant's sentence and are dominated by the judge rather than the prosecutors.
3. For example, Judge White explained his severe sentences for aggravated forgery: "I feel that once a fellow is a 'paper hanger' (that is, a check forger), he'll always be one. So the best thing is to get him off the street." In a comparison of the frequency with which the other Minneapolis judges grant probation for aggravated forgery, Judge White ranks last with 11.1 percent (11). All the judges' names in this study are pseudonyms that were chosen to reflect the actual ethnic and religious backgrounds of the judges.
4. Twelve of the seventeen judges feel that trials should not be used by the "guilty" to escape a conviction. Thus if a defendant pleads not guilty and is then convicted, they are critical of him because "he has put the state through the expense of a trial." They then feel that his plea indicated "a wrong attitude" or that he "wasn't repentant" and that he "deserves less consideration" in sentencing. Minneapolis defense attorneys are aware of the judges' attitudes and behavior concerning pleas of not guilty, and thus they usually discourage their clients from pleading not guilty. Only 14.4 percent of the defendants in this study's sample pleaded not guilty in Minneapolis, but 71.1 percent of the Pittsburgh sample pleaded not guilty.
5. For example, in the early 1960s the Minnesota Department of Correction requested that those defendants incarcerated by the Minneapolis judges receive uniform terms to achieve greater consistency and thus make prisoners more manageable. They specifically requested that all the incarcerated defendants receive maximum indeterminate terms because this would achieve consistency and would also give them the discretion to determine the prisoner's exact term. They argued that prison and parole officials were in the

best position to make these determinations because they could observe the prisoner closely and because of their professional expertise. Within a few years many of the Minneapolis judges began to comply with these requests to a great extent because they agreed with the Correction Department's view—they felt that sentences ought to be consistent, and they respected the professional expertise of the correction authorities.

6. For example, Judge Jensen said, "Many times those young fellows need the jolt that comes when the jail door closes behind them. So I give them probation coupled with six to twelve months in the workhouse."

7. Judge Edwards' view seems to be typical: "If the crime involves violence—like robbery or rape—then the defendant is a danger to society, and I won't place him on probation. For example, in a rape case I have no sympathy for the defendant because I have two daughters and I know the feeling I would have if they were attacked."

8. For example, Judge Swanson said, "In auto theft you always get such crummy people. It's not that they just drive the car around and abandon it—they do it as a steady practice. . . . Burglary is serious; it's just an awful experience to have someone in your house. I know people that have been burglarized, and it's terrible. Forgery is awful because if you can't trust another person's money (that is, check) then business couldn't be carried on. I probably feel this way because my (pre-judicial) office practice dealt with banking, real estate, trust, and corporate work."

9. For example, Judge Bloom told an interviewer, "A judge should feel a kinship with the people that come into criminal court. Through my thirty years of active political work I worked with Negroes and other poor persons, and I developed a kinship with them and an awareness of their problems."

10. Judge Guggliemi explained: "I was brought up in a semi-industrial neighborhood, and my father worked in the mills. I was a solicitor for the township, so I got to know people with problems more intimately. I learned that it's really tough for some people just to get along in this world. . . . You also see this inability to cope with life in the people in (criminal) court, particularly the minorities."

11. They penalize defendants who plead not guilty much less frequently than do the Minneapolis judges, and, on the whole, their decisions for such defendants are only slightly more severe than those for defendants who plead guilty. (In Pittsburgh, unlike Minneapolis, most defendants are not reluctant to plead not guilty. In the Pittsburgh sample, 71.1 percent pleaded not guilty, but only 14.4 percent pleaded not guilty in Minneapolis.) Also, eleven of the eighteen Pittsburgh judges state that they usually do not penalize defendants who plead not guilty. Most of the judges seem to view not-guilty pleas in terms of "fairness to the defendant" rather than "the expense to the state."

12. These informal sources focus almost exclusively on mitigating information. By contrast, the formal presentence report is made by a "third party," the probation officer, whose professional ethos stresses objectivity and it includes both mitigating *and* aggravating information. The informal sources—with the partial exception of the court staff—do not attempt to be objective.

13. Judge Bloom told an interviewer, "I don't feel bound to follow suggestions for uniform sentencing. An individual judge should not be obligated by another judge's system. For example, some send a sodomy case to jail, but I don't. If the legislature had wanted us to sentence all the same, it would have said so; it wanted the sentence determined by each individual judge. I was elected to exercise my discretion."

14. Some of these "special" relationships include prior acquaintance and sometimes strong ties (for example, as a relative, friend, or lover), the victim's physical or sexual provocation (for example, in assault or rape cases), monetary provocation (for example, in forged check or theft cases), or the "victim's" desire for revenge.

15. In crimes against person the nature of the offense tends to become the dominant criterion for the decisions of fourteen of the eighteen judges and thus tends to operate as a general standard. However, these judges significantly qualify the generality of this standard by making several distinctions—most of which are diffuse—among various types of crimes against person (for example, the degree of viciousness involved in the violence, the degree of aggressiveness, the degree of passion, whether a weapon was involved, the degree of

provocation involved, or whether the act caused an injury). For example, a comparison of the Pittsburgh and Minneapolis judges' sentencing decisions for armed robbery indicates that the Pittsburgh judges frequently qualify this general standard and the Minneapolis judges almost always adhere to it.

16. Four of the Pittsburgh judges are Jewish (two of whom were foreign-born), seven are Catholic (one of whom was foreign-born, three have Irish backgrounds, two Italian, one Polish, one Hungarian), one is black, and six are white Protestants. Eleven of the judges have working-class backgrounds and seven have middle-class backgrounds.

17. For example, most Pittsburgh judges contrasted the standards upon which they and the "visiting" judges base their decisions: " 'Visiting' judges have a different view because they come from smaller towns with homogeneous populations: ours [Pittsburgh's] is very heterogeneous; . . . it's a mill town." The view of a black defense attorney is also typical: " 'Visiting' judges come from the smaller rural counties . . . , and it affects their evaluations. They think that if a man is guilty, then he's guilty. Our [local] judges have different backgrounds, and they are more kindhearted; they make social judgments."

18. For example, in Pittsburgh a much higher proportion of the bench is Jewish (four of the eighteen judges) and Irish (three of the eighteen) than is the city's population. (Approximately 4 percent of the city's population is Jewish and 10 percent is Irish.) There are more Protestants than Catholics in Minneapolis, but the proportion of Catholics on the bench in Minneapolis (two of the eighteen judges) is much lower than that of the city's population (approximately 37 percent of the population).

19. M. A. Levin, "Policy Evaluation and Recidivism," *Law and Society Review,* August 1971. This analysis is based on studies of over twenty-two different court and prison jurisdictions, including several studies of recidivism in California's thirteen largest counties.

ARTICLE

19

Maintaining the Myth of Individualized Justice: Probation Presentence Reports

John Rosecrance

The presentence investigation has been justified so that judges can individualize sentences to fit the particular circumstances of the offender as well as the offense. In many states probation officers are required to submit presentence reports prior to sentencing in all felony cases. But what is the function of these reports in a system where plea bargaining is so dominant? Is justice really individualized, or are sentence recommendations actually influenced by the administrative context of the system?

The Justice Department estimates that over 1 million probation presentence reports are submitted annually to criminal courts in the United States. The role of probation officers in the presentence process traditionally has been considered important. After examining criminal courts in the United States, a panel of investigators concluded: "Probation officers are attached to most modern felony courts; presentence reports containing their recommendations are commonly provided and these recommendations are usually followed" (Blumstein, Martin, and Holt 1983). Judges view presentence reports as an integral part of sentencing, calling them "the best guide to intelligent sentencing" (Murrah 1963: 67) and "one of the most important developments in criminal law during the twentieth century" (Hogarth 1971: 246).

Researchers agree that a strong correlation exists between probation recommendations (contained in presentence reports) and judicial sentencing. In a seminal study of judicial decision making, Carter and Wilkins (1967) found 95 percent agreement between probation recommendations and sentence disposition when the officer recommended probation and 88 percent agreement when the officer opposed probation. Hagan (1975), after controlling for related variables, reported a direct correlation of .72 between probation recommendation and sentencing. Walsh (1985) found a similar correlation of .807.

Source: From John Rosecrance, "Maintaining the Myth of Individualized Justice: Probation Presentence Reports," *Justice Quarterly,* 5 (June 1988), pp. 235–256. Footnotes and some references deleted. Reprinted with permission of the Academy of Criminal Justice Sciences.

Although there is no controversy about the correlation between probation recommendation and judicial outcome, scholars disagree as to the actual influence of probation officers in the sentencing process. That is, there is no consensus regarding the importance of the presentence investigator in influencing sentencing outcomes. On the one hand, Myers (1979: 538) contends that the "important role played by probation officer recommendation argues for greater theoretical and empirical attention to these officers." Walsh (1985: 363) concludes that "judges lean heavily on the professional advice of probation." On the other hand, Kingsnorth and Rizzo (1979) report that probation recommendations have been supplanted by plea bargaining and that the probation officer is "largely superfluous." Hagan, Hewitt, and Alwin (1979), after reporting a direct correlation between recommendation and sentence, contend that the "influence of the probation officer in the presentence process is subordinate to that of the prosecutor" and that probation involvement is "often ceremonial."

My research builds on the latter perspective and suggests that probation presentence reports do not influence judicial sentencing significantly but serve to maintain the myth that criminal courts dispense individualized justice. On the basis of an analysis of probation practices in California, I will demonstrate that the presentence report, long considered an instrument for the promotion of individualized sentencing by the court, actually de-emphasizes individual characteristics and affirms the primacy of instant offense and prior criminal record as sentencing determinants. The present study was concerned with probation in California; whether its findings can be applied to other jurisdictions is not known. California's probation system is the nation's largest, however, and the experiences of that system could prove instructive to other jurisdictions.

In many California counties (as in other jurisdictions throughout the United States) crowded court calendars, determinate sentencing guidelines, and increasingly conservative philosophies have made it difficult for judges to consider individual offenders' characteristics thoroughly. Thus judges, working in tandem with district attorneys, emphasize the legal variables of offense and criminal record at sentencing. Probation officers function as employees of the court; generally they respond to judicial cues and emphasize similar variables in their presentence investigations. The probation officers' relationship to the court is ancillary; their status in relation to judges and other attorneys is subordinate. This does not mean that probation officers are completely passive; individual styles and personal philosophies influence their reports. Idiosyncratic approaches, however, usually are reserved for a few special cases. The vast majority of "normal" (Sudnow 1965) cases are handled in a manner that follows relatively uniform patterns.

Hughes's (1958) work provides a useful perspective for understanding the relationship between probation officers' status and their presentence duties. According to Hughes, occupational duties within institutions often serve to maintain symbiotic status relationships as those in higher-status positions pass on lesser duties to subordinates. Other researchers (Blumberg 1967; Neubauer 1974; Rosecrance 1985) have demonstrated that although judges may give lip service to the significance of presentence investigations, they remain suspicious of the probation officers' lack of legal training and the hearsay nature of the reports. Walker (1985) maintains that in highly visible cases judges tend to disregard the probation reports entirely. Thus the judiciary, by delegating the collection of routine information to probation officers, reaffirms its authority and legitimacy. In this context, the responsibility for compiling presentence reports can be considered a "dirty-work" assignment that is devalued by the judiciary. Judges expect probation officers to submit noncontroversial reports that provide a facade of information, accompanied by bottom-line recommendations that do not deviate significantly from a consideration of offense and prior record. The research findings in this paper will show how probation officers work to achieve this goal.

In view of the large number of presentence reports submitted, it is surprising that so little information about the presentation investigation process is available. The factors used in arriving at a sentencing recommendation, the decision to include certain information, and the methods used in collecting data have not been described. The world of presentence investigators has not been explored by social science researchers. We lack research about the officers who prepare presentence reports, and hardly understand how they think and feel about those reports. The organizational dynamics and the status positions that influence presentence investigators have not been identified prominently. In this article I intend to place probation officers' actions within a framework that will increase the existing knowledge of the presentence process. My research is informed by fifteen years of experience as a probation officer, during which time I submitted hundreds of presentence reports.

Although numerous studies of probation practices have been conducted, an ethnographic perspective rarely has been included in this body of research, particularly in regard to research dealing with presentence investigations. Although questionnaire techniques, survey data, and decision-making experiments have provided some information about presentence reports, qualitative data, which often are available only through an insider's perspective, are notably lacking. The subtle strategies and informal practices used routinely in preparing presentence reports often are hidden from outside researchers.

The research findings emphasize the importance of *typing* in the compilation of public documents (presentence reports). In this paper "typing" refers to "the process by which one person (the agent) arrives at a private definition of another (the target)." A related activity, *designating,* occurs when "the typing agent reveals his attributions of the target to others." In the case of presentence investigations, private typings become designations when they are made part of an official court report. I will show that presentence recommendations are developed through a typing process in which individual offenders are subsumed into general dispositional categories. This process is influenced largely by probation officers' perceptions of factors that judicial figures consider appropriate; probation officers are aware that the ultimate purpose of their reports is to please the court. These perceptions are based on prior experience and are reinforced through judicial feedback.

Methods

The major sources of data used in this study were drawn from interviews with probation officers. Prior experience facilitated my ability to interpret the data. Interviews were conducted in two three-week periods during 1984 and 1985 in two medium-sized California counties. Both jurisdictions were governed by state determinate sentencing policies; in each, the district attorney's office remained active during sentencing and generally offered specific recommendations. I did not conduct a random sample but tried instead to interview all those who compiled adult presentence reports. In the two counties in question, officers who compiled presentence reports did not supervise defendants.

Not all presentence writers agreed to talk with me; they cited busy schedules, lack of interest, or fear that I was a spy for the administration. Even so, I was able to interview thirty-seven presentence investigators, approximately 75 percent of the total number of such employees in the two counties. The officers interviewed included eight women and twenty-nine men with a median age of 38.5 years, whose probation experience ranged from one year to twenty-seven years. Their educational background generally included a bachelor's degree in a liberal arts subject (four had degrees in criminal justice, one in social work). Typically the officers regarded probation work as a "job" rather than a profession. With only a few exceptions, they did not read professional journals or attend probation association conventions.

The respondents generally were supportive of my research and frequently commented that probation work had never been described adequately. My status as a former probation officer enhanced the interview process greatly. Because I could identify with their experiences, officers were candid, and I was able to collect qualitative data that reflected accurately the participants' perspectives. During the interviews I attempted to discover how probation officers conducted their presentence investigations. I wanted to know when a sentencing recommendation was decided, to ascertain which variables influenced a sentencing recommendation decision, and to learn how probation officers defined their role in the sentencing process.

Although the interviews were informal, I asked each of the probation officers the following questions:

1. What steps do you take in compiling a presentence report?
2. What is the first thing you do upon receiving a referral?
3. What do you learn from interviews with the defendant?
4. Which part of the process (in your opinion) is the most important?
5. Who reads your reports?
6. Which part of the report do the judges feel is most important?
7. How do your reports influence the judge?
8. What feedback do you get from the judge, the district attorney, the defense attorney, the defendant, your supervisor?

In addition to interviewing probation officers, I questioned six probation supervisors and seven judges on their views about how presentence reports were conducted.

• • •

Findings

In the great majority of presentence investigations, the variables of present offense and prior criminal record determine the probation officer's final sentencing recommendations. The influence of these variables is so dominant that other considerations have minimal influence on probation recommendations. The chief rationale for this approach is "That's the way the judges want it." There are other styles of investigation; some officers attempt to consider factors in the defendant's social history, to reserve sentencing judgment until their investigations is complete, or to interject personal opinions. Elsewhere (Rosecrance 1987), I have developed a typology of presentence investigators that describes individual styles; these types include self-explanatory categories such as hard-liners, bleeding-heart liberals, and team players as well as mossbacks (those who are merely putting in their time) and mavericks (those who strive continually for independence).

All types of probation officers, however, seek to develop credibility with the court. Such reputation building is similar to that reported by McCleary (1978) in his study of parole officers. In order to develop rapport with the court, probation officers must submit reports that facilitate a smooth work flow. Probation officers assume that in the great majority of cases they can accomplish this goal by emphasizing offense and criminal record. Once the officers have established reputations as "producers," they have "earned" the right to some degree of discretion in their reporting. One investigation officer described this process succinctly: "When you've paid your dues, you're allowed some slack." Such discretion, however, is limited to a minority of cases, and in these "deviant" cases probation officers frequently allow social variables to influence their recommendation. In one report an experienced officer recommended probation for a convicted felon with a long prior record because the defendant's father agreed to pay for an intensive drug treatment program. In another case a probation officer decided that a first-time shoplifter had a "very bad attitude" and therefore recommended a stiff jail sentence rather than probation. Although these variations from normal procedure are interesting and important, they should not detract from our examination of an investigation process that is used in most cases.

On the basis of the research data, I found that the following patterns occur with sufficient regularity to be considered "typical." After considering offense and criminal record, probation officers place defendants into categories that represent the eventual court recommendation. This typing process occurs early in the course of presentence inquiry; the balance of the investigation is used to reaffirm the private typings that later will become official designations. In order to clarify the decision-making processes used by probation officers, I will delineate the three stages in a presentence investigation: (1) typing the defendant, (2) gathering further information, and (3) filing the report.

Typing the Defendant

A presentence investigation is initiated when the court orders the probation department to prepare a report on a criminal defendant. Usually the initial court referral contains such information as police reports, charges against the defendant, court proceedings, plea-bargaining agreements (if any), offenses in which the defendant has pleaded or has been found guilty, and the defendant's prior criminal record. Probation officers regard such information as relatively unambiguous and as part of the "official" record. The comment of a presentence investigator reflects the probation officer's perspective on the court referral:

> I consider the information in the court referral hard data. It tells me what I need to
> know about a case, without a lot of bullshit. I mean the guy has pled guilty to a

certain offense—he can't get out of that. He has such and such a prior record—there's no changing that. So much of the stuff we put in these reports is subjective and open to interpretation. It's good to have some solid information.

Armed with information in the court referral, probation officers begin to type the defendants assigned for presentence investigation. Defendants are classified into general types based on possible sentence recommendations; a probation officer's statement indicates that this process begins early in a presentence investigation.

Bottom line; it's the sentence recommendation that's important. That's what the judges and everybody wants to see. I start thinking about the recommendation as soon as I pick up the court referral. Why wait? The basic facts aren't going to change. Oh, I know some POs will tell you they weigh all the facts before coming up with a recommendation. But that's propaganda—we all start thinking recommendation right from the get-go.

At this stage in the investigation the factors known to probation officers are mainly legally relevant variables. The defendant's unique characteristics and special circumstances generally are unknown at this time. Although probation officers may know the offender's age, sex, and race, the relationship of these variables to the case is not yet apparent.

These initial typings are private definitions based on the officer's experience and knowledge of the court system. On occasion, officers discuss the case informally with their colleagues or supervisors when they are not sure of a particular typing. Until the report is complete, their typing remains a private designation. In most cases the probation officers type defendants by considering the known and relatively irrefutable variables of offense and prior record. Probation officers are convinced that judges and district attorneys are most concerned with that part of their reports. I heard the following comment (or versions thereof) on many occasions: "Judges read the offense section, glance at the prior record, and then flip to the back and see what we recommend." Officers indicated that during informal discussions with judges it was made clear that offense and prior record are the determinants of sentencing in most cases. In some instances judges consider extralegal variables, but the officers indicated that this occurs only in "unusual" cases with "special" circumstances. One such case involved a probation grant for a woman who killed her husband after she had been a victim of spouse battering.

Probation investigators are in regular contact with district attorneys and frequently discuss their investigations with them. In addition, district attorneys seem to have no compunction about calling the probation administration to complain about what they consider an inappropriate recommendation. Investigators agreed unanimously that district attorneys typically dismiss a defendant's social history as "immaterial" and want probation officers to stick to the legal facts.

Using offense and prior record as criteria, probation officers place defendants into dispositional (based on recommendation) types. In describing these types I have retained the terms used by probation officers themselves in the typing process. The following typology is community- (rather than researcher-) designated: (1) deal case, (2) diversion case, (3) joint case, (4) probation case with some jail time, (5) straight probation case. Within each of these dispositional types, probation officers designate the severity of punishment by labeling the case either lightweight or heavy-duty.

A designation of "lightweight" means that the defendant will be accorded some measure of leniency because the offense was minor, because the offender had no prior criminal record, or because the criminal activity (regardless of the penal code violation) was relatively innocuous. Heavy-duty cases receive more severe penalties because the offense, the offender, or the circumstances of the offense are deemed particularly serious. Diversion and straight-probation types generally are considered lightweight, while the majority of joint cases are considered heavy-duty. Cases involving personal violence invariably are designated as heavy-duty. Most misdemeanor cases in which the defendant has no prior criminal record or a relatively minor record are termed lightweight. If the defendant has an extensive criminal record, however, even misdemeanor cases can call for stiff penalties; therefore, such cases are considered heavy-duty. Certain felony cases can be regarded as lightweight if there was no violence, if the victim's loss was minimal, or if the defendant had no prior convictions. On occasion, even an offense like armed robbery can be considered lightweight. The following example (taken from an actual report) is one such instance: a first-time offender with a simulated gun held up a Seven-Eleven store and then returned to the scene, gave back the money, and asked the store employees to call the police.

The typings are general recommendations; specifics such as terms and conditions of probation or diversion and length of incarceration are worked out later in the investigation. The following discussion will clarify some of the criteria for arriving at a typing.

Deal cases involve situations in which a plea bargain exists. In California, many plea bargains specify specific sentencing stipulations; probation officers rarely recommend dispositions contrary to those stipulated in plea-bargaining agreements. Although probation officers allegedly are free to recommend a sentence different from that contained in the plea bargain, they have learned that such an action is unrealistic (and often counterproductive to their own interests) because judges inevitably uphold the primacy of sentence agreements. The following observation represents the probation officers' view of plea-bargaining deals.

> It's stupid to try and bust a deal. What's the percentage? Who needs the hassle? The judge always honors the deal—after all, he was part of it. Everyone, including the defendant, has already agreed. It's all nice and neat, all wrapped up. We are supposed to rubber-stamp the package—and we do. Everyone is better off that way.

Diversion cases typically involve relatively minor offenses committed by those with no prior record and are considered "a snap" by probation officers. In most cases, those referred for diversion have been screened already by the district attorney's office; the probation investigator merely agrees that they are eligible and therefore should be granted diversionary relief (and eventual dismissal of charges). In rare instances when there has been an oversight and the defendant is ineligible (because of prior criminal convictions), the probation officer informs the court, and criminal proceedings are resumed. Either situation involves minimal decision making by probation officers about what disposition to recommend. Presentence investigators approach diversion cases in a perfunctory, almost mechanical manner.

The last three typings generally refer to cases in which the sentencing recommendations are ambiguous and some decision making is required of probation officers. These types represent the major consequences of criminal sentencing: incarceration and/or probation. Those categorized as joint (prison) cases are denied probation; instead the investigator recommends an appropriate prison sentence. In certain instances the nature of the offense (for example, rape, murder, or arson) renders defendants legally ineligible for probation. In other situations, the defendants' prior record (especially felony convictions) makes it impossible to grant probation. In many cases the length of prison sentences has been set by legal statute and can be increased or decreased only marginally (depending on the aggravating or mitigating circumstances of the case).

In California, the majority of defendants sentenced to prison receive a middle term (between minimum and maximum); the length of time varies with the offense. Those cases that fall outside the middle term usually do so for reasons related to the offense (for example, using a weapon) or to the criminal record (prior felony convictions or, conversely, no prior criminal record). Those typed originally as joint cases are treated differently from other probation applicants: concerns with rehabilitation or with the defendant's life situation are no longer relevant, and proper punishment becomes the focal point of inquiry. This perspective was described as follows by a probation officer respondent: "Once I know so-and-so is a heavy-duty joint case I don't think in terms of rehabilitation or social planning. It becomes a matter of how long to salt the sucker away, and that's covered by the code."

For those who are typed as probation cases, the issue for the investigator becomes whether to recommend some time in jail as a condition of probation. This decision is made with reference to whether the case is lightweight or heavy-duty. Straight probation usually is reserved for those convicted of relatively innocuous offenses or for those without a prior criminal record (first-timers). Some probation officers admitted candidly that all things being equal, middle-class defendants are more likely than other social classes to receive straight probation. The split sentence (probation and jail time) has become popular and is a consideration in most misdemeanor and felony cases, especially when the defendant has a prior criminal record. In addition, there is a feeling that drug offenders should receive a jail sentence as part of probation to deter them from future drug use.

Once a probation officer has decided that "some jail time is in order," the ultimate recommendation includes that condition. Although the actual amount of time frequently is determined late in the case, the probation officer's opinion that a jail sentence should be imposed remains constant. The following comment typifies the sentiments of probation officers whom I have observed and also illustrates the imprecision of recommending a period of time in custody:

> It's not hard to figure out who needs some jail. The referral sheet can tell you that. What's hard to know is exactly how much time. Ninety days or six months—who knows what's fair? We put down some number but it is usually an arbitrary figure. No one has come up with a chart that correlates rehabilitation with jail time.

Compiling Further Information

Once an initial typing has been completed, the next investigative stage involves collecting further information about the defendant. During this stage most of the data to be collected consists of extralegal considerations. The defendant is interviewed and his or her social history is delineated. Probation officers frequently contact collateral sources such as school officials, victims, doctors, counselors, and relatives to learn more about the defendant's individual circumstances. This aspect of the presentence investigation involves considerable time and effort on the part of probation officers. Such information is gathered primarily to legitimate earlier probation officer typings or to satisfy judicial requirements; recommendations seldom are changed during this stage. A similar pattern was described by a presentence investigator:

> Interviewing these defendants and working up a social history takes time. In most cases it's really unnecessary since I've already decided what I am going to do. We all know that a recommendation is governed by the offense and prior record. All the rest is just stuffing to fill out the court report, to make the judge look like he's got all the facts.

Presentence interviews with defendants (a required part of the investigation) frequently are routine interactions that were described by a probation officer as "anticlimatic." These interviews invariably are conducted in settings familiar to probation officers, such as jail interviewing rooms or probation department offices. Because the participants lack trust in each other, discussions rarely are candid and open. Probation officers are afraid of being conned or manipulated because they assume that defendants "will say anything to save themselves." Defendants are trying to present themselves in a favorable light and are wary of divulging any information that might be used against them.

It is assumed implicitly in the interview process that probation officers act as interrogators and defendants as respondents. Because presentence investigators select the questions, they control the course of the interview and elicit the kind of responses that serve to substantiate their original defendant typings. A probationer described his presentence interview to me as follows:

> I knew what the PO wanted me to say. She had me pegged as a nice middle-class kid who had fallen in with a bad crowd. So that's how I came off. I was contrite, a real boy scout who had learned his lesson. What an acting job! I figured if I didn't act up I'd get probation.

A probation officer related how she conducted presentence interviews:

> I'm always in charge during the interviews. I know what questions to ask in order to fill out my report. The defendants respond just about the way I expect them to. They hardly ever surprise me.

On occasion, prospective probationers refuse to go along with structured presentence interviews. Some offenders either attempt to control the interview or are openly hostile to probation officers. Defendants who try to dominate interviews often can be dissuaded by reminders such as "I don't think you really appreciate the seriousness of your situation" or "I'm the one who asks the questions here." Some defendants, however, show blatant disrespect for the court process by flaunting a disregard for possible sanctions.

Most probation officers have interviewed some defendants who simply don't seem to care what happens to them. A defendant once informed an investigation officer: "I don't give a fuck what you motherfuckers try and do to me. I'm going to do what I fuckin' well please. Take your probation and stick it." Another defendant told her probation officer: "I'm going to shoot up every chance I get. I need my fix more than I need probation." Probation officers categorize belligerent defendants and those unwilling to "play the probation game" as dangerous or irrational. Frequently in these situations the investigator's initial typing is no longer valid, and probation either will be denied or will be structured stringently. Most interviews, however, proceed in a predictable manner as probation officers collect information that will be included in the section of the report termed "defendant's statement."

Although some defendants submit written comments, most of their statements actually are formulated by the probation officer. In a sociological sense, the defendant's statement can be considered an "account." While conducting presentence interviews, probation officers typically attempt to shape the defendant's account to fit their own preconceived typing. Many probation officers believe that the defendant's attitude toward the offense and toward the future prospects for leading a law-abiding life are the most important parts of the statement. In most presentence investigations the probation investigator identifies and interprets the defendant's subjective attitudes and then incorporates them into the report. Using this procedure, probation officers look for and can report attitudes that "logically fit" with their final sentencing recommendation.

Defendants who have been typed as prison cases typically are portrayed as holding socially unacceptable attitudes about their criminal actions and unrealistic or negative attitudes about future prospects for living an upright life. Conversely, those who have been typed as probation material are described as having acceptable attitudes, such as contriteness about the present offense and optimism about their ability to lead a crime-free life. The structuring of accounts about defendant attitudes was described by a presentence investigator in the following manner:

> When POs talk about the defendant's attitude we really mean how that attitude relates to the case. Naturally I'm not going to write about what a wonderful attitude the guy has—how sincere he seems—and then recommend sending him to the joint. That wouldn't make sense. The judges want consistency. If a guy has a shitty attitude but is going to get probation anyway, there's no percentage in playing up his probation problem.

In most cases the presentence interview is the only contact between the investigating officer and the defendant. The brevity of this contact and the lack of postreport interaction foster a legalistic perspective. Investigators are concerned mainly with "getting the case through court" rather than with special problems related to supervising probationers on a long-term basis. One-time-only interviews rarely allow probation officers to become emotionally involved with their cases; the personal and individual aspects of the defendant's personality generally are not manifested during a half-hour presentence interview. For many probation officers the emotional distance from offenders is one of the benefits of working in presentence units. Such an opinion was expressed by an investigation officer: "I really like the one-shot-only part of this job. I don't have time to get caught up with the clients. I can deal with facts and not worry about individual personalities."

The probation officer has wide discretion in the type of collateral information that is collected from sources other than the defendant or the official record. Although a defendant's social history must be sketched in the presentence report, the supplementation of that history is left to individual investigators. There are few established guidelines for the investigating officer to follow, except that the psychiatric or psychological reports should be submitted when there is compelling evidence that the offender is mentally disturbed. Informal guidelines, however, specify that in misdemeanor cases reports should be shorter and more concise than in felony cases. The officers indicated that reports for municipal court (all misdemeanor cases) should range from four to six pages in length, while superior court reports (felony cases) were expected to be six to nine pages long. In controversial cases (to which only the most experienced officers are assigned) presentence reports are expected to be longer and to include considerable social data. Reports in these cases have been as long as thirty pages.

Although probation officers learn what general types of information to include through experience and feedback from judges and supervisors, they are allowed considerable leeway in deciding exactly what to put in their reports (outside of the offense and prior-record sections). Because investigators decide what collateral sources are germane to the case, they tend to include information that will reflect favorably on their sentencing recommendation. In this context the observation of one probation officer is understandable: "I pick from the mass of possible sources just which ones to put in the report. Do you think I'm going to pick people who make my recommendation look weak? No way!"

Filing the Report

The final stage in the investigation includes dictating the report, having it approved by a probation supervisor, and appearing in court. All three of these activities serve to reinforce the importance of prior record and offense in sentencing recommendations. At the time of dictation, probation officers determine what to include in the report and how to phrase their remarks. For the first time in the investigation, they receive formal feedback from official sources. Presentence reports are read by three groups important to the probation officers: probation supervisors, district attorneys, and judges. Probation officers recognize that for varying reasons, all these groups emphasize the legally relevant variables of offense and prior criminal record when considering an appropriate sentencing recommendation. Such considerations reaffirm the probation officer's initial private typing.

A probation investigator described this process:

> After I've talked to the defendants I think maybe some of them deserve to get special consideration. But then I remember who's going to look at the reports. My supervisor, the DA, the judge; they don't care about all the personal details. When all is said and done, what's really important to them is the offense and the defendant's prior record. I know that stuff from the start. It makes me wonder why we have to jack ourselves around to do long reports.

Probation officers assume that their credibility as presentence investigators will be enhanced if their sentencing recommendations meet with the approval of probation supervisors, district attorneys, and judges. On the other hand, officers whose recommendations are consistently "out of line" are subject to censure or transfer, or they find themselves engaged in "running battles" with court officials. During the last stage of the investigation probation officers must consider how to ensure that their reports will go through court without "undue personal hassle." Most investigation officers have learned that presentence recommendations based on a consideration of prior record and offense can achieve that goal.

Although occupational self-interest is an important component in deciding how to conduct a presentence investigation, other factors are also involved. Many probation officers agree with the idea of using legally relevant variables as determinants of recommendations. These officers embrace the retributive value of this concept and see it as an equitable method for framing their investigation. Other officers reported that probation officers' discretion had been "short-circuited" by determinate sentencing guidelines and that they were reduced to "merely going through the motions" in conducting their investigations. Still other officers view the use of legal variables to structure recommendations as an acceptable bureaucratic shortcut to compensate partially for large case assignments. One probation officer stated, "If the department wants us to keep pumping out presentence reports we can't consider social factors—we just don't have time." Although probation officers are influenced by various dynamics, there seems little doubt that in California, the social history that once was considered the "heart and soul" of presentence probation reports has been largely devalued.

Summary and Conclusions

In this study I provide a description and an analysis of the processes used by probation investigators in preparing presentence reports. The research findings based on interview data indicate that probation officers tend to de-emphasize individual defendants' characteristics and that their probation recommendations are not influenced directly by factors such as sex, age, race, socioeconomic status, or work record. Instead, probation officers emphasize the variables of instant offense and prior criminal record. The finding that offense and prior record are the main considerations of probation officers with regard to sentence recommendations agrees with a substantial body of research.

My particular contribution has been to supply the ethnographic observations and the data that explain this phenomenon. I have identified the process whereby offense and prior record come to occupy the central role in decision making by probation officers. This identification underscores the significance of private typings in determining official designations. An analysis of probation practices suggests that the function of the presentence investigation is more ceremonial than instrumental.

I show that early in the investigation probation officers, using offense and prior record as guidelines, classify defendants into types; when the typing process is complete, probation officers essentially have decided on the sentence recommendation that will be recorded later in their official designation. The subsequent course of investigations is determined largely by this initial private typing. Further data collection is influenced by a sentence recommendation that already has been firmly established. This finding answers affirmatively the research question posed by Carter (1967: 211):

> Do probation officers, after "deciding" on a recommendation early in the present-ence investigation, seek further information which justifies the decision, rather than information which might lead to modification or rejection of that recommendation?

The type of information and observation contained in the final presentence report is generated to support the original recommendation decision. Probation officers do not regard defendant typings as tentative hypotheses to be disproved through inquiry but rather as firm conclusions to be justified in the body of the report.

Although the presentence interview has been considered an important part of the investigation, I demonstrate that it does not significantly alter probation officers' per-ceptions. In most cases probation officers dominate presentence interviews; inter-action between the participants is guarded. The nature of interviews between defen-dants and probation officers is important in itself; further research is needed to identify the dynamics that prevail in these interactions.

Attitudes attributed to defendants often are structured by probation officers to reaffirm the recommendation already formulated. The defendant's social history, long considered an integral part of the presentence report, in reality has little bearing on sentencing considerations. In most cases the presentence is no longer a vehicle for social inquiry but rather a typing process that considers mainly the defendant's prior criminal record and the seriousness of the criminal offense. Private attorneys in grow-ing numbers have become disenchanted with the quality of probation investigations and have commissioned presentence probation reports privately. At present, however, such a practice is generally available only for wealthy defendants.

The presentence process that I have described is used in the great majority of cases; it is the "normal" procedure. Even so, probation officers are not entirely pas-sive actors in this process. On occasion they will give serious consideration to social variables in arriving at a sentencing recommendation. In special circumstances offi-cers will allow individual defendants' characteristics to influence their report. In addition, probation officers who have developed credibility with the court are allowed some discretion in compiling presentence reports. This discretion is not unlimited, however; it is based on a prior record of producing reports that meet the court's approval, and is contingent on continuing to do so. A presentence writer said, "You can only afford to go to bar for defendants in a few select cases; if you try to do it too much, you get a reputation as being 'out of step.' "

This research raises the issue of probation officers' autonomy. Although I depict presentence investigators as having limited autonomy, other researchers contend that probation officers have considerable leeway in recommendation. This contradictory evidence can be explained in large part by the type of sentencing structure, the pro-fessionalism of probation workers, and the role of the district attorney at sentencing. Walsh's study (1985), for example, which views probation officers as important actors in the presentence process, was conducted in a jurisdiction with indeterminate sentencing, where the probation officers demonstrated a high degree of profession-alism and the prosecutors "rarely made sentencing recommendations." A very dif-ferent situation existed in the California counties that I studied: determinate sen-tencing was enforced, probation officers were not organized professionally, and the district attorneys routinely made specific court recommendations. It seems apparent that probation officers' autonomy must be considered with reference to judicial jurisdiction.

In view of the primacy of offense and prior record in sentencing considerations, the efficacy of current presentence investigation practices is doubtful. It seems ineffective and wasteful to continue to collect a mass of social data of uncertain relevance. Yet an analysis of courtroom culture suggests that the presentence investigation helps maintain judicial mythology as well as probation officer legitimacy. Although judges generally do not have the time or the inclination to consider individual variables thoroughly, the performance of a presentence investigation perpetuates the myth of individualized sentences. Including a presentence report in the court file gives the appearance of individualization without influencing sentencing practices significantly.

Even in a state like California, where determinate sentencing allegedly has replaced individualized justice, the judicial system feels obligated to maintain the appearance of individualization. After observing the court system in California for several years, I am convinced that a major reason for maintaining such a practice is to make it easier for criminal defendants to accept their sentences. The presentence report allows defendants to feel that their case at least has received a considered decision. One judge admitted candidly that the "real purpose" of the presentence investigation was to convince defendants that they were not getting "the fast shuffle." He observed further that if defendants were sentenced without such investigations, many would complain and would file "endless appeals" over what seems to them a hasty sentencing decision. Even though judges typically consider only offense and prior record in a sentencing decision, they want defendants to believe that their cases are being judged individually. The presentence investigation allows this assumption to be maintained. In addition, some judges use the probation officer's report as an excuse for a particular type of sentence. In some instances they deny responsibility for the sentence, implying that their "hands were tied" by the recommendation. Thus judges are taken "off the hook" for meting out an unpopular sentence. Further research is needed to substantiate the significance of these latent functions of the presentence investigation.

The presentence report is a major component in the legitimacy of the probation movement; several factors support the probation officers' stake in maintaining their role in these investigations. Historically, probation has been wedded to the concept of individualized treatment. In theory, the presentence report is suited ideally to reporting on defendants' individual circumstances. From a historical perspective this ideal has always been more symbolic than substantive, but if the legitimacy of the presentence report is questioned, so then is the entire purpose of probation.

Regardless of its usefulness (or lack of usefulness), it is doubtful that probation officials would consider the diminution or abolition of presentence reports. The number of probation workers assigned to presentence investigations is substantial, and their numbers represent an obvious source of bureaucratic power. Conducting presentence investigations allows probation officers to remain visible with the court and the public. The media often report on controversial probation cases, and presentence writers generally have more contact and more association with judges than do others in the probation department.

As ancillary court workers, probation officers are assigned the dirty work of collecting largely irrelevant data on offenders. Investigation officers have learned that emphasizing offense and prior record in their reports will enhance relationships with judges and district attorneys, as well as improving their occupational standing within probation departments. Thus the presentence investigation serves to maintain the court's claim of individualized concern while preserving the probation officer's role, although a subordinate role, in the court system.

The myth of individualization serves various functions, but it also raises serious questions. In an era of severe budget restrictions, should scarce resources be allocated to compiling predictable presentence reports of dubious value? If social variables are considered only in a few cases, should courts continue routinely to require presentence reports in all felony matters (as is the practice in California)? In summary, we should address the issue of whether the criminal justice system can afford the ceremony of a probation presentence investigation.

References

BLUMBERG, ABRAHAM (1967). *Criminal Justice.* Chicago: Quadrangle.

BLUMER, MARTIN (1979). "Concepts in the Analysis of Qualitative Data." *Sociological Review* 27:651–77.

BLUMSTEIN, ALFRED J., S. MARTIN, AND N. HOLT (1983). *Research on Sentencing: The Search for Reform. Washington, D.C.: National Academy Press.*

CARTER, ROBERT M. (1967). "The Presentence Report and The Decision-Making Process." *Journal of Research in Crime and Delinquency* 4:203–11.

CARTER, ROBERT M., AND LESLIE T. WILKINS (1967). "Some Factors in Sentencing Policy." *Journal of Criminal Law, Criminology, and Police Science* 58:503–14.

CLEAR, TODD, AND GEORGE COLE (1986). *American Corrections.* Pacific Grove, Calif.: Brooks/Cole.

HAGAN, JOHN (1975). "The Social and Legal Construction of Criminal Justice: A Study of the Presentence Process." *Social Problems* 22:620–37.

——— (1977). "Criminal Justice in Rural and Urban Communities: A Study of the Bureaucratization of Justice." *Social Forces* 55:597–612.

HAGAN, JOHN, JOHN HEWITT, AND DUANE ALWIN (1979). "Ceremonial Justice: Crime and Punishment in a Loosely Coupled System." *Social Forces* 58:506–25.

HOGARTH, JOHN (1971). *Sentencing As a Human Process.* Toronto: University of Toronto Press.

HUGHES, EVERETT C. (1958). *Men and Their Work.* New York: Free Press.

KINGSNORTH, RODNEY, AND LOUIS RIZZO (1979). "Decision-Making in the Criminal Courts: Continuities and Discontinuities." *Criminology* 17:3–14.

MARQUART, JAMES W. (1986). "Outsiders As Insiders: Participant Observation in the Role of a Prison Guard." *Justice Quarterly* 3:15–32.

McCLEARY, RICHARD (1978). *Dangerous Men.* Beverly Hills, Calif.: Sage.

McCLEARY, RICHARD, BARBARA NIENSTADT, AND JAMES ERVEN (1982). "Uniform Crime Reports as Organizational Outcomes: Three Time Series Experiments." *Social Problems* 29:361–73.

McHUGH, JOHN J. (1973). "Some Comments on Natural Conflict between Counsel and Probation Officer." *American Journal of Corrections* 3:15–32.

MICHALOWSKI, RAYMOND J. (1985). *Order, Law and Crime.* New York: Random House.

MURRAH, A. (1963). "Prison or Probation?" In B. Kay and C. Vedder (eds.), *Probation and Parole.* Springfield, Ill.: Charles C. Thomas, pp. 63–78.

MYERS, MARTHA A. (1979). "Offended Parties and Official Reactions: Victims and the Sentencing of Criminal Defendants." *Sociological Quarterly* 20:529–46.

NEUBAUER, DAVID (1974). *Criminal Justice in Middle America.* Morristown, N.J.: General Learning.

ROSECRANCE, JOHN (1985). "The Probation Officers' Search for Credibility: Ball Park Recommendations." *Crime and Delinquency* 31:539–54.

―――― (1987). "A Typology of Presentence Probation Investigators." *International Journal of Offender Therapy and Comparative Criminology* 31:163–77.

SUDNOW, DAVID (1965). "Normal Crimes: Sociological Features of the Penal Code." *Social Problems* 12:255–76.

WALSH, ANTHONY (1985). "The Role of the Probation Officer in the Sentencing Process." *Criminal Justice and Behavior* 12:289–303.

The Effect of Race on Sentencing:
A Reexamination of an Unsettled Question

Cassia Spohn/John Gruhl/Susan Welch

Questions about racial bias in the sentencing process have been a major concern for decades, but past studies on this issue have had methodological problems. Cassia Spohn, John Gruhl, and Susan Welch attempted to overcome these problems by using a large number of cases, a large number of offenses, and other research controls. They show that race does not have a direct effect on sentence severity, but that blacks are more likely than whites to be sent to prison.

Observers have noted that black criminal defendants tend to receive more severe sentences than white defendants do. For years social scientists have examined this disparity (Sellin 1928) and have put forth three explanations to account for it. Some researchers have suggested that it is due to racial discrimination. Others have emphasized wealth discrimination resulting from poor defendants' inability to obtain a private attorney or pretrial release. As the effect of wealth discrimination on black defendants is likely to be greater than on white defendants, since blacks are more likely to be poor, it amounts to indirect racial discrimination. Still others have suggested that this disparity is due to the effect of legal factors, such as the seriousness of the charge or prior criminal record. Since blacks are more likely to have a serious charge or prior criminal record, they are also likely to receive a more severe sentence.

Early studies often concluded that this disparity in sentencing was due to racial discrimination (see studies cited in Hagan 1974). But in his review of these studies, Hagan found that most employed inadequate controls or improper statistical techniques and were thus methodologically unsound. The evidence of racial discrimination in capital cases in the South could be supported, but little else could.

More recent sentencing studies by social scientists sometimes concluded that the continued disparity in sentencing is due to racial discrimination (Pope 1975; Levin 1977; Uhlman 1977; Sutton 1978a; Unnever et al. 1980) or wealth discrimination (Lizotte 1978), but these studies more often concluded that the disparity is due to

Source: Law and Society Review 16 (1981–1982): 71–88 (footnotes deleted). Reprinted by permission of the Law and Society Association.

the effect of legal factors (Baab and Furgeson 1967; Engle 1971; Cook 1973; Burke and Turk 1975; Chiricos and Waldo 1975; Tiffany et al. 1975; Clarke and Koch 1976; Eisenstein and Jacob 1977; Lotz and Hewitt 1977; Gibson 1978; Sutton 1978b). These recent studies generally corrected the obvious methodological defects of the earlier research. Nevertheless, many of them had less obvious defects which cast some doubt on their findings. These defects include:

1. Use of a relatively small number of cases (Clarke and Koch 1976; Bernstein et al. 1977; Unnever et al. 1980). Presumably to avoid this problem, some researchers lumped numerous federal or state jurisdictions together (Tiffany et al. 1975; Sutton 1978a, 1978b; Pope 1975). Given different regional perspectives toward racial matters, this approach risks obscuring discrimination which may exist in some jurisdictions but not in others. Some studies included both men and women defendants but did not provide adequate controls for gender (Unnever et al. 1980). Given the potential for different treatment of men and women, this approach too risks distorting the amount of racial discrimination which may exist.

2. Use of a relatively small number of offenses (Cook 1973; Tiffany et al. 1975; Clarke and Koch 1976). No particular offenses are so "typical" that just one or two or three or four of them can be analyzed to ascertain the existence of a pattern of discrimination. Certainly draft evasion (Cook 1973) is not necessarily generalizable to other crimes, and neither are auto theft, bank robbery, and forgery (Tiffany et al. 1975).

3. Use of inadequate controls for relevant "legal" and "extralegal" variables. Some researchers failed to control adequately for the seriousness of the charge when they collapsed disparate offenses into broad categories (Baab and Furgeson 1967; Burke and Turk 1975; Pope 1975; Gibson 1978). Collapsing offenses into categories of "violent crimes," "theft crimes," or "vice crimes" (Burke and Turk 1975) does not adequately control for the seriousness of the charge. Collapsing offenses into categories based upon some statutory classification, when the result is a single category encompassing driving while intoxicated, auto theft, rape, and murder (Baab and Furgeson 1967), also does not adequately control for the seriousness of the charge. Some researchers failed to control for prior criminal record (Uhlman 1977), and some failed to control for such extralegal variables as type of attorney or pretrial bail status (Pope 1975; Levin 1977; Gibson 1978).

4. Use of one sentence decision rather than two. The sentence is actually a product of two decisions—the decision whether to incarcerate and the decision on length of sentence. These are separate decisions based upon different criteria; the seriousness of the prior criminal record may be the best predictor of the decision to incarcerate, while the seriousness of the charge may be the best predictor of length of sentence (Sutton 1978a). Consequently, it is necessary to analyze the two decisions separately in order to avoid masking discrimination which may exist (Nagel 1969). Very few recent studies have done this (but see Eisenstein and Jacob 1977; Levin 1977; Sutton 1978a; 1978b).

5. Use of an inadequate measure of sentence severity. Most researchers employed a scale to measure severity. Some of these scales do not distinguish sufficiently between degrees of severity (Bernstein et al. 1977; Lotz and Hewitt 1977; Lizotte 1978). The range is quite wide, but certainly a scale which has three cate-

gories of fines, one category of probation, and just one category of incarceration (Bernstein et al. 1977) does not make fine enough distinctions between degrees of severity.

6. Use of inadequate statistical techniques. Some researchers did not use adequate multivariate analysis or tests of significance (Greenwood et al. 1973; Chiricos and Waldo 1975; Clarke and Koch 1976; Levin 1977). Failure to control for other factors influencing sentence may allow spurious relationships between race and sentence to be interpreted as valid ones.

The findings of prior studies, even recent ones, are contradictory and often inconclusive because of the methodological problems we have noted. The findings of these studies are not necessarily invalid, but additional research on this unsettled question is needed.

The Study

Our study of the relationship between race and sentencing replicates and elaborates upon the research conducted by Uhlman (1977), who concluded that there seemed to be evidence of racial discrimination in "Metro City." His study was one of the most sophisticated yet done in its use of an appropriate scale to measure sentence severity and in its use of path analysis. However, it had two serious defects. One, which Uhlman himself pointed out, was its failure to control for prior criminal record; this information was not available to him. Another, in our judgment, was its failure to divide sentencing into two decisions and analyze them separately.

We examine the sentences imposed on 2,366 black ($N = 1,939$) and white ($N = 427$) defendants in Metro City. Although we analyze data from the same city studied by Uhlman, we expect that our findings, unlike his, will show no direct relationship between race and sentencing once we control for the seriousness of the charge and prior criminal record. Accordingly, we hypothesize that we will find no direct racial discrimination either in the decision to impose a more or less severe sentence or in the decision to incarcerate.

The Data

The data for this project were drawn from a file of nearly 50,000 felony cases heard between 1968 and 1979 in Metro City, a city in the Northeast which is one of the largest cities in the United States. The initial data file consisted of a stratified random sample of all felony cases disposed of during this time period. From this sample we selected those cases where the "maximum charge" was one of the fourteen most common offenses appearing in the sample: murder, manslaughter, rape, robbery, assault, minor assault, burglary, auto theft, embezzlement, receiving stolen property, forgery, sex offenses other than rape, drug possession, and driving while intoxicated. We then eliminated cases where all charges were dismissed.

Our master data file included information on the race and sex of the defendant; the charges against the defendant; and, for each charge, the type of plea entered, whether or not the defendant was convicted, and, when the defendant was convicted, the sentence imposed. Information on the amount of bail set and whether or not the defendant made bail also was included in this data file. Data on the prior criminal record of the defendant and on the type of attorney representing the defendant were not included in the master data file but instead were contained in a separate file. Due to the difficulty and expense of adding this information to the master file for all defendants, we randomly selected over 4,000 defendants for whom to code this information. After eliminating defendants who were not convicted, and thus not sentenced, and defendants for whom there was missing data on one or more variables, we had a base of about 2,700 cases. To eliminate one possible source of variation, we then dropped all cases with female defendants. This left us with 2,366 cases.

The Variables

Two dependent variables measuring sentence severity were used in the analysis. The first measures sentence severity on a 93-point scale which ranges from a suspended sentence at one end to life imprisonment at the other. The second measures sentence severity by focusing on the decision to incarcerate or not; this decision is measured by a dichotomous prison/no-prison variable. This variable reflects the important distinction between sanctions involving suspended sentences, fines, or probation, on the one hand, and those involving prison terms, on the other hand.

Eight independent variables were employed: the defendant's race, charge, prior criminal record, type of attorney, type of plea, evidence of charge reduction, bail amount, and pretrial bail status. The prior-criminal-record variable was chosen from thirteen separate measures of prior record for each defendant. The measure of prior record selected—the number of times the defendant had been sentenced to prison for more than one year—was the one that had the strongest relationship with the sentence given for the current charge, controlling for type of crime. The dependent and independent variables and their codes are summarized in Table 1.

The Analysis

Our analysis includes correlation, regression, and path analysis. Path analysis, based on multiple regression, allows one to examine both the direct and indirect effects of an independent variable on a dependent variable. Thus, for example, we can analyze not only the direct effects of race on sentence controlling for other factors, as we could with multiple regression, but also the indirect effects of race on sentence resulting from the effect of race on other factors related to sentencing (see Asher 1976 for a good discussion of path analysis). In this path analysis, the impact of our group of dummy variables measuring type of charge was handled through the block variable approach suggested by Heise (1972).

Because of precautions taken in the design and execution of this study, we believe we have been able to avoid the most troublesome methodological problems of previous studies. Our study includes a large number of cases and a large number of offenses. It controls for relevant legal and extralegal variables. It examines two sentence decisions—the decision to impose a more or less severe sentence and the decision to incarcerate or not. It uses a 93-point scale to distinguish between more or less severe sentences, and it employs path analysis.

T A B L E   1 / **Independent and Dependent Variables Included in the Study**

Variable	Description	Code
Defendant race	Whether the defendant was black or white; persons of other racial groups were eliminated from the analysis	1 = black 0 = white
Charge	Fourteen felonies were included (see text)	Dummy variables were used to measure the charges
Prior criminal record	Number of times the defendant had been sentenced to prison for more than one year	A number ranging from 0 to 9
Type of attorney	Representation by either a private attorney or a public defender	1 = private attorney 0 = public defender
Type of plea	Plea of guilty or not guilty	1 = guilty plea 0 = not-guilty plea
Evidence of charge reduction	Sentencing on either the most serious charge or a lesser charge	1 = sentencing on lesser charge 0 = sentencing on most serious charge
Bail amount	Amount of bail requirement in dollars	Dollar amount
Pretrial bail status	Released or detained prior to trial	1 = pretrial release 0 = pretrial detention
Sentence severity	Severity of the sentence imposed on the defendant	Measured by a 93-point scale
Prison/no prison	Whether or not the defendant was sentenced to prison	1 = sentenced to prison 0 = not sentenced to prison

Findings

Data from Metro City reveal consistent differences between black and white male defendants on both the dependent and the independent variables utilized in this study. Table 2, which presents the zero-order correlations between the variables, shows an absolute disparity in the sentences imposed on black and white defendants. Black males receive harsher sentences than white males; more specifically, they are more likely than whites to receive prison terms. These black and white defendants also differ in terms of legal factors (prior criminal record and charge) and extralegal factors (type of attorney, charge reduction, bail amount, pretrial status). Blacks have more serious criminal records and are charged with more serious crimes. They also are more likely than whites to be represented by a public defender, to engage in plea bargaining, to have high bail set, and to be detained prior to trial.

These findings are in accord with previous reseach. They also indicate the plausibility of the earlier noted explanations of racial disparities in sentencing. Blacks

TABLE 2 / **Matrix of Intercorrelations**

	Sentence severity	Prison/no prison	Race	Prior record	Charge	Type of attorney	Type of plea	Charge reduction	Bail amount	Pretrial status
Sentence severity	—									
Prison/no prison	.79[a]	—								
Race	.09	.14	—							
Prior record	.07	.14	.12	—						
Charge	.58	.54	.17	-.25	—					
Type of attorney	.20	.13	-.12	-.06	.31	—				
Type of plea	-.09	-.12	.00	-.01	.20	-.02	—			
Charge reduction	-.12	-.14	-.06	.01	.72	-.03	.01	—		
Bail amount	.23	.22	.04	.08	.27	.08	.00	.06	—	
Pretrial status	-.22	-.32	-.17	-.25	.31	.12	.03	.05	-.18	—

[a] All correlations are Pearson's r except with charge variable, whose correlations are multiple R. Coding: See Table 1.

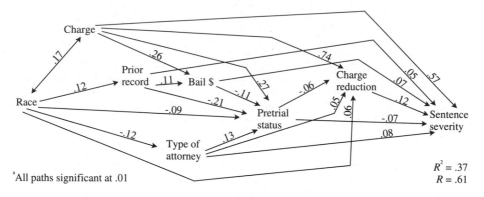

Figure 1   The impact of race and other variables on sentence severity[a]

may receive harsher sentences than whites (1) because of racial discrimination within the criminal justice system, (2) because of wealth discrimination, or indirect racial discrimination, resulting from their inability to obtain a private attorney or pretrial release, or (3) because they are charged with more serious crimes and have more serious criminal records.

Race and Sentence Severity

We expected to find no direct relationship between race and sentence severity, as measured by the 93-point sentence scale, once we controlled for the charge against the defendant and the defendant's prior criminal record. The data presented in Table 3 and in Figure 1 confirm this hypothesis.

As shown in Table 3, the bivariate relationship between race and sentence severity (Pearson's r = .092) is statistically significant. Controlling the seriousness of the charge against the defendant reduces the correlation substantially (beta = 45), but the relationship between the two variables is still significant. Adding a control for the seriousness of the defendant's prior criminal record, however, further reduces the correlation (beta = .017) to the point where the relationship between race and sentence severity no longer is significant.

These findings illustrate the importance of the legal factors, including prior criminal record, in explaining sentence severity. Merely controlling for the seriousness of the charge against the defendant, without taking into account the seriousness of the defendant's prior criminal record, might lead one to conclude, incorrectly, that racial disparities in sentencing are due to racial discrimination. Instead, it appears that these disparities can be attributed to racial differences in the seriousness of the charges against the defendants and to racial differences in the seriousness of the defendants' prior criminal records.

Our hypothesis was tested further using path analysis. We defined and operationalized a causal model that would allow us to explore the direct and indirect influences of race on sentence severity. We began with a fully defined model, one in which all of the relevant paths linking race to sentence were identified and all of the correlations were calculated. We then eliminated paths which were not significant ($p \leq .01$). The reduced model is presented in Figure 1.

TABLE   3 / **Relationship of Race to Sentence Severity with Various Controls[a]**

	Sentence
No controls	.092*
Control for charge	.025*
Controls for charge and prior record	.017
Controls for charge, prior record, and extralegal factors[b]	.009

[a]The measure of the bivariate relationship between race and sentence is Pearson's r. All of the other measures are betas.

[b]The extralegal factors include type of attorney, type of plea, charge reduction, pretrial bail status, and bail amount.

*$s \leq .05$.

The data presented in Figure 1 substantiate the lack of direct racial discrimination in determining sentence severity in Metro City. After removing the effects of the six other independent variables, no direct path remains between race and sentence. Judges in Metro City apparently do not take the defendant's race into consideration when determining sentence severity.

From this alone, however, we cannot conclude that race has *no* effect on sentence severity. As Figure 1 clearly reveals, there are a number of significant indirect relationships between these variables. The most important compound paths, measured by the percentage of the total variance in sentence severity explained by the path, are those from race to the legal factors to sentence. After controlling for all other factors included in the model, we still find that blacks' harsher sentences can be attributed, first and foremost, to the fact that they are charged with more serious crimes and have more serious prior criminal records. But Figure 1 also reveals that race affects sentence length in other, less explicable, ways. There are a number of indirect paths from race to extralegal factors to sentence. Although these paths clearly are less important than those involving the legal factors, they nonetheless are statistically significant. While space limitations prohibit analyzing each of these paths, the nature of the relationships can be illustrated by examining the two most significant of them:

- Black males are less likely than white males to be released prior to trial and thus receive harsher sentences than whites.
- Black males are less likely than white males to be represented by private attorneys, who are more likely than public defenders to get their clients released prior to trial. Because they are less likely than whites to be released, blacks receive harsher sentences.

These findings are a futher indication of indirect racial discrimination in Metro City. A defendant's socioeconomic status influences, at least to a moderate degree, the sanction imposed. Defendants who cannot obtain a private attorney or pretrial release receive slightly harsher sentences than those who can.

To put our findings thus far in perspective, we again emphasize that race has no direct effect on sentence severity in Metro City. Rather, black males receive harsher

T A B L E   4 / **Relationship of Race to Incarceration with Various Controls**[a]

	Prison/no prison
No controls	.144*
Control for charge	.074*
Controls for charge, and prior record	.061
Controls for charge, prior record, and extralegal factors	.042[b]

[a]The measure of the bivariate relationship between race and incarceration is Pearson's *r*. All of the other measures are betas.

[b]The *b* here is .048 (S.E. = .020), which means that blacks are incarcerated about 5 percent more than whites.

*$s \leq .05$.

sentences than white males primarily because of legal factors but secondarily because of extralegal factors.

Race and the Decision to Incarcerate

In addition to exploring the relative severity of sentences imposed on black and white male defendants, we also examined the frequency with which defendants of each race were sentenced to prison. For most defendants this is probably the critical decision. As Uhlman (1977: 22) has noted, "Qualitatively, there is almost an incalculable jump between nonprison sanctions . . . and a jail term."

In accord with our first hypothesis, we expected to find no direct relationship between race and the decision to incarcerate once we controlled for the seriousness of the crime and prior record. But as shown in Table 4 and Figure 2, this hypothesis was not confirmed. A statistically significant relationship between race and incarceration remains after controlling for both legal and extralegal factors. After entering all controls in the regression equation, the *b*-value is .048, indicating that black males are incarcerated about 5 percent more often than white males. Twenty-nine percent of convicted blacks, but only 24 percent of convicted whites, were sent to prison. Thus, black defendants are 20 percent more likely than white defendants to be incarcerated.

That judges do discriminate against black males in deciding whether or not to sentence defendants to prison is confirmed further by the causal model presented in Figure 2. We should point out, however, that the direct path from race to incarceration is not as predictive as the indirect path from race to charge to incarceration. The correlation of the indirect path, obtained by multiplying the individual coefficients that comprise the path (Asher 1976), is .09, while the correlation of the direct path is only .04. Thus, black males receive prison sentences more often than white males because they are charged with more serious crimes *and* because they are black.

Since both dependent variables are based on the same sentence severity scale, it might seem inconsistent that the first hypothesis was confirmed but the second hypothesis was not. The data presented in Table 5, however, reconcile this seeming inconsistency.

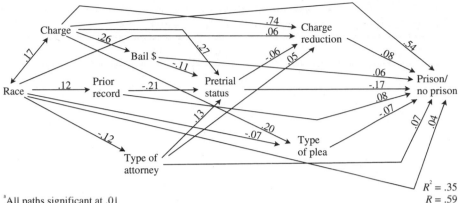

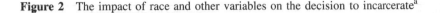

[a]All paths significant at .01

$R^2 = .35$
$R = .59$

Figure 2 The impact of race and other variables on the decision to incarcerate[a]

We divided all defendants into two groups—those not sentenced to prison and those sentenced to prison—and, controlling for the legal and extralegal factors, compared the severity of sentences imposed on defendants of each race within each group. We found that within each group blacks received *lighter* sentences than whites and that the differences between the races were statistically significant in the "not-incarcerated" group.

Thus, while black males *are* more likely than white males to receive prison terms, those who do are, as a group, given lighter sentences than their white counterparts. We interpreted this to mean that in "borderline cases"—cases where the judge could either decide to impose a lengthy (eight to nine years) probation sentence or a short (one to two years) prison sentence—the judge selected the probation option for whites more than blacks, the prison option for blacks more than whites. Consequently, more whites than blacks are found at the upper end of the "not-incarcerated" category, while more blacks than whites are found at the lower end of the "incarcerated" category. Our findings, therefore, are not inconsistent. The way in which black and white male defendants were distributed along the 93-point sentence scale, and the comparison of defendants across the entire continuum, tended to mask important differences.

Conclusion

We expected to find no direct relationship between race and sentence severity once we controlled for the seriousness of the charge and prior criminal record. Accordingly, we hypothesized that we would find no direct racial discrimination either in the decision to impose a more or less severe sentence, or in the decision to incarcerate.

Our first hypothesis was confirmed. Black males did receive harsher sentences than white males, but this disparity was due primarily to the fact that blacks were charged with more serious offenses and had more serious prior criminal records. We found no statistical evidence of direct racial discrimination in determining sentence

T A B L E   5 / **Comparison of the Effect of Race on Sentence Severity among Defendants Not Incarcerated and Incarcerated**[a]

	Not incarcerated	Incarcerated
Pearson's r	−.10	.07
Beta	−.05	− .02
b	−.82	−1.31
S.E.	.41	2.18
F	4.08*	0.36
N	1,767	599

[a] All of the legal and extralegal factors were controlled for in calculation of the beta, b, and standard error.
*$s \leq .05$.

severity. We did, however, find some evidence of wealth discrimination. Defendants who could not obtain a private attorney or pretrial release received harsher sentences than those who could. Since blacks are more likely than whites to be poor, this type of discrimination affects blacks more than whites. It can, therefore, be seen as a possible source of indirect racial discrimination.

Our second hypothesis was not confirmed. Even after controlling for both legal and extralegal factors, black males still were sentenced to prison 5 percent more often than white males, resulting in a 20 percent higher rate. Race by itself accounted for 4 percent of the variation in this sentencing decision. Thus, judges in Metro City apparently do discriminate against black males in deciding between incarceration and lengthy probation. White males are more likely to receive probation, black males a short prison term. This is consistent with the findings of Nagel (1969), Pope (1975), Levin (1977), and Unnever and colleagues (1980), all of whom concluded that blacks were less likely than whites to receive probation. These earlier findings, then, hold up even when given a more rigorous test.

One might question whether a 5 percent difference between blacks and whites in the rate of incarceration is substantively significant. As we noted earlier, however, this 5 percent difference means that blacks are 20 percent more likely than whites to be incarcerated. We have been so sensitized to racial discrimination that the absence of a glaring disparity may seem trivial (see Hagan 1974). But as Nagel (1977: 189) has pointed out, the relationship between race and sentence severity should not be treated "as if it were just another statistical relationship like the relation between the religion of voters and whether they vote Democratic or Republican." Even though race accounts for "only" 4 percent of the variation in our study in the decision to incarcerate, the tremendous difference between being confined and being free makes it a difference which is both "substantial and disturbing" (Nagel 1977: 194). Our study examined only the most visible aspect of the criminal justice process. It says nothing about the well-documented and pervasive discrimination elsewhere in the process—the police officer's decision to arrest, the prosecutor's decision to charge, the judge's or jury's decision to convict, and the parole board's decision to grant parole (see Black 1974).

We think that our findings are an advance over previous work on race and sentencing. The large number of cases and offenses, controls for relevant legal and extralegal factors, the division of the sentencing decision, and the use of multivariate analysis have contributed to somewhat more refined conclusions about the influence of race on sentencing. But our study also has its limitations. It only examined sentences imposed on male offenders in one large city in the Northeast. And there is other evidence that the patterns found here might not apply to females (Spohn et al. 1981; see also Kruttschnitt 1980). In short, our findings support, but certainly do not prove, the existence of racial discrimination in sentencing.

References

ARNOLD, WILLIAM R. (1971). "Race and Ethnicity Relative to Other Factors in Juvenile Court Dispositions." 77 *American Journal of Sociology* 211.

ASHER, HERBERT B. (1976). *Causal Modeling.* Sage University Paper Series on Quantitative Applications in the Social Sciences, No. 07-003. Newbury Park, Calif.: Sage Publications.

BAAB, GEORGE WILLIAM, AND WILLIAM ROYAL FURGESON, JR. (1967). "Texas Sentencing Practices: A Statistical Study." 45 *Texas Law Review* 471.

BERNSTEIN, ILENE NAGEL, WILLIAM R. KELLY, AND PATRICIA A. DOYLE (1977)."Societal Reaction to Deviants: The Case of Criminal Defendants." 42 *American Sociological Review* 743.

BLACK, CHARLES L. (1974). *Capital Punishment: The Inevitability of Caprice and Mistake.* New Haven: Yale University Press.

BURKE, PETER J., AND AUSTIN T. TURK (1975). "Factors Affecting Postarrest Decisions: A Model for Analysis." 22 *Social Problems* 313.

CHIRICOS, THEODORE G., AND GORDON P. WALDO (1975). "Socioeconomic Status and Criminal Sentencing: An Empirical Assessment of a Conflict Proposition." 40 *American Sociological Review* 753.

CLARKE, STEVENS H., AND GARY G. KOCH (1976). "The Influence of Income and Other Factors on Whether Criminal Defendants Go to Prison." 11 *Law and Society Review* 57.

COHEN, LAWRENCE E., AND JAMES R. KLUEGEL (1978). "Determinants of Juvenile Court Dispositions." 43 *American Sociological Review* 162.

COOK, BEVERLY B. (1973). "Sentencing Behavior of Federal Judges: Draft Cases— 1972." 42 *University of Cincinnati Law Review* 597.

EISENSTEIN, JAMES, AND HERBERT JACOB (1977). *Felony Justice: An Organizational Analysis of Criminal Courts.* Boston: Little, Brown.

ENGLE, CHARLES DONALD (1971). *Criminal Justice in the City: A Study of Sentence Severity and Variation in the Philadelphia Criminal Court System.* Ph.D. dissertation, Temple University.

FARRELL, RONALD A., AND VICTORIA LYNN SWIGERT (1978). "Prior Offense Record as a Self-Fulfilling Prophecy." 12 *Law and Society Review* 437.

GIBSON, JAMES L. (1978). "Race as a Determinant of Criminal Sentences: A Methodological Critique and a Case Study." 12 *Law and Society Review* 455.

GREENWOOD, PETER C., SORREL WILDHORN, EUGENE C. POGGIO, MICHAEL J. STRUMWASSER, AND PETER DELEON (1973). *Prosecution of Adult Felony Defendants in Los Angeles County: A Policy Perspective.* Santa Monica: Rand Corporation.

GRUHL, JOHN, CASSIA SPOHN, AND SUSAN WELCH (1981). "Women as Policy Makers: The Case of Trial Judges." 25 *American Journal of Political Science* 308.

HAGAN, JOHN (1974). "Extra-Legal Attributes and Criminal Sentencing: An Assessment of a Sociological Viewpoint." 8 *Law and Society Review* 357.

HAGAN, JOHN, AND ILENE N. BERNSTEIN (1979). "Conflict in Context: The Sanctioning of Draft Resisters, 1963–76." 27 *Social Problems* 109.

HEISE, DAVID R. (1972). "Employing Nominal Variables, Induced Variables, and Block Variables in Path Analysis." 1 *Sociological Methods and Research* 147.

KRUTSCHNITT, CANDACE (1980). "Social Status and Sentences of Female Offenders." 15 *Law and Society Review* 247.

LEVIN, MARTIN A. (1977). *Urban Politics and Criminal Courts.* Chicago: University of Chicago Press.

LIZOTTE, ALAN J. (1978). "Extra-Legal Factors in Chicago's Criminal Courts: Testing the Conflict Model of Criminal Justice." 25 *Social Problems* 564.

LOTZ, ROY, AND JOHN D. HEWITT (1977). "The Influence of Legally Irrelevant Factors on Felony Sentencing." 47 *Sociological Inquiry* 39.

NAGEL, STUART S. (1964). *The Legal Process from a Behavioral Perspective.* Homewood, Ill.: Dorsey Press.

NAGEL, STUART S., AND MARIAN NEEF (1977). *The Legal Process: Modeling the System.* Newbury Park, Calif.: Sage Publications.

POPE, CARL E. (1975). *Sentencing of California Felony Offenders.* Washington, D.C.: United States Department of Justice, Law Enforcement Assistance Administration, Criminal Justice Research Center.

SCARPITTI, FRANK, AND RICHARD STEPHENSON (1971). "Juvenile Court Dispositions: Factors in the Decision Making Process." 17 *Crime and Delinquency* 142.

SELLIN, THORSTEN (1928). "The Negro Criminal: A Statistical Note." 140 *Annals of the American Academy of Political and Social Science* 52.

SPOHN, CASSIA, SUSAN WELCH, AND JOHN GRUHL (1981). "Women Defendants in Court: The Interaction between Sex and Race in Convicting and Sentencing." Unpublished paper.

SUTTON, L. PAUL (1978a). *Federal Sentencing Patterns: A Study of Geographical Variations.* Albany, N.Y.: Criminal Justice Research Center.

——— (1978b). *Variations in Federal Criminal Sentences: A Statistical Assessment at the National Level.* Albany, N.Y.: Criminal Justice Research Center.

SWIGERT, VICTORIA LYNN, AND RONALD A. FARRELL (1977). "Normal Homicides and the Law." 42 *American Sociological Review* 16.

TERRY, ROBERT (1967). "Discrimination in the Handling of Juvenile Offenders by Social-Control Agencies." 4 *Journal of Research in Crime and Delinquency* 218.

THOMAS, CHARLES W., AND ROBIN J. CAGE (1977). "The Effect of Social Characteristics on Juvenile Court Dispositions." 18 *Sociological Quarterly* 237.

THORNBERRY, TERENCE P. (1973). "Race, Socioeconomic Status, and Sentencing in the Juvenile Justice System." 64 *Journal of Criminal Law, Criminology, and Police Science* 90.

TIFFANY, LAWRENCE P., YAKOV AVICHAI, AND GEOFFREY W. PETERS (1975). "A Statistical Analysis of Sentencing in Federal Courts: Defendants Convicted after Trial, 1967–1968." 4 *Journal of Legal Studies* 369.

UHLMAN, THOMAS M. (1977). "The Impact of Defendant Race in Trial Court Sentencing Decisions." In John A. Gardiner, ed., *Public Law and Public Policy.* New York, Praeger.

UNNEVER, JAMES D., CHARLES E. FRAZIER, AND JOHN C. HENRETTA (1980). "Race Differences in Criminal Sentencing." 21 *Sociological Quarterly* 197.

WELLFORD, CHARLES (1975). "Labelling Theory and Criminology: An Assessment." 22 *Social Problems* 332.

PART SIX

Corrections

Few citizens of the United States realize that their country gave the world the modern prison system, and still fewer know that our prison system came about in response to concern for humanitarian treatment of criminals. During the first decades of the nineteenth century, the creation of penitentiaries in Pennsylvania and New York attracted the attention not only of legislators in other states but also of observers from Europe. In 1831, France sent Alexis de Tocqueville and Gustave Auguste de Beaumont, England sent William Crawford, and Prussia dispatched Nicholas Julius. And even travelers from abroad who had no special interest in penology made it a point to include a penitentiary in their itineraries, just as they would want to see a Southern plantation, a textile mill in Lowell, or a frontier town. The U.S. penitentiary had become world-famous by the middle of the nineteenth century.

During the colonial and early postrevolutionary years, Americans used physical punishment, a legacy from Europe, as the main criminal sanction. Together with the fine and the stocks, flogging was a primary means of controlling deviancy and maintaining public safety. For more serious crimes, the gallows was used frequently. In New York criminals were regularly sentenced to death, with about 20 percent of all offenses being capital ones, including picking pockets, burglary, robbery, and horse stealing. Especially for recidivists, hanging was the preferred sanction in the early days of the republic. Jails throughout the country served only the limited purpose of holding people awaiting trial or unable to pay their debts.

With the spread of the humanistic ideas of the Enlightenment during the latter part of the eighteenth century, the concept of criminal punishment was revised. Part of the impetus came from the postrevolutionary patriotic fervor that blamed recidivism and criminal behavior on the Englishlaws. To a greater degree, however, the new correctional philosophy coincided with the ideals of the Declaration of Independence, stressing an optimistic view of human nature and a belief in its perfectibility. The conviction followed that social progress and advancement were possible through reforms carried out according to the dictates of "pure reason." Further, emphasis shifted from the assumption that deviance was inherent in human nature to a belief that crime was a result of forces operating in the environment.

The Invention of the Penitentiary

Reform of the penal structure became the goal of a number of humanist groups, the oldest of which was the Philadelphia Society for Alleviating the Miseries of Public Prisons, formed in 1787. Under the leadership of Dr. Benjamin Rush, a signer of the Declaration of Independence, this group, which included a large number of Quakers, urged that capital and corporal punishment be replaced with incarceration. The Quakers believed that criminals could best be reformed if they were placed in solitary confinement so that, in the isolation of their cells, they could consider their deviant acts, repent, and make changes in themselves. The word *penitentiary* comes from the Quaker idea that criminals needed an opportunity for penitence and repentance.

Through a series of legislative acts, Pennsylvania made provision in 1790 for the solitary confinement of "hardened and atrocious offenders" in the existing three-story Walnut Street Jail in Philadelphia. Pressed by the reformers, the legislature also decided to build additional institutions: Western Penitentiary on the outskirts of Pittsburgh, and Eastern Penitentiary near Philadelphia. Eastern's opening in 1829 marked the culmination of forty-two years of reform activity by the Philadelphia Society. The first prisoners were assigned to a cell 12 by 8 by 10 feet, with an individual exercise yard some 18 feet long. In the cell was a fold-up steel bedstead, a simple toilet, a wooden stool, a workbench, and eating utensils. Light came through an 8-inch window in the ceiling. Solitary labor, Bible reading, and reflection were the keys to the moral regeneration that was to occur within the prison walls. Although the cell was larger than most currently in use today, it was the only world the prisoner would see for the duration of the sentence. The only other human voice heard would be that of a clergyman who would visit on Sundays. Nothing was to distract the penitent from the path to reformation.

Eastern Penitentiary provided an example for reform efforts in other states. In 1823 the "Auburn System" of New York evolved as a rival to Pennsylvania's system. The Auburn System did not question the use of incarceration, only the regimen to which the prisoners were exposed. Rather than the complete isolation espoused by the Philadelphians, New York's reformers urged that criminals be kept in individual cells at night but be together in workshops during the day. The inmates were forbidden to talk with one another or even to exchange glances while on the job or at meals. In a sense, Auburn reflected the spirit of the Industrial Revolution: inmates were to have the benefits of both labor and meditation. They were to live under tight control, on a spartan diet, according to an undeviating routine.

During this period of reform, advocates of the Pennsylvania and Auburn plans debated on the public platforms and in the periodicals of the nation. Although the approaches seem very similar in retrospect, an extraordinary amount of intellectual and emotional energy was spent on the argument. Often the two have been contrasted by noting that the Quaker method sought to produce honest people, whereas that of New York intended to mold obedient citizens. Advocates of both the congregate and solitary systems agreed that the prisoner must be isolated from society and placed in a disciplined routine. They believed that deviance was a result of corruptions pervading the community and that institutions such as the family and the church were not providing the counterbalance. Convicts were not inherently depraved but rather were the victims of a society that had not protected them from vice. Only removing these temptations and substituting a steady and regular regimen could make the offenders useful citizens.

By the middle of the nineteenth century, reformers had become disillusioned with the results of the penitentiary movement. They believed that deterrence and the reclamation of prisoners had not been achieved in either the Auburn or Pennsylvania systems. A new approach, advocated by Zebulon Brockway, took effect in Elmira, New York, in 1877. According to Brockway, the key to rehabilitation was education; he persuaded the legislature to provide for indeterminate sentences and the release of inmates on parole when there was evidence that they had been reformed. At Elmira attempts were made to create a schoollike atmosphere, with courses in both academic and moral subjects. Inmates who performed well were placed in separate categories so that they could progress to a point where they were ineligible for parole.

By 1900 the reformatory movement had spread throughout the nation, yet by World War I it was already in decline. In most institutions the architecture, the demeanor of the guards, and the emphasis upon discipline differed little from the custodial orientation of the past. Too often, education and rehabilitation took a back seat to the punitive ideology. Even Brockway admitted it was difficult to distinguish between inmates whose attitudes had changed and inmates who only superficially conformed to prison rules. As before, "being a good prisoner" became the way to win parole in most of these institutions.

Although the declaration of principles adopted by the National Prison Association in 1870 declared that "reformation, not vindictive suffering, should be the purpose of penal treatment," the fortress prison emphasizing custody and discipline remained the dominant type of institution for most of the twentieth century. Until the end of World War II, the "big house" dominated the penological landscape. These walled prisons, holding an average of 2,500 men, with large cell blocks containing stacks of one- or two-man cells in three or more tiers, could be found in most states by the 1920s. The "big house" was the image that most Americans conjured up when they thought of prison; however, this type of institution did not prevail throughout the country. In the South there was a much greater emphasis upon using prisoners as agricultural workers, and thus prisons were run on the "plantation" model, with gangs being taken each day into the field to tend crops.

Beginning in the 1940s some states began to implement the rehabilitative philosophy first advocated in 1870. Emphasis was shifted to the treatment of criminals, offenders whose social, intellectual, or biological deficiencies had caused them to engage in illegal activity. Using a model analogous to the medical concept of disease, rehabilitation theorists blamed such conditions as poverty, unstable family relations, and limited mental capacity for producing maladjusted individuals who were unable to live by society's rules. Vocational and educational training, individual counseling and psychotherapy, honor farms, group therapy, work-release programs, chemotherapy, behavior modification—all were incorporated into the modern penal system. California became the standard-bearer for this movement; by 1960 correctional rehabilitation had become the preeminent theme in penology. But the failure of these new techniques to stem crime, changes in the characteristics of the prison population, and misuse of the discretion required by the treatment model prompted another cycle of correctional reform. By 1970 rehabilitation as a goal had been discredited.

It is important to emphasize that each of the reform movements was the work of well-intentioned people who had pushed for change in the name of humanity. Unfortunately, the reformers' ideals were never achieved, and the changes that were made often produced unsatisfactory results. The assumptions underlying one correctional period proved to be unfounded in the next period. In the 1980s reform appeared to be so fruitless that many penologists threw up their hands in despair. By 1990 new records for size of the prison population in the United States were being set, and correctional officials became concerned primarily with making custody in overcrowded institutions as humane as possible.

The Modern Prison: Legacy of the Past

For someone schooled in criminal justice history, entering one of today's U.S. penitentiaries is like entering a time machine. Elements of each of the major penology reforms may be seen within the walls of today's prisons. Conforming to the early notion that the prison should be located away from the community, most correctional facilities are still in rural areas, far from the urban homes of the inmates' families. The architecture of the typical prison is like that of a fortress. Prison industries, founded on the principles of Auburn, remain an important activity. Treatment programs are available, including vocational education, group therapy, and counseling, with participation rewarded. Although the lexicon of modern penology stresses corrections, "a prison remains a prison whatever it's called." The overriding emphasis of most prisons still appears to be on the time-honored goal of custody and punishment.

Prison Organization

Prison is different from almost any other institution or organization in modern society. More than its physical features set it apart; it is a place where a group of free people devote themselves to managing a group of captives. Prisoners do not commit themselves voluntarily, as do hospital patients, for instance. Prisoners are brought forcibly through the gates and prevented from leaving by guards, walls, and fences. Prisoners are required to live according to the dictates of their keepers, and their movements are greatly restricted.

Over and above these features of the prison, three important organizational characteristics dictate the administrative structure, and these factors influence the nature of prison society. First, the prison, like the mental hospital and monastery, is a closed institution. Whatever the inmates do or do not do begins and ends in the prison; every minute behind bars must be lived according to the rules of the institution, as enforced by the staff. Second, the administrative structure of the prison is organized down to the lowest level. However, unlike the factory or the military, where there are separate groups of supervisors and workers, the lowest-status prison employee—

the guard—is both a supervisor and a worker. Guards are seen as workers by the warden but as supervisors by the inmates. Guards must face the problem that their efficiency is being judged by the warden, on the basis of their ability to manage the prisoners. Because this can be achieved only if there is some degree of cooperation from the inmates, the guard must often ease up on enforcement of some rules in order to secure compliance with other rules. Third, the prison exists to carry out a number of functions related to the keeping (custody), the using (working), and the serving (treatment) of the inmates. Employees are divided into groups to perform these functions, but since the goals are often at cross-purposes, the administration of the correctional institution is often filled with conflict and ambiguities.

A view widely held by the public is that prisons are operated in an authoritarian manner. In such a society of captives, guards are taught to give orders and inmates to take orders. Forcing people to follow commands is, however, basically an inefficient way to make them carry out tasks. In addition, the threatened use of physical force by correctional officers has many limitations. As a result, prisons can be said to conform to an authoritarian model of control only in a formal sense. In reality, the prison society, like society at large, operates through an informal network of social and exchange relationships among the administrators, guards, prisoner leaders, and general population of captives. Changes in the leadership of the institution, attempts to shift from custodial to treatment goals, and pressures to "tighten up" discipline have all been cited as forces that can create instability in the system.

Prison Culture

In an institutional setting, the social distance between staff and inmates works to enhance the prison subculture. Powerful inmates may dominate others through a system of friendships, mutual obligations, intimidation, deception, and violence. The norms of the subculture may reflect the belief that prisoners should have as little as possible to do with the guards. "Do your own time," "Play it cool," "Mind your own business" are slogans that express this aloofness from and indifference to the interests of the staff and of other inmates.

Subculture leaders tend to be persons with extensive prison experience who have been tested through their relationships with other inmates—they are neither "pushed around" by their peers nor distrusted as "stool pigeons." Because they can be trusted by the staff, they serve as the essential middlepersons in communication between the inmates and the authorities. Because of their ability to acquire "inside information" and their access to decision makers, the inmate leaders are in a position to command deference from other prisoners. In many institutions, this aspect of the subculture is used as a means for the staff to maintain control.

Given the conflicting purposes and the complex set of role relationships, it is amazing that prisons do not degenerate into a chaotic "mess of social relations that have no order and make no sense." Although the U.S. prison may not conform to the enunciated goals of treatment and rehabilitation, and the formal organization of the staff with respect to the inmates may have little resemblance to the ongoing reality of their informal relations, order *is* kept and a routine is followed.

Violence

The following might be an ideal recipe for violence. Confine in cramped quarters a thousand men, some of whom have a history of engaging in violent interpersonal acts; restrict their movement and behavior; allow no contact with women; guard them by using other men; and keep them in this condition for indefinite periods of time. Although collective violence like the riots at Atlanta, Attica, and Santa Fe has become well known to the public, little has been said about the interpersonal violence that exists in U.S. prisons. Each year more than a hundred inmates die and countless others are injured through suicides, homicides, and assaults. Still others live in a state of constant uneasiness, always on the lookout for persons who might subject them to homosexual demands, steal their few possessions, and in general increase the pangs of imprisonment.

Too often, explanations of prison violence merely recite the deprivations and injustices of life in penal institutions. Mention is usually made of the rules enforced by brutal guards, the loss of freedom, and the boredom. Incarceration is undoubtedly a harsh and painful experience, but it need not be intensified by physical assault or death at the hands of fellow inmates. Prisons must be made safe places. Because the state puts offenders there, it has a responsibility for preventing violence and maintaining order.

Prison Management

Most of the scholarship on prison operations has been written by sociologists who have focused on the inmate society. From that perspective has come the belief on the part of many correctional officers that "the cons run the joint." One would get the impression that management is almost powerless to run prisons without working through offender leaders to get the cooperation of the general inmate population.

Recent scholarship by political scientist John J. DiIulio, Jr., has challenged the assumptions found in the correctional literature. He has argued that the quality of prison life as measured by levels of order, amenity, and service is mainly a function of management. He believes that prisons can be governed, violence can be minimized, and services can be offered to the inmates if leadership is provided by correctional executives and wardens. This means that prison directors must be able to manage those political and other pressures that engender administrative uncertainty and instability. In particular, he argues, wardens must be in their jobs long enough to learn the job, make plans, and implement them. Wardens must be hands-on and proactive, paying close attention to details. Wardens must provide leadership to a wide range of people both inside and outside the institution. From this perspective making prisons work is a function of administrative leadership and the application of management principles.

Prisoners' Rights

Until the 1960s the courts generally took the position that the internal administration of prisons or the conditions within the prisons did not fall within the courts' purview.

A hands-off policy existed, on the ground that such concerns belonged to the executive branch of government, not the judicial branch. With the civil rights movement and the expansion of due process rights by the Warren Court, prisoner groups and their supporters pushed to secure inmate rights. Prisoners mounted cases that reached the U.S. Supreme Court, arguing that their rights under the First Amendment (freedom of speech, assembly, petition, and religion), the Fourth Amendment (forbidding unreasonable searches), and the Eighth Amendment (forbidding cruel and unusual punishment) had been violated. Many of these actions were brought under the provisions of Section 1983 of the United States Code, which have been interpreted to allow prisoners to sue public officials in the federal courts over the conditions of their confinement.

The prisoners' rights movement has been responsible for some changes in corrections during the past decade, changes that resulted from court orders to bring prison conditions up to constitutional standards. Religious practices have been protected, legal assistance has been provided, and due process requirements have been upheld. Federal judges in a number of states have ordered renovation of existing facilities and construction of new facilities. To ensure implementation of their orders, judges have taken over administration of some correctional institutions through the appointment of special masters. The judicial intervention has generally led to increased correctional budgets, reformulation of policies, and creation of new organizational structures. The impact of the prisoners' rights movement on the behavior of correctional officials has not yet been measured, but the evidence suggests that court decisions have had a broad effect. Because prisoners and their supporters have been asserting their rights, wardens and their subordinates may be holding back from traditional disciplinary actions that might result in judicial intervention.

Community Corrections

During the social and political turmoil of the late 1960s there was a change of direction with regard to the way offenders should be handled. Referred to as "community corrections," this shift in policy emphasized the reintegration of the offender into society. Although probation and parole had long been parts of the criminal justice system, the new direction has supplemented these efforts. The community corrections movement attracted the attention of penological groups and was broadly supported in the 1967 report of the President's Commission on Law Enforcement and Administration of Justice. The commission stated that crime results from disorganization in the community and the inability of some persons to receive and to be sustained by the stable influences and resources that are necessary for living as productive members of society.

The goal of community corrections is reintegration of offenders into society by building ties between them and the community: restoring family links, obtaining employment and education, and securing a sense of place and pride in daily life. This model of corrections focuses attention both on the offender and on the community, for it not only assumes that the offender must change but also recognizes that factors within the community that might encourage criminal behavior (unemployment, for example) must change as well.

With the de-emphasis of rehabilitation as the major goal of the criminal sanction, community corrections has changed. Surveillance and supervision, rather than the provision of treatment, educational, and vocational services, has become dominant. But this shift has not diminished the importance of corrections in the community, as evidenced by the fact that even though the number of people incarcerated has grown dramatically during the past decade, there has been an even greater growth in the number of people under correctional supervision in the community. The new forms of intermediate sanctions such as house arrest, community service, intensive probation supervision, and electronic monitoring have the potential of further increasing the role of community corrections.

Release from Incarceration

Parole is the conditional release of adult prisoners from incarceration, but not from the legal custody of the state. Not the product of any single reformer or movement, parole evolved in the United States during the nineteenth century under a variety of influences. Among these were the work of Zebulon Brockway at Elmira, the earlier British practice of allowing prisoners to become indentured servants in its colonies, and the Australian system, begun in the 1840s, whereby a "ticket-of-leave" was given convicts who had earned credits for satisfactory performance while incarcerated. By 1900 some system of parole existed in twenty states; by 1922, in forty-four states, the federal system, and Hawaii. At first the approach was used primarily for young and first offenders, who were released with little supervision. Gradually, eligibility for parole was broadened and supervision by professional agents was added. After World War II, parole was incorporated into every state correctional system. With the movement away from rehabilitation and toward definite sentencing, the discretionary power of parole boards to release convicts has been restricted or abandoned in twenty-nine states, the District of Columbia, and the federal system.

With the passage of determinate sentencing laws and parole guidelines in some jurisdictions during the past decade, it is necessary to distinguish mandatory release from discretionary release. Where parole boards have been restricted or abandoned, felons reenter the community through mandatory release mechanisms that allow correctional authorities little leeway to consider whether the offender is ready for community supervision. Release is mandated at the end of a certain period of time, as stipulated by the sentencing judge, minus good time and other reductions. Discretionary release prevails where the parole board has extensive authority to consider the prisoner's behavior, participation in a treatment program, and readiness for a return to the community.

A major criticism of release by parole boards is that it shifts responsibility for many of the primary decisions of criminal justice from the judge, who holds legal procedures to be foremost, to an administrative board, where discretion rules. In states using discretionary release, parole decisions are made in secret hearings, with only the board members, the inmate, and correctional officers present. Usually, no published criteria are used to guide the decisions, and prisoners are given no reason for the denial or granting of their release. The question remains whether even good people should be trusted with such uncontrolled discretionary power.

Community Supervision

The concept of parole involves more than just release. It is assumed that the offender will go back into the community only under the supervision of a trained agent, who will assist in the adjustment and may continue some of the therapeutic endeavors begun in prison. Parole officers are asked to play two different roles: "cop" and social worker. As "cops" they are given the power to restrict many aspects of parolees' lives, to enforce conditions of release, and to initiate revocation proceedings if there are violations. As social workers they are responsible for helping parolees find jobs and restore ties with their families. The parole officer must develop the kind of relationship that will make the parolee feel comfortable about confiding his or her frustrations and concerns. This is a relationship that is difficult to maintain, because the parolee recognizes the parole officer's ability to send him or her back to prison.

The Future of Corrections

Crime control policies have dominated the correctional landscape for the past twenty years. Where once rehabilitation of the offender was emphasized, retributive policies now dominate. The new correctional orientation has been justified as helping to reduce crime by keeping offenders under tighter supervision either in prison or in the community. The War on Drugs and the problem of AIDS have brought new problems to correctional systems. Many correctional workers have become dispirited by the increase in the prison population, high probation caseloads, and the feeling that they are no longer members of a helping profession. Many correctional officers say that they are also serving time, but at eight hours a stretch.

Of the various subsystems of the criminal justice system, corrections appears to be going through the most sustained soul-searching. As incarceration rates climb, one can expect that public pressures will build to deal more effectively with the offender population. Intermediate sanctions—those punishments more severe than probation but less restrictive than prison—hold promise to relieve some of these pressures. However, ultimately the American people will have to decide the level of resources they want to allocate to punish offenders. Policy questions about the levels of incarceration, the role of community corrections, and the width of the criminal justice net all flow from this issue.

Suggestions for Further Reading

CLEAR, TODD R., AND GEORGE F. COLE. *American Corrections.* Pacific Grove, Calif.: Brooks/ Cole, 1990. A comprehensive look at the corrections system.

CLEAR, TODD R., AND VINCENT O'LEARY. *Controlling the Offender in the Community.* Lexington, Mass.: Lexington Books, 1983. Examination of risk assessment, classification, and supervision in the context of community corrections.

DIIULIO, JOHN J., JR. *Governing Prisons.* New York: Free Press, 1987. A critique of the sociological perspective on inmate society. DiIulio argues that the problems of prisons should be viewed as one of governance.

FOUCAULT, MICHEL. *Discipline and Punish.* Translated by Alan Sheriden. New York: Pantheon Books, 1977. An analysis of the philosophical and historical changes that took place in Europe during the seventeen and eighteenth centuries, as criminal behavior was viewed as resulting from the person rather than from the body.

FREEDMAN, ESTELLE B. *Their Sisters' Keepers.* Ann Arbor: University of Michigan Press, 1981. The role of female reformers in the creation of prisons for female offenders.

JACOBS, JAMES B. *Stateville.* Chicago: University of Chicago Press, 1977. A Study of Stateville Penitentiary, with emphasis upon the organization of the institution. It is one of the few sociological studies to look at the role of the guard.

JOHNSON, ROBERT. *Hard Time: Understanding and Reforming the Prison.* Pacific Grove, Calif.: Brooks/Cole, 1987. A significant contribution to an understanding of prison society.

LOMBARDO, LUCIEN X. *Guards Imprisoned.* New York: Elsevier, 1981. One of the few full-length treatments of the life of correctional officers. It describes the role complexity of the position in that the guard is both a "people worker" and a "bureaucrat."

ROTHMAN, DAVID J. *The Discovery of the Asylum: Social Order and Disorder in the New Republic.* Boston: Little, Brown, 1971. A history of the invention of the penitentiary. Rothman shows the links among the ideology of the 1830s, assumptions concerning corrections, and the design of institutions.

SHEEHAN, SUSAN. *A Prison and a Prisoner.* Boston: Houghton Mifflin, 1978. A fascinating description of life in Green Haven Prison and the way one prisoner "makes it" through "swagging," "hustling," and "doing time." It contains an excellent discussion of the inmate economy.

USEEM, BERT, AND PETER KIMBALL. *States of Siege: U.S. Prison Riots, 1971–1986.* New York: Oxford University Press, 1989. Analysis of collective riots in American prisons over the past two decades.

ARTICLE

21

The Society of Captives:
The Defects of Total Power

Gresham M. Sykes

In theory, prisons are organized in an authoritarian manner. In such a "society of captives," one might assume that guards have only to give orders and inmates will follow them. Because the guards have a monopoly on the legal means of enforcing rules, many people believe that there should be no question about how the prison is run. In reality, however, the relationship between the guards and the prisoners is based on a more fragile foundation. As this article shows, there are limitations on the ability of correctional officers to use total power.

"For the needs of mass administration today," said Max Weber, "bureaucratic administration is completely indispensable. The choice is between bureaucracy and dilettantism in the field of administration."[1] To the officials of the New Jersey State Prison the choice is clear, as it is clear to the custodians of all maximum security prisons in the United States today. They are organized into a bureaucratic administrative staff—characterized by limited and specific rules, well-defined areas of competence and responsibility, impersonal standards of performance and promotion, and so on—which is similar in many respects to that of any modern, large-scale enterprise; and it is this staff which must see to the effective execution of the prison's routine procedures.

Of the approximately 300 employees of the New Jersey State Prison, more than two-thirds are directly concerned with the supervision and control of the inmate population. These form the so-called custodian force which is broken into three eight-hour shifts, each shift being arranged in a typical pyramid of authority. The day shift, however—on duty from 6:20 A.M. to 2:20 P.M.—is by far the largest. As in many organizations, the rhythm of life in the prison quickens with daybreak and trails off

Source: Selection from Gresham M. Sykes, *The Society of Captives: A Study of a Maximum Security Prison* (copyright © 1958 by Princeton University Press; Princeton Paperback, 1971), pp. 40–first 2 paragraphs p. 53. Reprinted by permission of Princeton University Press. Portions of this article concerning the corruption of the guards' authority are to be found in Gresham M. Sykes, *Crime and Society* (New York: Random House, 1956). Reprinted by permission of Random House, Inc.

in the afternoon, and the period of greatest activity requires the largest number of administrative personnel.

In the bottom ranks are the wing guards, the tower guards, the guards assigned to the shops, and those with a miscellany of duties such as the guardianship of the receiving gate or the garage. Immediately above these men are a number of sergeants and lieutenants, and these in turn are responsible to the warden and his assistants.

The most striking fact about this bureaucracy of custodians is its unparalleled position of power—in formal terms, at least—vis-à-vis the body of men which it rules and from which it is supposed to extract compliance. The officials, after all, possess a monopoly on the legitimate means of coercion (or, as one prisoner has phrased it succinctly, "They have the guns and we don't"); and the officials can call on the armed might of the police and the National Guard in case of an overwhelming emergency. The twenty-four-hour surveillance of the custodians represents the ulti- mate watchfulness, and presumably noncompliance on the part of the inmates need not go long unchecked. The rulers of this society of captives nominally hold in their hands the sole right of granting rewards and inflicting punishments and it would seem that no prisoner could afford to ignore their demands for conformity. Centers of opposition in the inmate population—in the form of men recognized as leaders by fellow prisoners—can be neutralized through the use of solitary confinement or exile to other state institutions. The custodians have the right not only to issue and administer the orders and regulations which are to guide the life of the prisoner, but also the right to detail, try, and punish any individual accused of disobedience—a merging of legislative, executive, and judicial functions which has long been regarded as the earmark of complete domination. The officials of the prison, in short, appear to be the possessors of almost infinite power within their realm; and, at least on the surface, the bureaucratic staff should experience no great difficulty in con- verting their rules and regulations—their blueprint for behavior—into a reality.

It is true, of course, that the power position of the custodial bureaucracy is not truly infinite. The objectives which the officials pursue are not completely of their own choosing and the means which they can use to achieve their objectives are far from limitless. The custodians are not total despots, able to exercise power at whim, and thus they lack the essential mark of infinite power, the unchallenged right of being capricious in their rule. It is this last which distinguishes terror from govern- ment, infinite power from almost infinite power, and the distinction is an important one. Neither by right nor by intention are the officials of the New Jersey State Prison free from a system of norms and laws which curb their actions. But within these limitations the bureaucracy of the prison is organized around a grant of power which is without an equal in American society; and if the rulers of any social system could secure compliance with their rules and regulations—however sullen or unwilling— it might be expected that the officials of the maximum security prison would be able to do so.

When we examine the New Jersey State Prison, however, we find that this expectation is not borne out in actuality. Indeed, the glaring conclusion is that despite the guns and the surveillance, the searches and the precautions of the custodians, the actual behavior of the inmate population differs markedly from that which is called for by official commands and decrees. Violence, fraud, theft, aberrant sexual behav- ior—all are commonplace occurrences in the daily round of institutional existence in spite of the fact that the maximum security prison is conceived of by society as the ultimate weapon for the control of the criminal and his deviant actions. Far from being omnipotent rulers who have crushed all signs of rebellion against their regime, the custodians are engaged in a continuous struggle to maintain order—and it is a struggle in which the custodians frequently fail. Offenses committed by one inmate against another occur often, as do offenses committed by inmates against the officials and their rules. And the number of undetected offenses is, by universal agreement of both officials and inmates, far larger than the number of offenses which are discovered.

Some hint of the custodial bureaucracy's skirmishes with the population of prisoners is provided by the records of the disciplinary court which has the task of adjudicating charges brought by guards against their captives for offenses taking place within the walls. The following is a typical listing for a one-week period:

Charge	*Disposition*
1. Insolence and swearing while being interrogated	1. Continue in segregation
2. Threatening an inmate	2. Drop from job
3. Attempting to smuggle roll of tape into institution	3. 1 day in segregation with restricted diet
4. Possession of contraband	4. 30 days loss of privileges
5. Possession of pair of dice	5. 2 days in segregation with restricted diet
6. Insolence	6. Reprimand
7. Out of place	7. Drop from job. Refer to classification committee for reclassification
8. Possession of homemade knife, metal, and emery paper	8. 5 days in segregation with restricted diet
9. Suspicion of gambling or receiving bets	9. Drop from job and change Wing assignment
10. Out of place	10. 15 days loss of privileges
11. Possession of contraband	11. Reprimand
12. Creating disturbance in Wing	12. Continue in segregation
13. Swearing at an officer	13. Reprimand
14. Out of place	14. 15 days loss of privileges
15. Out of place	15. 15 days loss of privileges

Even more revealing, however, than this brief and somewhat enigmatic record are the so-called charge slips in which the guard is supposed to write out the derelictions of the prisoner in some detail. In the New Jersey State Prison, charge slips form an administrative residue of past conflicts between captors and captives and the following accounts are a fair sample:

This inmate threatened an officer's life. When I informed this inmate he was to stay in to see the Chief Deputy on his charge he told me if he did not go to the yard I would get a shiv in my back. Signed: Officer A _____

Inmate X cursing an officer. In mess hall inmate refused to put excess bread back on tray. Then he threw the tray on the floor. In the Center, inmate cursed both Officer Y and myself.   Signed: Officer B _____

This inmate has been condemning everyone about him for going to work. The Center gave orders for him to go to work this A.M. which he refused to do. While searching his cell I found drawings of picks and locks.   Signed: Officer C _____

Fighting. As this inmate came to 1 Wing entrance to go to yard this A.M. he struck inmate G in the face.   Signed: Officer D _____

Having fermented beverage in his cell. Found while inmate was in yard.
                                                 Signed: Officer E _____

Attempting to instigate wing disturbance. When I asked him why he discarded [sic] my order to quiet down he said he was going to talk any time he wanted to and _____ me and do whatever I wanted in regards to it.   Signed: Officer F _____

Possession of home-made shiv sharpened to razor edge on his person and possession of 2 more shivs in cell. When inmate was sent to 4 Wing officer H found 3″ steel blade in pocket. I ordered Officer M to search his cell and he found 2 more shivs in process of being sharpened.   Signed: Officer G _____

Insolence. Inmate objected to my looking at papers he was carrying in pockets while going to the yard. He snatched them violently from my hand and gave me some very abusive talk. This man told me to _____ myself, and raised his hands as if to strike me. I grabbed him by the shirt and took him to the Center.
                                                 Signed: Officer H _____

Assault with knife on inmate K. During Idle Men's mess at approximately 11:10 A.M. this man assaulted Inmate K with a home-made knife. Inmate K was receiving his rations at the counter when Inmate B rushed up to him and plunged a knife in his chest, arm, and back. I grappled with him and with the assistance of Officers S and V, we disarmed the inmate and took him to the Center. Inmate K was immediately taken to the hospital.   Signed: Officer I _____

Sodomy. Found inmate W in cell with no clothing on and inmate Z on top of him with no clothing. Inmate W told me he was going to lie like a _____ _____ _____ to get out of it.   Signed: Officer J _____

Attempted escape on night of 4/15/53. This inmate along with inmates L and T succeeded in getting on roof of 6 Wing and having home-made bombs in their possession.   Signed: Officer K _____

Fighting and possession of home-made shiv. Struck first blow to Inmate P. He struck blow with a roll of black rubber rolled up in his fist. He then produced a knife made out of wire tied to a toothbrush.   Signed: Officer L _____

Refusing medication prescribed by Doctor W. Said "What do you think I am, a damn fool, taking that _____ for a headache, give it to the doctor."
                                                 Signed: Officer M _____

Inmate loitering on tier. There is a clique of several men who lock on top tier, who ignore rule of returning directly to their cells and attempt to hang out on the tier in a group.   Signed: Officer N _____

It is hardly surprising that when the guards at the New Jersey State Prison were asked what topics should be of first importance in a proposed in-service training program, 98 percent picked "what to do in event of trouble." The critical issue for the moment, however, is that the dominant position of the custodial staff is more fiction than reality, if we think of domination as something more than the outward forms and symbols of power. If power is viewed as the probability that orders and regulations will be obeyed by a given group of individuals, as Max Weber has suggested, the New Jersey State Prison is perhaps more notable for the doubtfulness of obedience than its certainty. The weekly records of the disciplinary court and charge slips provide an admittedly poor index of offenses or acts of noncompliance committed within the walls, for these form only a small, visible segment of an iceberg whose greatest bulk lies beneath the surface of official recognition. The public is periodically made aware of the officials' battle to enforce their regime within the prison, commonly in the form of allegations in the newspapers concerning homosexuality, illegal use of drugs, assaults, and so on. But the ebb and flow of public attention given to these matters does not match the constancy of these problems for the prison officials who are all too well aware that "incidents"—the very thing they try to minimize—are not isolated or rare events but are instead a commonplace. The number of "incidents" in the New Jersey State Prison is probably no greater than that to be found in most maximum security institutions in the United States and may, indeed, be smaller, although it is difficult to make comparisons. In any event, it seems clear that the custodians are bound to their captives in a relationship of conflict rather than compelled acquiescence, despite the custodians' theoretical supremacy, and we now need to see why this should be so.

In our examination of the forces which undermine the power position of the New Jersey State Prison's custodial bureaucracy, the most important fact is, perhaps, that the power of the custodians is not based on authority.

Now power based on authority is actually a complex social relationship in which an individual or a group of individuals is recognized as possessing a right to issue commands or regulations and those who receive these commands or regulations feel compelled to obey by a sense of duty. In its pure form, then, or as an ideal type, power based on authority has two essential elements: a rightful or legitimate effort to exercise control on the one hand and an inner, moral compulsion to obey, by those who are to be controlled, on the other. In reality, of course, the recognition of the legitimacy of efforts to exercise control may be qualified or partial and the sense of duty, as a motive for compliance, may be mixed with motives of fear or self-interest. But it is possible for theoretical purposes to think of power based on authority in its pure form and to use this as a baseline in describing the empirical case.

It is the second element of authority—the sense of duty as a motive for compliance—which supplies the secret strength of most social organizations. Orders and rules can be issued with the expectation that they will be obeyed without the necessity of demonstrating in each case that compliance will advance the subordinate's interests. Obedience or conformity springs from an internalized morality which transcends the personal feelings of the individual; the fact that an order or a rule is an order or a rule becomes the basis for modifying one's behavior, rather than a rational calculation of the advantages which might be gained.

In the prison, however, it is precisely this sense of duty which is lacking in the general inmate population. The regime of the custodians is expressed as a mass of commands and regulations passing down a hierarchy of power. In general, these efforts at control are regarded as legitimate by individuals in the hierarchy, and individuals tend to respond because they feel they "should," down to the level of the guard in the cell block, the industrial shop, or the recreation yard. But now these commands and regulations must jump a gap which separates the captors from the captives. And it is at this point that a sense of duty tends to disappear, and with it goes that easily won obedience which many organizations take for granted in the naïveté of their unrecognized strength. In the prison, power must be based on something other than internalized morality, and the custodians find themselves confronting men who must be forced, bribed, or cajoled into compliance. This is not to say that inmates feel that the efforts of prison officials to exercise control are wrongful or illegitimate; in general, prisoners do not feel that the prison officials have usurped positions of power which are not rightfully theirs, nor do prisoners feel that the orders and regulations which descend upon them from above represent an illegal extension of their rulers' grant of government. Rather, the noteworthy fact about the social system of the New Jersey State Prison is that the bond between recognition of the legitimacy of control and the sense of duty has been torn apart. In these terms the social system of the prison is very similar to a *Gebietsverband,* a territorial group living under a regime imposed by a ruling few. Like a province which has been conquered by force of arms, the community of prisoners has come to accept the validity of the regime constructed by their rulers but the subjugation is not complete. Whether he sees himself as caught by his own stupidity, the workings of chance, his inability to "fix" the case, or the superior skill of the police, the criminal in prison seldom denies the legitimacy of confinement.[2] At the same time, the recognition of the legitimacy of society's surrogates and their body of rules is not accompanied by an internalized obligation to obey and the prisoner thus accepts the fact of his captivity at one level and rejects it at another. If for no other reason, then, the custodial institution is valuable for a theory of human behavior because it makes us realize that men need not be motivated to conform to a regime which they define as rightful. It is in this apparent contradiction that we can see the first flaw in the custodial bureaucracy's assumed supremacy.

Since the officials of prison possess a monopoly on the means of coercion, as we have pointed out earlier, it might be thought that the inmate population could simply be forced into conformity and that the lack of an inner moral compulsion to obey on the part of the inmates could be ignored. Yet the combination of a bureaucratic staff—that most modern, rational form of mobilizing effort to exercise control—and the use of physical violence—that most ancient device to channel man's conduct— must strike us as an anomaly and with good reason. The use of force is actually grossly inefficient as a means for securing obedience, particularly when those who are to be controlled are called on to perform a task of any complexity. A blow with a club may check an immediate revolt, it is true, but it cannot assure effective performance on a punch-press. A "come along," a straightjacket, or a pair of handcuffs may serve to curb one rebellious prisoner in a crisis, but they will be of little aid in moving more than 1,200 inmates through the mess hall in a routine and orderly fashion. Furthermore, the custodians are well aware that violence once unleashed is not easily brought to heel and it is this awareness that lies behind the standing order that no guard should ever strike an inmate with his hand—he should always use a nightstick. This rule is not an open invitation to brutality but an attempt to set a high threshold on the use of force in order to eliminate the casual cuffing which might explode into extensive and violent retaliation. Similarly, guards are under orders to throw their nightsticks over the wall if they are on duty in the recreation yard when a riot develops. A guard without weapons, it is argued, is safer than a guard who tries to hold on to his symbol of office, for a mass of rebellious inmates may find a single nightstick a goad rather than a restraint and the guard may find himself beaten to death with his own means of compelling order.

In short, the ability of the officials to physically coerce their captives into the paths of compliance is something of an illusion as far as the day-to-day activities of the prison are concerned and may be of doubtful value in moments of crisis. Intrinsically inefficient as a method of making men carry out a complex task, diminished in effectiveness by the realities of the guard–inmate ratio,[3] and always accompanied by the danger of touching off further violence, the use of physical force by the custodians has many limitations as a basis on which to found the routine operation of the prison. Coercive tactics may have some utility in checking blatant disobedience—if only a few men disobey. But if the great mass of criminals in prison are to be brought into the habit of conformity, it must be on other grounds. Unable to count on a sense of duty to motivate their captives to obey and unable to depend on the direct and immediate use of violence to ensure a step by step submission to the rules, the custodians must fall back on a system of rewards and punishments.

Now if men are to be controlled by the use of rewards and punishments—by promises and threats—at least one point is patent: The rewards and punishments dangled in front of the individual must indeed be rewards and punishments from the point of view of the individual who is to be controlled. It is precisely on this point, however, that the custodians' system of rewards and punishments founders. In our discussion of the problems encountered in securing conscientious performance at work, we suggested that both the penalties and the incentives available to the officials were inadequate. This is also largely true, at a more general level, with regard to rewards and punishments for securing compliance with the wishes of the custodians in all areas of prison life.

In the first place, the punishments which the officials can inflict—for theft, assaults, escape attempts, gambling, insolence, homosexuality, and all the other deviations from the pattern of behavior called for by the regime of the custodians—do not represent a profound difference from the prisoner's usual status. It may be that when men are chronically deprived of liberty, material goods and services, recreational opportunities, and so on, the few pleasures that are granted take on a new importance and the threat of their withdrawal is a more powerful motive for conformity than those of us in the free community can realize. To be locked up in the solitary-confinement wing, that prison within a prison; to move from the monotonous, often badly prepared meals in the mess hall to a diet of bread and water; to be dropped from a dull, unsatisfying job and forced to remain in idleness—all, perhaps, may mean the difference between an existence which can be borne, painful though it may be, and one which cannot. But the officials of the New Jersey State Prison are dangerously close to the point where the stock of legitimate punishments has been exhausted and it would appear that for many prisoners the few punishments which are left have lost their potency. To this we must couple the important fact that such punishments as the custodians can inflict may lead to an increased prestige for the punished inmate in the eyes of his fellow prisoners. He may become a hero, a martyr, a man who has confronted his captors and dared them to do their worst. In the dialectics of the inmate population, punishments and rewards have, then, been reversed and the control measures of the officials may support disobedience rather than decrease it.

In the second place, the system of rewards and punishments in the prison is defective because the reward side of the picture has been largely stripped away. Mail and visiting privileges, recreational privileges, the supply of personal possessions— all are given to the inmate at the time of his arrival in one fixed sum. Even the so-called good time—the portion of the prisoner's sentence deducted for good behavior—is automatically subtracted from the prisoner's sentence when he begins his period of imprisonment. Thus the officials have placed themselves in the peculiar position of granting the prisoner all available benefits or rewards at the time of his entrance into the system. The prisoner, then, finds himself unable to win any significant gains by means of compliance, for there are no gains left to be won.

From the viewpoint of the officials, of course, the privileges of the prison social system are regarded as rewards, as something to be achieved. That is to say, the custodians hold that recreation, access to the inmate store, good time, or visits from individuals in the free community are conditional upon conformity or good behavior. But the evidence suggests that from the viewpoint of the inmates the variety of benefits granted by the custodians is not defined as something to be earned but as an inalienable right—as the just due of the inmate which should not turn on the question of obedience or disobedience within the walls. After all, the inmate population claims these benefits have belonged to the prisoner from the time when he first came to the institution.

In short, the New Jersey State Prison makes an initial grant of all its rewards and then threatens to withdraw them if the prisoner does not conform. It does not start the prisoner from scratch and promise to grant its available rewards one by one as the prisoner proves himself through continued submission to the institutional regulations. As a result a subtle alchemy is set in motion whereby the inmates cease to see the rewards of the system as rewards, that is, as benefits contingent upon performance; instead, rewards are apt to be defined as obligations. Whatever justification might be offered for such a policy, it would appear to have a number of drawbacks as a method of motivating prisoners to fall into the posture of obedience. In effect, rewards and punishments of the officials have been collapsed into one and the prisoner moves in a world where there is no hope of progress but only the possibility of further punishments. Since the prisoner is already suffering from most of the punishments permitted by society, the threat of imposing those few remaining is all too likely to be a gesture of futility.

Unable to depend on that inner moral compulsion or sense of duty which eases the problem of control in most social organizations, acutely aware that brute force is inadequate, and lacking an effective system of legitimate rewards and punishments which might induce prisoners to conform to institutional regulations on the grounds of self-interest, the custodians of the New Jersey State Prison are considerably weakened in their attempts to impose their regime on their captive population. The result, in fact, is, as we have already indicated, a good deal of deviant behavior or non-compliance in a social system where the rulers at first glance seem to possess almost infinite power.

Yet systems of power may be defective for reasons other than the fact that those who are ruled do not feel the need to obey the orders and regulations descending on them from above. Systems of power may also fail because those who are supposed to rule are unwilling to do so. The unissued order, the deliberately ignored disobedience, the duty left unperformed—these are cracks in the monolith just as surely as are acts of defiance in the subject population. The "corruption" of the rulers may be far less dramatic than the insurrection of the ruled, for power unexercised is seldom as visible as power which is challenged, but the system of power still falters.

Now the official in the lowest ranks of the custodial bureaucracy—the guard in the cell block, the industrial shop, or the recreation yard—is the pivotal figure on which the custodial bureaucracy turns. It is he who must supervise and control the inmate population in concrete and detailed terms. It is he who must see to the translation of the custodial regime from blueprint to reality and engage in the specific battles for conformity. Counting prisoners, periodically reporting to the center of communications, signing passes, checking groups of inmates as they come and go, searching for contraband or signs of attempts to escape—these make up the minutiae of his eight-hour shift. In addition, he is supposed to be alert for violations of the prison rules which fall outside his routine sphere of surveillance. Not only must he detect and report deviant behavior after it occurs; he must curb deviant behavior before it arises as well, as when he is called on to prevent a minor quarrel among prisoners from flaring into a more dangerous situation. And he must make sure that the inmates in his charge perform their assigned tasks with a reasonable degree of efficiency.

The expected role of the guard, then, is a complicated compound of policeman and foreman, of cadi [judge], counselor, and boss all rolled into one. But as the guard goes about his duties, piling one day on top of another (and the guard too, in a certain sense, is serving time in confinement), we find that the system of power in the prison is defective not only because the means of motivating the inmates to conform are largely lacking but also because the guard is frequently reluctant to enforce the full range of the institution's regulations. The guard frequently fails to report infractions of the rules which have occurred before his eyes. The guard often transmits forbidden information to inmates, such as plans for searching particular cells in a surprise raid for contraband. The guard often neglects elementary security requirements and on numerous occasions he will be found joining his prisoners in outspoken criticisms of the warden and his assistants. In short, the guard frequently shows evidence of having been "corrupted" by the captive criminals over whom he stands in theoretical dominance. This failure within the ranks of the rulers is seldom to be attributed to outright bribery—bribery, indeed, is usually unnecessary, for far more effective influences are at work to bridge the gap supposedly separating captors and captives.

In the first place, the guard is in close and intimate association with his prisoners throughout the course of the working day. He can remain aloof only with great difficulty, for he possesses few of those devices which normally serve to maintain social distance between the rulers and the ruled. He cannot withdraw physically in symbolic affirmation of his superior position; he has no intermediaries to bear the brunt of resentment springing from orders which are disliked; and he cannot fall back on a dignity adhering to his office—he is a *hack* or a *screw* in the eyes of those he controls and an unwelcome display of officiousness evokes that great destroyer of unquestioned power, the ribald humor of the dispossessed.

There are many pressures in American culture to "be nice," to be a "good Joe," and the guard in the maximum security prison is not immune. The guard is constantly exposed to a sort of moral blackmail in which the first sign of condemnations, estrangement, or rigid adherence to the rules is countered by the inmates with the threat of ridicule or hostility. And in this complex interplay, the guard does not always start from a position of determined opposition to "being friendly." He holds an intermediate post in a bureaucratic structure between top prison officials—his captains, lieutenants, and sergeants—and the prisoners in his charge. Like many such figures, the guard is caught in a conflict of loyalties. He often has reason to resent the actions of his superior officers—the reprimands, the lack of ready appreciation, the incomprehensible order—and in the inmates he finds willing sympathizers. They, too, claim to suffer from the unreasonable irritants of power. Furthermore, the guard in many cases is marked by a basic ambivalence toward the criminals under his supervision and control. It is true that the inmates of the prison have been condemned by society through the agency of the courts, but some of these prisoners must be viewed as a success in terms of a worldly system of values which accords high prestige to wealth and influence even though they may have been won by devious means; and the poorly paid guard may be gratified to associate with a famous racketeer. Moreover, this ambivalence in the guard's attitudes toward the criminals nominally under his thumb may be based on something more than a sub-rosa respect for the notorious. There may also be a discrepancy between the judgments of society and the guard's own opinions as far as the "criminality" of the prisoner is concerned. It is difficult to define the man convicted of deserting his wife, gambling, or embezzlement as a desperate criminal to be suppressed at all costs, and the crimes of even the most serious offenders lose their significance with the passage of time. In the eyes of the custodian, the inmate tends to become a man in prison rather than a criminal in prison, and the relationship between captor and captive is subtly transformed in the process.

In the second place, the guard's position as a strict enforcer of the rules is undermined by the fact that he finds it almost impossible to avoid the claims of reciprocity. To a large extent the guard is dependent on inmates for the satisfactory performance of his duties; and like many individuals in positions of power, the guard is evaluated in terms of the conduct of the men he controls. A troublesome, noisy, dirty cell block reflects on the guard's ability to "handle" prisoners and this ability forms an important component of the merit rating which is used as the basis for pay raises and promotions. As we have pointed out above, a guard cannot rely on the direct application of force to achieve compliance nor can he easily depend on threats of punishment. And if the guard does insist on constantly using the last few negative sanctions available to the institution—if the guard turns in charge slip after charge slip for every violation of the rules which he encounters—he becomes burdensome to the top officials of the prison bureaucratic staff who realize only too well that their apparent dominance rests on some degree of cooperation. A system of power which can enforce its rules only by bringing its formal machinery of accusation, trial, and punishment into play at every turn will soon be lost in a haze of pettifogging detail.

The guard, then, is under pressure to achieve a smoothly running tour of duty not with the stick but with the carrot, but here again his legitimate stock is limited. Facing demands from above that he achieve compliance and stalemated from below, he finds that one of the most meaningful rewards he can offer is to ignore certain offenses or make sure that he never places himself in a position where he will discover them. Thus the guard—backed by all the power of the state, close to armed men who will run to his aid, and aware that any prisoner who disobeys him can be punished if he presses charges against him—often discovers that his best path of action is to make "deals" or "trades" with the captives in his power. In effect, the guard buys compliance or obedience in certain areas at the cost of tolerating disobedience elsewhere.

Aside from winning compliance "where it counts" in the course of the normal day, the guard has another favor to be secured from the inmates which makes him willing to forgo strict enforcement of all prison regulations. Many custodial institutions have experienced a riot in which the tables are turned momentarily and the captives hold sway over their quondam captors; and the rebellions of 1952 loom large in the memories of the officials of the New Jersey State Prison. The guard knows that he may some day be a hostage and that his life may turn on a settling of old accounts. A fund of goodwill becomes a valuable form of insurance and this fund is almost sure to be lacking if he has continually played the part of a martinet. In the folklore of the prison, there are enough tales about strict guards who have had the misfortune of being captured and savagely beaten during a riot to raise doubts about the wisdom of demanding complete conformity.

In the third place, the theoretical dominance of the guard is undermined in actuality by the innocuous encroachment of the prisoner on the guard's duties. Making out reports, checking cells at the periodic count, locking and unlocking doors—in short, all the minor chores which the guard is called on to perform—may gradually be transferred into the hands of inmates whom the guard has come to trust. The cell block runner, formally assigned the tasks of delivering mail, housekeeping duties, and so on, is of particular importance in this respect. Inmates in this position function in a manner analogous to that of the company clerk in the armed forces and like such figures they may wield power and influence far beyond the nominal definition of their role. For reasons of indifference, laziness, or naïveté, the guard may find that much of the power which he is supposed to exercise has slipped from his grasp.

Now power, like a person's virtue, once lost is hard to regain. The measures to rectify an established pattern of abdication need to be much more severe than those required to stop the first steps in the transfer of control from the guard to his prisoner. A guard assigned to a cell block in which a large portion of power has been shifted in the past from the officials to the inmates is faced with the weight of precedent; it requires a good deal of moral courage on his part to withstand the aggressive tactics of prisoners who fiercely defend the patterns of corruption established by custom. And if the guard himself has allowed his control to be subverted, he may find that any attempts to undo his error are checked by a threat from the inmate to send a *snitch-kite*—an anonymous note—to the guard's superior officers explaining his past derelictions in detail. This simple form of blackmail may be quite sufficient to maintain the relationships established by friendship, reciprocity, or encroachment.

It is apparent, then, that the power of the custodians is defective, not simply in the sense that the ruled are rebellious, but also in the sense that the rulers are reluctant. We must attach a new meaning to Lord Acton's aphorism that power tends to corrupt and absolute power corrupts absolutely. The custodians of the New Jersey

State Prison, far from being converted into brutal tyrants, are under strong pressure to compromise with their captives, for it is a paradox that they can ensure their dominance only by allowing it to be corrupted. Only by tolerating violations of "minor" rules and regulations can the guard secure compliance in the "major" areas of the custodial regime. Ill-equipped to maintain the social distance which in theory separates the world of the officials and the world of the inmates, their suspicions eroded by long familiarity, the custodians are led into a *modus vivendi* with their captives which bears little resemblance to the stereotypical picture of guards and their prisoners.

The fact that the officials of the prison experience serious difficulties in imposing their regime on the society of prisoners is sometimes attributed to inadequacies of the custodial staff's personnel. These inadequacies, it is claimed, are in turn due to the fact that more than 50 percent of the guards are temporary employees who have not passed a Civil Service examination. In 1952, for example, a month and a half before the disturbances which dramatically underlined some of the problems of the officials, the deputy commissioner of the Department of Institutions and Agencies made the following points in a report concerning the temporary officers of the New Jersey State Prison's custodian force:

1. Because they are not interested in the prison service as a career, the temporary officers tend to have a high turnover as they are quick to resign to accept more remunerative employment.
2. Because they are inexperienced, they are not able to foresee or forestall disciplinary infractions, the on-coming symptoms of which the more experienced officer would detect and take appropriate preventive measures against.
3. Because they are not trained as the regular officers, they do not have the self-confidence that comes with the physical training and defensive measures which are part of the regular officers' pre-service training and, therefore, it is not uncommon for them to be somewhat timid and inclined to permit the prisoner to take advantage of them.
4. Because many of them are beyond the age limit or cannot meet the physical requirements for regular employment as established by Civil Service, they cannot look forward to a permanent career and are therefore less interested in the welfare of the institution than their brother officers.
5. Finally, because of the short period of employment, they do not recognize the individual prisoners who are most likely to incite trouble or commit serious infractions, and they are at a disadvantage in dealing with the large groups which congregate in the cellblocks, the mess hall, the auditorium, and the yard.

The fact that the job of the guard is often depressing, dangerous, and possesses relatively low prestige adds further difficulties. There is also little doubt that the high turnover rate carries numerous evils in its train, as the comments of the deputy commissioner have indicated. Yet even if higher salaries could counterbalance the many dissatisfying features of the guard's job—to a point where the custodial force consisted of men with long service rather than a group of transients—there remains a question of whether or not the problems of administration in the New Jersey State Prison would be eased to a significant extent. This, of course, is heresy from the viewpoint of those who trace the failure of social organizations to the personal failings of the individuals who man social organizational structure. Perhaps, indeed, there is some comfort in the idea that if the budget of the prison were larger, if higher salaries could be paid to entice "better" personnel within the walls, if guards could be persuaded to remain for longer periods, then the many difficulties of the prison bureaucracy would disappear. From this point of view, the problems of the custodial institution are rooted in the niggardliness of the free community and the consequent inadequacies of the institution's personnel rather than flaws in the social system of the prison itself. But to suppose that higher salaries are an answer to the plight of the custodian is to suppose, first, that there are men who by reason of their particular skills and personal characteristics are better qualified to serve as guards if they could be recruited; and second, that experience and training within the institution itself will better prepare the guard for his role, if greater financial rewards could convince him to make a career of his prison employment. Both of these suppositions, however, are open to some doubt. There are few jobs in the free community which are comparable to that of the guard in the maximum security prison and which, presumably, could equip the guard-to-be with the needed skills. If the job requirements of the guard's position are not technical skills, but turn on matters of character such as courage, honesty, and so on, there is no assurance that men with these traits will flock to the prison if the salary of the guard is increased. And while higher salaries may decrease the turnover rate—thus making an in-service training program feasible and providing a custodial force with greater experience—it is not certain if such a change can lead to marked improvement. A brief period of schooling can familiarize the new guard with the routines of the institution, but to prepare the guard for the realities of his assigned role with lectures and discussions is quite another matter. And it seems entirely possible that prolonged experience in the prison may enmesh the guard deeper and deeper in patterns of compromise and misplaced trust rather than sharpening his drive toward a rigorous enforcement of institutional regulations.

We are not arguing, of course, that the quality of the personnel in the prison is irrelevant to the successful performance of the bureaucracy's task, nor are we arguing that it would be impossible to improve the quality of the personnel by increasing salaries. We are arguing, however, that the problems of the custodians far transcend the size of the guard's paycheck or the length of his employment and that better personnel is at best a palliative rather than a final cure. It is true, of course, that it is difficult to unravel the characteristics of a social organization from the characteristics of the individuals who are its members, but there seems to be little reason to believe that a different crop of guards in the New Jersey State Prison would exhibit an outstanding increase in efficiency in trying to impose the regime of the custodians on the population of prisoners. *The lack of a sense of duty among those who are held captive, the obvious fallacies of coercion, the pathetic collection of rewards and punishments to induce compliance, the strong pressures toward the corruption of the guard in the form of friendship, reciprocity, and the transfer of duties into the hands of trusted inmates—all are structural defects in the prison's system of power rather than individual inadequacies.*

The question of whether these defects are inevitable in the custodial institution—or in any system of total power—must be deferred. For the moment it is enough to point out that in the New Jersey State Prison the custodians are unable or unwilling to prevent their captives from committing numerous violations of the rules which make up the theoretical blueprint for behavior and this failure is not a temporary, personal aberration but a built-in feature of the prison social system. It is only by understanding this fact that we can understand the world of the prisoners, since so many significant aspects of inmate behavior—such as coercion of fellow prisoners, fraud, gambling, homosexuality, sharing stolen supplies, and so on—are in clear contravention to institutional regulations. It is the nature of this world which must now claim our attention.

Notes

1. Max Weber, *The Theory of Social and Economic Organization,* Talcott Parsons (New York: Oxford University Press, 1947), p. 337.
2. This statement requires two qualifications. First, a number of inmates steadfastly maintain that they are innocent of the crime with which they are charged. It is the illegitimacy of their particular case, however, rather than the illegitimacy of confinement in general, which moves them to protest. Second, some of the more sophisticated prisoners argue that the conditions of imprisonment are wrong, although perhaps not illegitimate or illegal, on the grounds that reformation should be the major aim of imprisonment and the officials are not working hard enough in this direction.
3. Since each shift is reduced in size by vacations, regular days off, sickness, and so on, even the day shift—the largest of the three—can usually muster no more than ninety guards to confront the population of more than 1,200 prisoners. The fact that they are so heavily outnumbered is not lost on the officials.

The Prison Experience: The Convict World

John Irwin

What is it like to be incarcerated? Because the population of a prison is made up of felons, one might expect that chaos would prevail if it were not for the discipline imposed by the authorities. John Irwin, a former convict who is now a sociologist, describes how offenders adapt to the world of the prison. He finds that a complete social organization exists on the "inside," with norms, role relationships, and leadership patterns functioning within the parameters of the formal organization set by correctional officials. Some scholars have argued that prisons are really microcosms of society: with some exceptions, they reflect the conflicts and tensions of the larger world.

Many studies of prison behavior have approached the task of explaining the convict social organization by posing the hypothetical question: How do convicts adapt to prison? It was felt that this was a relevant question because the prison is a situation of deprivation and degradation, and, therefore, presents extraordinary adaptive problems. Two adaptive styles were recognized: (1) an individual style—withdrawal and/or isolation—and (2) a collective style—participation in a convict social system which, through its solidarity, regulation of activities, distribution of goods and prestige, and apparent opposition to the world of the administration, helps the individual withstand the "pains of imprisonment."

I would like to suggest that these studies have overlooked important alternate styles. First let us return to the question that theoretically every convict must ask himself: How shall I do my time? or, What shall I do in prison? First, we assume by this question that the convict is able to cope with this situation. This is not always true; some fail to cope with prison and commit suicide or sink into psychosis. Those who do cope can be divided into those who identify with and therefore adapt to a broader world than that of the prison, and those who orient themselves primarily to the prison world. This difference in orientation is often quite subtle but always

Source: From John Irwin, *The Felon,* © 1970, pp. 67–85. Reprinted by permission of Prentice-Hall, Inc., Englewood Cliffs, New Jersey.

important. In some instances it is the basis for forming very important choices, choices which may have important consequences for the felon's long-term career. For example, Piri Thomas, a convict, was forced to make up his mind whether to participate in a riot or refrain:

> I stood there watching and weighing, trying to decide whether or not I was a con first and an outsider second. I had been doing time inside yet living every mental minute I could outside; now I had to choose one or the other. I stood there in the middle of the yard. Cons passed me by, some going west to join the boppers, others going east to neutral ground. The call of rep tore within me, while the feeling of being a punk washed over me like a yellow banner. I had to make a decision. *I am a con. These damn cons are my people.... What do you mean, your people? Your people are outside the cells, home, in the streets. No! That ain't so.... Look at them go toward the west wall. Why in hell am I taking so long in making up my mind? Man, there goes Papo and Zu-Zu, and Mick the Boxer; even Ruben is there.*[1]

This identification also influences the criteria for assigning and earning prestige—criteria relative to things in the outside world or things which tend to exist only in the prison world, such as status in a prison social system or success with prison homosexuals. Furthermore, it will influence the long-term strategies he forms and attempts to follow during his prison sentence.

It is useful to further divide those who maintain their basic orientation to the outside into (1) those who for the most part wish to maintain their life patterns and their identities—even if they intend to refrain from most lawbreaking activities—and (2) those who desire to make significant changes in life patterns and identities and see prison as a chance to do this.

The mode of adaptation of those convicts who tend to make a world out of prison will be called "jailing." To "jail" is to cut yourself off from the outside world and to attempt to construct a life within prison. The adaptation of those who still keep their commitment to the outside life and see prison as a suspension of that life but who do not want to make any significant changes in their life patterns will be called "doing time." One "does time" by trying to maximize his comfort and luxuries and minimize his discomfort and conflict and to get out as soon as possible. The adaptation made by those who, looking to their future life on the outside, try to effect changes in their life patterns and identities will be called "gleaning."[2] In "gleaning," one sets out to "better himself" or "improve himself" and takes advantage of the resources that exist in prison to do this.

Not all convicts can be classified neatly by these three adaptive styles. Some vacillate from one to another, and others appear to be following two or three of them simultaneously. Still others, for instance the noncopers mentioned above, cannot be characterized by any of the three. However, many prison careers fit very closely into one of these patterns, and the great majority can be classified roughly by one of the styles.

Doing Time

When you go in, now your trial is over, you got your time and everything and now you head for the joint. They furnish your clothing, your toothbrush, your toothpaste, they give you a package of tobacco, they put you up in the morning to get breakfast. In other words, everything is furnished. Now you stay in there two years, five years, ten years, whatever you stay in there, what difference does it make? After a year or so you've been . . . after six months, you've become accustomed to the general routine. Everything is furnished. If you get a stomachache, you go to the doctor; if you can't see out of your cheaters, you go to the optician. It don't cost you nothing.[3]

As the above statement by a thief indicates, many convicts conceive of the prison experience as a temporary break in their outside career, one which they take in their stride. They come to prison and "do their time." They attempt to pass through this experience with the least amount of suffering and the greatest amount of comfort. They (1) avoid trouble, (2) find activities which occupy their time, (3) secure a few luxuries, (4) with the exception of a few complete isolates, form friendships with small groups of other convicts, and (5) do what they think is necessary to get out as soon as possible.[4]

To avoid trouble the convict adheres to the convict code—especially the maxims of "do your own time" and "don't snitch," and stays away from "lowriders"—those convicts engaged in hijacking and violent disputes. In some prisons which have a high incidence of violence—knifings, assaults, and murders—this can appear to be very difficult even to the convicts themselves. One convict reported his first impression of Soledad:

> The first day I got to Soledad I was walking from the fish tank to the mess hall and this guy comes running down the hall past me, yelling, with a knife sticking out of his back. Man, I was petrified. I thought, what the fuck kind of place is this. [Interview, Soledad Prison, June 1966.]

Piri Thomas decided to avoid trouble for a while, but commented on the difficulty in doing this:

> The decision to cool myself made the next two years the hardest I had done because it meant being a smoothie and staying out of trouble, which in prison is difficult, for any of a thousand cons might start trouble with you for any real or fancied reason, and if you didn't face up to the trouble, you ran the risk of being branded as having no heart. And heart was all I had left.[5]

However, except for rare, "abnormal" incidents, convicts tend not to bother others who are "doing their own number." One convict made the following comments on avoiding trouble in prison:

> If a new guy comes here and just settles down and minds his business, nobody'll fuck with him, unless he runs into some nut. Everyone sees a guy is trying to do his own time and they leave him alone. Those guys that get messed over are usually asking for it. If you stay away from the lowriders and the punks and don't get into debt or snitch on somebody you won't have no trouble here. [Interview, San Quentin, July 1966.]

To occupy their time, "time-doers" work, read, work on hobbies, play cards, chess, and dominoes, engage in sports, go to movies, watch television, participate in some group activities, such as drama groups, gavel clubs, and slot car clubs, and while away hours "tripping" with friends. They seek extra luxuries through their job. Certain jobs in prison, such as jobs in the kitchen, in the officers' and guards' dining room, in the boiler room, the officers' and guards' barber shop, and the fire-house, offer various extra luxuries—extra things to eat, a radio, privacy, additional shows, and more freedom. Or time-doers purchase luxuries legally or illegally available in the prison market. If they have money on the books, if they have a job which pays a small salary, or if they earn money at a hobby, they can draw up to $20 a month which may be spent for foodstuffs, coffee, cocoa, stationery, toiletries, tobacco, and cigarettes. Or using cigarettes as currency, they may purchase food from the kitchen, drugs, books, cell furnishings, clothes, hotplates, stingers, and other contraband items. If they do not have legal access to funds, they may "scuffle": sell some commodity which they produce—such as belt buckles or other handicraft items—or some commodity which is accessible to them through their job—such as food items from the kitchen. "Scuffling," however, necessitates becoming enmeshed in the convict social system and increases the chances of "trouble," such as conflicts over unpaid debts, hijacking by others, and "beefs"—disciplinary actions for rule infractions. Getting into trouble is contrary to the basic tenets of "doing time," so time-doers usually avoid scuffling.

The friendships formed by time-doers vary from casual acquaintanceships with persons who accidentally cell nearby or work together, to close friendship groups who "go all the way" for each other—share material goods, defend each other against others, and maintain silence about each other's activities. These varying friendship patterns are related closely to their criminal identities.

Finally, time-doers try to get out as soon as possible. First they do this by staying out of trouble, "cleaning up their hands." They avoid activities and persons that would put them in danger of receiving disciplinary actions, or "beefs." And in recent years, with the increasing emphasis on treatment, they "program." To program is to follow, at least tokenly, a treatment plan which has been outlined by the treatment staff, recommended by the board, or devised by the convict himself. It is generally believed that to be released on parole as early as possible one must "get a program." A program involves attending school, vocational training, group counseling, church, Alcoholics Anonymous, or any other special program that is introduced under the treatment policy of the prison.

All convicts are more apt to choose "doing time," but some approach this style in a slightly different manner. For instance, doing time is characteristic of the thief in prison. He shapes this mode of adaptation and establishes it as a major mode of adaptation in prison. The convict code, which is fashioned from the criminal code, is the foundation for this style. The thief has learned how to do his time long before he comes to prison. Prison, he learns when he takes on the dimensions of the criminal subculture, is part of criminal life, a calculated risk, and when it comes he is ready for it.

> Long before the thief has come to prison, his subculture has defined proper prison conduct as behavior rationally calculated to "do time" in the easiest possible way. This means that he wants a prison life containing the best possible combination of a maximum amount of leisure time and maximum number of privileges. Accordingly, the privileges sought by the thief are different from the privileges sought by the man oriented to prison itself. The thief wants things that will make prison life a little easier—extra food, a maximum amount of recreation time, a good radio, a little peace.[6]

The thief knows how to avoid trouble; he keeps away from "dingbats," "lowriders," "hoosiers," "square johns," and "stool pigeons" and obeys the convict code. He also knows not to buck the authorities; he keeps his record clean and does what is necessary to get out—even programs.

He occasionally forms friendships with other criminals, such as dope fiends, heads, and possibly disorganized criminals, but less often with square johns. Formerly he confined his friendship to other thieves with whom he formed very tight-knit groups. For example, Jack Black, a thief in the last century, describes his assimilation into the "Johnson family" in prison:

> Shorty was one of the patricians of the prison, a "box man," doing time for bank burglary. "I'll put you in with the right people, kid. You're folks yourself or you wouldn't have been with Smiler."
>
> I had no friends in the place. But the fact that I had been with Smiler, that I had kept my mouth shut, and that Shorty had come forward to help me, gave me a certain fixed status in the prison that nothing could shake but some act of my own. I was naturally pleased to find myself taken up by the "best people," as Shorty and his friends called themselves, and accepted as one of them.
>
> Shorty now took me into the prison where we found the head trusty who was one of the "best people" himself, a thoroughgoing bum from the road. [The term "bum" is not used here in any cheap or disparaging sense. In those days it meant any kind of traveling thief. It has long since fallen into disuse. The yegg of today was the bum of twenty years ago.]
>
> "This party," said Shorty, "is one of the 'Johnson' family." (The bums called themselves "Johnsons" probably because they were so numerous.) "He's good people and I want to get him fixed up for a cell with the right folks."[7]

Clemmer described two *primary* groups out of the fourteen groups he located, and both of these were groups of thieves.[8]

Presently in California prisons, thieves' numbers have diminished. This and the general loosening of the convict solidarity have tended to drive the thief into the background of prison life. He generally confines his friendships to one or two others, usually other thieves or criminals who are "all right"; otherwise he withdraws from participation with others. He often feels out of place amid the changes that have come about. One thief looking back upon fifteen years in California prisons states:

> As far as I'm concerned their main purpose has been in taking the convict code away from him. But what they fail to do when they strip him from these rules is replace it with something. They turn these guys into a bunch of snivelers and they write letters on each other and they don't have any rules to live by. [Interview, Folsom Prison, July 1966.]

Another thief interviewed also indicated his dislocation in the present prison social world:

> The new kinds in prison are wild. They have no respect for rules or other persons. I just want to get out of here and give it all up. I can't take coming back to prison again, not with the kind of convicts they are getting now. [Interview, Soledad Prison, June 1966.]

Like the majority of convicts, the dope fiend and the head usually just "do time." When they do, they don't vary greatly from the thief, except that they tend to associate with other dope fiends or heads, although they too will associate with other criminals. They tend to form very close bonds with one, two, or three other dope fiends or heads and maintain a casual friendship with a large circle of dope fiends, heads, and other criminals. Like the thief, the dope fiend and the head tend not to establish ties with squares.

The hustler in doing time differs from the other criminals in that he does not show a propensity to form very tight-knit groups. Hustling values, which emphasize manipulation and invidiousness, seem to prevent this. The hustler maintains a very large group of casual friends. Though this group does not show strong bonds of loyalty and mutual aid, they share many activities such as cards, sports, dominoes, and "jiving"—casual talk.

Square johns do their time quite differently from the criminals. The square john finds life in prison repugnant and tries to isolate himself as much as possible from the convict world. He does not believe in the convict code, but he usually learns to display a token commitment to it for his own safety. A square john indicated his forced obedience to the convict code:

> Several times I saw things going on that I didn't like. One time a couple of guys were working over another guy and I wanted to step in, but I couldn't. Had to just keep moving as if I didn't see it. [Interview, Soledad Prison, June 1966.]

He usually keeps busy with some job assignment, a hobby, cards, chess, or various forms of group programs, such as drama groups. He forms friendships with one or two other squares and avoids the criminals. But even with other squares there is resistance to forming *close* ties. Square johns are very often sensitive about their "problems," and they are apt to feel repugnance toward themselves and other persons with problems. Besides, the square usually wants to be accepted by conventional people and not by other "stigmatized" outcasts like himself. So, many square johns do their time isolated from other inmates. Malcolm Braly in his novel *On the Yard* has captured the ideal-typical square john in prison:

> Watson had finally spoken. Formerly a mild-mannered and mother-smothered high school teacher, he had killed his two small sons, attempted to kill his wife, cut his own throat, then poisoned himself, all because his wife had refused a reconciliation with the remark, "John, the truth is you bore me."
>
> Watson stood with culture, the Republic, and motherhood, and at least once each meeting he made a point of reaffirming his position before launching into his chronic criticism of the manner in which his own case had been, was, and would be handled. ". . . And I've been confined almost two years now, and I see no point in further imprisonment, further therapy, no point whatsoever since there's absolutely no possibility I'll do the same thing again. . . ."
>
> "That's right," Red said softly. "He's run out of kids."
>
> And Zeke whispered, "I just wish he'd taken the poison *before* he cut his throat."
>
> Watson ignored the whispering, if he heard it at all, and went on, clearly speaking only to Erlenmeyer. "Surely, Doctor, as a college man yourself you must realize that the opportunities for a meaningful cultural exchange are sorely limited in an institution of this nature. Of course, I attend the General Semantics Club and I'm taking the course Oral McKeon is giving in Oriental religions, but these are such tiny oases in this desert of sweatsuits and domino games, and I can't understand

why everyone is just thrown together without reference to their backgrounds, or the nature of their offense. Thieves, dope addicts, even sex maniacs—"

Zeke threw his hands up in mock alarm. "Where'd you see a sex maniac?"

"I don't think it cause for facetiousness," Watson said coldly. "Just yesterday I found occasion to step into the toilet off the big yard and one of the sweepers was standing there masturbating into the urinal."

"That's horrible," Zeke said. "What'd you do?"

"I left, of course."

"Naturally. It violates the basic ideals of Scouting."[9]

The lower-class man, though he doesn't share the square john's repugnance toward criminals or the convict code, usually does not wish to associate closely with thieves, dope fiends, heads, and disorganized criminals. In his life outside he has encountered and avoided these persons for many years and usually keeps on avoiding them inside. He usually seeks a job to occupy himself. His actual stay in prison is typically very short, since he is either released very early and/or is classified at minimum custody and sent to a forestry camp or one of the minimum-custody institutions, where he has increased freedom and privileges.

Jailing

Some convicts who do not retain or who never acquired any commitment to outside social worlds tend to make a world out of prison.[10] These are the men who

seek positions of power, influence, and sources of information, whether these men are called "shots," "politicians," "merchants," "hoods," "toughs," "gorillas," or something else. A job as secretary to the captain or warden, for example, gives an aspiring prisoner information and consequent power, and enables him to influence the assignment or regulation of other inmates. In the same way, a job which allows the incumbent to participate in a racket, such as clerk in the kitchen storeroom where he can steal and sell food, is highly desirable to a man oriented to the convict sub-culture. With a steady income of cigarettes, ordinarily the prisoner's medium of exchange, he may assert a great deal of influence and purchase those things which are symbols of status among persons oriented to the convict subculture. Even if there is not a well-developed medium of exchange, he can barter goods acquired in his position for equally desirable goods possessed by other convicts. These include information and such things as specially starched, pressed, and tailored prison cloth-ing, fancy belts, belt buckles or billfolds, special shoes, or any other type of dress which will set him apart and will indicate that he has both the influence to get the goods and the influence necessary to keep them and display them despite prison rules which outlaw doing so. In California, special items of clothing, and clothing that is neatly laundered, are called "bonaroos" (a corruption of *bonnet rouge,* by means of which French prison trustees were once distinguished from the common run of prisoners), and to a lesser degree even the persons who wear such clothing are called "bonaroos."[11]

Just as doing time is the characteristic style of the thief, so "jailing" is the characteristic style of the state-raised youth. This identity terminates on the first or second prison term, or certainly by the time the youth reaches thirty. The state-raised youth must assume a new identity, and the one he most often chooses, the one which his experience has prepared him for, is that of the "convict." The prison world is the only world with which he is familiar. He was raised in a world where "punks" and "queens" have replaced women, "bonaroos" are the only fashionable clothing, and cigarettes are money. This is a world where disputes are settled with a pipe or a knife, and the individual must form tight cliques for protection. His senses are attuned to iron doors banging, locks turning, shakedowns, and long lines of blue-clad convicts. He knows how to survive, in fact prosper, in this world, how to get a cell change and a good work assignment, how to score for nutmeg, cough syrup, or other narcotics. More important, he knows hundreds of youths like himself who grew up in the youth prisons and are now in the adult prisons. For example, Claude Brown describes a friend who fell into the patterns of jailing:

> "Yeah, Sonny. The time I did in Woodburn, the times I did on the Rock, that was college, man. Believe me, it was college. I did four years in Woodburn. And I guess I've done a total of about two years on the Rock in about the last six years. Every time I went there, I learned a little more. When I go to jail now, Sonny, I live, man. I'm right at home. That's the good part about it. If you look at it, Sonny, a cat like me is just cut out to be in jail.
>
> "It could never hurt me, 'cause I never had what the good folks call a home and all that kind of shit to begin with. So when I went to jail, the first time I went away, when I went to Warwick, I made my own home. It was all right. Shit, I learned how to live. Now when I go back to the joint, anywhere I go, I know some people. If I go to any of the jails in New York, or if I go to a slam in Jersey, even, I still run into a lot of cats I know. It's almost like a family."
>
> I said, "Yeah, Reno, it's good that a cat can be so happy in jail. I guess all it takes to be happy in anything is knowin' how to walk with your lot, whatever it is, in life."[12]

The state-raised youth often assumes a role in the prison social system, the system of roles, values, and norms described by Schrag, Sykes, and others. This does not mean that he immediately rises to power in the prison system. Some of the convicts have occupied their positions for many years and cannot tolerate the threat of every new bunch of reform-school graduates. The state-raised youth who has just graduated to adult prison must start at the bottom; but he knows the routine, and in a year or so he occupies a key position himself. One reason he can readily rise is that in youth prison he very often develops skills, such as clerical and maintenance skills, that are valuable to the prison administration.

Many state-raised youth, however, do not tolerate the slow ascent in the prison social system and become "lowriders." They form small cliques and rob cells, hijack other convicts, carry on feuds with other cliques, and engage in various rackets. Though these outlaws are feared and hated by all other convicts, their orientation is to the convict world, and they are definitely part of the convict social system.

Dope fiends and hustlers slip into jailing more often than thieves, due mainly to the congruities between their old activities and some of the patterns of jailing. For instance, a central activity of jailing is "wheeling and dealing," the major economic activity of prison. All prison resources—dope, food, books, money, sexual favors, bonaroos, cell changes, jobs, dental and hospital care, hot plates, stingers, cell furnishings, rings, and buckles—are always available for purchase with cigarettes. It is possible to live in varying degrees of luxury, and luxury has a double reward in prison as it does in the outside society: first, there is the reward of consumption itself, and second there is the reward of increased prestige in the prison social system because of the display of opulence.

This prison lifestyle requires more cigarettes than can be obtained legally; consequently, one wheels and deals. There are three main forms of wheeling and dealing for cigarettes: (1) gambling (cards, dice, and betting on sporting events); (2) selling some commodity or service which is usually made possible by a particular job assignment; and (3) lending cigarettes for interest—two for three. These activities have a familiar ring to both the hustler and the dope fiend, who have hustled money or dope on the outside. They very often become intricately involved in the prison economic life and in this way necessarily involved in the prison social system. The hustler does this because he feels at home in this routine, because he wants to keep in practice, or because he must present a good front—even in prison. To present a good front one must be a success at wheeling and dealing.

The dope fiend, in addition to having an affinity for wheeling and dealing, may become involved in the prison economic life in securing drugs. There are a variety of drugs available for purchase with cigarettes or money (and money can be purchased with cigarettes). Drugs are expensive, however, and to purchase them with any regularity one either has money smuggled in from the outside or he wheels and deals. And to wheel and deal one must maintain connections for securing drugs, for earning money, and for protection. This enmeshes the individual in the system of prison roles, values, and norms. Though he maintains a basic commitment to his drug subculture which supersedes his commitment to the prison culture, and though he tends to form close ties only with other dope fiends, through his wheeling and dealing for drugs he becomes an intricate part of the prison social system.

The head jails more often than the thief. One reason for this is that the head, especially the "weed head," tends to worship luxuries and comforts and is fastidious in his dress. Obtaining small luxuries, comforts, and "bonaroo" clothing usually necessitates enmeshing himself in the "convict" system. Furthermore, the head is often vulnerable to the dynamics of narrow, cliquish, and invidious social systems, such as the "convict" system, because many of the outside head social systems are of this type.

The thief, or any identity for that matter, *may* slowly lose his orientation to the outside community, take on the convict categories, and thereby fall into jailing. This occurs when the individual has spent a great deal of time in prison and/or returned to the outside community and discovered that he no longer fits in the outside world. It is difficult to maintain a real commitment to a social world without firsthand experience with it for long periods of time.

The square john and the lower-class man find the activities of the "convicts" petty, repugnant, or dangerous, and virtually never jail.

Gleaning

With the rapidly growing educational, vocational training, and treatment opportunities, and with the erosion of convict solidarity, an increasing number of convicts choose to radically change their lifestyles and follow a sometimes carefully devised plan to "better themselves," "improve their mind," or "find themselves" while in prison.[13] One convict describes his motives and plans for changing his lifestyle:

> I got tired of losing. I had been losing all my life. I decided that I wanted to win for a while. So I got on a different kick. I knew that I had to learn something so I went to school, got my high school diploma. I cut myself off from my old YA buddies and started hanging around with some intelligent guys who minded their own business. We read a lot, a couple of us paint. We play a little bridge and talk a lot of time about what we are going to do when we get out. [Interview, Soledad Prison, June 1966.]

Gleaning may start on a small scale, perhaps as an attempt to overcome educational or intellectual inferiorities. For instance, Malcolm X, feeling inadequate in talking to certain convicts, starts to read:

> It had really begun back in the Charlestown Prison, when Bimbi first made me feel envy of his stock of knowledge. Bimbi had always taken charge of any conversation he was in, and I had tried to emulate him. But every book I picked up had few sentences which didn't contain anywhere from one to nearly all of the words that might as well have been in Chinese. When I just skipped those words, of course, I really ended up with little idea of what the book said. So I have come to the Norfolk Prison Colony still going through only book-reading motions. Pretty soon, I would quit even these motions, unless I had received the motivation that I did.[14]

The initial, perfunctory steps into gleaning often spring the trap. Gleaning activities have an intrinsic attraction and often instill motivation which was originally lacking. Malcolm X reports how once he began to read, the world of knowledge opened up to him:

> No university would ask any student to devour literature as I did when this new world opened to me, of being able to read and *understand*.[15]

In trying to "improve himself," "improve his mind," or "find himself," the convict gleans from every source available in prison. The chief source is books: he reads philosophy, history, art, science, and fiction. Often after getting started he devours a sizeable portion of world literature. Malcolm X describes his voracious reading habits:

> I read more in my room than in the library itself. An inmate who was known to read a lot could check out more than the permitted maximum number of books. I preferred reading in the total isolation of my own room.
>
> When I had progressed to really serious reading, every night at about 10 P.M. I would be outraged with the "lights out." It always seemed to catch me right in the middle of something engrossing.
>
> Fortunately, right outside my door was a corridor light that cast a glow into my room. The glow was enough to read by, once my eyes adjusted to it. So when "lights out" came, I would sit on the floor where I could continue reading in that glow.[16]

Besides this informal education, he often pursues formal education. The convict may complete grammar school and high school in the prison educational facilities. He may enroll in college courses through the University of California (which will be paid for by the Department of Corrections), or through other correspondence schools (which he must pay for himself). More recently, he may take courses in various prison college programs.

He learns trades through the vocational training programs or prison job assignments. Sometimes he augments these by studying trade books, correspondence courses, or journals. He studies painting, writing, music, acting, and other creative arts. There are some facilities for these pursuits sponsored by the prison administration, but these are limited. This type of gleaning is done mostly through correspondence, through reading, or through individual efforts in the cell.

He tries to improve himself in other ways. He works on his social skills and his physical appearance—has his tattoos removed, has surgery on physical defects, has dental work done, and builds up his body "pushing iron."

He shys away from former friends or persons with his criminal identity who are not gleaners and forms new associations with other gleaners. These are usually gleaners who have chosen a similar style of gleaning, and with whom he shares many interests and activities, but they may also be those who are generally trying to improve themselves, although they are doing so in different ways.

Gleaning is a style more characteristic of the hustler, the dope fiend, and the state-raised youth than of the thief. When the former glean, though they tend to associate less with their deviant friends who are doing time or jailing, they are not out of the influence of these groups, or free from the influence of their old subculture values. The style of gleaning they choose and the future life for which they prepare themselves must be acceptable to the old reference group and somewhat congruent with their deviant values. The life they prepare for should be prestigious in the eyes of their old associates. It must be "doing good" and cannot be "a slave's life."

The state-raised youth who gleans probably has the greatest difficulty cutting himself off from his former group because the state-raised values emphasize loyalty to one's buddies:

> I don't spend much time with my old YA [Youth Authority] partners and when I do we don't get along. They want me to do something that I won't do or they start getting on my back about my plans. One time they were riding me pretty bad and I had to pull them up. [Interview, Soledad Prison, June 1966.]

He also has the greatest difficulty in making any realistic plans for the future. He has limited experience with the outside, and his models of "making it" usually come from the mass media—magazines, books, movies, and television.

The dope fiend and the head, when they glean, tend to avoid practical fields and choose styles which promise glamor, excitement, or color. Most conventional paths with which they are familiar seem especially dull and repugnant. In exploring ways of making it they must find some way to avoid the humdrum life which they rejected long ago. Many turn to legitimate deviant identities such as "intellectual outsiders," "bohemians," or "mystics." Often they study one of the creative arts, the social sciences, or philosophy with no particular career in mind.

The hustler, who values skills of articulation and maintained a good "front" in his deviant life, often prepares for a field where these skills will serve him, such as preaching or political activism.

The square john and the lower-class man, since they seldom seek to radically change their identity, do not glean in the true sense, but they do often seek to improve themselves. The square john usually does this by attacking his problem. He is sat-isfied with his reference world—the conventional society—but he recognizes that to return to it successfully he must cope with that flaw in his makeup which led to his incarceration. There are three common ways he attacks this problem: (1) he joins self-help groups such as Alcoholics Anonymous, (2) he seeks the help of experts (psychiatrists, psychologists, or sociologists) and attends the therapy programs, or (3) he turns to religion.

The lower-class man is usually an older person who does not desire or deem it possible to carve out a radically new style of life. He may, however, see the prison experience as a chance to improve himself by increasing his education and his voca-tional skills.

The thief tends to be older and his commitment to his identity is usually strong, so it is not likely that he will explore other lifestyles or identities. This does not mean that he is committed for all time to a life of crime. Certain alternate conclusions to a criminal career are included in the definitions of a proper thief's life. For instance, a thief may retire when he becomes older, has served a great deal of time, or has made a "nice score." When he retires he may work at some well-paying trade or run a small business, and in prison he may prepare himself for either of these acceptable conclusions to a criminal career.

The Disorganized Criminal

In the preceding discussion of prison adaptive modes, the "disorganized criminal" was purposely omitted. It is felt that his prison adaptation must be considered sep-arately from the other identities.

The disorganized criminal is human putty in the prison social world. He may be shaped to fit any category. He has weaker commitments to values or conceptions of self that would prevent him from organizing any course of action in prison. He is the most responsive to prison programs, to differential association, and to other forces which are out of his control. He may become part of the prison social system, do his time, or glean. If they will tolerate him, he may associate with thieves, dope fiends, convicts, squares, heads, or other disorganized criminals. To some extent these associations are formed in a random fashion. He befriends persons with whom he works, cells next to, and encounters regularly through the prison routine. He tends not to seek out particular categories, as is the case with the other identities. He does not feel any restraints in initiating associations, however, as do the square john and the lower-class man.

The friendships he forms are very important to any changes that occur in this person. Since he tends to have a cleaner slate in terms of identity, he is more sus-ceptible to differential association. He often takes on the identity and the prison adap-tive mode of the group with which he comes into contact. If he does acquire a new identity, however, such as one of the deviant identities that exist in prison, his com-mitment to it is still tentative at most. The deviant identities, except for that of the convict, exist in the context of an exterior world, and the more subtle cues, the responses, the meanings which are essential parts of this world cannot be experienced in prison. It is doubtful, therefore, that any durable commitment could be acquired in prison. In the meantime, he may be shaken from this identity, and he may continue to vacillate from social world to social world, or to wander bewildered in a maze of conflicting world views as he has done in the past.

Race and Ethnicity

Another variable which is becoming increasingly important in the formation of cleavages and identity changes in the convict world is that of race and ethnicity. For quite some time in California prisons, hostility and distance between three segments of the populations—whites, Negroes, and Mexicans—have increased. For several years the Negroes have assumed a more militant and ethnocentric posture, and recently the Mexicans—already ethnocentric and aggressive—have followed with a more organized, militant stance. Correspondingly, there is a growing trend among these two segments to establish, reestablish, or enhance racial-ethnic pride and identity. Many "blacks" and "Chicanos" are supplanting their criminal identity with a racial-ethnic one. This movement started with the blacks.[17] A black California convict gives his recently acquired views toward whites:

> All these years, man, I been stealing and coming to the joint. I never stopped to think why I was doing it. I thought that all I wanted was money and stuff. Ya know, man, now I can see why I thought the way I did. I been getting fucked all my life and never realized it. The white man has been telling me that I should want his stuff. But he didn't give me no way to get it. Now I ain't going for his shit anymore. I'm a black man. I'm going to get out of here and see what I can do for my people. I'm going to do what I have to do to get those white motherfuckers off my people's back. [Interview, San Quentin, March 1968.]

Chicanos in prison have maintained considerable insulation from both whites and blacks—especially blacks—toward whom they have harbored considerable hostility. They possess a strong ethnic-racial identity which underpins their more specialized felonious one—which has usually been that of a dope fiend or lower-class man. This subcultural identity and actual group unity in prison has been based on their Mexican culture—especially two important dimensions of Mexican culture. The first is their strong commitment to the concept of "machismo"—which is roughly translated manhood. . . . The second is their use of Spanish and Calo (Spanish slang), which has separated them from other segments. Besides these two traits there are many other ethnic subcultural characteristics which promote unity among Chicanos. For instance, they tend to be stoic and intolerant of "snitches" and "snivelers" and feel that Anglos and blacks are more often snitches and snivelers. Furthermore, they respect friendship to the extreme, in fact to the extreme of killing or dying for friendship.

Until recently this has meant that Chicanos constituted the most cohesive segment in California prisons. In prison, where they intermingle with whites and Negroes, they have felt considerable distance from these segments and have maintained their identification with Mexican culture. However, there have been and still are some divisions in this broad category. For instance, various neighborhood cliques of Chicanos often carry on violent disputes with each other which last for years.

Furthermore, Los Angeles or California cliques wage disputes with El Paso or Texas cliques. Many stabbings and killings have resulted from confrontations between different Chicano groups. Nevertheless, underpinning these different group affiliations and the various criminal identities there has been a strong identification with Mexican culture.

Recently the Chicanos, following the footsteps of the Negroes in prison and the footsteps of certain militant Mexican-American groups outside (for example, MAPA and the Delano strikers), have started organizing cultural-activist groups in prison (such as Empleo) and shaping a new identity built upon their Mexican ancestry and their position of disadvantage in the white society. As they move in this direction, they are cultivating some friendship with the Negroes, toward whom they now feel more affinity.

This racial-ethnic militance and identification will more than likely become increasingly important in the prison social world. There is already some indication that the identity of the black national and that of the Chicano is becoming superordinate to the criminal identities of many Negroes and Mexican-Americans, or at least is having an impact on their criminal identities.

> A dude don't necessarily have to become a Muslim or a Black National now to get with Black Power. He may still be laying to get out there and do some pimping or shoot some dope. But he knows he's a brother and when the shit is down we can count on him. And maybe he is going to carry himself a little differently, you know, like now you see more and more dudes—oh, they're still pimps, but they got naturals now. [Interview, San Quentin, April 1968.]

The reassertion or discovery of the racial-ethnic identity is sometimes related to gleaning in prison. Frequently, the leaders of blacks or Chicanos, for example, Malcolm X and Eldridge Cleaver, have arrived at their subcultural activism and militant stance through gleaning. Often, becoming identified with this movement will precipitate a gleaning course. However, this is not necessarily the case. These two phenomena are not completely overlapping among the Negro and Chicano.

The nationalistic movement is beginning to have a general impact on the total prison world—especially at San Quentin. The blacks and Chicanos, as they focus on the whites as their oppressors, seem to be excluding white prisoners from this category and are, in fact, developing some sympathy for them as a minority group which itself is being oppressed by the white establishment and the white police. As an indication of this recent change, one convict comments on the present food-serving practices of Muslim convicts:

> It used to be that whenever a Muslim was serving something (and this was a lot of the time, man, because there's a lot of those dudes in the kitchen), well, you know, you wouldn't expect to get much of a serving. Now, the cats just pile it on to whites and blacks. Like he is giving all the state's stuff away to show his contempt. So I think it is getting better between the suedes and us. [Interview, San Quentin, April 1968.]

The Convict Identity

Over and beyond the particular criminal identity or the racial-ethnic identity he acquires or maintains in prison, and over and beyond the changes in his direction which are produced by his prison strategy, to some degree the felon acquires the perspective of the "convict."

There are several gradations and levels of this perspective and attendant identity. First is the taken-for-granted perspective, which he acquires in spite of any conscious efforts to avoid it. This perspective is acquired simply by being in prison and engaging in prison routines for months or years. Even square johns who consciously attempt to pass through the prison experience without acquiring any of the beliefs and values of the criminals do to some extent acquire certain meanings, certain taken-for-granted interpretations and responses which will shape, influence, or distort reality for them after release. . . .

Beyond the taken-for-granted perspective which all convicts acquire, most convicts are influenced by a pervasive but rather uncohesive convict "code." To some extent most of them, especially those who identify with a criminal system, are consciously committed to the major dictum of this code—"do your own time." As was pointed out earlier, the basic meaning of this precept is the obligation to tolerate the behavior of others unless it is directly affecting your physical self or your possessions. If another's behavior surpasses these limits, then the problem must be solved by the person himself; that is, *not* by calling for help from the officials.

> The convict code isn't any different than stuff we all learned as kids. You know, nobody likes a stool pigeon. Well, here in the joint you got all kinds of guys living jammed together, two to a cell. You got nuts walking the yard, you got every kind of dingbat in the world here. Well, we got to have some rules among ourselves. The rule is "do your own number." In other words, keep off your neighbors' toes. Like if a guy next to me is making brew in his cell, well, this is none of my business. I got no business running to the man and telling him that Joe Blow is making brew in his cell. Unless Joe Blow is fucking over me, then I can't say nothing. And when he is fucking over me, then I got to stop him myself. If I can't, then I deserve to get fucked over. [Interview, San Quentin, May 1968.]

Commitment to the convict code or the identity of the convict is to a high degree a lifetime commitment to do your own time—that is, to live and let live, and when you feel that someone is not letting you live, to either take it, leave, or stop him yourself, but never call for help from official agencies of control.

At another level, the convict perspective consists of a more cohesive and sophisticated value and belief system. This is the perspective of the elite of the convict world—the "regular." A "regular" (or, as he has been variously called, "people," "folks," "solid," a "right guy," or "all right") possesses many of the traits of the thief's culture. He can be counted on when needed by other regulars. He is also not a "hoosier"—that is, he has some finesse, is capable, is levelheaded, has "guts" and "timing." The following description of a simple bungled transaction exemplifies this trait:

> Man, you should have seen the hoosier when the play came down. I thought that that motherfucker was all right. He surprised me. He had the stuff and was about to hand it to me when a sergeant and another bull came through the door from the outside. Well, there wasn't nothing to worry about. Is all he had to do was go on like there was nothin' unusual and hand me the stuff and they would have never suspected nothing. But he got so fucking nervous and started fumbling around. You know, he handed me the sack and then pulled it back until they got hip that some

play was taking place. Well, you know what happened. The play was ranked and we both ended up in the slammer. [Field notes, San Quentin, February 1968.]

The final level of the perspective of the convict is that of the "old con." This is a degree of identification reached after serving a great deal of time, so much time that all outside-based identities have dissipated and the only meaningful world is that of the prison. The old con has become totally immersed in the prison world. This identification is often the result of years of jailing, but it can result from merely serving too much time. It was mentioned previously that even thieves after spending many years may fall into jailing, even though time-doing is their usual pattern. After serving a very long sentence or several long sentences with no extended period between, any criminal will tend to take on the identity of the "old con."

The old con tends to carve out a narrow but orderly existence in prison. He has learned to secure many luxuries and learned to be satisfied with the prison forms of pleasure—for example, homosexual activities, cards, dominoes, handball, hobbies, and reading. He usually obtains jobs which afford him considerable privileges and leisure time. He often knows many of the prison administrators—the warden, the associate wardens, the captain, and the lieutenants, whom he has known since they were officers and lesser officials.

Often he becomes less active in the prison social world. He retires and becomes relatively docile or apathetic. At times he grows petty and treacherous. There is some feeling that old cons can't be trusted because their "head has become soft" or they have "lost their guts" and are potential "stool pigeons."

The convict identity is very important to the future career of the felon. In the first instance, the acquiring of the taken-for-granted perspective will at least obstruct the releasee's attempts to reorient himself on the outside. More important, the other levels of the identity, if they have been acquired, will continue to influence choices for years afterward. The convict perspective, though it may become submerged after extended outside experiences, will remain operative in its latency state and will often obtrude into civilian life contexts.

The identity of the old con—the perspective, the values and beliefs, and other personality attributes which are acquired after the years of doing time, such as advanced age, adjustment to prison routines, and complete loss of skills required to carry on the normal activities of civilians—will usually make living on the outside impossible. The old con is very often suited for nothing except dereliction on the outside or death in prison.

notes

1. Piri Thomas, *Down These Mean Streets* (New York: Alfred A. Knopf, 1967), p. 281. Reprinted by permission.
2. "Gleaning" is one term which is not natural to the prison social world, and the category itself is not explicitly defined. Convicts have recognized and labeled subparts of it, such as "intellectuals," "programmers," and "dudes on a self-improvement kick," but not the broader category which I have labeled gleaners. However, whenever I have described this category to convicts, they immediately recognized it and the term becomes meaningful to them. I chose the term *gleaning* because it emphasizes one very important dimension of this style of adaptation, the tendency to pick through the prison world (which is mostly chaff) in search of the means of self-improvement.

3. David W. Mauer, *Whiz Mob* (Princeton: Princeton University Press, 1964), p. 196.
4. Erving Goffman has described this mode of adaptation, which he calls "playing it cool." *Asylums* (Garden City, N.Y.: Doubleday, 1961), pp. 64–65.
5. Thomas, *Down These Mean Streets,* p. 280.
6. John Irwin and Donald Cressey, "Thieves, Convicts, and the Inmate Culture," *Social Problems,* Fall 1962, p. 150. Reprinted by permission of the Society for the Study of Social Problems and of the authors.
7. Black, *You Can't Win,* pp. 104–105.
8. Donald Clemmer, *The Prison Community* (New York: Holt, Rinehart & Winston, 1966), pp. 123, 127.
9. Malcolm Braly, *On the Yard* (Boston: Little, Brown, 1967), pp. 106–107.
10. Fifteen percent of the 116 ex-prisoners were classified as "jailers."
11. Irwin and Cressey, "Thieves, Convicts, and the Inmate Culture," p. 149.
12. Claude Brown, *Manchild in the Promised Land* (New York: Macmillan, 1965), p. 412. Reprinted by permission.
13. In the sample of 116 ex-prisoners, the records indicated that 19 percent had followed a gleaning course in prison.
14. Malcolm X and Alex Haley, *The Autobiography of Malcolm X* (New York: Grove Press, 1966), p. 171. Reprinted by permission of Hutchison as U.K. and Commonwealth publisher.
15. Ibid., p. 173.
16. Ibid., pp. 173–174.
17. This movement was foretold by Malcolm X (ibid., p. 183).

23

Well-Governed Prisons Are Possible

John J. DiIulio, Jr.

Political scientist John DiIulio challenges the view of Sykes and other sociologists that prisons should be analyzed from the perspective of the inmate society. He argues that because of the dominance of the view that "the cons run the joint," the importance of good management has been neglected.

Although a disputatious lot, public management scholars tend to agree strongly (if implicitly) on one thing: public management matters. They share a belief ("faith" might be a better word) that how public organizations are managed has a significant bearing on how, and how well, those organizations perform. They assume that how public executives, managers, and line workers behave affects significantly what and how much their organizations produce in the way of public safety, health, education, environmental protection, national security, and so on. This assumption undergirds every public administration text and many books and articles on the organization of the White House, Congress, and the lesser bodies that form each institution.

For example, many studies now suggest that student performance on standardized tests and other measures of educational attainment is largely a function of school management, which is defined in terms of such hard-to-measure factors as how teachers structure their classes, how principals lead their teachers, and how superintendents coordinate their principals. In popular and scholarly discourse, these works are often lumped together and called the "effective-schools" literature.[1] This literature deepens one's faith in the efficacy of the public management variable. Broadly stated, if society's goal is to make students literate and social, then it matters

Source: This is the first publication of "Well-Governed Prisons are Possible," by John J. DiIulio, Jr.

Author's Note: Portions of this article have been adapted from my previously published works, including "Recovering the Public Management Variable: Lessons from Schools, Prisons, and Armies," *Public Administration Review* (March/April) 1989): 127–133; *No Escape: The Future of American Corrections* (New York: Basic Books, 1991), Chap. 1.; and "Understanding Prisons: The New Old Penology," *Law and Social Inquiry* 16 (Winter 1991): 65–86.

greatly how the schools are managed. The studies indicate that simply paying teachers more, "tinkering" with testing devices, or "fiddling" with pupil-to-teacher ratios does not work.

Well-Governed Prisons

No literature is available on prisons that parallels the "effective-schools" literature. Most of the research on prisons has been done by sociologists and focuses heavily on the social order of the cell blocks.[2] The "ineffective-prisons" literature might be the most fitting label for the past five decades of research on prisons.

Most works on prisons by sociologists and penologists embody grave doubts about the efficacy of prison management. Indeed, most of this literature suggests that prison managers can do virtually nothing to improve conditions behind bars: if prisons develop a distinctive social system along racial and ethnic lines, reinforced by an informal but powerful distribution of authority, then policy makers can do little more than take notice, while prison managers must compromise their formal authority. To the extent that any of these studies relate prison management practices to the quality of life behind bars, the results are maddening: prisons that are managed in a tight, authoritarian fashion are plagued by disorder and inadequate programs; prisons that are managed in a loose "participative" fashion are equally troubled; and "mixed" cell block management regimes do no better.

But general faith in the efficacy of public management, the existence of numerous (though admittedly laughable) "prison administrator" textbooks and former wardens' "how to" memoirs, and a few quite recent empirical studies of prison management conspire to challenge this perplexing view of these "barbed-wire bureaucracies."

My *Governing Prisons: A Comparative Study of Correctional Management* reports on three years of exploratory research on prison management in the Texas, Michigan, and California departments of corrections.[3] In sum, that book analyzed intersystem, intrasystem, and historical variations in the quality of life, which were measured in terms of three criteria: order (rates of individual and collective violence and other forms of misconduct), amenity (availability of clean cells, decent food, and so on), and service (availability of work opportunities, educational programs, and so forth).

Using the simplest sort of approach and having weighed the possibility of problems in the data, I found no evidence that levels of order, amenity, and service varied directly with any of these factors: a "better class" of inmates; greater per capita spending; lower levels of crowding; lower inmate-to-staff ratios; greater officer training; more modern plant and equipment; more elaborate systems to sensitize official decision makers to the views (especially the grievances) of inmates; more elaborate systems to improve inmate–staff and inmate–inmate race relations (including the existence of a more racially "representative" officer force); and a more routine use of repressive measures, including official and quasi-official beatings of "troublemakers" by officers or by designated inmate "trusties."

All roads, it seemed, led to the conclusion that the quality of prison life depended mainly on the quality of prison management. This conclusion was teased from a close analysis of the history, politics, penological credo, and administration of each system and was bolstered by two natural experiments in the data. To simplify greatly, prison organizations that were led strongly by a stable team of like-minded executives, structured in a paramilitary, security-driven, bureaucratic fashion, and coordinated proactively in conjunction with the demands of relevant outside actors (including key legislators, community activists, judges, and overseers) had higher levels of order, amenity, and service than prison organizations that were managed in other ways, *even when* the former institutions were more crowded, spent less per capita, had higher inmate–staff ratios, and so on. The research supported this conclusion: *"The only findings of this study that, to me at least, seem indisputable, is that . . . prison management matters."*[4]

Other recent studies are part of what might be termed the emerging "well-governed prisons" literature. Bert Useem, analyzing major prison riots in the United States between 1971 and 1986, provides ample evidence that the riots were due mainly to a breakdown in security procedures—the daily routine of numbering, counting, frisking, locking, contraband control, and cell searches that is the heart of administration in most prisons.[5] The main determinants of prison riots are obvious and proximate factors related to the quality of prison management. Crowding, underfunding, court intervention, festering inmate–staff or inmate–inmate racial animosities, and other widely cited causes of prison disorders may make riots more likely, but only failed security management makes them "inevitable."[6] In short, how prisons are managed may increase or decrease the probability of an inmate living out his term in a safe, lawful environment.

Similarly, my *Principled Agents: Leadership, Administration, and Culture in a Federal Bureaucracy* shows how efficacious prison management can be.[7] The Federal Bureau of Prisons is recognized far and wide as one of the nation's most successful correctional agencies. Almost without exception, its prisons have been safe and humane; they have improved every decade since the agency came into being. There are two popular but false explanations for the bureau's success relative to state prison systems. The first explanation is that the bureau has always gotten "a better class of criminals." Historically, however, the bureau has never held only white-collar offenders; in mid-1988, for example, 46 percent of its prisoners had a history of violence; and each year the states transfer many of their "too-hard-to-handle" inmates to "the Feds." The second explanation is that the bureau's annual per-inmate expenditures far exceed the states'; in fact, historically the agency has spent almost exactly at the national median. Furthermore, like many states systems, the bureau has had overcrowding, poorly designed cell houses, staff shortages, and other problems that adversely affect the quality of prison life. But the bureau has met these challenges better, and with greater consistency, than any other correctional agency in the land.

The reason: bureau management. In sum, unlike most state prison systems, the bureau has had stable and talented executive leadership (only four directors in its first fifty-seven years of existence); a progressive inmate classification system; an elaborate system of audits, transfers, and other internal "checks and balances"; a positive, closely knit organizational culture; and many other positive features. State and local agencies that have copied bureau management practices have improved. For example, recent analysis of intrasystem differences in the New York City system documents the comparative strengths of "unit management," a form of correctional administration pioneered by the bureau in which security staff and noncustodial personnel are given responsibility for a wing of an institution and trained to work cohesively.[8] In these and other recent studies, prison management emerges as the crucial variable in determining the quality of life behind bars.

General Principles of Good Correctional Leadership

Successful correctional leaders differ in many ways, from their own penological credos to their personal styles. However, in certain crucial aspects, they and the organization they lead are the same.

One important trait shared by successful correctional leaders is devotion to building or maintaining an organizational culture. James Q. Wilson has defined *organizational culture* as "a persistent, patterned way of thinking about the central tasks of and human relationships within an organization. Culture is to organization what personality is to an individual. Like human culture generally, it is passed on from one generation to the next."[9] As Wilson has observed, unlike students of business administration, students of public administration have not puzzled much over "creating the right organizational culture," and little is known about how government executives "define tasks and motivate workers to perform those tasks."[10]

While the literature of public administration includes nothing of note about the relationship between correctional leadership and organizational culture, certain interlocking patterns are clear. In *No Escape: The Future of American Corrections,* I identified six general principles of good leadership drawn from my observations of correctional managers in both state and national agencies.[11] Let us examine these principles closely.

1. *The successful leaders focus, and inspire their subordinates to focus, on results rather than process, on performance rather than procedures, on ends rather than means.* Managers are rewarded (or not) according to whether the cell blocks are clean, the inmates safe, the classes orderly, the industry productive, the staff turnover rate low, the escape rate zero, and so on. A warden who fails to deliver these goods cannot excuse himself by reciting budget woes, crowding problems, red tapes, too many "heavies," or anything else.

Some of the successful correctional leaders have concentrated more or less exclusively on results, but all of them have stressed results in accordance with their sense of the organization's mission and primary objectives. But in each case, a clear mission statement existed and the institutions were organized and managed around it.

2. *Organizational culture is custodial at core.* Doctors, nurses, secretaries, counselors, accountants, and other nonuniformed institutional staff are trained to think as correctional officers first, and the primary responsibility of every employee is to protect the inmates and to keep them from escaping. Leaders have made institutional safety and security their top priority and have worked hard to see to it that the organization's formal and informal (peer group) incentive structure mirrored this emphasis.

In the Federal Bureau of Prisons, for example, all staff members have undergone the same basic training. They have been required to take target practice and are expected to join shoulders with uniformed officers in the event of a major disturbance. The spectacle of middle-aged secretaries in skirts toting guns on the perimeter of a prison amazed (and distressed) some on-site observers of the 1987 hostage incident at the bureau's Atlanta Penitentiary—but it was an example of the kind of management that has made the bureau a close-knit family organization with high esprit de corps and little of the workaday tension between treatment and custodial personnel that has harmed other corrections agencies. Similarly, a Michigan prisons research analyst was amused when he telephoned his counterpart in the Texas Department of Corrections and was told that the fellow was out hunting down escapees. Such practices accounted for the once-healthy staff morale and good relations among Texas prison workers at all levels.

As Wilson points out, public organizations that have strong management and a concomitantly strong sense of mission sometimes suffer from resistance to needed administrative changes, slowness in adapting to new political circumstances, and other problems.[12] The net effect, however, is almost always positive, and correctional organizations that have been led in ways that promote a strong custodial culture have everywhere been more safe and humane than those that have not.

3. *Leaders of successful institutions follow the MBWA principle; management by walking around.* "Walking" George Beto, director of the Texas Department of Corrections from 1962 to 1972, takes the prize for this approach to management, but his successful peers come in as close seconds.

New Jersey's William Fauver, for example, began his practice of "feet-on" leadership when he was the warden of Trenton State Prison. As he later recalled: "When I first came to Trenton, a warden walking around without a bodyguard was unheard of. I felt it was necessary—a symbolic thing that says you're in charge." He has continued this practice as commissioner, making regular visits (not "tours" or "inspections") to each of his facilities.

The same has been true for other successful leaders. None are strangers to the cell blocks; each knows the facilities almost as well as he knows his own home, and he is always on the scene (often in the center of things) when major trouble erupts. MBWA keeps correctional managers from becoming hostages to (often distorted or incomplete) reports from the field and helps them escape the iron bars of paperwork. Moreover, it gives the staff greater personal respect for their chief and also enhances his reputation among the inmates.

In prison and jail settings, one's personal reputation is crucial: inmates who lie about their criminal exploits or "punk out" when challenged physically by their peers are not respected; and officers who are easily intimidated, break their word, or do not act in a "firm but fair" manner are not taken seriously. Everyone "looks through" the uniform to the person inside it. Of senior officers who have weak personal reputations, one often hears comments such as "He's just a paper captain," or "His bars aren't for real," or (from inmates) "He's Major No-Balls."

Correctional leaders who have not practiced MBWA have not made a reputation; instead, staff and inmates have made one for them. In most cases, the reputation they fastened to the director was not flattering ("removed," "chickenshit," "out of touch," "head up his ass," and so on). Leaders who have practiced MBWA have not always done so successfully, but most have.

4. *Successful leaders make significant alliances with key politicians, judges, journalists, reformers, and other outsiders with the ability to affect the organization's fiscal health, statutory authority, and public image.* Among the strategies employed by successful correctional leaders are throwing parties for key outsiders (in some cases at the executive's personal expense), responding quickly and cordially to legislative inquiries for information, lecturing in public, attending conferences, freely granting interviews, publishing articles and essays, and developing good personal relationships with top officials in other law-enforcement agencies—or, when that failed, creating interagency procedures to "force" and routinize cooperation.

Above all else, important outsiders are invited into the facilities to see for themselves what conditions are like and how things operate. Often, events are staged; for example, an inmate college graduation ceremony. Just as often, however, the outsiders (including judges) are invited to take a long, hard look at what is going on. Sometimes they like what they see; other times they do not. In some instances, the resultant political fallout, press coverage, and public attention is favorable; in other cases, it causes fresh headaches for the director and his staff.

But successful correctional leaders follow a policy of openness and alliance building, and in the long run they are better than leaders who do not. Leaders who try to keep the outsiders out, or who simply ignore them, are more likely to wind up fired, burned out, or forced to resign, even when their institutions do not fare as badly as those of other systems where leaders are more open.

Successful leaders take it as axiomatic that the general public can neither know nor care enough about correctional staff (or the unpopular people they supervise) to furnish anything like sturdy political support for their institutions. Instead, they have made such broad appeals only one component, and by no means the largest one, of the strategy for handling outside "coaches, customers, and critics."[13] They consciously manage their agency's external relations with as much zeal as they have managed their cell blocks.

5. *Successful leaders rarely innovate, but their innovations are far-reaching and the reasons for them are made known in advance to both inmates and staff.* Changes are made slowly, allowing staff and inmates plenty of time to learn the new ways and "get on board." For the most part, the innovations address a current or potential problem that most of those who live and work in the facilities already acknowledge as serious. As often as not, the innovations represent a fundamentally new way of achieving an old mission, rather than being a new mission itself. And in most cases, the old practices are abolished without any implication that they (and hence those who followed and believed in them) failed or were misguided; rather, they are presented as necessary or unavoidable responses to changed circumstances and "sold" to inmates and staff accordingly.

Correctional line staff are notoriously sensitive to what their leaders "do for the inmates" versus "what they do for us." Signs of appreciation, tangible and symbolic, for the public service that line staff perform tend to be few and to come from within the organization. As one warden stated, at times it is almost as though there were a sibling rivalry between inmates and line officers. Thus, to give inmates a new athletic facility without making a commensurate gesture toward line staff, or to enhance inmates' eligibility for college and vocational courses without improving (or at least attempting to improve) the educational benefits of staff, can erode staff loyalty to "the brass," harm labor–management relations in other areas, and cost a director much of whatever personal and professional capital with line workers he may have accumulated over the years. Thus, many "innovations" in correctional settings are in actuality attempts to correct this sort of real or perceived imbalance.

6. *Successful leaders are in office long enough to understand and, as necessary, to modify the organization's internal operations and external relations.* Most correctional leaders who are successful serve for at least six consecutive years in one position; some, for over a decade. With respect to length of service, there have been four kinds of correctional leaders, which I classify (with shameless alliteration) as flies, fatalists, foot soldiers, and founders.

Over the past two decades, corrections officers have served an average of only three years before quitting, getting fired, or moving on to another agency; several have stayed in office less than a year. These flies of summer have either come and gone unnoticed or have attempted to reform the agency in one fell swoop. The former flies are inconsequential; the latter buzzed loudly and were a nuisance until they were swatted down by reality.

The fatalists served similarly brief terms that began and ended with their complaining about the futility of incarceration and the hopelessness of institutional reform. Often, they had little or no previous experience managing correctional institutions. In some cases, they were talented and energetic people who convinced key decision makers that their institutions were beyond repair; several brought about deinstitutionalization schemes of one sort or another. Whatever the results of these schemes (usually the results have been poor to mixed), the fatalists did nothing to achieve institutional reform but did succeed in abolishing some institutions.

Compared to the flies and most of the fatalists, the foot soldiers served long terms. Whether they inherited their job from a fly, a fatalist, or a founder, they worked in the trenches to make whatever incremental improvements they could, usually in a pragmatic spirit unleavened by a commitment to any particular penological theory. When what they inherited was good, they tried to preserve as much of it as they could and to consolidate new administrative measures around old routines. W. J. Estelle in Texas, Steve Bablitch in Wisconsin, and Orville Pung in Minnesota would rank among the foot soldiers.

The founders were those who created an agency or reorganized it in major and positive ways. Generally, like directors James V. Bennett and Norman A. Carlson of the Federal Bureau of Prisons, and New Jersey's William Fauver and William Leeke, they served long terms.

Not every leader who served a long term has done good things organizationally. And some leaders are hard to classify meaningfully. But the record suggests that foot soldiers and founders are a boon to the quality of institutional life; indeed, if I were forced to choose between one mediocre leader for ten years and a succession of four talented ones over the same period, I would probably entrust the institutions to the former.

Summary

Throughout the nineteenth century and the early part of the twentieth, studies of prisons focused more on the administrators than on the inmates. Prison governance was the central and abiding focus of these studies. To permit prisoners to associate freely was to abandon them to criminal mischief and corruption and to raise the likelihood of criminal disorders behind bars.

Beginning in the 1940s with the publication of research by sociologists, there was a shift in focus from sympathy for the work of prison administrators to sympathy for prison inmates. Whereas the "old penology" maintained that prisons must be governed strictly by duly appointed officials, the "new penology" maintained that prisons must be governed by the prisoners themselves.

In the 1960s the prison population became increasingly black and Hispanic. In a spate of studies, a second generation of new penologists documented the rise of a younger, more aggressive, more politicized breed of convict chieftains. These new inmate leaders were far less willing and able to get other inmates to go along with even the most basic wishes of the administration. Prison populations became fractionalized along racial and ethnic lines. The pliable con-boss was succeeded by the inflexible prison gang leader. The society of captives, it seemed, was about to run out of control.

The old penology, of course, had a cure for this virus of inmate dominance: namely, rigorous internal controls, rule enforcement, and the atomization of the "prison community." And in the few corrections agencies where old penologists remained at the helm, that is precisely the medicine they administered.

To old penologists, prison administrators were admirable public servants, inmate associations behind the walls were to be restricted and minimized, and any form of inmate self-government was considered a nightmare. To new penologists, prison administrators were damnable ogres, prisoners were responsible souls, and complete inmate self-government was a pleasant dream. By the mid-1980s, the new penologists' dream had come true in many places, but with precisely the ill consequences that the old penologists would have predicted.

Publication in 1987 of *Governing Prisons* gave rise to what has been called the "new old penology," a shift of attention from the society of captives to the government of keepers.[14] In that book I presented empirical evidence and arguments that tight administrative control was often more conducive to decent prison conditions (and possibly rehabilitation) than loose administrative control; highlighted the moral and practical sophistry of inmate self-government schemes; and otherwise restored some, though by no means all, of the claims of the old penology. This approach to understanding prisons pushes administrators back to the bar of attention, is inclined to treat them at least as sympathetically as it treats their charges, and attempts to translate empirically grounded research on prisoner behavior into ideas about how to manage toward more safe and humane conditions behind bars.

The "new old penology" posits as central that, other things being equal, correctional leaders who follow the precepts discussed above produce more in the way of safe and humane conditions behind bars than leaders who do not. It is time to stop treating correctional management as an impossible job. And it is long past time to stop offering lame sociological excuses for real failures of administration. What Sykes called the "society of captives" can be governed well or ill.

Notes

1. Edward B. Fiske, "New Look at Effective Schools," *New York Times,* April 15, 1984, Section 12.
2. Major works in this large literature include Donald Clemmer, *The Prison Community* (New York: Holt, Rinehart & Winston, 1940); Gresham M. Sykes, *The Society of Captives: A Study of a Maximum Security Prison* (Princeton: Princeton University Press, 1958); Donald R. Cressey (ed.), *The Prison: Studies in Institutional Organization and Change* (New York: Holt, Rinehart & Winston, 1961); John Irwin, *The Felon* (Englewood Cliffs, N.J.: Prentice-Hall, 1970); John Irwin, *Prisons in Turmoil,* (Boston: Little, Brown, 1980).
3. John J. DiIulio, Jr., *Governing Prisons: A Comparative Study of Correctional Management* (New York: Free Press, 1987).
4. Ibid., p. 256.
5. Bert Useem, *States of Siege: U.S. Prison Riots, 1971–1986* (New York: Oxford University Press, 1988).
6. Contrary to much of the "ineffective-prisons" literature, Useem's carefully documented work provides no support for the theory that security-driven management and prison violence vary inversely. The idea that the more prison authorities do to control inmates, the more inmates will run out of control is intriguing, counterintuitive, and wholly without empirical evidence to support it. For a discussion of this theory, see DiIulio, *Governing Prisons,* pp. 22–23, and Useem, *supra.*
7. John J. DiIulio, Jr., *Principled Agents: Leadership, Administration, and Culture in a Federal Bureaucracy* (New York: Oxford University Press, forthcoming).
8. John J. DiIulio, Jr., *Interim Report on Corrections in New York City* (New York: New York City Board of Corrections, September 10, 1987); and Richard J. Koehler, Memo to First Deputy Mayor Stanley Brezenoff, New York City Department of Corrections, April 19, 1988.
9. James Q. Wilson, *Bureaucracy: What Government Agencies Do and Why They Do It* (New York: Basic Books, 1989). p. 91.
10. Ibid.
11. John J. DiIulio, Jr., *No Escape: The Future of American Corrections* (New York: Basic Books, 1991), Chap. 1.
12. Wilson, *Bureaucracy.*
13. This alliterative phrase is from Richard A. McGee, *Prisons and Politics* (Lexington, Mass.: Lexington Books, 1981). McGee directed the California penal system for several decades.
14. The term was coined by Bert Useem in "Correctional Management: How to Govern Our 'Cities,'" *Corrections Today* (February 1990): 88.

24

Judicial Reform and Prisoner Control:
The Impact of *Ruiz* v. *Estelle*
on a Texas Penitentiary

James W. Marquart

Ben M. Crouch

During the past two decades, federal courts have become increasingly involved in upholding the rights of prisoners in state correctional facilities. Judicial decisions ordering administrators to implement procedures and standards that meet constitutional requirements have often had widespread and unintended consequences.

In the 1960s a "due process revolution" occurred in which the judiciary addressed and attempted to remedy aspects of many of this society's institutional ills. Almost since the start of this revolution jails and prisons have been an important focus of judicial attention. In general, the courts have expanded the constitutional rights of prisoners at the expense of the so-called "hands-off" doctrine (Calhoun 1978; Jacobs 1980). That is, the courts have rejected the traditional view that prisoners were socially "dead" and managed at the discretion of the prison staff. Courts for the past fifteen years have responded sympathetically to prisoners' grievances and have issued as well as administered many rulings forcing prison organizations to modify or cease numerous institutional policies and procedures. To illustrate, as of December 1983 thirty state prison systems were operating under court order or consent decrees designed to alleviate prison overcrowding (U.S. Department of Justice 1984). This change in court posture has made possible the fuller integration of the penitentiary within the central institutional and value systems of the society (Shils 1975: 93; Jacobs 1977).

Despite the proliferation of "prisoner rights" cases, there exists relatively little empirical research on the impact of judicially mandated reforms on prison structures and operations. The sociology of confinement literature typically describes court-ordered reforms as part of or ancillary to changes wrought by shifts in prison administration (Carroll 1974; Jacobs 1977; Colvin 1982), goals (Carroll 1974; Stastny and Tyrauner 1982), or inmate populations (Irwin 1980; Crouch 1980). When researchers have directly examined court-ordered reforms (for example, Kimball and Newman

Source: Law and Society Review 19 (1985): 557–586. Reprinted by permission of the Law and Society Association.

1968; *UCLA Law Review* 1973; Champagne and Haas 1976; Turner 1979), their analyses have been narrowly focused and do not assess the long-term effects of intervention on the prison community. Because systematic empirical research is lacking, we have only some general ideas about what happens in prisons when courts intervene and alter an established order. Jacobs (1980) summarizes those general ideas and notes that court-ordered reforms often lead to a demoralized staff, a new generation of prison administrators, a bureaucratic prison organization, a redistribution of power within the prison, and a politicized and often factionalized inmate society.

The most general observation made about the consequences of judicial intervention has been that prisons have become increasingly bureaucratized (Jacobs 1977; Turner 1979). Authority in prisons is no longer unrestricted but based instead on formal procedures and policies. The days of the autonomous "big house" warden are history. Bureaucratization has also affected prisoner control. The harsh disciplinary measures of the past have been replaced with a legalistic due process model, similar, in some respects, to hearing procedures in nonprison settings. We do not know, however, how the bureaucratization of prisons and prisoner control that judicial intervention has engendered has affected day-to-day life within the prison community. We need to know what transpires within prisons after court-ordered reforms have been implemented by the administrators. In particular, we need to know more about the consequences of court-ordered reforms for prison control systems and for relationships among the parties—inmates, guards, and administrators—on whom control ultimately depends.

This paper is a case study and institutional analysis that examines the impact of legal intervention on a Texas penitentiary—the Eastham Unit. This study, unlike many legal impact studies, is not primarily concerned with the "gap" question— whether or not compliance has been achieved. Rather, it analyzes the institutional implications of a judicial remedy that has been implemented in good faith. The case in question is *Ruiz v. Estelle* (1980), a massive class action suit against the Texas Department of Corrections (TDC) in which a federal district judge ordered TDC to make wholesale organizational changes (for example, in health care, overcrowding, inmate housing). Our focus is on a central feature of *Ruiz* which ordered TDC and Eastham to abandon certain official and unofficial methods of prisoner control. Our objective is to analyze the prisoner control structure at Eastham prior to this case, the specific changes that were ordered, and how these changes affected the prison community. In the last section, we contrast several organizational elements of the old order with the emerging bureaucratic-legal order and discuss the implications of this shift in structure and philosophy for daily control. In effect, this analysis examines a penitentiary before, during, and after the implementation of a legal reform.

The Setting and Method of Study

The research site was the Eastham Unit of the Texas penal system. Eastham is a large maximum security institution located on 14,000 acres of farmland, which housed, in 1981, nearly 3,000 inmates (47 percent black, 36 percent white, 17 percent Hispanic). Inmates assigned to this prison were classified by the Texas Department of Corrections as recidivists over the age of twenty-five, all of whom had been in prison (excluding juvenile institutions) three or more times. Eastham has a reputation for tight disciplinary control and so receives a large number of inmate troublemakers from other TDC prisons. Structurally, the prison has eighteen inside cell blocks (or tanks) and twelve dormitories which branch out from a single central hall—a telephone pole design. The Hall is the main thoroughfare of the prison and is almost one-quarter of a mile long, measuring 16 feet wide by 12 feet high.

The data for this paper were collected in two phases through participant observation, interviews with guards and inmates, searching documents and inmate records, and informal conversations resulting from the participant observation. In phase one, the first author entered the penitentiary as a guard and collected dissertation data on social control and order for nineteen months (June 1981 through January 1983). He worked throughout the institution (for example, in cell blocks, shops, dormitories) and observed firsthand how the guards cultivated "rats" and meted out official and unofficial punishments. In addition, he cultivated twenty key informants among the guards and inmate elites, with whom he discussed control and order as a daily phenomenon. The first author's close relationship with these informants and their "expert" knowledge about prison life and prisoner control were essential to the research (see Jacobs 1974b; Marquart 1984). Most important, his presence allowed observation and documentation of the control structure before, during, and for a short period after the reform measures were implemented.

In the second phase of research, the authors returned to Eastham and collected data from late September 1984 until January 3, 1985. Data collection procedures involved intensive observation and open-ended structured interviews (tape-recorded) with a cross section of thirty officers and sixty inmates. The inmate interviews addressed such issues as race relations, gang behavior, violence, relations with guards, and prison rackets. The officer interviews focused on such topics as morale, violence, gang behavior, unionism, and relations with inmates. While formal and taped interviews were conducted, the researchers also obtained valuable insights from daily observations of and informal conversations with guards on and off duty throughout the prison as well as from inmates at work, recreation, meals, and in their cells. Furthermore, we closely interacted with seventeen key informants—ten inmates and seven officers—who provided a constant source of support and information. Available official documents (for example, memos, inmate records, solitary-confinement logbooks) were used to substantiate and corroborate the interview and observational data.

The Change Agent: *Ruiz v. Estelle*

In December 1980 Judge William W. Justice (Eastern District of Texas) delivered a sweeping decree against the Texas Department of Corrections in *Ruiz v. Estelle*. That decree, a year in the writing following a trial of many months, was the culmination of a suit originally filed with the court in 1972. The order recited numerous constitutional violations, focusing on several issues. First, TDC was deemed overcrowded. Prison officials were ordered to cease quadruple and triple celling.[1] To deal with the overcrowding problems, TDC erected tents, expanded furloughs, and in May 1982 even ceased accepting new prisoners for approximately ten days. Moreover, a "safety valve" population control plan passed by the legislature in 1983 and a liberalized "good time" policy have been used to expand parole releases. Nevertheless, over-crowding continues. A second issue was TDC's security practices. The judge ordered the prison administrators to sharply reduce and restrict the use of force by prison personnel. He also demanded the removal and reassignment of special inmates known as "building tenders" since the evidence clearly indicated that these inmates were controlling other inmates. To further increase security, the decree called for TDC to hire more guards and to develop a much more extensive inmate classification plan. Third, the judge found health care practices, procedures, and personnel in need of drastic upgrading. A fourth shortcoming involved inmate disciplinary practices. Problems included vague rules (for example, "agitation," "laziness"), the arbitrary use of administrative segregation, and a failure to maintain proper disciplinary hear-ing records. Fifth, the court found many problems with fire and safety standards in TDC. Finally, TDC was found to have unconstitutionally denied inmates access to courts, counsel, and public officials.

To implement this sweeping decree, Judge Justice appointed Vincent Nathan to serve as special master. Because TDC encompassed twenty-three units in 1981 (it now has twenty-seven), a group of monitors was hired to visit the prisons regularly and gauge compliance. The nature and extent of noncompliance with each aspect of the decree are contained in a series of lengthy monitors' reports and have served as the basis for ongoing negotiation and policy changes by the prison system.

Since our concern in this paper is with the official and unofficial means of pris-oner control that were ruled unconstitutional by the court, we limit our analysis to those parts of the court order (for example, removal of building tenders and changes in security practices and personnel) relevant to that concern. To appreciate the effects of the order, we must first understand how Eastham was organized and how it oper-ated prior to the court's intervention.

Prisoner Control Under the Old Order

The control of older, hard-core criminals presents special problems in any prison. At Eastham, the staff maintained tight discipline and control through a complex system of official rewards and punishments administered by an elite group of prison officers. Basically, this control system rewarded those inmates who had good prison records with such privileges as good time, furloughs, dormitory living instead of a cell, and jobs other than fieldwork. On the other hand, the staff severely punished those inmates who challenged the staff's definition of the situation. The most unusual and important element in controlling the prisoners in the old order centered on the staff's open and formal reliance upon a select group of elite inmates to extend their authority and maintain discipline. It was this latter system of prisoner control, called the "building tender (BT) system,"[2] that the court ordered TDC to abolish.

The Building Tender/Turnkey System

The staff employed a strategy of co-opting the dominant or elite inmates with special privileges (for example, separate bathing and recreational periods, better laundered uniforms, open cells, clubs or knives, "friends" for cell partners, craft cards) in return for aid in controlling the ordinary inmates in the living areas, especially the cell blocks. The use of select inmates to control other inmates is ubiquitous and has been documented in such various prison settings as the Soviet Union (Solzhenitsyn 1974; 1975), India (Adam, n.d.), Australia (Shaw 1966), and French Guiana (Charriere 1970), as well as in Nazi concentration camps (Bettelheim 1943; Kogon 1958) and the management of slaves (Blassingame 1979). The most notable as well as notorious use of pro-staff-oriented inmates (convict guards) has occurred in the Mississippi, Arkansas, and Lousiana prison systems (see McWhorter 1981; Murton and Hyams 1969; Mouledous 1962). In these prisons, selected inmates were issued pistols and carbines to guard the other inmates. However, these elite inmates, unlike the inmate agents at Eastham, were housed in separate living quarters.

Structure and Work Role   The BT system at Eastham involved three levels of inmates. At the top of the hierarchy were the "head" building tenders. In 1981, each of the eighteen blocks had one building tender who was assigned by the staff as the "head" BT and was responsible for all inmate behavior in "his" particular block. Indeed, "ownership" of a block by a head BT was well recognized: inmates and officers alike referred informally but meaningfully to, for example, "Jackson's tank" or "Brown's tank." Essentially, the head BT was the block's representative to the ranking officers. For example, if a knife or any other form of contraband was detected in "his" living area, it was the head BT's official job to inform the staff of the weapon's whereabouts and who had made it, as well as to tell the staff about the knife maker's character. In addition, these BTs would help the staff search the suspected inmate's cell to ferret out the weapon. Because of their position, prestige, and role, head BTs were the most powerful inmates in the prisoner society. They acted as overseers and frequently mediated and settled disputes and altercations among the ordinary inmates. This role frequently called for the threat of or use of force. They stood outside ordinary prisoner interaction but by virtue of their position and presence kept all other inmates under constant surveillance.

At the second level of the system were the rank and file building tenders. In every cell block or dormitory, there were generally between three and five inmates assigned as building tenders, for a total of nearly 150 BTs within the institution. These inmates "worked the tank," and their official role was to maintain control in the living areas by tabulating the daily counts, delivering messages to other inmates for the staff, getting the other inmates up for work, cleaning, and reporting any serious misbehavior by inmates to the head BT who, in turn, told the staff. Another important duty of the BTs was the socialization of new inmates into the system. When new inmates arrived at a living area, BTs informed them of the "rules," which meant "keep the noise down, go to work when you are supposed to, mind your own business, and tell us [the BTs] when you have a problem." In addition to these tasks, the BTs broke up fights, gave orders to other inmates, and protected the officers in charge of the cell blocks from attacks by the inmates.

The BTs also unofficially meted out discipline to erring inmates. For example, if an inmate had to be told several times to be quiet in the dayroom (the living area's television and recreation room), stole another inmate's property, or threatened another inmate, he was apt to receive some form of physical punishment. If this initial encounter did not correct the problem, the BTs, with tacit staff approval, would severely beat the inmate (sometimes with homemade clubs) and have him moved to another cell block. This process, called "whipping him off the tank" or "counseling," was not uncommon, and some inmates were moved frequently throughout the prison. Although the BTs were "on call" twenty-four hours a day, the head BT assigned the other BTs to shifts (morning, evening, and night) to provide the manpower needed to manage the block. The living areas were their turf, and the staff basically left the management of these areas in their hands.

The third level of the building tender system consisted of inmates referred to as runners, strikers, or hitmen. Runners were not assigned to work in the blocks by the staff; rather, these inmates were selected by the BTs for their loyalty and willingness to act as informants. They also worked at regular jobs throughout the prison. Runners performed the janitorial work of the block, sweeping and dispensing supplies to the cells. They also served as conduits of information for the BTs since they had more contact with the ordinary inmates than BTs and picked up important information. More important, runners served as the physical backups for the BTs. If a fight or brawl broke out, the runners assisted the BTs in quelling the disturbance. As a reward for their services, runners enjoyed more mobility and privileges within the block than the other inmates (but less than the BTs). The BT crew in each tank recruited their runners, and selection was based primarily on the inmate's ability to work and willingness to inform. Moreover, many runners were friends of or known by the BTs in the free world; some runners were also the homosexual partners of their BT bosses. Some tanks had three or four runners, while others had seven, eight, or even nine. The numbers of runners totaled somewhere in the vicinity of 175 to 200 inmates.

The final aspect of the building tender system consisted of inmates referred to as turnkeys, who numbered seventeen in 1981. As mentioned earlier, the prison contained a large corridor known as the Hall. Within the Hall were seven large metal barred doors, or riot barricades. Turnkeys worked in six-hour shifts, carrying on long leather straps the keys that locked and unlocked the barricades. They shut and locked these doors during fights or disturbances to prevent them from escalating or moving throughout the Hall. In addition to operating the barricades, turnkeys routinely broke up fights, assisted the BTs, and protected the prison guards from the ordinary inmates. These doorkeepers also passed along information to the BTs about anything they heard while "working a gate." More important, turnkeys assisted the cell block guards by locking and unlocking the cell block doors, relaying messages, counting, and keeping the Hall free of inmate traffic. In fact, the block guards and turnkeys worked elbow to elbow and assisted one another so much that only their respective uniforms separated them. When off duty, the turnkeys, who lived in the blocks, assisted the BTs in the everyday management of the block. In terms of power and privileges, turnkeys were on the same level as the regular BTs.

The building tender system functioned officially as an information network. Structurally, the staff was at the perimeter of the inmate society, but the building tender system helped the staff penetrate, divide, and control the ordinary inmates. BTs and turnkeys in turn had snitches working for them, not only in the living areas but throughout the entire institution. Thus, the staff secured information that enabled them to exert enormous power over the inmate's daily activities. As mentioned earlier, the BTs and turnkeys were handsomely rewarded for their behavior and enjoyed power and status far exceeding that of ordinary inmates and lower ranking guards. Unofficially, these inmates maintained order in the blocks through fear, and they physically punished inmates who broke the rules.

Selection of BTs and Turnkeys   These inmate "managers" of the living areas performed a dangerous job for the staff. Vastly outnumbered, BTs and turnkeys ruled with little opposition from the ordinary inmates. In reality, most of the ordinary inmates justifiably feared their "overseers" because of their status and physical prowess. The BTs and turnkeys were selected through an official appointment procedure to perform a "formal" job within the living areas. The selection procedure began with the staff at Eastham (and the other TDC prisons), who recommended certain inmates as BTs/turnkeys to the Classification Committee (a panel of four TDC officials, all with prison security backgrounds). This committee then reviewed each inmate's record and made the final selections. Recommendations to the Classification Committee from the staff were not always honored, and fewer than half of those recommended were selected for BT/turnkey jobs. One supervisor who was an active participant in the recruitment process at Eastham expressed his preference, which was typical:

> I've got a personal bias. I happen to like murderers and armed robbers. They have a great deal of esteem in the inmate social system, so it's not likely that they'll have as much problem as some other inmate because of their esteem, and they tend to be a more aggressive and a more dynamic kind of individual. A lot of inmates steer clear of them and avoid problems just because of the reputation they have and their aggressiveness. They tend to be aggressive, you know, not passive.

The majority of the individuals selected for BT and turnkey positions were the physically and mentally superior inmates who appeared to be natural leaders. Generally, BTs and turnkeys were more violent and criminally sophisticated than the regular inmates. For example, of the eighteen head BTs at Eastham, eight were in prison for armed robbery, five for murder (one was an enforcer and contract-style killer), one for attempted murder, one for rape, one for drug trafficking, and two for burglary. Their average age was thirty-nine and their average prison sentence was thirty-two years. Of the seventeen turnkeys, there were three murderers, three armed robbers, six burglars, two drug traffickers, one rapist, one car thief, and one person in for aggravated assault. Their average age was thirty-one and their average sentence was twenty-two years. In contrast, the average TDC inmate in 1981 had a twenty-one-year sentence, with a modal age category between twenty-two and twenty-seven. These data clearly show that the BTs and turnkeys were older than most inmates and more likely to be violent recidivists. This is consistent with the patterns noted by others who have described inmate leaders (for example, Clemmer 1940; Schrag 1954).

Race   Most of the regular BTs/turnkeys came from the black and white inmate populations. Only a handful of Hispanic inmates were ever recruited for these positions. The staff distrusted most Hispanic inmates, perceiving them as dangerous, clannish, and above all "sneaky." Hispanic inmates, primarily for cultural reasons, were tight-lipped and generally avoided any voluntary interaction with the staff or other inmates. They feared being labeled as pro-staff because physical reprisals from other Hispanics for snitching were common inside as well as outside the prison world. Moreover, Hispanic inmates were generally not as imposing physically as inmates of other races.

Although black and white inmates both served as BTs, power was not equally distributed between the races. The predominantly rural, white, ranking guards kept the "real" power in the hands of the white BTs. That is, of the eighteen head BTs, there were fourteen whites, three blacks, and one Hispanic. The ranking staff members were prejudiced and "trusted" the white BTs more than members of the other two races. In short, with the help of the staff, a "white con" power structure similar to a caste system dominated the inmate society in the same way the "old con" power structure ruled Stateville (Joliet, Illinois) in the 1930s through the 1950s (see Jacobs 1977).

The Staff and Unofficial Control

The staff at Eastham did not leave control of the prison totally in the hands of their inmate agents. In addition, the guards actively enforced "unofficial" order through intimidation and the routine use of physical force. Rules were quickly and severely enforced, providing inmates with clear-cut information about where they stood, what they could and could not do, and who was boss (see McCleery 1960). The unification or symbiotic relationships of these two groups—that is, guards as inside outsiders and inmate agents as elite outside insiders—precluded revolt at practically every level.

Intimidation   Inmates who challenged a guard's authority (for example, by insubordination, cursing at him, or "giving him a hard time") were yelled at by guards or supervisors (sergeants, lieutenants, and captains). Racial epithets, name-calling, derogation, threats of force, and other scare tactics were common. These methods, though physically harmless, ridiculed, frightened, or destroyed the "face" of the offending inmate. The following remarks by one ranking officer are an example. "You stupid nigger, if you ever lie to me or to any other officer about what you're doing, I'll knock your teeth in." On another occasion, a supervisor made this typical threat: "Say, big boy, you're some kind of motherfucker, aren't you? I oughta just go ahead and whip your ass here and now."

Verbal remarks such as these were routine. In some cases, inmates were threatened with extreme physical force (for example, "You'll leave here [the prison] in an ambulance") or even death ("Nobody cares if a convict dies in here; we'll beat you to death"). Such threats of physical force were scare tactics meant to deter inmates from future transgressions.

Physical Force   Coercive force is an important means of controlling people in any situation or setting. At Eastham, the unofficial use of physical force was a common method of prisoner control. Inmates were roughed up daily as a matter of course. Within a two-month period, the first author *observed* over thirty separate instances of guards using physical force against inmates. Key informants told the researcher that this number of instances was not surprising. Indeed, as Marquart (1985) notes, fighting inmates was an important value in the guard subculture. Guards who demonstrated their willingness to fight inmates who challenged their authority were often rewarded by their supervisors with promotions, improved duty assignments, and prestigious labels such as "having nuts" or being a "good" officer. The willingness to use force was a rite of passage for new officers, and those who failed this test were relegated to unpleasant jobs such as cell block and gun tower duty. Those who refused to fight were rarely promoted, and many of these "deviant" officers eventually quit or transferred to other TDC prisons.

Generally, the physical force employed by ranking officers was of two kinds. First, some inmates received "tune-ups" or "attitude adjustments." These inmates were usually slapped across the face or head, kicked in the buttocks, or even punched in the stomach. The intent of a "tune-up" was to terrorize the inmate without doing physical damage. More serious, but still a "tune-up," was the "ass whipping" in which the guards employed their fists, boots, blackjacks, riot batons, or aluminum flashlights. These were meant to hurt the inmate without causing severe physical damage. Like simple "tune-ups," "ass whippings" were a common and almost daily form of unofficial control. Both were "hidden" in that they were conducted in private settings free from inmate witnesses.

The second form of force was beatings. Beatings occurred infrequently and were reserved for inmates who violated certain "sacred" rules by, for instance, attacking an officer verbally or physically, inflicting physical harm on other inmates, destroying prison property, or attempting to lead work strikes, to escape, or to foment rebellion against the rules or officers. Inmates who broke these rules were defined as "resisting" the system and were severely injured—often suffering concussions, loss of consciousness, cuts, and broken bones. Although beatings were rare, many were conducted in front of other inmates (always in the name of "self-defense") and served to make examples of those inmates who dared to break important norms.

The threat and use of force were an everyday reality under the old order, and the guards routinely used force to subdue "unruly" inmates (see *Ninth Monitor's Report* 1983). Although rewards and privileges served as important official means of control, the prison order was ultimately maintained through the "unofficial" use of fear and terror. The staff ruled the penitentiary with an iron hand and defined most situations for the inmates. Those inmates who presented a serious challenge (for example, threatening or attacking officers, fomenting work strikes) to the system were harassed, placed in solitary confinement, and sometimes beaten into submission. To the outsider, it might seem that this control structure would create enormous tension and foster mass revolt, but, as we have seen, the small number of guards did not face the inmates alone. The BTs and turnkeys with whom the guards shared power served as a first line of control and functioned as a buffer group between the staff and ordinary inmates.

This type of prisoner control can be referred to as internal because of the important official role given to insiders. It was proactive in nature since the elite inmates knew when trouble was likely to arise and could move to forestall it. BTs and turnkeys functioned as the communication link between the officials and ordinary inmates. The BTs dealt with most of the inmate problems within the living areas and thereby insulated the staff from the multitude of petty squabbles arising in the course of prison life. Riots and mob action were obviated by this relentless BT surveillance and control. Problem situations were passed upward to the guards. In this old order, the staff, BTs, and turnkeys maintained an alliance that ensured social order, peace, the status quo, and stability. But the institutional arrangement that made for such a "well-working" prison fostered an atomistic inmate community fraught with fear and paranoia.

Eastham in Transition

Although there were some efforts to ease overcrowding and to reform prison operations such as medical services, the dominant posture of TDC in 1981 and most of 1982, at all levels, was to resist the court order both through legal action and by noncompliance. Prison officials rejected the intrusion of the court as a matter of principle and particularly feared the consequences of relinquishing such traditional control measures as the BT system. Initially, TDC fought the BT issue. However, additional court hearings in February 1982 made public numerous examples of BT/turnkey perversion and brutality.[3] In late May 1982, attorneys for the state signed a consent decree agreeing to dismantle the decades-old inmate-guard system by January 1, 1983.

Compliance

To comply with the decree, the staff in September 1982 reassigned the majority of the BTs to ordinary jobs (for example, laundry, gym, showers) and stripped them of all their former power, status, and duties. Even BTs reassigned as orderlies or janitors in the living areas were not permitted to perform any of their old BT duties. Court-appointed investigators, called monitors, oversaw the selection of orderlies and kept close tabs on their behavior. These outside agents periodically visited Eastham and asked their own inmate informants to make written statements about any orderly misbehavior. Consequently, several inmate orderlies lost their jobs for fighting with and giving orders to the ordinary inmates; they were replaced by less quarrelsome ordinary inmates.

   To reduce the chances of violence against the former BTs, the staff moved many of them into several blocks and dormitories for mutual protection. While some former BTs were indeed fearful, most did not fear retaliation. As one former BT stated:

> Man, I've been doing this [prison] for a long time and I know how to survive. I know how to do it. I'm not going to stab nobody, I'm going to cut his fucking head off. I'm doing seventy years and it doesn't make a bit of difference and I'm not going to put up with any of that shit.

These inmates all spoke of their willingness to use force, even deadly force, in the event of attacks from the ordinary inmates. The ordinary inmates were well aware of the BTs' reputations and propensity for violence. They did not seek revenge. In short, the ordinary inmates were glad to be "free" from the BT system and stayed away from the BTs, whom they still feared. As a general rule, when an inmate exemplifies his courage and willingness to fight and stand up for his rights under adverse conditions, he is left alone. Turnkeys were formally removed from their jobs and reassigned elsewhere during the last week of December 1982. These inmates were moved in with their BT counterparts and did not experience any retaliation from the ordinary inmates.

In addition to removing the BTs and turnkeys, TDC was ordered to hire more officers to replace the former inmate-guards. Eastham received 141 new recruits during November and December 1982. The guard force was almost doubled. Guards were assigned to the barricades and had to learn from the former turnkeys how to operate them (for example, how to lock and unlock the doors, what to do when fights broke out). More important, a guard was assigned to every block and dormitory. For the first time in Eastham's history (since 1917), guards had assignments within the living areas. Also for the first time, the guards maintained the security counts.[4]

Compliance with the court order also required the TDC to quit using physical force as an unofficial means of punishment and social control. At Eastham, in early 1983, ranking guards were instructed to "keep their hands in their pockets" and refrain from "tuning up" inmates. In fact, guards were told that anyone using unnecessary force—more force than was needed to subdue an unruly inmate—would be fired. The staff at first believed this rule would be "overlooked" and that the TDC administration would continue to support a guard's use of force against an inmate. But in this they were disappointed. In March 1983, a ranking guard was fired and two others were placed on six months' probation for beating up an inmate. Another incident in April 1983 led to the demotions and transfers of three other ranking guards. These incidents were investigated by TDC's Internal Affairs, which was organized in November 1982 to investigate and monitor all inmate complaints about guards' use of force. The termination and demotions had their intended effect, for they spelled the end of the guards' unofficial use of force (see *Houston Chronicle*, January 28, 1984). This series of events sent a message to the guards and inmates at Eastham (as well as throughout the TDC) that noncompliance with the court order would be dealt with harshly.

In sum, within six months the staff (aided by the BTs) changed the prisoner control system by abolishing the decades-old building tender/turnkey system without incident. Although the guards initially attempted to resist complying with the decree's restrictions on the use of force, a firing and several demotions broke their will to resist. These changes in response to the reform effort were substantial, and they set in motion a series of further changes that fundamentally altered the guard and inmate societies.

The New Order

Once the BTs/turnkeys were removed from their jobs and the guards finally quit using unofficial force, the highly ordered prison social structure began to show signs of strain. The balance of power and hierarchical structure within the prisoner society were leveled, and the traditional rules governing inmate behavior, especially in the living areas, were discarded. That is, the ordinary inmates no longer had to act according to the BTs' rules or fear physical reprisals from BTs. The guards' use of physical force as a means of punishment was abolished, and a new system of prisoner discipline/control was established that emphasized due process, fairness, and pris-

TABLE   1 /   **Selected Disciplinary Cases Resulting in Solitary Confinement: Direct Challenges to Authority from 1981 to 1984**[a]

	1981	1982	1983	1984
Striking an officer	4	21	38	129
	(1.3)	(6.5)	(12.0)	(49.4)
Attempting to strike an officer	7	9	18	21
	(2.3)	(2.7)	(5.7)	(8.0)
Threatening an officer	4	5	38	109
	(1.3)	(1.5)	(12.0)	(41.8)
Refusing or failing to obey an order	90	65	72	213
	(30.6)	(20.1)	(22.8)	(81.7)
Use of indecent/vulgar language (cursing an officer)	11	14	89	94
	(3.7)	(4.3)	(28.2)	(36.0)
Total	116	114	255	566
Population levels	2,938	3,224	3,150	2,607

[a]Numbers in parentheses indicate the rate per 1,000 inmates. The population figures are based on the average monthly population at Eastham.

oners' rights. The implementation of these reforms resulted in three major changes within the prison community.

Changes in Interpersonal Relations between the Guards and Inmates

The initial and most obvious impact of the *Ruiz* ruling has been on the relations between the keepers and the kept. Formerly, inmates were controlled through relentless surveillance and by a totalitarian system that created a docile and passive ordinary inmate population. In all interactions and encounters, the guards and their agents defined the situation for the ordinary inmates. The penitentiary's social structure was in effect a caste system, whereby those in the lowest stratum (the ordinary inmates) were dictated to, exploited, and kept in submission.

Now, however, with the abolition of the BT/turnkey system and the disappearance of "tune-ups" and "beatings," a new relationship between keepers and kept has emerged. It is characterized by ambiguity, belligerence, confrontation, enmity, and the prisoners' overt resentment of the staff's authority (see, for example, Carroll 1974). Inmates today no longer accept "things as they are." They argue with the guards and constantly challenge their authority. Moreover, the guards now find themselves in the position of having to explain and justify the rules to the inmates. The guards no longer totally define situations for the inmates.

Disciplinary reports show the contrast between the new (1983 and 1984) and old (1981 and 1982) orders.[5] We see from Table 1 that reported inmate threats toward and attacks on the guards increased by 500 percent and more over two years. The data do not precisely mirror behavior since some challenges to authority that would have been dealt with by unofficial coercion under the old order had to be reported or ignored under the new one. Nevertheless, it is clear from these data, as well as from interviews and observations, that the behavior of inmates toward the staff became increasingly hostile and confrontational. Simple orders to inmates (for example, "tuck your shirt in," "get a haircut," "turn your radio down") were often followed by protracted arguments, noncompliance, and such blistering verbal attacks from inmates as "Fuck all you whores, you can't tell me what to do anymore," "Get a haircut yourself, bitch," "Quit harassing me, you old country punk," or "Get your bitchy ass out of my face. This is my radio not yours." Not surprisingly, the number of cases for using indecent and vulgar language also steadily rose from 1981 to 1984. Indeed, the experience of verbal abuse became so commonplace that many officers overlooked this rule violation. On one occasion, for example, one author observed an officer ask an inmate why he was leaving his living area. The inmate walked past the officer and gruffly responded, "I'm going to work, so what the hell are you fucking with me for? If you got any other questions, call the kitchen." The officer turned around and walked away.

There are several reasons for this drastic change in interpersonal relations between guards and prisoners. First, there are simply more guards, which translates into more targets for assaults, verbal abuse, and disciplinary reports. Second, the guards are restricted from physically punishing "agitators," so fear of immediate physical reprisals by the guards has been eliminated. Third, the guards no longer have their inmate-agents to protect them from physical and verbal abuse or challenges to their authority by the ordinary inmates. By and large, the inmates feared the BTs more than the security staff. Purging the BT system eliminated this buffer group between the guards and ordinary inmates. Today the guards are "alone" in dealing with the prisoners, and the inmates no longer fear physical retaliation from the officials.

In addition to, and perhaps as important as, these changes in the control structure, the social distance between the guards and prisoners has diminished. The "inmates-as-nonpersons" who once inhabited our prisons have become citizens with civil rights (see Jacobs 1980). In the past, inmates at Eastham, subjected to derogation and physical force and ignored by extramural society, saw little to gain from challenging the system. Recent court reforms, however, have introduced the rule of law into the disciplinary process. Inmates now have many due process privileges. They can present documentary evidence, call witnesses, secure representation or counsel, and even cross-examine the reporting guard. They are in an adversarial position vis à vis their guards, which at least in some procedural senses entails a kind of equality. Moreover, the inmates' moral status has been improved because the guards can no longer flagrantly abuse them without fear of retaliation—verbal, physical, and/or legal. Although the guards ultimately control the prison, they must now negotiate, compromise, or overlook many difficulties with inmates within the everyday control system (see for example, Sykes 1958; Thomas 1984).

Reorganization within the Inmate Society

The second major change concerns a restructuring of the inmate social system. The purging of the BT/turnkey system and the elimination of the old caste system created a power vacuum. The demise of the old informal or unofficial rules, controls, and status differentials led to uncertainty and ambiguity. In such situations, as Jacobs (1977) and Irwin (1980) suggest, realignments of power in prison often mean the heightened possibility of violence.

T A B L E   2 / **Selected Inmate–Inmate Offenses Resulting in Solitary Confinement: Weapons Offenses 1981–1984**

	1981	1982	1983	1984
Fighting with a weapon	25	31	46	31
	(8.5)	(9.6)	(14.6)	(11.8)
Striking an inmate with a weapon	21	25	40	57
	(7.1)	(7.7)	(12.6)	(21.8)
Possession of a weapon	40	25	59	134
	(13.6)	(7.7)	(18.7)	(51.4)
Homicide	0	1	0	3
	(0)	(.3)	(0)	(1.1)
Total	86	82	145	225
Population levels	2,938	3,224	3,150	2,607

The Rise of Inmate–Inmate Violence   Prior to *Ruiz* and the compliance that followed, inmate–inmate violence at Eastham was relatively low, considering the types of inmates incarcerated there and the average daily inmate population. Table 2 illustrates the trends in inmate–inmate violence at Eastham. The data in this table clearly document a rise in serious violence between inmates. The most remarkable point here is that the incidence of violence increased while the prison population decreased by over 300 inmates.

Prison overcrowding raises constitutional problems, but it is extremely difficult for a judge to decide when population levels constitute cruel and unusual punishment barred by due process or the Eighth Amendment. To make this decision, judges attempt to link population levels with various major forms of institutional violence (that is, assaults, homicides, suicides). Cox and colleagues (1984) maintain that high degrees of overcrowding (especially in large institutions) have a variety of negative psychological and physical side effects, including higher death and disciplinary infraction rates. However, Ekland-Olson (1985: 32) tested the overcrowding–tension–violence model and concluded, among other things, that "there is no supportable evidence that institutional size or spatial density is related to natural death, homicide, suicide, or psychiatric commitment rates in prison. . . . There is evidence to support the idea that crowding is not uniformly related to all forms of prison violence." While the Eastham data do not allow us to choose between these views, they are consistent with Ekland-Olson's position and suggest that there is no simple relationship between crowding and violence. They also suggest that the social organization of a prison is a more important predictor of violence than crowding per se.

When the BTs were in power, one of their unofficial roles was to settle disputes, disagreements, and petty squabbles among the inmates in the living areas. Inmates came to the BTs not only for counsel but to avoid discussing a problem with the guards. The disputes often involved feuding cell partners, love affairs, petty stealing, or unpaid debts. The BTs usually looked into the matter and made a decision, thereby playing an arbitrator role. Sometimes the quarrelers were allowed to "fight it out" under the supervision of the BTs and without the staff's knowledge. Inmates rarely took these matters into their own hands by attacking another inmate in a living or work area. To do so would invite a serious and usually injurious confrontation with the BTs. Fistfights were the primary means for settling personal disputes or grudges. Weapons were rarely used because the BTs' information network was so extensive that it was difficult for an inmate to keep a weapon for any length of time. Furthermore, any inmate who attacked another inmate with a weapon was usually severely beaten by the BTs and/or the guard staff. Although the BTs ruled through fear and terror, their presence helped restrain serious violence among the inmates.

To avoid the labels of punk, rat, or being weak, inmates involved in personal disputes shy away from telling guards about their problems. With the BTs gone, this leaves the inmates on their "own" to settle their differences. The inmates' sense of justice—a revenge and machismo-oriented system with characteristics of blood feuds—is given full sway (see Ekland-Olson 1985). The system means that inmates are virtually "cornered" and forced to use serious violence as a problem-solving mechanism. Physical threats, sexual come-ons, stealing, and unpaid debts are perceived as similarly disrespectful and as threats to one's "manhood." For example, not paying a gambling debt is a form of disrespect, and in a maximum security prison being "disrespectful" can lead to physical confrontations. Not *collecting* a gambling debt or *submitting* in the face of threats is also seen as weak or unmanly behavior. Inmates who are labeled weak are often preyed upon by inmates anxious to maintain or establish their reputations as "strong."

Fistfights, the "traditional" dispute-settling mechanism in the old order, are no longer an effective means of settling a problem. One inmate, whose response was typical, described the transition from fistfights to serious violence:

> Used to, you could fight on the tank |block] or in the field. You know, they'd [BTs and/or staff] let you settle it right then and there. After a fight, they'd make you shake hands. Yeah, grown men shaking hands after a fight. But it was over, you didn't have to worry about the dude creeping [sneak attack] on you. Now, oh man, there's more knifings and less fistfights. If somebody has trouble, they're gonna try to stick the other guy. Whoever beats the other to the draw wins. See, their attitude has changed. They don't believe in fistfights anymore, it's kidstuff to them. If you got a problem with a dude today, you better stick him. It wasn't like that when I was here in the sixties and seventies.

To the inmates, using a weapon proves more effective because if a "tormentor" is seriously wounded he will be transferred to another prison hospital and, when recovered, to another Texas prison. Furthermore, an inmate who uses serious violence for self-protection obtains a reputation for being "crazy" or dangerous, which reduces the possibility of other personal disputes.

To many inmates, killing or seriously wounding a tormentor in response to a threat is justifiable behavior. At Eastham, violent self-help has become a social necessity as well as a method of revenge. Rather than lose face in the eyes of one's peers and risk being labeled weak, which is an open invitation to further victimization, many inmates see assaultive behavior as a legitimate way to protect their "manhood" and self-respect. This is a dangerous situation for all, and especially for genuinely "weak" inmates who feel trapped and may use extreme violence as a last resort.

The Emergence of Inmate Gangs   As personal violence escalated, inmate gangs developed, partly as a response to the violence but chiefly to fill the void left by the

BTs. Prior to 1982, only one inmate gang, the Texas Syndicate, or TS, existed at Eastham. This group, which evolved in California prisons (see Davidson 1974), consisted of Hispanic inmates primarily from San Antonio and El Paso. It was estimated to have had about fifty full-fledged members and is reputed to have carried out "hits" or contracts on other prisoners at other TDC prisons.

Since 1983 a number of cliques or gangs have appeared at Eastham. Several white groups (Aryan Brotherhood or AB, Aryan Nations or AN, Texas Mafia or TM) and several black groups (Mandingo Warriors, Interaction Organization, Seeds of Idi Amin) have gained a foothold within the inmate society. All of these groups have a leadership structure and recruitment procedures, such as "kill to get in and die to get out" for the AB. Like the TS, these are systemwide organizations. Top-ranking guards at Eastham estimate the number of prisoners who are members at between 8 and 10 percent of the prison population. Of the various groups, the TS and AB are the largest and best organized groups at Eastham.

The presence of the gangs was not really felt or perceived as a security problem until late 1984. Prior to this time, the staff had identified and kept tabs on the gang leaders as well as on recruiting trends. The staff also uncovered several "hits," but violence did not erupt. Then, in November 1984, two ABs stabbed two other ABs; one victim was the AB leader. Early December saw four TS members stab another TS in a cell block. Shortly thereafter, several members of the Texas Mafia murdered another TM in an administrative segregation block, a high-security area housing inmates with violent prison records, known gang leaders, and many gang members. In the final incident a TS leader at Eastham murdered a fellow TS member, in the same segregation block as the previous murder, on January 1, 1985. Thus, gang-related violence has emerged at the prison, but within the gangs themselves. In short, the gangs are locked in internal power struggles.

The rise of inmate–inmate violence has created a "crisis" in self-protection. Some inmates have sought safety in gangs, as we have seen. The staff is perceived—with justification—as unable to maintain control. Interviews with inmates reveal that gang membership offers identity, a sense of belonging, and a support system for the member. Revenge is also a powerful drawing card (see Jacobs 1974a). Gang members know that if they are threatened, assaulted, or stolen from, they will have assistance in retaliating against the offender. On the other hand, nonmembers who fear for their personal safety feel they must rely on themselves. These inmates have felt it increasingly important to obtain weapons (see Table 2). In short, violence has almost become an expectation, both as a threat and as a means of survival.

Reactions of the Guards

The reforms have upset the very foundations of the guard subculture and work role. Their work world is no longer smooth, well ordered, predictable, or rewarding. Loyalty to superiors, especially the warden, the job, and/or organization—once the hallmark of the guard staff at Eastham—is quickly fading. The officers are disgruntled and embittered over the reform measures that have "turned the place over to the convicts."

Fear of the Inmates Part of the *Ruiz* ruling ordered TDC to hire hundreds of guards to replace the BTs. Eastham received 150 new guards between November 1982 and January 1983. For the first time guards were assigned to work in the living areas. It was hoped this increase in uniformed personnel would increase order and control within the institution. Contrary to expectations, the increase in inexperienced personnel and the closer guard–inmate relationships resulted in more violence and less prisoner control. As indicated earlier, assaults on the staff skyrocketed between 1981 (4) and 1984 (129). In addition, one officer was taken hostage and three guards were stabbed by inmates at Eastham in 1984.

Fear of the inmates is greatest among the rank and file guards, most of whom are assigned to cell block duty and have close contact with the inmates. These personnel bear the brunt of the verbal abuse, assaults, and intimidation that have increased since the new system was implemented. The new guards are hesitant to enforce order, and this is evidenced in the officers' less authoritative posture toward the inmates. One guard put it this way: "Look, these guys [prisoners] are crazy, you know, fools, so you gotta back off and let them do their thing now. It's too dangerous around here to enforce all these rules." Previously, guards were not subjected to verbal abuse, threats, and derogation. Compliance was effected through fear and physical force. Today, the guards cannot physically punish "troublemakers" and must informally bargain with the inmates for control. Many officers have stated that they try to enforce the rules but to no avail, since their supervisors overlook most petty rule violations to avoid clogging the prison's disciplinary court docket.[6]

The traditional authoritarian guarding style at Eastham has been replaced with a tolerant, permissive, or "let's get along" pattern of interaction. Furthermore, the guards, especially new officers,[7] fear retaliation from inmates and officials to the point of not enforcing the rules at all. The attitude currently prevailing among the guards is summed up by the following guard's statement: "I don't give a damn about what they do, as long as they leave me alone. I'm here to do my eight hours and collect a pay check, and that's it."

"We've Lost Control" The rise in inmate–inmate violence, the emergence of violent gangs, the loss of traditional control methods, the combative nature of guard–inmate interactions, the derogation of guards, and the influx of inexperienced guards have contributed to a "crisis in control" for the guards (Alpert et al. 1985). Many of the guards, especially the veterans, perceive the changes wrought in the wake of *Ruiz* as unjustified and undermining their authority. They feel they can no longer maintain control and order within the penitentiary. This is not because they have not tried the new disciplinary system. Indeed, as we see in Table 3, the total number of solitary-confinement cases has skyrocketed since 1981.

These data reveal that the rate of serious disciplinary infractions (violence and challenges to guards' authority) rapidly increased after the reforms in 1983 despite a decrease in the inmate population. The rapid increase in rule violations has demoralized the guard staff to the point of frustration and resignation. Interviews with guards and inmates revealed that most inmates are no longer afraid of being "written up," losing good time, and spending time in solitary confinement.[8]

T A B L E   3   /   **Inmates Sentenced to Solitary Confinement from 1981 to 1984**

	1981	1982	1983	1984
All offenses	487	404	889	1,182
	(165.7)	(175.3)	(282.2)	(453.0)
Population levels	2,938	3,224	3,150	2,607

The traditional means of dealing with "unruly" prisoners have been abolished and replaced with more official, due process methods. Standards and guidelines for the guards' use of force have been implemented. Whenever a guard uses force to control an inmate for whatever reason (for example, breaking up fights, taking an inmate into custody), the officer must submit a written report detailing all phases of the incident. When a use of force involves a scuffle, all parties are brought to the prison's hospital to photograph any injuries or abrasions. Forced cell moves are also videotaped. Documentation and accountability are musts for the guard force today. Furthermore, whenever physical force is used against inmates, Internal Affairs investigates the incident. Their investigation of a guard taken hostage on October 15, 1984, involved interviews with thirty-eight prison officials and twenty-one inmates. Twenty-four polygraph tests were also administered (*Houston Chronicle*, February 14, 1984). This investigation revealed that unnecessary force was used to quell the disturbance. Eleven guards and two wardens were reprimanded, and two guards were demoted and transferred to other prisons. Thus, the disciplinary process itself frustrates the line officers—so much so that they often "look the other way" or simply fail to "see" most inmate rule violations. Moreover, the implementation of the new disciplinary process has strained the once cohesive relations between the guards and their superior officers. Not only do the latter sometimes fail to back up the guards' disciplinary initiatives because of the pressures of crowded dockets, but they may also initiate investigations that result in guards being sanctioned.

Some Conclusions on Court Reforms and Prisoner Control

The *Ruiz* ruling sounded the death knell for the old prison order in Texas. Legal maneuverings and a new prison administration have given increasing substance to the new order that *Ruiz* initiated. Table 4 summarizes the distinctions between the old, or inmate-dependent, order and the new, bureaucratic-legal order. We have included only those elements of each order that are directly relevant to prisoner control.

We do not mean by our headings to suggest that prior to the court ruling Eastham was not bureaucratically organized. Indeed, all of the trappings (for example, rules, records, accountability) were present. Under the old order, however, those trappings rarely penetrated the daily operations of the prison. Eastham officials enjoyed considerable autonomy from the central prison administration. Guards, particularly those in the midranks, exercised much discretion in their dealings with inmates. The inmate-dependent order openly recognized the importance of informal relations

T A B L E   4 / **A Summary Depiction of Eastham Before and After** *Ruiz*

	Inmate-dependent order *Pre-Ruiz era*	*Bureaucratic-legal order* *Post-Ruiz era*
Decision-making power	Decentralized. Warden establishes many policies and procedures at the prison. Prison administrators enjoy a high degree of autonomy.	Centralized. Warden carries out directives established in central TDC office. Less unit flexibility; prison officials allowed little autonomy.
Staff/inmate relations	Based on paternalism, coercion, dominance, and fear. The majority of the inmates are viewed and treated as nonpersons. Guards define the situation for the inmates.	Based on combative relations wherein guards have less discretion and inmates challenge the staff's authority. Guards fear the inmates.
Prisoner control apparatus	Internal-proactive control system based on information. Guards penetrate the inmate society through a system of surrogate guards. Organized violence, riots, mob action, and general dissent are obviated. Punishment is swift, severe, certain, and often corporal. Control is an end in itself.	External-reactive control system in which the guard staff operates on the perimeter of the inmate society. Loss of information prevents staff from penetrating inmate society; thus they must contain violence. Punishment is based on hearings and due process considerations. Control mechanisms are means-oriented.
Inmate society	Fractured and atomistic due to the presence of BTs—official snitches.	Racially oriented with the emergence of violent cliques and gangs.

between officers and inmates and the manipulation by staff of a subrosa reward system. The old regime fostered particularistic relations (the "major's boy," BTs, and other institutionalized snitches), which were important to control and kept the inmate community fractured and atomistic. The elite inmates were a reliable source of information about inmate activities that could threaten order. Finally, the control mechanisms consistent with this regime were ends-oriented. That is, order and the dominance of staff over the inmates were maintained by pragmatic means selected over time to achieve these ends. Where force and other sanctions were used by BTs and guards, they were employed immediately following a transgression. This strategy engendered fear among both the offenders and those who observed the punishment.

The transition toward a bureaucratic-legal order at Eastham permits much less autonomy. To increase central office control over TDC's many prisons, the new TDC administration (under Raymond Procunier) established, in 1984, regional directors to supervise more closely the wardens of individual units. As elsewhere, new policies to carry out court-ordered reforms have also reduced the discretion of all unit officials (Glazer 1978). Written directives regarding disciplinary or supervisory procedures emphasize legal standards more than the traditional, cultural values that once defined prison objectives. The precedence of legal standards is especially evident in the "use of force" policy. Each time some physical means of control is used, a "use of force" report (a series of statements and photographs) must be completed and filed with the central office. Whenever a physical confrontation is anticipated (for example, forced cell moves), the action is videotaped. The watchword is documentation. The bureaucratic-legal order also discourages informal relations between officers and inmates. Yet fewer staff–inmate links limit organizational intelligence and thus the ability to anticipate trouble. Officers regularly complain, "We don't know what's going on back there [in the tanks]." At the same time, prison relations are universalistic; all inmates are to be treated alike, and unless they are officially found to have violated some prison rule, they are due equal benefits and freedom regardless of demeanor or attitude. Last, control mechanisms are more means-oriented. The focus is as much on how the control is effected as it is on whether or to what extent it is effective. The legality of the means appears to many staff members to take precedence over the deterrent effect of the control effort. One consequence of this focus is a disciplinary procedure that effectively distances the punishment from the offense in both time and place. Thus, the staff's authority rests not on threat of force or other informal means of domination but on explicit rules.

Although court intervention has made Eastham's operations more consistent with constitutional requirements of fairness and due process, the fact remains that life for the inmates and guards at Eastham is far less orderly than it was before. Authority has eroded, and the cell blocks and halls are clearly more dangerous. Our observations and the data presented in Tables 1 through 3 suggest that the push toward the bureaucratic-legal order, at least in the first few years after the decree, lessened control to the point that many are increasingly at risk behind the walls.

The court-prompted reforms have created for prison officials a dilemma analogous to that experienced by police (Skolnick 1966). Guards, like police, must balance two fundamental values: order and rule by law. Clearly, order can be maintained in a totalitarian, lawless manner. In a democratic society, order must be maintained under rules of law. Having been mandated to maintain control by constitutional means, Eastham prison officials face a problem that pervades our criminal justice system today. Specifically, as Jacobs and Zimmer (1983: 158) note: "[T]he great challenge for corrections is to develop an administrative style that can maintain control in the context of the legal and humane reforms of the last decade."

Officials at Eastham certainly feel this challenge. They feel pressure to comply with the court and the central office directives designed to operationalize that compliance. Yet the unanticipated consequences of today's reforms have jeopardized the staff's ability to maintain and enforce order. While prisoners in many institutions now have enhanced civil rights and are protected by many of the same constitutional safeguards as people in the free society, they live in a lawless society at the mercy of aggressive inmates and cliques. The dilemma apparently facing society and prison administrators revolves around the issues of rights versus control. Should prisons be managed through an authoritarian structure based on strict regimentation, fear, few civil rights, and controlled exploitation, in which inmates and guards are relatively safe? Or should prisons be managed within a bureaucratic–due process structure espousing fairness, humane treatment, and civil rights, in which inmate and guard safety is problematic—and where uncontrolled exploitation is likely? One would like to believe that civil rights and personal safety goals within prison settings are not incompatible, but we may ultimately have to confront the fact that to some extent they are. At the very least, the experience at Eastham suggests that reforms, especially in maximum security prisons, should be: (1) phased in gradually rather than established by rigid timetables, (2) implemented with a fundamental appreciation of the entire network of relationships and behaviors involved, and (3) undertaken with a healthy sensitivity to the unanticipated negative consequences that have often surrounded attempts to "do good" (Glazer 1978; Rothman 1980).

Notes

1. The order also called for an end to double celling, but this element was later vacated by the Fifth Circuit Court of Appeals.
2. For a more detailed analysis of the BT system, see Marquart and Crouch (1984).
3. The news media extensively covered these hearings, and press releases provided grisly examples of BT/turnkey brutality and perversions (see the numerous *Houston Post* and *Houston Chronicle* articles between February 16, 1982, and July 1, 1982).
4. The former BTs had to show the guards how to keep the living area counts. Thus, the staff adopted a system of counting that the BTs had developed.
5. The data presented in the three tables reflect only disciplinary infractions resulting in solitary confinement. We recognize the limitations here and know our data are quite conservative. The TDC's record keeping on all disciplinary cases (minor and major) was nonsystematic, and we had to rely on Eastham's disciplinary logbooks. However, our interviews and observations are consistent with the rise in violent and other behavior reflected in the tables.
6. This is like the situation in many large cities, where police and prosecutors have relationships of accommodation with minor criminals. Some crimes must be prosecuted, whatever the cost to the system. Other crimes are not worth the trouble, so agents of justice ignore them or find ways to handle them simply.
7. Interviews with ranking guards indicated that the rise of inmate–guard and inmate–inmate violence has contributed to the turnover of new guards. Of the 246 guards assigned inside the building, 125, or 51 percent, have less than one year of experience, and these numbers include ranking guards.
8. A guard's threat to seek solitary confinement has also become less intimidating since *Ruiz* because of the due process protections imposed and limitations on the good time that can be forfeited. Also, the guard who seeks solitary confinement for an inmate knows he is triggering a hearing in which his own actions may be questioned. The increase in solitary-confinement cases should be read in light of these disincentives.

References

ADAM, H. L. (n.d.). *Oriental Crime.* Clifford's Inn, London: T. Werner Laurie.

ALPERT, G., B. M. CROUCH, AND C. R. HUFF (1985). "Prison Reform by Judicial Decree: The Unintended Consequences of *Ruiz v. Estelle.*" *Justice System Journal* 291.

BETTELHEIM, BRUNO (1943). "Individual and Mass Behavior in Extreme Situations." 38 *Journal of Abnormal and Social Psychology* 417.

BLASSINGAME, JOHN W. (1979). *The Slave Community.* New York: Oxford University Press.

CALHOUN, EMILY (1978). "The Supreme Court and the Institutional Rights of Prisoners: A Reappraisal." 4 *Hastings Constitutional Law Quarterly* 219.

CARROLL, LEO (1974). *Hacks, Blacks, and Cons.* Lexington, Mass.: Lexington Books.

CHAMPAGNE, ANTHONY, AND K. C. HAAS (1976). "Impact of *Johnson v. Avery* on Prison Administration." 43 *Tennessee Law Review* 275.

CHARRIERE, HENRI (1970). *Papillon.* New York: Basic Books.

CLEMMER, DONALD C. (1940). *The Prison Community.* Boston: Christopher Publishing House.

COLVIN, MARK (1982). "The 1980 New Mexico Prison Riot." 29 *Social Problems* 449.

COX, V. C., P. B. PAULUS, AND G. MCCAIN (1984). "Prison Crowding Research: The Relevance for Prison Housing Standards and a General Approach Regarding Crowding Phenomena." 39 *American Psychologist* 1148.

CROUCH, BEN M. (1980). "The Guard in a Changing Prison World." In B. M. Crouch, ed., *The Keepers: Prison Guards and Contemporary Corrections.* Springfield, Ill.: C. H. Thomas.

DAVIDSON, R. T. (1974). *Chicano Prisoners: Key to San Quentin.* New York: Holt, Rinehart & Winston.

EKLAND-OLSON, SHELDON (1985). "Judicial Decisions and the Social Order of Prison Violence: Evidence from the Post-*Ruiz* Years in Texas." Unpublished manuscript.

GLAZER, NATHAN (1978). "Should Judges Administer Social Services?" 50 *Public Interest* 64.

IRWIN, JOHN (1980). *Prisons in Turmoil.* Boston: Little, Brown.

JACOBS, JAMES B. (1974a). "Street Gangs, Behind Bars." 21 *Social Problems* 395.

———— (1974b). "Participant Observations in Prison." 3 *Urban Life and Culture* 221.

———— (1977). *Stateville: The Penitentiary in Mass Society.* Chicago: University of Chicago Press.

———— (1980). "The Prisoners' Rights Movement and Its Impact, 1960–1980." 2 *Crime and Justice: An Annual Review of Research* 429.

JACOBS, JAMES B., AND L. ZIMMER (1983). "Collective Bargaining and Labor Unrest." In J. Jacobs, ed., *New Perspectives in Prisons and Imprisonment.* Ithaca, N.Y.: Cornell University Press.

KIMBALL, EDWARD L., AND DONALD J. NEWMAN (1968). "Judicial Intervention in Correctional Decisions: Threat and Response." 14 *Crime and Delinquency* 1.

KOGON, E. (1958). *The Theory and Practice of Hell.* New York: Berkley Publishing.

MARQUART, JAMES W. (1984). "Outsiders as Insiders: Participant Observation in the Role of a Prison Guard." Unpublished manuscript.

———— (1985). "Prison Guards and the Use of Physical Coercion as a Mechanism of Prisoner Control." Unpublished manuscript.

MARQUART, JAMES W., AND BEN M. CROUCH (1984). "Co-opting the Kept: Using Inmates for Social Control in a Southern Prison." 1 *Justice Quarterly* 491.

MCCLEERY, RICHARD H. (1960). "Communication Patterns as Bases of Systems of Authority and Power." In R. A. Cloward et al., *Theoretical Studies in Social Organization of the Prison.* New York: Social Science Research Council.

MCWHORTER, WILLIAM L. (1981). *Inmate Society: Legs, Halfpants, and Gunmen: A Study of Inmate Guards.* Saratoga, Calif.: Century Twenty-One Publishing.

MOULEDOUS, J. C. (1962). "Sociological Perspectives on a Prison Social System." Master's thesis, Department of Sociology, Louisiana State University.

MURTON, TOM, AND JOE HYAMS (1969). *Accomplices to the Crime: The Arkansas Prison Scandal.* New York: Grove Press.

NINTH MONITOR'S REPORT OF FACTUAL OBSERVATIONS TO THE SPECIAL MASTER (1983).

ROTHMAN, DAVID (1980). *Conscience and Convenience.* Boston: Little, Brown.

SCHRAG, CLARENCE (1954). "Leadership among Prison Inmates." 19 *American Sociological Review* 37.

SHAW, ALAN G. L. (1966). *Convicts and the Colonies.* London: Faber & Faber.

SHILS, EDWARD A. (1975). *Center and Periphery: Essays in Macrosociology.* Chicago: University of Chicago Press.

SKOLNICK, JEROME H. (1966). *Justice without Trial.* New York: John Wiley.

SOLZHENITSYN, ALEKSANDR I. (1974). *The Gulag Archipelago.* New York: Harper & Row.

———— (1975). *The Gulag Archipelago II.* New York: Harper & Row.

STASTNY, CHARLES, AND GABRIELLE TYRAUNER (1982). *Who Rules the Joint?* Lexington, Mass.: Lexington Books.

SYKES, GRESHAM M. (1958). *The Society of Captives.* Princeton: Princeton University Press.

THOMAS, J. (1984). "Some Aspects of Negotiated Order, Loose Coupling, and Mesostructure in Maximum Security Prisons." 4 *Symbolic Interaction* 213.

TURNER, WILLIAM BENNETT (1979). "When Prisoners Sue: A Study of Prisoner Section 1983 Suits in the Federal Courts." 92 *Harvard Law Review* 610.

UCLA LAW REVIEW (1973). Note, "Judicial Intervention in Corrections: The California Experience—An Empirical Study." 20 *UCLA Law Review* 452.

U.S. DEPARTMENT OF JUSTICE (1984). "Prisoners in 1983." *Bureau of Justice Statistics Bulletin.* Washington, D.C.: U.S. Government Printing Office.

Intermediate Punishment and the Piling Up of Sanctions

Thomas Blomberg

Karol Lucken

Intermediate punishments—sanctions that are more restrictive than nominal probation but less restrictive than incarceration—have been promoted as a means of increasing sentencing options. The authors argue that Florida's intermediate-punishment program has resulted in the "piling up of sanctions" on participating offenders, with the result that many violate the provisions of their sentence.

Introduction

Entering the decade of the 1990s, a major crime control strategy is emerging in response to escalating jail and prison populations and associated costs. This strategy is variously termed intermediate punishment, regional corrections, or community-based intermediate sanctions. Intermediate punishment can be administered at the local, state, or federal level and may include work release, restitution centers, vocational and educational services, community service, substance abuse treatment, juvenile services, electronic surveillance, home confinement, probation, and so on. Specifically, this strategy is designed to offer an alternative that falls between traditional reliance on nominal probation and incarceration.

The multiple purposes, applications, and components of intermediate punishment have been summarized by Morris and Tonry (1990). They specify that intermediate punishments can be applied to many offenders currently in prison or jail, as well as those serving probation or even suspended sentences. They contend that to be effective, intermediate punishments must be rigorously enforced. Further, the authors stipulate that the use of fines and community service orders should be greatly expanded, either alone or as part of a punishment package. Morris and Tonry (1990: 11) conclude:

> Intensive probation is a mechanism by which reality can be brought to all intermediate punishments. Allied to house arrest, buttressed by electronic monitoring

Source: This is the first publication of "Intermediate Punishment and the Piling Up of Sanctions" by Thomas Blomberg and Karol Lucken.

where appropriate, and paid for by fees for service by the offender where that is realistic, intensive supervision has the capacity both to control offenders in the community and to facilitate their growth in crime-free lives.

In essence the underlying reasoning is that by providing offenders with a package of various intermediate punishments, coupled with rigorous enforcement of program conditions, more accountable, more effective, and less expensive crime control can be realized.

This reasoning is being used to promote intermediate punishment throughout the United States. With the 1991 legislative passage of the Community Corrections Partnership Act, Florida began its efforts to establish intermediate-punishment systems throughout the state. This paper provides a preliminary assessment of a Florida county's program that is recognized as a prototype intermediate-punishment system. A primary purpose of the assessment is to explore some of the consequences associated with intermediate punishments' effort to administer multiple sanctions to participating offenders, or what will be termed "the piling up of sanctions."

To elaborate, proponents of intermediate punishment contend that this strategy should not be viewed as merely an alternative to incarceration. They claim that when intermediate punishments are introduced into a binary system in which the only choices are incarceration or nominal probation, the new punishments will tend to draw more heavily from those offender groups previously subject to probation rather than those previously subject to incarceration. As a result, they argue that intermediate sanctions will not contribute to "net widening." Specifically, the concept of "net widening" has been used to describe the capacity of sentencing reforms to be implemented as supplements rather than as alternatives to previous practices. This results in the widening, as opposed to the redistribution, of social control to a larger portion of the base population. For example, in the 1970s diversion programs were intended to reduce the numbers of defendants being formally prosecuted through the court system. Instead, the programs drew the bulk of their clients from groups previously not subject to court contact.

The rush to provide new and more proportionate intermediate punishments to those offenders who formerly received suspended sentences, probation, and incarceration may initiate a series of events that go beyond mere net widening. Specifically, in addition to widening the net, the imposition of intermediate punishments may result in the "piling up of sanctions" by subjecting offenders to multiple and simultaneous punishments capable of producing unknown consequences.

Program Components

The County Corrections Division consists of two major components, namely, the county jail and the Community Corrections Department (CCD). The County Corrections Division provides a comprehensive network of community-based programs coupled with a county jail facility. These components serve a county comprised of over six cities and/or municipalities. This metropolitan area has experienced rapid and consistent population growth over the past two decades. Since 1970, the county population has increased from 344,311 to 674,600 as of 1990. Projections for the future indicate a county population of 767,700 by 1995. Between 1975 and 1989, the county experienced an 87 percent increase in arrests. Moreover, during this fourteen-year period the county jail's average daily population increased by 245 percent. The development of the Community Corrections Department has largely been in response to the escalating jail population. The CCD serves the county court system in the handling of misdemeanor cases and the circuit court system for select felony cases. The following provides a brief description of the targeted offenders and operations of the various CCD program components.

The Probation Program supervises primarily misdemeanor offenders but also felony cases that have been reduced to misdemeanor status. The most frequently encountered felony cases reduced to misdemeanors include aggravated battery, simple battery, assault on a law-enforcement officer, criminal mischief, possession of a controlled substance, burglary, and trespassing on an unoccupied dwelling. The program also maintains a specialized unit for domestic violence and severe substance abuse cases (that is, multiple DUI offenders). In these instances, the probationers are supervised by officers with special training and/or certification in the appropriate fields. The department supervises approximately 8,400 probationers with an average caseload of 230.

The Pre-Trial Diversion Program (PTD) is designed to provide an alternative to prosecution and adjudication for first-time offenders with charges up to third-degree felonies. Often-encountered examples of third-degree felonies include burglary, auto burglary, criminal mischief, grand theft, and obtaining drugs by fraud or forgery. First-time drug offenders became eligible for this program in 1990. A special unit of PTD is the Bad-Check Diversion caseload, which handles only worthless-check offenses. This unit is focused upon restitution collection and offender instruction on financial management techniques. The PTD program supervises approximately 600 offenders.

The Pre-Trial Release Program (PTR) is designed to reduce jail overcrowding by releasing those offenders, prior to court appearances, who are judged to pose no apparent threat to the community. Offenders are required to maintain weekly telephone contact with a PTR officer until they are sentenced.

The Pre-Sentence Investigations Unit prepares presentence reports at the request of judges for either misdemeanor cases or felony cases reduced to misdemeanor status.

The Work Release Center is a residential facility for selected inmates of the county jail. Eligible inmates include female/male, pre/postsentence, misdemeanor, or felony offenses. Those not qualifying are offenders with extensive and/or violent criminal backgrounds. Residents of the center are required to work, obtain a GED, and often attend substance abuse counseling. A resident may be returned to jail for disciplinary reasons, drug use, or new arrests.

The Home Confinement Program provides another alternative to jail. All offenders on home confinement are subject to electronic and manual surveillance. Participants may be male/female, pre/postsentence, or misdemeanor/felony offenders. Inmates with extensive or violent criminal backgrounds do not qualify for this program. Misdemeanors or felony offenders with sentences of up to one year or less in the county jail may serve their sentences on home confinement. Additionally, home confinement provides another option for judges in the event that pretrial release or release on recognizance (ROR) are not considered appropriate. For example, offenders incarcerated due to violations of probation may be released to home confinement pending their court date. Offenders are returned to jail for failure to comply with regulations or new arrests. The current maximum caseload size for home confinement is 150.

The Alternative Community Service Program (ACS) is utilized by both the county courts and the circuit court as an alternative sentence. However, community service is frequently imposed in combination with other sanctions such as probation, fine, or jail. Another function for the ACS program is to provide offenders with the option of performing community service in lieu of a fine.

The Mental Health Unit is designed to provide services to potentially all offenders under the supervision of the County Corrections Division. Major services include crisis intervention and psychological evaluations and referrals. A primary function of this unit is the screening of high-risk inmates admitted to jail and the tracking of inmates in need of psychological treatment while incarcerated.

Operational Features and the Piling Up of Sanctions

Several distinct features have resulted from the operations of the Community Corrections Department. For example, probation, work release, home confinement, and, to some degree, alternative community service were developed to either divert or remove offenders from the incarceration system—or, in the case of pretrial diversion, allow for deferred prosecution. However, in the split-sentencing and/or piling-up-of-sanctions process, these programs are used as supplements to each other, so that an offender receives multiple sanctions (for illustration, see Figure 1). In this process, it is common for an offender to receive a period of incarceration (A on Figure 1), to be followed by a term of probation (D), community service (E), and/or a fine. When a period of incarceration and probation are imposed and the offender qualifies for work release (C) or home confinement (B), the offender will then be supervised simultaneously by a probation officer and work-release counselor or home confinement officer. Split sentences and/or the piling up of sanctions are most likely to occur with repeat offenders, which constitute a major proportion of the department's clientele. In these instances, offenders not only are supervised by two officers but also are required to adhere to the conditions of each program. Furthermore, many offenders are serving terms of probation for both the state and the county and are therefore subject to what are frequently overlapping conditions.

Moreover, placement in various community corrections programs often result in offender surveillance and/or control beyond that administered by the original placement program(s). For example, referrals to various treatment centers and other private counseling organizations (F) may be made at the discretion of a community corrections officer if not already stipulated by the court as a condition of the sentence. Participation and completion of a substance abuse program or domestic violence counseling program may be court-ordered or agency-ordered, as well as any follow-up treatment if deemed necessary by the initial referral agency. The collective use of community treatment agencies underlies the philosophy of intermediate pun-

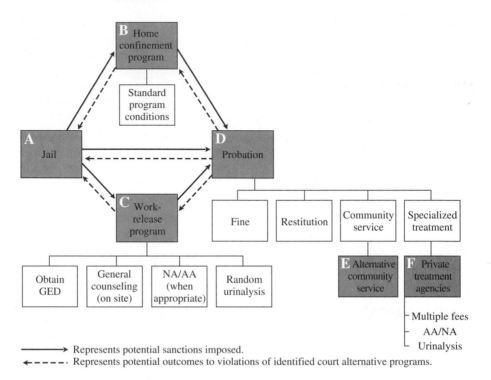

Represents potential sanctions imposed.
Represents potential outcomes to violations of identified court alternative programs.

Figure 1   Process flow of the piling up of sanctions

ishment—namely, that offenders will benefit from an exposure to a range of program services falling between traditional probation and incarceration.

The following scenario illustrates the series of events that often follow an offender's referral to a treatment program. While on probation (or any community corrections program), the offender is referred to a substance abuse center. During the course of the treatment program, it is determined that the offender needs more intense treatment. The agency counselor justifies his or her decision based on broadly interpretive test results (such as MAST, Michigan Alcohol Screen Test) and subjective observations influenced by such criteria as smoking too much, being late to a session, sexual peculiarities, refusal to submit a urine sample (often due to cost), or expressing concerns that treatment sessions interfere with one's work schedule. In this respect, the proposed benefit of treatment becomes problematic, as successful completion of probation (or any CCD program) is contingent upon compliance with the recommendations of outside agencies, private, nonprofit organizations whose funding and survival is derived solely from the number of clients served and services provided. Such agencies often develop in response to offender types targeted for community placement and, as such, pattern their counseling services accordingly (that is, spouse abuse, sexual offenses, drug- and alcohol-related offenses).

Often this piling up of sanctions and the rehabilitative posture employed by the system leads to the offender's exposure to numerous forms of control and scrutiny, culminating in frequent violations of the terms of sentence. For example, a first-time offender on pretrial diversion for petit theft can be required to attend an impulse control seminar, perform community service, seek career counseling, and obtain a GED. Further, for a first-time DUI offender, Florida law mandates a one-year term of probation, fifty hours of community service, fine and court costs totaling nearly $600, a treatment awareness program, and any additional treatment deemed necessary by that program. As a result, many of these DUI offenders violate the conditions of their probation and become subject to more probation and/or additional sentences. To reiterate, the likelihood of a successful completion of the sentence is jeopardized because of extensive supplemental-program involvement and entangling requirements for these offenders.

Failure to complete the requirements of these various other programs results in a return to court, at a minimum, followed by a range of potential sanctions. This may include the original sentence conditions' being reimposed, often coupled with an additional term of community supervision, which may also be supplemented by a period of incarceration. This type of sentencing often has the effect of recycling an offender through the system two or three times.

Home confinement is another program designed as an alternative to incarceration. However, revocation from this program for technical reasons (not including new arrests or escape) can prolong the offender's involvement in the system. Specifically, if an offender is of pre- or postsentence status and is terminated from the program for technical reasons, the offender may be charged at the judge's discretion with the additional offense of violation of home confinement. If this occurs, the offender can be sentenced to an additional period of incarceration. For a complete illustration of the split-sentencing and the piling-up-of-sanctions process and consequences (that is, violations), see Figure 1.

Given the consequences associated with the piling up of sanctions, the program's diversion impact on the county jail is unclear. It appears that, at best, the various community-based programs serve only as temporary alternatives to incarceration and may, in fact, generate a need for expanded jail facilities. Offenders placed on probation, in particular, often make the request, "Can I just do the jail time now because I know I won't make it and will be right back in?" Offenders frequently ask their probation officer to return them to the judge to request removal from the community program in exchange for straight jail time. Further, many offenders are left with the impression that the jail time concludes their sentence—"I just did jail time, how come I have to do probation and pay a fine?" "Probation keeps us in business" is one statement made by a correctional officer in recognizing that incarceration for violations of probation represent a significant proportion of the overall jail population.

The potential of intermediate punishment to increase jail populations, as associated with program violations, is illustrated by one county judge who stated that "as a prosecutor, if you want to set someone up, offer probation knowing full well that he will be unable to make it." On the other hand, the judge noted that for "certain offenses, a majority of individuals placed on probation did not require supervision, but they were required by law to impose that sanction" (that is, DUI sentences). Probation officers as well recognize that for certain offenses (namely, petit theft) approximately 50–100 offenders per month could be referred to Pre-Trial Diversion with adjudication of guilt withheld, and for minor public disorder crimes no program placement at all is necessary. However, for reasons such as being unable to contact the defendant, individuals who would otherwise qualify for Pre-Trial Diversion may be placed on probation. This reflects, in part, the tendency to overrely on probation as a sentencing option.

Sanction Agent Perceptions

Evaluation studies of correctional programs are typically focused upon program outcomes to determine program success or failure. However, the roles of "sanctioning agents"—namely, program administrators, community corrections officers, judges, and private treatment personnel—are rarely studied in connection with the program and the offender, despite their direct role in the program's processes. As a result, an important question concerns how the various professional ideologies and organizational interests guiding the decision making of sanctioning agents contribute to an offender's involvement and experiences with intermediate punishment's piling up of sanctions.

An examination of these various sanctioning agents reveals that, while many share perspectives regarding the role of corrections, they do not represent a homogeneous group of actors. Rather, important distinctions exist between the various "sanctioning agents" with regard to the primary interests that influence their decision making. Consequently, in the process of pursuing these distinctive interests (that is, ideological and organizational), various program and offender conflicts can be introduced. The following discussion focuses on some of the factors influencing the decisions of the various sanctioning agents.

In the county studied, intermediate punishment, or what correctional administrators identify as innovative methods of offender management, has been promoted with great optimism and expectations of success. Reservation or criticism regarding the program's outcomes is rarely expressed. Instead, a confident, supportive, and often defensive posture is maintained by the administrators despite evidence of escalating offender populations under correctional supervision. To illustrate, the director of the County Corrections Division views the expansion of in-jail services and subsequent community program involvement as the "accurate diagnosis to the jail crowding issue," and as a means to "break the cycle of recidivism." However, the Corrections Division has experienced exponential growth in both its components. Administrators and most "sanctioning agents" account for this growth as a natural consequence of increasing arrest rates and/or increasing populations at risk. Consequently, they confine their responses for curbing high incarceration rates to variations of traditional correctional methods, namely more and somewhat modified treatment or punishment practices.

The prevailing ideology guiding administrators of the County Corrections Division is that the coupling of treatments while under institutional or community supervision offers the most ideal environment for modifying offender behavior, thus ultimately reducing jail overcrowding and recidivism. The administrators favor a "systems approach" to correcting the offender, beginning with incarceration and followed by community-based programs, in order to establish a "continuum of care" that is viewed as essential to an effective crime control strategy. Therefore, the advancement of program goals, through the proliferation of programs and services, requires little justification by the administrators other than a professional response to the needs of offenders.

In contrast, judges indicated that they must reconcile competing interests and system limitations unique to their position. While maintaining their sentencing goals and correctional philosophies, judges must often adapt these to the various demands from the public, private community organizations, and correctional sources. To illustrate, program administrators promote the use of their in-jail and community programs as the solution to jail overcrowding and the prior neglect by the system to provide offenders with skills to function as productive members of society. Private agencies intervene as well, by promoting the necessity of specialized treatment to the prevention of repeated antisocial behavior once the offender is released into the community.

While it is the judges that most often impose the conditions and programs that result in the piling up of sanctions, they do so, in part, because it allows for punishment through incarceration, when appropriate, as well as reintegration and restitution through the use of community-based alternatives. Subsequently, in attempting to exact "just desserts," individualize punishment, and alleviate jail overcrowding, judges may incidentally impose sanctions of unrealistic proportions (that is, jail, then work release, followed by probation, fines, counseling, restitution, community service, GED).

Once the offender is sentenced to the Community Corrections Department, staff from each program focus upon their respective goals, responsibilities, and operations. For example, community correctional officers from work release, home confinement, probation, and alternative community service have independently established their own agenda for the offender and, therefore, concentrate on the daily decision making necessary to realize that agenda. While these sanctioning agents may be aware of the sometimes overwhelming program involvement and conditions, they tend to ultimately assign priority to what is required of the offender for the completion of their particular program and compliance with the court order.

These sanctioning agents typically observe only the benefits to be gained from the multiple programs, conditions, and referrals to counseling rather than any possible detriments. In the desire to transform the offender, sanctioning agents seldom consider the potential for accelerated and prolonged involvement in the system. In fact, most agents do not view extended and/or repeated involvement in the system as necessarily good or bad but as a matter of course for accepting and complying with the penalty imposed. Therefore, frequent program violations, and the associated negative consequences (namely, increasing jail and community programs populations), are not attributed to the excessive nature of the piling up of sanctions but, rather, to the failure on the part of the offender to comply with the obligations of the sentence.

If the defendant is ordered to complete some form of counseling, private treatment agencies becomes involved as well in the supervision and reform of the offender. However, unlike community correctional officers, they are influenced by an additional organizational-survival interest. As indicated previously, these private treatment agencies obtain their funding strictly from the number of clients served. Therefore, the offender/client is overwhelmed with costs consisting of initial evaluation fees, late fees, rescheduling fees, counseling fees, and aftercare fees, which, when imposed, are justified as rehabilitative in terms of being held accountable for one's behavior. Given that the treatment counselor's employment is often contingent upon the agency's survival and expansion, he or she may also be required to participate in practices used for securing funds, which may include questionable recommendations for extended treatment.

The preceding discussion suggests that sanctioning agents constitute a diverse group of actors with unique and multiple interests that guide their decision making. However, they do share some basic assumptions regarding corrections and the offender. In particular, sanctioning agents appear to be consistent in their expectations of offenders. For full compliance with the piling up of sanctions, a level of competency and responsibility is required that is characteristic of the law-abiding citizen with higher education, stronger community ties, and greater financial resources. In essence, a "middle-class measuring rod" underlies what offenders are expected to accomplish as part of their punishment and rehabilitation.

The following scenario provides a brief profile of the county offender typically exposed to the piling up of sanctions. This scenario illustrates how the various sanctioning agents' expectations and decisions in effect set the stage for offender program failure.

While many offenders have received a high school diploma or a GED, a substantial number have only elementary or junior high school levels of education, and many offenders are illiterate. The majority of offenders are employed in construction, a construction-related industry, or a service industry (namely, restaurants or hotels). In short, offenders are often employed in positions with relatively little job security, no insurance, and, at times, inconsistent wages. In particular, given the nature of the construction market, offenders are either overemployed or unemployed. For example, while employed for a certain project, the offender may work a sixty-hour workweek, including weekends, and often out of town. Once the project is completed, the offender must move on to another construction project for employment. Meanwhile, the offender may be unemployed for a month or more. Also, an overwhelming majority of offenders do not possess a driver's license (given their usual history of DUIs or DWLSs) nor have convenient or emergency access to transportation. Frequently, the offenders must rely on employers or friends and family, who are often in the same situation with respect to lack of transportation and/or a driver's license.

If the offender is employed, he or she may have the money to enroll in treatment programs but no time to attend and complete the several meetings required each week. If unemployed, the offender now has the time to attend the various programs but not enough money to participate. In essence, with the piling up of sanctions, offenders must spread what little resources they possess over several costly conditions and programs. In sum, critical factors for completing multiple conditions and programs—money, reliable transportation, and an above-average sense of responsibility—are often absent from the typical county offender.

While the sanctioning agents are aware of these obstacles and conditions, they understandably cannot excuse the offender from the consequences of violating the law. Moreover, because these circumstances are common to most offenders, they are not viewed as unusual or exceptional and therefore deserving of any special consideration. Nevertheless, such obstacles are frequently perceived as manifestations of the offender's lack of responsibility and criminality. Strict enforcement is therefore viewed as a significant step in redirecting the offender toward a law-abiding lifestyle. To accommodate or sympathize with the offender's haphazard lifestyle is often labeled as being a victim of the offender's manipulations, too lenient, or an "enabler" to the offender's antisocial behavior. Furthermore, inflexibility on the part of the sanctioning agents is likely to intensify with the cynicism or "hardening" that often develops with time and experience in the criminal justice system.

Nevertheless, a community corrections officer's style of supervision appears to provide the most immediate means to minimizing the negative aspects associated with the piling up of sanctions. While these particular sanctioning agents do not shape the ideological directives and organizational interests of the County Corrections Division, the Community Corrections Department, or private treatment agencies, they are in the position to modify and somewhat temper the conditions and policies that they or judges have set forth. If the officer is willing, this can be accomplished through formal procedures or, unofficially, through their own creativity and style of supervision. Most notably, judges have been agreeable to altering sentences upon request by community corrections officers who identify conditions and/or circumstances that are consistently problematic for offenders. However, the majority of community correctional officers, and sanctioning agents as a whole, do not foresee the potential negative effects associated with the piling up of sanctions on the correction system. However, some officers do realize that, on occasion, rigid enforcement may need to be relaxed for practical purposes in order to offset some of the impractical aspects associated with an ideology of "more is better." This approach often provides correctional administrators and private treatment agencies the opportunity to advance organizational interests that, in turn, present more hardship than value to either the offender or the system as a whole.

Summary and Discussion

The purpose of this paper has been to provide an assessment of a program movement that is quickly spreading across the country. The paper demonstrates the need for a tempered approach to the implementation of intermediate punishment. Specifically, the findings on this county's program, while preliminary, demonstrate once again how seemingly well-intentioned reforms can produce results that are in contradiction to their stated purposes. It is important to note that these reported consequences are not the only possible results produced from the county's program. Specifically, a number of offender groups may well be benefiting from receiving multiple services from the County Corrections Division. Consequently, more comprehensive and systematic evaluation of this program is necessary before definitive conclusions are reached about what this program strategy can and cannot do and for whom. Nonetheless, it should be clear that these programs may be capable of not only operating as organizational supplements to jail or prison but also generating an accelerated demand for jail and prison services for those offenders unable to comply with intermediate punishment's multiple-program requirements.

Morris and Tonry (1990) contend that two major implementation obstacles facing the intermediate-punishment movement are net widening and evaluation accountability. However, with regard to the net-widening obstacle, they contend that such an outcome may well be positive in relation to the issue of proportionality in sentencing. Morris and Tonry (1990: 226–227) state:

> Concern for fairness compels concern for proportionality in punishment, both in the sense that punishments should in some meaningful way be commensurate with the severity of the offender's crime and in the sense that relatively more severe offenders should in general receive relatively more severe punishment. Under current practice in most states, proportionality in either sense has been a possibility only for that minority of offenders who receive incarcerative sanctions. There has been little proportionality in punishment for those who are not bound for prison. When all of these people receive "mere probation" there is no feasible way to make punishments proportionate. Intermediate punishment would provide the successive steps for a ladder of scaled punishments outside prison.

Morris and Tonry conclude that when punishments are administered on the basis of a range of programs that vary in their levels of control or punitiveness, the question of net widening changes. The question is not, "Is the program being used for only those who would have been incarcerated?" but "Is the program being used by those for whom it was intended?" Their point is that intermediate punishment can appropriately serve as an in-between punishment to both incarceration and nominal probation, which in turn can contribute to net widening. The associated question that emerges concerns evaluation of intermediate punishment to definitively establish under what program conditions and offender characteristics net widening is desirable or undesirable.

The present study demonstrates, however, that focusing concern only on intermediate punishment's capacity to produce net widening, whether intended or unintended, desirable or undesirable, may miss a more salient outcome of the program movement. To elaborate, the process of providing offenders with new and more proportionate intermediate punishments may initiate events that go beyond net widening. As indicated for this county, the practice of blurring offender punishment and treatment is resulting in a piling up of sanctions that can bring about failures in program compliance and a return to court, often followed by jail—and upon jail release, a return to the same multitude of community program requirements, with the potential for additional program violations and a return to court again.

A recurring theme in the history of correctional alternatives has been the tendency by policy makers and criminologists alike to respond in a pendulumlike fashion to what has been perceived as failures among various reform movements. In contrast, the intermediate-punishment movement has adopted an eclectic approach to corrective techniques. Instead of embracing one approach to the exclusion of the other (for example, punitive versus treatment, incarceration versus community-based), intermediate punishment has all but eliminated the concept of alternatives. This philosophy of "using all available resources" was supported in a statement issued by the director of the County Corrections Division. His contention was that once an offender had been through the incarceration system and had been exposed to the various vocational/educational, life skills, and substance abuse programs, he would then return to the community as "a better probationer." What may be emerging, then, in the implementation of intermediate punishment is a standard acceptance of imposing supplements to incarceration rather than alternatives.

With regard to specific policy questions and issues, several points warrant mentioning. First, given this paper's findings, what recommendations can be made to judges concerning the imposition of intermediate punishments? Clearly, judges need to recognize that when several simultaneous sanctions are imposed, the potential for program failure is enhanced. However, in contrast, split sentences (that is, a jail term followed by community program involvement) or multiple intermediate sanctions can be useful for certain offender groups. While we are unable to specify what works best and for whom, identification of offender groups—for example, those with tendencies for violating programs—is possible. Efforts to address enhanced violation potentials can begin with increased interaction between judges and community corrections officers. Moreover, because community corrections officers most often act as the primary coordinator for the offender's activities and sentence requirements, they are privy to information that can provide some guidelines for more appropriate matching of offenders to specific program sanctions.

Further, it is expected that different jurisdictions will operate with considerable variation when implementing intermediate punishments. As a result, the piling up of sanctions may not be as relevant across jurisdictions. Nevertheless, given the problems associated with multiple-program sentences, jurisdictions should be tempered in their selection, implementation, and utilization of intermediate punishments. In short, jurisdictions should be mindful that "more is not always better" when attempting to successfully implement and operate intermediate-punishment systems.

References

ARROWHEAD REGIONAL CORRECTIONS (1988). *1988 Comprehensive Plan.* Duluth, Minn.

BLOMBERG, T. (1983). "Diversion's Disparate Results and Unresolved Questions: An Integrative Approach." *Journal of Research in Crime and Delinquency* 30(1):24–38.

BLUE RIBBON COMMISSION ON INMATE POPULATION MANAGEMENT (1990). State of California.

CHEN, H., AND P. H. ROSS (1980). "The Multi-Goal, Theory Driven Approach to Evaluation: A Model Linking Basic and Applied Social Science." *Social Forces* 59(1):100–120.

COMMUNITY CORRECTIONS DEPARTMENT, COUNTY CORRECTIONS DIVISION (1990). Administrative document outlining Pre-Trial Diversions, Youthful Offender Program.

————. Monthly statistical summary reports.

COUNTY CORRECTIONS DIVISION, OFFENDER SERVICES. *Statistical Reports on Inmate Populations and Admissions.*

DIRECTOR, COUNTY CORRECTIONS DIVISION (1990). *Revisioning the Role of Corrections and Its Effect on Crowding.* County Corrections Division Document.

FLORIDA DEPARTMENT OF LAW ENFORCEMENT. *Uniform Crime Reports, State of Florida, 1975–1990.* Tallahassee: Florida Department of Law Enforcement.

Florida Statistical Abstract, 1975–1989. Gainesville: Bureau of Economic and Business Research, College of Business Administration, University of Florida.

MORRIS, N., AND M. TONRY (1990). *Between Prison and Probation.* New York: Oxford University Press.

NORTHWEST COMMUNITY CORRECTIONS SYSTEM (1983). *Administrative Overview.* Crookston, Minn.

PARENT, DALE (1990). *Day Reporting Centers for Criminal Offenders—A Descriptive Analysis of Existing Programs.* Washington, D.C.: U.S. Department of Justice, Office of Justice Programs, National Institute of Justice.

U.S. CENSUS OF POPULATION, UNIVERSITY OF FLORIDA BUREAU OF ECONOMICS AND BUSINESS RESEARCH (1990). *Population Studies 92.* Gainesville, Fla.

PART SEVEN

Policy Perspectives

Crime and the administration of justice have been prominent on the public policy agenda for more than a quarter of a century. During this period, Congress has created and abolished the Law Enforcement Assistance Administration (LEAA), two presidential commissions have made extensive suggestions for reform, and billions of dollars have been spent in attempts to reduce crime and improve the justice system. Initially, an air of certainty about the causes of crime and the way to reform criminals characterized official and scholarly statements on the problem. But only during the past few years have the true dimensions of crime and the potential for dealing with it been viewed with a new realism. As James Q. Wilson, a leading exponent of this realistic stance, stated, our efforts to understand and curb the rise in crime have been frustrated by "our optimistic and unrealistic assumptions about human nature." This view is a far cry from the previously prevalent belief that crime, like poverty, could be ended if only there were enough money to apply the techniques of the social and behavioral sciences to the "root causes"—poor housing, unemployment, and racial prejudice.

During the early period of activity by the LEAA, it was apparently assumed that, because the criminal justice system had been given a low public resources priority for such a long time, there was a need for "more of everything." The states were given generous grants to purchase new equipment (especially for the police), to encourage education and training, and to experiment with a variety of programs. Battles over the distribution of federal money seem to have taken on more importance than the development of a systematic and comprehensive approach to the problem to be solved: how to control crime yet maintain due process values. Programs tried out new approaches to crime prevention, court efficiency, and offender rehabilitation in a scattershot manner. The accent was on implementing the experiment; less attention was paid to theoretical foundations, testable hypotheses, or methods of evaluation. Because of the nature of the congressional mandate, the interest groups waiting to stake their claim to portions of the funds, and the philosophy that multiple approaches should be used in order to discover "what works," the LEAA soon was charged with being a captive of political forces and with making no headway in dealing with crime. Congress abolished the LEAA in 1982.

In the past twenty years, research has provided a glimmer of hope for those who believe that the social sciences have the analytical tools to understand crime and to contribute to formation of public policies to deal with it. This research appears to be more systematic, to be based on empirical findings, and to challenge much of the "conventional wisdom" about crime, criminal behavior, and the administration of justice. There is a new appreciation of the complex dimensions of criminal behavior and of the fact that the law-enforcement function is only one role of the police. The courts are increasingly viewed as organizations composed of small groups, and it is recognized that rehabilitative techniques have had a low success rate. In addition, the dominant approach has been that criminal justice is a system.

Research should be the essential activity on which public policies are built. If government decisions were not influenced by politics, one might be able to show how the findings of social scientists could be directly applied to solving a public problem. However, public decisions are made in the political arena, where negotiation among relevant interest groups and political leaders is the way policy is formed. The solutions discussed by experts usually have little relation to the operational plans that emerge from the policy process.

For many Americans the goal of the criminal justice system appear to be obvious: control crime within the context of due process. There is undoubtedly widespread agreement among citizens that these should be the goals, but such broad terms do not tell us how the goals are to be achieved. Debate over criminal justice policies may be daily noted in the press, in legislative assemblies, and in private conversations. Should the police be allowed to detain suspects without bail? Should sentences emphasize incapacitation or rehabilitation? Should efforts be undertaken to improve neighborhoods that breed crime? Should the War on Drugs be continued?

Discussion of these and similar questions get to basic questions about crime and justice policies in a democracy. During the past quarter of a century one can detect a shift in public opinion and policy direction. Until the mid-1970s the recommendations of the 1967 report of the President's Commission on Law Enforcement and Administration of Justice seemed to hold sway at both the federal and state levels of government. The commission declared that crime was caused essentially by disorganization in American society; that agencies engaged in enforcement, adjudication, and corrections lacked sufficient resources; and that rehabilitation had been insufficiently emphasized in the treatment of offenders. The writers of the report recommend eliminating social conditions that bring about crime, doing away with social and racial injustices in order to achieve the ideals of the American ethic, and reintegrating those who commit crime into their communities.

The middle of the 1970s saw a shift in criminal justice policies that mirrored the ascendance of conservative political leaders. Since that time the conservative critique of the liberal policies of the 1960s has been constant. The critique gained credence during the 1970s in part because research cast doubt on many previous policies. Debate about "what works" sparked a reconsideration of the role of rehabilitative programs. Committees of the National Academy of Sciences recommended that greater weight be given to policies of incarceration and deterrence. Questions were raised about the dangers posed by the practice of allowing bail to repeat offenders, the prosecution of career criminals, lengths of incarcerative sentences, and the broader efforts to reduce crime through social reform.

The election of Ronald Reagan in 1980 consolidated the shift in crime control policies. Actions taken during the Reagan and Bush administrations, and copied in most states, placed greater emphasis upon increasing resources for police and prosecutors, raising sentence lengths, increasing the use of incarceration, tightening the insanity defense, and abolishing parole release.

Now that we have experienced almost twenty years of harsher crime control policies, have they made a difference? Some will point to the leveling off of the crime rate during the mid-1970s and argue that the tougher policies have worked. Opponents point to the doubling of the incarcerative population during the past decade as proof that these policies have failed. Is another shift in crime and justice policies in the offing? Will the costs of the War on Drugs and increased use of prison cause taxpayers to raise questions about the future of these policies? Will concerned citizens again call for policies that emphasize justice over crime control?

Suggestions for Further Reading

CULLEN, FRANCIS T., AND KAREN E. GILBERT. *Reaffirming Rehabilitation.* Cincinnati: Anderson Publishing Company, 1982. A defense of the rehabilitative goal of correction and a critique of the justice model.

FEELEY, MALCOLM M. *Court Reform on Trial.* New York: Basic Books, 1983. Examination of programs designed to reform the courts and the problems of bringing about innovations.

GARLAND, DAVID. *Punishment and Modern Society.* Chicago: University of Chicago Press, 1990. Examination and critique of some of the leading modern theorists on punishment. Garland argues for a social approach to punishment.

GORDON, DIANA R. *The Justice Juggernaut.* New Brunswick, N.J.: Rutgers University Press, 1990. Argues that recent approaches to street crime have amounted to uncontrolled growth in state coercion without a corresponding reduction in violence and thievery.

MORRIS, NORVAL, AND MICHAEL TONRY. *Between Prison and Probation: Intermediate Punishments in a Rational Sentencing System.* New York: Oxford University Press, 1990. Urges development of a range of intermediate punishments that can be used to sanction offenders more severely than nominal probation but less severely than incarceration.

VON HIRSCH, ANDREW. *Doing Justice.* New York: Hill & Wang, 1976. The best statement of the philosophy of the "just deserts" model, with recommendations for implementing it.

WALKER, SAMUEL. *Sense and Nonsense about Crime: A Policy Guide.* 2nd ed. Pacific Grove, Calif.: Brooks/Cole, 1989. Examination of crime control policies that don't work (the nonsense) and those that appear to have some potential (the sense).

26

Ten Deadly Myths about Crime and Punishment in the United States

Charles Logan

John J. DiIulio, Jr.

During the past two decades conservatives have mounted a challenge to the liberal crime and justice policies that dominated the 1960s and early 1970s. The crime control approach is well outlined by Logan and DiIulio. What are the implications of these views for future crime and justice policies?

False ideas can have tragic consequences. For the last quarter-century, a network of anti-incarceration, pro-prisoner analysts, activists, lawyers, lobbyists, journalists, and judges has perpetuated a number of false ideas about crime and punishment in the United States. For average law-abiding American citizens, if not for predatory street criminals and elite penal reformers, the consequences of these false ideas have been quite tragic indeed. As these ideas have been carved into federal, state, and local penal codes, they have succeeded in making it easier for the criminals to hit, rape, rob, burglarize, deal drugs, and murder with impunity. Worse, they have succeeded in concentrating such criminal mischief in economically distressed inner-city neighborhoods, inviting the criminal predators of these areas to repeatedly victimize their struggling underclass neighbors.

In this essay, we propose to identify and rebut ten deadly ideas about crime and punishment in the United States. Before we do so, however, three cautions are in order.

First, we refer to these ideas as "myths." In the *The American Heritage Dictionary,* myth is defined in four ways, including a "fiction or half-truth, especially one that forms part of the ideology of a society"; for example, "the myth of racial superiority." The false ideas about crime and punishment in the United States that we wish to challenge are myths in that sense. As we will show, in some cases the ideas are flatly untrue; in other cases, they are more or less skillful, more or less well-publicized exaggerations of half-truths. But, in all cases, they are by-products

Source: From Charles H. Logan and John J. DiIulio, Jr., "Ten Deadly Myths about Crime and Punishment in the U.S.," *Wisconsin Interest* 1 (Winter/Spring 1992), pp. 21–35. Reprinted with permission.

of an ideological vision in which punishing all save the most vicious chronic criminals is considered either morally illegitimate or socially counterproductive, or both. For the purposes of the present essay we shall confine ourselves to the discussion of ten particular myths about crime and punishment in the United States, driving our points through the gaping empirical and other holes in each of them, and suggesting what a truer, or at least a more balanced, vision of the realities in question might be.

Second, our list of ten is by no means exhaustive. There are other myths that could as easily come in for critical scrutiny, such as the myth that building new prisons encourages the courts to fill them up, while a moratorium on prison construction will prevent that outcome. Tempted though we are to try and clean up each and every myth, data availability, interpretive range, and space have limited us to rounding up the ten "worst offenders" below.

Third, we do not believe that most of those who have perpetrated these myths have done so with any sort of malicious intent. Instead, we believe that their intentions have been good, but that they have been blinded by ideology to the connection between the false ideas they have pushed, and the dire human and financial consequences that have resulted.

Myth One: *Crime in the United States is caused by poverty, chronic unemployment, and other socioeconomic factors.*

Many academic criminologists, most of whom are sociologists, believe that capitalism produces pockets of poverty, inequality, and unemployment, which then foster crime. The solution, they believe, is government intervention to provide jobs, stimulate the economy, and reduce poverty and other social ills. There certainly is a correlation between the geography of crime and the geography of certain socioeconomic factors, but to interpret the correlation as evidence that poverty causes crime is to get it just about backwards.

As James K. Stewart, former director of the National Institute of Justice, has pointed out, inner-city areas where crime is rampant have tremendous potential for economic growth, given their infrastructure of railways, highways, electric power, water systems, and large supply of available labor.[1] There is every reason for these areas to be wealthy and, indeed, many of them have been rich in the past. But crime takes a terrible toll on physical, fiscal, and human capital, making it difficult to accumulate wealth and break out of the cycle of poverty. Criminals steal and destroy property, drive away customers and investors, reduce property values, and depreciate the quality of life in a neighborhood. Businesses close and working families move away, leaving behind a vacuum of opportunity. As Stewart says, crime "is the ultimate tax on enterprise. . . . The natural dynamic of the marketplace cannot assert itself when a local economy is regulated by crime."[2] What these areas need most from government is not economic intervention but physical protection and security. The struggling inner-city dwellers whom sociologist William Julius Wilson has dubbed "the truly disadvantaged" deserve greater protection from their truly deviant neighbors.

People who are poor, uneducated, unskilled, and unemployed may need and deserve help, but not because of their alleged propensity toward crime. In high-crime urban areas, most poor people do not commit serious crimes. Fighting poverty and other problems only where, when, and because they are associated with crime would be an injustice to those who are neediest. It also would not succeed; that was the lesson of the 1960s and 1970s, when the Great Society and its massive War on Poverty stemmed neither inner-city poverty nor crime.[3]

Economists, like sociologists, see a relation between economic conditions and crime, but the connection they make is much more straightforward. They see criminal behavior, like all behavior, as a rational response to incentives and opportunities. Statistical analyses have provided only mixed and limited evidence that levels of arrest and imprisonment may have deterrent effects, but as a matter of both theory and common sense, the belief that criminal behavior is responsive to reward and punishment has considerable strength.

Crime rates rose during the 1960s and early 1970s, then fell during the 1980s. In contrast, imprisonment rates as a percentage of crimes fell during the 1960s and early 1970s, then rose during the 1980s.[4] A deterrence-minded economist looking at these mirrored trends would say that crime rose and fell in response to its expected cost in terms of punishment.[5] An interpretation more favored by sociologists is that crime rose and fell as the "baby boom" cohort of young men in the population moved through their most crime-prone years. Economist Bruce Benson notes, however, that this "alternative" interpretation still requires some further explanation of why it is that young men are more prone to commit crimes. He provides an economist's answer: the opportunity costs of crime are lower for this group than for others. "Wages for young people are low, and their unemployment is always substantially higher than for the older population. In addition, punishment for young criminals tends to be less severe, particularly for those under eighteen who are prosecuted as juveniles. Even for those over eighteen, punishment may be less severe in a relative sense."[6]

Myth Two: *In the 1980s, the United States enacted all sorts of "get tough on crime" legislation and went on an incarceration binge.*

Prison populations have risen sharply over the last decade; that much is true. The myth is that this is due to an unprecedented and purely political wave of punitivity sweeping the nation, as epitomized by the War on Drugs and by legislative demands for longer and mandatory sentences. Several elements of this myth are shattered by a meticulous and authoritative article published recently in *Science* by Patrick A. Langan, a statistician at the Bureau of Justice Statistics.[7]

Langan examined the tremendous increase in state prison populations from 1973 to 1986. He determined that the growth was due to increases in prison admissions, rather than to (alleged but nonexistent) increases in sentence length or time served. He estimated that about 20 percent of the growth in admissions could be accounted for by demographic shifts in age and race. Increases in crime were offset by decreases in the probability of arrest, with the result that combined changes in crime and arrest rates accounted for only 9 percent of admissions growth. Increased drug arrests and imprisonments contributed only 8 percent.[8] By far the strongest determinant, explaining 51 percent of growth in prison admissions, was an increase in the postarrest probabilities of conviction and incarceration.[9] Prosecutors convicted more felons, judges imposed more prison sentences, and more violators of probation or parole were sent or returned to prison. The data suggest that the system may have gotten more efficient but not harsher.

A column in the *Washington Post* captures well the form and spirit of the "imprisonment binge" myth.[10] In "The Great American Lockup," Franklin E. Zimring, a professor of law at Berkeley, claims that we are more punitive now than ever before in history, that the rising tide of imprisonment is a matter of overzealous policy rather than a response to need, and that we must come to our senses and reverse an essentially irrational imprisonment policy.

When Professor Zimring says that we are experiencing a "100-year peak in rates of imprisonment," he does not inform the reader that this is true only when you measure imprisonment on a crude per capita basis. If, however, you wish to describe the *punitivity* of our imprisonment rate, you need to measure the amount of imprisonment relative to the number of crimes for which people may be sent to prison. To get an even more complete measure of punitivity, you should multiply this probability of imprisonment by the length of time served. When just such an index is examined for all the years in which it is available, 1960 through 1986, it becomes clear that we have not been marching steadily forward to an all-time high in punitivity. Instead, this index of "expected days of imprisonment" fell steadily from its high in 1959 (ninety-three days) to about one-seventh of that figure in 1975 (fourteen days). From 1975 through 1986 it returned to about one-fifth (nineteen days) of its 1960 level.[11] Even if we ignore the factor of time served and look only at prison commitments divided by crimes, we see much the same pattern. In 1960 there were sixty-two prison commitments per 1,000 Uniform Crime Index offenses; that number fell to twenty-three in 1970, remained relatively stable during the 1970s, then climbed from twenty-five back to sixty-two between 1980 and 1989.[12]

Thus, when we look at imprisonment per crime rather than per capita, and over thirty rather than ten years, we see that our punishment level is not rocketing to a new high but recovering from a plunge. The myth of the imprisonment binge requires that we focus only on punishment and not on crime, and that we ignore all data prior to about 1980.

Myth Three: *Our prisons hold large numbers of petty offenders who should not be there.*

Tom Wicker, writing in the *New York Times,* asks: "Why does our nation spend such an exorbitant amount of money each year to warehouse petty criminals?"[13] He takes his question, and its underlying assumption, from a study by the National Council on Crime and Delinquency (NCCD), which he summarizes as finding "that 80 percent of those going to prison are not serious or violent criminals but are guilty of low-level offenses: minor parole violations, property, drug and public disorder crimes." Neither Wicker's account nor the NCCD's own summary, however, is supported by the data.[14]

The NCCD study involved interviews with 154 incoming prisoners in three states.[15] Based primarily on "facts" related by these new convicts, their crimes were classified as "petty," "medium serious," "serious," or "very serious." While the NCCD claims in its summary that the "vast majority of inmates are sentenced for petty crimes," we discover in the body of the report that "inmates" refers to just the entering cohort and not all inmates, that "vast majority" refers to 52.6 percent, and that "petty crimes" refers to acts that most Americans believe it is appropriate to punish by some period of incarceration.

Since more serious offenders receive longer sentences (and therefore accumulate in prison), the profile of incoming offenders differs significantly from that of the total population. The NCCD study is based on this distinction, but obscures it by referring always to "inmates," rather than "entering inmates."

A careful reader will find buried in the NCCD report sufficient information to calculate that 25.4 percent of the sample were men whose conviction offense was categorized by the researchers as "petty" but who revealed to the interviewers that they were high-rate offenders who were committed to a criminal lifestyle. If that fact was revealed also to the judge, in the form of a prior criminal record, it would have been a valid factor in sentencing. In any case, shouldn't these 25.4 percent have been added to the 47.4 percent whose crimes were in some degree "serious" (that is, more than "petty")? Then the study would show that nearly three-quarters of new admissions are either serious or high-rate offenders. And that does not even count 21 percent of the sample who, while not identified as high-rate offenders, were described as having been on a "crime spree" at the time of their commitment offense.

The major fallacy in the NCCD study, however, was in concluding that certain property crimes are "petty"—and therefore undeserving of punishment by imprisonment—merely because they score low on a scale of "offense severity" developed in 1978. For example, burglary of a home resulting in a loss of $1,000 received a relatively low score on the severity scale, albeit higher than some descriptions of robbery, assault requiring medical treatment, bribery, auto theft for resale, embezzlement of $1,000, and many other offenses. A severity score, however, does not tell us what punishment is proper for any particular crime. In a recent survey, an overwhelming majority (81 percent) of Americans said that some time in jail or prison was a proper punishment for a residential burglary with a $1,000 loss. A clear majority (57 percent) thought jail or prison was appropriate even for a nonresidential burglary resulting in only a $10 loss.[16]

What the American public seems to understand, but NCCD does not, is that it is not just the amount of money or other material harm that makes a property crime like burglary or robbery serious rather than petty. It is the breach of an individual's security and the violation of those rights (to property and person) that form the foundation of a free society. Moreover, the NCCD dichotomy of crimes into "serious" and "petty" omits several factors that are very important both legally and morally. These include the number of counts and the offender's prior record, both of which the law recognizes as legitimate criteria in determining the culpability of offenders and the gravity of their acts.

Comprehensive national data from the Bureau of Justice Statistics show that U.S. prison populations consist overwhelmingly of violent or repeat offenders, with little change in demographic or offense characteristics from 1979 to 1986.[17] There may be individuals in prison who do not deserve to be there, and there may be some crimes now defined as felonies that ought to be redefined as misdemeanors or decriminalized altogether (some would argue this for drug crimes). But most people now in prison are not what most of the public would regard as "petty" offenders.

Myth Four: *Prisons are filthy, violence-ridden, and overcrowded human warehouses that function as schools of crime.*

There are two popular and competing images of American prisons. In one image, all or most prisons are hellholes. In the other image, all or most prisons are country clubs. Each image fits some prisons. But the vast majority of prisons in the United States today are neither hellholes nor country clubs. Instead, most American prisons do a pretty decent job of protecting inmates from each other, providing them with basic amenities (decent food, clean quarters, recreational equipment), offering them basic services (educational programs, work opportunities), and doing so in a way that ensures prisoners their basic constitutional and legal rights.

It is certainly true that most prison systems now hold more prisoners than they did a decade ago. The Federal Bureau of Prisons, for example, is operating at over 160 percent of its "design capacity"; that is, federal prisons house 60 percent more prisoners than they were designed to hold. When the federal prison agency's current multibillion-dollar expansion program is completed, it will still house about 40 percent more inmates than its buildings were designed to hold. That is by no means an ideal picture, and much the same picture can indeed be painted for dozens of jurisdictions around the country.

Contrary to the popular lore and propaganda, however, the consequences of prison crowding vary widely both within and between prison systems, and in every careful empirical study of the subject, the widely believed negative effects of crowding—violence, program disruption, health problems, and so on—are nowhere to be found. More broadly, several recent analyses have exploded the facile belief that contemporary prison conditions are unhealthy and harmful to inmates.

For example, in a study of over 180,000 housing units at 694 state prisons, the Bureau of Justice Statistics reported that the most overcrowded maximum security prisons had a rate of homicide lower than that of moderately crowded prisons and about the same as that of prisons that were not crowded.[18] By the same token, a recent review of the prison-crowding literature rightly concluded that "despite familiar claims that crowded prisons have produced dramatic increases in prison violence, illness, and hostility, modern research has failed to establish any conclusive link between current prison spatial and social densities and these problems."[19] Even more compelling was the conclusion reached in a recent and exhaustive survey of the empirical literatures bearing on the "pains of imprisonment." This conclusion is worth quoting at some length:

> To date, the incarceration literature has been very much influenced by a pains of imprisonment model. This model views imprisonment as psychologically harmful. However, the empirical data we reviewed question the validity of the view that imprisonment is universally painful. Solitary confinement, under limiting and humane conditions, long-term imprisonment, and short-term detention fail to show detrimental effects. From a physical health standpoint, inmates appear more healthy than their community counterparts.[20]

Normally, those who for ideological or other reasons are inclined to paint a bleaker portrait of U.S. prison conditions than is justified by the facts respond to such evidence with countervailing anecdotes about a given prison or prison system. Perhaps because good news is no news, most media pundits lap up these unrepresentative prison horror stories and report on "powder keg conditions" behind bars.

And when a prison riot occurs, it is now de rigueur for "experts" to ascribe the incident to "overcrowding" and other "underlying factors." For selfish and short-sighted reasons, some prison officials are all too willing to go along with the farce. It is easier for them to join in a Greek chorus about the evils of prison crowding than it is for them to admit that their own poor leadership and management were wholly or partially responsible for the trouble (as it so often is).

Indeed, recent comparative analyses of how different prison administrators have handled crowding and other problems under like conditions suggest that the quality of life behind bars is mainly a function of how prisons are organized, led, and managed.[21]

Overwhelmingly, the evidence shows that crowded prisons can be safe and humane, while prisons with serious problems often suffered the same or worse problems before they were crowded. In short, the quality of prison life varies mainly according to the quality of prison management, and the quality of prison life in the United States today is generally quite good.

More specifically, contrary to the widely influential "nothing works" school of prison-based criminal rehabilitation programs, correctional administrators in a number of jurisdictions have instituted a variety of programs that serve as effective management tools and appear to increase the probability that prisoners who participate in them will go straight upon their release. Recent empirical studies indicate that prisoners who participate in certain types of drug abuse, counseling, and work-based programs may be less likely than otherwise comparable prisoners to return to prison once they return to the streets, as over 95 percent of all prisoners eventually do.[22]

Unfortunately, the recent spate of analyses that support this encouraging conclusion remain empirically thin, technically complex, and highly speculative. Moreover, each of the successful programs embodies a type of highly compassionate yet no-nonsense management approach that may be easier to describe in print than to emulate in practice or export widely. But, taken together with the more general facts and findings mentioned above, these studies—and the simple reality that most of those released from prison never return there—rebut the notion that most or all prisons in the United States are little better than crowded human warehouses that breed crime and other ills.

Myth Five: The U.S. criminal justice system is shot through with racial discrimination.

Most law-abiding Americans think that criminal sanctions are normally imposed on people who have been duly convicted of criminally violating the life, liberty, and property of their fellow citizens. Many critics, however, harbor a different, ostensibly more sophisticated view. They see prisons as instruments of "social control." To them, America is an oppressive, racist society, and prisons are a none-too-subtle way of subjugating the nation's poor and minority populations. Thus are roughly one of every nine adult African-American males in this country now under some form of correctional supervision—in prison, in jail, on probation, or on parole. And thus in the "conservative" 1980s was this "net of social control" cast over nearly a quarter of young African-American males in many jurisdictions.

There are at least three reasons why such race-based understandings of the U.S. criminal justice system are highly suspect at best. First, once one controls for socioeconomic and related factors, there is simply no empirical evidence to support the view that African-Americans, or the members of other racial and ethnic minorities in the United States, are far more likely than whites to be arrested, booked, indicted, fully prosecuted, convicted, be denied probation, incarcerated, disciplined while in custody (administrative segregation), or be denied furloughs or parole.

In one recent study, for example, the RAND Corporation found that "a defendant's racial or ethnic group bore little or no relationship to conviction rates, disposition times" and other adjudication outcomes in fourteen large urban jurisdictions across the country.[23] Instead, the study found that such mundane factors as the amount of evidence against a defendant, and whether or not a credible eyewitness testified, were strongly related to outcomes. This study echoed the findings of several previous empirical analyses.[24]

Second, the 1980s were many things, but they were not a time when the fraction of African-Americans behind prison bars skyrocketed. In a recent report, the Bureau of Justice Statistics revealed that the number of African-Americans as a percentage of the state prison population "has changed little since 1974; 47 percent in 1974, 48 percent in 1979, and 47 percent in 1986."[25] It is certainly true that the imprisonment rate for African-Americans has been, and continues to be, far higher than for whites. For example, in 1986 the rate of admission to prison per 100,000 residential population was 342 for African-Americans and 63 for whites.[26] But it is also true that crime rates are much higher for the former group than for the latter.

Finally, it is well known that most crime committed by poor minority citizens is committed against poor minority citizens. The typical victims of predatory ghetto criminals are innocent ghetto dwellers and their children, not middle- or upper-class whites.[27] For example, the best available data indicate that over 85 percent of single-offender crimes of violence committed by blacks are committed against blacks, while over 75 percent of such crimes committed by whites are committed against whites.[28] And if every credible opinion poll and victimization survey is to be believed, no group suffers more from violent street crime, "petty" thefts, and drug dealing, and no group is more eager to have courts, cops, and corrections officials crack down on inner-city criminals, than the predominantly minority citizens of these communities themselves.

The U.S. criminal justice system, therefore, may be biased, but not in the ways that elite, anti-incarceration penal reformers generally suppose. Relative to whites and more affluent citizens generally, the system now permits poor and minority citizens to be victimized readily and repeatedly: the rich get richer, the poor get poorly protected against the criminals in their midst. The system is thus rigged in favor of those who advocate community-based alternatives to incarceration and other measures that return violent, repeat, and violent repeat offenders to poor, drug-ravaged, minority communities far from the elites' own well-protected homes, offices, and suites.

Myth Six: *Prisons in the United States are prohibitively expensive.*

Certainly, no sane citizen relishes spending public money on prisons and prisoners. A tax dollar spent to confine a criminal is a tax dollar not spent to house the homeless, educate the young, or assist the handicapped. There are many intrinsically rewarding civic ventures, but the imprisonment of wrongdoers is hardly at the top of anyone's list.

Nevertheless, it is morally myopic, and conceptually and empirically moronic, to argue that public money spent on prisons and prisons is public money wasted. That, however, is precisely what legions of critics have argued.

To begin, nobody really knows how much the United States now spends each year to construct, renovate, administer, and finance prisons. Widely cited estimates range from $20 billion to over $40 billion. Corrections expenditures by government have been growing rapidly of late; in New Jersey, for example, the corrections budget has increased fivefold since 1978, and corrections threatens to become the largest single item in many state budgets. But viewed as a fraction of total government spending, in the 1980s the amount spent on corrections was trivial; for example, despite enormous growth in the Federal Bureau of Prisons, less than one penny of every federal dollar went to corrections. Just the same, estimating the costs of corrections in general, and of prisons in particular, is an exceedingly complex business to which competent analysts have given only scant attention.[29] Still, it is possible to get a conceptual and empirical handle on the financial costs and benefits of imprisonment in the United States today.

When critics assert that we are spending "too much" on imprisonment, we must ask "too much relative to what?" Is it the case, for example, that the marginal tax dollar invested in low-income housing, inner-city high schools, or programs for the disabled poor would yield a greater social benefit than the same dollar invested in constructing or administering new prison cells? The heart says yes, but the answer is far from obvious. Meaningful benefit–cost analyses of such competing public purposes are hard to conduct, and great difficulties attend any serious effort to quantify and compare the costs and benefits of this versus that use of public money. It is somewhat easier, but still problematic, to ask what benefits we would forgo if we did not use public money for a given purpose. For example, U.S. taxpayers now spend somewhere between $14,000 and $25,000 to keep a convicted criminal behind bars for a year. What would they lose if they chose instead to save their money, or apply it elsewhere, and allowed the criminals to remain on the streets rather than paying to keep them behind bars?

At least one thing they would lose is personal and property protection against the criminals. In simplest terms, if the typical street criminal commits X crimes per year, then the benefit to society of locking him up is to be protected against the X crimes he would have done if he were free. Thus, if the typical offender committed only one petty property crime per year, then paying thousands and thousands of dollars to keep him confined would be a bad social investment. But if he committed a dozen serious property or violent crimes each year, then the social benefits of keeping him imprisoned might well exceed the social costs of doing so.

Is imprisonment in the United States today worth the money spent on it? While critics assert that it is not, only a few serious efforts have been made to grapple with this question.[30] The first such effort was made in 1987 by National Institute of Justice economist Edwin W. Zedlewski.[31] Zedlewski surveyed cost data from several prison systems and estimated that the annual per-prisoner cost of confinement was $25,000. Using national crime data and the findings of criminal victimization surveys, he estimated that the typical offender commits 187 crimes per year, and that the typical

crime exacts $2,300 in property losses and/or in physical injuries and human suf-
fering. Multiplying these two figures (187 times $2,300), he calculated that, when
on the streets, the typical imprisoned felon was responsible for $430,000 in "social
costs" each year. Dividing that figure by $25,000 (his estimate of the annual per-
prisoner cost of confinement), he concluded that incarceration in prison has a benefit–cost ratio of just over 17. The implications were unequivocal. According to Zedlewski's analysis, putting 1,000 felons behind prison bars costs society $25 million
per year. But not putting these same felons behind prison bars costs society about
$430 million per year (187,000 crimes times $2,300 per crime).

There were, however, some flaws in Zedlewski's study. For example, he used
dated data from a RAND prisoner self-report survey of prison and jail inmates in
Texas, Michigan, and California. The inmates in the survey averaged between 187
and 287 crimes per year, exclusive of drug deals. He opted for the lower bound of
187. But the same RAND survey also found that half the inmate population committed fewer than 15 crimes per year, so that the median number of crimes committed
was 15. There are plenty of good analytical reasons for using the median rather than
the average in a benefit–cost study of this type. Making this one adjustment (using
15 rather than 187 for the number of crimes averted through incapacitation of an
offender) reduces the benefit–cost ratio to 1.38—still positive, but more credibly and
realistically so.

Last December one of us published a report on corrections in Wisconsin that
featured an analysis of the benefits and costs of imprisonment.[32] The analysis was
based on one of the largest and most recent scientific prisoner self-report surveys of
inmates in a single system ever conducted. Among a host of other interesting results,
the survey indicated that the prisoners committed an average of 141 crimes per year,
exclusive of drug deals. The median figure was 12. Using the median to calculate,
the study estimated the benefit–cost ratio to be 1.97.

In an attempt to satisfy the more reasonable critics, the Wisconsin data were
reanalyzed and the results of the reanalysis were published in a recent edition of *The
Brookings Review,* journal of The Brookings Institute.[33] But even after factoring in
a host of assumptions that would be likely to deflate the benefits of imprisonment,
the study reported a benefit–cost ratio of 1.84. This does not prove that "prison
pays"; indeed, the Brookings study suggested that, for the lowest-level offenders,
imprisonment probably is not a good social investment. But it does indicate that the
net social benefits of imprisonment could well meet or exceed the costs.

At a minimum, the studies discussed above cast grave doubts over the notion
that prisons clearly "cost too much," either in absolute terms or relative to alternate
uses of the public monies that now go to build and administer penal facilities. What
we simply do not know at this point is whether any given alternative to incarceration
yields as much relative to costs as imprisonment apparently does. Recent studies have
put question marks over several strictly supervised community-based correctional
programs that might well represent a better investment than imprisonment for certain
categories of low-level offenders.[34] Still, further research on the costs and benefits
of imprisonment and other correctional sanctions is badly needed.

Myth Seven: *Interventions by activist judges have improved prison and jail
conditions.*

In 1970, not a single prison or jail system in America was operating under judicial orders to change and improve. For most of our legal and constitutional history, prisoners were "slaves of the state," and judges followed the "hands-off" doctrine by normally deferring to the policies and practices of legislators and duly appointed corrections officials.

Today, however, over three dozen correctional agencies are operating under "conditions of confinement" court orders; many have class action suits in progress or population limits set by the courts; and several have court-mandated early-release programs that put dangerous felons right back on the streets before they have served even one-tenth of their sentences in confinement. Despite the proliferation of Reagan- and Bush-appointed judges on the federal bench, activist federal judges continue to be the sovereigns of the nation's cell blocks, issuing directives on a wide range of issues, including health care services, staff training procedures, sanitation standards, food services, and the constitutionality of conditions "in their totality." Indeed, in some prison systems, the texts of court orders and consent decrees are now used as staff training manuals and inmate rule books, and everything from inmate disciplinary hearings to the exact temperature of the meat served to prisoners at supper is governed by judicial fiat.

There are at least three general points that can be safely made about the course and consequences of judicial intervention into prisons and jails. First, especially in the South, but in many jurisdictions outside the South as well, judicial involvement has substantially raised the costs of building and administering penal facilities.[35] Second, many of the most significant expansions in prisoners' rights, and most of the actual improvements in institutional conditions, made over the last two decades were conceived and implemented by professional correctional administrators, not coerced or engineered by activist judges.[36] Third, in the small but significant fraction of interventions that have succeeded at a reasonable human and financial cost, judges have proceeded incrementally rather than issuing all-encompassing decrees. In conjunction, they have vacated the serenity of their chambers for the cell blocks to get a firsthand understanding of things, working with and through the professionals who must ultimately translate their orders into action, rather than relying solely on self-interested special masters and neatly typed depositions.[37]

Even taking into account the human and financial accidents caused by judges driving at breakneck activist speed through the intersection of corrections and the Constitution, the net of judicial involvement in this area is arguably positive. But there is at least as much evidence here for the thesis, articulated well by Nathan Glazer, Lon Fuller, and other scholars, that judges should limit themselves to doing what they are schooled to do; namely, to gather and weigh legal evidence, to analyze factual and legal issues, and to apply precedent standards in resolving disputes between parties.[38] At most, the idea that activist judges have helped to make prisons and jails more safe and humane is a half-truth.

Myth Eight: *The United States has the most punitive criminal justice system in the world.*

Over a decade ago, the National Council on Crime and Delinquency foisted on the media a statistic it produced in a 1979 report: in terms of severity of punishment, as measured by the number of prisoners per capita, only two countries in the world—

the Soviet Union and South Africa—were more ruthlessly repressive than the United States. The media have been parroting this claim ever since, never asking the NCCD why they were so willing to accept Soviet figures at face value, nor why they did not include the 4 or 5 million prisoners held captive in the forced labor camps that have been indispensable to the Soviet economy.[39]

Well, maybe a sloppy attitude toward data didn't matter before; we merely would have been a more distant third. But now the NCCD, the Soviets, and the South Africans have all been trumped. According to The Sentencing Project, a Washington-based research group, the United States has moved into first place, with 426 prison and jail inmates per 100,000 population, compared to 333 in South Africa and 268 in the Soviet Union.[40] The media, including commentators as diverse as Tom Wicker and William Raspberry, have reacted just as uncritically to the new figures as they did to the old ones.

While gullibility toward Soviet statistics is the most glaring, it is not the most fatal flaw in this comparison, which also shows American incarceration rates to be much higher than, say, those of European countries, for which we have more reliable figures. The fatal flaw is very simple and very obvious: to interpret incarceration as a measure of the punitivity of a society, you have to divide, not by the population size, but by the number of crimes.

More competent comparative studies have discovered that when you control for rates of serious crime, the difference between the United States and other countries largely, and for some crimes completely, disappears.[41] For example, after controlling for crime rate and adjusting for differences in charge reduction between arrest and imprisonment, the United States in the early 1980s had an imprisonment rate virtually identical to Canada and England for theft, fell between those two countries in the case of burglary, and lagged well behind each of the others in imprisonments for robbery.[42]

In addition to the myth of the United States as the world's most punitive nation, The Sentencing Project perpetuates in its report several of the other myths we discuss in this essay. It notes that African-American males are locked up at a rate four times greater than their counterparts in South Africa. A fleeting reference to the very high crime rate among black males is immediately buried in an avalanche of references to root causes, poverty, diminished opportunities, the gap between rich and poor, and the failure of schools, health care, and other social institutions—all wrapped up as "the cumulative effect of American policies regarding black males." The report calls for increased spending on supposed "prevention policies and services" such as education, housing, health care, and programs to generate employment. In a truly wacky expression of faith in social engineering, the report urges the General Accounting Office "to determine the relative influence of a range of social and economic factors on crime."

Most of all, The Sentencing Project advocates the expanded use of alternatives to incarceration, but with a unique twist: they recommend racial quotas in the distribution of criminal justice. Independent of any preceding reduction in criminal behavior, the "Justice Department should encourage the development of programs and sanctions designed specifically to reduce the disproportionate incarceration rate of African-American males."[43] The Sentencing Project endorses the language of one such program designed to reduce the incarceration "of ethnic and minority groups where such proportion exceeds the proportions such groups represent in the general population." Methods recommended for such reduction include diversion from prosecution, intensive probation, alternative sentencing, and parole release planning, among others.

That crime rates are very high in this country, particularly among black males, is an unhappy fact. When that fact is taken into account, it exposes as a myth the argument that we are excessively punitive, relative to other countries, in our imposition of imprisonment. A related myth is that we have failed to consider sanctions other than incarceration.

Myth Nine: *We don't make enough use of alternatives to incarceration.*

According to this myth, we could reduce prison crowding, avoid new construction, and cut our annual operating costs if we would just take greater advantage of intensive probation, fines, electronic monitoring, community service, boot camps, wilderness programs, and placement in nonsecure settings like halfway houses.

It is important to distinguish the myth of a supposed need for "alternative" sanctions from the more valid assertion of a need for "intermediate" sanctions. Norval Morris and Michael Tonry, among others, argue that, for the sake of doing justice and achieving proportionality between crime and punishment, we need a greater variety of dispositions that are intermediate in punitivity between imprisonment and simple probation.[44] Most people will find that argument perfectly sensible, even if they disagree about what crimes deserve which intermediate punishments.

The myth that we need more sanctions to use as *alternatives* to imprisonment is used on the false premise that we do not already make the maximum feasible use of *existing* alternatives to imprisonment. Consider, however, the following figures for the most recent available years:[45]

2,356,486	(63%)	On probation
407,977	(11%)	On parole
771,243	(21%)	In state and federal prisons
195,661	(5%)	In jails, postconvicted
3,731,367	(100%)	Total

It is true that about two-thirds of convicted felons are sentenced to at least some period of incarceration.[46] (A felony, by definition, is punishable by a year or more in prison.) However, at any time after sentencing and prior to final discharge from the criminal justice system, the great majority of those under correctional supervision (74 percent in the figures above) will be in the community and not incarcerated. In other words, they will be experiencing an "alternative sanction" for at least some part of their sentence.

If one-third of convicted felons receive no incarceration at all, and three-quarters receive at least some time on probation or parole, how much room is left for expanding the use of alternatives to imprisonment? Some, perhaps, but probably not much, especially if you look at offenders' prior records when searching for additional convicts to divert or remove from prison. Two-thirds of inmates currently in state prisons were given probation as an alternative sanction one or more times on prior convictions, and over 80 percent have had prior convictions resulting in either probation or incarceration.[47] After how many failures for a given offender do we say that alternatives to imprisonment have been exhausted?

In sum, the idea that we have not given alternatives to imprisonment a fair chance is a myth. Any day of the week you will find three times as many convicts under alternative supervision as you will find under the watchful eye of a warden. And most of those in the warden's custody probably are there at least partly because they did not do well under some prior alternative.

Myth Ten: Punishment is bad.

Underlying all the myths we have discussed so far, and motivating people to believe them, is the biggest myth of all: that punishment itself is inherently wrong. It is largely because they are opposed to punishment generally and to imprisonment in particular that many people argue so strongly that we must address the root causes of crime, that our criminal justice system discriminates, that we are overly punitive and haven't considered alternatives, that prisons are too costly and overcrowded, and that we must look to the courts for reform.

The "Big Myth" is that punishment has no value in itself; that it is intrinsically evil, and can be justified as a necessary evil only if it can be shown to be instrumental in achieving some overriding value, such as social order. Even retributivists, who argue that the primary purpose of the criminal sanction is to do justice by imposing deserved punishment (rather than to control crime through such strategies as rehabilitation, deterrence, or incapacitation), can find themselves caught up in utilitarian terminology when they speak of the "purpose"—rather than the "value"—of punishment.

Andrew von Hirsch provides the major contemporary statement of the justice model in his book *Doing Justice*.[48] Following Immanuel Kant, von Hirsch calls for penal sanctions on moral grounds, as the "just desserts" for criminally blameworthy conduct. Unlike Kant, however, von Hirsch sees deservedness only as necessary, but not sufficient, to justify punishment. There is supposedly a "countervailing moral consideration"—specifically, "the principle of not deliberately causing human suffering where it can possibly be avoided."[49] Accepting this principle, von Hirsch argues that for punishment to be justified, it must also be shown to have a deterrent effect. A utilitarian element has been added.

Von Hirsch's compromise is internally inconsistent, and this is weaker than a purely retributivist justification. The principle that punishment for wrongdoing is deserved, and the principle against all avoidable suffering, are logically incompatible. To say that *some* suffering (that is, punishment) is deserved is to say that we do *not* believe that *all* avoidable infliction of pain *should* be avoided. The justice model is stronger when the utilitarian requirement of deterrence is dropped.[50]

The best defense of punishment is not that it upholds the social order, but that it affirms important moral and cultural values.[51] Legal punishment is a legitimate and, if properly defined and administered, even a noble aspect of our culture. Imprisonment, in order to be respectable, does not need to be defined as "corrections," or as "treatment," or as "education," or as "protection of society," or as any other instrumental activity that an army of critics will forever claim to be a failure.

We must reject the false dichotomy between punishment and "humanitarianism." It is precisely within the context of punishment that humanistic concepts are most relevant. Principled and fair punishment for wrongdoing treats individuals as persons and as human beings, rather than as objects. Punishment is an affirmation of the autonomy, responsibility, and dignity of the individual.

Punishment in the abstract is morally neutral. When applied in specific instances and in particular forms—including imprisonment—its morality will depend on whether or not it is deserved, justly imposed, and proportionate to the wrongfulness of the crime. Where these conditions are met, punishment will not be a necessary evil, tolerable on utilitarian grounds only when held to the minimum "effective" level. Rather, under those conditions, it will have positive moral value.

Notes

1. James K. Stewart, "Urban Crime Locks People in Poverty," *Hartford Courant,* July 15, 1986.
2. Ibid.
3. See Charles Murray, *Losing Ground: American Social Policy, 1950–1980* (New York: Basic Books, 1984); and James Q. Wilson, *Thinking About Crime* (New York: Basic Books, 1975).
4. See Myth Two, below.
5. Morgan Reynolds, *Crime in Texas,* NCPA Policy Report No. 102 (Dallas: National Center for Policy Analysis, February 1991).
6. Bruce Benson, *The Enterprise of Law: Justice without the State* (San Francisco: Pacific Research Institute, 1990), p. 258.
7. Patrick A. Langan, "America's Soaring Prison Population," *Science* 251 (March 29, 1991): 1568–1573.
8. The war on drugs probably had a greater effect on state prisons after 1984 and undoubtedly has had a great effect on federal prisons, where over half of last year's admissions were for drug offenses.
9. Ibid., p. 1572.
10. Franklin E. Zimring, "The Great American Lockup," *The Washington Post,* February 28, 1991.
11. Mark Kleiman et al., *Imprisonment-to-Offense Ratios* (Washington, D.C.: Bureau of Justice Statistics Report, November 1988), p. 21; we are using his figures without adjustment for underreporting by the UCR, since that adjustment is only possible from 1973 on.
12. Robyn L. Cohen, *Prisoners in 1990* (Washington, D.C.: Bureau of Justice Statistics, 1991), p. 7
13. Tom Wicker, "The Punitive Society," *The New York Times,* January 12, 1991, Section 1, p. 25.
14. James Austin and John Irwin, *Who Goes to Prison?* (San Francisco: National Council on Crime and Delinquency, 1990). The discussion here draws on Charles H. Logan, "Who Really Goes to Prison?" *Federal Prisons Journal* (Summer 1991): 57–59.
15. See Logan, op. cit., for a critique of the study's methodology, including the sample.
16. Joseph E. Jacoby and Christopher S. Dunn, *National Survey on Punishment for Criminal Offenses* (Bowling Green, Ohio: Bowling Green State University, 1987).
17. Christopher A. Innes, *Profile of State Prison Inmates, 1986* (Washington, D.C.: Bureau of Justice Statistics Special Report, 1988).
18. Christopher A. Innes, *Population Density in State Prisons* (Washington, D.C.: Bureau of Justice Statistics, December 1986).
19. Jeff Bleich, "The Politics of Prison Crowding," *California Law Review* 77 (1989):1137.
20. James Bonta and Paul Gendreau, "Reexamining the Cruel and Unusual Punishment of Prison Life," *Law and Human Behavior* 14 (1990):365.
21. For example, see Bert Useem and Peter Kimball, *States of Siege: U.S. Prison Riots, 1971–1986* (New York: Oxford University Press, 1989); and John J. DiIulio, Jr., *Govern-

ing Prisons: A Comparative Study of Correctional Management (New York: Free Press, 1987).

22. For an overview, see DiIulio, *No Escape,* ibid., Chapter 3.

23. Stephen P. Klein et al., *Predicting Criminal Justice Outcomes: What Matters?* (Santa Monica, Calif.: RAND Corp., 1991), p. ix.

24. For example, see Stephen Klein et al., "Race and Imprisonment Decisions in California," *Science* 247 (February 1990): 769–792.

25. Patrick A. Langan, *Race of Prisoners Admitted to State and Federal Institutions, 1926–86* (Washington, D.C.: Bureau of Justice Statistics, May 1991), p. 8.

26. Ibid., p. 7.

27. See Stewart, op. cit.; and DiIulio, "Underclass," op. cit.

28. Joan Johnson et al., *Criminal Victimization in the United States, 1988* (Washington, D.C.: Bureau of Justice Statistics, December 1990), p. 48.

29. For a good overview, see Douglas C. McDonald, *The Cost of Corrections: In Search of the Bottom Line* (Washington, D.C.: National Institute of Corrections Research in Corrections Report, February 1989).

30. In addition to the efforts to be described in the remainder of this section, see the following: David P. Kavanaugh and Mark A.R. Kleiman, *Cost-Benefit Analysis of Prison Cell Construction and Alternative Sanctions* (Cambridge, Mass.: Biotec Analysis Corp., June 1990); Tara Gray et al., "Using Cost-Benefit Analysis to Evaluate Correctional Sentences," *Evaluation Review* 15 (August 1991): 471–481; and Peter W. Greenwood et al., *The RAND Intermediate-Sanction Cost Estimation Model* (Santa Monica, Calif.: RAND Corp., September 1989).

31. Edwin W. Zedlewski, *Making Confinement Decisions* (Washington, D.C.: National Institute of Justice Research in Brief, 1987). The material in the remainder of this section is adapted from John J. DiIulio, Jr., *Crime and Punishment in Wisconsin: A Survey of Prisoners* (Milwaukee, Wis.: Wisconsin Policy Research Institute, December 1990), and John J. DiIulio, Jr., and Anne Morrison Piehl, "Does Prison Pay?" *The Brookings Review* (Fall 1991).

32. See DiIulio, *Crime and Punishment,* op. cit.

33. DiIulio and Piehl, op. cit.

34. For example, see Joan Petersilia and Susan Turner, *Intensive Supervision for High-Risk Probationers: Finding from Three California Experiments* (Santa Monica, Calif.: RAND Corp., December 1990).

35. Malcolm M. Feeley, "The Significance of Prison Corrections Cases: Budgets and Regions," *Law and Society Review* (1990).

36. Clair A. Cripe, "Courts, Corrections, and the Constitution: A Practitioner's View," in DiIulio, *Courts,* op. cit., Chapter 10.

37. John J. DiIulio, Jr., ed., *Courts, Corrections, and the Constitution: The Impact of Judicial Intervention on Prisons and Jails* (New York: Oxford University Press, 1990), especially Chapter 11.

38. Nathan Glazer, "Towards an Imperial Judiciary," *The Public Interest* (1978); Lon Fuller, "The Forms and Limits of Adjudication," *Harvard Law Review* (1978).

39. See Ludmilla Alexeyeva, *Cruel and Usual Punishment: Forced Labor in Today's U.S.S.R.* (Washington, D.C.: AFL-CIO Department of International Affairs, 1987); see also various editions throughout the 1980s of the State Department's annual *Country Reports* on human rights practices of governments around the world.

40. Marc Mauer, *Americans Behind Bars: A Comparison of International Rates of Incarceration* (Washington, D.C.: The Sentencing Project, January 1991).

41. James Lynch, *Imprisonment in Four Countries* (Washington, D.C.: Bureau of Justice Statistics Special Report, February 1987); see also Alfred Blumstein, "Prison Populations: A System Out of Control?" in Michael Tonry and Norval Morris, *Crime and Justice: A Review of Research,* vol. 10 (Chicago: University of Chicago Press, 1988).

42. Lynch, op. cit., p. 2.

43. Mauer, op. cit., p. 12.

44. Norval Morris and Michael Tonry, *Between Prison and Probation: Intermediate Punishments in a Rational Sentencing System* (New York: Oxford University Press, 1990).

45. Figures are taken from the following Bureau of Justice Statistics bulletins: *Probation and Parole 1988* (November 1989); *Prisoners in 1990* (May 1991); *Jail Inmates, 1990* (June 1991).

46. Jacob Perez, "Tracking Offenders, 1988" *Bulletin* (Washington, D.C.: Bureau of Justice Statistics, June 1991); a study of offenders convicted of felonies in fourteen states.

47. Christopher A. Innes, *Profile of State Prison Inmates, 1986* (Washington, D.C.: Bureau of Justice Statistics Special Report, January 1988), combining information from Tables A and 8.

48. Andrew von Hirsch, *Doing Justice: The Choice of Punishments* (New York: Hill & Wang, 1976).

49. Ibid., p. 553.

50. Charles H. Logan, *Private Prisons: Cons and Pros* (New York: Oxford University Press, 1990), pp. 243, 298.

51. This discussion draws on Charles H. Logan and Gerald G. Gaes, "The Rehabilitation of Punishment," (unpublished, 1991).

27

Putting Justice Back into Criminal Justice: Notes for a Liberal Criminal Justice Policy

Samuel Walker

The 1967 report of the President's Commission on Law Enforcement and Adminis-tration of Justice recommended crime policies that attacked the causes of crime, that rehabilitated offenders, and that upheld civil rights. Many of these ideas have been criticized by conservatives as not effectively dealing with crime control. Samuel Walker argues that the policies of the past two decades have not reduced crime and that liberal policies are more likely to achieve justice.

I. Introduction

The principal thrust of criminal justice policy for the last twenty years has been the effort to enhance crime control: to arrest, prosecute, convict, and punish more offend-ers—or at least those who are guilty of serious crimes. That effort, which should be seen as a vast social experiment, has failed. We do not control crime any more effec-tively now than we did before. The time has come for a new direction in criminal justice policy. It is time to put an emphasis on justice back into criminal justice.

The conservative domination of criminal justice policy is the result of several forces. Persistently high crime rates have produced deep public frustration about crime. Fear of crime, moreover, is inextricably bound up with issues of race—fears that were exploited in the "Willie Horton" issue in the 1988 presidential election. Evidence of the conservative mood on crime policy is everywhere. The philosophy of rehabilitation has been abandoned in favor of a new interest in punishment, ret-ribution, incapacitation, and deterrence. There has been particular interest in identi-fying and punishing the so-called career criminal or high-rate offender.[1] The death penalty returned after a ten-year moratorium in 1977. Public support for capital pun-ishment is at the highest level in history.[2]

The Supreme Court has followed the popular mood as expressed in national elections. The present Court is dominated by a solid conservative majority. Unlike

Source: This is the first publication of "Putting Justice Back Into Criminal Justice: Notes for a Liberal Criminal Justice Policy," by Samuel Walker.

the Warren Court in the 1960s, the Court today is willing to side with the asserted claims of law-enforcement officials. It has sanctioned drunk driving checkpoints, a public safety exception to the *Miranda* warning, and a good-faith exception to the exclusionary rule, and it has drastically limited the use of habeas corpus as an avenue of relief for convicted offenders—to cite only a few recent decisions.

This, at any rate, is the conventional wisdom about national crime policy over the past twenty years. Upon closer inspection, however, the matter is a lot more complex. Change in the criminal justice system has not been completely dominated by a conservative agenda. There have been a number of very important changes that reflect the traditional liberal values of due process and equal protection. A surprising number of reforms have in fact achieved their stated goals.[3] These successes form the building blocks for a new direction in national criminal justice policy.

II. Two Deadly Myths about Criminal Justice Policy

Creating a liberal criminal justice policy has to begin by demolishing two prevalent myths about national crime policy.

The first is that liberal reforms don't work. While many reforms reflecting liberal social values did prove to be failures, others have succeeded and represent significant improvements in criminal justice policy. The second myth is that conservative "get-tough" crime-fighting policies do work. There is no evidence to support this belief. We can view the past twenty years as a vast social experiment in which conservative crime policies have been tried and found wanting.

III. The Foundations of a Liberal Criminal Justice Policy

A liberal criminal justice policy begins with a renewed commitment to the traditional liberal values of fairness and equality. These values are embodied in the constitutional principles of due process, equal protection of the law, and protection against cruel and unusual punishment. In many, but not always all, cases, liberal values are consistent with civil libertarian principles. The criminal justice system has two basic goals: to control crime and ensure justice. The time has come to put a renewed emphasis on justice for people who are the victims of discrimination at the hands of the system.

A renewed commitment to a national policy based on liberal values does not mean that every proposal cloaked in the garb of justice and fairness is a good idea. Good intentions alone do not make for good crime policy. Some of the well-intentioned reforms of the 1960s did fail. Nor does a commitment to liberal values mean that criminal behavior is excused. Wrongdoing should be punished. There is nothing inconsistent between liberal values and punishing those people found guilty of a serious crime. Liberal values, however, do require that use of the most serious penalties be carefully limited and tailored to the crime involved.

The second key element in a liberal criminal justice policy is a sober appreciation of the limits of the criminal justice system. We should not ask it to do things it cannot do. Criminal justice officials need to learn how to "just say no." When the public and elected officials ask it to do things that are beyond its power, responsible officials have a professional and social obligation to explain why they cannot. Already, for example, some police chiefs have been willing to publicly say that more arrests will not solve the nation's drug problem. The evidence on the limits of some of the more popular crime control programs is explored in detail later in this essay.[4]

The third element of a liberal approach to crime would be to direct public attention to the social problems that underly criminal behavior. This point flows inexorably from a recognition of the limits of the criminal process. The problems the criminal justice system is asked to handle (murder, robbery) are the end product of larger forces, which, in turn are influenced by social policies related to employment, housing, race relations, transportation, social welfare, and so on.

The limits of the criminal justice system are best symbolized by the police officer called for the third time to a domestic disturbance. The people involved have a lot of problems: unemployment, alcohol abuse, psychological problems, and so on. The officer cannot solve those problems. At best, he or she can do a professional job of resolving the immediate dispute. Policies based on liberal values should attempt to enhance that professionalism. But the ultimate solution to this particular domestic incident lies elsewhere, outside the justice system.

The Myth of Liberal Failure

The conservative mood that began in the mid-1970s and reached its peak with the election of Ronald Reagan as president in 1980 was based in part on a reaction against the liberal social programs of the 1960s. According to the conventional wisdom, those policies failed. With respect to criminal justice policy, that indictment is partly true. The task of policy analysis at the moment is to sort out the failures and the successes.

The proper point of reference for this analysis is the 1967 report of the president's crime commission, *The Challenge of Crime in a Free Society.*[5] The commission's recommendations had two broad thrusts. The first was that more money needed to be spent on criminal justice. The administration of justice would be substantially improved by hiring more police, raising their salaries, subsidizing their education, expanding their training, developing more sophisticated communications technology, expanding pretrial services for arrestees, creating more community-based treatment programs for convicted offenders, funding research, and so on. This approach was consistent with liberal social policy generally: investing in programs to deal with social problems (for example, the so-called War on Poverty). Furthermore, the commission recommended that the federal government undertake, for the first time, comprehensive assistance to state and local criminal justice agencies.

In many respects, this goal was achieved. Spending on criminal justice did increase substantially. The federal government did initiate a comprehensive program of financial assistance. Whether or not all this spending improved the administration of justice, however, is another question altogether. Much of the increase in spending has been a result of inflation and rising crime rates. It is not clear that the spending has improved either the crime control effectiveness of the system or the quality of justice.

The second general element of the crime commission's recommendations was a general belief in rehabilitation. This consisted of several different parts. The first was the optimistic belief that criminal offenders would be rehabilitated (or corrected, or treated, or resocialized) into productive law-abiding lives. The second element was the belief that this could be more effectively achieved in a community-based setting. There was a strong anti-institutional current in the commission's recommendations. Diversion was better than prosecution; probation was better than imprisonment; parole was better than long imprisonment.

It is the commitment to rehabilitation that has been the target of the strongest reaction over the past twenty years. The concept of rehabilitation fell into disrepute and is, today, the object of much derision. The reaction against rehabilitation was summed up by Robert Martinson's survey of correctional treatment programs. Asking the basic question, "What works?" he found that few programs could persuasively demonstrate their effectiveness.[6] Although he did find that some programs were more effective than alternatives, the public translated his findings into the conclusion that "nothing works."

The idea that nothing works has, on occasion, been inflated into a general indictment of criminal justice reform, particularly reforms reflecting liberal values. Some analysts argue that well-intentioned reforms backfire and aggravate the problem they set out to correct.[7] Other analysts argue that reforms are simply negated by the informal resistance of criminal justice officials.[8]

The most extreme versions of the nothing-works argument arise from the literature on correctional programs. Martinson's report seemed to indict all rehabilitation programs. One widely cited example of failure is the so-called "net-widening" phenomenon. Some evaluations indicated that programs designed to divert offenders from the criminal justice system actually brought more people under some form of official control.

With respect to the issue of rehabilitation, the critics have a good point. Few correctional treatment programs have persuasively demonstrated that a convicted offender is less likely to recidivate because he or she received a particular kind of "treatment" as opposed to a conventional form of punishment or treatment. Thus, the prisoner who participated in group therapy sessions is no less likely to recidivate than the offender who did his time in prison and was released at the same time; intensive parole supervision is no more successful than normal supervision. The list could be extended.

The Hidden Successes of Criminal Justice Reform

Not all of the crime commission's recommendations failed, however. A number of them have had considerable vitality and are responsible for significant improvements in the administration of justice. Nearly all are consistent with liberal values. The most important of these goals are (1) the control of discretion, (2) the reduction of official misconduct, and (3) equal employment opportunity. In addition, there is a new goal, (4) community renewal, which is an indirect result of the crime commission's work.

Controlling Discretion

Perhaps the most important recommendation made by the crime commission was one that did not receive much attention at the time: the control of discretion by criminal justice officials. In fact, it is largely hidden in the commission's report, buried among innumerable other recommendations. It was most explicit with respect to the police, where the commission recommended that "police departments should develop and enunciate policies that give police personnel specific guidance for the common situations requiring exercise of police discretion."[9] It also recommended that departments develop "a comprehensive regulation" on officer use of firearms.[10] With respect to plea bargaining, the commission recommended the "establishment of explicit policies for the dismissal or informal disposition" of cases,[11] along with a written record for guilty pleas (pp. 337–338). Correctional agencies, meanwhile, were advised to adopt "explicit standards and administrative procedures" for decisions affecting prisoners.[12]

The commission's recommendations were part of a broader recognition of the phenomenon of discretion. The pioneering field research by the American Bar Foundation had identified discretion as one of the key elements of a new paradigm of the administration of justice. This paradigm was embodied in the now-famous flowchart of the criminal justice system. It not only provided a graphic representation of the "system" but also focused attention on the many decision points in the system.

In the intervening twenty-five years, the control of discretion has become one of the central issues in criminal justice policy. Every decision point in the system has been subject to new controls. The police department SOP (Standard Operating Procedure) manual has become a large document and the principal instrument of contemporary police management. Bail decisions have been subject to controls by several different types of bail reform. Prosecutors' decisions to charge and to accept guilty pleas have been subject to both legislative and administrative controls. Sentencing, through mandatory provisions and sentencing guidelines have been instituted to limit discretion. Prisoners' rights litigation produced an intricate network of controls over correctional decisions, particularly disciplinary actions against inmates.

There are several notable examples of positive gains resulting from new controls over discretion. Restrictive deadly force policies have reduced the number of citizens shot and killed by the police. This has been accomplished without endangering police officers or contributing to an increase in the crime rate. Even more important, Lawrence W. Sherman's and Ellen G. Cohn's data indicates that the limits on shootings have reduced the racial disparity in persons shot and killed, from about 6:1 to 3:1.[13] Given the urgent nature of the race issue in American society, this reduction in police shootings is extremely important.

There are also new police department policies attempting to control officer discretion with respect to domestic violence and high-speed pursuits. It is still to early, however, to say whether these policies have had a significant effect on routine police practices.

Other attempts at discretion control have also produced some modest gains. The bail reform movement of the 1960s, which sought to guide bail-setting decisions of judges, did reduce the number of pretrial detainees in many cities, thereby reducing discrimination against defendants because of their economic status. Some analysts, however, suggest that this reduction might have occurred even without the benefit of "reform." There is also some evidence that administrative controls over plea negotiations, in the form of written standards about dismissals and charge reductions, have resulted in greater consistency in case disposition.

The results of attempting to control judicial sentencing discretion through sentencing guidelines are even more dramatic. The greatest success appears to have occurred in Minnesota, where formal guidelines have significantly limited the use of imprisonment and have reduced, although not eliminated, racial and economic disparities in sentencing.[14] Minnesota has the second-lowest imprisonment rate in the entire country. Moreover, it maintained a very low rate through the 1980s while other states were drastically increasing their prison populations. As will be discussed below, limiting the use of imprisonment yields additional benefits in terms of maintaining humane conditions within prisons.

These successes represent building blocks for a more comprehensive effort to control discretion. One of the principal items on the agenda of a liberal criminal justice policy should be to continue the effort to control discretion for the purpose of reducing and eliminating racial and economic injustice. Formal controls over discretionary decision making should be extended to those decision points that remain free of controls. The most important of all is the arrest decision. Apart from the new policies on domestic violence, the decision of the police officer to take a suspect into custody is unregulated. A second extremely important area involves the complex relationship between the various decisions that constitute plea bargaining and sentencing.

Reducing Official Misconduct

A second major goal should be the elimination or reduction of official misconduct. The control of discretion is one means of achieving this goal, although there are several other means as well.

In the 1960s the most important attacks on official misconduct came through Supreme Court decisions. The exclusionary rule (*Mapp v. Ohio*) was essentially an attempt to eliminate illegal searches and seizures. The *Miranda* warning was an attempt to eliminate or reduce coercive interrogations. The *Gault* decision imposed some minimal standards of due process in juvenile court proceedings. The many prisoners' rights decisions have reduced some of the more barbaric practices in prisons.

One of the most important corollary effects of these Supreme Court decisions was a transformation of the working environment of policing. A study of narcotics detectives in Chicago found that court decisions had forced significant improvements in training and supervision. At the same time, a new generation of officers had come to accept the principles underlying court decisions protecting individual rights. Many stated that formal, externally imposed limits on police powers were a necessary means of controlling police conduct.[15]

Another important area of police misconduct involves the unjustified use of physical force and abusive language directed at citizens. The crime commission recommended that police departments create a formal process for handling citizen complaints.[16] As a part of that, it also recommended that every department have a separate internal-affairs unit. To a large extent these recommendations have been fulfilled. Formal complaint procedures are now standard items in virtually all big-city departments. Despite this progress, the problem of police misconduct continues—as the 1991 beating of Rodney King by the Los Angeles police clearly indicated. Public attention has now focused on the effectiveness of police disciplinary procedures. The belief that they are inadequate has led to the creation of civilian review procedures in thirty-two of the fifty largest cities.[17]

One of the most important consequences of the Rodney King incident in Los Angeles has been the new focus on the phenomenon of the "problem-prone" officer. Investigations in Los Angeles, Kansas City, Boston, Houston, and elsewhere have consistently found that a small percentage of officers are involved in a disproportionate number of citizen complaints.[18]

The U.S. Civil Rights Commission identified this problem in 1981 and recommended that police departments create "early-warning systems" to identify these officers and take appropriate remedial steps.[19] Apparently, no department followed this recommendation. In the wake of the Rodney King incident, however, several police departments have begun to address the problem. A liberal criminal justice program would emphasize the reduction of police misconduct through the development of "early-warning" procedures in all police departments.

A major part of a liberal criminal justice program would be to continue the movement to instill respect for legal principles in criminal justice agencies and to encourage the growth of self-regulation. One form of self-regulation is accreditation. Litigation against police misconduct led to the creation of the Commission on Accreditation for Law Enforcement Agencies, which has now accredited 195 agencies.[20] Administrative rule making—controls over deadly force, handling of domestic violence, and high-speed pursuits—may be the most promising avenue for controlling police behavior in the immediate future.

Another significant area of official misconduct involves the abuse of prison inmates: physical brutality, prolonged sentences to solitary confinement, absence of due process in disciplinary procedures, and the violation of other individual rights such as access to reading material, visits, mail, and so forth. The crime commission called for "explicit standards and administrative procedures" regarding decisions affecting prisoners, but it did not give the matter a great deal of attention.[21] The commission's report was published before the modern prisoners' rights movement began. Since then, litigation based on constitutional principles has created a vast body of prisoners' rights, including physical facilities, services and programs, and the rights and privileges of inmates.

This litigation has had a far-reaching impact on American prisons. Many of the grossest abuses have been eliminated. Formal disciplinary procedures have been established. Also, litigation stimulated the correctional accreditation movement, which has resulted in the development of minimum standards for institutions. As is the case with the police, these developments represent a step in the direction of self-regulation and a transformation of the working environment of institutions. This is an important and overdue development that a liberal criminal justice program would continue to foster.

Many of the gains of the prisoners' rights movement began to be eroded in the 1980s, however. The dramatic increase in prison populations resulted in severe overcrowding, which, in turn, aggravated tensions among inmates, overloaded prison programs, and made routine supervision and discipline far more difficult.

The key to maintaining humane conditions in prisons—and in the process reducing both misconduct by officials and violence by inmates—is to limit the use of imprisonment. The state of Minnesota has shown that this can be done. The use of sentencing guidelines to control judicial discretion is a viable technique for limiting imprisonment. By limiting prison populations, states will be able to maintain humane conditions inside prisons within the constraints of limited state budgets.

Providing Equal Employment Opportunity

The crime commission also recommended the hiring of more racial minorities and women in policing. The commission produced devastating data on the underrepresentation of African-Americans (then referred to as Negroes) in big-city police departments. They represented 38 percent of the population of Atlanta but only 9.3 percent of the police force; 23 percent of the population of Oakland but only 2.3 percent of the police; 29 percent of the population of Detroit but only 3.9 percent of the police force.[22] Significantly, the employment of Hispanic Americans was not even mentioned.

In the intervening twenty-five years, there has been considerable progress in minority employment. Nationally, the percentage of African-Americans as sworn officers has increased from 3.6 percent in 1960 to 12.3 percent by 1988.[23] In some departments African-American and Hispanic officers are now the majority. Several departments approach the theoretical ideal where the percentage of minority officers on the force equals the presence of minorities in the community. There is also evidence of recent progress in the employment of Hispanic Americans as police officers.[24]

Increased racial-minority employment has furthered several important goals. Most important, it represents a commitment to the principle of equality. In the process it has created real employment opportunities for thousands of people of color. It also has some positive impact on police–community relations. A more diverse police force does not appear to be an all-white occupying army. Diversity also alters the police subculture such that, today, national organizations representing African-American officers offer a different point of view on such issues as civilian review and police brutality. Together with the growing number of female officers, minority officers have shattered the once-homogeneous police subculture.

At the same time, however, increased minority employment has not fulfilled all the objectives of reformers. The impact on police–community relations is indirect at best. Studies of police behavior have found no significant differences between white and black officers. Thus, minority employment does not automatically translate into improved police work.

With respect to women in policing, there has been a revolution in social policy since the mid-1960s. At that time, women represented an estimated 1 percent of all sworn officers and were relegated to second-class status in police work: excluded from patrol work and restricted to juvenile, clerical, or other peripheral tasks. In some departments they were barred from promotion to the highest ranks as a matter of official policy. The *Task Force Report* (but not the main report) delicately raised the question of recruiting more women officers and assigning them to patrol duty.[25]

Following the crime commission's recommendation, the Police Foundation conducted an experiment on women on patrol in 1973. This was followed by similar experiments. Evaluations of these experiments reached consistent conclusions: despite minor differences, women officers performed just as well as male officers in routine patrol duty. The formal barriers to female recruitment quickly fell, in large part because of federal civil rights laws. The presence of women in policing increased to about 8.8 percent of all sworn officers by 1986. Informal barriers to employment, however, have remained.[26]

As has been the case with racial-minority employment, the addition of female officers has enhanced the principle of equality, provided real job opportunities for many women, and diversified the police subculture. At the same time, the addition of female officers has not fulfilled all reform expectations. The performance of female officers is essentially the same as male officers; thus, they are not fundamentally better able to mediate disputes. This notion rested on an inverse sexist stereotype of women as more verbal and nurturing than men.

There has also been progress in terms of the employment of women in other parts of the criminal justice system. The enrollment of women in law schools has increased substantially, and more women are securing jobs as prosecutors and defense attorneys, as well as election and appointment as judges. Women are also being employed as correctional officers in male institutions.

The increase in racial-minority and female employment in criminal justice represents a good beginning. But it is only a beginning. In every occupation category, both groups remain underrepresented. Even more ominous has been the hostility of the Supreme Court to affirmative action. The studies of employment in policing all conclude that affirmative action plans have been critical to increased racial-minority and female employment. Recent court decisions threaten to remove this remedy and undermine progress to date. A liberal criminal justice program would reaffirm the commitment to equal employment opportunity in all aspects of the criminal justice system.

Stimulating Community Renewal

Another important goal of a liberal criminal justice program is community renewal. Specifically, this refers to programs that criminal justice agencies might undertake to help communities resist the downward spiral of deterioration. This goal rests on the recognition that the criminal justice system cannot, by itself, control crime. It is a last-resort mechanism that comes into play only when all other instruments of social control have failed.

Some of the most creative thinking in policing over the past decade argues that the police might play a vital role in community renewal. This idea has been given the label "community policing." The essence of community policing is that the police should de-emphasize traditional crime fighting in favor of attention to long-range problem solving and attention to small signs of disorder in the community.

Community policing is an indirect result of the crime commission's work. First, the commission's *Task Force Report: The Police* was the first full statement of the idea that the police have a diverse and complex role, with only a small part of their work being devoted to crime fighting.[27] This point was reinforced by the field studies of policing sponsored by the commission.[28] Subsequent studies found that increased patrol presence did not reduce crime[29] and that faster response time did not result in more arrests. All of this research demolished the "crime fighter" image of the police role.

Drawing upon this accumulated research, first Herman Goldstein and then James Q. Wilson and George Kelling sketched out new models of policing. Wilson and Kelling argued that the capacity of the police to control crimes was very limited and that, instead, they should concentrate on the less serious problems of disorder (which they identified by the metaphor of "broken windows").[30] This was designed to accomplish two things. First, it would enhance feelings of community safety. Second, it would help to arrest the process of community deterioration at an early stage and, thus, help prevent neighborhoods from sinking into serious crime. Wilson and Kelling's "Broken Windows" article was enormously influential and, more than anything else, launched the community policing movement.

Herman Goldstein, meanwhile, had already developed the concept of "problem-oriented policing."[31] He argued that the police should disaggregate the different aspects of their role and develop strategies to address particular ones. Problem-oriented policing is really a planning process. It does not tell the police what to do; it tells them only how to approach their mission in a different fashion. Community policing, at least as defined by Wilson and Kelling, did have a specific content. By de-emphasizing crime fighting, however, both approaches involved a very different conception of the police role.

In the first major experiment of problem-oriented policing in Newport News, Virginia, police officers attacked crime in a public housing project by organizing community residents and bringing pressure to bear on both public and private agencies.[32] This illustrated the important components of problem-oriented policing. First, police officers played a very different role, acting as community organizers and brokers of government services. Second, the police department addressed the underlying causes of crime: in this instance, the failure of both government agencies and private businesses to fulfill their obligations in a public housing project.

The jury is still out on community policing. There is the danger that it will be destroyed by its own early success. It has quickly become a fad, in some cases nothing more than a rhetorical phrase with no content. As was the case with team policing over twenty years ago, many departments are jumping on the bandwagon with no planning. In some instances, community policing has become a trendy label for putting more police on the streets in response to community fears about crime. Even under the best of circumstances—assuming careful planning, training, and supervision—there are serious limits to what community policing could accomplish in the way of community renewal. The key word here is *renewal*. Taking Wilson and Kelling at their word, the police might be able to help communities resist the downward spiral of deterioration. That, however, assumes the existence of a viable community. Yet in the most crime-ridden neighborhoods today, no such community exists. One of the main characteristics of economically devastated neighborhoods is the absence of the institutions and informal networks that make up a "community." Indeed, one could argue that drug gangs thrive because they fill that void, providing identity, protection, work, and income. In this respect, community policing has been oversold.

Nonetheless, community policing represents a bold new concept of the police role. It recognizes that the police cannot, by themselves, control crime, but that they might be able to help communities renew themselves and resist the forces that lead to high levels of crime.

The blunt fact is that the police cannot create a community where one does not exist. No amount of creative community policing can hope to overcome the devastating effect of massive unemployment and declining job opportunities—the conditions that affect today's inner cities. The real solution to the crime problem lies outside the realm of criminal justice policy: in the realm of economic policy and job creation. This conclusion is not based on liberal sentimentality about the "roots" of crime; it reflects a sober assessment of what the criminal justice system can and cannot do.

IV. The Failure of Tough Crime Control

For the past twenty years, national criminal justice policy has been dominated by a conservative "get tough with crime" approach. This represents a far longer period than the heyday of 1960s liberalism. We can now look back and evaluate it as we would any other social experiment.

In virtually every respect, the conservative experiment has failed. Crime is no more effectively controlled today than it was in the early 1970s. It is true that for many forms of predatory crime, the crime rate has declined. The National Crime Survey has found a 19.6 percent decrease in robbery and a 38.5 percent decrease in household burglary between 1973 and 1989.[33] This decline, however, can be attributed largely to demographic changes, particularly in the aging of the baby boom generation.[34]

In many other respects, however, the crime problem has worsened. The gravest crisis is in the poorest, most crime-ridden, drug-dominated neighborhoods. It is here that the murder rate has soared in recent years; that gangs have taken over community life; that the quality of life has deteriorated to the point where one regularly hears of families being afraid to turn on lights at night and of children sleeping in bathtubs because of random drive-by shootings. The War on Crime—and the War on Drugs, in particular—has utterly failed to stop this downward spiral. This failure is evident in every component of the criminal justice system.

It is now the conventional wisdom, even among conservatives, that traditional police crime control efforts will not reduce crime. Adding more patrol officers, increasing response time, and adding more detectives will not produce either fewer crimes or more arrests. The evidence is also overwhelming on the long-standing controversy over the exclusionary rule. Studies have convincingly found that the rule affects a tiny percentage of criminal cases at best.

In response to public alarm over drugs, some departments have resorted to massive "sweep" arrests. The Los Angeles police arrested over 1,000 alleged gang members in one weekend. These arrests are done entirely for their publicity value and have had no effect whatsoever on crime, drug trafficking, or gang membership. Evaluations of a much publicized drug crackdown in one section of New York City ("Operation Pressure Point") failed to prove that it produced any long-term reduction in drug dealing in the city—a point that is evident to every resident of the city.[35]

With respect to bail, the federal government and many states have adopted some form of preventive detention that is designed to allow judges to deny bail to allegedly dangerous offenders. The Supreme Court upheld the federal law in 1987. The impact of preventive detention on crime has been negligible. Prior studies indicated that serious crime by persons on pretrial release was confined to a small percentage of defendants and that it was impossible to identify exactly which ones they were. Evaluations of the federal preventive detention law have found little change in the total percentage of defendants being held before trial. Judges have always practiced a covert form of preventive detention. The new procedures have yielded no gain.[36]

With respect to the disposition of criminal cases, studies have persuasively demonstrated that plea bargaining is not a loophole by which dangerous people beat the system. Persons who have committed a serious crime against a stranger, who have a prior criminal record, and against whom there is solid evidence are charged with the top offense, convicted of that offense, and sentenced to prison. "Career criminal" prosecution programs have produced no net gain in the imprisonment of dangerous criminals because those people were being treated fairly harshly under normal conditions.[37]

With respect to sentencing, there has been an enormous increase in imprisonment. The total prison population more than tripled between 1973 and 1989. The result has been massive prison overcrowding but little, if any, direct gain in crime reduction. The decline in criminal incidents reported by the National Crime Survey can be attributed entirely to demographic change. Trends with respect to drug offenses dramatize the failure even further. In every state and the federal system the most dramatic change has been the increase in the number of convicted drug offenders. Yet there is no evidence that this has curbed the drug problem through either incapacitation or deterrence. In fact, the problem of drug gangs and gang-related violence worsened in the late 1980s—*after* more than ten years of increasing use of imprisonment. The much-publicized idea of *selective* incapacitation had no effect on policy, in large part because normal prosecution and sentencing practices were already highly selective.

Nor has the revival of the death penalty had any discernible effect on crime. The sudden upsurge in murders, almost all of them related to inner-city drug gang activity, occurred *after* a yearly average of more than twenty people were executed in the mid-1980s.

In short, the conservative criminal justice program of "getting tough" with crime has failed in all of its manifestations.

V. Conclusion

A sound criminal justice policy begins with a sober respect for the limits of what can be accomplished through the criminal justice system.

The first principle is that criminal justice agencies—police, courts, prisons—cannot make significant changes in the level of criminal behavior. This is where much of the liberal thinking of the 1960s went wrong. It assumed that the right kind of programs—diversion of minor offenders, community-based treatment programs, and the like—would affect the lives of offenders: resocializing them into law-abiding lives. There is no reason to believe that today. By the same token, it should be noted that many of the popular conservative crime control programs of the past twenty years assume an ability to change people's behavior. To cite one example: the concept of deterrence assumes that by raising the cost of crime, potential offenders will choose not to offend. Altering criminal justice programs, in short, has little effect on criminal behavior.

The crime commission also assumed that pouring more money into the justice system—for more personnel, better equipment, better training, more research—would enhance the crime control capacity of the system. There is no support for that assumption either.

This is not to say that many of the crime commission's proposals were entirely wrong. More money, resources, and research may not reduce crime but it can help to improve the *quality* of justice. And that is an important goal. By the same token, community-based programs for convicted offenders may not rehabilitate them, but they may well be cheaper and more humane forms of punishment.

If our capacity to affect the behavior of criminals and potential criminals is very limited, we can control the behavior of criminal justice officials. The evidence indicates that we can control their discretion, we can reduce misconduct, and we can eliminate employment discrimination. These goals, which reflect the liberal values of fairness and equality, are the proper goals of a national criminal justice policy.

Notes

1. Alfred Blumstein et al., *Criminal Careers and "Career Criminals"* (Washington, D.C.: National Academy Press, 1986).
2. Survey data is reported in Bureau of Justice Statistics, *Sourcebook of Criminal Justice Statistics—1990* (Washington, D.C.: Government Printing Office, 1991), pp. 199–200.
3. A full discussion of these developments is in Samuel Walker, *Taming the System: The Control of Discretion in Criminal Justice, 1950–1990* (New York: Oxford University Press, forthcoming).
4. The limits of the "get-tough" approach are examined in Samuel Walker, *Sense and Nonsense about Crime,* 2nd ed. (Pacific Grove, Calif.: Brooks/Cole, 1989).
5. U.S. President's Commission on Law Enforcement and Administration of Justice, *The Challenge of Crime in a Free Society* (Washington, D.C.: Government Printing Office, 1967).
6. Robert Martinson, "What Works?" Questions and Answers about Prison Reform," *Public Interest* 35 (Spring 1974): 22–54.
7. Eugene Doleschal, "The Dangers of Criminal Justice Reform," *Criminal Justice Abstracts* 14 (March 1982): 133–152.
8. Malcolm Feeley, *Court Reform on Trial* (New York: Basic Books, 1983).
9. President's Commission, *The Challenge of Crime,* p. 104.
10. Ibid., p. 119.
11. Ibid., p. 134.
12. Ibid., pp. 181–182.
13. Lawrence W. Sherman and Ellen G. Cohn, *Citizens Killed by Big City Police, 1970–1984* (Washington, D.C.: Crime Control Institute, 1986).

14. Terance D. Miethe and Charles A. Moore, "Socioeconomic Disparities under Determinate Sentencing Systems: A Comparison of Preguideline and Postguideline Practices in Minnesota," *Criminology* 23 (May 1985): 337–263. Minnesota Sentencing Guidelines Commission, *Guidelines and Commentary,* rev. ed. (St. Paul: August 1981).
15. "The Exclusionary Rule and Deterrence: An Empirical Study of Chicago Narcotics Officers," *University of Chicago Law Review* 54 (1987): 1016–1069.
16. President's Commission, *The Challenge of Crime,* p. 100.
17. Samuel Walker and Vic W. Bumphus, *Civilian Review of the Police: A National Survey of the 50 Largest Cities* (Omaha: University of Nebraska at Omaha, 1991).
18. *Report of the Independent Commission on the Los Angeles Police Department* (Los Angeles: Office of the Mayor, 1991). *Report of the Boston Police Department Management Review Committee* (Boston: Office of the Mayor, 1992).
19. U.S. Civil Rights Commission, *Who Is Guarding the Guardians?* (Washington, D.C.: U.S. Civil Rights Commission, 1981), pp. 81–86, 166.
20. Commission on Accreditation for Law Enforcement Agencies, *Standards for Law Enforcement Agencies* (Fairfax, Va.: CALEA, 1988).
21. President's Commission, *The Challenge of Crime,* pp. 181–182.
22. President's Commission, *Task Force Report: The Police* (Washington, D.C.: Government Printing Office, 1967), p. 168.
23. David L. Carter et al., *The State of Police Education* (Washington, D.C.: Police Executive Research Forum, 1989), p. 84.
24. Samuel Walker, *Employment of Black and Hispanic Police Officers, 1983–1988: A Five Year Follow Up Study* (Omaha: University of Nebraska at Omaha, 1989).
25. President's Commission, *Task Force Report: The Police,* p. 125.
26. Susan E. Martin, *On the Move?: The Status of Women in Policing* (Washington, D.C.: The Police Foundation, 1990).
27. President's Commission, *Task Force Report: The Police.*
28. Albert Reiss, *The Police and the Public* (New Haven, Conn.: Yale University Press, 1971).
29. George Kelling et al., *The Kansas City Preventive Patrol Experiment* (Washington, D.C.: The Police Foundation, 1974).
30. James Q. Wilson and George L. Kelling, "Broken Windows: The Police and Neighborhood Safety," *Atlantic Monthly* 249 (March 1982): 29–38.
31. Herman Goldstein, "Improving Policing: A Problem-Oriented Approach," *Crime and Delinquency* 25 (1979): 236–258; Herman Goldstein, *Problem-Oriented Policing* (New York: McGraw-Hill, 1990).
32. John E. Eck and William Spelman, *Problem-Solving: Problem-Oriented Policing in Newport News* (Washington, D.C.: Police Executive Research Forum, 1987).
33. Bureau of Justice Statistics, *Criminal Victimization 1989* (Washington, D.C.: Government Printing Office, 1990).
34. James Q. Wilson argues persuasively that about half of the increase in crime in the 1960s could have been predicted on the basis of demographic trends; see his *Thinking about Crime,* pp. 12–13.
35. Lynn Zimmer, "Proactive Policing against Street-Level Drug Trafficking," *American Journal of Police* IX (1990, No. 1): 43–74.
36. Thomas E. Scott, "Pretrial Detention under the Bail Reform Act of 1984: An Empirical Analysis," *American Criminal Law Review* 27 (1989, No. 1): 1–51.
37. Eleanor Chelimsky and Judith H. Dahmann, *National Evaluation of the Career Criminal Program: Final Report* (McLean, Va.: Mitre Corp., 1979).

TO THE OWNER OF THIS BOOK:

We hope that you have found *Criminal Justice: Law and Politics*, 6th Edition, useful. So that this book can be improved in a future edition, would you take the time to complete this sheet and return it? Thank you.

Instructor's name: _____

Department: _____

School and address: _____

_____

1. The name of the course in which I used this book is: _____

_____

2. My general reaction to this book is: _____

_____

_____

3. What I like most about this book is: _____

_____

_____

4. What I like least about this book is: _____

_____

_____

5. Were all of the chapters of the book assigned for you to read?   Yes   No

    If not, which ones weren't? _____

6. Do you plan to keep this book after you finish the course?   Yes   No

    Why or why not? _____

_____

7. On a separate sheet of paper, please write specific suggestions for improving this book and anything else you'd care to share about your experience in using the book.

Optional:

Your name: _____ Date: _____

May Wadsworth quote you, either in promotion for *Criminal Justice: Law and Politics*, 6th Edition, or in future publishing ventures?

Yes: _____ No: _____

Sincerely,

George F. Cole

FOLD HERE